W9-CAH-262

ISRAEL'S SECRET WARS

Published by Grove Weidenfeld
A division of Grove Press, Inc.
841 Broadway
New York, NY 10003-4793

First published in Great Britain in 1991 by
Hamish Hamilton Ltd, London

Library of Congress Cataloging-in-Publication Data

Black, Ian, 1953–
Israel's secret wars: a history of Israel's intelligence services / Ian Black and Benny Morris.
p. cm.
Includes bibliographical references and index.
ISBN 0-8021-1159-9 : $24.95
1. Intelligence services—Israel. 2. Secret service—Israel. 3. Military intelligence—Israel. 4. Israel. Mosad le-modi in tafkidim meyuhadim. 5. Israel. Sherut ha-bitahon ha-kelali. 6. Jewish-Arab relations—1949– 7. Israel-Arab conflicts. I. Morris, Benny, 1948– II. Title.
UB251.I78B55 1991
355.3'432'095694—dc20 90-49373
CIP

Manufactured in the United States of America

Printed on acid-free paper

First American Edition 1991

10 9 8 7 6 5 4 3 2 1

ISRAEL'S SECRET WARS

A History of Israel's Intelligence Services

Ian Black and Benny Morris

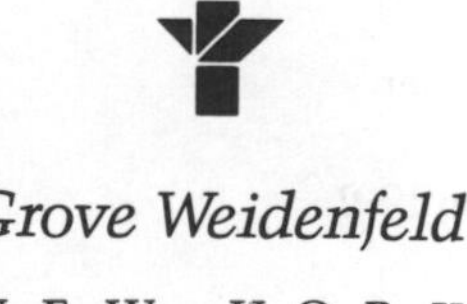

Grove Weidenfeld

NEW YORK

Contents

Authors' Note

Many people, especially those involved in the Haganah, the Jewish Agency or the Zionist establishment, Hebraized their names (sometimes first names as well as surnames) during the mandatory period and in the early years after independence in 1948. The practice followed throughout this book has been to give first the original name with the new one in brackets and then to use just the new name. Thus Reuven Zaslani (Shiloah) later becomes Reuven Shiloah, Moshe Shertok (Sharett) becomes Moshe Sharett.

Acknowledgements

In writing this book, we have tried to use as much original documentation as possible and have invariably indicated the source of our information (broadly document, interview, book or newspaper). Large parts of the narrative are based on interviews with former Israeli intelligence personnel from all three services. A surprisingly large number were willing to speak, although only a tiny handful agreed to be identified. Many were prevented by law from allowing their names to be published and expressed frustration that this was so. Some non-Israeli sources preferred anonymity.

We have also drawn heavily on Israeli and foreign newspapers, journals and books – but always carefully separating the wheat from the chaff. Throughout we have made strenuous efforts at verification from two or more independent sources. The bulk of the book has been read over by retired intelligence officers, although any errors of fact or interpretation that may have crept in are, of course, our own.

We have been handicapped by the irritating but unavoidable fact that whatever we wrote would ultimately have to pass through the sieve of Israeli military censorship. But the censors treated our finished product with far greater liberalism than we had expected or than anyone could have enjoyed only a few years ago. Surprisingly little had to be deleted from the original, finished manuscript (and this only after all possible appeal procedures had been exhausted).

Far too many people have helped with this project to be

mentioned by name. Many of those who can be have been credited in the notes at the end of the book; some of those whose assistance was priceless still cannot be publicly thanked. This is one of the unfortunate occupational hazards of being involved in, and writing about, intelligence.

Introduction

Just off Israel's Mediterranean coastal highway, a few miles north of Tel Aviv, a cluster of unremarkable grey-white concrete buildings can be made out through a line of dusty eucalyptus trees that runs roughly parallel to the main road. Turn left after the busy Glilot junction, past the soldiers waiting for lifts, and there, hidden in the centre of the cluster, yet clearly signposted for all the world to see, lies a fine public memorial to over 400 Israelis who died while serving in their country's intelligence services.

The monument, fittingly enough perhaps, is built in the form of a maze, an interlocking complex of smooth stone walls engraved with the names of the fallen, and by each name is the date of death. It is divided into five chronological sections, beginning in November 1947 – when the United Nations voted to partition British-ruled Palestine into separate Jewish and Arab states – and ending (so far) in February 1989. The section covering the last fifteen years is entitled 'the beginnings of peace' but it still lists more than 200 names. More blank walls, backing on to a grassy outdoor amphitheatre, are available for future use.

The monument should be a spycatcher's dream. But the hand of official secrecy lies heavily even on the dead. Names and dates yes, but there are no ranks, no units, no places, no hints of the circumstances in which these unknown soldiers lost their lives. Some died naturally after long years in the shadows, yet most of these are still as anonymous as the many others who fell on active service.

A few of their stories have been told, though most are covered in a heavy patina of heroic myth. There, from the early days, is Ya'akov Buqa'i, executed in Jordan in 1949 after filtering in disguise through the ceasefire lines together with hundreds of released Arab prisoners of war. There are Max Binnet and Moshe Marzuk, who died in Egyptian prison in the mid-1950s after the exposure of the famous Israeli sabotage network at the centre of the Lavon Affair. There are Eli Cohen, the legendary spy who penetrated the highest echelons of the Syrian government and was hanged, live on television, in Damascus in 1965; Baruch Cohen, the Mossad agent-runner shot dead in Madrid by a Palestinian gunman in 1973; Moshe Golan, a Shin Bet security service officer murdered by a West Bank informer in a safe house inside Israel in 1980; Ya'akov Barsimantov, a Mossad man assassinated in Paris weeks before the invasion of Lebanon in 1982; and Victor Rejwan, a Shin Bet man killed in a shoot-out with Muslim militants in Gaza just before the outbreak of the Palestinian uprising in 1987.

A little knowledge and imagination can help with the majority of names that are still unknown to the wider public. A cluster of men killed in June 1967 and a larger number who died between October and December 1973 are the losses of army field intelligence units during the Six Day and Yom Kippur wars. Another group who died on the same day in November 1983 comprised Shin Bet agents blown up by a Shi'ite Muslim suicide bomber in the southern Lebanese city of Tyre. But most of the names remain mysterious, impenetrable and unyielding as tombstones. Only the breakdown of the total fatalities (available until mid-1988) reflects the different roles – and degree of exposure to mortal danger – of the three separate services that make up Israel's intelligence community: army intelligence, 261; the Shin Bet, eighty; the Mossad, sixty-five.

Israel has many war memorials. Different military units – the paratroops, the air force and the tank corps – have all erected monuments to the men and women they have lost in five full-scale conventional wars (six if the 1968–70 'war of attrition' on the Suez Canal is counted) and four decades of cross-border incursions and anti-guerrilla operations. The memorial to the fallen of the intelligence community at Glilot was erected in 1984 as a result of pressure from bereaved families, who felt that the contribution of their relations to national security had not been given adequate public recognition. A few of the 415 men and women whose names are engraved on its walls are still buried in unmarked graves or under assumed names in the Arab countries where they operated.

The monument is as unique as it is bizarre, a taut compromise between the harsh demands of official secrecy and the need for recognition for those whose loved ones lived and died in anonymity. There is probably nowhere else on earth that, proportionate to its size and population, produces, analyses or consumes as much intelligence as Israel, a country of 4 million people that has been in a state of war for every moment of its forty-three-year existence and sees its future depending, perhaps more than ever before, on the need to 'know' its enemies, predict their intentions and frustrate their plans.

Intelligence is an expanding business. The British writer Phillip Knightley has calculated that in the mid-1980s over a million people, spending £17,500 million annually, were engaged worldwide in what he irreverently reminded spy buffs was called 'the second oldest profession'.[1]

Serious study of the subject is growing too. In the academic world intelligence is starting to receive attention as the 'missing dimension' without which politics, war, diplomacy, terrorism and international relations cannot be properly understood.[2] The United States, with a unique though often threatened tradition of relative openness in such matters, has taken the lead in the field. But there has been impressive progress elsewhere. In Britain historians like Christopher Andrew have shown that hard work and imaginative research methods can circumvent some of the more absurd restrictions of official secrecy, clumsy 'weeding' and censorship in the name of national security. Learned journals, symposia and multidisciplinary international conferences are proliferating like the intelligence and security bureaucracies themselves.

Exposure has brought with it more public interest. The British government's prolonged attempts to ban *Spycatcher*, the sensational memoirs of the former MI5 officer Peter Wright, were bound to fail in the end. Israel ignored this lesson, and in 1990 tried and also failed to halt publication – in the United States and Canada – of an embarrassing book about the Mossad by Victor Ostrovsky, a disgruntled former officer. Democratic societies cannot consistently withstand pressures for some measure of accountability and control of their secret services. This is especially true when intelligence efforts are directed against a country's own citizens, not at foreign armies, spies or terrorists. But unlike Israel, neither the United States nor Britain is at war.

Yet even Israel is not immune from the trend towards more exposure. Several recent security and espionage scandals have badly tarnished the halo of its secret services, although, as is the case with intelligence organizations everywhere, mistakes have become public knowledge far more quickly than successes. The Lavon Affair of the 1950s and 1960s, the intelligence failure that preceded the surprise Egyptian–Syrian assault of October 1973, the bungled killing of an innocent man in Lillehammer, Norway, in the Mossad's shadowy war against Palestinian terrorism and the 1984–6 Shin Bet scandals over the killing of prisoners and torture of suspects have all been documented far more completely than the impressive number of successes notched up by Israel.

Success is a problem too. Like other intelligence communities in other democratic societies, Israel's has become adept at cultivating selective links with journalists who are grateful for whatever snippets of secret information are released from the nether world. Israel has its equivalents of Nigel West and Chapman Pincher, two British writers who for years had a virtual monopoly of writing about their country's secret services on the basis of unattributable interviews. And Israel's stringent laws of military censorship and non-release of almost all intelligence material in government archives combine to ensure that exposure generally remains limited. That is why Victor Ostrovsky's damaging claims in his book, *By Way of Deception: The Making and Unmaking of a Mossad Officer*, came as such a grievous blow.

Thus any serious study of the subject is bound to be difficult. It is not necessary to subscribe to the rigid view that an event is true only if it is somehow documented to acknowledge that the existence of hard, written evidence is the exception rather than the rule in the field of intelligence and security. A substantial amount of original documentation is available – *if one knows how and where to look* – for the period up to about 1958; this material can provide remarkable insights into matters that were never intended to be made public, and, perhaps, should never have been committed to paper.

Secret reports on officially sanctioned assassinations and kidnappings survive from the chaotic period before the outbreak of the 1948 war. A declassified file of Mossad cable traffic detailing communications between Baghdad and Tel Aviv gives a fascinating glimpse of the nuts and bolts of clandestine operations, of the rising panic when an agent is blown and may be talking under torture; a mass of more mundane yet often thrilling material gives a sense of the scale and character of routine intelligence gathering. Records of interrogations of captured Palestinian infiltrators show how Israel built up a picture of its enemy. Foreign Ministry material reveals diplomats choosing to ignore intelligence facts when they contradicted the official propaganda line.

From the end of the 1950s contemporary documents are sporadic, non-existent or, in most cases, simply unavailable. Other historical evidence can be partial or unreliable: personal memoirs tend to suffer from self-censorship and a natural human tendency to be self-serving. Old men forget; but younger ones can have surprising lapses of memory as well – official censorship often demands it.

Yet if the obstacles to the study of Israeli intelligence are considerable, there are very powerful incentives. One is the glaring lack of balanced, factual work on the subject whereas the profusion of fictional or sensationalist 'factional' accounts and countless miles of newsprint suggest that interest in it is strong and growing.

John le Carré's bold excursion to the Middle East in *The Little Drummer Girl* remains the best literary treatment of Israeli intelligence and its continuing war against the Palestinians. *Agents of Innocence*, a gripping story by the American author David Ignatius, touches on the subject too. But these successful novels – and several recent, less well-known Hebrew works that have not been translated into other languages – are exceptions. The Arab–Zionist conflict has produced few memorable paperback heroes; many purportedly 'documentary' works owe far more to fantasy than reality.

Operation Uranium Ship,[3] for example, is billed as a 'true' account of how, in 1968, a team of Israeli agents hijacked a ship full of uranium for use in the country's clandestine nuclear programme. The book's dustjacket reveals tantalizingly that the team included:

> A handsome, sophisticated, ruthless Israeli super-agent . . . a beautiful young woman with exquisite sexual skills . . . a wire-thin, lethally efficient professional killer . . . a grizzled sea-captain pressed into perilous service . . . a mechanical genius who performed miracles with anything made of metal . . . and others . . . from the top levels of Israel's scientific and espionage elite to the outmost limits of her worldwide network of operatives.

The real world would be hard put to compete with such superlatives, yet if the truth is not actually stranger than fiction, it is certainly more complex. Secret agents have controllers, and controllers have department heads, just as intelligence chiefs are responsible to ministers, who in turn have diplomacy, budgets, public opinion and elections to think about.

One of the recurrent themes of the history of Israeli intelligence is how politicians keep intruding into the secret world, making demands, exercising control and then ducking responsibility when things go wrong. The fundamental question about the Lavon

Affair, which clouded the horizons of the Israeli intelligence community and intermittently rocked its political life for almost two decades, was 'Who gave the order?' The same deceptively simple question applied equally well to the scandal that erupted in 1986 over the Shin Bet's killing of Arab prisoners and to the recruitment and running of Jonathan Pollard, the American-Jewish spy for Israel whose capture and exposure briefly shook the cosy web of US–Israeli intelligence liaison and exchange.

Another incentive to studying Israeli intelligence is that it really matters. The conflict between the Jewish state and its Arab neighbours remains in some ways as bitter and insoluble today as it was in 1948, when independent Israel fought its way into the world out of the ruins of the British Mandate and the disarray of the Palestinians and the Arab governments which supported them.

When intelligence fails, both in its primary mode as a device intended to provide early warning of enemy strength and intentions, and in its secondary one as a supplier of raw information and considered assessments on the basis of which policies, strategies and tactics can be constructed, the results can be catastrophic. The bitter lessons of the October 1973 war, when much of the blame for the initial disaster was laid at the door of military intelligence, and of the grandiose and wrong-headed design that led to the 1982 invasion of Lebanon have not been forgotten. Yet for all its importance, intelligence does not exist in a vacuum; the advice of secret servants can be – and often is – ignored by the politicians. For it is they, not the spymasters, who must make policy.

The importance of accurate and reliable military and political intelligence has not been diminished by the considerable progress that there has been towards Israeli–Arab coexistence. The Sadat initiative in 1977 and the subsequent peace treaty with Egypt, the de facto peace with Jordan and the slackening of the PLO's 'armed struggle' in the wake of the Lebanon war do not mean that Israeli intelligence can rest on its laurels.

Yehoshafat Harkabi, the brilliant, and now outspokenly 'dovish', former head of military intelligence, has argued persuasively that a sea change has taken place in Arab attitudes towards Israel and that the onus is now on the Jewish state to take up the challenge. 'Knowing your enemy', Harkabi and others have insisted, must include knowing how to see that that enemy may be in the process of becoming a non-belligerant.

But the conflict, with its periodic outbreaks of full-scale warfare and tense, prolonged respites in between, continues. The political and human tragedy of the Palestinians has still not been resolved; without such a resolution, the conflict can only deepen or at best stagnate. Israel's intelligence services are still in the eye of the struggle – military intelligence, with its sensors focused on Syrian and Iraqi armaments and intentions; the Shin Bet as the cutting edge of Israeli rule in the West Bank and Gaza Strip; and the Mossad as the executive arm in the savage battle of terrorism and counter-terrorism in the Middle East and Europe. The Shin Bet's response to the Palestinian uprising – the intifada – in the occupied territories and the Mossad's assassination of Abu Jihad, the senior PLO military leader, in April 1988 have served as reminders of the centrality of these services.

Israel's controversial kidnapping of a militant Lebanese Shi'ite leader, Sheikh Obeid, in July 1989 to obtain a bargaining chip in negotiations to free its soldiers held by pro-Iranian groups in Lebanon provided another of many examples of daring based on precise intelligence and a hard-headed view of its foes. Powerful Arab states like Syria and Iraq continue to pose a military threat to Israel's hold on the occupied territories if not to Israel itself. Iraq's invasion of Kuwait in August 1990 turned the region upside down, breaking old alliances and forming new ones, creating previously unimagined uncertainties and dangers for the future. On different fronts, in the Middle East and beyond, the war goes on.

Israel's intelligence community has come a long way since its origins in the amateurish and improvised information-gathering begun by a handful of dedicated volunteers working for the Haganah militia in British-ruled Palestine of the 1930s. Today, IDF Intelligence Branch (Aman), the Mossad and the Shin Bet together employ thousands of people and spend hundreds of millions of dollars every year on defending Israel from its enemies, acquiring their secrets and penetrating their ranks. Neither are its friends immune. Whether the awesome reputation of Israeli intelligence is wholly deserved remains moot. It is clear, however, that in many Arab countries there is still a strong belief that Israel has a long and dangerous arm, controlled by a subtle and cunning mind.[4]

Too much is at stake in the Middle East conflict for the intelligence activity at the centre of it to be left solely to its anonymous practitioners. *Israel's Secret Wars* treats intelligence with the seriousness it deserves and tries to take spies, secret agents, terrorism and security out of the realm of popular fiction, deliberate leaks and excessive official secrecy and place them firmly where they belong – in the context of history, politics and international relations, and in the real, contemporary world.

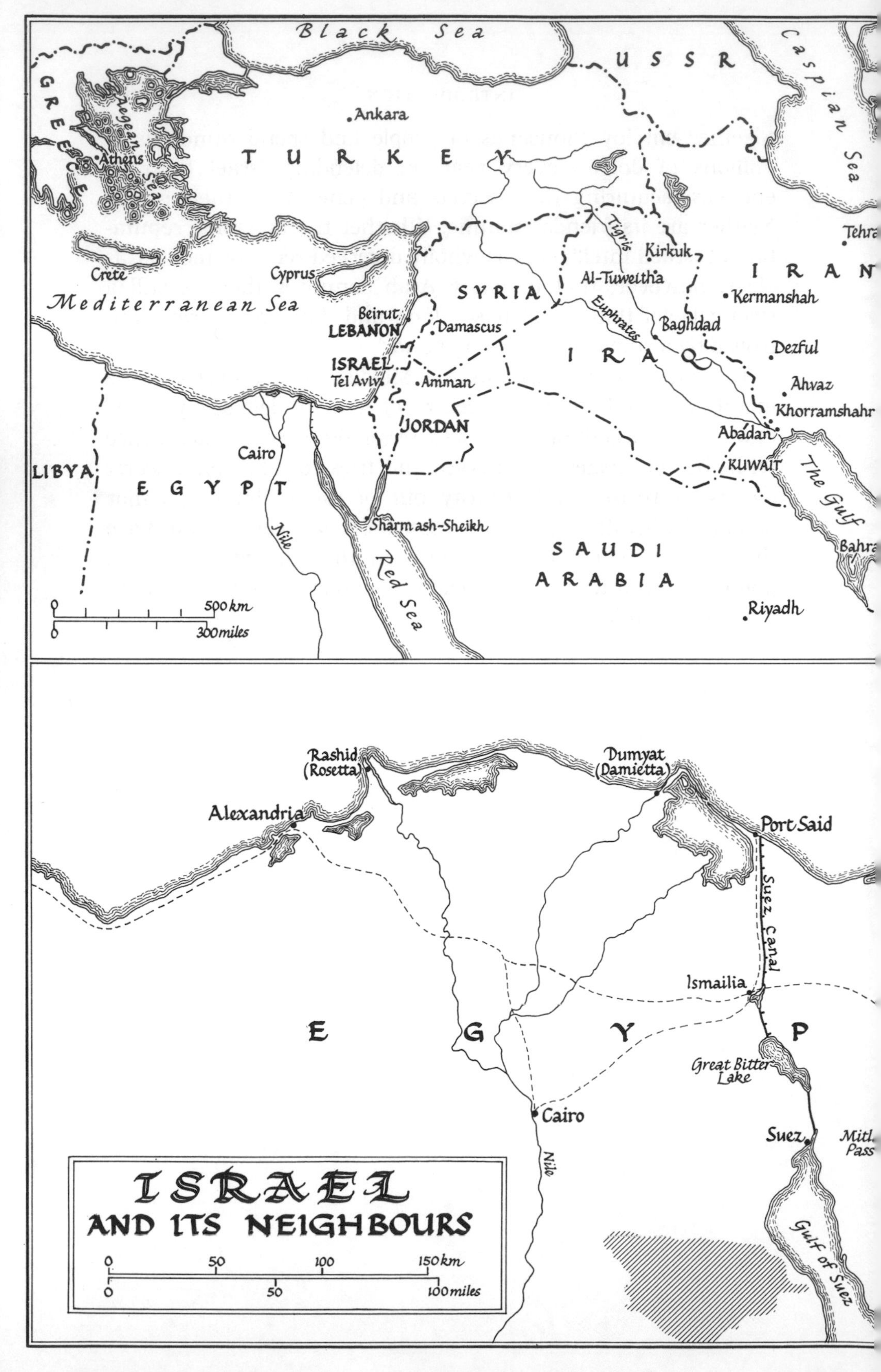
Black Sea
USSR
Caspian Sea
GREECE
Aegean Sea
Athens
Ankara
TURKEY
Tigris
Kirkuk
Tehra
Crete
Cyprus
SYRIA
Al-Tuweitha
IRAN
Kermanshah
Mediterranean Sea
Beirut
LEBANON
Damascus
Euphrates
Baghdad
Dezful
ISRAEL
Tel Aviv
Amman
IRAQ
Ahvaz
Khorramshahr
JORDAN
Abadan
Cairo
KUWAIT
The Gulf
LIBYA
EGYPT
Sharm ash-Sheikh
Nile
Red Sea
SAUDI ARABIA
Bahra
500 km
300 miles
Riyadh
Rashid (Rosetta)
Dumyat (Damietta)
Alexandria
Port Said
Suez Canal
Ismailia
EGYP
Great Bitter Lake
Cairo
Suez
Mitl. Pass
Nile
Gulf of Suez
ISRAEL AND ITS NEIGHBOURS
0
50
100
150 km
0
50
100 miles

Homs
Tripoli
LEBANON
Jounieh
Beirut
Zahle
Damour
Mediterranean
Sea
Sidon
Jezzine
Nabatiyah
Litani
Damascus
Mt Hermon
SYRIA
Tyre
GOLAN
Quneitra
Nahariya
'Akko (Acre)
Safad
CEASEFIRE LINES 1974
Haifa
GALILEE
Lake Tiberias
Jabal Druze
Mt Carmel
Zikhron Ya'akov
Hadera
Bet She'an
Irbid
Jenin
Netanya
Qabatiya
Tulkarm
ISRAEL
Nablus
Qalqilya
Tel Aviv-Jaffa
SAMARIA
WEST BANK
Jordan
Zarqa
Lod (Lydda)
Allenby Bridge
Rehovot
Ramallah
Jericho
Amman
Ashdod
Jerusalem
Ashkelon
JUDAEA
PALESTINE
GAZA STRIP
Gaza
Hebron
Dead Sea
ARMISTICE LINE 1949
Rafah
Khan Yunis
Beersheba
JORDAN
Yamit
El Arish
Sodom
Dimona
N
NEGEV
Ma'an
SINAI
Eilat
Aqaba
Gulf of Aqaba
Main roads
Land over 500m (1640 feet)

1

Origins: 1936–46

The Arab strike and the failure of Haganah intelligence

On the evening of Wednesday, 15 April 1936, several armed Palestinians blocked the narrow road between the little village of Anabta and the British detention camp at Nur Shams – a lonely and exclusively Arab area at the western end of the rolling Samarian uplands – and stopped about twenty vehicles to demand money to buy weapons and ammunition. One of them, a truck carrying crates of chickens to Tel Aviv, had a Jewish driver, Zvi Danenberg, and a Jewish passenger, a poultry-firm clerk of about seventy called Yisrael Hazan, a recent immigrant from Salonika in Greece. A third Jew was travelling in another car. The Arab bandits rounded up the three and shot them. Hazan was killed outright and the other two were injured. Danenberg died later of his wounds.

The next day, 16 April, two Jews – easily identifiable as such since they were bare-headed and wearing khaki shorts – drove up to a tin shack close to the road between Petah-Tikva and Sharona, in Palestine's fertile coastal plain east of Tel Aviv. The two, members of a dissident Zionist militia group called Irgun Bet, knocked on the door and fired inside, killing one Arab and badly wounding another. Before he died, the injured man managed to describe his assailants to British policemen. Both police and Arabs assumed at once that the attack was in retaliation for the previous day's incident in Samaria. 'If the perpetrators had imagined that they would thus put an end to the bloodshed in Palestine,' a mainstream Zionist historian commented dryly later, 'they were very soon to be disappointed.'[1]

On Friday, 17 April, Yisrael Hazan was buried in Tel Aviv. His funeral quickly turned into a large and angry demonstration against both British and Arabs, with members of the local Jewish community calling for revenge attacks against neighbouring Arab Jaffa. Shops in Allenby Street, the main commercial thoroughfare, were forced to close as thousands of mourners thronged round Hazan's flag-draped coffin while the cortège made its way from Hadassah Hospital to the city's old cemetery. Police used batons and fired into the air to control the swelling crowd. A passing Arab was badly beaten, as was a policeman who came to his assistance.

There was more unrest the next day, the Jewish Sabbath. Arab pedlars and shoeshine boys from Jaffa were beaten up by Jewish thugs, but calm returned towards evening. British troops who had been rushed in from nearby Ramle to reinforce the overstretched Tel Aviv police were sent back to camp, and the headquarters of the Jewish Haganah militia force cancelled the general alert declared a few days earlier.

On Sunday, 19 April, just four days after the ambush near Nur Shams, life in the Tel Aviv area returned to normal. Hundreds of Jews went to their offices and businesses in Jaffa, others to government departments in and around the Old Port behind the clocktower. The trouble started with a rumour: three Syrian labourers and a local Arab woman had been killed in Tel Aviv. It wasn't true. By 9.00 that spring morning a large crowd of Arabs had gathered outside the government offices in the old Turkish Serail building, demanding the bodies of the 'victims'. Dozens of Jews were stabbed or beaten up, although many were given shelter in Arab homes until the fury was spent. Others escaped via the port back to Tel Aviv. A British police officer shot and killed two Arabs who were attacking a Jewish car. The army was called back from Ramle and by the afternoon the authorities had more or less regained control. A curfew was imposed on both Jaffa and Tel Aviv and a state of emergency declared all over the country. Nine Jews had been killed and nearly sixty injured.

By the standards of both earlier and later conflicts in the Middle East in general and in Palestine in particular, the bloodshed in Jaffa that Sunday was on a relatively minor scale. But in the spring of 1936 the Holy Land was teetering on the edge of a volcano, its calm and prosperity precarious. And afterwards it would never be the same again.

After the previous spate of disturbances in 1929, triggered by the clashes over prayer rights at the Wailing Wall in the Old City of Jerusalem and general Arab fears of the expansionist nature of the Zionist enterprise, Palestine had been relatively quiet for nearly seven years. British troops had easily crushed a local rebellion in the Haifa area in 1933; its leader, the charismatic Sheikh Izzedin al-Qassem, was killed in a British ambush in November 1935, a revered martyr for a cause that seemed to be going nowhere fast.

Zionist land purchases continued apace and despite verbal protests there was little organized Arab opposition to the massive wave of Jewish immigration that began shortly after Hitler became German chancellor. In 1935 62,000 Jews entered Palestine, the highest annual number since 1920, when the British Mandate began over the territory captured from the Ottoman Turks in the First World War. By 1936 there were 400,000 Jews in the country, slightly more than a third of the total population. And 40 per cent of the Jews – about 150,000 – had been there for five years or less.

The British High Commissioner, Sir Arthur Grenfell Wauchope, was extremely popular with the Zionists, and the Yishuv (the Jewish community in Palestine) forged ahead in economic strength and social cohesion, despite acrimony and occasional violence between the Mapai-dominated Labour movement and right-wing Revisionist Zionists of various hues. The institutions of Jewish Palestine were modern, well planned and confident.

The Jewish Agency, founded in 1929, acted as a sort of parallel administration to the British government, coordinating immigration and settlement activities, with its key Political

Department monitoring developments in the Arab sector and maintaining contacts with Arab leaders inside and outside Palestine. The Haganah militia, closely linked to the powerful Histadrut labour federation, was already well developed and organized on a country-wide basis, despite the semi-clandestine conditions in which it had to operate.

The long-running debate over the creation of a Legislative Council had been shelved, thanks to a classic combination of British dithering, Zionist opposition and Arab disunity. But towards the end of 1935 financial insecurity and mounting political instability in the eastern Mediterranean put an abrupt end to Palestine's fat years. Mussolini's invasion of Abyssinia had badly damaged British prestige in the area and many Arabs looked to fascist Italy and Nazi Germany to liberate them from their colonial and mandatory yokes. The fall in investments in the lucrative citrus-fruit sector led to the dismissal of both Jewish and Arab workers, while riots and promises of constitutional change in both Egypt and Syria – keenly observed by the Palestinians – came as ominous warnings of trouble pending nearer home.

It is widely agreed that the outbreak of the riots in Jaffa caught the Yishuv unawares – perhaps the first of many occasions in Zionist and Israeli history when the Jews were taken aback by the timing or strength of Arab opposition. And even when the dead had been counted and buried it took time before the scale of the problem was fully appreciated. On 17 April, monitoring movements around the main Jaffa mosque, Haganah intelligence officers had seen no reason to report that anything was amiss.[2]

At the fortress-like headquarters of the Jewish Agency in Jerusalem's Rehavia neighbourhood, the Arab experts attached to the Political Department were not, at that early stage, unduly worried. One official reported on 22 April: 'The general impression at the office here – in particular also that of the Arab Division – is that while the possibility of some trouble tomorrow cannot be entirely ruled out, there is no ground for apprehending anything in the nature of a serious disturbance of the peace.'[3] The assessment was terribly wrong. Only three days later the heads of five different Arab political parties buried their differences and formed the Arab Higher Committee (AHC), under the presidency of the most powerful of the country's leaders, the Mufti of Jerusalem, Haj Amin al-Husseini. Its first decision was to continue the general strike already declared spontaneously and simultaneously by newly formed 'national committees' – local bodies mirroring the national coalition of the AHC – in Jaffa, Nablus and elsewhere.

In one sense, the Arab strike played right into the hands of the Jews. The stoppage by the stevedores in Jaffa port led to demands for the creation of a Jewish harbour in Tel Aviv. Jewish workers, often escorted by British troops, were introduced into sectors of the economy previously monopolized by Arabs. The peasantry, the vast majority of the Arab population, continued to harvest their spring crops. But the Jews quickly began to boycott Arab agricultural produce, deliberately using the strike and the accompanying disturbances as a tool with which to galvanize the Yishuv into a more nationalist spirit. 'Hebrew labour' and 'Hebrew produce', the subject of prolonged and often bitter struggle between the Labour movement and the private Jewish farming sector, advanced by leaps and bounds in this period. Where cheap and unorganized Arab day labourers had worked before, Jewish workers now stepped in. Moshe Shertok, head of the Political Department, was told of the reaction in the old wine-producing settlements of Atlit and nearby Zikhron Ya'akov when 'Hebrew labour' was introduced. 'One farmer worked out that Jewish grapes cost him only 3 mils [a few pennies] more per ton than Arab grapes,' Shertok noted in his diary, 'and as well as that he saves his health as he doesn't need to stand in the sun all day shouting "yallah" ["Come on"] at the Arab women.'[4]

But there were serious dangers as well. Immediately after the Jaffa riots Jews were attacked by Arabs all over the country, both in the other main cities and in isolated areas, where farms were raided and crops destroyed. Transport facilities were hit hard. For several months the main Zionist effort against the

Palestinians was political and diplomatic, trying to convince the British of the need to crack down hard on Arab offenders and strikers, persuading the Palestine government that they were faced with criminals and hooligans and not with a politically inspired rebellion against the Mandate and the Zionist enterprise. In mid-May, for example, Dr Chaim Weizmann, the Russian-born Anglophile who had headed the Zionist movement since before the Balfour Declaration in 1917, told the British prime minister, Stanley Baldwin, that 'Arab discontent was not really deep seated; the Arab peasant was not interested, but he was terrorized into it'.[5]

Ezra Danin: knowing the enemy

But the strike and the violence continued and security soon became an overriding concern. Ezra Danin, a native of Jaffa working as a citrus farmer and agricultural expert in Hadera, half-way between Haifa and Tel Aviv, had already been approached by the local Haganah commander and asked to use his extensive Arab contacts to try and solve the murders of two Jews killed in ambushes on the Haifa–Qalqilya road.[6] Danin, then aged thirty-three, recruited a young Arab from the village of Khirbet Manshieh, close to the kibbutzim Ein Hahoresh and Givat Haim. The Arab's family, typically, had previously been involved in land sales to the Jews. Danin saw the man regularly and began to submit written reports to the Haganah and to a young Jewish Agency official called Reuven Zaslani, one of the Political Department's experts on security and Arab affairs. 'As time went on,' Danin wrote in his autobiography, 'my senses got sharper and sharper. From a dedicated farmer, who had never thought before about problems of politics and security, I began to devote myself mostly to intelligence.'[7]

From these modest and haphazard beginnings in the early summer of 1936, Ezra Danin came to occupy a legendary position in the annals of Zionist and Israeli intelligence work. It was Danin who laid the foundations for the collection, interpretation and use of intelligence about the Arabs in the crucial years of the struggle for Palestine. And more than half a century later his ideas about 'knowing the enemy' could still be traced in Israeli policy towards the Palestinians.

Josh Palmon, who became a close friend and valued colleague, paid glowing tribute to Danin later:

> In the years between 1936 and 1940 we all talked about *the* enemy with the definite article. Ezra said: 'We are not confronting *the* Arabs, but a very specific Arab. We need to know who he is. Some lad sits up on a hill or down in a valley and fires – and we all scream and panic and leap into the trenches when all we're really talking about is Ali or Muhammad. We have to be able to identify him and act against him.'
>
> Ezra also said that we must analyse every fact and every incident, to look at things in depth and not see everything that glitters as gold. That was his decisive contribution. His was a critical, scientific approach, not one that made do with superficial impressions. Only thus, Ezra argued, will we be able to distinguish between an ally and an enemy . . . Thus Ezra laid the foundations for our Middle East intelligence work.[8]

Danin was not the only Jew working on intelligence matters in this early period, although he was quickly recognized as the most expert in the Arab field. Ephraim Krasner, a member of the British police in Tel Aviv, had extensive contacts in the force. In Haifa Emmanuel Wilensky, a Ukrainian-born architect and engineer, had been working for the Haganah and the Jewish Agency since 1933, gathering information about Britons, Jews and Arabs. Wilensky was a keen archaeologist who believed that intelligence work should be conducted on similar scientific principles and he disliked Danin's tendency to 'embroider' his reports in a dramatic way in order to persuade his 'customers' of their accuracy. Wilensky often complained that his dry and factual style of reporting could not compete with Danin's 'juicy letters'. He abandoned intelligence work in 1939.[9]

Danin's informer from Khirbet Manshieh was the first of many he worked with. As the violence continued that summer, he began to expand, recruiting not only other Arabs but Jews as well – both in rural settlements and in towns – to act as permanent 'collators'. In the early days they included a Jewish corporal serving in the British police station in Kfar Saba, north-east of Tel Aviv, and another man who dealt with Jewish butchers who bought cattle from Arabs. Eliahu Golomb, the commander of the Haganah, allocated Danin a monthly budget of £6, but it wasn't enough. Throughout the period from April to October 1936, when the Arab strike ended, Danin was spending an additional £15 a month of his own money on expenses and payments to informers. By 1939, the monthly budget had soared to £45.

As Danin wrote afterwards:

> The Arab informers got favours in return, and only rarely money, since financial reward was not the main reason they worked with us. Almost all of them were persecuted by their brothers because of ties of commerce or land-dealing with the Jews, or because of internal conflicts, and so they had strong personal reasons for wanting to harm, neutralize – or even get rid of – their persecutors. They all feared for their lives and wanted to be able to take refuge with us in time of trouble, or to defend their villages. We tried to exploit these situations and we made efforts to locate Arabs who were in need of assistance.[10]

Danin's intelligence reports were of varying quality and tended, inevitably, to concentrate on local information, but they also went beyond mere collection. A physically large man, Danin had a strong sense of his own expertise and authority, and he needed no one to tell him what to do – a characteristic which endeared him to many, but not to all who worked with him.

At the end of August 1936, for example, an informer identified as 'M.N.' reported to him that Arabs from 'Atil village were planning to lay mines on the road from Givat Haim to nearby Hadera. 'I told M.N.,' Danin recorded, 'to return to his village and tell them that if anything happened on the road then revenge would be taken against the boys.' At the same time he warned the local Haganah men to be on the alert for trouble.[11]

In the same period the Political Department's Arab Division tried various means to foment dissension within the enemy camp, combining straightforward bribery with simple disinformation. Groups of striking Arabs were paid to go back to work, and fake Arabic leaflets signed by non-existent organizations such as 'The Patriotic Drivers of Palestine' were produced, criticizing national leaders. Letters from Arab notables, such as Awni Abdel-Hadi, the Istiqlal party chief, were intercepted by the Zionists, giving the Jewish Agency experts a good idea of the way things were developing on the Arab side.[12]

Intelligence work became increasingly important as the Arab disturbances continued, claiming about eighty Jewish lives by the time they peaked in August. At the end of that month Danin wrote a memorandum proposing the creation of a formal Haganah intelligence service and explaining why such a service was needed. The remarkable two-page, handwritten document contains all the basic outlines of how modern intelligence work should be organized and conducted. He argued that:

> The attacks against us appeared to begin spontaneously and because we were unprepared we suffered many casualties at their start. Since the government is either also uninformed or doesn't want to crush the trouble we must find a solution by setting up our own Haganah intelligence service. The intelligence work must be carried out all the time, even when things are quiet, as happens in every country. Thus we will be able to predict and perhaps prevent future outbreaks.

Intelligence, Danin proposed, must keep tabs on post offices and telephone exchanges, maintain lists of Arab clubs, organizations and information on political activists, including their addresses, car licence numbers and the names of friends and relatives. Arab groups should be infiltrated by two independent agents (he used the word *balashim* – detectives) 'so they can [also] spy on each other'. Information should be exploited to create internal squabbles. The agents must not know whom they are working for and should be kept in a state of intimidation. Invisible ink should be used.[13]

Reuven Zaslani: born for intelligence

If Ezra Danin was one pillar on which the structure of the fledgling Zionist intelligence and security apparatus was to be built, Reuven Zaslani was the other. Zaslani, aged twenty-seven in 1936, was the Jerusalem-born son of an eminent Russian rabbi. He was well connected in the Mapai political establishment, had already had a varied career and showed promise in both Arab affairs and information-gathering. Zaslani was a graduate of a Jerusalem teacher-training college and the oriental studies faculty of the Hebrew University, whose Arabic prize he had won in 1931. He had spent a year teaching Hebrew in Baghdad and served as a part-time correspondent for the *Palestine Bulletin*, a Zionist-owned English-language weekly, and had reported informally to the Political Department on both Iraqi politics and the country's Jewish community. Returning home in 1934, he dealt with Arab affairs for the Histadrut, and began to work with the Political Department shortly after the April riots in Jaffa. He had also had contact with Royal Air Force intelligence, which was responsible for all British military intelligence activities in the Middle East.

In February 1937, during a lull in the disturbances, Zaslani's position became formalized and full-time. 'Intelligence on security matters' was how he defined his task when he wrote, early that month, to Haim Sturman and Nahum Horowitz in the north, two veteran and widely respected settlers, asking them to contribute occasional reports on Arab affairs in their vicinity.[14]

Zaslani was a young man of enormous energy, but he was difficult to work with. Frenetic, untidy, disorganized and obsessively secretive, he seemed to have been born for the world of intelligence. Teddy Kollek, who worked with him later in the Political Department, liked to tell the story of how Zaslani was so secretive, he once snapped, 'There's no need for you to know' at a taxi driver who asked where he wanted to go.[15] For Marcus Sieff, the British Jew who became an informal adviser to Ben-Gurion in 1948, Zaslani's appearance 'was that of a super-spy in a James Bond film'.[16]

Danin and Zaslani became a powerful team, their partnershp providing a badly needed point of contact and coordination between the Haganah and the Jewish Agency. Both men were well placed to cultivate useful contacts with Arabs. However, their work was very different from the more conventionally diplomatic activities of Elias (Eliahu) Sasson, the Political Department's Damascus-born Arab expert, and Eliahu Epstein, a brilliant Russian-born academic who became the department's resident specialist on the Muslim world and the Arab countries neighbouring Palestine. Diplomacy still had an important role to play, but in intelligence and security terms the Palestinians were simply becoming the enemy. The British authorities, in the form of the Royal Commission appointed in August 1936, recognized the way the winds were blowing.

Six wise men

The Peel Commission arrived in Jerusalem in mid-November 1936, shortly after the end of the Arab strike. It had been appointed 'to ascertain the underlying causes of the disturbances which broke out in Palestine in April', but was briefed also to inquire more widely into the implementation of the Mandate, British obligations towards Arabs and Jews, the existence of grievances and 'to make recommendations for their removal and the prevention of their recurrence'. Lord Peel, the chairman, had served twice as secretary of state for India and on many commissions of inquiry. His five colleagues were no less illustrious.

The six heard more than 100 witnesses at seventy sessions in the dining room of Jerusalem's opulent Palace Hotel, opposite the ancient Muslim cemetery of Mamilla. The Arab Higher Committee, led by the Mufti of Jerusalem, Haj Amin al-Husseini, boycotted the hearings until almost the end in early January 1937, because of the government's failure to suspend Jewish immigration to Palestine while work was in progress.

The Jews made by far the better impression. In his public

testimony Dr Weizmann set out his arguments powerfully, sketching the broad outlines of Jewish history, the rise of modern anti-Semitism, the plight of the Jewish masses in Eastern Europe and his own attempts to reach agreement with the Arabs, although this was, by all accounts, the weakest part of an otherwise masterly performance.

The British official witnesses took the Peel Commission through the weary and complex story of trying to run the Mandate between the conflicting pressures of 400,000 Jews and nearly 1 million Arabs, the questions of land sales and immigration being the thorniest issues and their cessation being the main Arab demands of the general strike and disturbances.

The Palestine government officials did not put it quite like this, but the overall effect must have been similar to the summary of a percipient Jewish observer who once explained the working of the Mandate in terms of a minor English public school. 'There was the headmaster, the High Commissioner, trying to be firm and impartial, but the assistant masters favoured the sporting stupid boarders (Arabs) against the clever swot dayboys (Jews) who had the deplorable habit of writing home to their parents on the slightest provocation to complain about the quality of the teaching, the food and so on.' Haj Amin kicked off the Arab testimonies on 12 January 1937, with sinister references to the 'Jews' ultimate aim' being to reconstruct the Temple of Solomon on the site of the Haram ash-Sharif (the Temple Mount or Mount Moriah) in Jerusalem. He again demanded a complete halt to Jewish immigration and said ominously that the question of whether or not these newcomers would be permitted to stay in an independent Muslim Palestine would have to be left to the future.

As they listened patiently to the rival claims, the idea of a territorial division began to take root in the commissioners' minds. Outside the dining room of the Palace Hotel (where the chandeliers had been bugged by Jewish technicians so that the secret hearings could be heard back in Jewish Agency headquarters on the other side of the Mamilla cemetery), they could not fail to be impressed by what the Zionists had achieved in the twenty years since General Allenby had driven the Turks out of the Holy Land.

After a short visit to the Emir Abdullah in Transjordan (a stenographic report of the meeting reaching the Jewish Agency a fortnight later), the commissioners left Palestine in the third week of January. Professor Reginald Coupland of Oxford, the most cerebral member of the team, was already being persuasive in pushing the partition idea. 'Jewish nationalism is as intense and self-centred as Arab nationalism,' he and his colleagues were to conclude in their famous report. 'Both are growing forces and the gulf between them is widening.'[17]

Zaslani and Danin were the first to appreciate the point made by the British commissioners. The end of the Arab strike had not deluded the Zionists that the struggle was over. When the violence resumed in earnest in September 1937, they were better prepared than before to meet the challenge, and this time the British authorities were more determined to crush the Arab unrest. When Arab rebels assassinated Lewis Andrews, the British district commissioner in Nazareth, the government was galvanized into action. Martial law was declared and the Arab Higher Committee and national committees declared illegal. Many Palestinian leaders, including Haj Amin, fled the country. Others were deported.

Rebellion in Palestine

By summer 1938, a fully fledged revolt was in progress. Zaslani was kept busy urging the British to provide greater protection for outlying Jewish settlements and to make better use of the forces at their disposal. A large-scale Arab attack on Givat Ada, near Zikhron Ya'akov, had caused particular concern. 'I said it was very essential for the government to act quickly and radically,' Zaslani told the head of the British Criminal Investigation Department (CID). 'It was vitally necessary that the government should punish the villagers involved in the attack on

Givat Ada in a spectacular form so that it should act as a deterrent against similar attacks.'[18]

At the end of July Zaslani obtained a *laissez-passer* from British police headquarters, allowing him to drive undisturbed to Haifa. Unbeknown to the authorities, the man named in the document as his driver, Mr E. Golomb, was none other than Eliahu Golomb, the commander of the Haganah.[19] The Arabs were doing well. Whole areas were under rebel control and police stations were regularly attacked. In September 1938 the British military commander, General Haining, reported gloomily to London that 'the situation was such that civil administration and control of the country was, to all practical purposes, non-existent'.[20]

One bright spot on an otherwise gloomy horizon came in the form of an eccentric British officer and fervent Christian Zionist called Captain Charles Orde Wingate. His Special Night Squads (SNS), composed of a mixed force of British soldiers and Haganah volunteers, scored significant successes against the Arab rebels in the lower Galilee and in the Jezreel Valley. The SNS operations encouraged the Haganah to be bolder, to use night ambushes and to go out and meet their Arab enemy on his own ground, without waiting for attacks on settlements. Wingate, who liked to read from the Bible while stark naked and munch raw onions, was eventually recalled to London; but 'HaYedid' (the friend), as he was known to the Zionists, left the Haganah with a taste for special operations and derring-do that was to stand it in good stead in the years of struggle to come.

A routine report Danin sent to Zaslani in early October gives a good idea of the concerns and methods of Zionist intelligence at this time. It contained details of internal 'courts' set up by the rebels: a new informer ('he works with great precision') had supplied details of a clandestine Arab centre for the production of mines and the use of gelignite to blow up electricity poles. The culprits were from the Qalqilya area. A platoon of Royal Hussars from Tulkarm had conducted ambushes in an area shown them by Danin. Arab dogs were a problem, since their barking provided warning of the British raids. It would be useful to persuade the government to declare an outbreak of rabies in the area so that all dogs could be put down. Various Arabs working for the British had links with the rebels and should be dismissed. Villagers whose houses had been blown up by the army were being helped to rebuild them by their neighbours. This should be stopped. Arab women, who were not searched by soldiers, had smuggled four revolvers aboard the Netanya–Tulkarm bus. When, the report concluded, would Zaslani send more money to cover mounting costs for paying informers?[21]

Danin's activities were known to the Palestinians. One of his later reports to Zaslani, which was based on the detailed interrogation of a rebel captured by the British army, contained the fascinating snippet that in Khirbet Manshieh, near Hadera, there was an Arab known as the 'mouse' who spied for 'Ezra', the Jewish citrus farmer. He had been caught and sentenced to death, but managed to escape to Syria.[22] The 'mouse' from Khirbet Manshieh was almost certainly the same informer whose recruitment in the summer of 1936 launched Danin on his new career as spymaster.

Both Danin and Zaslani had cultivated useful contacts in British military intelligence. Information gathered by the Jews about the movements, weapons and hiding places of the Arab bands was regularly passed to the authorities. Typically in this period, British troops would enter a village and Danin would supply Arab informers to sit safely inside an armoured car and identify known rebels. Some of those captured were hanged.

Danin always tried to make sure that Palestinians were severely punished. 'Bringing members of the gangs to court often involved complicated and sensitive preparation of the Arab witnesses giving evidence against them,' he wrote later. 'Our lawyer would prepare the witnesses before the trial in order to prevent possible mistakes that could lead to the acquittal of the criminals. The witnesses were real witnesses, but it was sometimes necessary to "smooth out" the details so there would be no contradictions and the gang members wouldn't escape justice because of "technical hitches".'[23]

The British police were often hostile and thought they were being taken for a ride by the Zionists. A sergeant at the Beit Lidd station, for example, said that 'all the information given by the Jews is false, and intended solely to kill Arabs'. Danin complained in November 1938 that Arabs he had named had been arrested by the police but then released.[24]

Relations with the army, which had made it a priority to crush the revolt, were far better and documents captured by the British from the rebels were handed over freely, giving Danin and the Jewish Agency Arabists a unique insight into both the social basis and *modus operandi* of the Palestinian fighters. The mounting signs of internal divisions in the Arab camp were readily exploited by both the Jews and British. The Arab opposition to the Mufti, which was headed by the prestigious Nashashibi family of Jerusalem, sought and received help from the Jewish Agency. Arab 'peace bands' were set up and the army, directed by RAF intelligence, supplied them with money and weapons and in return were given information about the location of rebel gangs. 'We encouraged the peace gangs,' Danin said, 'and tried to influence the police to let them carry on undisturbed. We also helped them to conceal their identities when they came to give information to the authorities.'[25]

By early 1939 the Arab rebellion was clearly waning. In March the commander-in-chief of the revolt, Abdel-Rahim al-Haj Muhammad, was killed by the army in a Samarian village after the British had received information about his whereabouts from a 'peace band' commander. Rebel gangs fled to Syria and the Palestinians were more deeply divided than ever before. By the summer it was all but over. The Zionists should have been pleased, but they were losing disastrously on the diplomatic front. The British government White Paper of May 1939 finally killed off all hopes of the partition scheme suggested by the Peel Commission. Worse still, Jewish immigration – the very lifeblood of the Zionist enterprise – was to be severely restricted, as was the sale of land to Jews. Within ten years an independent Palestinian state was to be set up.

The White Paper, war and the Shai

The gradual collapse of the Arab rebellion and the outbreak of the war in Europe in September brought an uneasy peace to Palestine. Despite the draconian White Paper, the Yishuv gradually began to enjoy a calm and prosperity it had not known since early 1936. It was not until 1942 that news of what was happening in the distant ghettos and death camps of Eastern Europe began to filter back to Palestine and there was a general feeling that the situation should be exploited to prepare the Yishuv in general and the Haganah in particular for the next stage of confrontation with both the Arabs and the British, whenever and in whatever form it came.

The existing intelligence system, such as it was, was rearranged in early 1940 after a wave of arrests of Haganah members by the British authorities, who were now determined to crack down on the organization. As early as June 1939 one of Zaslani's agents in Haifa had reported that the CID was suddenly displaying great interest in the structure of the Haganah and the activities of Jewish fishermen in illegal immigration, which began in earnest once the White Paper was published.[26]

Haganah national command set up a counter-espionage department (*rigul negdi*), which was mainly intended to operate as an internal security service to monitor Jews who collaborated with the British, as well as the right-wing dissidents of the Irgun. Shaul Meirov (Avigur) had overall responsibility for these matters, and the department was organized by David Shaltiel, a former French Foreign Legionnaire and travelling salesman known universally but rather obviously as 'Tsarfati' (the Frenchman). In June an Arab department was formally set up under Ezra Danin, although, in accordance with the British amateur tradition he so admired, Danin retained his independent status and was never formally employed by the Haganah.

In 1940 and 1941, however, most of the Haganah's intelligence efforts were directed against Jewish collaborators with the British. Investigations were conducted against criminals, underworld types or Jewish women who had formed liaisons with British soldiers or officials, and others suspected of being too close to the mandatory authorities. A special section was organized to monitor Jewish Communists. Some 200 people were put under surveillance, although many of the charges or suspicions eventually turned out to be groundless. Some got off with a severe warning or a beating. But in serious cases, involving arrests or the discovery of Haganah arms caches by the CID, counter-espionage would go to the national command and demand the death penalty. The official history of the Haganah is coy on numbers but it states baldly that 'several informers and traitors' were executed in this period.[27]

Time and effort were expended on the Zionist dissident groups too, especially when it became clear that the Irgun was trying hard to locate Haganah weapons stores and was using various ploys to try and sow dissension in the ranks of the larger, mainstream organization. Members of the smaller Stern Gang (Lehi) were captured and imprisoned by Shaltiel's counter-espionage men and forced under interrogation to reveal their own operational plans and the location of their arsenals.

In June 1940 Meirov submitted a proposal to the Haganah command and to Moshe Shertok, head of the Political Department, for the creation of a joint country-wide information service (*sherut yediot*), to be known by its Hebrew acronym as the Shai. The proposal went into effect that September, with counter-espionage becoming just one of the three departments of the new body. But it was not until March 1942, when Yisrael Zavlodovsky (Amir) replaced Shaltiel and was appointed overall head of the Shai, that the Haganah's various intelligence departments were finally united under one roof in a Tel Aviv office whose 'cover' was as premises for the Soldiers' Welfare Committee.

Amir, an expert on clandestine arms procurement (*rekhesh*), knew nothing about intelligence when he was given the job and anxiously devoured every book he could find on the subject. In its new form the Shai bypassed the normal military channels and answered directly to the Haganah command and to the Political Department. Broadly, it was composed of three departments: counter-espionage (or 'internal'), dealing with Jews; a British (or 'political') department, charged with infiltrating the armed forces, police and Palestine government; and Danin's Arab Department. Organizationally, the same format was retained until the Shai was finally disbanded in June 1948, a few weeks after Israel's independence.

Danin was naturally suspicious of high politics and was always happier chatting to a simple peasant than exchanging formal pleasantries with a sophisticated, tarbooshed, urban effendi. 'My interests remained first and foremost in reducing the daily friction between us and the Arabs,' he wrote later. 'Despite what was written in the Arab newspapers and what was said in the sermons in the mosques and in the politicians' salons, I favoured an effort to reduce the casualties of confrontation, to improve relations between Jewish settlements and Arab villages.'[28]

But he nevertheless began to work more closely with the Arab Division of the Political Department, headed by Eliahu Sasson. Ze'ev Sharef, a Jewish Agency official, was appointed to oversee the work of the Shai's Arab Department, again emphasizing its role as the servant of both the military and political wings of the Yishuv. Sharef's administrative abilities were a useful complement to Danin's unrivalled experience and instincts. They decided that Palestine was to be divided up into squares, and in each of the squares an intelligence collator appointed to report on local Arab affairs. Danin found £6 a month (then the salary of a policeman) out of his meagre budget to employ an assistant, a young watchman from Hadera called Shimshon Mashbetz. Together they scoured the country in Danin's car, looking for likely recruits, mostly among watchmen and mukhtars (headmen) of Jewish settlements. Jewish cattle traders and butchers were a favourite too, because of their regular contact with Arabs in outlying rural areas and the thin line that often divided their commercial activities from smuggling. Many of these contacts had worked with Danin since the 1936 troubles. 'We looked for anyone,' Mashbetz said later, 'who had connections with the Arabs.'[29]

When the system started to operate at full steam, Mashbetz would drive round on his motorbike once a fortnight with new questions and instructions from Danin, collecting the information and bringing it back to Hadera, where it was processed and sifted. Later, around the end of the war, Mashbetz was replaced by Benjamin (Binyamin) Gibli, who rose to head the Arab Shai in Jerusalem in 1948 and became the second head of the Israeli army's intelligence branch. The general quality of the agent reports was patchy and often unreliable at the beginning, but it improved with time.

The raw material that formed these reports is still classified, over forty years later, but the 'finished product' soon achieved wide circulation in both the Jewish Agency and the Haganah. In these reports the Shai agents were never identified by name, only by location. Thus Danin's man in Kibbutz Alonim in northern Galilee was identified as 'Aloni'; the agent in the Haifa Bay area (*Mifratz Haifa* in Hebrew) as 'Mifratzi'; the representative in Kibbutz Kfar Menachem in the south as 'Menachemi', and so on. By 1947 Danin had between thirty and fifty regular correspondents, all volunteers, as well as a handful of high-quality Arab sources, known only by their Hebrew codenames: the best was 'HaNoter' (the watchman), but HaIkar (the farmer), 'HaHazan' (the cantor) and 'HaPoel Ha'Aravi' (the Arab worker) were highly valued too.

'Menachemi', whose real name was David Karon, was one of Danin's best agents and in many ways a model for the others. In 1940, when he first met Danin, Karon was one of the founder members of Kfar Menachem, set up by the left-wing HaShomer HaTzair movement in barren countryside surrounded by Arab villages. For obvious security reasons, the new Jewish settlement – originally founded by a different group of pioneers in 1937 – was constructed, like all others in this period, in the distinctive 'stockade and watchtower' mode. Karon was a committed and inquisitive young man who had joined the Haganah shortly after arriving in Palestine from Russia in 1931 to study agriculture and had recently returned home unscathed from eighteen months' fighting with the Polish Battalion of the International Brigade in Spain.

Since Karon, still only in his mid-twenties, had already acquired considerable military experience, it was natural enough that he became the young kibbutz's watchman and security expert, a task which brought him into close and regular contact with his new Arab neighbours. He started to learn colloquial Arabic and generally absorb the experiences and customs of Palestinian rural life. And his long and distinguished career in secret intelligence began in earnest when a young peasant from the nearby village of Tina volunteered some interesting information about an incident towards the end of the rebellion the previous year. Six Jewish employees of the Palestine Electric Corporation, sent to repair power lines damaged by the rebels, had been murdered at Masmiya, a couple of miles away on the main road south to Gaza. The perpetrators had never been caught, but Karon's informant knew who and where they were. Karon quickly filed a detailed report to Haganah headquarters in Tel Aviv and it was not long before Ezra Danin arrived at Kfar Menachem, looking for him.

It was the beginning of a lifelong relationship founded on mutual admiration and personal trust. Karon then knew little or nothing of the fledgling Shai organization, but he was impressed by Danin and deeply interested in the Arabs. 'As far as I was concerned Ezra was the Haganah's representative for Arab intelligence,' Karon recalled years later. 'He told me what sort of things would be of interest and we became close friends.'[30]

Karon learned quickly to distinguish between the political affiliations and internal hierarchies of the Arab villages in the vicinity. Some were loyal supporters of the Nashashibi-led opposition (the *Mu'aridin*), which had its heartland in the Hebron area to the east. Others, especially Masmiya, which had links to Gaza, were pro-Mufti and therefore potentially very hostile. Any information which might be useful was gratefully received and filed away: conflicts between different families, personal rivalries and intrigues, debts and so on.

Some time in 1940 Danin asked Mashbetz to organize a

course in Haifa for Shai collators and the mukhtars of rural settlements, with the accent on dealing with local problems with Arab neighbours. 'We taught Arabic and customs,' Mashbetz said. 'We weren't trying to teach them intelligence work, but how to get information that would help us in guarding the fields. How to find whoever it was who was giving us problems. The stress was on local problems. What we were concerned about was the security of the settlements.' The following year David Karon attended a similar course, run jointly in Jerusalem by Danin's department and the Jewish Agency. Again, Arabic language and village customs were the keynote, the purpose being to prevent friction stemming from ignorance of Arab life. Karon proved his worth shortly afterwards when the guards at Kfar Menachem shot dead an Arab gathering hay in the kibbutz fields one night. The young Shai man, known by then to the Arabs as Daoud, played a key role in the formal *sulha* (reconciliation) with the dead man's family and village. Rice and meat for the festive meal were provided by the Jewish Agency and Eliahu Sasson came down from Jerusalem with a message of peace and good-neighbourliness.

Just wandering around the country was the best way of acquiring the sort of gossipy and basic intelligence the Shai wanted. Soon afterwards, Karon and three other young men from Kfar Menachem moved south towards the Negev with a tractor and a tent. The situation created by the White Paper moved the settlement authorities to organize what they called 'political ploughing' to demonstrate Jewish ownership of new land that had been bought before 1939 but not yet worked or settled because of the freeze imposed by the British. As Karon says:

> Wherever we were I would sit for hours with the Arab watchmen and chat to them about the area. I learned masses about their customs. That was my 'open university' and I exploited it to the full. And later, when we moved into thirteen new settlements in the Negev, I was asked by the Haganah to organize things on the Arab side. I found access routes without going through the Arab villages. And in the morning, when we'd set everything up, we'd open up a

tent and invite any Arab who passed to come in and have a cup of coffee and stressed that our intentions were peaceful.[31]

But peace and good-neighbourliness were only part of the story. Karon used his extensive Arab connections in the south to buy captured German and Italian weapons smuggled into the country by Australian troops who had been serving in the Egyptian Western Desert. And as the war in Europe dragged on, unimpeded by the British defeat of Rommel's Afrika Korps at El Alamein, Danin's Shai network gradually began to look more and more like a professional intelligence organization that was thinking seriously about a future conflict with the Arabs.

Ya'akov Shimoni, a Berlin-born intellectual and teacher who had become disillusioned with the restrictions of life in the young kibbutz of Givat Haim, near Hadera, was taken on by the Arab Department on the personal recommendation of David Shaltiel, whom he had met while on a Zionist training farm in France before arriving in Palestine in early 1936. Shimoni, with the thoroughness and dedication of a classic *yekke* (German Jew), had taught himself Arabic and was deeply interested in Arab affairs. He had hoped to be interviewed for the job by the great Shaul Avigur, the *éminence grise* of the Shai, but instead met a colourless bureaucrat called Ze'ev Sharef. Shimoni, engaged at £14 10s per month, began work in October 1941, setting up the Arab Department's first proper office in two back rooms of a bank on Lunz Street in central Jerusalem. The embryonic Shai archive, in keeping with the contemporary spirit of conspiracy and secrecy, was kept hidden in two suitcases under the bed of Eliahu Ben-Hur, the Haganah commander in the city, in his flat on nearby King George Avenue.

After Yisrael Amir's final reorganization of the Shai a few months later Shimoni, then aged twenty-six, moved the office down to Tel Aviv, first to 16 Melchett Street and then on to what became Shai headquarters in a four-room apartment on the second floor of 190 Ben-Yehuda Street. The suitcases with the swelling archives found a separate home, and his cover, appropriately enough for a serious young man with a penchant for paperwork, was as an employee of Am Oved, the Histadrut publishing company. 'I was told to get down to work and set up a department of Arab affairs, which meant at that time Palestinian Arab affairs,' he recalled afterwards.[32]

Shimoni began to get all the reports from the people in the field and quickly annoyed them by his rigorous standards and repeated requests for specific information for his swelling files. He was, by his own account, a hard taskmaster and took advice from no one but Danin.

As Shimoni reminisced years later:

Ezra was the only man I knew – and Josh Palmon also to a certain extent – who combined practical fieldwork experience in Arab affairs with a sound knowledge of Arabic as a language and Arab affairs as a discipline in the broader sense and who could talk to educated Arabs. Most of our fieldworkers were wonderful people, excellent people, but most of them were in that sense primitives who didn't know written, literary Arabic and I had a problem with the reports they sent. They couldn't write an Arab name properly. For them it was all the same. What does it matter to them if the man's name is Salah. It can be Saleh. It can be Hussein or Hassan or Ihsan or Muhsen. 'Ihsein,' they'd tell me. 'What does it matter whether its Hassan or Hussein or Muhsen?' Well, for me it matters because I had an index and he had to appear under the alphabet there. And their reporting, of course, was in most cases rather primitive. They were cultured people, but in this particular field their expertise was with the neighbouring Arab sheikh or the neighbouring village. They spoke Arabic but with very little background knowledge. Their reports exaggerated the significance of purely local affairs. For them the local chief baddy was the head of all the gangs. My job was to edit their reporting, to give it some kind of perspective, to incorporate it into a general report that I had to put out every week.[33]

The files were a mess. Shimoni took them to his home in the Tel Aviv suburb of Bat Yam and sorted them out. By the time he brought them back to a Shai safe house in Tel Aviv in the spring of 1943 he had the beginnings of an efficient and accessible reference system. His insistence on the correct transliteration of Arabic names – every orientalist's nightmare when confronted with amateurs – was not just pedantry. One part of the index was biographical, in the form of standardized questionnaires sent out to the fieldworkers, and the other geographical, with detailed information about specific villages entered on large green cards. Danin, who disliked paperwork and always refused to keep proper records, was especially keen on that. Some time in 1943, at the suggestion of Eliahu Sasson, the prolific Arabic press began to be systematically studied as a source of information on the Palestinians. Shimoni was embarrassed that he had not thought of this obvious idea himself. Under Shimoni's direction the Shai bulletins, codenamed 'Yediot Tene' ('Fruit Basket'), achieved a high level of professionalism and much wider distribution.

The lead taken by Shimoni was soon followed by the organization's other two main departments. Yosef Krakovsky (Karib), a teacher who was the first head of the Jewish (or Internal) Department, began to build up an orderly achive. In the summer of 1944 a physically short but determined young man called Isser Halperin (Harel) took it over and turned it into the pride of the Shai, with card index and coloured ribbons for speedy identification. Dr David Arian, a former Berlin policeman and bank clerk who dealt with communist affairs, did the same.[34]

The archive presented a serious problem of security. Under Harel's direction, a small apartment on Dov Hoz Street was rented from a well-known Tel Aviv actor and a small secret room constructed, complete with false wall, a special metal door that could be opened and closed quickly and a folding bed to camouflage the cracks in the wall. Haim Ben-Menachem, head of the Jerusalem Shai, had an even more novel and possibly more secure idea: he moved his files to a hut used for leprosy research on the Hebrew University campus on Mount Scopus.[35]

Organization and division of responsibilities became more precise and new talent was brought in. The Arab Department's most promising recruit was Josh Palmon. Palmon was born to a family of Russian origin in 1913 in Neve Tsedek, on the border between Tel Aviv and Jaffa, and he was a valuable acquisition.

He spoke good Arabic and had proved his worth, representing the Haganah in the harsh and isolated conditions at the Palestine Potash Company works at Sodom, at the southern end of the Dead Sea, throughout the previous round of disturbances. Palmon was as familiar with the local Bedouin tribes as he was with Hebron and the surrounding villages and was well placed to gather intelligence on arms smuggling across the long and lonely border with Transjordan. He already knew Danin, but his main contact in the second half of the 1930s was the Haganah commander in Jerusalem, Ya'akov Patt, to whom he would occasionally pass on whatever titbits of information came his way.

After the reorganization in 1940 Palmon's first job with Danin, logically enough, was as collator for the Hebron area, where, because there were almost no Jewish settlements, direct contact with Arab informants was crucial. But there was little work for him there, because of the calm that came with the fading of the rebellion, and he quickly expanded to cover the Jerusalem area and soon began to develop country-wide horizons and a broader perspective about the purpose of intelligence-gathering. 'I suggested that we change the name from information service (*sherut yediot*) to intelligence (*biyun*),' he recalled later. 'With an information service you work everywhere. What you catch you bring to the market whether there are buyers or not. What we tried to do was to go where it was important and interesting.'[36] Localized information-gathering, culled by a kibbutz watchman drinking coffee with an Arab mukhtar, or a butcher bantering with cattle traders, was fine as far as it went. But, Palmon realized, it did not go very far, and there was a need for greater precision and more forward planning. In Hebron, for example, Palmon – known to the Arabs as Abu Sabri – had a valuable contact called Najjar, who owned camel trains that plied the desert route to Transjordan. Najjar was also a paid and long-standing agent of RAF intelligence, which meant that he was already practised in keeping his eyes and ears open.

The increasingly 'scientific' direction taken by the Shai

Arabists reached a striking landmark in 1944, when Danin persuaded the Haganah to publish a collection of rebel documents captured during the 1936–9 disturbances. Danin had acquired most of the material from his contacts in British Military Intelligence, who passed them on to the Shai for translation and interpretation, apparently preferring to deal with the security-conscious Haganah rather than the notoriously leaky Palestine civil administration. Most of the material was captured from gangs operating in the Nablus–Jenin–Tulkarm area, close to Danin's home in Hadera.

The book, *Te'udot VeDmuyot* (*Documents and Personalities*), stands out as the first serious attempt by the Jews to record and analyse the motives and character of their Arab enemies and it remains a historical source of unique value. Danin's introduction to the collection looked at the sociological basis of the revolt, placing it firmly in the villages or in groups and individuals with strong rural links. He pointed out, for example, that both Zionists and British had tended to greatly exaggerate the standard and quantity of weapons and ammunition in rebel hands. As he wrote:

> The fact cannot be ignored that the military-technical training of the Arabs was not of a high standard. Their degree of expertise with modern weapons was almost nil. They mainly exploited the natural training of the Arab village: fighting for survival in the context of daily life – blood-feuds, fist-fights, ambushes, theft and retaliation, arson, destruction of orchards and crops, stabbing in the back, hunting and target shooting.

Te'udot VeDmuyot was not published commercially and was distributed in numbered copies only to Haganah commanders and a few political leaders; there was no mention in it of the Shai or intelligence work. But there were clearly important practical lessons for the future to be learned from studying the most recent clash with the Palestinians. As Danin wrote:

> We believe that one of the most effective weapons against the Arab rebel is knowing his mentality and likely reactions to various

situations. We must be aware of his mode of assembly, attack, defence, camouflage and escape; his childish love of power; his ability to withstand bribery; his sincerity; his tendency to be argumentative or to abandon a comrade in distress; the influence of social conflicts; his degree of readiness to betray a commander; his attitude towards an enemy or a neighbour. What are his rules for fair combat? What can rattle the nerves of an Arab fighter and what is the most effective way of hitting him? When is a physical attack effective and in what circumstances does an attack on his property work better?[37]

Questions of this kind soon began to be addressed to a wider audience. The Shai Arabists had always maintained a far more 'civilian' than military hue, and combat or field intelligence – based on patrols, observation or contact with the enemy – was largely ignored, developing only towards the end of the world war and the changes that signalled the eventual departure of the British and full-scale war with the Arabs. The Shai held a first intelligence course for Haganah men at Shefaya, near Zikhron Ya'akov, in 1944 and a larger second one, for thirty promising officer-grade types, in Hadera in 1946. Shimoni lectured on the Palestinians and Shaul Bar-Chaim gave them some instant Arabic.

Danin had suggested to Reuven Zaslani as early as April 1940 that the Shai should apply its resources to producing a comprehensive survey of Arab villages, and some enterprising individuals, like Zerubavel Arbel, had already done their own surveys in their particular areas. But it was not until 1945 that work on the 'village files' project got under way in earnest under a steering committee composed of Danin, Shimoni and Palmon. More than 600 of Palestine's 800 Arab villages were surveyed, using agent reports and aerial photographs obtained by light planes. The photographs served as a substitute for proper topographical maps, whose sale was forbidden in wartime. In 1948, when the British were about to leave, the Shai broke into the Government Survey Office in Tel Aviv and photographed the master copies of all official maps.[38]

The survey was the most striking example thus far of the application of intelligence activity to defined military ends. As the renewal of conflict with the Arabs approached it became a matter of some urgency to have centralized up-to-date information on possible targets. And all Arab villages were possible targets. As David Karon recalled:

The whole idea behind the Haganah in those days was that all retaliation by us had to be against the right target. In order to know what was the right target, you also needed to know what was the wrong one. So the Shai did an immense amount of work documenting villages, collecting information about their families, their internal conflicts. Say that a girl was raped somewhere: our response was always directed at a precise target. If you kept your finger on the pulse you knew very quickly who'd done what. And when you knew who'd done it, and you had detailed maps of the village and knew the approaches, you could point precisely to the house where the perpetrator lived.[39]

'As though there were no war . . .'

The 1939 White Paper, David Ben-Gurion had complained to the British High Commissioner, Sir Harold MacMichael, was 'a cruel and unjustifiable blow to the Jewish people in the most tragic hour of its history'. Yet the Yishuv and the Zionist movement could not afford to stand still. Ben-Gurion set the tone with a catchy and quotable line on 12 September 1939: 'We must support the army as though there were no White Paper,' he declared, 'and fight the White Paper as though there were no war.' It was a clever and timely formula that was honed into even sharper versions as the war dragged on. Implementing it wasn't that easy. Despite the progress both in numbers and in military expertise made by the Haganah during the three years of disturbances, the Yishuv was still basically dependent for its security on the presence of British forces. Concern as to what might happen should the British withdraw made it a priority for the Zionists to do as much for the general war effort – or at least for the defence of Palestine itself – as Whitehall would allow. But divergent interests were at work in London and Jerusalem.[40]

The British believed it was necessary both to implement the provisions of the White Paper and to do everything to avoid antagonizing the Arabs and were initially suspicious of doing anything that might increase Jewish military power. Circumstances changed radically in the spring of 1940, with the German occupation of Western Europe, the aerial attacks on the British mainland and Italy's entry into the war in June. The surrender of France and the declaration by the French army in Syria of its loyalty to the Vichy regime in early July altered the regional picture too, and the immediacy of the Axis threat was graphically underlined when Italian planes bombed Haifa and Tel Aviv. The Zionist leadership saw its chance and did everything it could to stress the degree of Arab animosity towards Britain to justify the increasingly voluble demand for a large-scale mobilization of the Yishuv.

Reuven Zaslani, who had developed close links with a wide range of British military and security officials since first coming into contact with RAF intelligence in 1933, was the ideal man for the liaison job. Contacts were made in both Palestine and London, especially with the newly formed Special Operations Executive (SOE), launched by Winston Churchill in July 1940 with the dramatic instruction to 'Set Europe ablaze'. Zionist representatives, notably Ehud Uberall (Avriel), who was working in Turkey on illegal Jewish emigration to Palestine, also cooperated with MI9, the organization that helped POWs who escaped from Germany. MI6 – also known as SIS – the British Secret Intelligence Service, was believed by the Jews to be too closely influenced by the pro-Arab Foreign Office and, like its political masters, too aware of the fact that after the war a Zionist–British confrontation was inevitable. Generally, as Zaslani was to recall later, it was easiest to work with ad hoc, essentially military British bodies set up solely for the duration of the war against Hitler, and to insist in contacts with them on the special status demanded by the Jewish Agency. The exchange of letters that established the secret relationship (there was no formal agreement) made clear what the Zionists were and were not prepared to do. 'We didn't agree to be subordinated to any

British military authority,' Zaslani said. 'We didn't want to say "yes sir, no sir". We weren't working for the British, we were allies.'[41]

Allied preparations for the invasion of Syria and Lebanon in spring 1941 marked the beginning of serious British–Zionist cooperation in intelligence and special operations. The Vichy takeover the previous summer had cut off the British from French intelligence resources on the spot, so approaches were made to the Yishuv to provide help both with informants and with sabotage and reconnaissance operations. The first major joint venture with the British ended in disaster in May. Twenty-three members of the Haganah, commanded by Zvi Spector and accompanied by an SOE observer, Major Anthony Palmer, set out from Haifa in a small motor launch on a mission to sabotage the oil refineries in the northern Lebanese port of Tripoli, thus denying fuel to the German planes that had begun to operate from Syria. Contact with the boat, the *Sea Lion*, was lost and the fate of the men remains unknown to this day. Other operations included smuggling Free French (Gaullist) officials to Palestine and forward reconnaissance missions before the actual invasion, which took place on 8 June 1941. In the last of these, on the night of 7 June, near Iskenderum in south Lebanon, a young Haganah officer named Moshe Dayan lost his left eye when a bullet fired by Senegalese troops smashed into the binoculars he was using. The increasing cooperation with SOE had done much to encourage the Haganah's decision, in mid-May, to form a new mobilized arm known as the Palmah (Plugot Mahatz – strike companies), which included a small unit known as the Syrian Platoon. Commanded by Yisrael Ben-Yehuda (codenamed Abdu) and Josh Palmon, whose expertise in intelligence had already made an important contribution to the development of the Shai, the platoon suffered from both a lack of suitable manpower and poor communications with Palestine, although the novel experience of working under deep cover in enemy territory was to prove invaluable for the Zionists.

One of its members, Yeruham Cohen, was quick to absorb the lessons of the period. As he wrote later:

> The time we spent in Syria and Lebanon taught us how great the difference was between the language and customs there and those in Palestine. We only had to open our mouths and we would be asked, 'Palestinians, hey?' But it wasn't only our speech that gave us away. I remember having my shoes cleaned in Tripoli one day and the shoeshine man said, 'These shoes are made in Haifa.' Those of us who were not originally from Syria and Lebanon looked and listened more than we talked. We had to learn the local dialect – and it was different everywhere, Beirut, Damascus, Aleppo – before we dared to say anything. It took months before we felt at home. We took care not to make ourselves conspicuous. None of us knew where the others lived.[42]

Members of the Syrian Platoon were drawn mostly from Jews who spoke Arabic as their mother tongue. They were preferably natives of the countries where they were to operate and were trained to be able to melt effortlessly into the milieu where they were working. Alongside the military training provided by SOE instructors at the unit's headquarters on Mount Carmel, the recruits were taught to absorb Arab customs, including singing and dancing, backgammon and other games of chance. Their cover did not always hold. After the invasion Yeruham Cohen and a colleague were caught by the Deuxième Bureau (the Vichy-run Syrian security service) in Damascus, wearing peasant clothes they had bought in the local flea market and carrying forged Lebanese identity papers. They were extricated from prison only by the efforts of Major Nick Hammond, the Syrian Platoon's liaison with SOE, in an elaborate charade according to which the two Palmah agents were described as deserters from the British army. The creation of the Platoon was the Jewish Agency's idea. 'Here,' Zaslani said later, 'was a clear question of our own goals. The British were not very enthusiastic and there was an element of us exploiting their weakness.'[43]

The British were deeply impressed by the Palmah scouts and their political masters. Julian Amery, who came to Mount Carmel with SOE's Balkan section from its headquarters at Rustum Buildings in Cairo, was to write later:

I worked closely with Shertok and Zaslani, the heads of the foreign and clandestine sections of the Jewish Agency. We had many mutual interests in the Balkans and were often able to help each other. I was impressed by their efficiency and by the originality of their operational thinking. They were quick to see our point of view but held tenaciously to their own. But when they made a deal they stuck to it.[44]

C. M. Woodhouse, another SOE man enamoured of 'mysterious organizations with inscrutable initials', left Palestine with similar positive views about Zionist talents in secret warfare.[45]

The next time the British were seriously interested in clandestine cooperation with the Jewish Agency was a few months later, when the British modified their plans for the defence of Palestine and Syria in the event of a German attack and drew up a plan called the Palestine Post-Occupation Scheme. In the tense summer months of 1942, before Rommel's Afrika Korps was finally beaten back at El Alamein, SOE was charged with creating a resistance movement to stay behind after an enemy occupation, collect intelligence, aid stragglers and escapees, help special forces and sabotage vital installations. SOE trained about 100 Palmah members in guerrilla warfare tactics and set up a network of radio operators and intelligence agents under Moshe Dayan, with most of the activity taking place at Kibbutz Mishmar HaEmek. The Yishuv welcomed the opportunities it was getting to acquire training and experience, and old British friends, especially the legendary, pro-Zionist Orde Wingate of the Special Night Squads of the late 1930s, tried to help argue the Jewish case in London. Zaslani saw Wingate briefly in Cairo on his way to Burma, where he was killed in an air crash while commanding his famous Chindits guerrilla group in action against the Japanese in 1944.

By 1943 the British–Zionist honeymoon was all but over. The theft of British weapons by the Palmah made a bad situation worse. The *raison d'être* of the Syrian Platoon was over anyway, although the same small pool of manpower proved invaluable when, in May that year, the Palmah decided to set up its own Arab Platoon, this time serving only Zionist not British interests. Other important areas of cooperation between the two sides included the formation of a Palmah German Platoon, composed of Jewish German speakers, commanded by Shimon Koch (Avidan). In 1944 Jewish volunteers were parachuted into Nazi-occupied Eastern Europe to try and encourage resistance and gather intelligence. Enzo Sereni and Hannah Szenes, the two most famous parachutists, were both captured and executed by the Germans.

In November 1944, as the war against Hitler drew to a close, Zaslani summarized four years of secret cooperation with the British. He pointed to the significance of the fact that the Allied intelligence services would continue to be active in Europe for years to come. 'We will have to operate in Europe because our immigrants will be coming from there, and we will have to create a Jewish state here and we will have to continue this cooperation,' he told senior Jewish Agency officials. 'Our intelligence must become better,' he said. 'It must become a permanent instrument of our political apparatus.'[46]

2
The Test of Battle: 1947–9

The Arab Platoon

At noon on Friday, 22 December 1947, shortly after the Muslim crowds had left the mosques of Jaffa, the largest Arab city in Palestine, two Jews called David Shemesh and Gideon Be'eri were taken to the nearby sands of Tel ar-Reish, shot and buried. No sign marked or marks the spot. Later the body of their colleague, Nissim Atiyah, who had been captured in Ramle to the south-east, was found in a ditch outside the town. The three, members of the Palmah's Arab Platoon – known in Hebrew as the Mist'Aravim, or by the unit's codename, the Shahar – were the first Israeli spies caught and killed in the 1948 war and the first to die in the Arab–Israeli conflict. They belonged to a five-man team infiltrated into the Jaffa–Ramle–Lydda area in the first weeks of the war as part of the Haganah's campaign to gauge Arab military preparations and the drift of public opinion in the enemy camp.

Shemesh and Be'eri were both Iraqi-born Jews but could pass easily as Arabs. In Jaffa they had taken up lodgings in a cheap hotel in the Manshieh quarter, bordering on Tel Aviv. They were picked up by members of the Jaffa security committee after they were overheard making telephone calls from the hotel to a contact in Tel Aviv, a mistake that was to cost them their lives.[1]

Under interrogation and torture the two stuck to their cover story that they were Arabs from Iraq, although they did admit that two of their friends were staying in Ramle. One of them, Nissim Atiyah, was arrested and executed shortly afterwards. A fourth Shahar agent, identified in Haganah intelligence reports as Sami Ibrahim Nimrod, was caught in Salameh village near Jaffa. Like the others, Nimrod carried an identity card that was clearly a forgery since the photograph on it had not, as required by British law, been properly endorsed with an official stamp. Nimrod was luckier than his colleagues. Although condemned to death by his captors, the sentence was revoked when 'Sami' impressed them by his devotion at Muslim prayers. He was released and lived to tell the tale.[2]

The Palmah's Arab Platoon, a small and initially amateurish unit, was the spearhead of the Yishuv's military intelligence gathering until the summer of 1948. From late 1947 onwards its members sortied repeatedly, disguised as Arabs, into the main population centres of Arab Palestine – Jaffa, Haifa, Nablus, Jerusalem and Hebron – and further afield to Transjordan, Syria and Lebanon, to collect political and military information.

The Arab Platoon was formed in May 1943 on the orders of Yitzhak Landsberg (Sadeh), the Polish-born founder and first commander of the Palmah. Sadeh, who had served as a company commander in the Red Army and emigrated to Palestine in 1920, instructed Yeruham Cohen, a veteran of the Palmah's Syrian Platoon, to find a dozen men who could pass for Arabs to carry out special operations. Cohen recruited from the communities of Sephardi (Oriental) Jews who lived in neighbourhoods that bordered on Arab districts. Many of them were barely literate although all were native Arabic speakers. They were trained in fieldcraft, sabotage, sniping, judo and communications as well as Muslim prayer rituals, the Palestinian Arabic dialect and local customs. The platoon was codenamed the Shahar and was based in Kibbutz Alonim in the Jezreel valley.

During the mid-1940s the unit's members, usually operating in teams of two or three, carried out dozens of reconnaissance, espionage and sabotage missions in the towns and villages of Arab Palestine. One of their more notorious exploits, in 1946, was the revenge kidnapping and castration of an Arab from Beisan who was suspected of having raped a Jewish girl from a nearby kibbutz. Early Shahar operations were local and short-range. Greater challenges were soon to come.

Countdown to war

From mid-1946 onwards, the Yishuv was gearing up for full-scale war. The conflict in Europe was finally over; the Allies had liberated the Nazi death camps in Europe and felt under immense moral pressure finally to grant the Jews a state of their own. The Yishuv, using its underground networks in Europe, organized a huge campaign of rescue and illegal immigration (*bricha*), running the British naval blockade to bring the emaciated survivors of the Holocaust to the shores of Palestine. The Jewish underground militias, the mainstream Haganah (with its elite Palmah units) and the dissident Irgun and Stern Gang launched a guerrilla campaign against the British, who still clung to Palestine out of vague pro-Arab sympathies combined with simple inertia. In spring 1946 an Anglo-American commission of inquiry visited the country and recommended that Britain permit the immediate entry of 100,000 Jewish refugees. Whitehall rejected the proposal. But by February 1947 the Labour government of Clement Attlee, under intense US pressure and discouraged by Britain's dual role of target for Jewish terrorists and umpire in a seemingly insoluble national conflict, decided to call it quits and let the United Nations solve the problem.

The UN General Assembly appointed a Special Commission on Palestine (UNSCOP), which recommended in November that the British withdraw and, following the example of the Peel Commission ten years earlier, the country be partitioned into separate Jewish and Arab states to be joined in an economic union. UNSCOP's recommendations were endorsed by the General Assembly on 29 November 1947. The Yishuv accepted the resolution; the Palestinian Arabs and the neighbouring Arab states all rejected it. The next day sporadic hostilities began. Jewish bypassers were stabbed; border neighbourhoods were shelled and sniped at; Jewish traffic was ambushed. The Haganah reacted slowly at first, assuming that the initial wave of Arab anger would pass. In the second half of December it adopted a posture of aggressive defence, occasionally launching massive retaliatory raids on Arab villages that harboured armed bands.

During January 1948 the first Arab 'volunteers' – mostly former or serving soldiers in the Iraqi, Syrian and Transjordanian armies – arrived in Palestine and, reinforced by Palestinian irregulars, launched the first large-scale attacks on outlying Jewish settlements. In February and March battles began on the main roads, with the Arab forces regularly ambushing Haganah supply convoys to isolated Jewish population centres, especially Jerusalem. The British, who were bent on withdrawal with as few casualties as possible, interfered only rarely.

In April and May, as the British gradually pulled out, the Haganah, assisted in certain areas by the far smaller Irgun, went on to the offensive, capturing large Arab centres – Haifa, Tiberias, Jaffa and parts of Jerusalem – and dozens of villages, triggering the main wave of the Palestinian Arab exodus. By 14 May, when the establishment of the State of Israel was announced by Ben-Gurion in a converted Tel Aviv cinema, some 300,000 Arabs had fled Palestine; by the war's end, in mid-1949, there would be a total of some 700,000 refugees.[3]

On 15 May, the day after the establishment of Israel, the armies of Egypt, Syria, Transjordan, Iraq and Lebanon invaded Palestine from the north, east and south. Their common aim was to nip the Jewish state in the bud, though Transjordan's King Abdullah, regarding this objective as unrealistic, probably desired primarily to gain for his kingdom the territory that the UN General Assembly had earmarked for Palestinian Arab statehood. Other Arab leaders spoke of 'throwing the Jews into the sea' or, like Azzam Pasha, the secretary-general of the Arab League, of a massacre that would rival those carried out by the

Mongol hordes. The leaders of the Yishuv, including the Haganah's operations chief, Yigael Yadin, gave the new state a 50 per cent chance of survival. Foreigners were even less optimistic. The British Field Marshal Bernard Montgomery, the victor of El Alamein, thought Israel might last three weeks. The war, in which 6,000 Jews, or one in every 100 Jews then in Palestine, would die, was seen as a battle for survival. The Jews won it with an initial stubborn and courageous defence, soon followed by successful lightning offensives in July, October to November and December to January 1949, beating back and then defeating the invading Arab armies and consolidating the state. But for weeks, perhaps months, it was touch and go.

Hazardous operations

By mid-1947, anticipating the coming war and the growing need for proper military intelligence, the Haganah proposed enlarging the Shahar and extending its operations beyond the borders of Palestine. In May that year Yisrael Galili, chief of the Haganah National Command – the Haganah's political steering committee – recommended the expansion of the Arab Platoon to the size of a company and the establishment of small, local Mist'Aravim units in the various districts.[4]

In July the chief of the Haganah General Staff – the Haganah's operational command – Ya'akov Dori, ordered a new mobilization of recruits for the Shahar.[5] But the drive moved slowly. Training a Mist'Arev required a great deal of time and effort and the Haganah's limited resources were already badly stretched. In August Yigal Allon, who had succeeded Yitzhak Sadeh as Palmah commander in 1945, recommended the establishment of permanent Mist'Aravim 'bases', manned by 'natives of those countries', in Beirut, Damascus or Baghdad.[6]

In November, just before the UN partition resolution, several agents were planted in Beirut and Damascus, but financial difficulties forced their early recall. One of the Beirut men reported – by mail – on his difficulties in settling in after managing to rent a shop. The unit's commander, Yeruham Cohen, complained that the Shahar men were forced to revert to a 'hazardous mode of operations', continuously crossing the lines between Jewish and Arab areas in Palestine and along its borders to obtain intelligence.[7]

A second effort to implant Mist'Aravim in Arab countries was made during the summer of 1948, following, and on the back of, the Palestinian exodus. The idea was that the agents would enter the enemy countries along with the fleeing masses of Arab refugees. But financial difficulties intervened again and Palmah HQ complained to Galili: 'Despite our efforts we have not been given any funds to cover the implementation of the penetration plan of Shahar men. Convenient opportunities are diminishing and we are doing nothing.'[8]

The Shahar distinguished between three types of missions: *hish-bazim, tayarim* and *mitbasesim*. The *hish-bazim* (fast falcons) were one-time, brief in-and-out missions – sometimes of only a few hours' duration – usually to pinpoint a specific target or acquire a specific piece of information for immediate military use. The *tayarim* (tourists) missions were one- to five-day sorties into Arab-held areas of Palestine or neighbouring Arab countries. The *mitbasesim* (settlers) were long-term missions, involving the implantation of an agent in an Arab city, usually a foreign capital, for years.

During the war, the expanded Shahar was commanded by Peretz Gordon, assisted by Yeruham Cohen. Another Haganah intelligence officer, an archaeologist from Kibbutz Na'an called Shmarya Guttman, served as a father figure and instructor. The unit was based in Jaffa and moved afterwards to an isolated two-storey house in an orange grove outside Ramle, once the headquarters of Hassan Salameh, a leader of the Arab irregulars.

Shahar operations were given a high priority. In February 1948 Yadin cabled all brigade and city commanders, ordering all assistance to be given to the Mist'Aravim.[9] Field intelligence work was combined with the dissemination of black propaganda among the Arab population. After a sortie to Quneitra on the

Syrian Golan Heights it was reported that: 'The Syrian soldier looks awful . . . he exudes misery . . . [he is] dirty . . . and very lazy.' The mission was also exploited to exaggerate Jewish military capabilities.[10] As the war progressed, Shahar men spent more time in the remaining Arab areas of Palestine, often accompanying the fleeing refugees and bringing back useful reports on enemy morale and military strength.

In summer 1948 the Shahar lost two men in Egyptian-occupied Gaza. David Mizrahi, a native of Jerusalem, had been a Mist'Arev since 1943. Ezra Horin, of Kibbutz Afikim, had joined up in 1945. He had repeatedly asked his comrades in the platoon to torture him so he would be ready if he fell into enemy hands. The two were infiltrated into the Gaza Strip on 7 May to gather intelligence on the Egyptian army, which was expected to enter the area the following week. Arrested at an Egyptian roadblock a few days later, they were interrogated and tortured, and, after a brief field court martial, which convicted them of trying to poison a well with typhus- and dysentery-infected water from their canteens, were executed by firing squad.[11] Other sorties were more successful, and several missions to Transjordan, Syria and Lebanon produced accurate intelligence about Arab military intentions on the eve of the invasion.[12] Two Mist'Aravim, equipped with a camera concealed in a cigarette lighter, spent a productive week in Syria early in May.[13]

Occasionally, intelligence-gathering was a bloody business. Late in January 1948 a Shahar team took an Arab taxi from Tiberias to Samakh, south of the Sea of Galilee, and discovered in conversation that their driver was an active member of the Arab irregular forces. 'Shimon', one of the agents, reported afterwards that they had tried but failed to strangle the Arab. When a British motorcycle approached, the driver was bundled into the vehicle's trunk. Later they killed him and threw the body into a gully. Other Arab vehicles were hijacked and their drivers 'liquidated'.[14]

The Mist'Aravim were often used for 'dirty tricks' missions, including sabotage and assassinations of Arab military and political leaders. On 28 February 1948 Shahar men blew up the Abu Sham garage in the downtown Arab area of Haifa after receiving information that a bomb that had been prepared on the premises was due to be planted in a 'crowded Jewish street' in a 'British' military ambulance. A Shahar reconnaissance team pinpointed the garage and the vehicle, packed a small car with 300 kilograms of explosives, drove freely through several Arab checkpoints and parked it by the garage. The front of the car had been smashed in to provide an excuse for repairs. One of the Mist'Aravim, Ya'akov ('Yakuba') Cohen, disguised as an Arab and speaking with the appropriate local accent, told the garage hand that the car had been in an accident and needed attention. 'In these bad times we don't serve people we don't know,' the worker replied. 'How do I know you don't have a bomb inside?' Cohen remonstrated with the garage hand. He would give his name to the local national committee for 'refusing to extend help to a fighter who had just driven through Jewish territory'. The garage worker, partially convinced, told Cohen to wait for the owner. The Jewish agent surreptitiously triggered the bomb's delayed-action detonator and drove away with his partner 'Yitzhak' in a back-up car towards the 'Fortified Triangle', a nearby British military area. A minute or so later, the bomb exploded, killing thirty Arabs and wounding seventy others. In the confusion, the Shahar escape car collided with a British army jeep. Two soldiers, armed with Sten guns, ordered the two agents out. Yitzhak smiled, and said in English: 'It is not polite to stop first without signalling, and you, as is known, are polite fellows.' The joke defused the tension. Although the British searched the car, they failed to find the guns hidden inside and let the Shahar men go. The British had thought they were Arabs.[15]

Their ability to move freely in Arab areas gave the Mist'-Aravim immense advantages in carrying out surveillance of enemy targets. The best-known assassination attempt carried out in the early weeks of the war was against Haj Muhammad Nimr al-Khatib, an important Haifa religious leader and a member both of the local national committee and of the Arab

Higher Committee. Two Shahar attacks were aborted but on 19 February two agents fired thirty-two bullets at a taxi in which al-Khatib was travelling north of the city, on his way back from Damascus. The aim, as spelt out clearly in the agents' subsequent report, was to kill him. But the operation failed. The preacher was hit by three bullets in the left shoulder and one in the lung; he spent the rest of the war out of commission and outside Palestine. Another passenger died and another was wounded in the attack.[16] Plans were also made to assassinate four other members of the Arab Higher Committee travelling in two cars from Jerusalem to Egypt, but this operation was called off for lack of information.[17]

In mid-August, with the war in full swing, the Shahar was integrated in the Shai's successor organization, the Israel Defence Forces Intelligence Service. (At the end of May 1948 the Haganah, the Yishuv's underground militia, formally became the IDF.) The IDF General Staff ordered Isser Be'eri, head of the newly created service, to integrate the Mist'Aravim into his organization.[18] Within weeks the Arab Platoon, renamed Shin Mem 18 (Sherut Modi'in 18), commanded by Guttman and Shimon ('Sam'an') Somekh, the unit's Iraqi-born expert on Arabic language and Muslim customs, was operating under Be'eri. For at least a decade afterwards it was responsible for the infiltration and implantation of Israeli agents in Arab countries. Its members provided a direct link between the amateurish, small-scale beginnings of Zionist intelligence work and the larger, more professional efforts made after 1948.

The Mist'Aravim played out their last role of the war in the spring of 1949, as the armistice agreement of 3 April (which formally ended the hostilities between Israel and Transjordan) went into effect. Among the thousands of prisoners of war and refugees transferred to Transjordan as part of the agreement were two Shin Mem 18 agents called 'Ephraim' and Ya'akov Buqa'i. Buqa'i, born in Damascus in 1930, emigrated to Palestine in 1945, working as an electrician at Kibbutz Ashdot Ya'akov. He joined the Arab Platoon in 1948 and was chosen, appropriately, to be a *mitbases* (long-term agent) in Syria. He was trained for the mission in Muslim customs, radio and communications techniques, secret writing and parachuting. His cover was as a refugee from Jaffa called Ibrahim Najib Hammouda.

To establish their new identities, Buqa'i and 'Ephraim' were imprisoned and then sent to the Sarafand POW camp, where they were regularly interrogated and beaten by their Israeli gaolers, along with their 'fellow' Arab prisoners. On 2 May 1949, bound for Damascus, they were sent across the border into Jordan at the Mandelbaum Gate crossing-point in Jerusalem, along with hundreds of bona fide released Arab prisoners of war. It was the last time Buqa'i's Shin Mem 18 controller, Ya'akov Nimrodi – a Shahar veteran who was to spend many years in Israeli intelligence – saw him. A subsequent investigation found that Buqa'i had fallen victim to an informant, probably a fellow prisoner in Sarafand who had noticed something odd about the agent's behaviour. Buqa'i was taken to the Kishle police station in Jerusalem's Old City and then transferred to prison in Amman, where he was tortured, tried and hanged on 3 August 1949 – as an Arab spy called Hammouda. Buqa'i himself thought he had been 'blown' by an Arab. In an emotional last letter smuggled to Israel before his execution, and which reached Shin Mem 18 in September, he wrote:

> I am not angry, and to this day I believe that the system was good but that some small things damaged the operation. I believe that the man I mentioned before I left was the one who informed on me. If I wanted to write all that was in my heart then all the paper in the world would not be enough to express my longing for you and the country. I have had enough of this miserable life on death row and every day I suffer torture and inhuman treatment.[19]

'Ephraim' apparently made it to Syria.[20]

The Shai, 1947–8

The Shai, the Haganah's intelligence service, entered 1947 ill prepared for the impending war. Its three departments, Arab,

British/Political and Jewish/Internal, still had a political rather than military focus. Ben-Gurion said in April that it 'lacked direction and systematic thinking'.[21] Despite the considerable improvements made in Yisrael Amir's reorganization in 1942, and the greater professionalism represented by Ya'akov Shimoni and others, the Shai remained a part-time and essentially amateur intelligence service.

It scored a notable coup in June 1946 when a British officer serving in the big army base at Sarafand handed over to Zvi Zehavi, the Shai commander in the Rishon LeTzion area, a copy of the plans for Operation Broadside, which was designed to arrest 5,000 leading members of the Haganah and almost the entire political leadership of the Yishuv. The document was over 600 pages long, and the Shai men, who took it to a nearby kibbutz to be photographed, had only enough paper to photograph 500. The remaining 100 pages were copied out in longhand by a group of Canadian Jewish volunteers. The British officer, 'G.G.', refused any payment but asked to be given a room in Rishon LeTzion where he could spend time with his Jewish girlfriend. Thus it cost the Shai just £8 per month to obtain most of the material gathered on the Haganah by the British army, police and intelligence since the early days of the mandate. 'G.G.' also warned the Shai exactly when Broadside was due to start. Almost all the leaders of the Haganah escaped capture by the British on what became known as the 'Black Sabbath'.[22]

Yet considering the importance of the coming struggle with the Arabs, a disproportionate amount of the Shai's manpower and energy was still devoted to keeping tabs on Jewish 'dissidents' – the Irgun, Stern Gang and Communists. From November 1946 this was the fiefdom of 'Little' Isser Harel, who, as head of the Internal or Jewish Department, had worked hard on building up his secret registry and making the most of the immense potential he saw in it. As he explained later:

I saw I could get far more out of the archive than by running agents. For example, I opened one file entitled 'Ginger-haired man of British appearance', a man who was suspected of being an intelligence agent. Afterwards I saw elsewhere that someone of such and such an appearance had been sighted, apparently pretending to be a Jew. So we already had two reports and maybe it was the same Ginger. And then we got another quite unconnected report about a certain officer in British intelligence. At some point I matched the name and then we'd managed to expose one of their most dangerous agents. Afterwards we got his picture and distributed it.[23]

In 1947 Harel became head of the Shai in Tel Aviv and later went on to even greater responsibilities.[24]

Arab intelligence was gathered largely by poorly paid or unpaid (and often unreliable) Arab agents run by Jewish officers and filed away on Shimoni's card index files. Far too much of the information was obtained from members of the Arab opposition rather than from the mainstream and better-informed Husseini leadership, which had returned to Palestine from exile after the end of the Second World War.

The Shai's budget for 1947 was 94,840 Palestine pounds (then roughly equivalent to pounds sterling). Salaries and office expenses accounted for 65 per cent; agents for 18 per cent; Arab informers for 15 per cent. It employed sixty-eight full-time staff and ran sixty British and Jewish agents and eighty Arabs. The Shai budget went up by nearly 50 per cent – to over 140,000 pounds – in 1948, but that had to be shared with the Jewish Agency's Political Department.[25]

An internal Haganah investigation of the Shai was conducted in May 1947, possibly by Vivian (Chaim) Herzog, the Belfast-born son of the chief rabbi of Ireland and later of Palestine. Herzog, then aged twenty-nine, himself a trained rabbi and lawyer, had been a major in British military intelligence in the Second World War and knew more about modern intelligence work than almost anyone in the Yishuv. The investigation found the Shai to be 'self-satisfied', plagued by 'pettiness and corruption' and too independent both of the Haganah General Staff and the Jewish Agency. Its manpower was both inadequate and below standard, the report concluded.[26]

The Shai's failure to give the Haganah advance warning of

Syrian military deployments along the border and its mistaken anticipation of Arab rioting in early October 1947 prompted Ben-Gurion to set up a committee of inquiry in November. The committee, composed of Yisrael Amir's successor as the Shai chief, David Shaltiel, and Eliahu Sasson and Reuven Zaslani of the Jewish Agency Political Department, concluded that the organization's veteran Arab 'stringers' were 'losing their value' and that new, well-placed informants were urgently needed, especially in Lebanon and Syria. Egypt and Transjordan were regarded as adequately covered.[27]

Listening in

When the Arabs of Palestine launched hostilities in early December 1947 the Shai used all its resources – and overspent its budget, Ben-Gurion complained – to try and determine the nature and aims of enemy operations. Wire-tapping was increased, usually by Jewish agents working in telephone exchanges. In early January 1948 the Shai recorded a series of conversations between a leading Jerusalem member of the Arab Higher Committee, Dr Hussein Khalidi, and the Mufti, Haj Amin al-Husseini, who was then living in exile in Heliopolis, outside Cairo.[28]

Ephraim Krasner (Dekel) and Ze'ev Grodzinsky of the Shai had begun to monitor British radio and telephone communications in the late 1930s, with priority given to the CID. They received help from some 'mathematically inclined' Haganah members, who set up a 'brains trust' and occasionally managed to crack the British codes, which were normally changed once a week. In 1942 the Jerusalem Shai chief had hired a Jewish worker in the central post office telegraph section to copy out all incoming cables to the High Commissioner's Office.[29] Things improved in 1944, when several British officers, motivated by sympathy for the Zionist cause, were persuaded to give the Shai the key to the weekly codes.

An important source of information was the CID's own

telephone-tapping centre in Jerusalem, where eighteen British policemen maintained round-the-clock surveillance on the phones of fifteen leading Arabs and five key Jewish Agency officials. One or more of the policemen copied out the transcripts of the conversations and forwarded them to the Shai on a daily basis. The Shai in Haifa also ran two permanent taps on telephone conversations from abroad – mostly from Amman, Damascus and Beirut – to local Arab leaders and British officials. The eavesdroppers were women secretaries who worked during the day in the city's Jewish Agency office and by night for the Haganah. In mid-March 1948 this operation gave the Haganah advance warning of the arrival of a large convoy of arms and ammunition from Beirut. The convoy was ambushed and destroyed and the commander of the Ḥaifa Arab militia, Muhammad ibn Hammad al-Huneiti, killed, with a telling effect on both the morale and military capabilities of the city's Arab population.

The most comprehensive Shai wire-tapping operation was in Jerusalem, where the lines into the British military headquarters at the Palace Hotel in Mamilla Street – where Jewish technicians had bugged the secret sessions of the Peel Commission a decade before – and to other British HQs, were monitored permanently. 'In 1947 we knew about every movement in the [Arab] Old City,' recalled Boris Gurevich (Guriel), head of the Shai's Political Department from late 1945. 'We had dozens of tappers and in June [1947], when UNSCOP came, we knew what every committee member said.' The Russian-born Guriel knew little about intelligence when he was given the job at the end of 1945, but he was good at it. One of his best sources was Yehuda Alhasid, a Jerusalem Jew who had worked for the British since the early days of the Mandate. Guriel cooperated with Ya'akov Eini, head of the Shai's Arab Department in the city, to find Arab agents who would betray their British employers. One of them, a Beit Jallah man, regularly provided the Haganah with copies of sensitive documents that were supposed to be destroyed.[30]

The Shai's attempts to penetrate the British administration in Jerusalem were stepped up in the summer of 1947. Shalhevet

Freier, a physics student at the Hebrew University, was put in charge. Freier, codenamed 'Uri', used a classic intelligence technique: he chose a soft target on the periphery of the British government, the Leasing Administration in Rehavia. Security was lax even though the office routinely received reports of troop movements and other highly classified material. Several Jewish employees were persuaded to cooperate with the Shai, whose agents used the old ploy of saying that they had the information already from other sources and simply wished to confirm it. Documents were 'borrowed' during the lunch hour and copied or photographed in Freier's basement headquarters nearby. Some Jewish secretaries made extra carbon copies of material they typed, or smuggled out the carbon itself, which was then read by using mirrors. Several women cooperated with the Shai in order to prove their loyalty to the Yishuv despite having British boyfriends. Valuable information about British strengths and plans was obtained in the same way from other ostensibly unimportant offices, such as the NAAFI or the Royal Army Pay Corps building in the Schneller barracks.[31]

In the Jaffa–Tel Aviv area, the Shai received copies of every cable reaching Jaffa until the end of 1947 – from Jewish employees at the city's central post office. When hostilities began in December and Jewish workers were unable to enter Jaffa, the Tel Aviv Shai, by then commanded by Isser Harel, dug a secret tunnel under a hut outside the Mikve Yisrael agricultural school and tapped the main underground telephone cable linking Jaffa to Ramle and Jerusalem. For weeks afterwards the Shai was able to listen in on conversations between the Jaffa Arab commanders and politicians and their colleagues in Jerusalem and Amman, although the main importance of the source was tactical rather than strategic.[32] 'I will never forget the face of the Arabic-speaking Shai man when he put on the earphones and recorded the first conversation,' Harel said later. 'It showed the immense potential of our secret monitoring station.'[33] On 14 November 1947 Shai wire-tappers recorded a conversation between Arthur Giles, deputy police commissioner for Palestine, and his brother in Cairo, which made clear that it was only a matter of time before the Mandate came to an end.[34]

During the countdown to war, the Shai also set up a station in Europe, which was headed from late 1947 by Haim Ben-Menachem. As the Shai's sources inside Palestine were steadily depleted, the feeling grew that the organization should transfer its HQ and operations to Europe, setting up a 'central international espionage office . . . in Rome or Paris'. Ben-Menachem's operation was devoted to 'European affairs', Zaslani complained. But what was needed was espionage against Arab activities – arms purchasing, political intrigues – in Europe. Sasson also favoured the establishment of such an office.[35] But months were to pass before Sasson himself was dispatched to the French capital to carry out this mission (as well as broader political tasks).

The networks collapse

In the first months of the war the Shai's Arab intelligence-gathering apparatus – local Jewish controllers running Arab agents – broke down almost completely. Despite the continued British presence, the war created insurmountable barriers between neighbouring Jewish settlements and Arab villages, between Jewish and Arab neighbourhoods in the 'mixed' cities and between adjacent Jewish and Arab districts. Border areas became front lines and free-fire zones and both the Jewish controllers and their Arab informants – who did not use radio communications – soon found it impossible to cross those lines to obtain or deliver information. The dangers of being caught grew enormously.

Shmuel Toledano, code-named 'Uzi', was one of the Shai Arab Department's agent controllers in the Jaffa area. Toledano, then in his mid-twenties, hailed from the mixed Arab–Jewish city of Tiberias, where his father was the chief rabbi, and he spoke fluent Palestinian Arabic. Since 1946, operating undercover as print workers at the *Davar* newspaper offices, he and three colleagues had recruited and run informers in a wide arc around the port city. Shmuel Gnizi, a former SOE wireless operator, served as liaison between the Jaffa controllers and Shai HQ in Tel Aviv, where the field reports were sent and evaluated. Toledano's best network consisted of five Jaffa prostitutes, whose business contacts with both British and Arabs provided useful snippets of raw intelligence. He had a couple of high-level political sources too, but nothing helped once the war started in earnest. 'When the roads were closed we couldn't get to Jaffa any more and the villages were impossible,' Toledano said later. 'We had serious problems of communication, so we improvised, holding meetings in no man's land. When the fighting began we simply became a burden. There was very little for us to do and we were overtaken by events.'[36]

Some Arab informants fled their villages and towns. And, for some, the outbreak of hostilities reawakened dormant national loyalties and many refused to continue working for the Jews. At the very moment the Yishuv needed all the intelligence it could get, the Shai's carefully cultivated sources of information simply dried up.

Ya'akov Shimoni, who had moved from the Shai to the Jewish Agency Political Department's Arab Division in 1945, summed up the problem in April 1948. As he reported:

> Contacts with Arabs have been severely damaged. The contacts were severed by the Arabs, who don't dare maintain them; the roads are closed; Jaffa and Tel Aviv are almost completely separated. Several Arabs linked to us have been caught [Lutfi Ya'akub in Jaffa; a Shai informant in Jenin]. But the greatest obstacle to continuing the contacts is from the Jewish side. Jewish troops have killed several Arab informants who wanted to get in touch with us. Many Arabs from the coastal plain who served as informers have been forced to emigrate because of Jewish attacks on Arab transport. The Irgun and Lehi have kidnapped several people connected with us.[37]

From the start of the fighting, senior Shai officers took part, along with Haganah commanders and Arab Division officials, in Ben-Gurion's consultative meetings about the general situation and the state and intentions of the Arab leadership. The meeting of 1–2 January 1948 was the most comprehensive. Danin and Sasson, the Yishuv's two leading Arabists, criticized various Haganah and Palmah operations, such as the one at Khisas in December 1947, in which civilians were killed and which had unnecessarily 'spread the fire' to hitherto quiet areas of Palestine. Ben-Gurion accepted their demand that Arab 'experts', to be drawn mostly from the Shai, be appointed to advise the regional brigade headquarters.[38]

Advisers – their powers limited by Yisrael Galili, head of the Haganah's National Command – were appointed. Emmanuel 'Mano' Friedman, Yosef Fein, Giora Zeid and Elisha Sulz, all veteran and respected Arabists in the north, were attached to the Golani Brigade in Galilee. Amnon Yanai went to the Carmeli Brigade in Haifa and Shimshon Mashbetz, who had worked closely with Danin in the mid-1940s, went to the Alexandroni Brigade on the coastal plain. But their advice was rarely heeded, Palmon complained only two months later. And Danin said that the Shai itself, theoretically still the servant of both the Haganah and the Jewish Agency, rarely took account of the guidelines laid down by the Arab Division experts.[39]

From the very start of hostilities it was clear to the Haganah that the organization needed a new intelligence unit, attached directed to the General Staff, to oversee the collation and analysis of military intelligence.[40] Yigael Yadin proposed setting up an Intelligence Department inside the Operations Branch of the General Staff (Agam 3) headed by an Old Shai hand, Ezra Helmer (Omer), assisted by Yehuda Ginsberg (Gidon). Over the following months this department created a network of intelligence officers who were attached to the Haganah's district (*nafot*) HQs, brigades and battalions. The unit intelligence officers, who worked closely with the Shai men in each area, were responsible for gathering field intelligence, preparing situation reports, supplying information for operations and for POW interrogations. 'The release or liquidation of prisoners requires the permission of the brigade commander,' Yadin ordered in January 1948.[41] That month a first training course for intelligence officers was held under the direction of Zerubavel Arbel, a Palmah reconnaissance unit veteran who had done his own work on the 'village files' project in the north. Chaim

Herzog and Aryeh Simon, another former British army intelligence officer, and Yitzhak Sheffer (Eiran), a Palmah man, were instructors.

The main test for both the Shai and the new Intelligence Department in 1948 concerned predicting the threatened invasion of Palestine by the regular Arab armies. Would they invade, on what date, which armies would participate, what routes would be used, how many troops would be deployed, what would be their objectives? From mid-April Shai agents began to pick up information about the prospective invasion. Most of it concerned Transjordan's Arab Legion, which was in Palestine on secondment to the British army until the end of the Mandate.[42] There was little expectation at this early stage of a concerted invasion by more than one Arab army. '. . . Information about the imminent intervention of the regular Arab armies . . . was, to a great extent, exaggerated and distorted,' wrote one Arab Division official, Shmuel Ya'ari, on 26 April 1948.[43]

Yet in the second half of the month the Shai started picking up hard information about Syrian and Iraqi movements and intentions. (On 30 April the Arab chiefs of staff met in Zarqa in Transjordan to discuss the size and composition of the invading forces.) In early May information about Arab armies massing near the borders began to appear regularly in Shai reports, but was generally buried in a welter of other material about the Arab Liberation Army – the volunteer force operating alongside the Palestinian militias inside the country – and the Palestinian collapse and flight. It was only on 9 May, six days before the actual invasion, that Haganah Operations Branch/Intelligence Department summarized everything that was known. The document outlined the proposed invasion routes of the Syrian, Lebanese and Transjordanian armies and their initial, intermediate and final objectives. 'The Arab armies will allocate 15,000 troops to this operation,' the report predicted. 'The aim of the attack is to defeat the Jews and force them to accept the status of a minority in an Arab state.' The Intelligence Department report was highly inaccurate.[44]

The Shai's assessments were more precise, with its informants more or less correctly estimating the numbers of the invading forces and the routes and objectives of the Arab Legion and the Iraqis.[45] The Shai's political 'twin', the Arab Division of the Political Department, produced fairly accurate information on the strength, training, equipment and structure of the Arab armies.[46]

In general, though, in the words of one official Israeli historian, the information about the invasion available to Zionist intelligence was 'general, vague and inaccurate'. Yigael Yadin, who bore the brunt of preparing for the impending attack in the Haganah operations branch, spoke of a feeling of 'great distress' stemming from fundamental intelligence 'blindness'. Broadly speaking, the Yishuv's intelligence community – the Shahar, the Shai, the Arab Division and the Haganah General Staff/Operations Intelligence Department – had failed to meet their most important challenge.[47]

Reform and reorganization

This failure, which was to tell in the initial Haganah defence against the Arab invasion, such as in the abortive battles in the Latrun salient and in the poor use of certain formations, underlay the massive shake-up of all the intelligence services in June and July 1948. The field commanders were almost unanimous about the shortcomings. 'There is no military intelligence,' said General Shlomo Shamir, commander of the 7th Brigade, 'and without it, it is difficult to fight.' Colonel Nahum Sarig, commander of the Negev Brigade, complained, 'There is no intelligence about the area or the enemy.' General Yitzhak Sadeh, commander of the newly formed 8th Brigade, said, 'Lack of intelligence about the enemy sabotages the war effort.'[48]

It was clear to Ben-Gurion that the intelligence apparatus of the new state had to be reformed and that there must be a clear separation between military and political matters. On 7 June, when independent Israel was just three weeks old and fighting for its life, he met Reuven Zaslani and Isser Be'eri, who had taken over from Shaltiel as overall Shai commander in February. It was agreed that:

a military Shai [information service] should be set up by the general staff under Isser [Be'eri] and Vivian Herzog. An internal Shai [was to be created] under Isser [Halperin–Harel] and Yosef Y[izraeli]. The military Shai in the general staff will be responsible for security . . . censorship and counter-intelligence. The external political Shai – Reuven will head it, and it will be under the Ministry of Defence until the end of the war and thereafter perhaps under the Foreign Ministry.[49]

A fortnight later Be'eri proposed to Ben-Gurion that military intelligence and internal security or counter-intelligence be separated, with Be'eri himself in charge of military intelligence and Isser Harel running security or counter-intelligence.[50] Ben-Gurion made his mind up at the end of the month. The Shai was dismantled, its functions devolving upon several new bodies. The new Intelligence Service (Sherut HaModi'in), functioning within the General Staff and headed by Be'eri with Herzog as his deputy, was given responsibility for 'battle intelligence, field intelligence and counter-intelligence; censorship and electronic monitoring'. Later, 'special duties' were added to these functions. The relationship between the new body and the existing Intelligence Department (in General Staff/Operations), headed by Ezra Omer, remained unclear for weeks. Omer's unit was eventually absorbed into the Intelligence Service.[51]

Members of the Shai's Arab section split up, some going to the Research Unit and Middle East Affairs Department of the Foreign Ministry and others, such as David Karon, the Shai man from Kfar Menachem, Binyamin Gibli and Shmuel Toledano, transferred to the Intelligence Service. Gibli, a handsome twenty-nine-year-old who had worked closely with Ezra Danin, and had been head of the Jerusalem Shai since April, became commander of Shin Mem 1, the service's combat intelligence unit. Karon, for example, continued to work in areas where he was an expert. In November that year he tried to persuade Bedouin sheikhs and their tribes in the Negev area either to move deeper into the desert away from Jewish areas or to leave Israel and resettle in Transjordan.[52] The Intelligence Service was beefed up by veterans of the British and US armies, and by a range of technical experts, including radio men, cryptanalysts, geographers and scientists. By early 1949 it comprised eleven departments, a structure that was to be maintained, with minor changes, for more than a decade:

Shin Mem 1 – combat intelligence, attached to front-line units to collect and interpret intelligence on the Arab armies, supply topographical data and analyse aerial photographs.
Shin Mem 2 – radio intelligence, monitoring enemy signals traffic.
Shin Mem 3 – field security.
Shin Mem 4 – military censorship.
Shin Mem 5 – research centre, serving both military intelligence and the other intelligence-gathering bodies.
Shin Mem 6 – mapping and topography of enemy countries.
Shin Mem 7 – central intelligence library and research branch dealing with foreign, non-Arab armies.
Shin Mem 8 – technical branch, providing the equipment and central laboratory for all intelligence services.
Shin Mem 9 – military attachés liaison branch, for foreign attachés in Israel and Israeli attachés abroad.
Shin Mem 10 – collection of intelligence from open sources and card index files on Arab subjects.
Shin Mem 18 – special operations branch, formerly the Palmah's Shahar unit (the Mist'Aravim).

In the summer of 1948 Isser Be'eri's Intelligence Service inherited the Shai's few remaining Arab agents and continued to run them into Arab-held areas of Palestine or on brief forays into Arab states proper. In July an agent codenamed Abu Zaki toured Amman and Irbid in Transjordan and Nablus in Iraqi-held eastern Palestine. Abu Zaki reported 'large demonstrations' in Amman, prompted by the defeat of the Arab Legion by the

IDF in Lydda and Ramle. There were desertions from the Legion and a popular ground swell against the continued employment of British officers in the Transjordanian army. (The Transjordanian Army, the Arab Legion, was largely led by British officers in 1948. Its commander was Major-General Sir John Glubb – 'Glubb Pasha'.) There was fear, too, of further Israeli air attacks, following raids on Amman and Cairo. The Legion was training able-bodied Palestinian refugees at Zarka in infantry tactics and the use of communications equipment. In Nablus an Arab had been detained on suspicion of spying for Israel; he was found to be in possession of a cheque from a Jewish bank. 'Later he confessed that he was spying for the Jews and informed on several other Arabs in Jenin who were working for us,' an Israeli report noted. 'Among those detained is an Arab named Raja . . . Apparently our Tubasi [an Arab from the town of Tubas] has been caught.'[53]

Raja's fate is unclear, but another Arab spy working for the Israelis, Muhammad Abu Filfel, of Ajjur, was arrested at the end of the year in Ramallah and sentenced to hang. He had reportedly worked for IL7 a month and had been caught 'suspiciously' snooping around the American School, where United Nations truce observers were housed.[54] Abu Zaki was sent on a second mission in August, again visiting the West Bank and Amman and providing useful information about both Iraqi and Jordanian troop deployments.[55]

During the second half of 1948 the Intelligence Service greatly expanded its electronic eavesdropping capabilities. The old Shai focus on the British mandatory authorities was switched to the Arab armies, now the chief target. In July the Intelligence Service picked up a series of messages that gave Israel an accurate picture of Jordanian morale after the Arab Legion defeat at Lydda and Ramle. The mayor of Ramallah, Hanna Khalaf, complained to King Abdullah that his town was flooded with 70,000 refugees from the two Arab cities on the plain. The situation, Khalaf said, was 'impossible' and he asked the king to order their eviction. Abdullah declined, urging Khalaf to 'have patience'.[56]

Other Jordanian messages monitored in this period showed the critical state of the Legion, which made urgent requests for more arms, ammunition, petrol, food and reinforcements.[57]

Another important source of intelligence during 1948 was POW interrogations. One captured legionnaire provided information on the results of the bombing of Amman in mid-July and the state of Palestinian refugees encamped in the Irbid area. The Israeli intelligence community also made efforts to 'turn' POWs so that they would serve either as spies or as propagandists for the Zionist cause. Shimoni secured agreement from the army, via Reuven Zaslani, to free a number of prisoners for such purposes.[58]

Be'eri's disgrace

In the final months of 1948 and in early 1949 it emerged that while the Intelligence Service was performing well in its military capacity, there was still a lack of clarity about the separation of powers and functions between the military and political intelligence services and between internal and external intelligence requirements. The demise of Isser Be'eri – known to all as 'Big' Isser because of his height – underlined the urgent need for further reorganization.

Be'eri, a naturally suspicious man with a penchant for security matters that had developed in his work in the Shai's Internal Department, had left the military core of his duties to his capable deputies, Herzog and Gibli. The other Isser – 'Little' Isser Harel from Tel Aviv – had been unhappy with Be'eri's replacement of Shaltiel, back in February, as the head of the Shai: 'We were in the middle of a war and he found time to deal with traitors, spies and black marketeers,' Harel complained. 'Most of the time he would deal with police matters rather than war duties. First he would decide that so-and-so was a traitor and a spy. The subsequent procedure was unimportant to him.'

'Big' Isser was not a popular man. Dressed always in plain khaki shorts and shirt, without insignia of rank, he looked to one contemporary 'like a Jesuit ascetic during the Inquisition'. His incessant hunt for the 'enemy within' proved his downfall. On 14 May 1948 his officers arrested a prosperous Haifa Jew named Yehuda (Jules) Amster. Be'eri suspected that the city's powerful Mapai party boss, Abba Hushi, a close friend of Amster's, was collaborating with the British. Be'eri's men tortured Amster for seventy-two hours in an attempt to extract evidence that could be used to incriminate Hushi. Blindfolded, Amster was subjected to Chinese water torture, beaten, drugged and burned with cigarettes, but he didn't crack and was finally freed. Be'eri later ordered Haim Waldner (Ya'ari) of the Shai laboratory to manufacture an exchange of three British CID cables implicating Hushi as an informer. Hushi complained to Ben-Gurion and the matter was dropped.

Then, in June or July, the bullet-riddled body of a wealthy Arab, Ali Qassem, of Sidna Ali, a village on the coast north of Tel Aviv, was found in a wadi near Mount Carmel. Qassem, a well-known land dealer, had been an informer for the IDF. The subsequent lackadaisical IDF investigation led to Be'eri, who admitted ordering the execution on the grounds that Qassem had been 'turned' and was spying for the other side. The Israeli justice minister, Pinhas Rosen, demanded that Be'eri be tried for murder. Ben-Gurion agreed to Be'eri's dismissal as head of the Intelligence Service, but decided that the charge should be manslaughter with 'extenuating circumstances'.

At his closed court martial, at the end of December 1948, Be'eri, facing three lieutenant-colonels as judges, declined the services of a defence counsel and argued simply that 'the moment an intelligence service begins to act according to the law, it will cease to be an intelligence service'. The court rejected his argument and in February 1949 convicted him of manslaughter and dismissed him from his post.[59]

There was more trouble to come. Shortly after the trial the IDF adjutant-general informed Ben-Gurion that the Hushi cables 'found' by Be'eri were forgeries. The former Intelligence Service commander was thrown out of the army with the rank of private. Doubly disgraced, Be'eri was arrested again in July

1949 and charged with the killing of Meir Tubiansky, a Jewish executive in the Palestine Electric Corporation and veteran Haganah member who had been accused by Be'eri of spying for the British and executed by a Palmah firing squad after a summary field court martial at Beit Jiz, west of Jerusalem, on 29 June 1948, the day before the Shai was disbanded. The court martial was composed of Be'eri, David Karon, another Shai man called Avraham Kremer (Kidron) – a South African Jew who later became Israel's ambassador to Britain – and Gibli. Be'eri was always to maintain that both the IDF commanders and Ben-Gurion had approved the court martial and the execution. Tubiansky's widow learned of her husband's arrest, trial and execution from a newspaper report three weeks afterwards. In 1949, after continuous representations by the widow, the IDF investigated the case and cleared Tubiansky of the espionage charges. Ben-Gurion awarded him the posthumous rank of captain and ordered that a state pension be given to his widow and their son.

Be'eri's trial began in October 1949. Privately, he continued to maintain that Tubiansky had been a British spy and that he had ample evidence to prove it. He declined to state this publicly or to produce the evidence, arguing that to do so would needlessly pain the dead man's family. He also refused to implicate Ben-Gurion, whom he admired greatly, in either the Amster or the Tubiansky cases, saying that this would harm the state. Be'eri was convicted and sentenced symbolically to 'one day in prison' from sunrise to sunset. He died, in 1958, and received a posthumous pardon – as Tubiansky had done – years later.[60]

On 8 February 1949, the day before the Ali Qassem trial judgement was delivered, Ben-Gurion met the IDF chief of staff, Ya'akov Dori, Be'eri and Herzog, and decided that henceforth Israel would have four clearly defined intelligence services. One would be within the police force and deal with criminals. The second would be a military intelligence service, directed against 'foreign enemies'. There would be an internal security service 'for now within the army' and a foreign intelligence service within the Foreign Ministry, 'to coordinate with the military service'.[61]

This second reorganization of Israel's intelligence community resulted in the establishment of the IDF Intelligence Department in March 1949. The Department, part of the IDF General Staff/ Operations, was headed by Chaim Herzog and his deputy was Binyamin Gibli. Unlike Be'eri, Herzog argued from the start that the reformed military Intelligence Department should not deal with internal security or counter-intelligence – except for field security within the armed forces. These, Herzog argued, should properly be handled 'by a special institution for security, subordinate to the minister of defence or the minister of the interior'.[62]

Spying in Cairo

Yolande Harmer was probably Israel's best spy in 1948, and she worked for neither the Shai and its successor, the IDF Intelligence Service, nor the Foreign Ministry's secret Political Division, the embryonic body that later became the Mossad. She was the most prominent and effective of the agents who had been run since the mid-1940s by the Arab Division of the Jewish Agency's Political Department in Arab countries and, after Israel's independence in May 1948, she continued to operate under the control of the Foreign Ministry's Middle East Department.

Yolande, a petite, fragile and attractive blonde who was later, in the fashion of the times, to Hebraize her name to Har-Mor, was the Yishuv's Mata Hari in Cairo. She ran through three husbands in almost as many years before taking on a succession of lovers, some of them simultaneously, mostly from among Egypt's rich and powerful and from the foreign diplomatic corps in Cairo. Under her journalistic cover – she contributed occasional pieces on Egyptian affairs to Paris journals – she moved effortlessly and successfully through Cairene high society. 'Her writing was very limited in scope,' Teddy Kollek said later. 'She was a socialite.'[63]

Yolande Gabai – her maiden name – was born in Egypt to a

Turkish–Jewish mother. First married at the age of seventeen, she was widowed when her third spouse, a wealthy South African businessman and the father of her only child, was killed in an air crash. Moshe Shertok, director of the Jewish Agency Political Department, recruited her as a secret agent for the Zionist cause at a cocktail party in 1945 or 1946. Her activities up to May 1948 were summarized that month by Eli Peleg, the Yishuv's clandestine emissary to Egypt's underground Zionist youth movement. Peleg reported to Shertok, by then Israel's foreign minister, that Yolande's contacts included Tak ed-Din as-Sulh, the chief assistant to Azzam Pasha, the secretary-general of the Arab League, and Mahmoud Mahlouf, son of the Grand Mufti of Cairo. Mahlouf freely volunteered information and promised to 'serve our interests' but needed 1,000 Egyptian pounds to finance his campaign to be elected to parliament. Yolande also had good contacts in the leading Cairo newspaper, *Al-Ahram*. Sulh, who later became prime minister of Lebanon, was infatuated with her. The Swedish ambassador to Egypt, Widar Bagge, had also fallen prey to her charms. 'Several months ago he was completely indifferent to our cause, but today he is an enthusiastic Zionist,' Peleg reported. 'Some of the information on the Egyptian army came from him.' Yolande could easily develop similar contacts with other diplomats, especially American and French, should she be so instructed. At the Polish Embassy in Cairo, Peleg told Shertok, 'We have a diplomat, a Jew, a former member of the Zionist movement who is unreservedly loyal to us. I had contact with him several times a week and received from him information on internal Egyptian problems, military matters and the functioning of the Foreign Ministry.'

But apart from these useful contacts, Zionist intelligence-gathering in Egypt was in a sorry state. The apparatus had been managed since December 1947 by an Egyptian–Jewish lawyer, a veteran Zionist called Filful, who had served British and French intelligence during the world war. In addition there were two paid informants in the Arab League. It was possible, Peleg reported, to hire the services of 'professional informants' for 'modest sums' and there were other Egyptian Jews 'who could be of use'. All of this, however, was hampered by 'lack of budget and lack of clear instructions'. Yolande had a radio transmitter but no one to operate it for her, so she was sending all her reports by mail via the United States, which meant that she was unable to 'keep up with the pace of developments'.[64] She did, however, have one notable success in this period, penetrating the US Embassy and obtaining copies of secret cables sent by Jefferson Patterson, the chargé d'affaires, to the State Department in Washington. One of them, which reached the Israeli Foreign Ministry in August, contained militarily useful information about the numbers of Tunisian and Algerian troops fighting with the Arab forces in Palestine.[65]

Azzam Pasha eventually suspected that she was working for the Israelis and when shortly afterwards, in July 1948, Yolande was arrested, her catalogue of codenamed contacts and lovers did little to help her. The 'Prophet' was 'acting very badly'; the 'Assistant' was 'worried about his own skin'; and despite his passion, Tak ad-Din as-Sulh 'was acting as if he "knew not Joseph"', one Israeli official complained.[66] In prison Yolande fell ill, but someone did manage to help because a month later, in August, she was freed and expelled from the country. Eliahu Sasson was unsure whether the release was due to his personal intercession with senior Egyptian officials or because 'she agreed to the proposal of the Arab League Secretariat "to go free and work for the Arabs"'.[67] Sasson ordered Yolande to come to Paris, where, from early October, she continued to meet and correspond with her Egyptian contacts and provided Tel Aviv with a stream of political intelligence.[68] Yolande had a nice habit of inserting in her letters to Cairo ideas and views suggested by the Foreign Ministry from Tel Aviv, and Shimoni expressed 'great pleasure' at one of them, but added pensively: 'Sometimes I doubt that Omar Bey and his friends are so ingenuous as to believe in Yolande's loyalty to their cause.' Ezra Danin suggested that in one of her future letters, Yolande should 'explain the need to resettle the refugees somewhere outside Israel'.[69]

By early 1949 Yolande had become one of the chief operatives of the Middle East Department's 'Paris Branch', which also included Sasson, Tuvia Arazi, a former Shai officer and Haganah arms procurer in Europe, Salim Bechor, who was in charge of Iraqi affairs, and Ziama Zeligson (soon to change his name to Shmuel Divon), who represented the Political Division. The Paris Branch defined its functions as 'establishing contacts with Arab countries in order to . . . follow developments . . . to propose peace negotiations ... to contact opposition groups with the aim of disrupting the Arab war effort'. Yolande's position was uncertain and some of her colleagues argued that she was ineffective. But Sasson believed she could be useful after the signing of the Israeli–Egyptian armistice agreement in February and prevented her dispatch to the United States, where she was slated to receive an Israeli diplomatic posting, 'to preserve her for future work in Egypt and keep her above suspicion in Egyptian eyes'.[70] Later, during the 1950s, Yolande worked for Israel in Madrid. She died in 1959.

Agents of influence

Throughout the 1940s the Arab Division of the Jewish Agency Political Department, and from 1948 the Middle East Affairs Department of the Foreign Ministry, maintained continuous discreet or clandestine contact with a variety of senior Transjordanian, Syrian, Lebanese and Egyptian officials, including the chief physician to King Abdullah and the Maronite archbishop of Beirut. These contacts, which had begun in earnest in the mid-1930s, were seen as channels through which the Yishuv's views could be conveyed to Arab rulers – agents of influence, in intelligence jargon. The long-standing relationship between the Agency and Abdullah was the most important of these relationships, but links with the Lebanese Christians – intensively exploited as long ago as 1937 to try and win their support for the Peel partition scheme – were of great value too. All of them served also as conduits through which Arab political intelligence reached the Zionist leadership.

Apart from Yolande, the Middle East Affairs Department ran a number of in-and-out agents in the second half of 1948 and in early 1949. One of them, Yusuf Sabbagh, was the French Consulate's 'agent' in the Galilee town of Safad, and he doubled up for both French and Israeli intelligence. Sabbagh reported to the Israelis at the end of June 1948, during the first truce, about the state of the roads and Lebanese troop and Palestinian guerrilla dispositions in the north. He identified Safad as the main objective of the Syrian army and Fawzi Qawuqji's irregular Arab Liberation Army when the truce expired. He had interesting political as well as military information. Palestinian refugees in Lebanon and Syria were anxious 'to end the war at any cost', although Lebanese and Syrian Muslims were more bellicose. The leadership in Damascus wanted 'to continue the war and to destroy the Jews', although Lebanese Christians were pleased by the creation of the Jewish state and saw it as a future ally. Sabbagh recommended a renewal of contacts with Bishop Mubarak in Beirut.[71]

Another important agent who worked for the Middle East Affairs Department in this period was Dr Kumran Ali Bedir-Khan, the European representative of the Kurdish national movement and a well-known chronicler of his people's neglected past. In late July 1948 the department sent him to Transjordan, Syria and Lebanon, and to Egypt to meet some of Yolande's contacts in Cairo and generally to study the situation at first hand. He returned carrying King Abdullah's 'conditions for an arrangement' with Israel and a report on Syrian attempts to obtain military and political support from France. One of Bedir-Khan's main proposals was that Israel should help organize revolts by discontented minorities in Syria and Lebanon, focusing on the Druse and the Maronites. Successful revolts, he and his Israeli supporters argued, would knock these states out of the war and perhaps, by example, indirectly help the Kurdish national cause.[72]

At the end of 1948 the Middle East Affairs Department activated one of its veteran informers, a middle-class Arab from Jerusalem, and sent him on a three-week boat trip, via Cyprus, to Egypt. He was briefed to report back on a strange variety of matters: 'the approximate distance at which the ship was met on arrival by the Suez Canal authority pilot at Port Said'; the nationality and business of warships anchored in Port Said; customs formalities; whether the ex-Mufti of Jerusalem, Haj Amin, was under house arrest; and the private lives of members of the so-called Palestine government-in-exile in Egypt. More seriously, the man was also told 'to endeavour to obtain employment with that government'.

Identifying his main informant in Egypt as Azmi Bey Neguib, a former Egyptian vice-consul in Jerusalem who was now working in the Foreign Ministry in Cairo, the agent reported that there was one (British) destroyer in Port Said; corruption was rampant among the customs inspectors; the Mufti was not under house arrest; and he, himself, was not offered a job with the Palestine government-in-exile. 'I must humbly apologize for not giving perhaps complete satisfaction from this mission,' the Arab spy reported after returning empty-handed to Cyprus. 'The officials I was in contact with (even Azmi) seemed to me very suspicious at the end.'[73]

Sasson, while in Paris, concentrated mainly on meeting Arab leaders and diplomats and exploring the prospects for Arab–Israeli coexistence or peace. But he also ran a fairly active military-intelligence-gathering operation. In September 1948, for example, he sent Shimoni (for onward transmission to 'the military authorities') lists of weapons and ammunition (including 10,000 rifles) Syria was trying to purchase in Western Europe.

Sasson was no spymaster, and he was careless enough to reveal something about the source of his information. Lieutenant-Colonel Fawzi Silalu of the Syrian army was in Paris at the head of a purchasing mission. Previously he had been in Czechoslovakia for several months, 'where he had bought 5million rounds of rifle ammunition but had so far failed to send them to Syria'. The mission included two other officers, named Colonel Fuad Mardam and Captain Faisal, who were living in the Mediterranean Hotel in Rome. Among the Syrian requirements, according to Sasson's extremely detailed list, were 25,000 battle dresses, 1,000 field binoculars, map-making equipment and 50-mm periscopes. Sasson described his source as 'reliable'.[74]

Apparently inadvertently, Sasson had got hold of the tail end of what was certainly one of the Shai's greatest successes in Europe during the 1948 war. The operation began in December 1947, when the Jerusalem Shai obtained a copy of an arms sales contract between the Syrian government and the Czechoslovak Skoda arms factory. Skoda contracted to supply Damascus with 8,000 rifles, 200 machine guns and 6 million bullets – a lot of weaponry in those days. The copy of the contract was obtained by a Jewish police officer named Lustig from the files of the British CID in Jerusalem. Efforts by Golda Myerson (Meir) and Moshe Shertok, the heads of the Jewish Agency Political Department, and by Chaim Weizmann himself, to persuade the Czech government, which was friendly towards the Yishuv, to cancel the contract failed. The Czechs, however, agreed, on the one hand, to delay implementation of the contract and, on the other, to also supply arms to the emergent Jewish state.

In late March 1948 the Syrian arms shipment was finally sent by rail to Yugoslavia, where it was loaded on to the steamer *Lino*, which then sailed for Beirut. But the ship developed engine trouble and docked in the southern Italian port of Bari. The European Shai and agents of the Yishuv's Mossad LeAliya Bet (Institute for Illegal Immigration) went into action. The actual plan was suggested by a Haganah agent in Italy, Ada Sereni, the beautiful widow of Enzo Sereni, a Haganah man who had been parachuted by the British SOE into Nazi-occupied Italy, been caught and had died at Dachau in 1945. A Palmah underwater demolitions team was mobilized and sent to Bari, where frogmen attached a limpet mine to *Lino*'s hull and sank it in the harbour in the early morning hours of 10 April. Neither the Italians nor the Syrians suspected Zionist sabotage.

But the Syrians did not despair. Colonel Mardam, who had handled the deal with the Czechs, organized an expensive salvage operation, and most of the weapons and ammunition were raised from the harbour bed, cleaned and stored in a Bari warehouse. Mardam eventually hired an old Italian corvette, the *Argiro*; he had been steered towards the hiring by Israeli agents. In early August the *Argiro* sailed for Bari, where the arms and ammunition were loaded, and the ship left for Beirut on 19 August. On board were two Italians who worked for the Mossad LeAliya Bet. At sea the *Argiro* was met by a fishing trawler with two Israeli agents, David Ben-Horin and Oved Sadeh, on board. They posed as Egyptian officers with instructions to accompany the *Argiro* to Alexandria. Having boarded the *Argiro*, together with the two Italians they took over the ship on 21 August. Within hours Israeli vessels drew up alongside. The arms (and the crewmen) were transferred to the Israeli ships and the *Argiro* was sunk. A few weeks later the rifles were distributed to soldiers of the Etzioni Brigade on the Jerusalem front. The Italian crewmen were repatriated in March 1949, save one, who died of tuberculosis in Israeli captivity.

The same month, in a bizarre sequel to the affair, the Syrian military authorities put Colonel Mardam on trial for treason after his return to Damascus. The charges stated that he had been seduced in Rome by a beautiful Czech (or, in another version, Yugoslav) Jewess working for Israeli intelligence and persuaded to divert the arms to 'the Zionists'. Mardam was also accused of making a personal profit out of the arms purchases and ship charter. He was sentenced to death. To save Mardam's life, the Israeli foreign minister, Moshe Shertok, issued a public denial of any connection between Israel and the unfortunate Syrian colonel.[75]

The test of battle

Israel was born and survived its trial by combat in 1948 despite the shortcomings of its intelligence services. Failures of both political and military intelligence attended both the British withdrawal from Palestine and the subsequent Arab invasion.

Until the very last moment, in mid-May, the Yishuv's political leaders remained unconvinced that the British were actually leaving and feared that the departure was part of an Anglo-Arab plot designed to usher in a British return. The intelligence services failed to inform or persuade Ben-Gurion and his colleagues of the new (post-1947) reality – that the British simply wanted out and had decided to wash their hands of Palestine.

At the same time, the Shai, the Arab Division of the Jewish Agency Political Department and the Palmah's Arab Platoon all failed to obtain definitive intelligence about enemy intentions and planning until a week or so before the invasion of 15 May. In part this was due to the nature of the beast – Arab irresolution. In mid- or even late April most if not all of the Arab leaders were still undecided about whether or not to invade. And it was the amateur, poorly planned and poorly coordinated character of the invasion that in great measure underlay its defeat.

Yet there had been Arab decision-making and planning, and the Zionist intelligence organizations virtually failed to obtain the details. The 1948 war underlined the fact that the Shai, a clandestine service run on a shoestring budget inside an underground militia, was far from adequate as the primary intelligence body of a state – and a state at war at that.

Since the late 1930s the Shai had developed a network of agents and sources among the Palestinian Arabs and had successfully penetrated the British Mandate government. It served the Yishuv well at the start of hostilities in late 1947. But once the front lines congealed and Arabs and Jews were physically separated, the controller–agent networks fell apart. And if intelligence on the Palestinians was to prove inadequate, how much more so was the Yishuv's intelligence directed against the Arab states.

In general, the Shai performed badly when it came to the collection or assessment of military intelligence; so did its successor organization, the IDF Intelligence Service. Ben-Gurion's realization that the war was being fought 'blind' underlay the two-stage shake-up of the intelligence bodies in the summer of 1948 and early 1949. The second stage also owed much to the case of Isser Be'eri, which highlighted – for the first but not the last time in Israeli history – the lack of ministerial, parliamentary or other controls over secret services.

On a tactical level, the Yishuv's intelligence bodies notched up some important successes. The Palmah's Arab Platoon brought back useful information about Arab morale and military preparedness. It managed, together with the Shai – albeit at the last minute – to divine the prospective routes of the invading Arab armies. The Foreign Ministry, through agents like Yolande Harmer and Bedir-Khan, was able to obtain some hard political intelligence from King Farouk's court in Cairo and Abdullah's in Amman. And the Shai's European branch had been able to keep tabs on and, in at least one case, scuttle enemy arms-acquisition projects. It was, all in all, an uneven beginning, but there were soon to be enough opportunities for improvement.

3

Birth Pangs: 1948–51

From the Political Division to the Mossad

In May 1948, though beset by myriad other problems, including an invasion by five Arab armies, Ben-Gurion, Shertok, the foreign minister and the heads of Israel's fledgling intelligence community set about organizing a foreign espionage service. Their model from the start, pushed by Chaim Herzog of IDF Intelligence, was Britain's legendary SIS, which was still considered – before the later exposure of so many Soviet 'moles' – as the best secret service in the world.

In May and June the Foreign Ministry in Tel Aviv set up the misleadingly named 'Political Division' (HaMahlaka HaMedinit, codenamed 'Da'at' or 'Bina') under Boris Guriel, who before the war had made his intelligence reputation as head of the Shai's British or Political Department. The Division's personnel came mostly from the Shai and from the disbanded Jewish Agency Political Department. The man appointed to head the key Operations Branch of the Political Division was Arthur (Asher) Ben-Natan, a colourful German-born Haganah operative with years of experience in organizing illegal immigration networks across Europe. In September Ben-Natan moved his headquarters to Paris, which before the war had served as the Shai's European centre. Ben-Natan retained the Paris station's codename, 'Yanai', calling it 'Yanai Centre'.

At home Guriel supervised the Division's domestic intelligence and counter-intelligence operations against foreign embassies and consulates and United Nations offices and personnel. Guriel saw this as a natural continuation of his pre-state intelligence-gathering work against the British. The operations included wire-tapping, radio monitoring and opening diplomatic bags as well as the surveillance and recruitment of diplomatic personnel and local employees. The Division had branches in Jerusalem and Haifa as well as its HQ in Tel Aviv.

Isser Harel, by now head of the Shin Bet (General Security Service – GSS), claimed angrily that Guriel had no authority to carry out such work. It came to 'Little' Isser's attention only after several East European missions complained of break-ins to their premises. Harel's first assumption, naturally enough, was that these operations were the work of Western intelligence services. But Shin Bet surveillance teams soon caught several Political Division agents red-handed.[1] After that, in July 1950, all local intelligence and counter-intelligence functions were transferred to the GSS.[2]

Guriel and Ben-Natan, who were often at odds, operated under the supervision of Reuven Shiloah, who by now bore the suitably mysterious title of Adviser on Special Duties to the Foreign Minister. Shiloah's function, besides overseeing the work of the Political Division, was to liaise, on the one hand, between the key departments of the Foreign Ministry – the Political Division, the Research Unit and the Middle East Affairs Department – and, on the other, between the ministry and the Defence Ministry, the IDF and the Intelligence Service.

From 1949 Shiloah also served as chairman of the Coordinating Committee of the Intelligence Services, a body created at Chaim Herzog's suggestion in an attempt to oversee and coordinate the work of the services and reduce the almost constant friction between them. The committee met for the first time in April that year and Shiloah headed it until March 1953. It was composed of the heads and deputy heads of the IDF Intelligence Department, the Political Division and the GSS. The inspector general of police and his deputy were also members.

The Political Division set up its first networks and stations abroad during the second half of 1948 and each station soon contained representatives of both army intelligence and the Shin Bet. During 1949, when the IDF concluded that the Division's Paris station was incapable of collecting the type of military information the army required, the IDF Intelligence Department opened its own office in the French capital. Its head, Major Haim Gaon, was ordered by Lieutenant-Colonel Binyamin Gibli, the deputy director of military intelligence, to create a complete information-gathering apparatus, with its own agents and independent communications links to Tel Aviv. IDF Intelligence Department officers set up shop in 1950 in other European capitals.[3]

A large Political Division station, based on the Mossad LeAliya Bet's efficient Italian network, was created in Rome. In late 1948 the Division also had stations or full-time operatives in Holland, North Africa, Belgium, Czechoslovakia and Germany. These, Ben-Gurion was told, collected information on 'Arab arms purchases, Arab activity [abroad] in general, economic relations between the Arab states and Europe, the policies of France and Italy [and the Vatican] and Belgium and Britain towards the Middle East . . .' The Israeli agents had formal links with the Italian and French intelligence services 'and were receiving information' from them. Altogether, there were fifteen full-time Israeli agents working abroad, and there were an undetermined number of 'volunteers' helping them. The entire operation cost some IL3,000 per month.[4]

Isser Harel was highly critical of the Political Division's *modus operandi*. As he wrote caustically later:

> Guriel and Ben-Natan saw secret services as an instrument for carrying out any illegal and immoral action. They saw intelligence work in Europe in a romantic and adventurous light. They pretended to be expert in the ways of the wide world . . . and sought to behave like international spies at home in the glory and the shadows on the fine line between law and licentiousness.

Smuggling and black-marketeering were necessary to finance their life style in the absence of a large enough official budget.[5] Harel told Ben-Gurion in June 1950: 'Israelis are smearing the country's name, trading on the black market and dealing in currency, and more.'[6]

Friendly spies

Early liaison with friendly foreign intelligence and security services was facilitated by the informal links that had been established with influential or rising individuals during and after the world war. By 1945 Shiloah and his deputy, Teddy Kollek, had worked with the US Office of Strategic Services (OSS) in Washington, Cairo and Istanbul. Kollek, a Viennese-born kibbutznik who was blessed with greater social gifts than his taciturn boss, even persuaded the US military attaché in Turkey to send cables in his own code to the US Consulate in Jerusalem, which then transferred them to the Jewish Agency.[7] Shiloah also got to know the head of the OSS counter-intelligence section X-2 in Italy, a young officer called James Jesus Angleton. Their relationship was to prove crucial in cementing ties with the CIA in later years.

Before the final, bitter struggle against the British, useful contacts were made with their people too. Kollek had been in close touch with Maurice Oldfield of SIME (Security Intelligence Middle East – MI5's cover name) in Cairo[8] and they worked together against the Irgun and the Stern Gang in the last years of the Mandate. 'After the murder of Lord Moyne by Jewish terrorists in 1944,' Kollek wrote later, 'the Jewish Agency worked in close cooperation with the British to demonstrate our disavowal of terrorism and prevent further incidents of that nature.'[9]

The Labour foreign secretary, Ernest Bevin, had been hostile to the idea of Jewish independence, but Britain's Secret Intelligence Service quickly and pragmatically recognized the benefits of working with the Israelis. 'From 1948 onwards,' according to an authoritative British source, 'the SIS station in Tel Aviv, its incumbent usually one of the few women officers, ensured a two-way flow of intelligence during years when overt relations between the two governments varied from cool to frigid.'[10] In France in 1946 and 1947, operatives of the Haganah's *bricha* (escape) organization had been helped by the left-wing officials of the powerful Ministry of the Interior. André Blimel, head of the French Zionist Federation, was the lawyer and close friend of Roger Wybot, a Gaullist resistance fighter and the then head of the Direction de la Surveillance du Territoire (DST) internal security service. When the DST located a secret Haganah transmitter in the Paris area, Wybot intervened and the personnel – French Jews and Palestinian emissaries – were released.[11] The Mossad was to inherit the Political Division's useful ties with the DST, but, ironically, it was IDF Intelligence that really established a strong French connection a few years later.

Birth pangs

Israel's bureaucratic birth pangs did not end in the summer of 1948. In the first months of independence sheer chaos often reigned as newly appointed officials and newly created agencies, services, departments and ministries jockeyed simultaneously for power, influence and a place in the sun. Friction, strain and duplication were the norm. Intelligence was no exception. The various Foreign Ministry departments were frequently at loggerheads; they repeatedly clashed, singly or collectively, with the Defence Ministry and the different branches of the IDF, especially the Intelligence Service. Who was responsible for collecting the military intelligence Israel needed? Who was to recruit and run spies abroad? Who needed to receive intelligence data? Whose job was it to analyse the raw data, assess it, and present the digested product to the political leaders? Many of these crucial questions remained unanswered for months. The fact that all these institutional births took place in circumstances of great chaos – of war, mass exodus of the Palestinians and mass Jewish immigration – only added to the confusion.

Ya'akov Shimoni of the Foreign Ministry Middle East Affairs Department summed up the situation accurately:

. . . the areas [of interest, authority] between us and Reuven [Shiloah and the Political Division] are a minor and simple problem compared with the [problem] of areas between us and Reuven together and, first and foremost, the military Intelligence Service . . . The truth is that our friend Isser [Be'eri, the head of the Service] continues to pursue a policy of gathering under his wing, and under his wing alone, the maximum activity and powers. In so far as this relates to intelligence work among the Arabs, this is Reuven's problem; and, in so far as this concerns, for example, activities among [Israel's] minorities, the mobilization of Druse companies [for the IDF] etc., then it is our problem. Reuven has taken upon himself to arrange matters definitively with the [IDF General] Staff . . . Meanwhile Ezra [Danin] has discussed the matter with [IDF chief of staff] Ya'akov D[ori] and there is hope that matters will be sorted out.[12]

My enemy's enemy is my friend

In the summer of 1948 Shimoni and his colleagues were greatly concerned by the Druse, the small and secretive sect who lived in the mountains of Galilee, Lebanon and Syria. Israeli officials hoped to be able to mobilize them against the Arabs, both politically and militarily. The Druse fell into that category of non-Arabs or non-Muslim peoples and religious minorities to whom Ben-Gurion and his advisers looked, both in the pre-state period and after independence in 1948, as natural allies of the 'minority' Jewish state in its confrontation with the surrounding Muslim Arab majority.[13] The concept that 'My enemy's enemy is my friend' was to serve for years as a guide to Israeli relations with Lebanon's Maronite Christians, with the Kurds of Iraq, with the black animists and Christians of southern Sudan, with non-Arab Iran and with the Druse both inside and outside Israel. And links with these 'enemy's enemy' peoples, parties and countries were later to be the responsibility chiefly of the Mossad.

In July 1948 a Druse company of about sixty soldiers, noting the turn in the tide of the Palestine war, had switched allegiance from the Arab cause to the Jews and had joined forces with the

IDF in Galilee. An old Shai hand, Giora Zeid, was appointed their commander. A dispute quickly sprang up between the IDF Intelligence Service and the Foreign Ministry Middle East Affairs Department over who would determine how the company should be employed. The department was also busy during those summer months trying to recruit a further company of Druse fighters from the Western Galilee villages of Yarka, Julis and Abu Snein, which at the time lay in no man's land between the IDF and Arab Liberation Army front lines. Josh Palmon, Mordechai Shachevitz and Zeid were involved in the clandestine negotiations, and in August Shimoni and Ezra Danin secretly visited Abu Snein to set the seal on the Druse–Israeli alliance.[14]

But the ambitions of the Middle East Affairs Department were more far-reaching. Its officials hoped for an alliance between Israel and the Syrian Druse that would trigger off a revolt against the Damascus government in Jabal Druse and thus knock Syria out of the war. In the summer of 1948 Shimoni and Danin sent out continuous feelers to Lebanese and Syrian Druse leaders to try to forge such an alliance and hammer out a plan of action. An Israeli agent named 'Labib' was sent to see the main Syrian Druse leaders. At one point, stuck in Hasbaya in southern Lebanon, Labib reported that he was 'under suspicion and being followed'.[15] He tried to set up a meeting to discuss, as Shimoni put it, 'linking up with potential rebellious forces in Syria, primarily the Druse, in order to create a serious diversion and stick a poisoned knife in the back of Arab unity . . .'

But Moshe Shertok cautioned Shimoni that Israel simply lacked the financial and military wherewithal to back such a revolt. The foreign minister, who was always suspicious of such grandiose schemes, was willing only to approve further 'feelers'. Shimoni drew heart from the prospect of further Syrian Druse defections to the IDF and of a switch of allegiance by Syrian Circassians to Israel.[16]

Yet the matter was never completely dropped. During the autumn lobbying by Bedir-Khan, the European representative of the Kurdish national movement, sparked off a lengthy discussion in the Israeli intelligence community of a possible Druse–Kurdish–Circassian revolt in Syria. But scepticism about its potential again quashed the idea of Israeli assistance. It was not the last time such ideas were raised.[17]

The issue of support for minority or opposition groups in the Arab world preoccupied Israeli intelligence for years to come. In January 1949 the senior officials involved – Shiloah, Shimoni, Danin, Sasson and the Foreign Ministry director-general, Walter Eytan – agreed that these contacts must be conducted 'only in a manner that does not implicate the State of Israel, or Israeli officials'. For the moment, the Arab section of the Political Division and the Middle East Affairs Department were expected to cooperate in this sensitive field.[18]

Secret arguments and secret problems

As time went on, the duplication of functions between the Political Division stations and IDF Intelligence Department offices in Europe continued to cause serious problems. One potentially promising operation begun by Asher Ben-Natan from his Paris headquarters – to plant an agent under foreign diplomatic cover in Egypt – ended in disaster when Binyamin Gibli insisted that the candidate for the mission be supplied by the army. The amateur spy was quickly caught.[19]

In February 1950 Reuven Shiloah engineered a compromise under which the Political Division stations were to be responsible for all military intelligence-gathering abroad while the IDF Intelligence Department's officers would be seconded to the Division for the duration of their foreign tours of duty. But the Intelligence Department continued to run independent agents.[20] And Shiloah's efforts to sort out the inter-agency feuds in September 1950 only earned him the anger of both Gibli and Isser Harel.

The organization, objectives and *modus operandi* of the Political Division, which were inherited by the Mossad less than a year later, were outlined with remarkable clarity by Shiloah in July 1950 at a meeting in Jerusalem with the heads of Israeli diplomatic missions abroad. A day in the week-long symposium was devoted to intelligence. Shiloah's detailed presentation set out some specifically Israeli problems as well as highlighting the eternally ambivalent relationship between diplomats and spies everywhere. Apart from the ambassadors and ministers, the conference was attended by the chief of staff, Yigael Yadin, and his deputy, Mordechai Makleff, the head and deputy head of the IDF Intelligence Department, Gibli and Yehoshafat Harkabi, and senior civilian officials, including Josh Palmon, who had left the Foreign Ministry to serve as adviser on Arab affairs to the prime minister.

Shiloah began by stating that rather than offering a comprehensive survey of Israel's foreign intelligence efforts after two years of Political Division operations, he would speak about specific problems of coordination and cooperation between Israeli diplomatic missions abroad and the Division.

He first defined the basic objectives of Israeli intelligence:

> We must penetrate these [i.e. Arab] countries ... We must collect economic, political and military information and be ready to warn the government, in time, of every hostile act. We must follow the activities of these countries around the globe, especially in Europe [and] South America ... where there is a large [Arab] population. We must lend a hand to acts of sabotage in order to frustrate their hostile plans.

Turning to Eastern Europe, Shiloah said:

> We have not so far begun serious work in the states of Eastern Europe. We hope to do this in the near future. There is a need to extend help to the [Israeli] missions dealing with the problems of the Jewish communities [in those countries] and the problems of immigration to Israel from those countries.

Manpower was a serious worry:

> We are suffering increasingly from lack of suitable people for intelligence work abroad. Before the establishment of the state, we could

rely on the help of loyal Jews and non-Jews, in addition to special units of Haganah personnel from [Palestine]. The supportive and special attitude towards us has changed since [1948] and it is difficult to rely on these [Jewish and non-Jewish] circles, who [now] see us as agents of a state who should be treated like agents of any other state.

Speaking more generally, Shiloah told his audience:

The experience gathered by our intelligence units before the establishment of the state is experience of operations underground which do not always suit present-day reality and could even endanger us and our legations. To rectify this situation we intend soon to open a training institution and every year train a number of people suitable for intelligence work and to send them to various legations abroad as additional manpower.

He then explained why foreign intelligence-gathering was carried out by the Political Division within the framework of the Foreign Ministry and its missions:

For financial, security and manpower reasons we have decided to make the Foreign Ministry alone fully responsible for carrying out various intelligence operations, and the country does not have separate intelligence services abroad [serving] the air force, the navy, etc. The collection of political, military, aerial, [and] economic intelligence is solely the preserve of the Political Division . . . The Division unreservedly accepts the assumption that the minister [i.e. the head of mission] himself must have complete authority over every operation of the Division abroad. The minister must be a partner in intelligence matters. On the other hand, it is clear to the Division that there is an urgent need for each mission to have one person whose job will be to deal only with intelligence matters.

In the discussion that followed, Eliahu Epstein (Elath), Israel's minister to London, complained that the status of the Division operatives in foreign missions was not sufficiently clear: he proposed that they be given the rank of second or third secretary, 'to help him make effective contacts'. Elath warned the Political Division not to regard all its work as clandestine. 'A large part of it can be done openly,' he argued, 'especially in the democratic countries, where there is no problem of . . . contacts with commercial, military, scientific and other circles.'

Elath's counterpart in Paris, Maurice Fischer, supported the idea of according the Political Division representative in each capital 'diplomatic title'. He praised the state of cooperation in his mission, where twice a week the minister saw the intelligence material collected 'and decides what [the Division operative] should continue to pursue and what not. He allows the representative of the Division a maximum of freedom, but directs his investigations and activities.'

Abba Eban, the ambassador to Washington, also praised the Division's work, singling out the help it had afforded Israel's mission to the United Nations by sending it material from Cairo dealing with the discussions of the Palestine Conciliation Commission. (The PCC was set up by the UN General Assembly in December 1948 to find ways to solve the Arab–Israeli dispute.) These documents had enabled the Israeli mission to confront the commission's proposals. Material about the churches' policy on the thorny question of Jerusalem was well received too, said Eban, alluding to another political intelligence coup. Eban also referred to the need to obtain information about Arab states through fellow UN members who had missions in the Arab world but were friendly towards Israel. Eban felt that the Political Division representative in each foreign capital should be accorded the rank of first secretary and should be integrated in the routine work of the embassy, so as to place him above suspicion.

The Israeli minister to Ankara, Eliahu Sasson, the veteran Arabist and former head of the Middle East Affairs Department, complained that despite the potential 'wide field of activity', there was still no Political Division operative in Turkey – which left Sasson himself in the awkward dual role of intelligence agent and diplomat. Moshe Ishai, the Israeli minister to Belgrade, insisted that the Division representatives in Eastern Europe could not function effectively without diplomatic cover.

Ehud Avriel, the minister to Bucharest, called for a clear distinction between the Division's work in Western and Eastern Europe. In the East, there was no free access to influential or knowledgeable people and, in any case, Israeli diplomats were under constant counter-intelligence surveillance. He suggested that the Division's operatives in Eastern Europe focus on studying and foiling Soviet Bloc counter-intelligence:

> Who are the people following us; what are the means they are using; what does the Cominform know about the Jews? . . . It is important to know at least several hours in advance about impending actions against Jews; it is important to know who are the people betraying us, who are trying to sabotage our activities, etc. . . . In these countries, the ministers themselves must serve as intelligence agents. They have contacts . . . In addition to the minister, there is room in each mission for a Political Division man . . . The best cover is the commercial [attaché's] job and it is best that whoever carries [the title] will be able to do the job properly.

Avriel singled out former Eastern European diplomats as good sources of intelligence. 'They should be exploited for this purpose,' he said.

Ya'akov Tsur, Israel's minister to Buenos Aires, complained (as did other participants) that not enough Political Division material was reaching them. Tsur asked specifically for intelligence about the Catholic Church and about Lebanon – because of the 400,000 Lebanese living in Argentina. The fact that Argentina had become a haven for Nazis and Fascists should be of special interest to the Division, he argued, and should compel it to keep tabs on developments. This could at some point affect the situation of Argentinian Jewry, and anything learned in good time could save not only Jews but also a lot of money. This dual interest in Argentina's Nazis and its large Arab community was to preoccupy the Mossad for years.

After the meeting, each ambassador and minister met the Political Division executives – Shiloah, Guriel and Ben-Natan – and discussed their mission's particular intelligence problems and needs.[21]

The Mossad is born

The Mossad – which was originally coyly christened HaMossad LeTeum (Institute for Coordination) and in 1963 renamed

HaMossad LeModi'in U'Letafkidim Meyuhadim (Institute for Intelligence and Special Duties) – was formally set up on 2 March 1951 on Ben-Gurion's order. It began operating, with Reuven Shiloah as its founder and first director, on 1 April 1951.

The initial moves to establish Israel's secret intelligence service were set in train by Shiloah in a letter to Ben-Gurion in July 1949. Shiloah had called for the establishment of a 'Central Agency for Problems of Security and Intelligence' (Mossad Merkazi LeBa'ayot Modi'in U'Bitahon) within the Prime Minister's Office.[22] After protracted haggling between Ben-Gurion and the various heads of services, the prime minister sent the following letter to foreign minister Sharett on 13 December 1949:

> On my instructions an institute [*mossad*] for the concentration and coordination of the activities of the intelligence and security services of the state (the Intelligence Department of the Army, the Political Division of the Foreign Ministry, the General Security Service, etc.) is being set up.
>
> I have appointed Reuven Shiloah, the adviser on special operations in the Foreign Ministry, to organize the Mossad and to serve as its head. Reuven Shiloah will work under me, will operate according to my instructions and will report to me constantly about his work; administratively, however, his office will function within the framework of the Foreign Ministry.
>
> I have instructed Reuven Shiloah to submit to the directorate of the Foreign Ministry a manpower and budget proposal for the year 1950–51 limited to IL20,000 in order that IL5,000 of this sum will be spent on special missions [but] only with my prior approval. You are herewith asked to add this budget to the Foreign Ministry budget for 1950–51.[23]

But fifteen months of bitter inter-departmental feuding – between Shiloah, the Political Division, IDF Intelligence and the General Security Service – were to elapse before Ben-Gurion's instructions were carried out and the Mossad finally became operational, replacing and taking over the duties previously performed by the Political Division, as well as other tasks.

At the end of 1950, against the backdrop of angry clashes between the Political Division and IDF Intelligence, Shiloah finally persuaded Ben-Gurion of the need to unify all intelligence gathering operations abroad under one – Mossad – roof. This followed a recommendation by a special three-man committee chaired by Isi Dorot, deputy head of the GSS, the deputy police commissioner and a senior Foreign Ministry official with an intelligence background.[24]

Once Shiloah had obtained the prime minister's agreement he summoned a meeting of the services coordinating committee in January 1951. He agreed with the complaint of IDF Intelligence that it was receiving insufficient and inadequate military intelligence from the Political Division's stations. But it was inappropriate that a number of agencies run spy operations abroad simultaneously. 'I cannot agree to the establishment of separate services abroad,' he said. All foreign espionage must be handled and coordinated by one agency. Ben-Gurion had agreed to this, and in future, Shiloah ruled, all spying abroad would be run by the Mossad HaMerkazi LeTeum (Central Institute for Coordination). The Mossad would have in its directorate representatives of the various 'client' and sister departments and services – the Foreign Ministry, the GSS and IDF General Staff – whose task would be to keep the Mossad informed of their specific intelligence needs.

A few days later, on 8 February 1951, Shiloah, Sharett and Ben-Gurion hammered out the details of the birth of the new agency. Intelligence-gathering would be taken out of the Foreign Ministry's control, the prime minister ruled; the Political Division would be disbanded after less than three inglorious years. Boris Guriel, the director, was summarily dismissed by Sharett and informed that his division was being disbanded.

The spies' revolt

The decision infuriated the Political Division. On 2 March 1951 its senior executives, including Asher Ben-Natan and most of the heads of stations abroad, submitted their collective resignation, the first move in a short but dramatic affair that became known in the folklore of the Israeli secret services as 'the spies' revolt'. The rebels warned that if Ben-Natan was not left in charge of foreign espionage operations, 'Israeli intelligence work will suffer very badly'. Shiloah reacted harshly to this extraordinary behaviour: the Political Division people were ordered not to meet or to discuss the matter in international telephone conversations. Personal files, accounts and other documents were then destroyed in what Harel called the Political Division's 'scorched earth' policy. Several of the rebels were dismissed and others were barred from future postings abroad. Shiloah even temporarily confiscated the passports of some of the executives.[25]

The rebels complained later that all they had wanted was a period of transition in which they could transfer their powers to their Mossad successors in an orderly fashion, but Shiloah, they claimed, had refused.[26] When the Mossad began operating, its personnel included former Political Division executives and former Mossad LeAliya Bet and Shai operatives. Several GSS and IDF Intelligence Department officers also joined the ranks of the new service.

The Political Division's Operations Branch was replaced in the Mossad from April 1951 by the Reshut LeModi'in BeHul (Foreign Intelligence Authority, usually codenamed 'Reshut' or 'Reshut Green' in Mossad cable traffic.) At its head stood Haim Ya'ari (Waldner), a Romanian-born former parachutist. He effectively took over Ben-Natan's job and the stations and agents that had been under his command.[27] Ya'ari (himself codenamed 'Green') had headed the technical section of the Shai and then of the IDF Intelligence Department. He was the man who, in 1948, on Isser Be'eri's instructions, had fabricated the three 'CID telegrams' that Be'eri tried to use to implicate Abba Hushi as an informer for the British.[28] Isi Dorot, Isser Harel's deputy at the GSS, was loaned by Harel to the Mossad, where he served for a year as Shiloah's deputy. Harel probably wanted to keep close tabs on the sister service and its new head. Akiva Levinsky, a Jewish Agency official, was appointed treasurer of the Mossad, and was also charged with various administrative duties.[29]

Haim Ya'ari headed Mossad operations for two years. After dealing with the mess left behind by the rebels, he inherited Political Division networks and stations in various countries, and took the initiative in increasing operations in the Arab states, which were still mainly the preserve of IDF intelligence. And it was in this sensitive area – specifically in Iraq – that the Mossad began its career with one of the worst setbacks in its history.

The Baghdad disaster

At noon on 22 May 1951 Yehuda Tajjar (codenamed 'Dan', then 'Gad') and Mordechai Ben-Porat (codenamed 'Dror', then 'Noah') were picked up by three Iraqi plain-clothes men as they emerged from Baghdad's busy Orozdi-Bek department store, bundled into a waiting car and rushed off to security police headquarters.

Tajjar, posing as an Iranian merchant called Ismail Salhon, was the representative of the Political Division/Mossad in Baghdad; the Iraqi-born Ben-Porat, whose cover was as a local Jew named Menashe Salim, was an emissary of the Mossad LeAliya Bet, which was responsible for organizing the emigration of Iraqi Jewry to Israel. The capture of the two men precipitated the collapse of the 'Iraqi ring', one of Israel's most successful espionage and illegal immigration networks.

It was also one of the most amateur clandestine operations in Israeli history. There was little compartmentalization between the network's three branches – espionage (handled by the Political Division/Mossad), emigration (handled by the Mossad LeAliya Bet) and the local Jewish self-defence organization (apparently handled by everyone). Jewish emigration, banned until 1949, became legal in 1950, but was still organized by (illegal) Israeli agents. Iraqi police had arrested Ben-Porat three times during the previous eighteen months – twice for attempting to illegally cross the border into Iran and once for knocking down an Arab cyclist and then punching an Iraqi army officer.

Ben-Porat's cover held, but only just. In 1951 he repeatedly cabled Tel Aviv that he wanted out, fast. And Tajjar, despite his cover, knew not a word of Persian. He also spoke Arabic with a distinct Palestinian accent.

The two agents were severely tortured but apparently held out. Ben-Porat was released within a few days, arrested again and released once more. In mid-June he fled Iraq in a dramatic, unscheduled midnight flight from Baghdad airport. (To this day the circumstances of Ben-Porat's release are puzzling.) Like all Mossad LeAliya Bet emissaries, Ben-Porat had been thoroughly vetted by the GSS. The Shin Bet report on him had described him as being 'stubborn, ambitious, but lacking in personal initiative and [able to] function only with detailed instructions'. He was also too talkative: 'Many of his acquaintances and neighbours know that he is about to go abroad on a mission', the security service found.[30]

Tajjar's telephone book provided the Iraqis with all the leads they needed. His fellow Mossad agent Robert Rodney ('Hodi', then 'Ehud') and seven Jews working in the emigration registration offices in the Mas'uda Shem-Tov synagogue were quickly picked up. A search of Rodney's and Tajjar's flats yielded secret ink, Hebrew-annotated documents about the private lives of Iraqi politicians and other political intelligence. More torture was followed by further arrests, and the exposure of the Baghdad Jewish community's self-defence network – the Haganah-trained Shura (line) or Babylonian Pioneer Movement. Its secret arms caches of more than 400 grenades, 200 pistols and several dozen sub-machine-guns were confiscated. Explosives, files, typewriters, printing presses and membership lists were also discovered hidden in synagogues or private homes.[31] At Baghdad airport policemen began to routinely stop and interrogate Jews who were about to leave for Israel. The situation was exploited by Iraqi officials for the extortion of bribes on a massive scale. By the end of June 1951 more than eighty Jews were under arrest.

The Shura had been set up in 1942, several months after the previous year's pogrom in Baghdad, in which hundreds of Jews were murdered during the pro-Axis revolt led by the Iraqi prime minister, Rashid Ali al-Kilani. Haganah emissaries – including Shaul Avigur, the Italian Enzo Sereni and Shmarya Guttman – had flown in from Palestine, picked out a core of young Zionists who were regarded as potential leaders and started training schemes and a clandestine arms acquisition programme. From 1943 the Shura was in constant radio communication with Mossad LeAliya Bet headquarters in Tel Aviv. By 1951 it had sixteen branches and 2,000 members around the country. Some 300 of them had undergone military training.

During the immediate post-war years, the Mossad LeAliya Bet emissaries in Baghdad (the station was codenamed 'Berman', then 'Dekel', then 'Oren') and Tehran (codenamed 'Goldman', then 'Nuri', then 'Allon') ran a large-scale, clandestine immigration line, with hundreds of Iraqi Jews crossing the Shatt al-Arab or points north, and, moving through Abadan, Khorramshar and Ahvaz, or Dezful and Kermanshah, journeying to Tehran and then on to Tel Aviv. The trickle gradually turned into a full-scale operation, which within three years was to see 104,000 of Iraq's 110,000 Jews emigrate to Israel, under the stewardship of Mossad LeAliya Bet emissary Shlomo Hillel (who was based in Baghdad in 1947–8 and 1950, and in Tehran in 1949).

Hillel (codenamed 'Emil' or 'Shamai') was born in Baghdad in 1923 and brought up in Palestine. He had organized the first direct flights from Baghdad to Palestine in August 1947. In 1949–50, posing as an airlines executive, 'Charles Armstrong' of 'Near East Air Transport Incorporated', he successfully negotiated with the Iraqi leadership a two-year-long airlift of Iraqi Jewry to Israel. The agreement was anchored in a unique law denaturalizing Jews who wished to leave. No other Arab country gave its Jewish citizens such an irreversible choice about their nationality and destination.[32] This was all the more remarkable since Iraq, which had fought against Israel in 1948, was still technically at war with the Jewish state; the emigration of its Jewish community was criticized at the time by other Arab countries as a reinforcement of Israel and a betrayal of the Arab cause. But the Iraqi leadership gave more weight to economic considerations, chief of which was that almost all the property of the departing Jews reverted to the state treasury. Money was also made from the flights themselves and from the various exit procedures (landing and refuelling fees, visa fees, bribes and so on). An additional reason for the Iraqi decision was that the Jews were seen as a restive and potentially troublesome minority the country was best rid of.[33]

It was towards the end of this airlift, after Hillel had been succeeded by Ben-Porat, that the Baghdad ring collapsed. The first word the Mossad and the Mossad LeAliya Bet in Tel Aviv had of the capture of Tajjar and Ben-Porat was a cable from Baghdad station on 22 May 1951: 'Dan and Dror vanished before noon. Their car was found abandoned on the main street. The police entered the emigrants' camp in Mas'uda Shem-Tov [synagogue] and arrested seven important members, and conducted searches of their houses . . . Assume both Dror and Dan caught.'[34]

Next day the Mossad cabled urgent instructions to its Tehran station, which served as regional control for Baghdad. 'Dan and Dror have vanished, presumed captured. Look into reason for arrest,' headquarters ordered. '. . . Where are the prisoners? Who is conducting the investigation and who is responsible for their arrest?'[35]

The Israeli Foreign Ministry's Middle East Affairs Department assessed that the Iraqi police clampdown was probably part of Baghdad's effort to demonstrate to the Arab world that Iraq was not in cahoots with the Zionist enemy. 'For a while now our people feared that with the approach of the end of the *aliya* [emigration] the police would arrest its organizers,' Shmuel Divon wrote to Reuven Shiloah. 'It is possible that Iraq's activities in Syria [see below] . . . prompted her to take this "anti-Zionist" step which would give evidence of Iraq's war on Israel.' Divon proposed a wide range of means to help Tajjar and Ben-Porat, including mobilizing the help of Iraqi Jewish community leader Yehezkel Shem-Tov ('Amon'), requesting the help of the Iranian diplomatic representative in Baghdad (as Tajjar had an Iranian passport) and raising funds.[36]

For years afterwards Israeli security officials were to agonize over the source of the leak that had led to the initial, fateful arrests. According to an early report from Baghdad, 'one of the Jews informed [the police] that the [Iraqi Jewish] emigration officials were supervised by people from [Israel]'.[37] But a few hours later, Baghdad station reported that the information had originated in the British Legation.[38] Then, two days after that, Baghdad told Tel Aviv that the leak came from the Iraqi Legation in Iran.[39] The more prosaic and now commonly held explanation was that Tajjar was accidentally noticed and identified as an ex-IDF officer by a Palestinian refugee, possibly named 'Salim', who had been in Israeli captivity in 1948 and was now living in Baghdad.[40] Years later a special committee investigated the matter at length. The Mossad's conclusion was that 'the most reasonable assumption was . . . that an Arab refugee who had known [Tajjar] in Jerusalem . . . had noticed him and had referred the matter to the police'.[41]

The last important Israeli agent in Baghdad, the representative of the Jewish Agency's Department for Oriental Jewry (codenamed 'Yoav', later 'Dov') began bombarding Tel Aviv with requests for permission to leave the country immediately.[42] 'Dov' was advised to delay his departure 'for as long as possible'.[43]

Meanwhile, an ambitious Israeli salvage operation got under way. A sum of well over 5,000 Iraqi dinars was rushed by the Jewish Agency through Tehran to Baghdad for bribes and legal costs designed to secure Tajjar's and Ben-Porat's release.[44] Expensive lawyers were hired in the Iraqi capital; others were brought in from Tehran and London. Ronald ('Ronnie') Barnett (codenamed 'Boaz'), a British Jew who had worked for the Mossad LeAliya Bet, was sent in to see what he could do. A fortnight after the first arrests, contact was made in a third country with a senior Iraqi security police officer and 'he agreed in exchange for a large sum of money . . . to release the men [Tajjar, Ben-Porat and Rodney] on bail and to bring them to Iran'.[45] But nothing came of the contact, which was apparently an Iraqi effort to discover the names of other Israeli agents who were still at large.

Yet the Mossad did manage to save Tajjar's life. In late 1951 Barnett and Shiloah met representatives of Iraq's interior minister in Claridge's in London and at a Paris hotel and handed over £10,000 to the interior minister. But the Israelis were told that the lives of the two main Iraqi Jewish defendants, Shalom Salah Shalom and Yosef Ibrahim Basri, could not be spared.[46]

The wave of arrests produced three trials, beginning in October 1951 and ending in January 1952. Twenty-eight Jews and nine Arabs were charged with espionage and illegal possession of arms. Some of the accused were also charged with the bombing and grenade attacks on the Al Bayda coffee shop in Baghdad, in which four Jews were injured in April 1950; on the Jewish emigrants' registration office at the Mas'uda Shem-Tov synagogue, in which three Jews were killed in January 1951; on the US Legation's information office in March 1951; on a Jewish home in May 1951; and on a Jewish shop in June 1951. The prosecution maintained that the aim of the attacks was to undermine the regime, to give the regime a bad (anti-Semitic) name and to create bad blood between Iraq and the Western powers. Some Iraqi Jews maintained, then and for years afterwards, that the attacks on the Jewish targets, especially on the Mas'uda Shem-Tov synagogue, were organized by the Mossad and/or the Mossad LeAliya Bet in order to persuade hesitant Iraqi Jews that it was in their interest to leave their growingly anti-Semitic homeland and emigrate to Israel.

Wilbur Crane Eveland, a former adviser to the CIA who was in Iraq at the time, later gave classic expression to this view, and incidentally supported the accidental explanation for Yehuda Tajjar's arrest. As he wrote:

> Just after I arrived in Baghdad, an Israeli citizen had been recognized . . . his interrogation led to the discovery of fifteen arms caches brought into Iraq by the underground Zionist movement. In an attempt to portray the Iraqis as anti-American and to terrorize the Jews, the Zionists planted bombs in the US Information Service library and synagogues, and soon leaflets began to appear urging Jews to flee to Israel. Embarrassed, the Iraqi government launched a full-scale investigation, and shared its findings with our Embassy.[47]

Salah and Basri were condemned to death and hanged in January 1952; seventeen others were given long prison sentences and a further eighteen were freed. Tajjar was sentenced to life with hard labour. Rodney was given five years with hard labour.[48]

Rodney, whose real name was Peter Niv, had emigrated from Berlin to Palestine with his father in the early 1930s. During the Second World War he had served in the British Army, mainly in India (hence his Mossad codename 'Hodi' – 'Indian'), rising to the rank of major. He was subsequently recruited by Israeli intelligence and sent to Iraq. Niv returned to Israel at the end of the 1950s a broken man. His Indian wife divorced him while he was in prison. Eventually, he married a young Moroccan woman and emigrated to Germany, where he set up a small business in Frankfurt. He died there in 1968.[49]

As for Salah and Basri, many of the Iraqi Jewish immigrants in Israel, who lived for long periods in shabby tent camps with poor services, expressed either indifference or pleasure at their fate. 'This is God's revenge on the movement that brought us here,' some said. Many continued to believe that Salah and Basri had thrown the bombs 'in order to encourage the emigration from Iraq'.[50]

A daring plan was drawn up by military intelligence to try and spring Tajjar from his Iraqi gaol, but this was vetoed by Isser Harel when he succeeded Shiloah shortly afterwards. Tajjar was finally freed in 1960, after the Mossad used its close friendship with Iran's SAVAK secret service to pass on a warning to Iraq's General Qassem of a Nasserist plot against him.[51]

After Tajjar's release Harel appointed a committee of three – Haim Ya'ari and Ya'akov Caroz of the Mossad, and Shmuel M. of the Shin Bet – to investigate the widely held belief that the Mossad, the Mossad LeAliya Bet or Iraqi Jews had been responsible for the grenade attacks of 1950–51. After questioning twelve witnesses (three Israeli emissaries to Baghdad and nine Iraqi Jews) and examining the documentary evidence (the cable traffic between Tel Aviv and Baghdad, and Mossad and Mossad

LeAliya Bet memoranda), the inquiry decided that there was 'no evidence' to prove that the bombs were thrown by Jews or a Jewish organization. Nor did it discover any 'logical reason' that could have motivated any Jewish organization or individual Jews to throw bombs. The committee noted that most of the witnesses questioned suggested that the bombs had been thrown by Jews. Some of these witnesses, it concluded somewhat vaguely, 'reached this view . . . out of considerations that are unclear to the committee'. It attributed these mistaken views to the effects of Iraqi propaganda, 'the coincidence between the throwing of the first bombs and the fluctuations in the Jews' readiness to emigrate', and 'the behaviour of Shalom Salah at his interrogation'.

The committee was 'convinced that the order [to throw the bombs] had not come from any agency in Israel' and that 'even if there was a grain of truth in the view of the witnesses [that local Jews had thrown the bombs], it is clear to the committee beyond any doubt that no orders to commit these acts were given by an Israeli agency or a local [Jewish] agency'.[52]

The Baghdad disaster, which happened in the very first months of the Mossad's life, helped give the Mossad LeAliya Bet a final push towards oblivion. It was understood that the duplication of duties and the multiplication of agents in the field worked against efficient operation. Many tricks of the trade that were developed and refined by the Mossad LeAliya Bet were adopted afterwards by the new service (including the highly successful operation of dummy shipping and airline companies) and some key operatives of the Mossad LeAliya Bet were absorbed in the Mossad.

But the new agency was thwarted in its desire to purchase the Mossad LeAliya Bet's successful clandestine shipping company ('Oniot U'Sfinot Ba'am'). The Israeli national shipping line, Zim, bought up the ships instead – and at bargain prices – before the secret service could get in its bid.[53] Zim's victory may have owed something to the resentment of the Mossad LeAliya Bet executives against their Mossad usurpers.

The damage caused by the exposure of the Baghdad ring was enormous: Tajjar and Rodney appear to have divulged information to their interrogators about Israeli intelligence's very successful penetration of the Iraqi military. That penetration was masterminded by the IDF Intelligence Department's station chief in Tehran, Max Binnet, whose name and role surfaced in the trials in Baghdad, a fact which was to cost him dearly in Egypt only a few years later. Binnet had sent Tel Aviv a great deal of high-grade intelligence originating in the Iraqi military attaché's office in the Iranian capital.

On 20 May 1951, for example, two days before the fall of the Iraqi network, Tehran station sent Tel Aviv first details about the dispatch of an Iraqi fighter squadron to Damascus, to reinforce the Syrians, who were at that time skirmishing with Israel along the Golan–Galilee border. The Iraqis first sent a colonel for secret talks in Damascus. On his return to Baghdad, the Iraqi air force's Seventh Squadron was put on alert. 'There was a secret meeting of the [Iraqi] cabinet whose results were not yet known,' Binnet reported.[54] A further cable that day from Tehran station reported an 'urgent and important meeting in the [Iraqi] General Staff'. The source believed that it was 'decided [there] to send aerial assistance to Syria. The commander of the [Iraqi] air force, Sami Fatah, was recalled from America . . .'[55] Four days later Tehran cabled Tel Aviv that on 17 May 200 Iraqi soldiers and fifteen officers of the First Royal Battalion had reached Damascus. 'The objective of the company is to guard the aircraft of the Seventh Squadron when they arrive.' A battery of Iraqi anti-aircraft guns had also reached the Syrian capital that day. The Seventh Squadron's Fury Fighters left for Damascus on 17 May '. . . with orders to guard Syrian cities and settlements against Israeli air attacks'.[56] On 27 May Tehran station sent a meticulously detailed inventory of the Seventh Squadron's arms and equipment.[57]

The grim story of the Iraqi network provides important insights into both the priorities and methods of Israel's non-military foreign intelligence during the first decade or so of independence. High on the agenda for the secret servants during those heady, nation-building days was the promotion of immigration of masses of Diaspora Jews to their newborn homeland.

Ben-Gurion believed that the 650,000-strong Jewish community of Palestine – now Israel – could not long survive the hostility of the surrounding Arab world unless it was substantially reinforced by large-scale Jewish immigration. He determined that the state's first vital task was to double and even triple its Jewish population, and within a decade this is what happened.

All the state's political, economic and human resources were committed to this objective, with the Mossad LeAliya Bet, the Mossad, the Jewish Agency and the Foreign Ministry playing the main roles. Helping build up exit and escape routes and arranging transportation for Jewish emigrants bound for Israel from 'countries of distress' – countries in which Jews were persecuted and/or with which Israel had no open ties – was one of the two primary functions of the Mossad in those early years.

Indeed, what was to emerge later as one of the Mossad's main tasks – the establishment and maintenance of covert ties with countries with which Israel had no formal relations – owed much to the illegal immigration campaigns of the 1950s. The semi-covert political relationship with Iran, which later became a close and mutually beneficial alliance, was based upon ties established and maintained initially to facilitate the emigration to Israel of Iraqi and Iranian Jewry. The same was true later of Morocco.

The Gross Affair

One of the worst setbacks for Israeli intelligence in this formative period was the Gross Affair, which Isser Harel, for one, saw as vindication of his belief in the endemic adventurism and corruption of the Political Division. Ted (Theodore) Gross, who was named David Magen in Hebrew and Cross in English, was taken on as an agent by the Division's Rome station. According to Harel, he was regarded by Boris Guriel as 'the jewel in the crown, the Division's best agent'. The Hungarian-born Gross, whose family had emigrated to South Africa, had passed himself off to his Division recruiters as a former South African intelligence officer who had liaised during and after the Second World War with various Italian and Allied secret agencies. When the Mossad replaced the Political Division, Gross was passed on as an important agent to the new agency. In fact, he was working, for money, for the Egyptians.

The Shin Bet cottoned on to him in late 1951 or early 1952. But when Harel confronted Boris Guriel with the evidence, Guriel angrily dismissed it, defended Gross and accused Harel of waging a vendetta. 'Little' Isser then took the matter directly to the Committee of the Heads of the Services, where he quickly persuaded the members of Gross's guilt. 'They – including Shiloah – decided that Gross should be eliminated,' Harel said later. 'I objected vigorously and said he must be brought back and tried.'

It was feared that Gross was about to flee to Egypt, where, Harel believed, he would be thoroughly debriefed by his controllers. So Harel travelled to Europe – his first trip abroad as the head of the Shin Bet – and personally handled the matter. It was decided in Tel Aviv to bring Gross back, either by persuasion or by force. Harel somehow managed to trick him into coming home voluntarily. Gross was secretly tried, convicted and gaoled for fifteen years. Guriel, by then already retired, testified in his defence. Gross died in prison.[58]

Reuven Shiloah's tenure as head of the Mossad lasted until September 1952. In March 1953 he resigned from his additional post of chairman of the Intelligence Services Coordinating Committee. Friends as well as rivals explained that he had never suited the job; they defined him as an 'ideas man' rather than an organization man immured in the brass tacks of clandestine operations. It was said later that the collapse of the Baghdad network, the Gross Affair and other problems had simply worn him down.

In mid-1952 Shiloah received serious head injuries in a traffic accident and this also contributed to his decision to step down. But the main reason for his double resignation was the subtle campaign waged against him by Isser Harel. Throughout Shiloah's brief stewardship of the Mossad, the ambitious Harel had kept close tabs on his associate through Isi Dorot, who had been seconded from the GSS, ostensibly to help the chaotic Shiloah with organizational matters. Harel had Ben-Gurion's ear and used his access to good effect. 'I believe that Reuven has failed in his task,' the prime minister noted in his diary after seeing the Shin Bet chief in May 1952.[59] Shiloah, who had showed such early promise, was in many ways a broken man. 'He fought the battle and dreamt the dream of Israel's resurgence only to burn himself out on the altar of his dream,' Abba Eban said after his colleague's untimely death in 1959. 'In Reuven there was a compulsive urge for self-exhaustion, and, alas, we failed to save him from himself.'[60]

Isser Harel became head of the Mossad in September 1952 and stayed in the job for eleven years. At Ben-Gurion's urging he retained overall control of the Shin Bet as well (a new head of the internal security service was appointed the following year), receiving the unusual title HaMemuneh (the responsible one or the appointed one) to indicate his overall responsibility for the two agencies.[61] Harel's enemies thought, unkindly perhaps, that the somewhat pompous phrase was his own. It was first used at a trial where 'Little' Isser was testifying. The judge asked him how he would describe himself. Harel didn't want to say the director of the Mossad and since he was also responsible for, though no longer the head of, the Shin Bet, he said: 'I am the "Memuneh" over the security services.' The title stuck.

4
From War to War: 1949–56

Spying on the Arabs

Israel had come into being in 1948 despite the wishes and strenuous – if poorly organized – efforts of its neighbours. As the years passed, and real or imagined opportunities for peace dissipated, the state's political and military leaders came to realize that Arab enmity was likely to remain constant for years to come and that the Arabs would make life as difficult as possible, both through economic and political sanctions and through low-level military harassment. Israel also believed that some combination of Arab countries, probably led by Egypt and/or Syria, would embark on a full-scale 'second round', with the aims of avenging the defeats of 1948 and crushing the Jewish state, as soon as they felt ready.

For reasons of tradition, size and 'vocation', IDF intelligence was given the primary responsibility for the intelligence effort against the Arab states, although the Mossad, the GSS and the police (Special Branch) all played auxiliary roles. The main concern of IDF intelligence was the threat posed by the Arab armies: what were their intentions, capabilities, weaponry, deployment, tactics and strategy? Were they really preparing to launch the 'second round' and, if so, when? The IDF attempted to answer these questions in its annual national intelligence assessment.

It was a period of transition to a more formal and efficient service. Shula Arazi-Cohen, an Israeli spy who operated in

Lebanon until the mid-1960s, first visited the IDF intelligence HQ in Jaffa in late 1948, when the expensive carved furniture of the original Arab owner stood side by side with rickety and improvised army tables covered with blankets. She noticed a striking difference when she next came, in autumn 1950. 'New procedures had been set up in the Green House. The casual atmosphere was lost. A wooden counter had been added to the front room where another woman soldier sat and recorded Shula's name and her time of arrival in a thick black notebook.'[1]

The Intelligence Department's Research Section, which was set up by Chaim Herzog in 1949, was expanded in the early 1950s, with separate 'desks' allocated to each Arab country. In 1951 and 1952 the section produced a thick annual report, entitled 'Mikre HaKol' ('The Complete Picture'), which described and analysed in very detailed fashion the political and military condition of the Arab states, their possible warlike intentions, their likely routes of advance and probable objectives in an all-out assault on Israel. Shin Mem 5, commanded by Shmuel Toledano, monitored the Arab press and radio stations and was also responsible for prisoner interrogations. Another section questioned recent Jewish immigrants from Arab countries.[2] Yet the IDF was far from omniscient about its Arab enemies in those early years. This was demonstrated on 23 July 1952, when the 'Free Officers' coup toppled the Egyptian monarchy and installed a vaguely socialist regime under General Muhammad Naguib; the driving force was a young colonel called Gamal Abdel Nasser. Israel was taken completely by surprise.[3]

But the main work of IDF intelligence concerned not the 'big picture' but daily, weekly and monthly local-level, country-by-country, area-by-area surveillance, monitoring and assessment. Changes were necessary to make this kind of comprehensive 'coverage' possible. In the course of the 1948 war the Shai's networks of agents, especially inside Palestine, had collapsed; after 1948 the intelligence needs of the IDF focused on the regular Arab armed forces, which had never been significantly penetrated by the Shai.

Lieutenant-Colonel Binyamin Gibli succeeded Herzog as director of the IDF Intelligence Department in 1950. (In December 1953 it was renamed the IDF Intelligence Branch, or Aman, the Hebrew acronym of Agaf Modi'in.) Gibli reorganized the Department's operations and networks: the Special Duties Officers (SDOs, or *katamim* in Hebrew) of Shin Mem 10, who ran Arab agents, were reinforced for cross-border intelligence work; the radio interception bases of Shin Mem 2 were expanded; the Air Force Intelligence Department, which dealt mainly with aerial photography, was developed; and Unit 131 – which operated against Egypt – was reactivated.

The Golan network

Typical of the SDO networks was the Syrian Druse spy ring, which fell in 1951. Most of its members came from the Golan Heights village of Majdal Shams, had been first recruited by the Shai in 1947–8 and were inherited by IDF intelligence after the establishment of the state.

It began with Raphael Grabli, a Tiberias telephone exchange operator who had joined the Shai in 1947. He eavesdropped on British and Arab conversations and reported to the local Shai commander, Aryeh Bibi. When the Shai was dismantled in June 1948, Bibi and Grabli were both inducted into the IDF Intelligence Service. Grabli's superior was Binyamin Shapira, of Kibbutz Amir. Shapira, together with Hillel Landsman, of Kibbutz Ayelet HaShahar, had cultivated ties with Druse villagers across the Syrian border.

In the course of 1948 Bibi and Grabli turned these contacts into a fully fledged spy ring, headed by Hamoud Safadi from Majdal Shams. Safadi's network consisted of a handful of Druse soldiers in the Syrian army, including a company commander and a sergeant in army HQ in Damascus. According to Grabli, the network members were motivated by a belief that Israel would one day conquer and occupy the Golan Heights and that it therefore made sense to work against Syria.

Bibi was the ring's controller until 1949, when he lost a leg in a land-mine explosion. Grabli took over. Members of the network crossed the border once a fortnight and handed over intelligence to Grabli or another officer. The headquarters sergeant, for example, brought over the Syrian military radio communications code. In 1950 the network supplied IDF intelligence with a ten-page document outlining the changes to be made in Syria's Golan Heights fortifications in line with the advice of German military experts in Syrian pay.[4] After the big Israeli–Syrian clash at Tel Mutilla in May 1951, one of the Safadi ring members informed IDF intelligence of the general call-up and state of alert in the Syrian army.

Usually it was Safadi himself who crossed the lines and Grabli would meet him in one of the border kibbutzim. One winter a network member froze to death trying to cross into Israel along the slopes of Mount Hermon. The ring also used a radio transmitter (the Druse operator was unimaginatively codenamed 'Golan') and messages were received by an IDF radio man who worked out of Grabli's home in Tiberias.

In 1951 one of the leading Druse notables on the Golan Heights, Kamal Kanj, crossed the border and offered his services to IDF intelligence. Grabli objected. He knew that the Kanj clan were enemies of the Safadis and suspected that Kanj had been sent by the Syrian authorities. A few days after Kanj was turned back, the Druse ring ceased operating. Newspapers in Damascus reported that the network had been rounded up; a show trial was held and Safadi was sentenced to death. His sentence was later commuted to life imprisonment but he died under torture in the infamous Tadmor gaol. The Safadi clan's lands were nationalized, although Israel returned them after it conquered the Golan Heights in 1967. According to Syrian documents discovered by the IDF in the Six Day War, it was information from Kamal that had led to the discovery of the Safadi ring. Only one of the network members managed to escape to Israel in 1951. He was recruited into IDF intelligence, 'replanted' in the Golan with a new identity and died in 1956. He was posthumously awarded the rank of first lieutenant in the IDF. Grabli left the army after the fall of his network and was succeeded as SDO north by Akiva Feinstein, an old Palmah Mist'Arev who had been in prison in Syria in 1948.[5]

'The Druse are willing'

The fall of the Golan network was the occasion for renewed inter-departmental feuding in Jerusalem. This was set off by Israeli efforts – or rather the lack of them – to help the imprisoned members of the spy ring, but it in fact concerned the broader problem of decision-making about a possible Israeli–Syrian Druse alliance against Damascus.

Throughout the early 1950s Israeli officials continued to toy with the idea of exploiting dissident elements within Syria to try and punch a hole in the wall of Arab hostility that surrounded the Jewish state. Interest focused largely on Iraq, which tried repeatedly in this period to topple successive regimes in Damascus. An intelligence report in Israeli files from January 1950 assessed that the Iraqi Military Mission in Syria was responsible for Baghdad's efforts to organize a 'counter-revolution' in Damascus. The Druse, the report stated, 'will be prepared to participate actively'.[6]

Israeli officials were divided over the desirability of supporting a coup against the generally anti-Western, pro-Egyptian administrations that ruled Syria from 1949 to 1951. The regime had, after all, generally adopted a pragmatic, non-aggressive stance along the border with Israel. In January 1950, for example, Moshe Sasson of the Foreign Ministry suggested informing the Syrians of the names of anti-government conspirators and of the role being played by the Iraqi Military Mission.[7] In the end, though, in late November 1951, it was not an Iraqi-backed group but a pro-Westerner, Colonel Adib Shishakli, who overthrew the short-lived Dawalibi government, to the ire of both Baghdad and Cairo.[8] The Shishakli coup temporarily put a damper on Israeli (and Iraqi) efforts to use the Druse to try to undermine or overthrow the Damascus government. But these efforts were renewed in 1954, as political chaos again engulfed Syria.

The Israelis were watching closely when the beginning of the end of the Shishakli regime came in late January 1954. Representatives of various opposition groups, with the Druse figuring prominently, had met secretly in Homs the previous July and resolved to overthrow the colonel.[9] Shishakli, who of course had his own informers, decided to pre-empt the plotters and struck at the Druse – 'the hard nut' among the rebel groups, according to IDF intelligence. Shishakli generally regarded the Druse 'as a treacherous community and collaborators with Israel'.

Mansour al-Atrash, son of the Druse leader Sultan al-Atrash, was arrested by the Syrian Deuxième Bureau. An attempt to detain his father quickly escalated into a fully fledged battle, with 6,000 Syrian soldiers, using tanks, armoured cars and artillery, 'invading' the Jabal Druse, often meeting fierce resistance. A paratroop company was dropped along the Syrian–Jordanian border to seal off possible escape routes from the Jabal. But Sultan al-Atrash, together with his family and entourage, managed to slip out and was granted political asylum in Jordan.

The punitive operation against the Jabal Druse created renewed Israeli interest in the Syrian opposition groups and in possible assistance that might help them to topple the Damascus government.[10] Shishakli, Hassan al-Atrash complained later, 'made much of the slanderous charge that we were hand in glove with Israel by displaying Israeli arms captured at the front as if they had been seized in the Jabal'.[11] Moshe Dayan, the chief of staff, had indeed suggested to the concerned representatives of Israel's own Druse community that the IDF equip some of them as 'saboteurs', but the community had declined, preferring an Israeli invasion. Moshe Sharett complained that the situation was unclear. 'It transpires that we really have no idea what is really happening on the Jabal or in Syria in general,' the premier wrote. 'This has revealed a serious shortcoming in our intelligence.'[12] All told, the four-day campaign cost the Syrian army 400 dead and 200 wounded; 150 Druse, including women and children, were killed and forty to fifty were wounded.[13] The Syrian push seemed to have succeeded.

But in less than a month, Shishakli was out. Syrian army units in the north of the country revolted; within days, the crack 6th Brigade, stationed in the Jabal Druse area, joined them. The Druse chief of staff of the Syrian army, Shawkat Shugayr, was at first neutral, but he then declared Hashem al-Atassi president. The opposition parties gathered in Homs and set up a coalition government. The Iraqis, according to IDF intelligence, 'apparently had no hand in the coup . . . The Iraqi Legation in Damascus lacked information about what was happening . . .' The acting director of Aman, Yehoshafat ('Fatti') Harkabi, assessed that the coup, and the return to parliamentary government, would render Syria less stable and its armed forces less ready to embark on a war with Israel.

But the defence minister, Pinhas Lavon, rejected Harkabi's analysis and argued that there was evidence indicating Iraqi involvement. Lavon was apparently basing himself on an intercept of a radio message from the rebel leaders to the Iraqis 'not to display too high a profile . . .' The defence minister implied that the Iraqis had organized the revolt 'not through the usual channels' (the Iraqi Legation in Damascus) and hence their machinations were picked up by neither IDF intelligence nor the Syrian regime. He defined Harkabi's assessment as a 'mistake'.[14] Lavon's position may have been a case of ignoring some decisive available intelligence and thinking wishfully and politically: he had tried forcefully to persuade the more cautious Sharett that the 'Iraqi intervention' provided Israel with a 'historic opportunity' to seize Syrian territory beyond the demilitarized zone.[15] Yet later evidence tended to support the view that the anti-Shishakli insurrection 'was encouraged and financed by Iraq'.[16]

Lebanon: intelligence and politics

IDF intelligence in the north did not focus only on Syria and was not restricted solely to espionage: the commander of the

Shin Mem 10 base in the north, Haim Auerbach, also involved himself in Lebanese politics. A general idea about his fields of activity is provided in a letter of 14 February 1951 to Intelligence Department HQ in Tel Aviv. Auerbach reported that three days before, Moshe Sasson and Shmuel Divon of the Foreign Ministry had visited his base in order to meet several of his Lebanese agents and informers. One agent, apparently a Palestinian refugee, codenamed 'Menachem', described the condition of the refugees in Lebanon. Sasson and Divon asked him to prepare reports on the possibility of influencing the Arab League to resettle the refugees in their host countries and on middle-class Lebanese who were interested in developing commercial ties with Israel.

Later the same day Sasson, Divon and Auerbach met a Lebanese agent codenamed 'Yael'. Yael was standing for parliament in the impending Lebanese elections and asked the Israelis to supply him with rifles and sub-machine-guns which would facilitate his election.

Auerbach recommended to his superiors that the IDF should supply 'Yael' with a small quantity of weapons. 'If he does not succeed in getting elected to the Lebanese parliament, he will without doubt try and perhaps succeed in getting an important government post which we will be able to exploit to our benefit.'[17]

Divon himself wrote a follow-up letter to Harkabi, the deputy director of Aman, supporting giving weapons to 'Yael' – 'taking into account the various possibilities "Yael" and his family have in Lebanon, and given our acknowledgement of the services that "Yael"'s family have rendered us. Moreover, our refusal could damage or end the ties with the man . . .'[18]

The SDOs of IDF intelligence worked closely with the police Special Branch and the GSS. In May 1951 both these agencies reported separately on aspects of the forthcoming elections in Lebanon and the content of their material suggests strongly that both were served by the same agent or informer.[19]

A few months later the police reported that the 10th Battalion of the Jordanian Arab Legion had been disbanded because of the discovery of a plot among its officers to kill the new Hashemite monarch, Talal.[20] The police also learned that Jordan intended to execute the four Palestinians arrested in connection with the assassination of King Abdullah, Talal's father.[21]

Most of the SDOs' information came from Arab agents. One of them, Ahmed Zut, was a native of Qaluniya, a small village west of Jerusalem captured by the Haganah and abandoned by its inhabitants in April 1948. He was recruited by the Jerusalem SDO and served repeatedly during the 1950s in Jordan and other Arab countries. At one point the Jordanians were on to him, but he managed to escape to Israel. In the early 1960s Zut returned to Israel, converted to Judaism, changed his name to Shlomo Amir, married and settled down. He was given a petrol station concession in Abu Ghosh, about two miles from the ruins of Qaluniya. He died in 1977.[22]

Another of the SDOs was Rafi Siton, who ran Arab agents in East Jerusalem and the West Bank for some two decades. Siton was born in Aleppo, Syria, emigrated to Israel in 1949 and soon found himself inducted into Aman. There he was trained as an SDO by Ya'akov Nimrodi, the veteran Mist'Arev, and by Yitzhak Shoshan. To get to know the ropes, he accompanied a veteran SDO named Havakuk to several rendezvous on the border with Arab agents. But Siton did not accompany Havakuk to his last meeting, in the Dead Sea area, in December 1951, when his colleague's agent pulled out a gun and shot his Israeli controller dead. 'It was a sobering introduction to the profession,' Siton recalled later.

Until 1965 the SDOs' office in Jerusalem was located in a nondescript apartment building near the YMCA, with a door plaque bearing a lawyer's name. It consisted of a staff of five professional field men, two vehicles, a driver and a secretary. To make up for the shortage in manpower, the intelligence officers often put in twenty-hour days and used their wits to keep their agents in line and overawe them. As Siton said:

We made sure we were always two levels above our agents. Thus we instilled in them the idea that they mustn't try to fob us off with exaggerations or lies . . . For example, we knew everything about East Jerusalem, better than Arab Jerusalemites. We knew in which alleys there were strips of concrete covering the steps so that vehicles could drive through, who sits with whom in which coffeeshop, and what colours the coffeeshop was painted in.

During the 1950s the Aman SDOs recruited agents from every level of society, from Bedouins to intellectuals. It was a time of border raiding by Arab infiltrators and Israeli retaliatory strikes into the West Bank. The SDOs spoke to potential recruits of their mutual interest in calming down the borders by bringing the infiltrations (and the Israeli responses) to an end.

'Afterwards, we always tried to transfer the continued connection on to a financial basis,' said Siton. The link could not be maintained for ever on an ideological basis only.

But we always tried not to spend too much. That is an important component . . . one mustn't give a villager sums above his station, even if he brings in a useful piece of intelligence . . . The minimal monthly [wage] was identical with that of a second lieutenant in the Arab Legion. We normally worked on a monthly wage basis, with bonuses for particularly good intelligence.

The SDOs also supplied the agents with special equipment needed for specific intelligence missions.

For example, we were asked to report on a new network of roads being built north of Nabi Samwil. We gave them [special] equipment and . . . taught them how to report on accurate scale. There was a problem with the Arab agents in accurately reporting distances, so we gave them a course on this in our area . . . We developed methods and instruments adapted to the level of the agents.[23]

Unit 131

Unit 131 – first known as Heker 2 (Research 2)[24] – was originally set up in 1948 as a super-secret section inside Boris Guriel's Political Division with the mission of conducting sabotage and black propaganda operations behind enemy lines.

After the war, over the Political Division's objections, Unit 131 was transferred to the IDF, which had successfully argued that its objectives were military.

A sister unit, 132, was charged with conducting psychological warfare. Before the Egyptian revolution of July 1952 its agents distributed anti-monarchy propaganda in Cairo. One of their more tasteless projects was a photomontage showing King Farouk in bed with a prostitute. An Iraqi-born Israeli called Eliahu Nawi was in charge of black propaganda radio broadcasts to Arab countries.[25]

From 1950 Unit 131 operations were overseen by a committee of two, Reuven Shiloah and the IDF deputy chief of staff, Mordechai Makleff. In 1951 the Unit 131 commander, Lieutenant-Colonel Motke Ben-Tsur, began to set up secret networks in Egypt. His choice to lead the operation, Major Avraham Dar, had been born in Palestine, worked in the Mossad LeAliya Bet in Europe after the Second World War and had operated in Arab countries during the 1948 war. He left the army afterwards, but re-enlisted in 1951. Dar's work was eventually to erupt into Israel's worst intelligence scandal ever.

Dar arrived in Egypt in the summer of 1951, carrying a British passport which identified him as 'John Darling'. Working with clandestine emissaries of the Mossad LeAliya Bet – on a cooperative basis similar to the abortive Iraqi venture of 1948–51 – Dar recruited a group of Egyptian Jewish youngsters and set up underground cells in Cairo and Alexandria. The objective of this network – Jewish self-defence, assistance to illegal emigration, espionage or anti-Egyptian sabotage – was not clear at first to Unit 131 HQ, Dar or the young Jews. The network's functions would be defined and set if and when a crisis arose in Israeli–Egyptian relations.

Dar departed from Egypt at the end of August 1951, leaving behind the two cells, each with an Israeli officer in command and with a radio transmitter for contact with Israel. The network members flew separately to Israel, via France, and were given concentrated – if superficial – courses in communications and sabotage, espionage (identifying ships) and naval demolitions. They were never instructed how to act if arrested; there was no compartmentalization inside the network; and the agents took few precautions against discovery. At the end of 1953, with the members all back in Egypt, the network purchased bomb-producing chemicals from Egyptian pharmacies; they set up an explosives workshop; and they reconnoitred possible targets for the event of war.

Aman decided to activate the network in the spring of 1954. Britain was about to sign an agreement with the Nasser regime to evacuate its troops from the Suez Canal Zone and hand it over to Egypt. Israel viewed this development as a serious threat: free of the British presence (which served as a physical buffer protecting Israel), with its prestige enhanced, Egypt might mount a 'second round' against the Jewish state. Aman wanted to delay the British departure by staging attacks on British targets in Egypt; the bad blood that would result between Cairo and London might torpedo the evacuation agreement.

On 26 May 1954 Motke Ben-Tsur flew to France to meet Avri (Avraham) Elad (Seidenwerg), an Aman agent who had already spent a few months in Cairo, getting to know the lie of the land (but without knowing anything about the Egyptian–Jewish network). Elad was born in Vienna in 1926 and came to Palestine in 1939. He had served with the British army in Europe, helping the Mossad LeAliya Bet transport Jews to Palestine, and had briefly been a driver in the Palmah and elsewhere in the IDF in 1948. He stayed on in the army, reaching the rank of major, before being cashiered and demoted to private for stealing a refrigerator that had belonged to an Arab. In 1952, unemployed, miserable and on the brink of divorce, he was recruited by Ben-Tsur to Unit 131.

In 1954 Elad was ordered to take command of the Egyptian network and activate it against Egyptian, British and American targets. After being briefed in Paris, Elad re-entered Egypt at the end of June on a German passport under the name of Paul Frank, a businessman. To the network he was known as 'Robert'.[26]

From the start Unit 131's functions were a source of controversy within the IDF. Moshe Dayan, the chief of staff, thought spending money and manpower on sideshows was wasteful; the army and, with it, Aman should concentrate on winning on the main prospective battlefields, he argued. Others, including the former chief of staff, Yigael Yadin, and his successor, Mordechai Makleff, thought otherwise. And a further dispute broke out between the Aman commander, Binyamin Gibli, and the Mossad chief, Isser Harel. 'Little' Isser argued that all foreign operations, including those of Unit 131, should come under the aegis of his organization. He also believed that the plans for Unit 131 were 'hasty and adventurous, and were lacking in judgement and political sense'. There was 'no coordination' between the Mossad and Aman concerning the Egyptian operation, Harel was to charge later.[27] Harkabi believed that 131 should not have been activated in peacetime. 'It was geared for use in war to make up for our weakness in the air,' he said later. 'Some in the IDF thought the networks would place bombs [against strategic targets]. That was what they were trained for, not for what happened.'[28]

Harel was told by Harkabi, who was standing in as head of Aman in Gibli's absence abroad, that the plans for Unit 131 were known to Dayan and to defence minister Lavon and had been worked out by Intelligence Branch with the complete approval of the two men. The Mossad chief was to insist later that he was certain that the prime minister, Ben-Gurion, had known nothing of the plans.

Harel demanded the reconstitution of the Committee of Two – the head of the Mossad and deputy IDF chief of staff – that had been set up to direct the work of Unit 131 in 1950. The IDF General Staff discussed the demand and then instructed Harkabi to inform Harel, in mid-February 1954, that the minister of defence had ruled that the IDF was to remain in control of Unit 131 (although IDF Intelligence must 'keep [the Mossad] in the picture').[29]

At a further meeting, towards the end of the month, Harel failed to shift Lavon. Relations between the Mossad and IDF intelligence deteriorated even further when Gibli returned from abroad in March 1954: 'Gibli exploited Lavon's support to alienate the Mossad and to arbitrarily cancel standing arrangements between [the two bodies],' 'Little' Isser complained. 'The cooperation of IDF intelligence with the intelligence-gathering bodies abroad, which were directed by the Mossad, reached a low ebb,' Harkabi agreed. 'Aman had many more Jewish agents in Arab countries than the Mossad did. The Mossad ran mainly Arab agents. Isser complained that we sent in third-rate agents. Maybe he was right. Generally we sent in people with problems. Who else would be willing to serve in an Arab country? What normal person?'[30]

The foul-up

Unimpeded by Harel, Unit 131's Egyptian network embarked on its bombing spree. On 2 July 1954 small firebombs were placed in several post-boxes in Alexandria. On 14 July small, harmless bombs exploded in the US cultural centres in Cairo and Alexandria. On 23 July network members set out to plant bombs in cinemas in Cairo and Alexandria and in a railway marshalling yard in Alexandria. A bomb went off prematurely in the pocket of one of the group, Philip Natanson, as he was about to enter the Rio cinema in Alexandria. Natanson was arrested and that night the Egyptian security police arrested the rest of the network: Dr Moshe Marzuk, Shmuel Azzar, Marcelle Ninio, Victor Levi, Robert Dassa, Meir Za'afran, Meir Meyuhas, Eli Ya'akov and Azzar Cohen. Ninio attempted to commit suicide but failed.[31]

The Egyptians also arrested Yosef Cremona, another Jew who had nothing to do with the network. Cremona died soon after in captivity. The Egyptians said it was suicide, Gibli thought otherwise. Shortly after the Egyptian press announced Cremona's death, the Aman chief reported to Harel and the Foreign Ministry: Cremona had 'stood up to many hours of blows and torture until he gave up the ghost. When [the Egyptians] saw that he had died, they hanged him in the bathroom and left him . . . [Later, the Egyptians] went to "look" for Cremona and "found" him hanging lifeless. The autopsy on Cremona's body determined that he had died before being hanged.'[32]

The Egyptians also picked up Max Binnet, a Unit 131 spy operating independently in Cairo, who had an indirect connection with the network. Binnet, in a basic breach of the rule of compartmentalization, had apparently been used by Aman, at least once, to convey funds to the Cairo Jewish network. Either his network contact, Marcelle Ninio, or Elad, had informed on him to the Egyptians. Isser Harel was to maintain that Elad had betrayed Binnet, although not all his colleagues agreed with this assessment.[33] Ninio, under torture, revealed the make and year of Binnet's car (though not his name as she did not know it). Harel maintained that Elad had already given Binnet away before Ninio made her confession.[34]

Born in Hungary in 1917 to German parents, Binnet had emigrated to Palestine in 1935. He worked as a seaman out of Jaffa and was quickly spotted by the Mossad LeAliya Bet. Binnet then worked for IDF Intelligence in Tehran and Baghdad. In 1951 he joined Unit 131, where his controller was Avraham Dar. In 1952 he was sent to West Germany to bolster his cover.

Binnet had entered Egypt as the representative of a German artificial limbs company. He later became the chief agent of Ford in Egypt, a position that enabled him to visit Egyptian military bases and to maintain close contact with the head of the Cairo military junta, General Muhammad Naguib. Before his arrest, Binnet managed to send his wife and daughter out of Cairo to West Germany. Elad, the network's commander, remained in Egypt for a further fortnight, and then left the country. For years afterwards Harel publicly accused Elad of betraying the network to the Egyptians.[35]

Soon after the fall of the network, Aman was forced to admit responsibility for what had happened, for the prisoners and for efforts to help them. At a top-level inter-departmental meeting in the Prime Minister's Office in Jerusalem in October 1954, Gibli agreed that:

Intelligence Branch was the body that took in these people, trained them for their duties, made some of them soldiers and charged them with certain missions. Therefore, it must take upon itself the handling of the families and relatives [of the prisoners], both morally and in material terms . . . Moreover, the Intelligence men's knowledge of the background and family circumstances of the [prisoners] means that it alone can, if need be, prevent extortion and unjustified demands [by family members].

It was decided that an Aman officer would be stationed for the duration of the affair in the Prime Minister's Office, and he would deal with the families.[36]

After this meeting Gibli activated a wide range of European contacts to try to improve the treatment or obtain the release of the Cairo defendants. Among those approached were French parliamentarians such as Couve de Murville and Daniel Maier and leading British and French lawyers. Gibli even persuaded the West German government to recognize Max Binnet's German citizenship and intercede on his behalf with the Egyptian authorities.[37]

The network's trial began in Cairo on 11 December 1954. Binnet committed suicide on 21 December. After his death, in a rare piece of inter-Arab intelligence cooperation, the Iraqis informed Cairo that Binnet, who had been mentioned in the 1951 Mossad ring trial in Baghdad, had 'headed the extensive spy network that had operated in Iraq and Iran . . .'[38] Marzuk and Azzar were sentenced to death and executed on 31 January 1955. The other agents were given prison sentences, ranging from seven years to life. Two members, Ya'akov and Cohen, were acquitted.

'Who gave the order?'

Disasters of this kind breed committees of inquiry, and the transparent attempt to cause bad blood between Egypt and the United States and Britain was no exception. Pinhas Lavon maintained that the activation of the Egyptian network had occurred without his authorization. The former IDF chief of staff, Ya'akov Dori, and the president of the Supreme Court, Yitzhak Olshan, were appointed to investigate what was henceforward to be known in Israeli politics as 'the affair' (*haparasha*) or 'the foul-up' (*ha'esek ha'bish*). The two-man committee encountered conflicting evidence, forged documents and a variety of suspected cover-ups, and ruled that it was unable to determine where the truth lay about the crucial question of who gave the order. Gibli's secretary, Daliya Goldstein, claimed years later that she had been ordered by her boss to forge one crucial document – a two-page letter from Gibli to Dayan dated 19 July 1954 – purportedly showing that Lavon was responsible for the fatal order to activate the Cairo cell.[39] Both the defence minister and the Aman chief emerged irreparably sullied.[40]

Despite Harel's suspicions, Elad was posted by Gibli to West Germany (according to Harel, in order to keep Elad from giving truthful evidence at the various inquiries being conducted in Tel Aviv). Elad was instructed to recruit agents and set up dummy import–export companies. He made contact with Colonel Osman Nuri, the Egyptian military attaché in Bonn, whom he had met in Cairo when Nuri was deputy director of Egyptian military intelligence. Elad proposed to Tel Aviv that he sign on with Nuri, intending to launch himself on a career as a 'double agent'. Aman toyed with the idea but Harel firmly quashed it and demanded Elad's immediate return to Israel. Elad came back but was soon allowed by Unit 131 to return to Europe. Early on during his stay in Germany Elad was asked to provide Tel Aviv with a list of ten or so possible German recruits. He included in the list a young West German whom he later brought in as a partner in a dummy company. (The German did not know that Elad was an Israeli, let alone a spy.)

But Elad apparently forgot about the list, for in 1956 Elad sent the young German as an intermediary to Colonel Nuri with an offer to sell documents and secrets about Unit 131. By chance a young British-born Mossad operative called David Kimche then began going through the list of potential recruits provided by Elad. He invited Elad's German partner for a drink and, under a false (NATO) flag, sounded him out on possible recruitment. Kimche mentioned Colonel Nuri as a possible target. The young German said: 'Yes, I know the man. My partner [Elad] is trying to sell him something.' Thus the game was up.[41] Elad was lured back to Tel Aviv, interrogated, tried and jailed for ten years for unauthorized contacts with Egyptian intelligence. On his release he emigrated to California, where he proceeded to write *The Third Man* (*Ha'Adam HaShlishi*), a lively, subjective account of his part in the '*parasha*'.

Lavon resigned on 17 February 1955 (and was succeeded at the Defence Ministry by his predecessor, Ben-Gurion, who was soon also to reassume the premiership. Ben-Gurion had been on leave since December 1953, when Moshe Sharett became prime minister). Heads rolled. In April Gibli was removed from command of Aman and Ben-Tsur from command of Unit 131. Gibli was succeeded by Harkabi. Avraham Dar resigned from IDF intelligence in 1957 in protest against Israel's failure to force Egypt to release the Cairo network members in an exchange of prisoners following the Sinai campaign of November 1956. Unknown to the Israelis, among those POWs was General Mohammed Digwi, the governor of Gaza, who had served in 1955 as president of the Egyptian tribunal that had condemned the two Cairo spies to death.

The remaining four prisoners – Marcelle Ninio, Victor Levi, Philip Natanson and Robert Dassa – along with two other Israeli spies – Wolfgang Lotz and his wife – were all freed in 1967. The release was engineered by Harel's successor as Mossad head, Meir Amit, who took the extraordinary step of sending a personal appeal to Nasser.

At the end of the 1967 war, Israel had 6,000 Egyptian POWs; Egypt held seven Israeli soldiers and the six agents. Nasser adamantly refused to include the agents in a prisoner exchange. Amit prevailed on the prime minister, Levi Eshkol, not to go ahead with an exchange that did not include the network agents. Eshkol and the cabinet gave Amit 'a few months'.

At first the Mossad chief tried psychological warfare. He

addressed the officers among the POWs, telling them that Nasser's refusal to free the agents was the obstacle to a general POW release. He then freed two of the officers and 1,000 soldiers as a goodwill gesture. But still no word came back from Cairo.

Amit, pressed for time, then gathered his Arab affairs experts and a group of psychologists to hammer out a personal message to Nasser. Amit proposed a public exchange of the POWs. As to the imprisoned agents, the Mossad chief said that Israel would 'rely upon' Nasser's integrity and sensitivity to their suffering. Israel, for its part, would keep secret Egypt's agreement to release the agents. When no answer was received, Amit renewed his appeal via the commander of the United Nations Truce Supervision Organization (UNTSO), General Odd Bull, who was requested to ask Nasser to promise to release the six 'at a later date'. The Egyptian leader gave Bull his agreement and, a few weeks after the POW exchange, the six were flown to Switzerland. Their release papers identified 'Geneva' as their 'final destination'.[42]

Damage assessment

The Unit 131 prisoners in Cairo, and Lavon and the intelligence bosses in Tel Aviv, were not the only casualties of the affair. Far worse was the damage it, and the harsh sentences, did to the then renascent, though clandestine, Israeli–Egyptian peace process.

Since the Free Officers coup of 1952 and Nasser's later emergence as the new ruler of Egypt, Israeli officials and politicians had looked to Cairo as the most promising candidate for renewed Israeli–Arab peace efforts. Hopes of a separate Israeli–Jordanian peace or non-belligerency treaty had died in the Al-Aqsa Mosque in East Jerusalem on 20 July 1951, when a Palestinian assassin had cut down Jordan's King Abdullah. Since 1947 Abdullah had toyed with the idea of concluding a separate peace with Israel, only to shy away from the brink whenever the signing seemed imminent. His murder put an end to the long Hashemite dalliance with the Jews; Abdullah's successor, Talal, was far from willing to jump in where his more majestic father had in the end feared to tread. Jerusalem now turned to Nasser.

But secret Israeli–Egyptian contacts during 1953–4, which at one point looked promising, were dashed by the bombing campaign and the fall of the Unit 131 network. Israel had demanded that Egypt refrain from imposing harsh sentences on the imprisoned agents and received 'an explicit Egyptian promise not to impose the death penalty'. Nasser personally repeated this assurance to Western diplomats. So when the death sentences were announced, and then carried out, there was a feeling in Jerusalem that Nasser had gone back on his word. 'It is clear that the results of the trial have for the time being blocked any possibility of proceeding on the path that Nasser [himself] outlined, on his own initiative,' commented one senior Israeli diplomat. 'The hostility will increase . . . and one may assume that the period of our restraint in face of Egyptian provocation will also come to an end at the first sign of Egyptian hostility.'[43]

The subsequent assessment of Gideon Rafael, adviser on Middle East affairs to the Foreign Minister, was that the trial had strengthened the hand of those Israeli officials who wanted military action. 'On the other side,' he wrote, 'the Egyptian military and intelligence services increased their vigilance and activities out of fear that Israel would activate its threats.' Eventually, as Rafael put it, 'the blow was delivered'. It came on 28 February 1955, with the massive IDF retaliatory raid against the Egyptian army camp in Gaza. The operation, code-named 'Hetz Shahor' (black arrow), was carried out by two paratroop companies, led by Lieutenant-Colonel Ariel ('Arik') Sharon. It resulted in the deaths of thirty-six Egyptian and Palestinian soldiers and irregulars. Eight Israelis were killed.[44]

Fedayeen

The Gaza raid was an announcement that Israel had taken off the gloves in its relations with Egypt. But it was less a consequence of the death sentences in Cairo than of years of raiding by Palestinian and Egyptian irregulars across the frontiers of the Gaza Strip and West Bank. The Arab marauding, often as close as ten miles from Tel Aviv and on the outskirts of Jerusalem, turned large stretches of the border into virtual combat zones and the fear of sudden attack was the main concern of many Israelis.

Fighting the Arab raiders, who were soon referred to universally as 'fedayeen', and preparing for the 'second round' against the regular Arab armies were the two main preoccupations of the IDF between 1949 and 1956, and, therefore, of IDF intelligence. The Arab attacks prompted an Israeli strategy based on ambushes and patrols and on offensive retaliatory strikes directed either at the infiltrator 'bases', at Arab border villages or at Egyptian or Jordanian army positions. The attacks were designed to pressure the relevant Arab governments into clamping down themselves on the marauders.

Starting spontaneously during the final months of the 1948 war, small groups of Palestinian refugees or individual refugees from among the 700,000 or so who had fled the area that became Israel began to infiltrate the new state's highly pregnable borders. Hundreds of infiltrations occurred each month. Some infiltrators wanted to return and resettle – illegally, in Israeli eyes – in their former homes. Some wished to visit relatives on the Israeli side of the border. Most were bent on material gain – at first by trying to collect possessions and crops in abandoned villages, later by stealing from Jewish farmers or by smuggling drugs or currency. Infiltrators cut telephone wires and damaged irrigation equipment. Some of them clashed with Israeli troops or settlers. A small number of infiltrations were intended to kill Israelis, sabotage Israeli targets or gather intelligence.

By April 1952 Arab infiltrators had committed '4,000 crimes' – mostly theft – on Israeli territory. About 6,000 were captured and almost all were sent back across the border after serving prison terms. Some 100 Israelis were killed by infiltrators during this period and about 200 more were killed up to the 1956 war. One of the high points of the campaign occurred on 17

March 1954, when a gang of raiders ambushed an Israeli civilian bus at Ma'ale Akrabim in the central Negev, slaughtering eleven passengers.[45]

At the beginning the infiltrations were disorganized, but by early 1954 the ḥand of Arab political and military organizations – the Moslem Brotherhood, the Arab Higher Committee and the almost defunct Egypt-based All-Palestine Government – could be seen in some of the more murderous sorties. Jordanian intelligence, for example, identified Sheikh Tawfiq Ibrahim al-Ghalaini ('Little Abu Ibrahim'), a gang leader active in the Jenin area, as an agent of the Arab Higher Committee.[46] Egyptian military intelligence was clearly behind some of the 1954 raiding.

'Creating fear'

In mid-1955, following the big Israeli retaliatory strike in Gaza, the fedayeen operations turned into a full-scale guerrilla campaign that was financed and directed by Egyptian military intelligence, with the Syrian and Jordanian military becoming increasingly active accomplices. According to the Jordanian military attaché in Cairo, Egypt's intention was 'to create an . . . atmosphere of fear and loss of security within Israel which would . . . shake . . . confidence in the government and army'. Emigration would increase, immigration would drop, and 'the morale both of the Egyptian army and the Palestinians in the Gaza area would improve.'[47]

The challenge that faced the Israeli intelligence community was complex: to identify the infiltrators, their commanders and their accomplices; to pinpoint the infiltration bases, routes and targets; to trace the political management and strategic aims, if any, of the operations; and to advise on ways in which the IDF, the Mossad and the Shin Bet could combat the fedayeen. Occasionally, IDF intelligence also turned operational in its own right, sending its agents to attack the infiltrators or their controllers.

The fedayeen were the bread and butter of the operational and research departments of Aman – and, to a lesser extent, of the GSS and police Special Branch until 1956. Arab informers – villagers on both sides of the border and refugees in the camps – were a vital source of information. So were interrogations of captured infiltrators. Less important were IDF intelligence-gathering patrols, telephone-tapping and radio interception.

Typical of the informers was an agent codenamed 'Gadi', who in early 1954 told his Israeli controller, the Aman SDO in the Jerusalem area, about a conversation he had had with a resident of Beit Likiya, a West Bank village west of Jerusalem, concerning a killing in a nearby Jewish settlement. According to 'Gadi's' source, three Palestinians, armed with a Schmeisser and a Tommy gun, had infiltrated the Beit Mahsir area in order to steal goats and cows. In the village of Kessalon they had shot a Jew armed with a Sten gun and taken his weapon. The agent's informant also described the exact route to and from Kessalon used by the gang.[48]

Captured infiltrators were usually cooperative under interrogation. Hussein Hassan Faraj al-Abid, a twenty-one-year-old Gaza vegetable hawker, was caught by Israeli police on 29 September 1954 about fifteen miles north of the Gaza Strip. After interrogation his captors presented him to a UN observer as part of a complaint to the Egyptian–Israeli Mixed Armistice Commission. (Complaints about border violations – infiltrations, exchanges of fire – were submitted in their hundreds every year by Israel and the Arab states to each bilateral armistice commission, which was chaired by a UN officer. The MACs tried to pacify the borders through negotiated local agreements and ruled on who was to blame for violations of the armistice.) Abid said he had entered Israel in mid-September. He said he did not know the purpose of the mission but had been personally instructed by Colonel Mustafa Hafez, the head of Egyptian military intelligence in the Gaza Strip, at the Gaza police station to go with one 'Abed Rabu' to Julis, near Ashkelon. Abid refused: 'Hafez threatened me that if I would not work with them they would beat me and throw me in gaol and cut off my rations and my family's [rations] . . . [So] I did not have any other alternative.' He was promised one Egyptian pound.

Abid described the ten-day sortie. He claimed that he was unarmed but that his companions carried Sten guns. The group's main task was apparently intelligence-gathering. As well as his Sten gun and ammunition, Abed Rabu had been issued with 'paper and a pencil'. In the course of their wanderings, the infiltrators exchanged fire with Israeli guards, blew up a tractor, stole clothes off a washing line on the edge of a settlement, kidnapped two donkeys and two geese, and finally encountered a patrol. Abid was shot in the leg and taken prisoner, although his three companions managed to escape.[49]

Intelligence-gathering against the infiltrators was difficult until 1954, because the infiltrator operations were largely disorganized and uncoordinated and there were no obvious targets against which to retaliate.[50] The work of Israeli intelligence became simpler as the various Arab military organizations became involved in, and then began actually to run, the fedayeen operations.

Until 1954 the IDF told 'the outside world' (as well as senior Israeli officials) that the infiltration on the Jordanian–Israeli border was 'sponsored, inspired, guided or at least utilized by the [Arab] Legion'. But privately the IDF knew better. IDF intelligence reports repeatedly stated explicitly that the Arab Legion and, occasionally, the Egyptian army as well, were making efforts to curb infiltration.[51] At the start of 1954, when Foreign Ministry officials asked Harkabi for some 'documentary proof' of the 'Legion's complicity', the deputy Aman chief responded – twice – that no such proof existed. Indeed, Harkabi concluded, the Jordanians were 'doing their best' to prevent infiltration. 'Listening to Fatti [Harkabi] or his colleagues these days, one could almost mistake them for the British Foreign Office,' one Israeli Foreign Ministry official commented wryly. The official went on to explain the problem thus created, after repeated statements to the contrary by Ben-Gurion, Sharett and Abba Eban. 'If Jordanian complicity is a lie, we have to keep lying. If there is no proof [of such complicity], we have to fabricate it,' he wrote. 'Notwithstanding the recent "discoveries" of the army we, I think, [should] continue to press the point of complicity and we can do so with a clear conscience.'[52]

It was certainly clear to most Israeli officials, at least until the end of 1955, that the Arab Legion's British Commander, General John Glubb (Pasha), was dead set against the raiding because it brought Israeli reprisals against Jordan and complicated the Legion's duties. In early 1954, for example, Glubb complained to the Jordanian defence minister that infiltrators into Israel were 'not being punished'. Glubb argued that 'all infiltration activities entail enemy response'. The Israel Foreign Ministry Research Division commented on this: 'This information dovetails with other reliable intelligence, proving that the Jordanian government is not interested in infiltration and, on the contrary, is taking steps to curb the phenomenon. On the other hand, it appears that there is a huge gap between the general order [to curb infiltration] and its effective implementation by those in charge along the borders.'[53] A few weeks later, after the Ma'ale Akrabim bus massacre, Glubb was reported by Israeli intelligence to be making 'great efforts' to identify and locate the perpetrators.[54]

But Glubb did not represent all currents of opinion in the Hashemite kingdom. Jordan soon followed Egypt in taking an active role in encouraging and then organizing the fedayeen operations. From mid-1955 Aman was – rightly – to regard the fedayeen campaign as part of a coordinated Arab 'softening up' strategy in preparation for the 'second round' against Israel. The campaign, Harkabi said, was run by Egypt, which in September had shifted the focus of operations from the Gaza Strip northwards, to Jordan, Syria and Lebanon, where the operations were run by Egyptian military attachés. Some local operatives were sent to Egypt for commando training. 'We know that the saboteurs raiding from Gaza have been ordered to retreat to the Hebron area and on no account to return to Gaza, in order to blur their tracks and divert the blame [away from Egypt],' Harkabi revealed. He identified the local fedayeen centres – Irbid in Jordan, Maroun al-Ras and Bint Jbail in

Lebanon – and said that 'the names of some of the organizers of the gangs and their modus operandi are known, and we are keeping our eye on them'.[55] Despite this solid evidence, Aman had to wait for more than six months before it received cabinet approval to mount an assassination campaign against the main controllers of the fedayeen operations.

Death in Gaza

Colonel Mustafa Hafez was the director of Egyptian military intelligence in the Gaza Strip. He was also responsible for all of Egypt's fedayeen activities against Israel. On the evening of 11 July 1956, three months before Israel, Britain and France invaded Egypt, Hafez was sitting in the garden of his Gaza headquarters when an agent from Palestine arrived. Hafez and a colleague, Major Imru al-Haridi, went to see the man – Muhammad al-Talalka. Talalka had been in Israel six times in the past two months on missions for Hafez. Using Israeli Bedouin relatives as intermediaries, Talalka had volunteered his services to Israeli intelligence, and reported back regularly to Hafez. On the face of it, Talalka seemed to be well on his way to a successful career as a double agent. But Aman had seen through him (after monitoring a conversation between Talalka and a relative, who also doubled for the Egyptians). It was to be his last mission.

Talalka's Israeli controllers – he knew them only as 'Sadek', 'Abu Nisaf' and 'Abu Salim' – gave him a top-priority assignment from which he expected to earn a fitting bonus. He was ordered to deliver a book, wrapped in brown paper, to Gaza's inspector of police, Lutfi al-Akawi. Talalka was deliberately given to understand that the book contained a secret message to Akawi from Israeli intelligence. He hid the book and, as expected, crossed the border and made directly for Hafez's HQ, where he told Hafez and Haridi what had happened. Talalka – apparently still with his eye on the Israeli bonus – pleaded that he be allowed to deliver the book to Akawi personally. But

Hafez's curiosity was too great. He pulled off the wrapping. A piece of paper fell to the floor, Hafez bent over to pick it up and the package, with its 400-gram bomb, exploded. In one version, Talalka was sent out of the room by Hafez before he opened the package but the agent, also curious, stared into the room through a window or a keyhole. Hafez, Haridi and Talalka were all severely injured. Hafez died a few hours later; Talalka was blinded for life. Akawi was subsequently arrested but a later Egyptian investigation cleared him. Talalka was also cleared. The Egyptian report, presented to President Nasser, stated:

> The attack on Hafez . . . was the result of satanic Israeli intelligence planning. The Israelis exploited the stupidity of the Egyptian agent Talalka and used him as an instrument in the base conspiracy . . . He thought he was handing over to Hafez a dangerous spy [Akawi] . . . Hafez's mistake was, that, despite his usual exaggerated caution and his rich experience, he personally opened the package.[56]

The Egyptian military attaché in Amman, Lieutenant-Colonel Salah Mustafa, was even more careless. Mustafa was Hafez's man in Jordan, via which many of the fedayeen attacks on Israel's border settlements were routed. Mustafa must have heard of Hafez's death the day before. Yet on 12 July, the day after the Gaza assassination, Mustafa's driver collected from the central post office a package sent from East Jerusalem, ostensibly from the headquarters of the UN truce observers. The driver brought the package – which contained a biography of the German Field Marshal von Rundstedt – back to the car and handed it to Mustafa. When the Egyptian attaché opened the parcel it exploded in his face. Mustafa died several hours later.

Both bombings were the work of Aman, with its director, Yehoshafat Harkabi, taking personal charge of the operation. The previous October Harkabi had publicly named Hafez as the mastermind of the fedayeen activities and Salah Mustafa as their organizer in Jordan. Both should have regarded the public statement as a warning – as was intended.[57]

The bombings were the initiative of Haim Levakov, a veteran Palmah intelligence officer. Several months later, after the

Israeli conquest of the Gaza Strip in November 1956, Levakov went to look for Talalka. He found him in a miserable house in a refugee camp, a long scar cutting across his face. He was completely blind. 'He offered us tea, but we declined,' Levakov recalled later. 'Talalka said: "Don't worry, I won't poison you."'[58]

Target Jordan

Aman closely monitored Jordan's changing role in the fedayeen operations, at first resistant, then passive, then active as an accomplice and finally active independently in organizing raids. Up to mid-1955 the Jordanian authorities – particularly the Arab Legion and the courts – tried to halt anti-Israeli infiltration from Jordanian territory. 'According to all the information in our hands . . . the Jordanians are truly interested in blocking the infiltration from their country to Israel, and they are trying . . . to end it,' one Research Department official wrote in mid-1953. 'It is quite clear that the infiltration is not organized, directed and/or encouraged by the responsible Jordanian authorities.'[59]

An IDF Intelligence Branch memorandum from mid-1956 traced this gradual shift from passivity to activism:

> Since autumn 1955 we have been witnessing the activity of irregular elements from Jordan, organized by the Egyptian and Syrian authorities . . . This activity took place until recently without the knowledge of the Jordanian central authorities and was largely underground in character . . . In April 1956 the situation changed for the worse, with increasing cooperation . . . of the Jordanian authorities in the organization of irregular groups [fedayeen] geared to terrorism against Israel . . . The Jordanian authorities then . . . in organized fashion hosted the groups of fedayeen who arrived . . . from the Gaza Strip . . . numbering at least seventy [fighters] . . . [They] were received with honour by units of the Arab Legion and were accorded festive welcomes in the Arab cities, especially in Hebron and Bethlehem, and were lodged in Arab Legion camps . . . Immediately afterwards, the

Jordanian authorities began themselves to initiate the formation ... of groups of irregulars in order to attack Israel. During the past month there has been widespread recruitment of refugees and criminals ... The recruiting officers are battalion COs in the National Guard and the police district commanders ... The recruits are promised a salary to be paid by the Arab Legion ... Select volunteers are given training in sabotage in Arab Legion camps ... We have in our possession lists which include names of Arab Legion and Jordanian police officers organizing this recruitment ... In the past, our custom was to transmit such information to the UN and the Jordanian authorities, but in light of the participation of the Jordanian authorities in these activities, it appears that there is no point in handing over lists, as the upshot would be only to endanger our sources of information.[60]

Intelligence and the test of battle: 1956

The fedayeen raids against Israel and the cycle of counter-raids they precipitated were the main cause of the IDF invasion of the Sinai peninsula on 29 October 1956, the eastern flank of the Anglo–French–Israeli attack on Egypt known as the Suez Campaign. The immediate trigger for the Israeli offensive was the fear of Egypt's military capability, which, it was believed, would shortly be vastly increased as a result of the Egyptian–Czech arms deal of 1955. The IDF commanders feared that the dozens of modern, Soviet-made fighter aircraft, bombers, tanks and guns that began to pour into Egypt would dramatically tip the military scales against Israel within months, and that a pre-emptive strike was necessary for survival.

Israel's generals turned in desperation to France to provide countervailing Western equipment. At the same time, they pressed upon the government plans for a pre-emptive strike that would destroy the Egyptian army before it became too powerful for the IDF to tackle. Once the secret alliance with Britain and France was in place, Ben-Gurion gave IDF chief of staff Moshe Dayan the green light, and on 29 October 1956 the Sinai Campaign was launched.

The countdown to war began with a serious Israeli intelligence blunder. It was the infiltrator raiding that had prompted the IDF's assault on the Egyptian military camp in Gaza on 28 February 1955. Contrary to all Intelligence Branch expectations, that raid led to a large-scale Egyptian guerrilla campaign against Israel, and to the Czech arms deal.

According to Aman, the Gaza border had been relatively quiet in the months preceding the raid. But from the beginning of February, Egypt stepped up its cross-border reconnaissance, 'out of fear that Israel would exploit the inter-Arab crisis' (resulting from the signing of the Baghdad Pact) to attack Egypt. On 26 February these Egyptian scouts murdered an Israeli cyclist near Rehovot; the IDF struck two days later.

In assessing the possible repercussions of the Gaza raid, IDF intelligence argued that Egyptian military intelligence 'could cause tension along the border' or give support to 'local organizations'. The report did not suggest that the Egyptians, as one of their options, could launch a large-scale cross-border guerrilla campaign – which is exactly what they did. Nor did Aman, in this comprehensive twelve-page document, suggest that in response to Gaza, the Egyptians might turn to the Eastern Bloc for arms – which they also did. Indeed, in considering the international reactions to the raid, the intelligence assessment completely omitted mention of the Soviet Bloc.[61]

When Nasser publicly announced the Czech arms deal, on 27 September 1955, there was shock and consternation in Jerusalem. The IDF General Staff and Intelligence Branch immediately embarked on a major internal debate about the scope of the deal, about how long it would take the Egyptians to absorb and deploy the new arms and about how effective these arms were. As a result of the failures revealed by the Czech deal, Intelligence Branch set up two new sections: a Technical Section, under Zvi Reuter, which looked into the capabilities of the various new Soviet weapons introduced or about to be introduced into the region; and an International Section, within the Research Department, whose function was mainly to monitor Soviet political and military penetration of the Middle East.[62]

There was virtual unanimity in the IDF General Staff and in the higher reaches of Aman that Egypt was bent on war and that the arms deal was geared to a 'second round'. The only questions that remained were who would take the initiative and when.

Only at the end of January 1956 did the size of the deal become apparent to Israel, as Dayan noted in his war diary: 'The extent [of the deal] is much more than we supposed: 200 MiG-15s . . .; fifty Ilyushin bombers; sixty half-tracks equipped with 122mm cannon; 275 T-34 tanks . . .'[63] Dayan felt that the Egyptians would be in a position to attack Israel, with weapons more powerful than Israel possessed, within 'months'. Intelligence Branch took a 'less alarmist view of the situation'.

The failure to predict or even suggest the possible consequences of the Gaza raid was in a sense a fitting conclusion to five years of failure by IDF intelligence in assessing properly the likely results of Israel's response to the infiltration and fedayeen incursions. During the early 1950s small IDF units had attacked houses in or near villages that IDF intelligence had identified as the infiltrators' home bases or jump-off points. As often as not, the retaliatory raids – often as vicious as the Arab attacks that prompted them if not more so – struck at the innocent rather than the guilty or their accomplices. And if the aim of the policy was to cow the infiltrators or the Arab host countries into stopping the raids, it was an abysmal failure.

In October 1953, following the Qibya attack, in which more than fifty Arab villagers were killed by an Israeli raiding party, the IDF General Staff decided on a change of policy – to attack Arab military bases and posts rather than civilian targets that rightly or wrongly were considered fedayeen bases. The aim was to force the Arab armies to curb the infiltrators in order to avoid Israeli retaliatory strikes that could lead to a general conflagration, in which the IDF would win.

The fact that the retaliatory policy, in both its stages, failed to curb the infiltrations and, from 1955, itself provoked an increase in fedayeen attacks was never properly appreciated by Aman, or, at least, imparted forcefully to the IDF General Staff. But on the operative, field level, Intelligence Branch performed competently. It selected targets and produced maps and information on access routes and enemy dispositions. The basis of Aman's intelligence on potential targets in the West Bank and the Gaza Strip was 'the village files' – a hangover from the Shai days, when a card index system, with detailed data on every Arab village in Palestine, was the basis of Haganah and Palmah operations. Gideon Mahanaimi, the Paratroop Brigade's intelligence officer, was ordered by his commander, Ariel Sharon, to update the material. Soon there was a file containing ground and aerial photographs, observation and agent reports on every village and military and police post. Reconnaissance patrols, listening posts within enemy lines and prisoner interrogations contributed further information.

Target Egypt

During the course of 1956 the focus of Aman and Mossad information-gathering switched from fedayeen objectives in the West Bank and Gaza Strip to Egypt proper. The pinpricks of guerrilla warfare had been displaced by a preoccupation with Egypt's swelling and increasingly sophisticated arsenal, and by Cairo's repeated threats of launching a 'second' and 'final' round against Israel.

Nasser's announcement on 26 July 1956 of Egypt's nationalization of the Suez Canal made war more or less inevitable. Unit 131, including Avri Elad[64] and Avraham Dar, had for years gathered intelligence about the Egyptian armed forces and, specifically, about the Egyptian order of battle in Sinai. Field intelligence teams had repeatedly penetrated far behind Egyptian lines to gather information about axes of advance (especially ones suitable for tanks and half-tracks) and Egyptian deployments. This effort was stepped up as the invasion date – the night of 29 October – approached. The IDF armoured and infantry brigades went in relatively well prepared.

IDF intelligence had an extremely clear picture of the

Egyptian (and Jordanian, Syrian and Lebanese) order of battle, down to battalion and even company levels, on the eve of the assault on Sinai. On 15 September 1956 Ben-Gurion jotted down in full detail Aman's assessment (made four days earlier) of the order of battle of all the Arab armies.[65]

Dayan noted in February that Egypt had concentrated nine of its sixteen brigades in Sinai. (In 1955 there had been only one Egyptian brigade in Sinai.) The chief of staff believed – probably mistakenly – that the Egyptians were preparing for war in the spring. Though the Egyptian armed forces were far from ready for a successful war against Israel, Egyptian documents captured during the Suez Campaign clearly show that the 'second round' intentions of the Nasser regime had been broadcast throughout the Egyptian army.[66] The Mossad reported at the end of 1955 that 'authoritative and knowledgeable Western circles were convinced that Egypt will attack Israel in about eight months' time'.[67] The IDF assessments had solid foundations.

Many of the Egyptian units stationed in Sinai in early 1956 were withdrawn westwards during the summer to guard the Suez Canal after Nasser's dramatic announcement of the waterway's nationalization. Intelligence Branch kept accurate tabs on the changes of the Egyptian dispositions.

But Dayan continuously urged Ben-Gurion to make a preemptive strike against Egypt. Israel also pressed the United States for arms to offset the Czech weapons deal. Not everyone was so bellicose. The 'dovish' Moshe Sharett, the foreign minister, noted the mounting war hysteria with concern: 'The press is covered with screaming headlines about Egyptian troop concentrations "on the border" . . . [based on IDF briefings]. The impression left is that we are actually on the brink of war, but the sceptical reader can understand that we have artificially exaggerated [this impression in order to] buttress our demand for arms.'[68] Sharett felt that Aman was supporting the hysteria. 'Intelligence Branch suffers from clear tendentiousness and marshals facts to reinforce a political view,' he noted a few months later.[69]

Deception

Aman's main success in 1956, apart from accurately assessing the Arab order of battle, was the grand deception plan that was launched in the second half of October, in the final days before the invasion. Through the media and agents around the Arab world, Intelligence Branch spread the rumour that Jordan rather than Egypt was the prospective Israeli target.

Part of the deception involved disinformation about the entry of Iraqi army units into Jordan. Many IDF reservists were told that a clash with Jordan was imminent. Jerusalem had repeatedly announced that it would regard Iraqi troop movements into Jordan as a *casus belli*; spreading the rumour that this in fact had happened served to reinforce the belief in the neighbouring Arab states and in some Western capitals that Israel was about to attack Jordan. On 29 October 1956, only a few hours before an Israeli paratroop battalion dropped near the Mitla Pass, deep behind Egyptian lines in Sinai, a cable arrived in Jerusalem from President Eisenhower expressing concern at the Israeli mobilization and informing Israel that Iraqi troops had not entered Jordan. Jordan, for its part, reinforced its front-line deployments and Iraq deployed a full division close to its frontier with the Hashemite kingdom.

A secondary deception was launched by the Mossad, under the personal direction of Isser Harel.[70] This involved feeding misinformation to the Egyptians through an unsuspecting channel – possibly a known Arab or Soviet agent in Israel. The operation had been going on for months. As the IDF assault approached, Harel specifically fed this channel with information that he said later was 'the main factor in dissuading the Egyptians from launching air attacks on Israel's cities'.[71]

Israel's cities in 1956 lacked any serious air defences, and during the first, crucial days of the war the IAF's fighter squadrons were engaged almost completely in ground support roles or in aerial interception over the battlefield. Tel Aviv, Haifa and Jerusalem were largely undefended (except for a handful of aircraft the French stationed for the duration of the war at Lydda airport). Harel's deception helped keep the Egyptian bombers away. It is unclear what the misinformation was that persuaded Cairo to hold off its air attacks. It may have been false or exaggerated reports of a bolstering of air defences. Or perhaps it was hints that there was an American commitment to Israel to intervene if the Egyptians attacked her cities.

Another unwitting and complementary conduit for the Mossad deception appears to have been James Angleton, the CIA counter-intelligence chief, who maintained close and sympathetic liaison with the Israelis. According to Robert Amory, the CIA's deputy director of intelligence, Washington learned of the imminent Israeli attack when a US military attaché in Tel Aviv reported that his driver, a disabled Israeli reservist, had been called up. Amory concluded that a full-scale mobilization was under way. Angleton disagreed strongly. His Israeli contacts had told him emphatically that there would be no attack. An angry Amory called Angleton 'this co-opted Israeli agent', but years later Amory would argue that Angleton was 'duped and not duplicitous'.[72]

On the very eve of the war precise intelligence allowed the Israelis to strike a powerful preparatory blow against the Egyptians. During the night of 28 October, only hours before the paratroops dropped near the Mitla Pass, a lone IAF Meteor jet, using its wing cannons, shot down an Ilyushin-14 transport plane over the Mediterranean. It was carrying eighteen senior Egyptian general staff officers, who were returning to Cairo from Damascus after signing a mutual defence pact with Syria. Nasser's commander-in-chief, Marshal Abdel-Hakim Amer, was saved only because he stayed behind at the last minute. 'That's the first half of the war over,' Dayan told the Meteor pilot, Yoash Tsidon, when he returned to base. 'Let's go and drink to the second half.' Israel did not admit responsibility for downing the Ilyushin and Tsidon received a citation with the details of his exploit left blank for security reasons.[73]

The sensitivity of the coup was such that when the incident was first fully described, over thirty years later, IDF sources complained that the military censor had erred in approving the story for publication.[74] At the time the incident made a powerful impression on the Egyptians. Two years later, in 1958, when Nasser visited the Yugoslav leader Tito, he travelled in the official yacht *Hurriyeh* with an escort of two destroyers. 'The sea,' wrote Mohamed Heikal, the president's confidante, 'was thought to be a safer means of transport than the air because it was believed that on the eve of the Suez war the Israelis had managed to bring down a plane flying over the Mediterranean by some secret weapon.'[75]

5
Enemies Within: 1948–67

Beginnings of the Shin Bet

Israel's General Security Service (Sherut HaBitachon HaKlali, Shabak, or Shin Bet) was born as what Ben-Gurion called the 'Internal Shai' on 30 June 1948. Its commander, Isser Harel, set up headquarters in several abandoned buildings in Jaffa, where only weeks before, immediately after the Palestinian exodus, his men had scoured the deserted city, looking for Arab military and political documents. Most of the Shai staff were transferred to Isser Be'eri's new IDF Intelligence Service. The few who went with Harel had worked under him in Tel Aviv, or represented the Shai in Jerusalem, Haifa and elsewhere. Early in 1949, after the disgraced Be'eri was sacked as head of IDF intelligence, Ben-Gurion asked Harel to take over counter-espionage as well as his other duties; this brought a welcome windfall of new manpower. Shin Mem 3 was transferred wholesale from the IDF to the security service.[1]

Until 1950 the Shin Bet remained administratively within the framework of the IDF, which provided cover, services, military ranks and pay. Harel was made a lieutenant-colonel. His deputy was Isi Dorot (formerly Isidore Roth), a slight, fair-haired, Polish Jew who had come to Palestine in 1936, served as a sergeant in a POW interrogation unit of British military intelligence and then worked in the Tel Aviv Shai in the final days of the Mandate. Like others in this period, Dorot had helped organize Jewish self-defence and illegal immigration from liberated Europe.[2]

Harel believed strongly in the need for a purely civilian security service, and he pressed repeatedly to be removed from under the army's wing, which afforded only minimal shelter in the battle for budgets, premises and manpower. In early 1950 a compromise was reached and the Shin Bet was attached to the Defence Ministry, although a year later 'Little' Isser was still complaining to Ben-Gurion that there were difficulties in the relationship. Harel told him that fifteen Shin Bet men operating abroad had not been paid for eight months. Ben-Gurion ordered the immediate payment of the $70,000 owed.[3] Shortly afterwards the service became autonomous, answerable directly to the prime minister, an arrangement which persists to this day. In January 1951 Harel submitted two annual budget proposals: one (IL888,000) allowed for salaries for 600 employees; the second smaller one (IL717,940), for 420.[4]

Corruption and black-marketeering were a major preoccupation in the first post-independence years of austerity and rationing, and Ben-Gurion relied heavily on the notoriously puritanical Harel for reports of how this affected the national mood and especially the government's popularity. 'All the immigrants talk about nepotism [*protektsia*],' the prime minister noted in his diary, 'and there's hardly a family that doesn't buy on the black market. In Isser's house there's nothing to eat because he doesn't.'[5]

The Shin Bet's existence was not publicly announced, although its activities quickly attracted attention. In 1949 members of the right-wing opposition Herut Party, formed by veterans of Menachem Begin's Irgun, noticed they were being followed and told the police, who arrested two young men and a woman, but the agents were promptly released without explanation.[6] From September 1952, when Harel replaced Reuven Shiloah as head of the Mossad, Dorot – codenamed 'Dafni' – ran the Shin Bet for a year, a fact which became publicly known only when he died nearly thirty years later.[7]

By the autumn of 1953, with Shiloah out of the way in Washington (as Minister Plenipotentiary at the Israel Embassy) and the reorganized Mossad firmly under his control, Harel took the loyal Dorot back as his deputy in charge of liaison with friendly foreign intelligence services and agreed to the appointment of a new Shin Bet chief, Ben-Gurion had told Harel to pick his own candidate and 'Little' Isser threatened to resign – this became something of a habit until he finally did quit ten years later – when some of the prime minister's advisers expressed their doubts about his choice, Amos Manor.[8] 'Some people criticized Isser and dismissed Manor as just a new immigrant,' one colleague said. 'But he was brilliant and full of ideas, and the critics probably wanted the job for themselves.'[9]

Manor, who was born Arthur Mendelovitch to a large and wealthy family in Sighet in Hungarian Transylvania, had come to Israel in 1949 and risen quickly in government service despite his late arrival and unusual lack of any party affiliation. His Zionist father had taught him both Hebrew and football, which remained a lifelong passion. Manor was studying in Paris when the world war broke out and survived Auschwitz to serve in the Bricha organization. Throughout his decade-long tenure as head of the security service he remained unknown to the Israeli public at large but won the lasting respect of both his colleagues and political masters.

Before succeeding Dorot in 1953, Manor made his name and reputation as head of the Soviet Bloc section of the Shin Bet's Counter-Espionage Division. New Jewish immigrants from behind the Iron Curtain, Israeli diplomatic missions and Jewish communities in Eastern Europe all served as valuable sources of intelligence. And, more important, they provided Israel with an invaluable asset in its dealings with friendly foreign secret services, especially the CIA and its own counter-intelligence chief, the legendary James Jesus Angleton. 'Manor came with excellent recommendations,' Harel said later. 'He had a lot of experience with the Soviet Bloc because that was where he came from. He was a very talented man with good judgement, and he proved himself fully. Our relations were always correct, but we were never friends.'[10]

In September 1963, when prime minister Levi Eshkol accepted the resignation 'of a senior government official who has headed a vital state service for over ten years', as Manor was coyly described, he was flatteringly profiled – still anonymously – by one newspaper:

> He has done his job without getting his name and pictures in the press and with only the rarest of official appearances, which is not in accordance with his ebullient spirits and general inclination to like people despite an exceptionally shrewd eye for their weaknesses. He is tall, striking-looking and the possessor of an energetic stride that blows papers off the table as he enters a room, but his good humour had to survive all the tribulations of European Jewry under the Nazis.[11]

He never spoke about his work. 'I don't care if you're Herodotus,' he wittily told a historian who wanted to interview him a quarter of a century after he resigned. 'I am not a source for the period when I was head of the security service.'[12]

Manor's introduction to the secret world may have been through Ehud Avriel, who knew him from the Bricha period. He spoke Hebrew with a heavy Hungarian accent, but was cosmopolitan, spontaneous and outgoing, and was very different from Isser, who was never accused of being a man of the world. Harel felt comfortable with Manor, but there was never any doubt about who carried more weight. 'When he appointed Amos at the beginning, Isser certainly kept an eye on him,' one Shin Bet man said later, 'not because he didn't trust him, but simply because Isser was like that.'[13]

Other Shin Bet personnel in these early years included many who, like Manor himself, had been in Bricha or the British army. One early recruit who served in both was Yosef Harmelin. He had emigrated to Palestine from Vienna in 1939, risen to the rank of captain in the Jewish Brigade and had briefly been in Shin Mem 3, the field security section of the IDF Intelligence Service, before he was transferred, along with the unit's other counter-intelligence staff, to the security service. Avraham Kidron of the Shai – one of Meir Tubiansky's judges – was another. Zvi Aharoni, a kibbutznik born in Germany as Hermann Arendt, had worked as a POW interrogator with British military intelligence in the Middle East and liberated Europe. He was approached by Dorot (who had served in the same British unit) in 1949 and headed the Shin Bet's Investigations Branch for ten years from early 1950.[14] Aharoni was recruited by Harel during a meeting at Kapulski's Café. The Shin Bet chief put several general questions and then asked: 'What is your opinion of the dissidents?' (the Irgun and Stern Gang – '*porshim*' in Hebrew). Aharoni's Hebrew was poor at the time and he had no idea what '*porshim*' meant. But he noticed that 'Little' Isser had placed great emphasis on the question, as if the answer was crucial. 'It sounded to me like *posh'im* [criminals],' he reminisced later. 'So I said: "I am definitely against." Isser seemed happy.' And Aharoni was recruited.[15]

Dan Lichtenstein (Laor), commander of the Haifa regional office, stayed with the service for five years until 1955; Pinhas Kopel, until transferring to the police in 1953. Others, like Meir Novick, son of an aristocratic Jewish family from Warsaw, had worked under Harel in the late 1940s as a senior member of the Internal Department of the Shai. Novick went on to become head of the police special branch.[16]

Recent Jewish immigrants from Middle Eastern countries, especially Iraq, were useful recruits for dealing with Arab affairs, even though Harel generally made sure that the executives in this area were Ashkenazim. These Sephardi field men sometimes had difficulty in explaining matters of Middle Eastern pace, style and timing to their East European bosses: Arabs expected, they insisted, to be pursued slowly and rigorously and their confidence won gradually. Quick and formal recruitment techniques did not work well.[17] The only Sephardi in a senior position before 1967 was the Damascus-born 'V.', who arrived in Israel in 1950 and worked briefly in the Foreign Ministry before joining the Shin Bet, rising to succeed Zvi Aharoni as head of the Investigations Branch in the 1960s. 'Little' Isser also disliked the veteran Arabists of 'the old school' – people like Ezra Danin – whose personal ties with and efforts on behalf of some Arabs, he believed, were often motivated by private considerations.[18] Harel mistrusted the assessments of professional orientalists who claimed to 'know' the Arabs and their mentality.

Ya'akov Caroz, another Hungarian, had served as a British censor in Syria, had run agents in the Tel Aviv Shai and had worked with the Mossad LeAliya Bet in North Africa before joining the Shin Bet in July 1949. Like Aharoni, he was summoned to meet Harel at a café near the service's headquarters in Jaffa and was immediately appointed commander of the Tel Aviv region, where the profusion of foreign embassies and legations – and their spies – provided a heavy workload for the counter-espionage officers. The Shin Bet took over these functions from Boris Guriel's Political Division in July 1950. United Nations personnel were targeted too: Melody's Bar in Haifa and the Kaete Dan Hotel in Tel Aviv, where the Shin Bet installed hidden microphones, were favourite hang-outs for members of the peace-keeping forces.[19] Caroz later served briefly as the commander of the Jerusalem area before taking over the service's important Arab Branch in 1952. An academically trained Hebraist, Caroz made a valuable contribution to the service's professionalism by compiling a classified Hebrew glossary of espionage and counter-intelligence terminology: he invented the neologisms *midur* (compartmentalization), *bodel* (cutout), *mishlash domem* (dead-letter box) and *beit mivtachim* (safe house).[20]

An atmosphere of pioneering and improvisation permeated the fledgling service. 'Trial and error', Harel called his method.[21] 'We were trying to build up something from scratch,' one of his senior officers said.

> We were trying to learn, trying to improve, trying to build a tradition of excellence and being second to none. It was a great challenge but on the other hand we had the great advantage of starting from zero. We were not handicapped by inherited traditions or outmoded fashions. True, we had to learn, we had to build up a tradition of our own, but our minds were free and the sky was the limit.[22]

Manor enjoyed regular access to Moshe Sharett, who replaced Ben-Gurion as prime minister from November 1953 to November 1955. Sharett's long and detailed political diary is full of references to the novelty, which he sometimes found irritating, of being constantly escorted by Shin Bet bodyguards. The service also saved him from grave embarrassment when one of its officers retrieved a briefcase full of secret documents that the prime minister had inadvertently lost on his way from Jerusalem to Tel Aviv.[23] The routine physical security of classified information and of government and defence establishment premises was the responsibility of the Shin Bet from the very beginning.

Priorities

The rest of the security service's work was divided roughly between counter-espionage and domestic subversion, with particular attention devoted to Israel's Arab minority. In November 1948 the Arab population was estimated at 156,000 – about 18 per cent of the total population. By 1951, because of mass Jewish immigration, it was down to around 11 per cent. By the mid-1950s Israel had about 200,000 Arab citizens, and most of them were still living, as they would until the system was finally abolished in 1966, under military administration, complete with curfews, pass laws and residence permits. 'The military government,' a foreign visitor to Nazareth was told by Arabs in 1958, 'was only a smokescreen, to hide the real security work done in secret by the Shin Bet.'[24]

Behind the scenes, though, as time went on, the Shin Bet's northern region, which was responsible for the vast majority of Arab citizens, found the apparatus of the military government unnecessarily oppressive and began to argue that it should be abolished. In the early years, the service used the system to apply pressure to Arabs by granting or withholding favours. But this aspect had its limits and was not sufficient argument to maintain the military government indefinitely.[25]

Arab Communists and their links outside the country were an early priority. In 1951 the security service asked the Foreign Ministry and the IDF Intelligence Department for more information about communist activities in the region and revealed that it knew the names of several Israeli citizens who planned to participate in clandestine meetings in Jordan and Lebanon.[26] Eliahu Sasson of the Foreign Ministry criticized the uneven analysis of a Shin Bet report on Jordan, but asked that the unnamed source for the material be encouraged, since he clearly enjoyed good access to political intelligence.[27]

Official monitoring of Arab activities had less to do with the danger of espionage and sabotage than with the authorities' fear of political radicalism among the minority. 'Consider what would happen if we abolished the restrictions,' argued Shmuel Divon, then adviser to the prime minister on Arab affairs.

> The Arabs who used to live in the empty villages, egged on and organized by the Communists, would go back and squat on their ruins, demanding their lands back. What good would that do? Their lands are in use. And then, when they have made as much trouble as possible about their own lands, they will start clamouring for the return of the refugees. They will form organizations, parties, fronts, anything to make trouble. That is the plan in Moscow. We have information. This 'Arab Front' they formed recently was all part of the grand design. They were out to create what I believe they call a 'revolutionary situation' – to make Israel a second Algeria [where an armed rebellion against French colonial rule had begun in 1954].[28]

The 'Arab Front', better known as 'Al-Ard' (The Land), was outlawed by the Defence Ministry in 1964 after a long legal struggle. Shin Bet lobbying was the main reason for the decision.[29]

Divon's argument accurately reflected the Shin Bet's view of the internal Arab danger. Harel reported to Ben-Gurion in December 1957 that the emerging split in the Communist Party between the Arab majority and the Jewish section, Maki, meant that Israel's Arabs intended to follow Moscow's instructions to demand self-determination and to turn the Triangle, the Galilee and the Negev into 'Algeria'.[30]

Security considerations were often cited publicly as a reason for the continued system of military rule in Arab areas. The cease-fire line with the Jordanian West Bank was long, ill defined and ill protected, and just beyond it lived hundreds of thousands of refugees. Rare cases of actual espionage were prominently reported, although, as a British journalist commented in 1958, 'for the most part they involved half-baked youths whose foolishness could be partly attributed to the frustrations of life under military rule. Nor was the apparatus of military rule often responsible for their apprehension: the secret service did that.'[31] Ya'akov Caroz agreed with this assessment many years later: 'We weren't really very worried about anything in particular,' he said. 'Everything was new and we behaved like a young man who is very sure of himself. Even the spies weren't very serious.'[32] Several enemy agents were caught with copies of *Ma'arachot* and *BaMahane*, magazines on military affairs published by the IDF which were sold freely to the public.[33]

Yet Arab spies captured by the Shin Bet were portrayed in a sensationalist and almost demonic light. A 1961 Defence Ministry anthology about espionage in the 1950s described the strange case of Nayifa Aqala, a Haifa woman with a 'pathological hatred for Jews and who worshipped the Egyptian dictator Nasser'. She carried out several unimportant missions for Jordanian intelligence (buying postcards to try and find pictures of army bases) and was caught with two male accomplices in June 1957 after having been seen crossing the border in Beit Safafa, a village south of Jerusalem that was half in Jordan and half in Israel.

Mahmoud Yasin, from Arraba village in the western Galilee, had the same problem: 'deep hatred for the State of Israel and blind admiration for Gamal Abdel Nasser'. He and a friend, members of a sports club run by the Israeli Communist Party, Maki, made their way to Quneitra on the Syrian Golan Heights. In Damascus they were questioned by a senior Syrian intelligence officer called Burhan Boulous, the head of the Deuxième Bureau's Israel section, and ordered to go back to Israel. A second hazardous attempt to cross the border from Israel into Syria failed when Yasin's brother, Ahmed, was injured in a tussle with a large porcupine. In July 1958 the network was activated when three more men, armed and led by a Palestinian who had fled Arraba during the 1948 war, turned up with instructions from Damascus to provide information about Israeli ports, airfields, army camps and radar stations. Thirteen Arabs were working for the group when the Shin Bet rounded them up later that summer. The few details released to the press contained all the traditional cloak and dagger elements of a good spy story: agents mingling with Israeli pilgrims who had crossed into the Old City of Jerusalem for the Christmas celebrations; armed Syrian couriers sneaking across the border to contact their agents; secret introductions by means of passwords; and a matchbox, of Syrian origin, dropped by a courier on the Israeli side of the frontier, which furnished the police and the Shin Bet with a vital clue.[34] The security service had professional respect for Syrian intelligence, although the Syrians often had exaggerated expectations of their agents' abilities: at the end of the 1950s two spies were sent to try and infiltrate Israel's nuclear reactor at Dimona, the single most sensitive site in the entire country.[35]

Manor's men scored several more successes by following Jews, often recent immigrants from Arab countries, who dutifully reported that they had been offered money by Arabs to spy for hostile intelligence services, especially the Jordanians. One such surveillance operation led to the discovery of a less patriotic Israeli citizen, a recent middle-aged immigrant from Iraq, who had agreed to work with enemy espionage.[36] In the second half of 1957 several Israelis who had inadvertently crossed the frontier into Jordan or had entered the country illegally for fun – a relatively common phenomenon at the time – reported that they had been interrogated by a Jewish-looking man who spoke Hebrew with a Moroccan-French accent. He was identified as Haim Avergil, a twenty-nine-year-old Moroccan-born Israeli who had disappeared from his home in Lod that summer. Jordanian intelligence had promised to help him return to his parents in Morocco if he cooperated with them. Avergil was arrested and imprisoned for four years when he returned to Israel in 1958.[37]

In the 1950s and 1960s Egypt had the most active and sophisticated of Arab intelligence services. In 1963 the Shin Bet captured an Egyptian spy called Kaburak Yacobian, who had been prepared thoroughly for his mission as a long-term agent and equipped with a false identity. Yacobian, an Egyptian-born Armenian, underwent basic training in espionage and was given detailed information about life in Israel and Jewish religious customs. His false identity was Yitzhak (Zaki) Kucuk, a native of Turkey. He was provided with photographs of relatives and even of his mother's grave. Towards the end of 1960 he acquired a refugee certificate from the United Nations in Cairo, and left for Brazil in March 1961. In Rio de Janeiro he obtained an identity card stating he was a Jew and made contact with the local Jewish community – a mirror image, curiously, of what the Israeli spy Eli Cohen, using the alias Kamal Amin Thabit, was doing in the Arab community of Buenos Aires at exactly the same time in preparation for his mission to Syria. In December 1961 Kucuk was helped by the Jewish Agency to emigrate to Israel.

Like any other new immigrant, Kucuk studied Hebrew in an *ulpan* (literally, studio; schools where Hebrew is taught intensively). But he failed to get into the IDF armoured corps, as instructed by his Egyptian controllers. The Shin Bet and IDF field security were suspicious, and he had a dull army career as a truck driver, which was virtually useless from an intelligence point of view. The evidence suggests that Yacobian was under surveillance for a long period. The security service knew he was using invisible ink to maintain contact with his controllers in Europe, but not that the material he used to decipher instructions he received from abroad was disguised as shoe polish. Yacobian was sentenced to eighteen years in prison, but released in March 1966, along with two other Egyptian agents, in return for three Israeli prisoners.[38]

Egyptian intelligence also ran a petty adventurer called Mordechai Luk, a Moroccan-born Israeli who had fled to Egypt, via Gaza, in 1961. His case came to light in a bizarre and much-celebrated manner in November 1964, when, concealed in a trunk, he was being bundled aboard a United Arab Airlines Comet at Rome's Fiumicino Airport. Luk had had doubts about his suitability as a spy, and was trying to evade the Egyptians.

An alert Italian porter saved his life, but the 'man in the suitcase' was sentenced to eleven years in gaol after being deported to Israel. Three Egyptian 'diplomats' were also expelled from Italy. According to Israeli sources, the Egyptians had planned to carry out plastic surgery on Luk to change his appearance, equip him with a false identity and send him to Israel to open a travel agency. 'This,' commented Ya'akov Caroz, 'provides an excellent cover for secret service work, since it permits regular contact with people from different walks of life, justifies varied links with foreign countries and is a convenient channel for transferring funds.'[39] Luk never had the makings of a successful agent, but the Egyptians kept him on, Caroz believes, because 'they were simply unduly dazzled by the fact of his being an Israeli Jew . . . who was willing to act against his own country'.[40]

Luk's exposure may have helped the Shin Bet net another Israeli traitor. Shmuel ('Sami') Baruch was a Jerusalem-born businessman from a well-known Sephardi family. He approached the Egyptians in Switzerland in September 1963, apparently because he needed financial help with a failing textile factory he had set up in the southern development town of Kiryat Gat. Egyptian intelligence personnel in neutral capitals were routinely monitored and Baruch was spotted almost immediately. His meetings were photographed and recorded. The Egyptians encouraged him to become politically active and by the summer of 1964 he was the treasurer of Yisrael HaTzeira (Young Israel), a new movement set up to advance the interests of Sephardi Jews and compete in the 1965 Knesset elections. The Kiryat Gat factory was supposed to provide the Egyptians with a foothold in the Negev area, which was deemed of strategic importance because of the large number of military installations there.[41] His Shin Bet watchers followed him night and day, the only bonus of their task being that Baruch had a young and beautiful girlfriend.[42] 'Had he succeeded in carrying out his plans on behalf of the Egyptians,' Caroz said, 'Baruch would have ranked as one of the major secret agents of his generation.'[43] As it was, he was arrested and gaoled for eighteen years in January 1965.

If Egyptian intelligence failed to establish Mordechai Luk as a travel agent in Israel, it may have succeeded with a better agent, who was not exposed until after his death. Rifa'at el-Gammal, an Egyptian from the Nile Delta, spent twenty years spying in Israel. He operated as Jack Bitton, who in 1956 founded the Citours travel agency in central Tel Aviv, until leaving the country for West Germany in 1968.[44]

Foreigners interested the Shin Bet too. Alcibiades Kokas, a Greek businessman who had made several trips to Israel, was arrested in August 1957 and sentenced to four years in prison for trying to set up a spy network on behalf of Egyptian intelligence. A particularly bizarre case that ended the same year was that of Orlich Schaeft, a German gentile who had served in the SS, circumcised himself while in a POW camp in Italy and emigrated to Israel as a Jew named Gabriel Zissman in 1949. He was first deported in 1954 after getting drunk and boasting publicly about his true identity. He made contact with Egyptian intelligence and returned to Haifa with a second new identity as a tourist. He was arrested and deported again.[45] Christian clergymen, who were allowed to cross the Mandelbaum Gate crossing-point between the Jordanian and Israeli sectors of Jerusalem, were closely watched. One, a Coptic priest from Jaffa, was given a twelve-year gaol sentence for collecting military information for the Egyptians.[46]

Red menace

Soviet Bloc embassies and personnel were obvious targets for Shin Bet surveillance in this period, when the Korean War was raging and the Cold War was at its height. Although Stalin had supported the crucial UN partition vote in November 1947 and Israeli relations with the United States were only a pale shadow of what they would become in the 1960s, the KGB quickly made the Jewish state an intelligence priority. Its penetration operations were facilitated by the large numbers of Soviet and East European Jews who had arrived in the country since independence, although according to Ilya Dzhirkvelov, who served in the KGB's Near and Middle East Department at the time, most of these immigrants were 'clean'. At the end of 1947, however, special groups of Soviet intelligence officers were formed to recruit, train and brief Jewish emigrants for work in Israel. These groups were headed by Lieutenant-Colonel Vladimir Vertiporokh, who had previously served in the KGB *rezidentura* in Tehran, and Colonel Aleksandr Korotkov, head of the KGB directorate in charge of 'illegals'. Both officers were later awarded government decorations in recognition of their success and promoted to the rank of general. Vertiporokh, who was known to his friends as Uncle Volodya, later became the first KGB *rezident* in Israel, where he was considered by his superiors, according to Dzhirkvelov, 'one of the most effective, both in gathering secret information and in the recruitment of new agents'.[47] But some Soviet Jewish immigrants told the Israeli authorities of the attempts to recruit them; and some, according to Isser Harel, then served as loyal and effective double agents.[48] 'Some of them would tell us as soon as they arrived,' Harel recalled. 'We said, "It's OK, calm down. Now that you've told us, what hold do they have over you? If they pressure you now you can tell them to go to hell."'[49]

By the mid-1950s the Soviet Embassy in Tel Aviv had a staff of sixty, and most of them, Harel believed, were involved in intelligence work. A team of Soviet archaeologists and scientists that came to Jerusalem and set up shop in the city's old Russian Compound in 1951 displayed more interest in the state of the exact sciences in Israel than in the country's ancient history. The Shin Bet repeatedly warned Israeli scientists of the dangers of friendship with and possible entrapment by Soviet and other Eastern Bloc 'diplomats'. The Czechs, Poles and Romanians were all active as well and won high marks for professionalism from their Israeli 'watchers'.[50]

A remarkably lurid book published in 1952 gives a contemporary view, albeit an American one, of the internal Red menace in Israel. As Ray Brock wrote in *Blood, Oil and Sand*:

> Despite the most rigorous screening the waves of immigrants into Israel contain men and women dedicated to the eventual anarchical overthrow of the Israeli government and the establishment of a desperate communist state in the heartland of the Middle East. Israel's swelling population is drawn from central and eastern European areas, where Communism alone afforded the organization and arms enabling limited resistance to the former enemy.[51]

Harel and Manor certainly had no doubts about the seriousness of the communist threat. The Kremlin's retreat from support for Israel to open hostility and friendly relations with the Arabs was designed, they believed, to isolate and control the Jewish minority in the Soviet Union. The wildly enthusiastic reception accorded by the Jews of Moscow to Golda Meir, the first Israeli representative to the Soviet Union, had surprised and worried the authorities. The KGB's main goal was military information, accompanied by serious attempts to penetrate the Israeli intelligence community.

Harel was aware of repeated efforts by the Soviets and their satellites to recruit and compromise Israeli officials serving abroad. One case that came to light in early 1956 was particularly shocking, because it turned out to involve a long-term KGB 'mole'. Ze'ev Avni of the Israeli Embassy in Belgrade was exposed as a Soviet spy and brought home to a secret trial.[52] Both Harel and Manor reported to a horrified Sharett on the investigation,[53] in the course of which Avni confessed fully, although Manor told the prime minister he believed that the attorney-general, Haim Cohen, had erred in not presenting evidence for the prosecution, presumably because of the immense sensitivity of the material.[54]

Avni, born Wolf Goldstein in Switzerland, where his parents had briefly sheltered the exiled Lenin, had emigrated to Israel in 1948 and had joined the foreign service. As a polyglot and trained economist, he was an invaluable recruit. He served as Israel's commercial attaché to the Benelux countries and took part in the reparations negotiations with West Germany in 1952. Avri Elad, the 'Third Man' in the Lavon Affair, met Avni in Ramle gaol shortly after his own incarceration in 1958.

Avni, Elad wrote, 'had quickly attracted the attention of the Mossad, joined the organization and within a short time could easily identify all the agents he encountered, since he served as a "postbox" between Mossad headquarters and the agents in the field'. Avni was sentenced to fifteen years in prison. Details of the case remain highly classified to this day.[55]

Another Israeli caught spying for an Eastern Bloc country was Yitzhak Zilberman, an engineer who had immigrated from Bessarabia in 1949. He was employed in the metals division of the Koor concern in Acre, where military contracts were carried out. Zilberman tried to swallow poison when he was arrested. He was sentenced to nine years in prison at his trial in autumn 1959.[56]

Enemies within

Spies and Arabs were not the Shin Bet's only area of interest. Mapai's total political dominance in the early years of independence was accompanied by deep suspicions of both the established opposition parties and small underground organizations of various, but mostly far-right or ultra-religious, persuasions. Menachem Begin's Herut, which grew out of the pre-state Irgun, was only one target. In January 1952, when Begin reached a peak in exploiting the emotional question of German reparations to attack Ben-Gurion and Mapai, Harel kept the prime minister supplied with secret information about Herut's plans.[57] Former Stern Gang activists, who moved both rightwards and leftwards after 1948, were another area of interest. Harel's first coup was the liquidation of the last organized traces of Lehi after the assassination of the Swedish UN mediator Count Bernadotte in September 1948. Bernadotte had been killed because his peace plan proposed the internationalization of Jerusalem, an idea which was unacceptable to the militants. A member of Lehi called Romek Greenberg approached the Shin Bet and struck a deal with Meir Novick: in return for immunity from prosecution, the informer was secretly set up in the Lempel Hotel in Tel Aviv and helped direct the search for the group's leader, Natan Yellin-Friedman, who was quickly arrested in the Haifa area.[58]

On the established left there was the new United Workers' Party, Mapam, with its shading off towards the Communist Party, Maki. Ben Gurion had decided that he would build his coalitions and rule 'without Herut or Maki'. Both were beyond the consensus; both, therefore, were to be watched especially carefully. Monitoring and penetrating these parties and groups was the job of Binyamin Hochstein, a highly intelligent, myopic man who was a veteran of the Shai's Internal Department and became the first head of the security service's Political Division.

Shin Bet surveillance of Mapam began in January 1951. Harel already had strong suspicions of the party's 'dual loyalty' to the new state and the Soviet Union. The previous summer he had reported to Ben-Gurion on the number of Mapam members or supporters working in the fledgling state-run military industry Ta'as.[59] The Shin Bet used the occasion of anti-government demonstrations over changes in the bread subsidy to photograph members of Maki; the task was given to the security service's Special Operations Unit, which had been transferred to Harel from the Palmah. The unit's commander, Gershon Rabinowitz, like many Palmah men, was a Mapam kibbutznik (from Ruhama in the Negev). Shortly afterwards, Rabinowitz asked to be relieved of his duties. Harel was then shocked to learn that the whole unit was functioning as an 'underground' inside the Shin Bet, passing classified information about the service to Mapam, which had its own independent 'security apparatus'. Harel's dismay may well have been disingenuous. He clearly wished to purge the Shin Bet of people he viewed as dangerous and potentially treasonable left-wingers; Rabinowitz provided the pretext.

Over the next two years the party veered sharply leftwards as Israel settled firmly into the anti-Soviet camp. The Slansky show trial in Prague, involving two prominent Mapam leaders then in Czechoslovakia, took place in December 1952, conjuring up an international Zionist conspiracy aimed at the heart of the communist world. And a month later nine Jewish doctors were arrested in Moscow and charged with planning the extermination of the Soviet hierarchy. Official Israel was shocked by what seemed to be an ugly manifestation of Soviet anti-Semitism. Ya'akov Hazan, the Mapam leader, used the occasion to attack his own country's 'reactionary' and pro-Western foreign policy. At the same time his left-wing rival, Moshe Sneh, moved closer to Maki.

It was against this turbulent background, in January 1953, that two Shin Bet agents were caught red-handed breaking into Mapam headquarters in Tel Aviv. The party had been aware for some time that details of its most secret meetings had unaccountably been leaked to the press, and officials found a small, US-made radio transmitter concealed under the desk of the secretary-general, Meir Ya'ari. The two security service men were ambushed when they came to change the transmitter's batteries. The government refused to admit responsibility for the affair, although Harel demanded a statement in the Knesset, arguing that if the existence of the Shin Bet were made public then Mapam would be unable to make political capital out of the affair and the country as a whole would understand the need for the surveillance.[60] But in a Knesset debate on the issue the following year the police minister insisted that there was nothing to investigate.

Other allegations of political bugging and surveillance by the Shin Bet surfaced occasionally in the mid-1950s. In June 1955 the minister of trade, a General Zionist called Peretz Bernstein, charged in the party newspaper *HaBoqer* that the 'letters of non-Mapai ministers and their telephone conversations are being monitored'. Sharett's response was that the claim had been investigated and found to be baseless. However, a year later further complaints led to an investigation by a specially appointed ad hoc subcommittee of the Knesset Interior Committee. Its findings confirmed several of the charges but its public statement simply urged meekly that unnamed 'services' restrict their activities to the country's essential security needs. The Shin Bet was clearly not impressed: just a month later

Menachem Begin complained that his flat had been broken into in an apparent attempt to install bugging devices. The Herut leader claimed to have been told by a friendly policeman that it was the work of the security service.

The existence of widespread surveillance was no secret among the Mapai leadership. Throughout the 1950s senior party officials received an unsigned, stencilled, monthly 'Information Bulletin', which reported on Mapam and Maki activities, especially meetings with Soviet Bloc diplomats and officials. The bulletin also covered occasional attempts by the extreme right to set up subversive underground organizations and ultra-Orthodox religious groups like the anti-Zionist Neturei Karta. In Jerusalem the document was always delivered by a special messenger who came by bicycle from the Prime Minister's Office, and it was common knowledge that it was the work of 'Little' Isser.[61] Ben-Gurion's official biographer has noted critically that Harel regularly advised the prime minister on purely political questions that had nothing to do with security, and that he often touched on developments within Mapai itself.[62]

Dealing with allegations of political monitoring was complicated by the fact that officially the Shin Bet did not exist. Yehezkel Sahar, the first police commissioner, had stated categorically: 'In this country there is no secret service and no political police.'[63] The pretence was finally dropped in June 1957 in a remarkable parliamentary statement by Ben-Gurion. Replying to motions proposed by Peretz Bernstein and Haim Landau of Herut, the prime minister put his cards on the table. Harel's fingerprints were all over the speech: 'The State of Israel has a security service, which has three purposes and three purposes only,' Ben-Gurion revealed. He explained that 95 per cent of the Shin Bet's budget and manpower was devoted to counter-espionage. The service was highly successful in this area, and in some cases there had been secret trials. Its other preoccupations were 'fragments of terrorist organizations' and a 'fifth column'. The prime minister made no mention of the country's Arab citizens, but his meaning was unmistakable: 'Unfortunately we are not yet living in peace with our neighbours,' he said. 'We had the Sinai campaign and we had other operations and we cannot know what will happen in the future. We must keep an eye on people and groups who form a fifth column, or could form a fifth column.'[64] Noting this landmark event in his diary that night, Ben-Gurion described the opposition as 'trying to depict the Shin Bet as a private detective agency of Mapai or the rulers'.[65]

Harel had already agreed, at the end of 1955, to the formation of a permanent ministerial committee – demanded by Mapam as a condition for joining a new Mapai-led government after that year's elections – that would be briefed on the work of the Shin Bet.[66] Ben-Gurion's first public comment on the activities of the security service led to a limited measure of parliamentary supervision of its budget. A month after the Knesset statement the prime minister and his military secretary, Nehemia Argov, worked out a proposal under which the Shin Bet would submit an annual report to the Knesset's Foreign Affairs and Defence Committee and a report on the service's total annual budget to a special subcommittee, with the whole being subject to the scrutiny of the state comptroller.[67] Harel didn't like such exposure. By the end of the year he was asking Ben-Gurion to amend the comptroller's law to exclude compulsory reporting on 'several areas of operation'.[68]

The 'apparatus of darkness'

The fact that Ben-Gurion made his Knesset statement at all owed much to a young anti-establishment journalist called Uri Avneri, editor of *HaOlam Hazeh* weekly magazine. Avneri, a former member of the Irgun, never named the Shin Bet but, rather, called it the 'apparatus of darkness' in order to avoid the restrictions of censorship. Throughout the first half of the 1950s he ran article after sensationalist article aimed at exposing the vice-like grip of Ben-Gurion and Mapai on the entire country. 'All instruments of government were subordinated directly to Ben-Gurion, and Ben-Gurion and the party were the same,' Avneri said later, 'and the Shin Bet was part of that.'[69]

HaOlam HaZeh tangled repeatedly with the authorities. The rest of the press was tame, and the struggling little magazine found itself the target of repeated verbal and physical attacks as it took on the government and Mapai party bosses, like Abba Hushi, the powerful mayor of Haifa. Avneri's cheeky, innovative style was utterly different from the staid, respectful prose of the rest of the media. He called Haifa 'Hushistan' and poked fun at everyone.[70]

'Little' Isser hated Avneri with a deep loathing. When, in December 1953, the paper's editor and his deputy, Shalom Cohen, were beaten up by unknown assailants, Avneri complained to Ben-Gurion: 'There is virtually no doubt that this was the work of the Shin Bet,' he told the prime minister, 'or at the very least its commander, Mr Isser Halperin, knew about it in advance and gave his approval.'[71] The dislike grew: in June 1955, when someone planted a bomb outside the magazine's offices, the Memuneh told Sharett that Avneri and his friends might have staged the whole thing to create the impression that they were 'martyrs',[72] although later he changed his mind and conceded that someone else might have done it. Avneri was sure the Shin Bet was out to get him.

The confrontation came to a head over the Kastner Affair, a turbulent, emotional episode that revived the traumatic memory of the Holocaust and the latent feelings of guilt that the Yishuv and the Jewish Agency, controlled by Mapai, had not done enough to save their brethren in occupied Europe. Dr Yisrael ('Rezo') Kastner was a senior Mapai Party official who during the war had been a leader of Hungarian Jewry and had held negotiations with the Nazis for the release of thousands of Jews. In 1953 a little-known right-winger called Malkiel Greenwald, himself a Hungarian Holocaust survivor, accused Kastner of collaborating with the SS in return for the freedom of a few hundred relatives and friends. The Sharett government, stung by both the political and emotional implications of the charge, joined Kastner in suing Greenwald for criminal libel, but in June 1955 a lower court substantiated the validity of the accusation and dismissed the case.

'The same Jewish Agency leaders who had tried to save Jews from the Holocaust (and obviously did not succeed) were now running the government,' said Teddy Kollek, 'and many asked to what extent they were capable of fulfilling such a task.'[73] The coalition fell on a motion of no confidence in its handling of the affair, and then, in March 1957, Kastner was murdered. 'The verdict of the court,' one historian has commented, 'opened a gaping wound in the fabric of Zionist moral and social cohesion. Kastner was assassinated as though in proof of the intolerable tension which the probing of Holocaust history could engender.'[74]

For 'Little' Isser, the case was less about guilt and the memory of the Holocaust than another worrying manifestation of the danger of fanatical underground groups pursuing their aims at the expense of the fragile institutions of the new state. Ze'ev Eckstein, one of the three nationalist extremists tried for killing Kastner, had links with the Shin Bet, although it is fairly clear that he was a paid informer rather than an *agent provocateur. HaOlam HaZeh*, ever alert for the machinations of the 'apparatus of darkness', suggested repeatedly that the security service was behind the murder, just as it had secretly organized attacks against the magazine, including the vicious 1953 beatings.[75] Avneri argued that the government wanted to prevent revelations about the Jewish Agency's policies during the Holocaust and that killing Kastner was the simplest way to do this. Harel was furious, and remained furious over thirty years later, when he wrote his own dense account of the affair. Avneri was 'cynical, evil and shameless', he wrote. 'Those who attempted in the 1950s to weaken the security services in their war against political terrorism were trying to weaken democratic institutions and to encourage terrorism.'[76]

HaOlam HaZeh was almost certainly wrong about the Shin Bet's role in the Kastner affair and Avneri was far more concerned about using the opportunity to lambast the government than to report 'objectively' on the case. But Avneri was quite right about being persecuted by the authorities. 'We were barely hanging on, with no money at all,' he recalled later. 'We were on the verge of bankruptcy in fact, and there was Isser painting a picture of the whole country being absolutely terrified of us as if we were public enemy number one and engaged in a sinister conspiracy like some fantastic version of *The Protocols of the Elders of Zion*.'[77] A well-known author was commissioned by the government to write a play attacking the sort of journalism represented by *HaOlam HaZeh*. It was called *Throw Him to the Dogs*, and the opening night at the HaBima Theatre in Tel Aviv was conspicuously attended by Ben-Gurion, his wife, Paula, and the entire cabinet.

Harel and Manor recruited a few loyal journalists and set up a rival weekly called *Rimon* (*Pomegranate*) that was designed specifically to undercut *HaOlam HaZeh*. Sharett, who was consulted throughout by his security chiefs, was aware that despite *Rimon*'s glossy appearance it was far too bland, although in August 1956 it had a circulation of 10,000 and by the following month was beating *HaOlam HaZeh*.[78] In September the magazine ran a flattering, illustrated profile of the prime minister, after Sharett had made a few minor corrections to the piece he felt was pleasant but utterly lacking in depth or brilliance. After the Sinai Campaign *Rimon*'s political line became much more obvious and it published articles praising the operation and attacking the US and Soviet positions.[79] But the magazine was a dismal failure. By September 1957 it had lost between 300,000 and 400,000 pounds without seriously denting the popularity of *HaOlam HaZeh*.[80] In June 1957 Avneri charged that 250,000 pounds had been invested in that 'foul publication whose sole task is to publish the revolting material supplied to it by agents of the Shin Bet'.[81]

Soviet spies

Soviet espionage remained a preoccupation in the late 1950s and early 1960s, and two of the Shin Bet's most famous and controversial coups were in the grey area between spying and the kind of legitimate left-wing political activity that Harel and Manor saw as a possible threat to Mapai's hegemony.

The case of Aharon Cohen began when an alert off-duty policeman spotted a car with diplomatic number plates loitering suspiciously outside the main gate of Kibbutz Sha'ar Ha'Amakim near Haifa in April 1958. A routine report was passed to the Shin Bet and the vehicle was found to be registered in the name of a Soviet diplomat called Sokolov, who was already known to the security service as an intelligence agent.

Amos Manor's Operations Branch people began surveillance and, after watching several more clandestine meetings at the kibbutz, they managed to identify the unknown man seen talking to the Russians as Aharon Cohen. Cohen, then aged fifty-three, was a senior Mapam leader, a former Shai man and his party's resident expert on Arab affairs. He had been in the country since 1929 and had devoted his life to study of the Arab world and the conflict with Israel.

A second Russian official seen meeting Cohen later was identified as Vitaly Pavlovski, a member of the Soviet scientific delegation in Jerusalem, which had long been an object of Shin Bet interest. Manor reported regularly to Harel on the results of the surveillance and it rapidly became clear to the Memuneh that something suspicious was afoot. Harel still disliked Mapam intensely, but since the party was a member of the ruling coalition he was concerned about the political implications of too public an arrest. He decided instead to talk privately to Cohen first.

The Mapam official was not perturbed. He told 'Little' Isser that his contacts with the Russians were of a purely academic nature and insisted that he had held no secret meetings with them. Manor tried the same tack but Cohen stuck to his story. In October 1958, after another meeting with a Soviet official, Cohen was arrested by an officer of the police special branch, which liaised closely with the Shin Bet and often carried out arrests on its behalf. Harel and Manor were both closely involved at all stages of the affair.[82] Pavlovski left the country suddenly; Cohen, who was released on bail, continued to protest his innocence; and Mapam charged vociferously that the arrest was politically motivated and that the security service was using trumped-up espionage charges to attack the party.

When Cohen's trial began in camera at the end of July 1961 he faced charges of unauthorized contacts with a foreign agent (though not of spying) and was sentenced to five years in gaol. Harel's main concern was that the Shin Bet had been cleared of the charge that the whole case was politically inspired, although Mapam continued to treat Cohen as a hero and to attack the security service as Mapai's private political police. The High Court reduced the sentence on appeal to two and a half years and Aharon Cohen was pardoned and freed in July 1963 after serving seventeen months of his term.[83]

'Little' Isser believed he was right. 'Aharon Cohen,' he wrote later, 'was no "Israeli Dreyfus". Cohen was an orientalist, a kibbutz member and an armchair Communist who fell into the net of Soviet espionage by his own doing and became entangled in his own lies.'[84] Mapam, said Harel, quoting the poet Abba Kovner approvingly, 'was born with a malignant growth in its belly – the Soviet Dybbuk'.[85] The Cohen case, and Mapam's reaction to it, strengthened the Memuneh's intense awareness of the dangers of KGB intelligence-gathering among Israeli left-wingers. His next catch in this field, Colonel Yisrael Beer, was much bigger.

The Yisrael Beer case

Beer, who was born in Vienna in 1912, had emigrated to Palestine in 1938 and immediately joined the Haganah, rising in 1948 to be chief assistant to Yigael Yadin, head of the Haganah Operations Branch. After the war he became head of the IDF Planning Department and expected to be appointed Yadin's deputy when the latter became chief of staff in 1949. When Mordechai Makleff got the job instead of him, Beer quit the army in disgust and went into the reserves. Later, from his prison cell, he accused Harel of trying to force his resignation.[86]

Colonel Beer was a left-winger and made no secret of this. He had joined Mapam on its foundation in 1948 and was close to its charismatic leader, Dr Moshe Sneh, the former head of the

Haganah National Command. Beer was a regular contributor to the party paper, *Al-Hamishmar*, and wrote on military affairs, including important international developments like the Korean War, with all the authority of a senior staff officer. Many other officers who were members of Mapam resigned soon after the 1948 war because they disliked the way the IDF was becoming a regular army and losing the élan of the Palmah period.

Beer boasted an impressive biography. He had been a member of the Schutzbund, the Austrian Social Democratic Party's defence organization, and had taken part in the Viennese workers' rising against the pro-Nazi Chancellor Dolfuss in 1934 (an event which had had a marked influence on a far more famous spy, the British traitor Kim Philby). In 1936 the party sent him to fight in the International Brigade in Spain under the *nom de guerre* of Colonel José Gregorio. A chance encounter with a biography of Theodor Herzl in early 1938 brought a sudden conversion to Zionism.[87]

He was an unusual figure in the Haganah in the 1940s. 'Beer was impressive compared with others,' recalled Ephraim Levy, who attended some of his lectures in the 1940s. 'He'd been in all these wars, he had lots of medals and had been an Austrian officer. His Hebrew was awful and he used to joke: "With my Hebrew I can't tell the difference between masculine and feminine, but in reality I can."'[88]

The colonel first came to 'Little' Isser's attention in the early 1950s, when he headed Mapam's Information Department, which was responsible for collecting material on security matters, including – through the good offices of Gershon Rabinowitz and his Special Operations Unit – the activities of the Shin Bet. Mapam was under close surveillance by the security service in that period, as the famous discovery of the microphone in its headquarters had shown. In 1953, when Sneh and other Mapam left-wingers quit the party for Maki because of disagreements over the Doctors' Trial in the Soviet Union, Beer moved sharply to the right and joined Mapai, and began writing for the party newspaper, *Davar*. This sudden political turnabout aroused Isser Harel's suspicions, and he ordered

Beer placed under limited surveillance. It was the beginning of a long obsession.

Moshe Sharett admired Beer's ability to combine military expertise with good writing. In early 1956 the foreign minister encouraged *Davar* to continue running Beer's pieces, despite a boycott of the paper by the IDF chief of staff, Moshe Dayan, who strongly disliked Beer.[89]

Beer used his new-found political respectability to try and return to the army, despite the opposition of both Dayan and Harel. In 1955, after Ben-Gurion replaced Pinhas Lavon as defence minister, Beer was commissioned to write the official history of the 1948 war, enjoyed regular access to the 'Old Man' and to classified IDF archives, and was given a secretary and an office in the ministry.

'Little' Isser already thought the colonel a 'spineless and unprincipled opportunist' and towards the end of the year, when there was mounting tension on the borders and the Egyptian–Czech arms deal was in the offing, he tried to sound Beer out. 'The excuse for our conversation was to hear Beer's views on Soviet penetration in the Middle East, but its real intention was to gauge his loyalty,' Harel wrote later. 'I remained convinced that Beer had not undergone a real political and ideological change and that he was a grave security risk.'[90]

During the second half of 1956, as the secret preparations for the Suez operation gathered momentum, Harel, who was responsible for security, worried about possible leaks. In September Beer was one of several people who were specifically warned to keep away from foreign agents, especially Russians. Beer dutifully reported that he had recently met Lusayev, the Tass representative in Israel, and had been told by Amos Manor to take care. Harel kept his mounting suspicions to himself. In 1957 the surveillance went a stage further: Rafi Eitan, the Shin Bet Operations Branch chief, burgled Beer's Tel Aviv apartment in search of incriminating evidence; there was none.

Beer went from strength to strength. He began writing columns for the independent liberal daily *Ha'Aretz* and in 1959 was appointed to the chair of military history at Tel Aviv

University. Beer was close to Shimon Peres, the ambitious young deputy minister of defence, and he began to go on regular visits to West Germany, touring NATO bases there. His fluent native German, solid academic reputation and close ties with the senior echelons of the defence establishment in Tel Aviv made him an honoured guest, and he was received in Bonn by the defence minister, Franz-Josef Strauss, the key figure in the evolving relationship between the two countries.

The relationship was controversial. In December 1957 non-Mapai ministers in the cabinet somehow heard of a planned trip to Bonn by Dayan and Peres, who were trying to buy two refurbished submarines, and then the news was leaked to the press. Beer was an obvious suspect. In the public outcry that followed, Ben-Gurion threatened to resign. For Harel's taste, Yisrael Beer simply knew too much. The Memuneh's suspicions mounted in mid-1958, when the colonel requested permission to meet the mysterious General Reinhard Gehlen.

Gehlen had been Hitler's espionage chief on the Eastern Front. After the war his semi-private organization was taken over by the OSS and then financed and run by the newly founded CIA, until it became the official West German external intelligence service, the BND, in 1956. Gehlen had global ambitions, and in the late 1950s shifted from his service's traditional focus on the Soviet Union and Eastern Europe, with an emphasis on military intelligence, to modern technical means of information-gathering.[91] Allen Dulles of the CIA had asked him to help inject 'life and expertise' into the Egyptian secret service, and some former SS and Gestapo officers had been supplied, with a first batch of about 100 being enlisted by Otto Skorzeny in 1953.[92] Equally, though, Gehlen 'recognized the political debt Germany owed to the Jews; we had to do what we could to contribute to the survival of Israel'.

After the Sinai campaign the BND chief wrote later:

> We began to take a more professional interest in the Israelis. We gave them expert advice on the development of their small but powerful secret service; we made facilities available to them and aided them in

placing key agents in the Arab countries, especially since Nasser was becoming increasingly involved with Moscow, and we recognized that Israel was as much an outpost of the free world as West Berlin.[93]

Yisrael Beer met Gehlen in May 1960 despite repeated refusals by Harel to permit him to do so. Isser was abroad for much of the first half of the year, preparing for the Eichmann kidnapping operation in Argentina. Harel was convinced that only a KGB agent would want to try so hard to meet the legendary German spymaster. He was also annoyed by Beer's efforts to convince the Germans of his own importance and present himself as an official conduit to the policy-makers in Tel Aviv. The Mossad, according to Harel, had only limited contact with the BND at the time. Gehlen wanted more.

Beer began to display signs of an ostentatious new life style. The balding, bespectacled academic started frequenting Tel Aviv nightclubs, drinking heavily and pursuing women. In early 1961 he was beaten up by the jealous husband of a young woman called Ora Zehavi and explained away his injuries by telling colleagues at the Defence Ministry that he had been in a car crash. Harel snapped at this point and finally reported his suspicions to Ben-Gurion, telling Beer: 'I think the Prime Minister is naive about you.'[94]

Harel banned Beer from leaving the country and stepped up the surveillance. When he was spotted early one morning making contact with several Soviet Embassy officials, the watch was intensified and a team of agents took up permanent position opposite his flat on Brandeis Street in Tel Aviv. Zvi Malchin, Rafi Eitan's successor as head of the service's Operations Branch, was put in charge.[95] On the evening of 30 March 1961 Beer was observed by the Shin Bet watchers behaving evasively and was thought to have handed over a briefcase full of documents to the Soviet diplomat Sokolov, who had already been positively 'flagged' as a KGB officer because of his contacts with Aharon Cohen.

Amos Manor was out of town, so Harel, who was by then obsessed with Beer and seems to have thought that the Shin

Bet chief was not pursuing the case with sufficient vigour, took personal charge of the operation. He may also have been intimidated by the suspect's close relationship with Ben-Gurion. A warrant was quickly obtained and Beer was arrested in the early hours of the morning. His briefcase, the contents of which were presumed to have been photographed by his controllers, contained parts of Ben-Gurion's personal diary and a report on a senior employee in a top-secret security establishment.

Beer's interrogation confirmed most of 'Little' Isser's worst suspicions, but not all of them. Some entries in Beer's personal diary contained three or four Xs, with a total number of Xs appearing at the end of every month. Harel was convinced that the entries were a coded summary relating to meetings with his KGB controllers. Beer insisted to his interrogators – who were privately impressed by his worldly manner and success with women – that the Xs were a register of his sexual acomplishments. Mrs Zehavi was naturally embarrassed by the Shin Bet's questions on this delicate matter, but had to admit that Beer's version was true.[96]

The Memuneh already knew that the colonel had been a regular visitor at Soviet Bloc embassies and now discovered that he had first met Sokolov secretly at the end of 1957. He had seen plans by the Israeli construction firm Solel Boneh for the building of NATO bases in Turkey and knew a great deal about the Alliance's defences. It was he, Harel believed, who had told Sokolov about Peres's secret arms-purchasing mission to Germany in 1957, the leak of which had led to Ben-Gurion's resignation.

Harel later dismissed suggestions that friendly security services helped the Shin Bet to expose Beer.[97] According to one report, Britain's MI5 alerted the Israelis when Beer's name was found among the papers of Gordon Lonsdale, the Soviet agent Conon Molody, who had been arrested in January 1961 and gaoled in connection with the famous Portsmouth spy ring.[98] Other sources suggest that Beer worked with Hugh Hambleton, a Canadian economist who was imprisoned in Britain 1982 for spying on NATO for the Russians from 1956 to 1961.[99]

Beer's relationship with the Soviet diplomat was a close and regular one. The spy and his controller met more than twenty times altogether and four times from the beginning of 1961 until Beer's arrest on 30 March. On 10 April, without knowing that Beer had been caught, Sokolov turned up at their usual rendezvous and then, like Pavlovski before him, left the country suddenly a few days later.

Beer's impressive curriculum vitae turned out to be completely bogus. The colonel had never been in the Schutzbund, never fought in Spain and had in fact been a lowly clerk in the Austrian Zionist Federation. He told his interrogators that his contacts with the Soviets had been intended to try and persuade Moscow to change its policy towards Israel. Harel concluded that Beer had made contact with the Soviets only in 1956 and had actually begun spying the following year. The discovery of his fake biography did not mean, as some sources have suggested, that he was a long-term 'mole' with a cover story to match.

The announcement of his arrest dropped like a bombshell. 'After Beer's arrest there were several weeks of investigation before the news was released,' one of the spy's two Shin Bet interrogators recalled later. 'There were no secrets in little Tel Aviv. But the name didn't leak. People were talking about some "senior official" who was a thief and all sorts of other rubbish. And you know everything and you can't move a muscle.'[100] Shimon Peres was especially concerned by the effect that the affair would have on the standing of the Defence Ministry and he and his aides tried their best to persuade Harel to let them 'deal' with the case quietly. 'Little' Isser would have none of it. At the end of March 1962 Beer was sentenced to ten years in prison and, after an appeal both by the defendant and by the state, the High Court increased the term to fifteen years in December 1962. He died in gaol on May Day 1966. His book *Israel's Security: Yesterday, Today, Tomorrow* was published posthumously and is deemed by historians of the war of independence to contain many original ideas and penetrating insights into the military and diplomatic realities of the period.[101]

The Beer Affair had an intriguing postscript over two decades later. In 1987, when the Ben-Gurion Archive admitted that all the prime minister's diary entries from January to July 1956 were inexplicably missing, Mordechai Bar-On, who served as an aide to Dayan at the time, suggested that the handwritten Hebrew volumes, scrawled in lined school exercise books, may have been given to the KGB by Beer.

Beer claimed that he had shown the Russians the diaries found in his possession to prove that Ben-Gurion was open to a constructive relationship with both Moscow and the Arab countries. Bar-On believed that the missing 1956 volumes may have been handed over at the same time, possibly because the Russians wanted to learn about the suspected collusion against Egypt. Bar-On remembered that before setting out with Ben-Gurion and Dayan for the crucial Sèvres talks that sealed the Franco–Israeli part of the Suez plot in October 1956, he and Dayan had seen Beer in the defence minister's bureau in Tel Aviv.

'It was a Friday afternoon and most of the office staff had already left,' Bar-On recalled. 'As we left we suddenly saw Yisrael Beer coming out of one of the rooms. We were surprised since Beer was known to be very lazy. On the way to the airport Moshe Dayan said to me: "What was he doing there at that time, that spy?" That was almost five years before he was arrested.'[102]

Ben Gurion was an obsessive diarist throughout his life. He noted himself, in the first notebook covering the second half of 1956, that the volumes for the previous six months were missing. But it is not clear when he discovered their loss, and there is no record of any explanation for why they were missing.

Dealing with Soviet Bloc and Arab espionage was a major preoccupation for the Shin Bet until the 1967 war, but the more honest of the service's counter-intelligence officers would admit afterwards, in the light of the IDF's Six Day War victory, that they had 'greatly exaggerated' the extent of the strategic threat posed by foreign agents.[103] And the capture of the archives of the Jordanian secret service, which included the files of Israelis who had spied for the Hashemite kingdom, showed that the Shin Bet had known about all of them.[104]

Changing the guard

According to the folklore of Isser Harel's resignation as Memuneh of the security and intelligence services in March 1963, Ben-Gurion had intended to ask Amos Manor to take charge of the Mossad, but when the Shin Bet chief could not be located (he was on his way to holiday in a kibbutz), the premier called instead Meir Amit, the head of IDF Intelligence Branch. Harel certainly thought that Manor was the obvious candidate. And so did Manor. He resigned from the security service in September 1963 and was replaced by his deputy, Yosef Harmelin, the Viennese-born veteran of the Jewish Brigade and Bricha.

Harmelin rose to the top job from within the service, enjoying a reputation for solidity rather than brilliance, great integrity and fiercely high standards of personal behaviour. He was called back from abroad to take over, although the outgoing head almost appointed Ya'akov ('Yanek') Ben-Yehuda, the Shin Bet director in northern Israel. Ben-Yehuda then resigned. Harmelin was a tall, powerfully built man and his colleagues tended to see him as the kibbutznik he had once been. Levi Eshkol, who served as premier from 1963 to 1968, admired his security chief greatly and consulted him often – although without ever managing to make him laugh.[105] Harmelin spoke only rarely about his work, although after he resigned he was slightly more voluble than his utterly silent predecessor. 'You cannot tell anyone what you are doing,' he said in an interview several years later. 'It's pretty hard not to be able to share even your successes with the people who are closest to you.'[106]

Harmelin's single most important act in the years before the 1967 war was his strong recommendation that the prime minister abrogate the military government in Arab areas of

Israel. Mishka Drori, head of the service's Arab Affairs Branch, had urged as early as 1958 that the system be abolished, although he insisted on the need to retain the Emergency Regulations inherited from the British Mandate.[107] The Shin Bet knew that if the regulations were abolished, nothing as draconian as them could ever be legislated again. And who knew when they might be needed?

Eshkol, freed from the towering influence of Ben-Gurion (who had wanted to maintain the military government), believed that a more liberal approach to the minority would send a positive message to the Arab states about the possibility of Arab–Jewish coexistence inside the country. Politically, it was no easy matter: from the opposition benches in the Knesset Menachem Begin's Herut and the new Rafi faction, which had broken off from Mapai in 1965, kept up a withering fire. Herut remembered how the British had brought in the Emergency Regulations to deal with their supporters in the Irgun underground days, and it also exploited the issue against Mapai.

The army, under chief of staff Yitzhak Rabin, opposed any change, and endless inter-departmental and ministerial debates brought the matter no nearer to conclusion. But Harmelin and the new head of the Arab Affairs Branch, Avraham Ahituv, were in favour. The Shin Bet had Israel's Arabs well 'covered', and the security service believed that only the radical Al-Ard group, which it had succeeded in having banned in 1964, represented a truly subversive threat. It submitted a list of 700 people whose activities would still be restricted. Shmuel Toledano, the former Mossad executive who became Eshkol's adviser on Arab affairs in 1966, also supported the abrogation. 'Avraham Ahituv saw the issue as one of national security, and not of whether Muhammad or Ahmed were being bad boys,' he said later.[108] Isser Harel, in his final days as special adviser on security and intelligence to the prime minister, agreed.[109]

6

Great Leaps Forward: 1956–67

Secrets from Moscow

Suez proved a watershed for Israel in many ways, and the standing and reputation of its intelligence services were no exception. The victory in Sinai ushered in a long period of peace on the borders, economic growth and widening international acceptance. Against this background Isser Harel's Mossad came to play a leading role in foreign policy, in the clandestine immigration of Jews and in a dazzling range of audacious secret operations. The dogged little spymaster dominated huge areas of national security, raising the prestige of the Israeli intelligence community to almost mythic proportions. In his unique role as Memuneh over both the Mossad and the Shin Bet, and with his close, jealously nurtured relationship with Ben-Gurion, he exercised far greater powers than the civilian intelligence chiefs of other democracies. It was a heroic age of great leaps forward.

In the months before the 1956 war the Mossad's acquisition of Nikita Khrushchev's historic speech to the 20th Soviet Communist Party Congress had done wonders for its already healthy relationship with the CIA. James Angleton ('Jim', to his Israeli friends) had ensured close liaison since the early 1950s. Although he was head of the agency's counter-intelligence department, and had no obvious business maintaining the Israeli 'account', Angleton knew that Israeli assets in the Soviet Union and Eastern Europe had provided the Americans with an invaluable source of information at a time when the Cold War demanded increasing their capabilities behind the Iron Curtain. 'Jim started out from the principle of "respect and mistrust" and became a zealous supporter of Israel from an American point of view,' said Meir ('Memi') de Shalit, who served in the Washington embassy in the early 1950s. 'He was a fanatical anti-Communist and he changed his attitude when he began to get to know people in Israel and became more and more convinced that the country wouldn't go Communist.'[1]

Angleton had arranged for Ben-Gurion to meet Walter Bedell-Smith, the CIA director, in May 1951. Shortly afterwards Reuven Shiloah went to Washington to draw up a formal US–Israeli agreement on intelligence cooperation. 'The main burden, indeed almost the sole one, fell upon the security service,' Isser Harel wrote later. 'It quickly transpired that Israel had a vast potential for information and manpower in the strategic field. This was a surprise for us, but mostly for our American collegues.'[2]

The Shin Bet's contribution to the burgeoning alliance with the US came in the form of a special, super-secret interrogations unit, responsible to the service's Investigations Department, that debriefed Jewish immigrants from Eastern Europe. Military installations, factories and railways behind the Iron Curtain were of no interest to Israel. For the CIA, the product was priceless. 'We knew much more than the Americans,' Harel said. 'We knew about the mood amongst the Jews and the mood in general, about the bitter disappointment, the queues, the shortages. We had a more accurate picture – not only of the Soviet danger but also of its limitations – than anyone else.'[3] Harel and Shiloah personally presented a progress report on the debriefing of the immigrants to Ben-Gurion in February 1952.[4]

That year the CIA hosted six senior Israeli intelligence officers for a course – 'rather poorly taught', according to one participant – on the basics of modern intelligence. Before leaving Israel the six were issued by the Shin Bet Operations Branch with a jacket, two ties and a raincoat instead of their usual khaki trousers and shirts. The clothes were so ill-fitting that, upon arrival, one of them was taken to a Washington tailor to be properly kitted out for the occasion.

Harel made his first official visit to the US as head of the Mossad in March 1954. Allen Dulles had taken over the CIA from Bedell-Smith in February 1953 and he gave his Israeli colleague a warm reception. Harel presented Dulles with an ancient dagger made by a Persian-Jewish craftsman and inscribed with the words from Psalms: 'The Guardian of Israel neither slumbers nor sleeps.'

'Little' Isser saw the secret cooperation as a way of overcoming American reservations about supporting Israel. 'From a psychological point of view the special relationship was a firm and appropriate answer to all those who had doubts about Israel's role – and the implications for American Jews who identified with the Jewish state,' Harel argued. 'Because of the Cold War, the aggression, subversion and global espionage activities of the Soviets and world Communism, the standing of the CIA had improved greatly. It is easy to guess what conclusions it would have reached about Israel had it not been for this special relationship.'[5] On another occasion he was even more specific: 'In the 1950s it was very important for us to create a positive image for Israel in the US against the background of the involvement of Jews from communist movements who had become enmeshed in the US in espionage cases on behalf of the Soviets and who thereby caused serious damage to Israel and the American Jews.'[6]

The Mossad's link with its American counterpart also provided a useful 'back channel' that could circumvent conventional diplomacy. Before Suez the CIA had helped (Operation Chameleon or Operation Mirage) to try and organize a secret meeting with Nasser, going behind the back of the State Department.[7]

According to one account, the Mossad's copy of Khrushchev's famous 'crimes of Stalin' speech originated with a Communist Party functionary in Poland.[8] Another claimed it came from a

Soviet Jew reporting to Israel. Teddy Kollek, perhaps wishing to disguise its true source, suggested that Jewish immigrants passing through Europe en route for Israel had helped the speech see the light of day.[9] Isser Harel kept the coup a closely guarded secret until the whole text had been handed over to the CIA and pronounced genuine. Moshe Sharett, the foreign minister, read it only after it had been leaked to *The New York Times* in early June.[10] Other Western intelligence agencies, including General Gehlen's BND in West Germany, obtained their own partial versions. The Israelis were the only ones to get the whole document. Many years later, although repeatedly pressed to reveal his source, Harel would say only that the speech had been obtained from behind the Iron Curtain.[11] 'We already had a very good relationship with the CIA,' another senior Mossad executive said later, 'but there is no doubt that acquiring the Khrushchev speech improved our standing with them.'[12]

The French connection

The United States was an attractive friend, but in the mid-1950s Israel's closest ally was still France, and there Isser Harel was less confident. Much to the annoyance of the Mossad, IDF intelligence conducted its own foreign liaisons in this period. The preparations for the 1956 war contributed considerably to the establishment of ties between Aman and the French and, to a lesser extent, the British intelligence services. Early in the year the IDF military attaché in Paris, Colonel Nishri, reported to Dayan, Yehoshafat Harkabi and his deputy, Yuval Ne'eman, about French interest in a 'secret link' with Aman.[13] At their first meeting in Paris a few weeks before the Suez invasion, Harkabi established a firm basis for cooperation with Pierre Bouriscot, the head of France's SDECE (Service de Documentation Extérieur et Contre-Espionage), but only after displaying detailed knowledge about the French service. As the Aman chief said later:

> At the beginning there was some confusion and suspicion. He thought I was the head of Israel's equivalent of the DST, the rival of the SDECE. I broke the ice by telling him that our (Aman) station chief in Djibouti had regular contacts with his station chief in that colony. He then opened the doors; he gave a dinner party with all his heads of divisions, and so on. From then on, Aman and the SDECE traded information. Almost everything. About Egypt, the Arab world. *Modus operandi*. Everything.[14]

The appointment of Ne'eman, who spoke fluent French, as the new Intelligence Branch representative in Paris consolidated the link. Shlomo Gazit took over shortly afterwards.

This relationship angered Harel, who felt that such inter-agency liaison was the sole purview of the Mossad, and he again threatened to resign. Yet Harel was not on firm ground. Mossad's French connection, cultivated by Ya'akov Caroz, was with the DST internal security service, a renewal of the friendship dating back to the period of illegal immigration in the late 1940s. Ben-Gurion rejected Harel's protests by arguing that the impending war necessitated Aman–SDECE links and cooperation. A compromise was eventually reached under which the Mossad would receive copies of any material obtained through this channel. Harkabi set up a new section within Intelligence Branch responsible for links with the Western intelligence agencies.[15]

The French connection continued well after Suez and built on the close cooperation that had been established before the war. The outbreak of the Algerian revolt in 1954 had created a considerable demand in Paris for good intelligence on the Arab world, especially the important question of Egyptian support for the FLN (Front de Libération Nationale) rebels.

French interest in the 'secret link' with Israel advanced by leaps and bounds as the Algerian war progressed. In May 1955 the SDECE had been charged with the 'neutralization' of the principal leaders of the FLN, but made little progress until the following year. In May 1956 Harkabi was informed that Aman had incidentally come across reports on the movements of 'several unknown and apparently insignificant people', who turned out on closer examination to include the FLN leader, Ahmed Ben Bella himself and Muhammad Khidr, the organization's political chief. The Aman source, a by-product of other intelligence-gathering, provided details of the travels of the Algerian leaders, their management of the revolt and arms smuggling to the guerrillas.

IDF intelligence now had an invaluable tool which could be used to increase French willingness to supply further types of armaments and could create the foundation for real intelligence cooperation. The French were asked to supply a list of FLN leaders because Israel had discovered a source of information about the guerrilla movement. French ears pricked up and the bait was quickly taken. Within weeks Israel was supplying real-time information about FLN movements and arms supplies, and Paris warmed to further Israeli arms requests. The Aman coup was a milestone on the road to Suez and a pillar of the Israeli–French relationship, which was to wane only with the 1967 war.[16]

Dramatic results followed quickly: in mid-October 1956, only weeks before the Suez operation, a Sudanese-flagged ship, the *Athos*, had been spotted after sailing from Alexandria on a suspiciously zig-zag course round the Mediterranean and had been intercepted with 70 tons of weapons on board – enough to equip 3,000 men – sent by Egyptian intelligence to the Algerians.[17] The *Athos* capture was mounted by the Cairo and Beirut stations of the SDECE, although the crucial initial intelligence probably came from the Aman source. A week later French aircraft hijacked Ben Bella's plane over Algeria on a flight from Morocco to Tunisia;[18] information about the flight may have been provided by Israel. Aman clearly had much to offer. 'I won't say we had the French eating out of our hands, but we did emphasize the Algerian thing,' Harkabi recalled.[19] 'Every Frenchman killed in North Africa, like every Egyptian killed in the Gaza Strip, takes us one step further towards strengthening the ties between France and Israel,' Shimon Peres had said in June 1955.[20]

Isser Harel did all he could to undermine Aman's links with

French intelligence. He made full use of an opportunity that came up in March 1961 when a disaffected former French army officer approached Yitzhak Baron, the deputy IDF military attaché in the Paris embassy, and suggested that Israel provide one of its Arab agents to assassinate de Gaulle. In return Israel would be supplied with whatever military equipment it wanted by the new French regime. The embassy reported back to Jerusalem on the approach and Harel and Ben-Gurion decided, over fierce objections from Aman, to warn de Gaulle at once.[21] The former officer was tried and executed. When Harel had published his own account of the affair,[22] Uzi Narkiss, the chief IDF attaché in Paris, said later: 'France was the only country in the world where links between the secret service and Israel were conducted via the IDF. Harel tried but failed to change this situation. He's still burning with jealousy.'[23]

The French connection also served Israel well in another context: the secret immigration from North Africa that was one of the Mossad's most important activities in this period.

The Moroccan aliya *campaign: 1955–62*

On the night of 11 January 1961 forty-two Moroccan Jews, a crewman and a Mossad wireless operator were drowned when their converted steamer, the *Pisces*, struck rocks and sank in a storm off the Moroccan coast. The 20-ton boat, flying a Honduran flag and renamed the *Egoz* (*Walnut*) by the Mossad, was ferrying illegal Jewish emigrants from Morocco to Gibraltar, on the first stage of their journey to Israel. Twenty-two bodies were eventually recovered and buried in the Jewish cemetery in the Moroccan fishing town of Al-Coseima. The mass drowning was both the low point and a turning-point in a seven-year-long Mossad-run operation which secretly brought tens of thousands of Moroccan Jews to Israel. It was the Mossad's biggest, longest and most successful clandestine immigration effort.

The operation was launched in the final years of Morocco's struggle for independence from France. In November 1954 a specially recruited Mossad agent, Shlomo Havilio, codenamed 'Louis', toured the Maghrib (Morocco, Algeria and Tunisia) and reported back to Jerusalem in early 1955 that the French Muslim territories would soon obtain independence, that the nationalist wave – backed by Israel's main enemy, Egypt's President Nasser – would probably endanger the countries' Jewish communities and that Israel must assist in setting up a self-defence and *aliya* organization for North African Jewry. In a long proposal submitted to Isser Harel, Havilio called for a three-country (Morocco, Algeria and Tunisia) organization, with headquarters in Paris and an independent branch in Tangier (until mid-1956 still an international territory). The plan proposed a staff of twenty Mossad agents, with eight of them centred in Morocco, which had the largest Jewish population in the Maghrib.[24]

On 27 April 1955 Ya'akov Caroz, the Mossad representative in Paris, met with France's high commissioner for Morocco, Francis Lacoste, in Casablanca to request French assistance in increasing Moroccan Jewish emigration to Israel. Because of the troubles, and wishing not to antagonize the Moroccans on a further front, the French were restricting Jewish emigration from the country. Lacoste and Caroz agreed on a new flexible ceiling of 700 immigrants per month.

Meanwhile, in Jerusalem the cabinet, under Ben-Gurion, approved Havilio's proposal and a team of Mossad operatives, with Havilio at its head, established an operational headquarters in Paris in August 1955. Mossad agents set up bases in Morocco. That month, a group of French settlers was massacred in Oued Zem by Moroccan nationalists. On 24 August rioters burst into the Mlah, the Jewish ghetto, in the town of Mazagan (El Jadida), near Casablanca, murdering eight Jews and injuring forty. Forty houses were also burned down.[25]

The Israelis had chosen a propitious moment. The threat to Moroccan Jewry was growing more obvious with the passing of each week and the community was naturally becoming more receptive to the Zionist message. At the same time, continued French rule in Morocco – until 2 March 1956 – assured a measure of protection for the establishment of the Misgeret (framework), as the Mossad-led, Jewish self-defence organization was called. Misgeret HQ, in Casablanca, had a commander, an administrative officer, an intelligence officer and a training officer. The defence-oriented part of the Misgeret (later code-named 'Lavi') was kept separate from the *aliya* part, which was eventually called Makhela (choir), but the 'Lavi' men selected jump-off points for the illegal emigrants and provided guards for the departees on their way to the beaches. Hundreds of Jewish volunteers were mobilized; over 100 went abroad – mostly to Israel – for military training, though some were trained in Morocco itself; cells and 'units' were organized in the main towns (eventually there were twelve local units); arms were bought and dispersed in underground caches ('*slikim*', in Haganah parlance, from the British Mandate days in Palestine). The members were trained in the use of pistols, sub-machine-guns and knives. At its height the Misgeret in Morocco had 600 members (and in Algeria and Tunisia, another 600 together). Some 470 of the Moroccan operatives went through training courses in France and Israel.

The expected blow fell in mid-1956. The Moroccan government, under the Sultan (later King) Muhammad V, responding to the anti-Zionist ground swell in the Arab world and in Morocco itself, shut down the emigrants' 'Kadima' transit camp, and on 27 September the head of the Moroccan secret police, Muhammad Lagazawi, issued 'Order No. 424', effectively forbidding emigration to Israel. About 110,000 Moroccan Jews had emigrated to Israel between 1948 and 1956, 60,000 of them in the last two years; well over 100,000 remained behind.

Israel's invasion of Sinai in October–November 1956 further undermined the position of the remaining half of the community. But the feared pogroms did not materialize. Until the Suez war, emigration of Moroccan Jews to Israel was handled by the Jewish Agency. From November to December the Mossad, using the Misgeret, took over that role, which had now become illegal and dangerous.[26]

The operation, like the Misgeret itself, was overseen by

'Jacques' (Caroz). Havilio was the Misgeret's direct commander. Another Mossad agent, based in Casablanca, was directly responsible for the Makhela. A separate section dealt with intelligence, which was vital to the success of the unfolding operation and served both Makhela and 'Lavi'.[27] The operation was run from Paris, using radio transmitters, receivers and couriers. The Misgeret operatives established contacts with various levels of Moroccan officialdom, police and army officers, and gathered information on police, army and secret police personnel and *modus operandi*. Their penetration of the Moroccan secret police was such that at one point an agent named 'Eppy' was able to tell 'Jacques' that the secret police were about to arrest four Misgeret operatives. The Misgeret managed to delay the implementation of the warrants by a few hours and the four were immediately smuggled out of the country.[28] Isser Harel revealed years later that some $500,000 – a large sum of money in those days – had been paid in bribes to Moroccans.[29] During the first months of the operation, the Misgeret managed to get about 500 Jews out of the country per month, mostly on old French or forged Moroccan passports. Some of the Mossad's best forgers, including Shalom Weiss (Dani), were put to work in Israel, Paris and Marseilles. Weiss, a Hungarian-born Holocaust survivor and Mossad LeAliya Bet veteran, was mobilized by the IDF in 1949, joined the Mossad in 1957 and was sent to Paris and Morocco. He collected North African art, painted and studied at the Beaux-Arts in Paris. He returned to Israel at the end of 1961, after participating in the Mossad's capture of Adolf Eichmann in Argentina, and died of cancer in 1963.[30]

Misgeret operatives assembled emigrants and ferried them at night to assembly points – safe houses near the exit ports. If the vehicles were stopped by police, the passengers had cover stories, such as 'We are on our way to a wedding' or 'to a football match'.

Problems in the ports resulted in a major change in 1957. Henceforward, the Misgeret took the emigrants across the border by land or in fishing boats, to the Spanish-governed enclaves of Ceuta and Melilla, with the knowledge and cooperation of the Spanish authorities. Occasionally, emigrant convoys also passed through Ifni and Tangier. Ferries would then take the emigrants to Gibraltar, where there was a Jewish Agency transit camp, or Algeciras, and from there to Marseilles and by boat or plane to Israel. 'The Spanish didn't ask for a penny and I never delved too much into their motives,' Harel said. 'But I thought all along they wanted to make a gesture to the Jewish people to make up for Spain's close ties with Hitler and Mussolini during the war. Without the aid of the Spanish government this secret operation would have been impossible to carry out.'[31]

The British authorities on the Rock, who were fully aware of what was happening, were as friendly and helpful as the Spanish in the enclaves. In the winter the police would often meet the immigrants with cauldrons of hot tea. The British also helped the immigrants with travel papers, eventually allowing into Gibraltar immigrants without passports.[32]

Despite occasional Moroccan crackdowns, prompted by swings in the king's foreign policy (which sometimes took a Nasserist or pan-Arab turn), the Misgeret continued functioning. The Moroccans, subjected to intermittent European and American pressures and themselves generally Western-oriented rather than 'non-aligned' or pro-Soviet, never wholeheartedly tried to stop the emigration. Isser Harel himself (code-named 'Pierre') secretly visited Morocco a number of times between 1958 and 1962, on one occasion spending a fortnight in the country, looking over the Misgeret's operations.[33]

The *Pisces*, used by the Allies in the Second World War to recover airmen who had ditched in the Mediterranean, was purchased by the Mossad in Gibraltar in 1960. That year Shlomo Havilio was replaced as commander of the Misgeret by a Mossad man codenamed 'Emile'. His real name was Olek Guttman (Alex Gatmon), still regarded by many as the unsung hero of the Moroccan operation. Gatmon, a Second World War Polish–Jewish partisan and a former IAF officer, was placed in charge of the Misgeret in Morocco, and took up residence in Casablanca.[34]

In late 1960, using the *Pisces*, the Misgeret began ferrying emigrants directly (bypassing Ceuta and Melilla) from Morocco to Gibraltar, lifting them off a beach outside Al-Coseima. On its thirteenth journey the *Pisces* sailed into a storm and was dashed against rocks just off Al-Coseima. Forty-two Jewish emigrants, the Mossad agent, 'Tzarfati', who had been the service's radio operator in the Marseilles station since 1957, and a crewman were drowned. In an act of open defiance, the Misgeret then distributed around Morocco a wall poster saying that the *aliya* effort would continue and attacked the Jewish community's 'persecutors'. The Moroccan secret police, under General Muhammad Oufkir, responded by arresting and torturing some twenty Misgeret members, though no Mossad operatives were caught. One of the members, Rafi Vaknin, was tortured so badly that he died in a Paris hospital a few months later. Vaknin was the only Misgeret member to have died in the seven-year operation.

The sinking of the *Pisces* and the arrest of the Misgeret activists resulted in massive pressure on Muhammad V to change his policy. Israel forswore secret diplomacy and launched a widespread public campaign on behalf of Moroccan Jewry. US President John Kennedy sent a personal message to King Muhammad; a group of American congressmen threatened to table a bill to stop US aid to Morocco unless the persecution stopped. French President Charles de Gaulle was also mobilized to exert pressure on Rabat.

The king was apparently in the process of bowing to these pressures and changing his policies when, on 25 February 1961, he died under a surgeon's knife. This, at least, was Harel's assessment five days before the king's death. Harel wrote to Alex Gatmon: 'There is no doubt that the king's and the interior minister's latest steps are a result of our actions and our information campaign around the world.' Harel wrote that he had never believed that the problem would be solved by the slow trickle of illegal immigrants to Israel but only by 'a political decision' by the Moroccans. The Misgeret operation, the sinking of the *Pisces* and the worldwide furore had all contributed to the evolving 'political decision' in Morocco. Harel pressed the commander to make sure that as many Jews as possible in Morocco immediately applied for passports (to put pressure on the Moroccan Ministry of Interior). Harel cautioned that there was no need to rush in with offers to the Moroccans of financial incentives to let their Jews out.[35]

King Muhammad's death was understood in Tel Aviv as marking a potential turning-point in the *aliya* campaign. Harel wrote again to Gatmon in Paris: 'One cannot know how the king's death will affect the internal situation in Morocco ... And the condition of the Jews of Morocco is greatly dependent on this internal situation ... It is unclear whether [Muhammad's successor] Hassan II will continue with the [pan-Arab] "Casablanca Conference policy" or whether he will revert to the previous pro-Western Moroccan orientation.' Harel proposed that Israel examine all its 'assets' vis-à-vis the new king and his advisers. It was advisable to 'try to find a direct link to the new ruler. If such a connection is established, there will be a need initially to feed him intelligence which will be of crucial interest to the new ruler ... We owe [Hassan's] opponents nothing.' The direction of Harel's thinking was obvious.[36]

And, indeed, under King Hassan II, Moroccan policy rapidly changed. Morocco eventually agreed to issue 'group passports' to the would-be Jewish emigrants. The first such passport was issued by the Interior Ministry on 27 November 1961; it covered 105 Jews. They left the country by plane the next day. During the next two years, almost all the remaining Moroccan Jewish community left for Israel. In 1961 there were 11,478 emigrants; in 1962, 35,758; in 1963, 36,874.[37]

The Mossad also had a hand in the emigration from North Africa to Israel of a number of other Jewish communities, including those of Port Said in Egypt and Bizerte in Tunisia.

On 9 November 1956 a three-man intelligence team, composed of Aryeh ('Lyova') Eliav, seconded for the occasion to the Mossad, Major Avraham Dar of Aman and Tommy Arieli, a communications expert, set out in a French Air Force Marauder aircraft for Port Said to join the French forces in the Canal zone, then under assault by the Anglo-French expeditionary force. The team was sent to liaise with the French on intelligence matters; to report (on the radio set they took with them) to Tel Aviv on the state and intentions of the French forces; to report on the state of Egypt's Jewish community; and, should the French march on Cairo, to help free from gaol the Jewish agents imprisoned in Cairo during the Lavon Affair.

Eliav and Dar spent the previous week beefing up on Egypt; their meetings included a long session with Shaul Avigur, the former head of the Mossad LeAliya Bet and Ben-Gurion's adviser on 'special matters', and sessions with former Egyptian Jews serving in Israel's intelligence community, including Binyamin Sidbon of the Mossad.

On 11 November Eliav and Dar, posing (in French uniforms) as Jewish soldiers of the French Foreign Legion, made contact with representatives of the 200-strong Jewish community in Port Said. The Jews were afraid that their Arab neighbours would set upon them in revenge after the departure of the Anglo-French expeditionary force. Eliav and Dar asked that a list of Jews interested in emigrating to Israel be drawn up. Meanwhile, they checked out the possibility of organizing a land convoy across Sinai for those interested in emigrating. But the idea was scrapped and Eliav decided on a sea route. He asked Tel Aviv for two small Israeli navy vessels to be sent to Port Fuad, on the east bank of the Canal, opposite Port Said. On 17 November French landing craft ferried about 100 Jews to Port Fuad, where they boarded the two Israeli vessels. The new immigrants reached Israel on 18 November.[38]

The Jewish emigration from Bizerte in September 1961 was prompted by the outbreak of hostilities between the Tunisian and French armies over possession of the big French naval base next to the town. During the initial fighting the French occupied Bizerte itself. The Tunisians had demanded French withdrawal; the French had refused. Hundreds of Arabs died. The 1,200-strong Jewish community was accused by the Arabs of collaborating with the French. Many of the Jews worked in the base or serviced it. All understood that the French would eventually withdraw. The Arabs threatened to take 'revenge' on the Jews.

Most of the Jews had French passports and so were able to leave easily immediately after the fighting. But about 300 had Tunisian passports or were stateless. The Jewish Agency, helped by the Mossad and Israel's military attaché in Paris, Colonel Uzi Narkiss, began organizing the community's departure. The French military cooperated. The Jews were ferried out of the town directly to France or via Algiers in French naval vessels. The departures were organized by Mossad representatives and guarded by French paratroops.[39]

Peripheral preoccupations

In the heady years after the Suez war Israel tried to formulate its foreign policy in a way that would reap the advantages of its military victory over Egypt. The method was to break through its regional isolation by forging links on the edges of the Middle East with non-Arab regimes that were deeply concerned, for their own reasons, by the spread of Nasserism and Communism. Isser Harel's Mossad played a significant part in this innovative strategy, developing and enhancing its own role as an instrument of Israel's clandestine diplomacy. 'My aim,' as Harel put it later, 'was to build a dam against the Nasserist–Soviet flood.'[40]

It was to fulfil this role that the Mossad set up its important Foreign Relations Division early in 1958. Headed by the able Ya'akov Caroz, who had been based in Paris since moving over from the Shin Bet in 1954, the branch quickly became a unique component of Israeli intelligence, serving as a sort of parallel secret foreign ministry to create and maintain links with countries which could not or would not establish formal ties with the Jewish state.[41]

Iran was the jewel in the crown of what became known as the 'periphery' doctrine and was to remain so for over two decades, until the fall of the Shah in 1979. Iran had recognized Israel *de facto* in 1950, shortly after Turkey, and there had been a low-level although unofficial presence in Tehran since then. Max Binnet had run the Aman station there in the early years of the decade, and it had served both as a base for intelligence operations against Iraq and in support of the clandestine exit of Iraqi Jews to Israel.

Relations between the two countries improved dramatically after Suez. In September 1957 General Taimour Bakhtiar, the first head of Iran's newly created SAVAK intelligence and internal security organization, met secretly in Paris with Caroz, who was serving as 'political counsellor' at the Israeli Embassy.[42] It was a vital breakthough. 'Isser took the matter straight to Golda [Meir, the Foreign Minister],' Caroz said later. 'It was the first time any Muslim state had expressed any interest in us.'[43] Bakhtiar, with whom Harel developed 'great personal friendship',[44] maintained contact with the Israelis and the CIA until he was sacked in 1961. He was later assassinated by SAVAK in Iraq while on a hunting expedition. Bakhtiar's eventual replacement, the notorious Lieutenant-General Nimatullah Nassiri, liaised closely with the Israelis until he was dismissed in 1978. In the spring of 1959 Chaim Herzog, head of Aman, was hosted in Tehran by his Iranian counterpart, General Alavi Kia, and they agreed, with the personal approval of both the Shah and Ben-Gurion, on military and intelligence cooperation.[45] Although the army and other Israeli bodies quickly became involved in the evolving relationship with the Shah, the Mossad remained the chief conduit. Harel wrote afterwards:

> Since Nasser's main instrument – like that of the Soviets and Communism – was subversion and organizing fifth columns, it was most essential and urgent to take effective measures in internal security. I therefore devoted considerable efforts to assist these countries in organizing efficient intelligence and security services and a military or police strike force that could resist any sudden internal or externally inspired coup attempt.[46]

The Iranian and Israeli secret services were soon cooperating closely: 'Mossad has engaged in joint operations with SAVAK over the years since the late 1950s,' said a CIA report written in 1976 and captured in Tehran in 1979. 'Mossad aided

SAVAK activities and supported the Kurds in Iraq. The Israelis also regularly transmitted to the Iranians intelligence reports on Egypt's activities in the Arab countries, trends and developments in Iraq and Communist activities affecting Iran.'[47]

Israel and Iran shared a common enemy in Iraq, although different circumstances sometimes dictated different approaches. Israeli calculations remained more or less constant. Iraq was the only Arab country that had not signed a ceasefire agreement with the Jewish state at the end of the 1948 war. And after the overthrow of General Qasem in 1963, when the new Aref regime in Baghdad allied itself with Nasser's Egypt, the Shah expressed a greater interest in trying to weaken Iraq internally. Assisting the country's Kurdish rebels, who had restarted their insurgency in 1961, was the simplest way to do that.

Israeli ties with the Iraqi Kurds began in earnest in 1964, when Meir Amit was running the Mossad and starting to increase its offensive operations against Arab targets. Shimon Peres, entrenched in his position as deputy minister of defence, met secretly with Kumran Ali Bedir-Khan, the old Kurdish leader who had spied for the Israelis back in the 1940s and 1950s. A first training course for Peshmerga officers – codenamed 'Marvad' (carpet) – began in August 1965 and lasted for three months.[48] The following summer Levi Eshkol and Amit asked Aryeh 'Lyova' Eliav, the Labour Party's energetic deputy minister for industrialization and development, to tour Iraqi Kurdish areas and meet Barazani. Haim Levakov, the veteran Palmah Arabist, was in charge of the Israeli assistance programme at that early stage, and one of the first non-military contributions was a field hospital.[49] Eshkol himself visited Tehran in June 1966, as did the foreign minister, Abba Eban, at the end of the year. Barazani was reportedly assisted by Israeli officers when his forces repulsed the big Iraqi offensive in June 1966.[50]

The secret relationship was given a high priority by the Jerusalem government, although some Israeli Middle East experts had their doubts about its wisdom. Ezra Danin was no longer involved in intelligence as such, but he worked on behalf of the Foreign Ministry on agricultural and water development programmes in Iran in the late 1950s and early 1960s, and he had grave reservations about the military aid to the Kurds. Danin wrote later:

> It was clear to me that the assistance we gave to the Kurdish fighters in Iraq could not but be interpreted as exploiting the Kurdish tragedy for our own ends, even though the assistance itself was a noble contribution and despite the fact that Israel gained military advantages by tying the hands of a considerable part of the Iraqi army by forcing it to deal with the Kurdish problem.[51]

Support for the Kurds also provided the Israelis with first-hand intelligence on the Iraqi army. One of the Mossad's most brilliant coups before the 1967 war, the painstakingly planned defection of an Iraqi air force MiG pilot – and his plane – in August 1966, was made possible with Kurdish help. It was in this period that the Mossad began to become even more influential with SAVAK than the CIA.[52] US sources say that the Israelis played an important role with respect to Department Three, SAVAK's hated internal security and surveillance apparatus. Relations with Iran developed slowly and cautiously, and although they were never formalized by an exchange of ambassadors, 'the amplitude of their substance outweighed the deficiency of their form', as the Foreign Ministry's Gideon Rafael put it.[53] It was an excellent summary of the whole policy.

The second side of the periphery 'triangle' was Ethiopia. Emperor Haile Selassie had first begun to put out feelers about establishing ties with Israel in 1955. Fears of Nasserist subversion and hopes for development and military assistance were his main motives. Asher Ben-Natan went to Addis Ababa at the end of the year, although Sharett doubted whether Haile Selassie was really prepared to establish formal diplomatic relations at that stage.[54]

Against the same background, similar contacts were made with Sudan, which was due to become independent in January 1956. In September 1955 Josh Palmon held secret talks in Istanbul with leaders of the Sudanese opposition Umma (Nation) party, which was pro-British, was keen to strengthen ties with the West and was opposed to the pro-Egyptian and leftist-neutralist orientation of other political groups. Palmon brought one of them – Omar – to see Ben-Gurion in August 1956. 'They speak Arabic and are Muslims,' the prime minister noted afterwards, 'but the Egyptians treat them scornfully and plan to dominate them.'[55]

Later, Israel was to change its clandestine policy towards Sudan. In the 1960s the Mossad gave limited support to the Anya Nya rebels in southern Sudan. The black, non-Arab southerners had first risen against the central government in Khartoum in 1955, and in later years, according to General Joseph Lagu, the Anya Nya leader, received arms, communications equipment and some training from the Israelis. Anya Nya documents captured by the Sudanese army showed that 'individual Israelis' had visited the rebel camps, although the assistance as a whole was on a relatively small scale. Political logic dictated a discreet and low-key approach. 'If any harm could be done to the Arab country, this, from the point of view of the Jewish state, was good . . . provided that other interests were not damaged . . . to an extent where the action designed to harm the Sudan became counter-productive,' a Western expert noted later. 'It was manifest to the Israelis that an open stand in favour of the south and a substantial aid operation for the benefit of the rebels would have made a disastrous impression in Black Africa.'[56]

Formal ties with Ethiopia were established shortly after the 1956 war.[57] Yosef Nahmias, who had been the Defence Ministry representative in Paris, went on some of these early exploratory missions. The Egyptian–Syrian union in the United Arab Republic in February 1958 strengthened Israel's belief that its periphery policy was both essential and workable.

Incoda, a wholly Israeli-owned company that exported Ethiopian beef, was a useful commercial front for intelligence activities. Yossi Harel, a former Aman officer, ran one of the firm's factories in Asmara on the Red Sea. 'Incoda was a station for Israeli intelligence in Africa,' one of its directors said later.

'We had a huge arms cache. It was there when we arrived. We just served as the cover. There was a military delegation, and they did their correspondence through us, with Israeli spies in Arab countries as well. We were only a cover in Mossad deals. When they had to send somebody to an Arab country, they did it through us.'[58]

In December 1960 the Israelis helped Haile Selassie crush a coup attempt by giving him information about his opponents and their dispositions when he was returning from a trip abroad.[59] The relationship was improved, rather than marred, when it turned out that the head of the Emperor's internal security service, which had been established with Israeli assistance, was one of the chief plotters.[60] The same month Ben-Gurion himself ignored the restrictions of military censorship and revealed that the IDF was helping to organize and train the Ethiopian army.[61] Further assistance was extended in 1962 when the secessionist Eritrean Liberation Front began fighting Haile Selassie, with the support of Egypt, Sudan and Syria. About forty Israeli advisers trained the Emergency Police, an elite counter-insurgency group of 3,100 men set up to operate in Eritrea.[62] The Eritreans later established links with Palestinian guerrilla organizations.

Turkey completed the periphery 'triangle', although as a member of NATO and the recipient of considerable US support, it was less exposed than Iran and Ethiopia. Starting in September 1957 Eliahu Sasson, then serving as ambassador in Rome, met regularly with the Turkish foreign minister, Fatin Zurlu. Reuven Shiloah, who had returned from the Washington embassy as a special adviser to Golda Meir, played an important part in the contacts too.[63] Events elsewhere in the Middle East helped the Israelis. The civil war in Lebanon and the landing of American marines, the overthrow of the Iraqi monarchy in July and the near collapse of the Hashemite regime in Jordan all bore the imprint of Nasserist subversion. When the Egyptian president flew to Damascus and announced his support for the revolutionary regime in Baghdad, the Turks overcame their hesitation about dealing with the Israelis.[64] At the end of

August, after seeking expressions of American support for the periphery plan, Ben-Gurion flew secretly to Ankara for talks with his Turkish counterpart, Adnan Menderes. Political, economic and military cooperation were on the agenda, and it was also agreed that there should be regular exchanges of intelligence.[65] According to the CIA report on Israel's secret services, the Mossad set up a triangular organization with the Turkish National Security Service (TNSS) and the Iranian SAVAK. The Trident agreement stipulated that the Mossad would monitor Soviet activities in Turkey and elsewhere and in return receive information about the UAR, presumably with special reference to its Syrian wing. The Israelis promised to give the TNSS training and technical advice on counter-intelligence matters, as they were doing with SAVAK.[66]

Nazi hunting

Hunting Nazis was not a priority for Israel in the first years of the state. At the end of the war in Europe small groups of soldiers in the Jewish Brigade and Holocaust survivors who called themselves Nokmim (Avengers) had secretly sought out and summarily executed several hundred SS and Gestapo men and other Nazi officials in Italy, Austria and Germany itself. The Nokmim were organized by Israel Carmi, later an IDF tank brigade commander, Chaim Laskov, later IDF chief of general staff, and Meir Zorea, later an IDF major-general, three serving soldiers in the Jewish Brigade of the British Eighth Army in northern Italy in May 1945. They operated for about half a year, identifying and locating Nazi war criminals, and summarily executing them. They operated in British uniforms, using British military documentation, equipment and vehicles.[67]

In the years following its establishment in 1948, Israel was busy with more pressing problems: state-building, immigrant absorption and Arab hostility. These left little time for exorcizing the ghosts from the past. But after Suez there was a revival of interest in the Nazi era. 'It was then,' Harel explained later, 'that we decided to give our attention to the Nazis. It was a bit late in the day I admit. But the first need had been to ensure the very life of the Jewish people.'[68]

Late in 1957 Harel received information about the whereabouts of Adolf Eichmann, the SS officer who, more than any other Nazi still known to be living, symbolized the cold bureaucratic horror of Hitler's 'final solution'. Harel has told his own gripping story of the capture in his book *The House on Garibaldi Street*. With certain omissions about operational details, a natural tendency to exaggerate his own role at the expense of his subordinates – who all appear under false names – and little mention of the Argentinian Jews who helped, it is an accurate account, although it was not until 1974 that the censor approved the book for publication.

The hunt did not go smoothly from the start. Two years passed after receipt of the first sketchy report about Eichmann living under an assumed name in Buenos Aires before the operation was finally mounted in May 1960. The definitive surveillance in Argentina was carried out by Zvi Aharoni, head of the Shin Bet's Investigations Branch, who had been loaned to the Mossad by Amos Manor. Aharoni, who appears in Harel's book as 'Yosef Kennet', was 'one of the best investigators in the country . . . a dedicated man who never let go once he got his teeth into an assignment'. Aharoni had been involved in the internal investigations of the Esek HaBish in Egypt and had interrogated the 'Third Man', Avri Elad.[69]

The Shin Bet supplied other valuable members of the kidnap team – who, because of the diplomatic sensitivity of operating illegally in a friendly foreign country, were described at the time as 'volunteers'. They included Rafi Eitan, head of the GSS Operations Branch, and his deputy, Avraham Shalom (Bendor), both Palmah veterans. Shalom Dani, the Mossad's top forger, who had been deeply involved in the Moroccan immigration operation and was himself a Holocaust survivor, was another. Eichmann was abducted on 11 May – he was physically grabbed on Garibaldi Street by Zvi Malchin,[70] a burly Shin Bet operations man who was also a technical wizard and master of disguise – and held in a safe house – one of seven rented throughout Buenos Aires – until he was flown to Israel nine days later on an El Al plane that had brought members of the Israeli delegation attending Argentina's 150th anniversary celebrations. His trial, which began on 11 April 1961, highlighted, in Hannah Arendt's famous words, the terrible 'banality of evil'. Eichmann was hanged on 31 May 1962, the only man ever judicially executed in Israeli history.[71]

Another notorious Nazi, Josef Mengele, the doctor who had conducted horrendous genetic experiments on Jewish inmates of Auschwitz, especially twins, was harder to find. The Israelis knew far less about him, and attempts to locate him in the final days of the Eichmann operation failed. Zvi Aharoni was given control of the hunt and transferred permanently to the Mossad. He set up headquarters in Paris, where he stayed until 1964. In the spring of 1962, after several abortive visits to Paraguay, Aharoni believed he was finally on Mengele's tracks. The breakthrough came from an informer, a former SS officer called Willem Sassen, who had interviewed Eichmann before his abduction and became convinced that everything the Jews said about the Holocaust was true and that German honour had been sullied. Sassen was approached in Uruguay in what Mengele's biographers have aptly called 'one of the most bizarre recruiting pitches in the history of espionage'.[72] Aharoni agreed to pay him $5,000 a month. Sassen and his contacts led the Mossad agent to a farm outside São Paulo and he saw a man who he was sure was Mengele himself. 'I've been involved in many operations,' Aharoni said later. 'I followed Eichmann on the bus before the kidnapping. I spent a night lying in the field opposite his house, but at that moment I was shaking with excitement.' Back in Paris, however, Harel waved aside his information because of another pressing case. 'I thought that now we would get down to planning the operation because I was convinced that the search stage was over,' Aharoni complained bitterly. 'When I looked for Isser to report to him, they told me he was busy, looking for Yossele! Isser wasn't interested and didn't have the time.'[73] Mengele died peacefully in Brazil in 1985. Harel always insisted that he had done as much as was possible to bring him to justice.[74] Aharoni disagreed.

Find Yossele

In March 1962, shortly before the sighting of Mengele and Eichmann's execution, Ben-Gurion asked Harel to take up the case of an eight-year-old child named Yossele Schumacher. He had been kidnapped from his parents two years earlier by ultra-Orthodox Jews who were opposed to Zionism and the State of Israel. The kidnappers were connected with the boy's grandparents, who wanted to give him a religious and anti-Zionist education. Ben-Gurion was deeply troubled by the case and its implications for relations between secular and religious Jews and the rule of law. Despite immense efforts, the police and the courts had failed to return Yossele to his distraught parents.

Harel at first doubted whether the secret services should get involved, but he quickly became convinced, like Ben-Gurion, that it was a mission of vital national importance. He became obsessed by the search and devoted massive resources to it. By the end more than forty agents were involved. 'At times,' he wrote later, 'it seemed that the state was losing control and . . . that the delicate balance between religious and secular, between civil and Halachic [Jewish religious] law would collapse over the bitter and painful dispute about one kidnapped child.'[75]

'Operation Tiger', as it was codenamed, was both unusual and complicated, and more than one senior officer, including the Shin Bet chief Amos Manor, was bitterly opposed to getting involved. 'Our greatest advantage,' said Shmuel Toledano, one of the many Mossad men assigned to the case, 'was always that we had people who could pass for any nationality, Arabs, Germans, whatever. When it came to the Schumacher case our files were bursting with pictures of rabbis but we had difficulties finding people who could pose as a Lubavitcher or a Satmarer Hasid.'[76]

But found they were. Avraham Ahituv, who was on loan to the Mossad and was later to become head of the Shin Bet, was kitted out with the black garb and grew the long sidelocks of the ultra-Orthodox; then he was ordered to penetrate the closed, secretive world of the Hasidim. Ahituv had grown up with a religious background, but he was not up to the rigours of the job. Hoping to glean intelligence on the missing boy in the Swiss town of Montreux, he asked a Jewish woman for food, only to be met with the shocked response that it was a minor fast day.[77] 'I felt as if I had landed on Mars,' another operative said, 'and had to get lost in a crowd of little green men without being noticed.'[78] Informers were recruited and agents dispatched as far afield as Antwerp, Paris and London. Complicated ploys were designed to draw out the main suspects, confront and pressure them. The child was eventually located in New York and returned to Israel with the help of the FBI.[79] Teddy Kollek of the Prime Minister's Office was one of those who had doubts about the wisdom of the operation. As he said later:

> Various other important activities had been neglected by the Mossad for lack of manpower. The alternatives had never been put to Ben-Gurion. It may well be that had he been told the search for Yossele would be at the cost of proper surveillance of enemy activities, he would have decided against it – or at least given it lower priority. When Yossele was finally found – and how could Isser afford not to find him after he had successfully traced Eichmann? – Isser was suddenly confronted with stories of German scientists in Egypt, and they frightened him.[80]

Rockets for 'Little' Isser

On 21 July 1962, at the traditional military parade marking the tenth anniversary of the Egyptian revolution, President Nasser revealed a new secret weapon in the struggle against Israel. The liquid-fuelled Al-Zafir and the longer range Al-Qahira rockets, could, he boasted, strike any target 'south of Beirut'. Harel was blamed for failing to foresee the development and there was much grumbling about him wasting Mossad time and resources hunting Nazis and chasing Yossele Schumacher round the world. Relations between Aman and the Mossad had been appalling for years. 'Little' Isser promised to update Ben-Gurion quickly and his agents soon reported that the rockets were being built by German scientists who had been working in Egypt since at least 1959.[81]

The Mossad's most stringent critic was General Meir Amit, the newly appointed chief of military intelligence. As he said later:

> We in Aman believed that the main problem was security, and not Yossele Schumacher and not even the Eichmann kidnapping. Bringing Eichmann to Israel, as distinct from bringing Yossele back, gave our intelligence professional expertise and a fine reputation. But Aman was struggling then with its own problems. These other operations took up so much effort that I had to tell my superiors I wasn't prepared to continue in this way when there was such a very severe shortage of information because of the diversion of our resources.[82]

Amit had accepted the request by the chief of staff, Zvi Tsur, that he take over Aman in early 1962, at a time when the destructive effect of the Lavon Affair was still being felt and relations with the Mossad were at an all-time low. Amit's own subordinates had warned him of reaching out to 'Little' Isser, but he ignored them and the atmosphere quickly deteriorated. Amit was soon complaining that the Mossad understood very little about either Arab armies or their war plans. Harel bristled as only he knew how. 'He really was the man "who knew everything",' Amit told a sympathetic colleague, 'but he couldn't bear any criticism.'[83]

Isser moved quickly. At the end of July 1962 the Mossad set up a special unit to deal with the missile question and other modern weapons. It coordinated closely with Aman's technical department. By mid-August he had already produced what was, by any standard, a tremendous intelligence coup. He showed Ben-Gurion a letter, dated 24 March that year, from a leading German scientist called Professor Wolfgang Pilz, to the

Egyptian director of a rocket factory codenamed 333. According to the document, 900 missiles were to be constructed, and there was additional, although flimsier, evidence of research work being carried out to fit the weapons with gas, chemical or biological warheads. The only bright spot was that there were grave doubts about the effectiveness of the missile guidance systems. The Germans had set up three secret factories, respectively working on jet planes, jet engines and medium-range liquid-fuelled missiles. Several dummy companies had been formed in Germany to provide cover for the logistics and thirty rockets had already been produced.[84] Pilz's activities were being monitored by Zvi Malchin and other members of Mossad surveillance teams operating in Germany. Malchin managed to break into Pilz's laboratory in Cologne and photograph blueprints and papers after first staging an elaborate ruse to remove a huge Dobermann guard dog.[85]

Harel believed that the German scientists were working on weapons that threatened the very existence of Israel. He suggested that Ben-Gurion formally ask the West German premier, Konrad Adenauer, to intervene to halt their work, arguing emotionally that the Bonn government had a moral duty to the Jewish state. But Ben-Gurion consistently resisted any action that might disrupt the steadily evolving cooperation between the two countries, and he preferred to ask Peres to deal with the matter quietly with Franz-Josef Strauss, the defence minister. Isser also angrily rejected charges that the Mossad should have known more.[86]

His men had first reported on Egyptian attempts to acquire unspecified technology in 1956, and then again in 1959, 1960 and 1961. The Mossad in that period conducted only intelligence-gathering and its raw material had been routinely passed on to the IDF and the Defence Ministry for evaluation. In September 1961 Aman had produced a first assessment on the development of ground-to-ground missiles in Egypt. A second Intelligence Branch evaluation in October 1962 predicted that about 100 rockets could be operational within a year to eighteen months.[87]

'Little' Isser felt his organization was being chosen as a whipping boy for other people's failures. He blamed Peres, whom he loathed, for the premature exposure of Israel's own fledgeling missile capability in July 1961 and argued that the launching of the Shavit-2 rocket on the eve of that year's general election was a political gesture that had backfired in alerting the Egyptians to the state of their enemy's technology.[88] No one believed the official explanation that the Shavit (Comet) was really intended for meteorological research. And no one bothered to ask what had happened to the Shavit-I. The truth was that there simply hadn't been one.

Harel rejected criticism that the Eichmann and Yossele operations had been a waste of resources: both had been personally approved by Ben-Gurion and both were seen as missions of utmost national importance. Peres, he wrote scornfully later, 'panicked' and 'infected' the prime minister with his exaggerated fears. He also believed that the ambitious deputy defence minister had fallen victim to his own inflated view of Israel's technological edge over the Arabs.[89]

What began as a bureaucratic disagreement about intelligence success and priorities rapidly took on clearly defined political contours. Harel – 'not a man to suffer doubters,' said one sceptical official[90] – won the support of the foreign minister, Golda Meir, who joined the Mossad chief in demanding all-out war against the scientists, as if they were still fully fledged Nazis and there was no such thing as a 'new' Germany making an immensely important contribution to Israel's financial and security situation. Amit, a career soldier, realized only later that the struggle was about internal Israeli politics and the war to succeed Ben-Gurion as much as anything else.[91]

'Operation Damocles'

The worrying reports about the scale of the Egyptian programme were reinforced catastrophically when a disaffected Austrian scientist called Otto Joklik approached the Israelis.

Once initial suspicions that he was a plant had been dispelled, he was brought secretly to Tel Aviv and interrogated. Joklik claimed that the Egyptians were preparing to fit their missiles with warheads containing radioactive waste in an operation codenamed Ibis I. Even more seriously, a project called Cleopatra was geared to producing nuclear warheads.

The Mossad operation, codenamed 'Damocles', went into high gear. Harel himself flew repeatedly to Europe to see his commander on the spot, a German-born Israeli called Joe Ra'anan (Reisman), who had joined the service from air force intelligence in May 1957. Isser, as always, was at his legendary best out in the field. 'Eat the cake,' the Mossad chief would order Ra'anan as they met repeatedly in cafés and tried their best to look normal, 'otherwise we'll look suspicious.'[92]

Another key figure in 'Damocles' was Yitzhak Shamir, a former Stern Gang leader whom Harel had recruited in 1955, as part of his policy of 'coopting' former dissidents who had acquired skills in clandestine activities during the underground struggle against the British. Shamir was given a room next to Harel and ran some *ad hoc* operations, usually involving assassinations, and was sent to Paris in 1956. He in turn brought in five former Sternists for 'low-grade' operations. One of them was Herzl Amikam, who joined in 1961 and stayed in the Mossad for eleven years.[93]

Dr Heinz Krug, director of a Munich-based Egyptian front-company called Intra, had disappeared mysteriously and was presumed murdered in September 1962. On 7 October Harel left for Europe 'to personally supervise authorized operations and the special collection programme'.[94] In November Aman sent several letter bombs to the rocket installations in Egypt and one of them, a large parcel that had been mailed by sea from Hamburg, killed five Egyptians. Someone with a black sense of humour dubbed the campaign 'post mortem'.[95]

In February 1963 a Mossad hit man provided by Shamir tried and failed to kill Dr Hans Kleinwachter, an electronics expert who had worked on Hitler's V2 project during the war. Harel was obsessed with eliminating him. The Mossad chief spent a whole night in a car with one of Shamir's killers, who held a sub-machine-gun under a blanket, outside Kleinwachter's house in Lorrach, but the target failed to arrive. The second hit man fired too soon and the bullet, deflected by a car window, lodged in the German's scarf. Then his weapon jammed. Threatening letters, posted in Egypt, were sent to the scientists and their families.[96]

Some of the letters were written and sent by an Israeli spy called Wolfgang Lotz, who was also the source of much of the Mossad's information about the German scientists in Egypt. Lotz was a German-born Israeli who had been operating from Cairo since early 1961, having first spent a year in Germany to establish his cover as a former Wehrmacht officer and wealthy horse-breeder. He was born in Mannheim in 1921 to a gentile father and a Jewish mother, who had brought him to Palestine in 1933. He had not been circumcised – 'a factor,' he wrote later, 'that was to prove vital in substantiating my cover story and saving my life'.[97]

Egyptian security was extremely tight and foreigners were routinely monitored by the Mukhabarat al-Amma and the secret police. 'The ubiquity of the intelligence apparatus on which Nasser had come to depend had disseminated an atmosphere of fear,' wrote a British diplomat serving in Cairo at the time. 'Telephones were liberally tapped, conversations eavesdropped and the Citadel was full of people who had allegedly offended against the state.'[98] But Lotz, an inveterate socialite and good-timer, made a number of powerful friends. He encouraged rumours that he had served in the SS rather than in the Wehrmacht and thus gained entry to the secretive clique of former Nazis living in Cairo. In August 1962, shortly after the unveiling of the new rockets at the Revolution Day parade, Lotz flew to Paris to meet his controller, 'Yosef', and was ordered to find out more about the weapons project.[99]

The Nazi-hunting being run from the French capital by Zvi Aharoni spilled over into 'Damocles'. Dealing with SS veterans was distasteful for the Israelis, but Willem Sassen had brought them closer to Mengele; they were clearly not a source that could be overlooked. More important information about the German scientists was provided by the Mossad's recruitment of Otto Skorzeny, the legendary commando colonel who had mounted a daring glider raid to rescue Mussolini from the hands of Italian partisans in September 1943. Skorzeny was living in Spain when he was approached by Mossad agents early in 1963. It is unclear whether the former Nazi knew he was dealing with Israelis. What is certain is that when one of Skorzeny's old comrades, who was working on the rocket project in Egypt, came to visit him, the German scientist met two Israelis masquerading as 'NATO officials'. This classic 'false flag' provided more valuable intelligence for 'Damocles'.[100]

Another Israeli agent operating in Egypt in this period was Aharon Moshel, a German-Jewish journalist who, according to his memoirs, in 1961 had been approached by the Mossad's David Kimche in a letter written on the notepaper of a Paris-based magazine called *L'Observateur du Moyen-Orient et de l'Afrique*.[101]

Moshel went to Cairo as a correspondent for German newspapers and disguised his intelligence reports as letters to an 'aunt' in Cologne. He lived close to the central telegraph office, which helped make his radio transmitter undetectable. His value as a spy is not clear from his bizarre account of his short espionage career, although he once stole an Egyptian secret police identity card from a hotel employee and passed it to the Mossad, allowing them to produce their own forgeries.

Like Lotz, Moshel was on the look-out for German scientists and technicians. He met some of them at a party given by the press attaché at the West German Embassy and overheard them discussing the problems they were encountering in the Egyptian aircraft- and rocket-building programmes, including a number of 'grotesque mistakes'.[102] Moshel left Cairo after Wolfgang Lotz was arrested. He quit espionage but the Mossad continued to help him when he moved to Luxembourg and published a Middle East news bulletin, which became popular with Arab embassies in Bonn.

The affair of the German scientists exploded publicly in March 1963. Joklik and a Mossad agent called Yosef Ben-Gal were arrested in Switzerland after threatening Heidi Goerke, the daughter of Dr Paul Goerke, an electronics expert who was working in Cairo. The Israelis had done their homework and were clearly hoping that they could use simple blackmail to persuade Goerke to go home: Ra'anan revealed later that Heidi herself was having an affair with a senior Egyptian official and that her father was conducting a clandestine liaison with the wife of a senior Egyptian engineer and kept a secret love-nest in the opulent Cairo suburb of Zamalek; several of his colleagues were practising homosexuals.

Ra'anan had been nervous about the ploy and briefed Ben-Gal carefully before he and Joklik went to see Heidi in a Basel hotel called the Drei Koenige on 2 March. But Heidi Goerke had alerted the Swiss police and the Mossad man and the Austrian scientist were followed and arrested. Ra'anan watched helplessly as Ben-Gal was picked up at Zurich railway station. Harel heard the bad news from Ra'anan and on 8 March the Memunch flew back to Israel to break it to Ben-Gurion.[103]

The crisis was getting badly out of hand. On 15 March the arrests were announced by the Swiss, and the German government demanded Ben-Gal's extradition. Ben-Gurion was furious and on his own initiative Isser began briefing senior Israeli journalists on the background to the affair. He gave them material on the condition that they filed their stories from Europe, in a transparent attempt to suggest that the leaks were emanating from there and not from Israel. The result was an intensive, hysterical press campaign that threatened to damage relations with Bonn seriously and to undermine the prime minister's controversial policy towards West Germany. There was talk of 'death rays' and other science-fiction weapons and of renewed German attempts to find a 'final solution' to the Jewish question.

Reassessment and resignation

Shimon Peres returned from France and took charge. He took Harel to task 'for his unconsidered action based on speculative reports'[104] and ordered the IDF and the Defence Ministry to 'reassess' the Egyptian rocket threat. The result was extraordinary. Almost overnight Aman changed its tune: the research department under Aharon Yariv concluded that there was no hard evidence that German scientists were working on chemical or biological weapons; Joklik was a crook or a charlatan; and the Ibis and Cleopatra projects were simply unworkable. On 24 March Ben-Gurion heard a report to this effect from Peres, Tsur and Amit. Harel was incensed. Peres, he told the prime minister, had presented a politically slanted version of indisputable intelligence facts. The next day, 'Little' Isser resigned.

Amit was touring the Dead Sea area on 25 March when he was ordered to contact the prime minister urgently in Tel Aviv. A plane was especially dispatched to collect him and Ben-Gurion showed him a letter he had just sent to the Memuneh accepting his resignation. Ben-Gurion ordered Amit to take over the Mossad at once until a successor to Harel could be found. The next day Amit presented himself at Isser's office, where the old spymaster, as Amit put it later, was 'sour as a lemon'. Harel said a few brusque words to his successor and left. Nearly all the employees were weeping.[105]

Despite the previous criticism, the campaign against the German scientists continued under Amit, providing Harel with a powerful argument that the Aman 'reassessment' had simply been part of the politically motivated 'conspiracy' to get rid of him. Joe Ra'anan resigned from his Mossad post in Europe and was replaced by Rafi ('the Stinker') Eitan, the Shin Bet operations chief who had led the Eichmann kidnap team in Argentina. The executive post that Ra'anan had been promised by 'Little' Isser went instead to Rehavia Vardi, a former SDO who had previously headed Aman's collection department under Amit.[106]

But Isser did not give up. His political allies called a meeting of the ministerial security committee so that he could present his case. Harel appeared with a bulging file and proceeded to quote at length from top-secret documents until Ben-Gurion cut him off furiously and stormed out of the room, complaining that he no longer had the right to possess classified material.[107] Isser's own account judiciously ignores that aspect of the meeting.

Harel allowed himself one last clandestine treat. Holidaying in Europe with his wife, he took time off in Paris to meet Yosef Ben-Gal, who had just been released from prison in Switzerland. They met at Yar, a little Russian restaurant Isser liked to frequent when he was in town.[108] 'Never before,' Harel wrote later in a rare personal aside, 'had I drunk alcohol in that restaurant, but the proprietor noticed that this was a special occasion and brought a bottle of vodka on the house. To his great surprise, I agreed and to his even greater surprise I thanked him in his mother tongue, Russian, which he had never guessed that I knew.'[109]

Not only in Aman was there satisfaction at Harel's departure. Teddy Kollek, who had been director-general of the Prime Minister's Office since 1952, had long objected to the way business was conducted between the Mossad chief and Ben-Gurion. 'Isser would report directly and confidentially to Ben-Gurion and to nobody else,' he wrote. 'There was no way of checking the validity of the intelligence evaluation since everyone else in the government – without exception – was kept in the dark. Even Ben-Gurion's unlimited faith in Isser did not seem to justify such a practice.'[110]

Gog and Magog

Isser Harel regretted his resignation and found it hard to accept his replacement by Meir Amit. According to many accounts, the former Memuneh wasted no opportunity to try to undermine the new Mossad chief, especially after the appointment became permanent in January 1964. Amit fought back, hesitantly at first and then tooth and nail. Yisrael Lior, Eshkol's military secretary, likened their rivalry to the biblical struggle of Gog and Magog – a titanic battle between two powerful forces. Harel had failed to prove that he was right to take a tough line over the German scientists but found a new opportunity to wage war on Amit when, in September 1965, Eshkol appointed him a special adviser on intelligence and security. The job had been proposed by the Yadin–Sharef Committee, set up in 1963 to look into the structure and functioning of the entire intelligence community in the light of the 'foul-up' in Egypt in 1954.

Amit, naturally enough, opposed Harel's appointment as adviser to Eshkol and threatened to resign if it went ahead. Amit believed that Harel was serving the interests of ministers like Golda Meir and Yigal Allon in their struggle against Ben-Gurion. Amit had to fight inside the Mossad as well as outside it. His deputy, Ya'akov Caroz, was one of Isser's most loyal supporters – 'his faithful servant', one disgruntled colleague complained[111] – and in October 1965, retaliating for Caroz's close relationship with Harel, Amit demanded that his deputy take leave of absence. When Caroz refused, Amit restricted his access to sensitive documents.[112] Amit handed over intelligence material to Harel, but made no attempt to conceal his reluctance to do so. Sometimes, during Amit's regular absences abroad, Harel would summon Mossad department heads to see Eshkol and give the premier their views of Amit. 'At meetings that were intended to approve Mossad operations, Harel rejected almost every proposal out of hand,' Lior wrote later. 'Amit was helpless.'[113]

The Ben Barka Affair

The confrontation came to a head late in 1965 against the background of the most serious crisis in the Israeli intelligence community since the Lavon Affair. The cause was the Mossad's involvement in the kidnapping and murder of Mehdi Ben Barka, the Moroccan opposition leader and publicist.[114]

The Ben Barka affair prompted internal cabinet-level investigations in Israel and France and a demand by Harel that Amit be dismissed or, alternately, that Eshkol himself resign. Harel tried to use the affair as the fulcrum which would at last enable him to topple his rival. It ended, though, with Harel's own final resignation in June 1966.

In his memoirs, constrained by the censor, Harel wrote cryptically of 'a very grave lapse'. Since King Hassan's succession to the throne of Morocco in 1961, Israeli intelligence had enjoyed a special relationship with his security service. The two countries had a common enemy in Egypt's President Nasser and a shared concern over his pan-Arab and republican aspirations. Harel had quickly seen the immense potential in this clandestine link and Israeli operatives helped the new king to reform his secret service and trained its agents on a regular basis.[115] In 1965 General Muhammad Oufkir, King Hassan's interior minister and the official responsible for the security service, was brought secretly to Israel by David Kimche of the Mossad.[116] In spring of that year Oufkir approached Amit and asked for the Mossad's help in finding and killing Ben Barka. Officers of the French counter-intelligence service, the SDECE, for whom Nasser and his Arab nationalist friends outside Egypt had been bugbears since their support for the FLN from the start of the Algerian War, were also brought in by the Moroccans.

Ben Barka, a former tutor of King Hassan's and ex-president of his country's National Consultative Assembly, had been involved in plots to topple the monarchy and had twice been sentenced to death – *in absentia* – by Moroccan courts. Israeli, French and Moroccan agents began tracking him from his home in Geneva. The exiled politician was lured to Paris – the Mossad was instrumental in fashioning the plan – where a mixed team of French and Moroccan agents abducted him on 29 October 1965. Ben Barka was driven to a villa owned by a French underworld figure in a prosperous Paris suburb, interrogated, tortured and killed in Oufkir's presence. He was buried in the villa's garden, disinterred and reburied a few weeks later on the banks of the Seine.

The howl that went up from the opposition parties in France following Ben Barka's kidnapping prompted President de Gaulle to launch a highly publicized investigation. He used the opportunity to cleanse the SDECE of right-wingers who were associated with the OAS during the 'Algérie Française' days. Two trials followed; in one of them, Oufkir was convicted and sentenced *in absentia*.[117]

The French were aware of the Israeli role in the affair but were persuaded by inter-service collegiality to keep the matter under wraps. But back in Jerusalem Harel found out about it from Ya'akov Caroz and raised a storm. The Mossad under Amit, Harel complained, had been used by another country to assassinate a political opponent. And the Mossad's actions, in obvious breach of local and international law, and on friendly foreign soil, had jeopardized Israeli–French relations, which had been the cornerstone of Israel's foreign policy since 1956. An important component of these relations was France's role as Israel's main arms supplier. This too had been endangered. Amit denied that Israeli agents had taken part in the actual kidnapping and killing and maintained that the Mossad's role had been 'marginal': the service had merely supplied the Moroccans with 'a passport' and 'several hired cars'.[118] Amit also maintained that he had received Eshkol's approval for the operation. Eshkol insisted later that he had known nothing about it until after the event. Not a word of Israel's role in the affair got out. As with the Lavon Affair, the question was, 'Who gave the order?'

Three investigations were launched; Eshkol appointed the Yadin–Sharef team to examine the matter 'privately'. The two-man committee blamed Eshkol for what had happened. A parallel, internal Mapai investigation called for Eshkol's resignation. But Harel persuaded Eshkol, on the basis of Mossad documentation made available to him by Caroz, 'that Amit had cheated him' and demanded that the premier sack the Mossad chief. 'The details of the incident,' one Israeli historian has written, 'remained as cloudy as the interpretation of the central document in the affair: a letter from Eshkol to Amit that might be read as agreeing to the Mossad assisting the Moroccans to kidnap Ben Barka.'[119]

Eshkol, desperately trying to avoid the embarrassment of a

do-or-die confrontation with Amit, which Amit had promised would be both noisy and messy, appointed another high-powered committee – foreign minister Golda Meir, justice minister Ya'akov Shimshon Shapira, minister without portfolio Yisrael Galili and former Mossad LeAliya Bet chief Shaul Avigur – to look into the affair. The committee demanded Amit's immediate resignation. The Mossad chief refused, saying he would go only together with Eshkol. With Ben-Gurion and his newly formed Rafi Party in the wings, waiting to pounce, the Mapai leadership and Eshkol declined to force the issue, which would have meant an open, public battle. A prolonged stalemate ensued. Harel demanded a decision. None came. Frustrated and bitter, his adviser's job emptied of all real content, he finally resigned in June 1966, and was quickly followed by Caroz. Eshkol and Amit successfully weathered the storm and kept the whole affair almost completely under wraps.[120]

There was one exception to the intense secrecy surrounding the affair. Just as the veteran Mapai politicians wanted to keep it quiet, so their rivals wanted to use it against Eshkol. In early September 1966 the story was leaked to *Bul*, a sensationalist, semi-pornographic weekly magazine. All copies of the magazine were confiscated and its two editors were charged under an espionage law and sentenced, in camera, to a year in prison. Despite the strict application of censorship, the truth came out. *The New York Times* published details in February 1967.[121]

Harel and Amit remained sworn enemies many years later. Responding to Isser's searing criticism of one account of their stormy relationship, Amit wrote:

> I have never encountered such a collection of half truths, facts taken out of context and brazen lies. My only explanation for this sad phenomenon is that Isser Harel, who slammed the door behind him when he left the Mossad, thought it was impossible to get along without him. And the amazing fact is that after he left, the Mossad's work improved immeasurably.[122]

7
Six Days in June: 1967

Stealing a MiG

On 16 August 1966 an Iraqi air force MiG-21, then the most advanced fighter plane supplied by the Soviet Union to the Arab states, landed at an air base in northern Israel, bringing to a successful conclusion one of the most complex and brilliant clandestine operations ever mounted by the Mossad. Israel and the United States were able to study at first hand the technology, flight and combat characteristics of the aircraft – knowledge that would stand the Israeli air force in good stead less than a year later, when it virtually annihilated the combined air forces of Egypt, Syria and Jordan in the first hours of the Six Day War in June 1967.

The operation began in mid-1963 with a characteristically flippant remark by the IAF commander, Ezer Weizman, to Meir Amit, who had just replaced Isser Harel as director of the Mossad. 'If you bring me a MiG-21, you will have done a good day's work,' Weizman said. The latest version of the aircraft, which first came off Soviet production lines in 1959, had recently been introduced into front-line service in Egypt, Syria and Iraq, and it was understood to constitute the chief potential aerial challenge to Israel in any future war.

Studying advanced enemy weapons systems is a priority of all intelligence services; actually obtaining them is extremely rare. The Mossad had tried to get hold of a MiG before and failed. Jean Thomas, an Israeli agent operating in Egypt in the late 1950s and early 1960s, was an Egyptian-born Armenian who had gone abroad after the 1952 revolution. He was probably recruited in West Germany and run by Joe Ra'anan, a Mossad officer operating in Europe, although it is unclear whether Thomas knew at first that he was working for Israel. His accomplices certainly believed they were employed by a Western embassy in Cairo, suggesting strongly that the initial recruitment was a 'false-flag' operation – a standard Mossad technique – designed to conceal the Israeli connection. The network had tried to find an Egyptian air force pilot who would fly a MiG-21 to Israel in return for $1 million. And it was that attempt that had led to their exposure by an air force officer named Adib Hanna. Thomas and five others were arrested in January 1961. Others charged included Thomas's father, another Armenian, who developed films for the alleged spy, and an official of the Egyptian War Ministry. Thomas and two accomplices were hanged in December 1962; the others received lesser sentences.[1]

The next attempt to acquire a MiG was no more successful. Two Iraqi pilots, one on a training course in the US, the other in Baghdad itself, were assaulted by Mossad agents to keep them quiet after rebuffing Israeli efforts to recruit them.

But the third try worked. Late in 1964 a new avenue for recruitment opened up when an Iraqi Jewish merchant, 'Yosef' – a diabetic in his sixties with connections in the Iraqi underworld – contacted Israeli officials in Tehran and Europe. His girlfriend's sister was married to an Iraqi air force pilot called Munir Radfa, a Catholic who was deputy commander of a MiG-21 squadron. Yosef told the Israelis that Munir had been passed over for promotion to command the squadron, was stationed at a base near Kirkuk, from where he flew attack missions against Kurdish rebels, rather than near his home in Baghdad, and was allowed to fly only with small fuel tanks, because he was a Christian. His commanders did not trust him and Munir felt frustrated. According to Yosef, Munir was ready to go over to Israel – with his MiG. To help plan the operation, a senior pilot and an air force intelligence officer were seconded to the Mossad.

Yosef was instructed to persuade Munir to agree to meet Israeli representatives in Europe. The meeting, which was attended by Munir, the IAF intelligence officer, Yosef and his girlfriend, took place in a Rome hotel room, with Meir Amit himself observing Munir through a peep-hole – itself a telling indication of the immense importance attached to the operation from the start. The main question was how Munir's family was to be extricated from Iraq, which the pilot made a condition of his defection. Munir wanted his parents, wife, children and other relatives to be smuggled out of the country just before his flight to Israel. It was also agreed that he would be paid over $1 million.

The main points were sorted out and everything waited upon the Iraqi's transfer to a base closer to Israel's borders. A team of Mossad agents was sent to Baghdad to keep tabs on the pilot and to prepare the family's departure. In mid-1966 Munir was transferred to the Rashid air base near Baghdad. The Mossad then began shipping out his family: one member flew to Europe 'for medical treatment,' another left the country as a tourist.

Munir himself was invited to Israel to see the airfield where he would be landing. A Mossad agent – described by some sources as a wealthy American woman – flew to Baghdad and accompanied Munir to Paris and then, after false travel documents had been obtained, to Israel. He met the IAF commander, General Mordechai ('Motti') Hod, who gave the Iraqi personal assurances about the planned flight path and the extrication of his family.

In early August 1966 Munir reported that he would soon be allowed on a long flight with fuel for a 900-kilometre run. On 16 August Jordanian air defence radar tracked a jet aircraft flying at high speed across northern Jordan. The Jordanians contacted the Syrian air force, who replied that the plane was probably a Syrian bomber on a practice run. The plane then landed in Israel.

At a press conference in Israel a few hours afterwards, Munir described his flight. On approaching Israeli air space he had been met by two IAF Mirage fighters and had tilted his wings and lowered his undercarriage in greeting before landing on his 'last drops of fuel'. One of the Mirage pilots said that they had been told nothing about the operation and had been ordered only to intercept but on no account to fire on the approaching Iraqi MiG.

The morning Munir took off, Mossad agents hired two large vans and picked up the remaining members of the pilot's family, who had left Baghdad ostensibly to have a picnic. They were driven to the Iranian border and guided across by anti-Iraqi Kurdish guerrillas. Safely in Iran, a helicopter collected them and flew them to an airfield, from where an airplane took them to Israel.[2] A few months later the MiG-21 was loaned to the United States for a period of testing. Two years later, and eleven months after the Six Day War, the plane led the traditional IAF Independence Day fly-past in May 1968.

After the war Israeli generals were to view the capture of the MiG-21 as an important contribution to IDF General Staff planning. It enabled the IAF to take exact measure of the Arab world's main front-line aircraft – fuel capacity, altitude, range, speeds, turnaround servicing time and armaments – in preparation for its assault on the morning of 5 June 1967 on the airfields of the neighbouring Arab states, the decisive opening gambit of the war.[3]

The CIA saw the capture of the Iraqi MiG in the same light even before the benefit of post-war hindsight. At a National Security Council meeting in Washington on 24 May 1967, agency director Richard Helms, rebutting Defence Secretary Robert McNamara's low assessment of the IAF's capabilities, said: '[The] Israelis had taken the MiG that defected from Iraq last year through all kinds of maneuvers . . . and had demonstrated in the 7 April air battle with Syria that they had learned their lessons well.'[4]

That battle, in which six Syrian MiG-21s were shot down by IAF Mirage IIIc interceptors with no Israeli losses, was a fitting prelude to the stunning aerial victory two months later. It was also the culmination of months of small-scale Syrian–Israeli clashes and Syrian-sponsored Palestinian guerrilla raids against

Israeli civilian and military targets along the Syrian–Israeli, Lebanese–Israeli and Jordanian–Israeli borders. It was these tensions, and Syrian and Soviet fears that Israel was bent on punishing the regime in Damascus for the Palestinian incursions, that set off the chain of miscalculations and errors that led to the Six Day War, a war which was neither desired nor really intended by either side, but turned out to have momentous consequences for the future.

Nasser's surprise

On 14 and 15 May 1967 lead units of two Egyptian divisions began rolling eastwards across the Suez Canal and taking up positions in the Sinai peninsula. Within three weeks seven Egyptian divisions – comprising about 100,000 troops and 900 tanks – would be deployed in the desert peninsula along the Israeli border. The Egyptian move, which was decided upon by Nasser and his high command on 13 May or early on 14 May, took Israel's intelligence services by complete surprise.

By mutual, UN-mediated agreement, Sinai was a *de facto* buffer zone between Egypt and Israel, albeit under Egyptian sovereignty. Its effective demilitarization (the Egyptians maintained only one division in the area before 1967) and the positioning of a United Nations peace-keeping force (UNEF) along the Egyptian side of the border were the preconditions for Israel's withdrawal from the peninsula following the 1956 war.

Once before, in February 1960, when Chaim Herzog was head of IDF intelligence, Egypt had surprised Israel and sent large forces into Sinai (the counter-operation was codenamed 'Rotem' by the IDF) with the aim of deterring Israel from attacking Syria. The Egyptian troop deployment had been unwarranted. Israel had no intention of attacking Syria, though continuous Israeli–Syrian skirmishing along the border had kept tension high for weeks. In any event, the Egyptian troops were quietly withdrawn from Sinai without incident or public attention.[5]

But in the mid-1960s the prevailing Aman assessment was that Egypt would not be ready for war at least until the end of 1970. This view was based on the state of Egypt's economy; the state of its armed forces (which had still to properly absorb a number of recently introduced Soviet weapons systems); and, most important, the continued deployment, in 1967, of Egyptian troops in Yemen, where they were propping up the republican side in the civil war with the Saudi-backed royalists. Aman argued generally that Egypt would not initiate a war against Israel so long as its forces were markedly inferior to Israel's. Throughout the 1960s, Aman believed that this was the case. But in 1967 IDF intelligence did not allow for the illogical and the unpredictable: it failed to appreciate that Nasser's assessment of the Egyptian–Israeli military balance might be different. In May Nasser apparently believed, perhaps basing himself on a quantitative comparison of Arab and Israeli troop strengths and weaponry, that if it came to war, Egypt could hold its own against the IDF.

Israel thought differently. In its semi-annual assessment of October 1964, for example, Intelligence Branch assessed that an Arab attack on Israel was not to be expected before 1968–70. 'No one,' wrote Ezer Weizman, head of the General Staff Division from 1966, 'predicted a full-scale war before 1969.'[6] In 1966–7 Aman failed, for technical reasons, to produce its regular annual assessment.[7] But the feeling in Aman, at the level of near certainty, was that war was 'far off'. In the preparatory drafts of the 1967 annual national intelligence appreciation, which was discussed in the General Staff in early May, Aman ruled explicitly that there was 'no chance' that war would break out in the coming year.[8]

Aharon Yariv, the Aman chief, said later:

> The evaluation was that in the foreseeable future – two to three years – a pan-Arab attack on Israel was unlikely. On the other hand, there was an assessment that Egypt could send forces to Sinai and hold on in a defensive war . . . In one of the [Aman] evaluations, in late 1965 or early 1966, we raised the possibility of an [Egyptian] closure of the

straits. But it is true that, regarding the actual entry of the [Egyptian] forces into Sinai [on 14–16 May], we had advance warning of no more than a few hours.[9]

But the Israeli prime minister, Levi Eshkol, had a different gut feeling, although this was probably more a function of character than of any hard intelligence. In February 1967, for example, he told a meeting of senior IDF officers that war could break out soon and urged that more tanks and aircraft be acquired.[10] Aman believed that should Israel undertake a major operation against Syria, the Egyptians could not but intervene. 'But we didn't take into account that both the Soviets and Egypt would act as if we really were about to mount a large-scale attack on Syria,' Yariv said later.[11]

Soviet warnings

The Egyptian thrust into Sinai on 14 May was triggered off by Soviet and Syrian reports that Israel was concentrating large armoured formations along the northern border and intended to attack Syria. According to Moshe Dayan, who was appointed Israel's defence minister shortly before the war, an intelligence officer in the Soviet Embassy in Cairo on 12 May gave the Egyptian military 'confirmation' of reports of the Israeli troop concentrations.[12] Reports of this kind, which stemmed from Syrian nervousness against the backdrop of persistent border clashes, had been emanating from Damascus for weeks. Whether the Soviets fuelled them or whether they were an independent Syrian invention is still unclear. Jordanian military intelligence, which 'had revealed no evidence of a build-up of Israeli troops on the Syrian borders', concluded that the Soviets were 'trying to inflame' tempers, perhaps with the ultimate aim of increasing Egyptian dependence upon them.[13]

Since 1965 Aman and the Mossad had persistently cautioned the government (and Washington) about renewed Soviet efforts to stir up trouble in the Middle East. According to James

Critchfield, the head of the CIA's Middle East division in the 1960s, Israeli estimates of the Soviet role expressed 'intense and growing alarm'. These estimates were usually passed on to the CIA by Mossad chief Meir Amit. CIA director Richard Helms recalled that the Israelis 'were getting scared in the early part of 1966 and became increasingly worried as the months passed. There was a note of rising anxiety in their estimates' regarding Soviet intentions and actions.[14]

In mid-May 1967, with no IDF troop concentrations along the Syrian border and with confusion about Moscow's role in the escalation, Eshkol invited the Soviet ambassador to Tel Aviv, Dmitri Chubakhin, to tour the Israeli side of the Syrian border to see the situation for himself. Chubakhin declined. On 14 May U Thant, the Burmese UN secretary-general, reported to the Security Council in New York that UN observers on the spot had found no evidence of an IDF build-up.

But the day before, 13 May, Soviet President Nikolai Podgorny told Anwar Sadat, Nasser's aide, who was then on a visit to Moscow, that Israeli troops were massing and intended to invade Syria. The Soviet leader had spoken of '11–13' IDF brigades; he may also have mentioned '17 May' as the prospective date of the putative IDF attack on Syria. Sadat quickly informed Nasser. Moscow had warned Damascus earlier of the impending Israeli assault. On 13 May Hafez Assad, the Syrian minister of defence, informed his Egyptian counterpart, Abdel Hakim Amer, of the Israeli build-up and asked for an Egyptian *démarche* to relieve the pressure on Syria. That day the Egyptian army's chief of staff, Muhammad Fawzi, flew to Damascus.[15]

The Soviet warnings and the Egyptian push into Sinai, while taking Aman by surprise, were firmly rooted in developments during the previous six weeks. In April and early May there had been an increase in public warnings to Syria by Israeli politicians and generals: these had been sparked off by an increase in Syrian-based Palestinian guerrilla raids against Israel, largely by Yasser Arafat's Fatah organization. 'The Syrians use this weapon of guerrilla activity because they cannot face us in open battle,' Yariv said at a briefing three weeks before the war.[16] But the troop concentrations were a figment of the Arab imagination and, perhaps, also of Soviet machinations. Moscow appears to have believed that if it came to a fight, the Egyptians would defeat Israel or at least fight the IDF in Sinai to a standstill. But the Soviets do not seem to have actually intended war. They pushed their clients towards a political success and a humiliation of Israel, America's ally, but they apparently believed that both Israel and the Arabs would stop short of the brink. Soviet intelligence miscalculated badly.[17]

Just how little thought Moscow had given to the prospect of actual war became clear only after the victory, when the leader of the Israel Communist Party, Moshe Sneh, told Aharon Yariv about a conversation he had had in May with Chubakhin, the Soviet ambassador to Tel Aviv:

Sneh: 'Israel will win the war.'
Chubakhin: 'Who will fight? The espresso boys and the pimps of Dizengoff Street [the main shopping thoroughfare of Tel Aviv]?'

The crisis

First reports from Intelligence Branch of unusual Egyptian troop movements eastward reached the premier's military secretary, Colonel Yisrael Lior, and Eshkol himself, on the evening of 14 May. Later that night the chief of staff, Yitzhak Rabin, gave the prime minister further details about the Egyptian move as Eshkol and other leading political and military figures were milling around the balcony of the Prime Minister's Office, overlooking the Hebrew University stadium, where the annual Independence Day military parade was about to start.

The following morning, 15 May, Rabin informed Eshkol that the Egyptian armed forces had been placed on a state of maximum alert. The Egyptians were moving into a defensive deployment and their chief of staff, Muhammad Fawzi, had spent 13–14 May in Damascus. 'We knew that Fawzi had demanded that the Syrians prevent actions against Israel [by Palestinian guerrillas], so that Israel would not have any cause to act,' said Lior. By the afternoon Rabin knew how many Egyptian tanks and how much artillery had moved into Sinai, and where the forces were deploying. On 16 May Intelligence Branch reported that there were now three full divisions in Sinai. Israel began mobilizing 15–18,000 reservists.[18]

Rabin's and Aman's immediate appreciation was that the Egyptians were re-enacting the 'Rotem' stratagem of 1960 to deter Israel from attacking Syria.[19] The 7 April air battle, which had ended with IAF mirages contemptuously overflying Damascus, may have persuaded Cairo and Damascus that further Israeli punishment of Syria was in the works. Bellicose statements directed against Syria by Israeli generals and politicians, including prime minister Eshkol himself, seemed to confirm this.[20]

Egypt's deployment in Sinai, rather than Syria, was Israel's main concern on 15 May. Yet Aman initially believed that the Egyptian move was little more than bravado and that the divisions would quickly be returned to their bases. Egypt had 'no offensive intentions', was the IDF General Staff assessment. The Israelis felt that the troop movements were a product of showmanship and bluff rather than genuine aggressive design. This appreciation was based mainly on the fact that Egypt's crack armoured unit, the 4th Division, was still deployed west of the Canal. But Yariv also pointed to some worrying signs, including the movement of a squadron of Ilyushin-28 bombers from Egypt proper to the frontline Bir Thamade airfield in Sinai.[21]

On 16 May Nasser asked U Thant to withdraw the United Nations Emergency Force (UNEF) from the Israeli–Egyptian border. Even this failed to set off the alarm bells in Jerusalem. At the General Staff meeting in Tel Aviv on 17 May the prevailing view was that the Egyptian move was designed to deter an Israeli attack on Syria. Yariv said: 'The Egyptians will argue that they are acting . . . according to their agreement with the Syrians and are coming to their aid in time of distress. Thus the Egyptians express their leadership of the Arab world.'

The Aman chief's assessment was largely based on the defensive deployment of the Egyptians in Sinai, especially of the 2nd Division, on the El Arish–Kusseima line.[22] More ominously, Yariv also reported that the Egyptian forces were equipped with poison gas.[23]

Intelligence Branch's Research Department changed its tune dramatically on the evening of 17 May, when news of U Thant's precipitate capitulation to the Egyptian demand reached Jerusalem: 'If the UN forces withdraw from the area a new situation could arise, which would give the Egyptian [deployment] an offensive – and not only defensive – character,' the new appreciation stated. Aman assessed that the Egyptians themselves had been surprised – and perhaps troubled – by the speed of the UN secretary-general's acquiescence in their demand. But Aman argued that, having taken the plunge, the Egyptians could not, for reasons of face, now pull back from the brink.

Yet at the security consultation on the morning of 18 May – attended by Eshkol, foreign minister Abba Eban and generals Rabin, Yariv and Meir Amit of the Mossad, the daily intelligence estimate remained that war was still 'a remote possibility'.[24]

At the General Staff meeting the next day, 19 May, with the Egyptians already deploying a full six divisions in Sinai, Yariv continued to argue that Nasser's intentions were not necessarily aggressive and that, although the situation had radically changed as a result of the UN agreement to withdraw, the Egyptians would hold back so long as they had not reached full strategic cooperation with the other Arab states and so long as their main forces were still divided between the two banks of the Suez Canal. Later that day Yariv assessed that Egypt now had four options: (1) to initiate a provocation to draw Israel into a full-scale conflict; (2) to maintain the new status quo and to do nothing further; (3) to launch an all-out assault across the border into the Negev; and (4) to begin a static campaign of attrition, in order to wear down Israel, which by now was largely mobilized, in preparation for an eventual ground assault.[25] Amit proposed that Israel publish abroad aerial reconnaissance photographs of the massive Egyptian deployment in order to justify Israel's own mobilization. But the idea was rejected.[26]

Intelligence branch learned that the Egyptians had ordered three of their brigades stationed in Yemen to return home and, on 20 May, had taken over Sharm ash-Sheikh, at the southern tip of the peninsula, thus controlling the entrance to the Gulf of Aqaba, Israel's commercial gateway to Africa and Asia. Aman now argued that while the 15 May entry into Sinai had been an ad hoc affair, with little prior planning and limited deterrent aims, the Egyptian president had been swept up by his own moves and their unfolding repercussions into a grand design with far-reaching political if not immediate military aims. On 21 May Nasser declared a general mobilization of the Egyptian army.

At a further IDF General Staff meeting, on 22 May, Yariv anticipated that the following day Egypt would complete its deployment of forces in the peninsula. The possibility that it would next close the Straits of Tiran – thus blocking the Gulf of Aqaba – was raised, but Intelligence Branch assessed that this was unlikely. At midnight that night Nasser announced the closure of the straits to Israeli shipping and an Egyptian battalion was parachuted into Sharm ash-Sheikh. The die was cast. Israel had always regarded the closure of the straits as a *casus belli*.

Yariv's reaction, at the General Staff meeting the following morning in Tel Aviv, which was also attended by Eshkol, was determined and dramatic: 'The post-Suez period is over,' he said, 'It is not merely a question of freedom of navigation. If Israel does not respond to the closure of the straits, there will be no value to its credibility or to the IDF's deterrent power, because the Arab states will interpret Israel's weakness as an excellent opportunity to assail her security and her very existence.' The Aman chief called for immediate Israeli military action; Ezer Weizman seconded the motion.

Yariv's view carried a great deal of weight, partly because of the high esteem in which he was held by generals and politicians alike and partly because he headed 'the only body capable of providing strategic-military intelligence and assessment'.[27]

Yariv was born in Moscow in 1920, arrived in Palestine as a child and joined the Haganah in 1939. During the Second World War he served as a captain in the British Eighth Army and afterwards worked with Mossad LeAliya Bet in Europe. In 1948 he had been a battalion commander in the Carmeli Brigade. In 1954 he was appointed the first head of the IDF Staff and Command College and three years later became Israel's military attaché in Washington. He was appointed director of IDF intelligence in 1964, a post he was to hold until 1972. Before, during and after the 1967 war, Yariv held a pre-eminent position in the intelligence community, far overshadowing the other service chiefs. His stature and record were such that he regularly participated in cabinet meetings, even some dealing with non-military matters. Both inside the General Staff and, even more strikingly, in the dealings of ministers with the army, Yariv emerged as the number-two military authority after Yitzhak Rabin, the chief of staff.

With some reservations, Rabin supported Yariv and Weizman at the meeting of 23 May. The army's recommendation, to go to war immediately, had been made. Now it was up to the cabinet.[28] But the ministers, who were dominated by Eshkol's natural hesitancy and by a desire to allow the Western powers – primarily the United States – time to solve the problem by diplomatic means, postponed a decision.

During the following days, Intelligence Branch concluded that the previous days' successes had gone to Nasser's head and that he now intended to launch an assault.[29]

Arab feelings of exhilaration and victory over 'the Zionist entity' – themselves a significant component in the escalation towards war – reached a crescendo on 30 May, when King Hussein of Jordan paid a surprise visit to Cairo, where he and Nasser, veteran rivals, signed a mutual defence agreement. IDF intelligence was again caught unawares. Arab leaders and radio stations, from Baghdad to Tunis, now daily proclaimed Israel's imminent destruction. The Arab noose, it was felt in Jerusalem, was tightening.

In the days before the war Intelligence Branch almost committed another serious blunder of misprediction. The veteran head of Aman's Jordanian desk, Ze'ev Bar-Lavi, known to his colleagues as 'Biber', stuck stubbornly to his assessment that Hussein would keep out of the war, 'Biber, wake up,' Yariv told him. 'It's a different ballgame now.'[30]

Predicting Jordanian behaviour on the ground was difficult in the period immediately before the war. According to Rafi Siton, an Aman Special Duties Officer (Katam) in Jerusalem, intensive intelligence-collection and agent-running continued until two days before fighting started, but then it became impossible, because the military deployments along the front lines were simply too dense. 'Although they [the Jordanians] had deployed, we didn't believe that they'd go to war,' he recalled. 'Their deployment was a mixture of the offensive and the defensive.'[31] From 25 May, anticipating war, but not against Jordan, officers of the Shin Bet security service deployed with army units only on the southern front, in preparation for the capture of the Gaza Strip.[32]

Throughout the 15–30 May period, Aman had proved itself unable to anticipate Nasser's moves accurately – the push into Sinai, the expulsion of UNEF and the closure of the straits. Later it was explained by Gazit, Amit and others that the multiple failures of May 1967 had been due to the fact that everything had been dictated by the will of one man who had acted out of character and irrationally, and, at least in part, had been guided in his actions by unpredictable external factors (such as the Soviet 'warning' about Israeli troop concentrations and U Thant's fatal decision to withdraw UNEF from Sinai).[33]

The two-week delay, characterized by fruitless diplomatic shuttling and exchanges of telegrams between Jerusalem and Washington, and grave anxiety in Israel over abandonment and a possible second Holocaust, approached its end on 2 June, when a joint meeting of the full cabinet and the IDF General Staff decided in principle on war. Aharon Yariv was again the main speaker on the military side. He argued that postponement of action would only strengthen Egypt's hand: more troops would arrive from Yemen, more equipment would arrive from the Soviet Union and more fortifications would be built in Sinai. 'Every day that passes substantially lessens the chances of Israel attaining air superiority,' he said. On the political front, the Aman chief argued, each passing day reduced Israel's deterrent capability and diminished the West's position in the Middle East. 'Our view is that the US does not seriously intend to break the naval quarantine [against Israel in the Straits of Tiran] by force . . . the US understands that we must act.'[34]

In trying to persuade the cabinet of the urgency of a pre-emptive attack, Yariv revealed something of the remarkable extent of Aman's knowledge of enemy deployment and morale. He told the ministers that the Egyptians were still busy pushing units across the canal and were doing so in such haste that some of their troops had been left without food and water for two days running. In one case reservists arrived at the front still wearing their galabiyas (the traditional, sweeping Arab robes), as there had not been time to issue them with uniforms.[35] The rest of the General Staff officers who spoke pressed the cabinet in a similar vein. 'What are we waiting for'? asked Quartermaster-General Mattityahu Peled.

Yet Eshkol still tarried. The final decision to go to war was taken at the cabinet meeting in Jerusalem on 4 June. The prime minister, who was worried about the superpowers' attitude to an Israeli pre-emptive strike and concerned about the contours of the political aftermath of the war, was finally persuaded by Meir Amit, who had secretly spent the previous three days in Washington, sounding out America's leaders specifically on these points. Amit, accompanied by Israel's ambassador to Washington, Avraham Harman, arrived at Eshkol's house at midnight, 3 June. All the country's senior political and military leaders – Eshkol, Eban, Dayan, Rabin, Allon, Yadin and others – were waiting for him.[36]

Amit began by reiterating his instructions. He had been sent to Washington '(a) to clarify, check and compare with the American intelligence community information and assessments regarding the military forces . . . and . . . political developments.

(b) To clarify what would be the mission of the special [naval] task force to handle Middle East affairs. (c) To clarify what would be the American reaction if we decide to act [militarily] . . .' Amit had also been charged with bringing back a set of the latest US satellite surveillance photos and reports on the deployment of the Arab armies along Israel's borders.

The Mossad chief had held long talks with his opposite number, the head of the CIA, Richard Helms, and with several senior Pentagon figures. Amit found 'no differences' between the Israeli and US appreciations of the military situation. The proposed US or Western naval task force that was intended to break the Egyptian blockade of the Straits of Tiran would not materialize. And he argued that the Americans 'will bless an operation if we succeed in shattering Nasser'. This bold statement appeared to contradict the stream of recent US public declarations and the cables arriving from Israeli diplomats in Washington and elsewhere, and it surprised the assembled Israeli leaders. Apparently, as the crisis dragged on into early June, the Americans had despaired of a political solution and resigned themselves to the inevitability of war – while continuing to publicly espouse the ways and virtues of diplomacy.

Abba Eban, the foreign minister, had arrived separately at the same conclusion as Amit on the basis of a secret report transmitted to him by a leading US official on 1 June. 'The United States would now back Israel,' was the bottom line of the message.[37]

But now, if it seemed that the die had finally been cast, Amit had a surprise in store. He suggested that Israel should wait a further week, testing the Egyptians and the sincerity of their blockade by sending a flotilla of its own ships through the Straits of Tiran. But the cabinet in Jerusalem rejected the idea.

The Mossad–CIA talks had two-way results: Amit reached the conclusion that the United States would support a preemptive IDF strike, while his US interlocutors came away feeling that Israel was indeed on the brink of launching that strike. The meetings with Amit had reinforced US perceptions of Israel's determination to go to war. On 2 or 3 June Helms sent

President Lyndon Johnson an 'eyes only' message, assessing that Israel would launch its attack within a few days.[38] Jordan had apparently also reached the same conclusion at about the same time. Jordanian military intelligence, noting new IDF concentrations west of the Latrun salient and in the Afula area, opposite the West Bank town of Jenin, reported on 3 June that hostilities were imminent. King Hussein declared at a press conference on 4 June that war was only 'a few days away'.[39]

Israel's generals and ministers had had enough of patient diplomacy. Eshkol, Dayan, Allon and Rabin had decided on war. The full cabinet was summoned for 8.15 a.m. on 4 June. Yariv again briefed the ministers: two Egyptian commando battalions had been flown to Jordan; Israel could expect the imminent start of terror and sabotage operations across the border. 'A process of the Egyptians moving over to the offensive is apparent in Sinai and the activation of Egyptian commando [units] in the Eilat area to cut off [the town] and conquer it can be expected,' the intelligence chief reported.[40] Dayan agreed fully with the bleak picture Yariv painted. Eshkol told his cabinet that, reluctantly, he too felt that there was no further point in postponement. The ministers voted for war, leaving the exact timing up to the prime minister, the defence minister and the generals.[41]

The battle

From IAF commander Motti Hod's briefing to the joint meeting of the cabinet and IDF General Staff on 2 June 1967, it was clear, as Yisrael Lior recorded at the time, that 'the Israeli air force knew accurately ... where every Egyptian aircraft was located, what it was doing, what it could do'.

The key to the Israeli victory was the assault of 5 June on the air forces of Egypt, Syria and Jordan. The IAF, flying modern Mirage IIICs and superannuated Super Mystères, Ouragans and Vautours, destroyed, mostly on the ground, 304 Egyptian aircraft (out of a total strength of 419), fifty-three Syrian aircraft (out of 112) and twenty-eight Jordanian aircraft (out of twenty-eight, mostly British-made Hawker Hunters): these made up 70–80 per cent of the front-line Arab air strength. The Israeli planes also managed to temporarily knock out most of these countries' military airfields. The first day's assault ended with a long-range attack on Iraq's westernmost airbase, H-3, in which ten aircraft were destroyed on the ground. The destruction of H-3 was prompted by the Iraqi bombing of several targets in Israel a few hours before.[42]

The main attack, which was carried out in two separate waves, was launched during the morning of 5 June against Egypt's seventeen air bases and radar installations. The IAF left only twelve combat aircraft behind to guard Israeli air space. The third wave, launched at 12.15 p.m. against Syria and Jordan, followed strafing attacks on Israeli targets about twenty minutes earlier by Syrian and Jordanian aircraft. (Nasser had informed neither Damascus nor Amman that his air force had already been virtually demolished.)

The secret of this multiple aerial assault, one of the most devastating and decisive first strikes in military history, was accurate intelligence – about the Egyptian air force and aircraft (capabilities, routines, command structure etc.), airfields and anti-aircraft defences (radar, missiles, guns). As King Hussein, an airman himself, put it later: 'Their pilots knew exactly what to expect . . . their pilots had a complete catalogue of the most minute details of each of the thirty-two Arab air bases, what objectives to strike, where, when and how. We had nothing like that.'[43]

The Egyptians, perhaps through their Soviet advisers, had a rough idea of Israel's possible strategy, should it take the offensive. Hussein later claimed that in his meeting in Cairo with Nasser on 30 May, he had 'alerted Nasser against an Israeli attack . . . I had explained . . . that if Israel decided to attack, its first objective would be the Arab air forces, and that its first assault would quite naturally be directed against the Egyptian air force.' Hussein recorded that Nasser had answered: 'That's obvious. We expect it . . .'[44] Addressing his generals two days before battle was joined, Nasser specifically cautioned them against a pre-emptive Israeli air strike.[45]

But the timing and in some cases the direction of the air assault came as immense shocks to Cairo. The timing owed everything to accurate Israeli intelligence, especially that provided by the IAF's own intelligence department. For weeks the Egyptian air bases had been on dawn alert, with reinforced interceptor patrols constantly in the air in anticipation of an Israeli attack between 4.00 or 5.00 and 7.00 a.m. According to King Hussein, the Egyptians sent up four patrols of twelve planes each from 4.00 a.m. until 7.00 round the clock, along the Israeli border, the Suez Canal and over the Mediterranean. Afterwards the Egyptians stood down, returning to base, with the pilots and ground control teams going off to breakfast. This was the point of maximum Egyptian vulnerability. As Motti Hod explained to Rabin on 4 June: 'For the past two weeks, we have been keeping a watch on the precise movements of the Egyptian air force ... At first light they take off on patrol, staying up for about an hour. Then they return to base and go off for breakfast. Between seven and eight, everything is dead, and 7.45 in the morning is the ideal timing for us.'[46] The Israeli pilots, who had enjoyed a good night's sleep, struck at 7.45 a.m. at the largely undefended Egyptian air bases.

Many of the first strafing and bombing runs were carried out from west to east or from north to south rather than from the more obvious and anticipated east. The Israeli formations, taking cognizance of Egyptian radar capabilities and deployment, which focused eastwards, towards Israel, at least initially came in low over the Mediterranean, flew south over Lower Egypt and, turning east, hit the airbases from the west or north. This may have contributed to the initial (baseless) Egyptian charge that American (Sixth Fleet) and British (Cyprus-based) aircraft had carried out or at least participated in the assault.

The Israeli pilots also benefited from a major, unplanned bonus: on the morning of 5 June Egyptian defence minister Abdel Hakim Amer and his air force commander, General Mohammed Sidki, had set out in an Ilyushin-14 transport plane from Cairo to Sinai to inspect their main bases. Fearing a mishap by jittery troops, the high command had ordered the Egyptian anti-aircraft batteries along the canal and in parts of the peninsula not to fire at any overflying aircraft.[47] It is not clear when, if at all, Aman learned of this order.

On the morning of 5 June the IAF pilots were issued with target sheets which accurately protrayed the real and fake targets – aircraft, runways, AA guns, etc. The main assault on the Egyptian air force was over by 11.00 a.m. The attacks on the Jordanian and Syrian air forces and Iraq's H-3 air base began about an hour later, after Jordanian, Syrian and Iraqi aircraft had launched several largely ineffectual attacks on targets inside Israel. Within two hours the Jordanian and Syrian air forces had been destroyed.[48]

Humint

Humint (human intelligence) and Sigint (signal intelligence), as well as Photint (photographic intelligence), combined to give the General Staff and the commanders of the IAF an accurate picture of the Arab, and primarily the Egyptian, air forces. Spies run by both Intelligence Branch and the Mossad had spent years photographing and collecting intelligence on the Arab airfields and air-defence systems. Shortly after the war the Egyptian press reported the capture of an Israeli agent (an Arab) who lived near Alexandria harbour. The implication was that the agent had supplied Israel with details about Egyptian naval facilities, craft and routine in Alexandria harbour, which was indeed raided by Israeli navy frogmen during the war.[49] Stories also circulated about another Israeli agent, an Egyptian army signals major, who died during the war in an Israeli bombing raid in Sinai. The major, recruited in Cairo and run by Intelligence Branch for three to four years, had given the IDF accurate information on the Egyptian order of battle and on senior commanders. He was ordered to contact the Israelis only if and when he was transferred to Sinai. His first message was broadcast on 17 May.[50]

Humint was largely responsible for the IAF's ability, come the day of reckoning, to distinguish between real and fake targets on the ground.

After the war Samir ar-Rifa'i, an aide to King Hussein, told Western reporters that a lone IAF Super Mystère had attacked King Hussein's office in the Royal Palace in Amman on the afternoon of 5 June. The Israeli plane 'machine-gunned the King's office at point-blank range with a precision and knowledge of its target that was stupefying,' Rifa'i said.[51]

Eli Cohen

Until 1964 the placing and running of Israeli spies in Arab countries bordering directly on Israel was carried out mainly by IDF intelligence; the Mossad's agents in Arab states were dispatched and controlled from third countries, usually Western Europe, with Paris serving as regional headquarters.

Spies were run all over the Arab world from the French capital. The short-lived union of Egypt and Syria in the United Arab Republic between 1958 and 1961 provided a brief but welcome opportunity for false-flag recruitments. The Mossad men were superbly equipped for this method: Israelis posing as Egyptians could persuade Syrian nationals to work for President Nasser far more easily than for the Zionists – that was a different matter altogether. One senior officer, Shmuel Toledano, spoke fluent, native Palestinian Arabic. In the summer of 1965, on a mission in Switzerland, he met a childhood friend from Tiberias, Fayez Sayegh, who was an important official in the newly formed Palestine Liberation Organization. The Mossad man invited Sayegh – a refugee – to visit his homeland. The ploy failed because Sayegh refused, saying he would return only to a liberated Palestine. 'I imagine he knew what my job was and I knew his,' Toledano said later. 'Each of us was wanted by the other's organization.'[52] David Kimche, the agent-runner who had stumbled across the treachery of Avri Elad – the 'Third Man' in the 'foul-up' in Egypt – spoke English as his mother tongue. The Polish-born Eliahu Ben-Elissar could pass easily as a Frenchman or a Belgian (he later worked in Ethiopia and East Africa and in 1979 became Israel's first ambassador to Egypt); Joe Ra'anan and Wolfgang Lotz as Germans, and so on. Shaltiel Ben-Yair, a Stern Gang veteran who followed Yitzhak Shamir into the Mossad, spoke fluent Arabic and French. He operated in Egypt under the deep cover of a Belgian cattle expert, providing valuable details about military bases and other sensitive installations. Many other Mossad spies in the first half of the 1960s were non-Jewish Europeans: two Italians and a Dutchman were caught by the Egyptians and 'turned' into double agents.[53]

In 1964, when Amit and Yariv took over the Mossad and Aman respectively, Aman's Unit 188 (the successor to the ill-starred Unit 131 of the Lavon Affair), which was responsible for planting and running Israeli spies in Arab countries, was transferred to the Mossad. The two service chiefs agreed that the Mossad would run both Israeli and Arab agents in Arab countries while Aman would control only Arab agents in the front-line enemy states. The new arrangement, which had brought Aman executives – the heads of Unit 188 as well as Amit himself – into the Mossad, helped neutralize the traditional IDF complaint that the civilian agency failed to supply the army with enough purely military intelligence.[54]

One of the most promising agents transferred from Aman to the Mossad in 1964 was Eli Cohen, who was caught and hanged by the Syrians the following year. During the three years he spent in Damascus Cohen provided Tel Aviv with a mass of high-grade political and military intelligence, including a great deal of detail about the front-line belt of Syrian fortifications on the Golan Heights, which were conquered by the IDF in June 1967.

Cohen, who was the first Israeli spy caught and executed as an Israeli, was born in Alexandria, Egypt, in 1924 and emigrated to Israel in 1957, after the expulsion of active Zionists from Egypt following the Suez war. In 1955 he had come secretly to Israel for a short sabotage and communications course after the Lavon Affair arrests and trial. After emigrating to Israel, Cohen briefly served in the IDF as a translator and was recruited by Unit 188 in May 1960.

In February 1961, armed with forged papers identifying him as Kamal Amin Thabit, a Syrian-Argentinian, Cohen flew to Buenos Aires, where he began to mix with the local Syrian and Lebanese immigrant communities, fleshing out his cover and making contacts. The notional 'Thabits' were a Syrian family that had moved to Egypt in 1933 and then to Argentina in 1948. 'Kamal' was born in Beirut in 1930. He told his new friends in Argentina that he was a wealthy businessman and was about to return to his ancestral homeland, Syria. Cohen arrived in Damascus in January 1962.

Cohen was a promising agent from the start. When he made his first radio transmission, by Morse, to Tel Aviv on 25 February, a bottle of champagne was opened in Unit 188 HQ. 'Menashe', as he was codenamed, used invisible ink for longer reports, smuggling them out to a contact in Europe in hidden compartments in the damascene furniture which he began to export. As a prosperous businessman with a wide range of South American, European and Middle Eastern connections, Cohen was able to mix with senior Syrian financial, military and political figures and managed to establish particularly close relations with several key Ba'ath party leaders.

In July 1962 he flew to Tel Aviv, via Europe, on home leave. Aman officers spent days debriefing him on Syrian military and political affairs. Back in Syria in September, a friend took Cohen on a guided tour of the Golan Heights fortifications. The importance of this – part of the heroic myth that has grown up around Cohen in Israel – may have been exaggerated: some intelligence experts argued that information about these defences was easily available from ground and aerial reconnaissance. He also got first sight of various new Soviet weapons systems. Cohen's value to Tel Aviv soared after the Ba'ath took control of Damascus in the March 1963 *coup d'état* and some of his closest friends were given important government posts. A few weeks later Cohen again paid a brief visit to Tel Aviv, where he met the new Mossad chief, Meir Amit. He was back in Damascus in May.

Cohen was not a perfect spy. During his home visits his superiors repeatedly warned him against transmitting too often and being frivolous on the airwaves. He once sent a message expressing disappointment about a defeat of the Israel national soccer team and often sent regards to his wife, Nadia, and other personal messages. Cohen's brother, Maurice, was working at the time in the Mossad's communications section and quickly guessed 'Menashe's' identity. Some of his customers in the intelligence community believed at the time that he was playing a dangerous game. 'He was too good an agent,' said Aharon Yariv, 'in the sense that he became too close to important Syrians and, as such, stuck out too much.'[55] Rafi Eitan, the veteran Mossad agent-runner, thought Cohen 'a very poor spy' who had simply behaved stupidly in Damascus.[56]

Cohen used his radio like a telephone. 'We'd ask him a question in the morning and by the afternoon you already had the answer,' one of his controllers said later. Between 15 March and 29 August 1964, for example, he transmitted some 100 messages, each averaging about nine minutes. Between 2 December and his capture on 18 January 1965, he sent thirty-one, all at 8.30 a.m. While technically rated a good radio man, overuse of the airwaves represented a cumulative security lapse and was almost certainly the cause of his capture. Radio-finding vans manned by Syrian security policemen and Soviet advisers eventually noticed the repeated transmissions and pinpointed their origin – Cohen's flat.

Israel's 'man in Damascus' returned twice more on home leave – from December 1963 to March 1964 and during October and November 1964. During the second visit, for extra security, he was questioned by Aman officers from behind a cloth screen, partly because there was a feeling at HQ – and by then shared by Cohen himself – that his luck was about to end.[57]

Sigint in 1967

Besides Humint, Israel's single most important method of gathering order-of-battle intelligence was Photint or aerial photography. Photography of potential targets in Sinai and in Egypt proper before 1967 had always been problematic, lest it spur military tension, a Western diplomatic backlash and even hostilities. But aerial photography and reconnaissance missions were flown over the years against specific, high-priority targets. Through most of May 1967 the cabinet curbed the IDF's natural desire to step up aerial reconnaissance missions. But in the final days before 5 June the air force was at last permitted to carry out repeated short- and long-range reconnaissance missions to obtain an accurate picture of the evolving Arab military deployments.

Sigint also contributed significantly to the victory, and specifically to the success of the initial IAF air strike. King Hussein was later to record that 'the Israelis intercepted [our radio messages] often, both in the air and on the ground'.[58] Sigint also provided some important political-strategic benefits. A good illustration – and the best-known example – of the quality of Israeli Sigint capabilities was the interception and recording, early on the morning of 6 June, of a radio telephone call between Nasser and Hussein. The conversation, according to the king, took place 'over the regular public telephone system'.[59]

Nasser: How are you? The brother [Nasser referring to Hussein] wants to know if the fighting is going on all along the front . . . Do you know that that the US is participating alongside Israel in the war? Should we announce this? . . . Should we say that the US and Britain [are participating] or only the US? [Nasser later did broadcast that the Americans had taken part in the initial, decisive air assault, in order to explain away the defeat.]
Hussein: The US and England.
Nasser: Does Britain have aircraft carriers?
Hussein: [Unclear]
Nasser: Good. King Hussein will make an announcement and I will

make an announcement . . . we will make sure that the Syrians [also] make an announcement that American and British aircraft are using their aircraft carriers against us . . . [Meanwhile], our aircraft have been attacking Israel's airfields since the morning.[60]

The intercept was carried out in a base near Tel Aviv by two veteran Aman officers using Second World War vintage equipment. The two had spent the previous day, 5 June, 'following' the retreat of various Egyptian units in Sinai. Neither were at first aware of the full importance of their intercept, but they were quickly enlightened by the officer in charge, who told them, 'It's worth millions. Make four copies.'

Though somewhat unclear, the purport of the Nasser–Hussein conversation seemed to be that Nasser was trying to persuade Hussein that the 5 June air strike had been carried out jointly by Israeli, US and British aircraft. It is even possible that the two Arab leaders at the time believed this to be the case.[61] And so, apparently, did a senior Soviet officer stationed at Ismailia, on the Suez Canal.[62]

Yariv opposed the publication of the Nasser–Hussein conversation to avoid revealing the extent of Israel's Sigint capabilities and operations. But he was overruled by Dayan and Eshkol, and the recorded conversation was released by Israel the following day, while the war was still raging, with telling political effect.

Publication of the monitored conversation prompted the Arabs to considerably upgrade their communications security, rendering Aman's electronic eavesdropping much more difficult. One senior Israeli intelligence officer said later that the publication cost Israel 60 per cent of its Sigint interception capability in the Arab states.[63] The feeling in Arab capitals was that if such a high-level, intimate exchange could be picked up by the Israelis, who knew what else Aman's Sigint units were capable of? Promoting this concern, of course, had been one of the precise purposes of the publication. Another motive was to try to drive a wedge between Egypt and Jordan by bringing home Nasser's duplicity to the king. (Nasser had not admitted to the destruction of his air force and, indeed, had told Hussein – on 6 June – that his planes were still busy attacking Israel's airfields.)

From the early morning of 6 June Egyptian, Jordanian and Syrian radio stations broadcast the news of the Anglo-US 'conspiracy' with Israel and the participation of British and US squadrons in the bombing runs over Egypt's airfields. Angry crowds stormed and burned down the US consulate in Alexandria, and wild appeals went out from Cairo and Damascus to the rest of the Arab world to attack US installations. The Arab states *en masse* broke off relations with the United States. Publication of the conversation deeply embarrassed Nasser and Hussein.[64]

In terms of operations on the ground, even more important was the interception, at around 2.00 p.m. on 6 June, of Nasser's general order to his forces in Sinai to fall back to the Suez Canal, following the major breakthroughs by Israeli divisions led by General Israel Tal (on the northern Sinai axis) and General Ariel Sharon (southern axis) early that day. This enabled the IDF General Staff to decide on opening an offensive against Syria in the southern Golan Heights three days later.[65]

Before the war an Aman officer named Shaul Shamai[66] had broken the Egyptian army code, with considerable effect. During the fighting Intelligence Branch repeatedly confused Egyptian commanders and units by issuing false orders. Later the Soviet press reported one such incident, in which Israeli Sigint officers ordered an Egyptian MiG pilot to release his bombs over the sea instead of carrying out an attack on Israeli positions. When challenged to prove their bona fides, the Israelis gave the pilot, named 'Mortaji', details about his wife and children. He eventually abandoned both bombs and plane over the sea and parachuted to safety.[67]

In the weeks before the war, Intelligence Branch on the southern front stage-managed a major deception operation whose aim was to persuade the Egyptians that Israel's main offensive thrust would be on the southern Sinai axis and even further southwards, near Kusseima, rather than along the more obvious northern coast road. Aman utilized a special dummy unit to this end. The Egyptians swallowed the bait and redeployed their forces, including General Saad ad-Din Shazli's elite armoured task force, in accordance with the presumed threat along the southern axis.

During the fighting itself, Intelligence Branch was relatively insignificant, as the IDF armoured formations in Sinai outstripped expectations with the rapidity and success of their advance. And the Egyptians disintegrated and fled westwards so quickly that field intelligence units were hard pressed to keep tabs on them. Aerial photography and reconnaissance was abandoned during the crucial first two days as the IAF's resources were completely mobilized for attack and interception missions. Only on 7 June did a squadron of eleven Piper Cub aircraft, with Aman officers, join the advancing Israeli ground columns, as forward spotters for artillery and armoured units.

Benefits

In intelligence terms the 1967 war proved a major boon to Aman. The IDF obtained extensive knowledge about the three Arab armies that it had defeated – their structures, weaponry, combat doctrine and personnel. Aman units spent months questioning POWs and combing through captured documents – of Egyptian military intelligence and secret police in the Gaza Strip and Sinai, of Arab Legion intelligence and of the Jordanian Mukhabarat security service in Jerusalem, Ramallah and Nablus, and of Syrian military intelligence HQ in Quneitra. The Jordanian material was to be of use in the exposure and destruction of PLO and especially Communist Party infrastructure and cells in the West Bank in the early months of the post-June 1967 Israeli occupation.

The war naturally left bad blood between the Soviets and their Arab clients. Nasser and the Syrians laid much of the blame for their defeat on the poor quality of Soviet equipment and on the inadequacies of both Soviet military doctrine and the training given by Soviet advisers. Israel acted quickly to widen this rift. In July 1967, only weeks after the battles, IDF Intelligence Branch published a Syrian military intelligence report from 1965, showing that its agents had kept close tabs on the Soviet advisers stationed in Damascus and Quneitra. The report was somewhat unkind to the Russians: 'They are miserly even towards each other,' wrote Major Mohammed Sharif al-Saoud.[68]

Aman also rushed into print with another Syrian intelligence document – this time hoping to blacken Syria in the eyes of UN personnel. The document, an order by the commander of the 6th Brigade, Colonel Muhammad Ziad al-Hariri, dating from 1962, instructed the Syrian garrisons on the Golan Heights to conceal the heavy weaponry and excess units whose presence was a violation of the forces limitation provisions of the 1949 Israeli–Syrian armistice agreement, which was monitored by UN military observers.[69]

Thieves in the night

The Six Day War marked the beginning of the end of the Israeli–French alliance, one of whose chief components was arms sales. The relationship had been forged in the mid-1950s against the background of the Algerian revolt, common hostility to Nasser's Egypt and the valuable intelligence that Israel supplied on the movements of the FLN rebel leaders. But Algeria became independent in 1962 and by the middle of the decade President de Gaulle found it more prudent to resuscitate French–Arab ties. During the crisis of May 1967 he warned Israel not to launch a pre-emptive strike. And when this advice was ignored he took it as a personal insult.

France retaliated by imposing an embargo on the further sale to Israel of Mirages – the aircraft that had proved so effective on 5 June. And after the IDF commando raid on Beirut Airport in December 1968, in which thirteen empty civilian planes were blown up on the tarmac in retaliation for Beirut-based PLO attacks on Israeli air traffic, the embargo was tightened to include all types of weaponry. The French had for decades maintained a special, protective attitude towards Lebanon. De Gaulle vetoed the transfer to Israel of the five remaining missile boats (out of twelve ordered) being constructed in Cherbourg harbour by CCM (Chantiers de Construction Mécanique de Normandie).

Israel responded to the French embargo on two levels: the government launched a campaign to persuade the United States to replace France as Israel's main arms supplier; and on the immediate, practical level, the intelligence and armed services were ordered to make good the losses, by hook or by crook.

In Switzerland, where French aircraft were being produced under licence, the Mossad, the IAF and Lakam – the Defence Ministry's technological espionage unit – jointly organized the acquisition of the Mirage IIIC construction blueprints, eventually enabling Israel to build its own Mirage replicas, the Nesher and the Kfir. A Swiss engineer, Alfred Frauenknecht, was arrested in 1969 and sentenced in 1971 by a Swiss court to four and a half years in prison – but only after he had transferred to Mossad agents some 200,000 blueprints and the specifications for the precision machine tools used in the Mirage's construction.[70]

The five Cherbourg boats, which were considered by Israel a vital part of its new missile craft flotilla, were smuggled out of France on Christmas Eve 1969 and sailed into Haifa harbour on New Year's Eve. The operation, which used a dummy third-country company and Israeli crews brought into France in civilian clothes, was organized by Admiral Mordechai ('Mokka') Limon, the head of Israel's military purchasing mission in France and a retired commander of the Israel Navy. The French government was hoodwinked into believing that the boats were being purchased by a Norwegian oil exploration company. (Lower-echelon French officials understood well before the flight from Cherbourg what was happening but failed to pass the information upwards, or were ignored by their superiors.) The Mossad was not involved in the operation in any significant way.[71]

8
Palestinian Challenges: 1967–73

The price of victory

Although the six-day military victory was stunning, Israel was unprepared for its consequences. The Palestinians had been consigned by history and geography to the wings of the Arab–Jewish struggle since the disaster of 1948; now the bulk of them were at centre stage again, almost 1 million people, shocked and embittered by the new catastrophe that had overtaken them. By 10 June 1967, with the West Bank, East Jerusalem and the Gaza Strip under full Israeli control, one of the first tasks of the conquerors was to work out how they were going to control a large and potentially hostile Arab population for the foreseeable future, pending whatever peace settlement might – or might not – arise from the ashes of war. The captured Syrian Golan Heights and the vast wastes of the Egyptian Sinai desert presented different problems.

Shlomo Gazit, the Intelligence Branch colonel appointed that summer as the government's first 'coordinator of operations' for the occupied territories, defined the main security goal of the new system: 'To isolate the terrorist [the Hebrew word generally used for terrorist is *mehabel*, although its more precise and original meaning is saboteur] from the general population and deny him shelter and assistance even though the natural sympathy of that population is with the terrorists and not the Israeli administration.'[1]

Gazit, a sober but somewhat ponderous officer who had served under Aharon Yariv as head of Aman's Research Department for the previous three years, argued later that, despite some early hitches, the Israeli security system in fact worked surprisingly well. IDF intelligence, the Shin Bet and the Mossad maintained their pre-war functions but simply expanded their regular activities to meet the requirements of the new situation.

Aman retained its overall responsibility for national intelligence, and thus set collection and research priorities for the two other main components of the intelligence community. The Shin Bet was given control of operational intelligence in the occupied territories, and the Mossad was ordered to increase its targeting and penetration of Palestinian organizations abroad. These had not been a top priority before the war: since 1948 new Palestinian nationalist groups had often disappeared as quickly as they emerged, and over the years Israeli intelligence had paid only scant attention to them. Aman's Research Department subsumed Palestinian affairs – largely Ahmed Shuqairi's Palestine Liberation Organization – under other headings and there was some opposition from Intelligence Branch officers to setting up what Gazit named the Hostile Sabotage Activity (FAHA by its Hebrew acronym, HSA in English) desk in 1965, the first year of military operations by Yasser Arafat's Fatah movement.[2] Until then, Palestinians as intelligence targets had been monitored together with the countries – Egypt, Syria, Jordan – which assisted them. In 1964, when Yariv had taken over Intelligence Branch from Meir Amit, he had been told that the PLO 'should not cause Israel concern'.[3]

Before the 1967 war Fatah, which was the largest and most homogeneous of the Palestinian organizations, seemed a far greater threat to Jordan than it did to Israel, and King Hussein's extensive security apparatus – which Israeli intelligence had come to admire for professional expertise[4] – had dealt with it thoroughly. In April 1966, for example, the Jordanians arrested about 200 'subversives', including most of the staff of the PLO office in Amman, which was closed down completely two months later. Between October and mid-November that year, six of eleven raids by Syrian-backed Palestinians into Israel took place through Jordanian territory, creating the danger of massive Israeli retaliation against West Bank villages. That was exactly what happened on 13 November 1966, when Samu, south of Hebron, was attacked by the Israeli army in its largest engagement since the Suez war. At the time of the Samu raid King Hussein made it clear to Israel that he had not yet managed to suppress Fatah activities in the Hebron area.[5] It was in this period that Jordan accepted from Israel lists of West Bankers collaborating with fedayeen groups, and on several occasions extensive arrests were carried out on the basis of such information.[6]

Shin Bet takes charge

In the immediate aftermath of the war the Shin Bet, like everyone else, was just not prepared for the magnitude of the task it faced. Although all the service's reserve manpower – especially Arabic speakers – had been mobilized, it took time before it was able to recruit and train the necessary new personnel to deploy operationally.[7] 'The service just wasn't ready to take over such a large area and such a large number of people,' a senior Shin Bet officer said. 'Our only previous experience was in the Gaza Strip in 1956, and we assumed that the same would happen, that it would all be over and we'd be leaving in a few months.'[8]

'I was quite relieved that the GSS took it all,' Aharon Yariv, the Aman chief, said later. 'We had enough on our plate.' In the eleven quiet years since the Suez war, the Shin Bet had evolved into a small and highly professional security and counter-espionage organization whose two main tasks had been the control of the country's relatively docile Arab minority and meeting the threat of hostile foreign intelligence operations on Israel soil, mostly from the Soviet Bloc and the Arabs. The abolition of the military government in the Arab areas inside the 'green line' in 1966 had not meant less work for its

Arabists. The closure of all Soviet Bloc embassies after the wholesale rupture of diplomatic relations in 1967 had freed some of the service's counter-intelligence personnel for other duties, although Russian or Czech speakers were of little use in the West Bank or Gaza.

For the first few weeks after the end of hostilities, the Palestinians remained in a state of collective shock. But by mid-July 1967 the Shin Bet was reporting to Eshkol that dismay was giving way to anger and that there were signs of readiness to begin a campaign of civil disobedience against the occupation authorities.[9] One factor in bringing the Palestinians face to face with the new reality was the large number of Israelis who started to go out to see the sights and hunt for bargains in the souks of East Jerusalem, Nablus and Hebron.

The security service was in on the act from the start. The idea for the government's inter-ministerial coordinating committee, which Dayan asked Gazit to chair in mid-August, came from Shmuel Toledano, the former Mossad officer and then adviser to prime minister Eshkol on Arab affairs. But it was Yosef Harmelin, head of the Shin Bet since 1963, who drew up the organizational proposal. Harmelin explained to Dayan how government operations dealing with Israeli Arabs were coordinated, and suggested a similar framework for the West Bank, the Gaza Strip and East Jerusalem.[10] Avraham Ahituv, head of the Shin Bet's Arab Affairs Branch, represented the service on the committee.

The new situation required new men and new methods: the shooting war was over but the real struggle was only just beginning. Harmelin gave Yehuda Arbel, the Hungarian-born director of the service's small Jerusalem regional office, responsibility for the West Bank and East Jerusalem. Immediately after the ceasefire a forward headquarters was set up in the Ambassador Hotel in the city's Sheikh Jarrah neighbourhood, where the army's central command was also based.[11]

Before the war Jerusalem had been the smallest and quietest of the Shin Bet's regions and it had had very little to do with Arab affairs. Apart from Abu Ghosh and three smaller villages (including the Israeli half of divided Beit Safafa) there were no Arabs in the area. Arbel had conducted much of his business from the Café Peter, a popular restaurant run by two Hungarian widows in the picturesque German Colony neighbourhood. At one point in the early 1960s, he had considered leaving the service because the work was so boring.[12] Arbel had been recruited in 1958 by his fellow Transylvanian, Amos Manor, after several years in the police force. Manor nicknamed him 'the Gypsy'. From 1959 to 1962, the period of operations against Nazi war criminals and scientists working in Egypt, he was on loan to the Mossad in Germany.[13] Arbel was a wiry, charismatic little man with piercing blue eyes, and a taste for wild parties and attractive woman; he looked like a thin version of Richard Burton. 'I am the result of a night of love between a Tatar King and a gypsy women,' he liked to tell his friends.[14] He could be seen in public occasionally in those early post-war days, wearing army uniform and accompanying Dayan and other senior political and military figures on tours of the area. During one trip to Hebron Arbel's twelve-year-old daughter helped satisfy the defence minister's archaeological curiosity by agreeing to be lowered into a small space in the Cave of Machpelah.[15] The real work, however, was done behind the scenes.

Escalating the struggle

Fatah, which had taken no part in the war itself, now made militant noises. 'Our organization has decided to continue struggling against the Zionist conqueror,' its military wing, Al-Asifa (The Storm), announced in Damascus on 22 June 1967. 'We are planning to operate far from the Arab states so they will not suffer Israeli reprisals for fedayeen actions. It will therefore be impossible to hold the Arab people responsible for our war. Our organization is the organization of the Palestinian people and we are united in our resolve to free our stolen homeland from the hands of the Zionists.'[16]

These were brave words, but the Palestinians were far from prepared for the sort of popular guerrilla struggle they envisaged, seeking inspiration from the anti-colonial liberation movements in Algeria and Vietnam. Arafat's deputy, Khalil al-Wazir, better known as Abu Jihad, sent recruiting officers into the West Bank and Gaza. Some 500 volunteers went through three-week military and ideological training courses at Fatah camps in Syria, first being screened by a 'security committee' to make sure they were not Israeli agents. At the same time about 500 more Palestinians who had been studying in Europe and Egypt, and had undergone brief training in Algiers, were dispersed to their home towns and villages in the occupied territories, having entered Jordan disguised as Iraqi troops.[17] But these crash courses were not enough. And the Fatah security screen was hopelessly ineffective.

When the first fedayeen arrived in the West Bank and Gaza that summer they were often careless about concealing their tracks and identities. The efficiency and ruthlessness of the Jordanian and Egyptian security services had made it difficult for the fledgling Palestinian national movement to build up much of an infrastructure before the war.[18] Early operations were amateurish and compartmentalization – the holy writ of all clandestine activity – almost non-existent. Cells were far too big. As one Israeli journalist has written:

> It was a simple matter to identify these people. At times the security services simply waited for the underground agents in the cafés and arrested them as they approached their table. And when one member of the underground did not show up in a particular café, the whole village knew who the leader of his cell was and there was always someone ready to point him out. As a rule, the arrest of one member was sufficient to fold up the whole cell.[19]

Both sides agree on this important point: another of Arafat's deputies, Salah Khalaf (Abu Iyad), attributed these PLO setbacks to the twin factors of 'the efficiency of the Israeli secret services and the carelessness of our fighters'.[20] Arafat himself had arrived in the West Bank secretly in mid-July or August, and set up headquarters first in Qabatiya, north of Nablus, and then in Nablus itself. But the Fatah leader was impatient and pressed for immediate action when he would have been wiser to establish bases and build up gradual support. He managed to do little more than talk to his supporters to test the waters and raise morale. One of those he met was Faisal Husseini, who was given two guns and arrested and imprisoned by the Israelis shortly afterwards.

Arafat was forced to leave the area, disguised as a woman, in the second half of December after almost being surprised by a Shin Bet raid, led by Yehuda Arbel, on a safe house where he was staying in Ramallah, only yards from the military government headquarters.[21] The mattress on which the Fatah leader had been sleeping was still warm, and it was confiscated, serving a security service officer stationed in the town for years to come. Arafat fled back to Nablus and from there to the Syrian capital, where his Fatah colleagues were meeting to discuss future prospects for resistance. (Arafat claimed later to have again visited the occupied territories, and Tel Aviv, in 1968, but Israeli sources deny this.)

From these modest beginnings in the first flush of victory, the Shin Bet rapidly became a power to be reckoned with. The Israelis had the advantage of putting their counter-measures into effect while Fatah was in the first stage of organization, before the onset of actual sabotage operations. Eshkol authorized the recruitment of large numbers of new personnel for the security service, as well as the Mossad and the police and border police.[22] Every available Arabist was drafted into the territories, badly depleting the service's northern region, where most of them were based. 'We took anyone who could chat in Arabic and put him straight to work,' one executive said later. 'It was an immense job. We had to get to know every village, and some of our people just couldn't stand the pace, especially those who'd left their families behind in the north.'[23]

Setting the pace

Although the heavy hand of the military censor masked its role from the Israeli public, the Shin Bet's name quickly became a source of fear among the Palestinians it ruled. Early friction with some IDF officers – military governors, battalion commanders and so on – quickly gave way to close cooperation. 'The Shin Bet began to set the pace, methods and timing,' one security service officer said, 'The big change was that we were no longer just collecting intelligence. We went operational in our own right.'[24]

A huge hoard of secret files captured from bases of the Jordanian Mukhabarat in East Jerusalem and Hawara, near Nablus, was a useful asset as the organization gingerly felt its way into the new reality, recruiting its own informers and getting the feel of its fiefdom,[25] although the information was quickly outdated[26] and there was little of value directly pertaining to fedayeen support.[27] One of the files contained the gossipy but interesting fact that a well-known public figure from Nablus had cheated in his high school matriculation exams. This sort of material provided priceless leads for the Shin Bet: Palestinians who had been monitored by Jordanian intelligence because of their nationalist or communist activities were highly likely to be of interest to the Israelis as well.

Yehuda Arbel was the driving force, conjuring new methods out of thin air and firing his subordinates with his legendary enthusiasm. He placed great emphasis on recruiting the best people he could find. A decade later his protégés all occupied key positions in the service. Soon the Jerusalem region was given greater powers of decision than the other Shin Bet regions, obviating the cumbersome need for approval from headquarters in Jaffa for every arrest or operation. The pace was simply too fast so the newcomers were trained on the job.

IDF intelligence, which was relieved that someone else was bearing the burden, handed over to the Shin Bet Palestinian agents who had been run by Aman's SDOs (*katamim*) in the West Bank and East Jerusalem before the war. Rafi Siton, a veteran Jerusalem-based SDO, described the immense change that had taken place in just six days. 'After the war we were doing a completely different job,' he said later. 'The border had gone, and however funny that might sound, we couldn't survive without the border, like a fish that's thrown up on dry land.'[28]

Yet Aman continued to use its own well-tried assests on the other side of the ceasefire line. One of Siton's best agents, a Palestinian resident of Jordan who was codenamed 'Edmond', produced the complete original Arabic Protocol of the Emergency Arab Summit Conference which began in the Sudanese capital, Khartoum, on 29 August. 'Edmond's' emissary swam across the Jordan with the thirty-eight-page transcript, which was translated into Hebrew and placed on Eshkol's desk in Jerusalem on 4 September, the day after the summit ended with its famous 'Three Noes' – no peace, no negotiation, no recognition of Israel. Edmond was paid the princely sum of 500 Jordanian dinars.[29]

The Border had simply shifted. A former Jordanian Mukhabarat officer, Azmi al-Sughayr, was sent by the Israelis on an espionage mission to the East Bank, where he turned himself over to the guerrillas. After explaining how much the new rulers knew about PLO structure and activities, Sughayr was rehabilitated into Fatah ranks and was killed in Lebanon during the 1982 invasion.[30] Another ex-Mukhabarat man in the Tulkarm area provided useful leads in the hunt for Yasser Arafat.[31]

Palestinian leaders agreed later that Fatah's operational security was virtually non-existent, but they enlisted an additional argument to explain why their performance was so poor. Hani al-Hassan, a close confidant of Arafat, blamed the Mossad's efficient monitoring of Palestinian students in Western Europe, especially in Germany and Austria. As the Fatah official explained:

> As a result of the Mossad's work the Israeli military authorities had a dossier on each of us at the time we were ready to begin our military activities. They knew our names and addresses and they had photo-

graphs of us. And I must say the Israeli intelligence people were very thorough. We came to know that there were two photographs with each of our files. One was a copy of the original picture – that is to say how we looked when we entered the universities and colleges in Europe. The other was the same picture but with a drawing of a kaffiyeh on the head. By wearing the kaffiyeh you can easily transform your appearance. The Israelis were obviously expecting us to do that. Once the Israelis had all this information about us it was not so difficult for them to track us down when the action started.[32]

Israeli sources dismiss al-Hassan's claims as self-serving nonsense. Explicable, perhaps, in terms of the devastating scale of the PLO's failure, but nonsense nevertheless. For the fact is that in the early years of the occupation – at least until 1970 – the Mossad devoted very little attention to Palestinians abroad. Almost all information about fedayeen activities was gathered on the ground, in the West Bank and Gaza.

But although the Israelis did have good intelligence, it was not their only advantage. As a British journalist noted at the time:

Whatever guerrilla doctrine might teach, the West Bank is not Vietnam. The mountains of Judaea and Samaria, though wildly beautiful, are empty and stony. Movement is easy to spot and control. Crossing the river Jordan, infiltrators have to climb out of the deep valley, to labour up rocky slopes carrying any arms and equipment. Then they had to be able to rely on West Bankers (who might after all be their families and friends) for food, shelter and disguise.[33]

Topography was not always on the side of the occupiers either. The barren area round Hebron, for example, was honeycombed with hundreds of caves, perfect hiding places for fedayeen, especially if they had local knowledge or assistance. Large army sweeps often failed to discover fugitives: only precise information worked.

Fatah military operations began in earnest in September, but the Israelis were still more concerned by civil disobedience at that stage. September and October, Dayan said later, were Israel's most difficult months since the ceasefire.[34] Palestinian political and religious leaders met in Nablus and raised the banner of rebellion. General strikes were declared. But by November the worst was over. In the last three months of 1967, networks of fedayeen were captured *en masse*. The Israelis were confident – and condescending – about their Palestinian enemy. General Uzi Narkiss, the military commander of the West Bank, spoke about the fedayeen, David Pryce-Jones noted perceptively, 'as if they were good boys gone astray'. Narkiss had realized that the tide was turning in Israel's favour.

For every guerrilla captured in action, the general said, forty were rounded up through denunciation. Nothing could be kept secret in a society criss-crossed with family or clan allegiances and enmities which kept everyone on the watch. Some of the tip-offs were simply to settle an old feud, or to start a new one, or for the sake of earning a few pounds . . . The Israeli security forces had planted an informer in a village to contact some known guerrillas. Within twenty-four hours the man had been denounced by his own brother, blown for getting on with the job, as it were.[35]

Michael Sassar, spokesman for the West Bank military government in the first years after the war, noted in his diary at the time that many such denunciations were of dubious value. A lawyer from Ramallah submitted an 'arrest list' with four names. Two of them were lawyers – his professional rivals. In another case, an old man who wanted to marry a younger woman but was opposed by his prospective brother-in-law, told the Israelis that the spoiler of his happiness was a member of Fatah.[36] Shin Bet officers insist that their information was in fact far more reliable.

Other Palestinian betrayals were more subtle. Sheikh Muhammad Ali Ja'abari, the veteran and highly conservative mayor of Hebron, knew well that PLO activities could bring ruin and suffering to his city. Once in the summer of 1967 he hinted heavily to the local Shin Bet representative – a veteran Arabist of the old school who used the name 'Nur' and had been based before the war in Beersheba – that a recently arrived stranger was worth investigating. 'Nur' was pleased, but not surprised, when the stranger turned out to be a wanted Fatah man.[37]

Denunciations of this kind were only one source for the Shin Bet; the sheer amateurishness of the Palestinians and their failure to observe clandestine operating procedures were still their worst enemy. In December 1967 the Israelis rounded up no fewer than forty-two Fatah men by observing who approached a dead-letter box situated close to a soft-drinks stand in Hebron. Since the drop was used only on Fridays, it was a simple matter to wait, watch and then quietly arrest whoever turned up. One man quickly led to others.[38] A stranger spotted buying food or cigarettes in an isolated village could quickly start a trail that ended in mass arrests.

In the first months the Israelis could count on one dependable ally in their war against the PLO: Jordan. Tahar Sa'adi, born in Jaffa in 1946, had fought with the Iraqi army during the Six Day War and fled across the river to Amman, joining Fatah just as it was starting its commando raids in the West Bank. As Sa'adi recalled later:

> My first operation was a reconnaissance job, to photograph the Ghor el-Safi potash plant south of the Dead Sea. On our way back, the Jordanian intelligence service caught us and beat us up. Then they turned their headlights on us, forcing us at gunpoint to cross the Jordan so that the Israelis would get us. That was on 15th November 1967. Jordan to me is no different from the United States.

Sa'adi and his companions were lucky twice. They managed to get across the river without being spotted by the Israeli patrols and got food from a peasant in Tubas, east of Nablus. They crossed back over the river two nights later and returned to base. Others were less fortunate. In those early days, the few commandos who did make it west across the Jordan found little local support.[39]

The natural barrier created by the river was reinforced by the IDF's fixed and mobile protective measures, which became more sophisticated as time went on. These included 'smudge paths' of ploughed earth in which footprints are easily visible, barbed-wire fences separated by minefields, booby traps and electronic surveillance devices. Irregular patrols along the whole front line – from south of the Sea of Galilee to north of the Dead Sea and then down the length of the Arava desert to Eilat – were supplemented by occasional ambushes on known fedayeen routes.

The infiltrators tried hard to breach the Israeli defences: the simplest and most imaginative approach involved wearing shoes the wrong way round so that tracks would appear to show people leaving rather than entering the area. One man would carry another on his back to mislead the Israelis as to the number of infiltrators; pepper was scattered on the ground to try to throw tracker dogs off the scent. If the army failed to catch the fedayeen within a few hours, the Shin Bet would start making inquiries in the villages in the hills above the Jordan Valley. Once the infiltrators had been captured and interrogated, the security service reported back to the IDF on how and where they had crossed the lines. Thus defences were constantly improved.[40]

Sources and methods

Starting in August and intensifying in September, a determined effort was made to recruit Arab agents who could provide information about the guerrillas. The problem was urgent and the solution was borrowed from the West German BND, which had once found itself without adequate intelligence coverage of the area on both sides of the Berlin Wall and had mounted a successful large-scale 'trawl' to recruit a mass of informers on a hit-or-miss basis. The theory was that if a sufficiently large number of people were approached, some, simply by the law of statistical averages, would be likely to turn out to be useful sources. The Israelis had their own experience: 'Suleiman', a Shin Bet man working on the Golan Heights, had run a similar operation along the Lebanese border before the 1967 war, and he was called to Jerusalem by Arbel to consider applying the model in the West Bank. 'Operation Flood', as the new recruiting drive was codenamed, worked simply. 'Suleiman' and a unit of soldiers spent two weeks scouring the edges of the Judaean desert, paying particular attention to places on known infiltration routes from the river Jordan. The Shin Bet officer would spot likely informers, question and photograph them, and then hand out one half of a Jordanian ten-dinar banknote, promising that the other, matching, half would be forthcoming if the recipient provided useful intelligence. If the agents delivered the goods, and seemed to have long-term potential, they would then be handed over for permanent contact with the regional security service representative. In early November 1967, in one of the first of several successes for 'Flood', a farmer from Shuyukh, near Hebron, reported on a seven-man fedayeen squad hiding in a cave. All seven were killed in an IDF assault hours after the farmer reported to 'Nur' in the Shin Bet office in Hebron, hopefully clutching his half of the ten-dinar banknote. He was given the missing half, and an additional ten dinars as a bonus.[41]

It was a period of excitement and improvisation on the Israeli side. Ya'akuba Cohen, a veteran Arabist who had begun his career as a Palmah Mist'Arev in the late 1940s and had later been sent on undercover missions to Egypt, rounded up a whole group of infiltrators by disguising himself as a Palestinian and pretending to be one of the members of a Fatah group. Yehuda Arbel led many operations and interrogations himself, speaking his few words of Arabic with a heavy Hungarian accent. Once, in 1968, he overcame the language barrier when questioning a group of Palestine Liberation Army (PLA) guerrillas who had learned German while being trained in East Germany.[42] Arbel was greatly helped by his deputy and eventual successor, a stolid and experienced Arabist who had spent years in the Shin Bet's northern region.

From the outset, the security service proved that it was adept at dealing with terrorism of the classic mould. An important Fatah cell operating in the Jerusalem area was rounded up quickly after an explosion at the Fast Hotel in September and an abortive bomb attempt at the crowded Zion Square cinema on 8 October. No one was injured, but the cinema attack set a dangerous and very worrying precedent: this was the first time that the Palestinians had tried to attack a purely civilian target; had they been successful, large numbers of people could have been hurt. The cell's commander, Omar Audah Khalil, or 'Dr Nur', as he was known in the underground, was a Palestinian refugee from Lebanon. He had recruited about thirty people, including Jerusalem residents and saboteurs who had been trained in Syria and had crossed the Jordan when operations began. Many were members of Jerusalem's African community, descendants of Muslim pilgrims who had settled in the Old City. So when two young black women were arrested immediately after the cinema bomb attempt, the Israelis had an obvious lead. It was fairly amateurish stuff: the first suspects gave everything away, providing the Shin Bet with the names of their comrades and their whereabouts, and precise information about their training in Syria, their infiltration routes and the organization of other cells in the West Bank. Within forty-eight hours the whole cell had been rounded up and the Shin Bet had uncovered arms, explosives and vehicles.[43]

But the security service was less obviously successful when it came to the sort of broad-based popular resistance that was to plague the Israelis, with differing degrees of seriousness, for years to come. In September 1967 it was decided to deport Sheikh Abdel Hamid al-Sayih, leader of the newly formed National Guidance Committee and head of the Supreme Muslim Council. It was a sign of the times. Organizations like the Union of Palestinian Pupils and the General Union of Arab Women were difficult to deal with. Only when political opposition merged with actual sabotage was it possible to round people up. Political activists were logged and watched, so suspects could be quickly arrested and questioned after any attack. Sayih, like many prominent deportees in the early years of the occupation, went on to occupy an important position in the PLO abroad. The Shin Bet saw speedy deportation as its most useful weapon: when a stage of appeal – to a military review board and then to the High Court of Justice – was introduced in later years, it lost much of its effectiveness. At that early stage Israel still hoped that Palestinian leaders in the occupied territories would serve as a moderating influence on the all-Arab position. A routine Shin Bet report circulated to ministers in December 1967 noted that messages being sent to Arab countries from prominent people in Nablus were urging the adoption of a more realistic attitude towards Israel.[44]

By the end of the first year of occupation the West Bank was relatively quiet, but there was more always to be done. The Shin Bet estimated that there were still between 100 and 200 Palestinian activists hiding in the warren of houses built round the narrow alleyways of the old Casbah in Nablus. Harmelin and Arbel pressed for action. But Dayan was unhappy. 'If the security service and the military government were incapable of searching a few houses in the Casbah and arresting the suspects, and only the suspects, he preferred the saboteurs not to be caught at all, rather than disturb the peace and punish a whole community by curfew and search,' one official commented at the time. The Shin Bet feared that if the nucleus of fedayeen was not broken up, they would be able to train and organize uninterruptedly and begin operating when the weather improved. Shlomo Gazit came under mounting pressure from the security service to persuade Dayan to approve the Nablus operation, codenamed 'Ring'. The defence minister gave the go-ahead only after a Palestinian was assassinated for collaborating with Israel. On 13 February 1968 the Casbah was surrounded; thousands of men were placed in compounds and paraded *en masse* in front of masked informers provided by the Shin Bet. Two arms caches were found and seventy-four people identified as belonging to guerrilla organizations.[45]

Dayan could be impatient with the security service and the way its *modus operandi* developed to suit – or rather bypass – a legal system which was often unwilling to convict simply on the basis of informers' reports or confessions which might have been obtained in dubious circumstances or unacceptable ways. At one staff meeting he asked about the practice of placing

Palestinians in administrative detention when they could be charged, brought to court and properly sentenced. He complained to Avraham Ahituv:

> Someone confessed he was a member of a group that threw a grenade. So why isn't he brought to trial? Or there's another case of someone who was tried and acquitted, and was then put in administrative detention by the Shin Bet. I don't think that's right. It makes a mockery of the judicial system. A large proportion of the cases you've shown me confessed, so why aren't they tried? It says: 'The interrogators formed a bad impression of him.' I'm sure that anyone who interrogated me could form either a good or a bad impression, but, between us, every interrogator will form a good impression of someone who kisses his boots and a bad one of someone who says that this is his homeland.

Ahituv protested: 'We may sometimes make mistakes when we carry out arrests,' he said, 'but not very often.'[46] Dayan's reticence usually gave way when he was shown the classified evidence – too sensitive for the courts – against administrative detainees. The Shin Bet took a hard line on other matters too, criticizing the chief IDF censor for adopting too liberal an approach to the Arabic press in East Jerusalem.[47]

Karameh and after

The focus of the action shifted in the first months of 1968. The Palestinian guerrillas had been pushed back across the Jordan after suffering heavy casualties and maintained their pressure on Israel from bases in Jordan, Syria and Lebanon. Repeated attempts were made to cross the river and move back into the hills of the West Bank, but most groups were discovered soon after crossing and were either killed or taken prisoner. Israel responded to attacks with reprisal raids – from the ground and air – on Jordanian army positions and border areas, a strategy which had the desired effect of increasing strains between King Hussein and the Palestinians. Early in March both Arafat's own agents in the occupied territories and Jordanian army intelligence began to receive reports that the Israelis were preparing a big military operation.[48]

The incident that provided the immediate trigger for the large-scale Israeli raid on the Fatah base at Karameh, on 21 March 1968, occurred when a schoolbus ran over a mine in the Arava desert, killing two adults and wounding several children. The IDF attack, the largest since the war, was designed, in part, to discourage the new and increasingly dangerous Jordanian support for Palestinian popular resistance, which until February had been banned by King Hussein and his ministers. Yitzhak Rabin's successor as IDF chief of staff, Chaim Barlev, said the goal of the operation was 'to help Hussein screw Fatah'.[49] Karameh was a turning-point in more ways than one.

A three-pronged assault, with 15,000 men, tanks, artillery and aircraft in close support, was mounted against the guerrilla base. Israel lost twenty-eight men and the Palestinians 150, with 130 captured. Intelligence played a vital role in planning for the operation. A Shin Bet officer and a captured guerrilla who had trained at Karameh accompanied each one of the three columns.[50]

A flood of volunteers queued up to join Fatah. According to Abu Iyad:

> After Karameh the Israelis dumped hundreds of agents and spies on us – Palestinians they recruited on the West Bank and in Gaza mainly by intimidation and blackmail ... Undoubtedly some of the agents and spies who were among us did give vital information which enabled Israel's air force to make very accurate attacks on our bases. But we also came to know that many of our people were being forced to act as traitors.[51]

The true scale of Israeli penetration of Fatah and other fedayeen organizations will never be known, but its main purpose was clearly short-range: to eliminate networks before they could carry out their operational plans. The Israelis were facing what they perceived to be an immediate, not a long-term problem. They were interested in getting information, not creating moles, especially when Fatah was so naturally suspicious of new recruits arriving from the West Bank.

As early as September 1967 a captured infiltrator said at his trial that there were already thirty-seven Palestinians, charged with spying for Israel, imprisoned in Fatah's main training base in Syria.[52] 'A special effort was made to plant informers in terrorist bases in Jordan and to infiltrate them into networks operating inside Israeli-administered territories,' one Israeli expert wrote later.[53]

Agents and double agents

The Palestinians themselves believed that penetration was extensive and they continued, over the years, to worry about it. Abu Iyad said of the agents:

> They came and told us that they had been taken to such and such a place and taught how to use invisible inks for preparing their secret messages. But as a result of Israel's game we also had our opportunity. We told some of our people to continue to spy for the Israelis, but only to give the information we prepared, so we created many double agents. In this way we were able to feed the Israelis wrong information and some of the information we received back from our double agents helped us to anticipate Israel's moves.[54]

Injured pride may well play a role in such Palestinian claims. Israeli sources insist that Abu Iyad's 'double agents' were a figment of his imagination, or at the very least their numbers were vastly exaggerated. Feeding false information to the Shin Bet about Palestinian plans was one thing, but there were no known PLO penetrations of Israel's own security service.

The Shin Bet was certainly quick to exploit Palestinian suspicions. A common technique, and one which had been used to great effect by the French in Algeria, was to 'casually' name a 'collaborator' in front of a prisoner and then to release or deport him. In many cases, the freed Palestinian would denounce his colleagues as traitors, fuelling the already intense fear of Israeli penetration and creating internal purges by 'remote control'.[55]

According to one senior officer:

Our great achievement was creating a distinct barrier between the population at large and the terror organizations. People knew that anyone who helped the terrorists would have his house blown up, be deported or arrested. We also showed them that captured terrorists were the first to inform. We created the impression that those who were supposed to be liberating the people were the most likely to betray those who helped them. This was a deliberate decision. We'd go to a village, impose a curfew and put all the men in the square and then file them past one of our prisoners – a captured terrorist – sitting in a car with a hood over his head. Now whether or not the prisoner actually identified any suspects, we'd pretend that he had done. The cumulative effect of all this was that when terrorists came to a village the locals would say: 'Get out of here. We know that you'll inform on us.' We even tested this once by sending a group of soldiers, dressed as terrorists, into a village to ask for help. And they got exactly that answer.[56]

One serious gap in Palestinian security helped the Shin Bet immeasurably. Until the end of the decade most of the PLO factions – especially Fatah – conducted large-scale training courses at their camps in Jordan and Syria. One big group of fedayeen recruits was kitted out with the same distinctive canvas, crepe-soled boots and foolishly continued to wear them once they had crossed into the West Bank.

In this situation the sheer numbers made the Israelis' work much easier: one captured guerrilla could do immense damage. The Shin Bet would take a captive, dress him up in IDF uniform and dark glasses and tour the West Bank from north to south as the prisoner pointed out faces he had seen in the camp on the other side of the river. When the security service officers felt the Palestinian had exhausted his usefulness he would simply be returned to prison. On the chain-letter principle, one name could lead quickly to many others. The Shin Bet always took elaborate care to disguise the identity of its informers: this in turn increased Palestinian suspicions of Israeli penetration.

Another well-tried method was to mount a search for someone who was known not to be in a certain village, obviously failing to find him and thus lulling the true suspect – who could be observed quietly – into a sense of false security. He would then stay put and could be detained later.

One of the service's most effective informers in that crucial autumn and winter of 1967 was a PLA man called Abu Sab'a. The guerrilla had entered the West Bank soon after the end of the war, was captured trying to return to Jordan and proved to be highly cooperative under interrogation by 'Haroun', the Shin Bet man responsible for the Jericho area. Abu Sab'a was freed – inadvertently, according to an Israeli source – and managed to flee to the East Bank. In the PLA camp he was arrested on suspicion of being an Israeli spy, but was eventually allowed to return to the occupied territories on condition that he kill 'Haroun'. Abu Sab'a gave himself up on 1 September and immediately led the Shin Bet to a cave near Tubas where twelve other heavily armed infiltrators were hiding. As a reward for this and other services rendered, the Palestinian double agent was 'inducted' into the Shin Bet in a mock ceremony held in a Jerusalem safe house. Yehuda Arbel presided, solemnly swearing Abu Sab'a on a Koran and promising a regular salary in addition to the handsome bonuses he had already received.[57]

As time went on, the PLO learned its lesson and training was conducted on a much smaller scale, reducing the danger of any leak. The more sophisticated the Palestinians became, the more they tightened up operational security by decreasing the size of training groups and infiltrations. By the early 1970s much of it was carried out on an individual basis. It became standard procedure to keep fedayeen squads in isolation until an operation began.[58]

Fatah was so concerned by the penetration phenomenon that at the end of 1967 it set up a special counter-intelligence unit called Jihaz al-Rasd (literally, Surveillance Apparatus), designed to foil espionage, eliminate enemy agents and 'turn' some of them back on the Israelis. Its first head, Faruq Qaddumi, was replaced by Abu Iyad, who later asked a young man called Ali

Hassan Salameh to take charge.[59] The nucleus of the group was reinforced later by ten Fatah members, including Abu Daoud, who took part in a six-week intelligence course in Cairo starting in August 1968.[60] But there was still no coordination between the different guerrilla groups: if Fatah observed that the Shin Bet and the IDF had adopted some new counter-measure, the information was rarely passed on to the Popular Front for the Liberation of Palestine, or vice versa. The Israelis were able to build quickly and constantly on experience. The fedayeen were much slower. It was an unequal struggle.

Palestinian sources claimed that Israeli penetration of their ranks was deliberately designed to help create the confrontation with King Hussein. This remains a moot point, but there is no doubt that the mounting tension between the guerrillas and the Jordanians was a welcome development for Israel. Violent clashes between the fedayeen and the Jordanian army began in November 1968, when twenty-eight Palestinians and four Jordanians were killed.[61]

Less than two years later, in the autumn of 1970, the Palestinians suffered a grievous blow when King Hussein, infuriated by the creation of an increasingly cocky and independent PLO state within his own kingdom, turned his army on the Palestinians, slaughtering thousands of them in what became known as Black September. The trigger for that confrontation was provided by Dr George Habash's PFLP, which brought three hijacked international airliners to a desert airstrip called Dawson's Field.

Israel followed that hijacking very closely. Dayan ordered the Shin Bet to ensure that the planners of the PFLP operation learned quickly that hundreds of their relatives who lived in the occupied territories were, in effect, being held hostage; scores of these relatives were ordered to cross the bridge to Jordan, which was opened specially on a Saturday for this purpose, to make the position clear. The passengers on the three planes were released unharmed. The aircraft were blown up.[62]

Scores of fedayeen fled from the East Bank during the second and final confrontation with King Hussein in July 1971.

Seventy-two surrendered to the Israelis in four days rather than continue the bloody confrontation with the Jordanian army.[63] Some of these guerrillas, grateful for their lives, were 'turned', at considerable risk, and used to make contact with other groups, which were then rounded up by the Israelis. Members of at least one Fatah cell were promised large amounts of money and tickets to South America if they agreed to operate as a 'tracer' to existing guerrilla units hiding in the West Bank.[64] The fedayeen were allowed to keep their weapons, uniforms and equipment, and the food and supplies they had brought with them across the river, and were followed by the Shin Bet and the army. Several successes followed: a big arms cache was found in Nablus on 25 July and the Israelis announced they had exposed the Fatah network responsible for bomb blasts in Haifa and Tel Aviv between July 1969 and September 1970. On 30 September 1971, in one of the biggest, longest and most complex operations of its kind, ninety Fatah suspects were detained in the Hebron area. Typically, that round-up began with the arrest of just two fedayeen and quickly snowballed. In the course of the investigation the Israelis stumbled across a plan, then in its final operational stages, to set off a car bomb in Jerusalem.

The Shin Bet's successes in the early years of the occupation proved that hard work, cunning and luck, combined with the weakness of the enemy, were a powerful recipe for success. Formally, the service was not supposed to run agents outside the West Bank or Gaza Strip, but its assets in the occupied territories were exploited to the full to bring back short-term tactical intelligence on PLO operations. Technically, running agents abroad was still the responsibility of Aman (against military targets) and the Mossad (political and military), although for both agencies the Palestinian organizations were still a very low-priority target.

IDF intelligence was extremely unhappy when the security service proposed changing these arrangements, as it made clear in the course of long and weary bureaucratic discussions. Inter-agency liaison had sometimes been difficult in the first years of the occupation, but after the 1973 war, with the entire intelligence community in disarray, the scope for reform was never satisfactorily exploited. Precise divisions of responsibility for running agents and intelligence-gathering against Palestinian targets were drawn up in 1974 by the new Aman chief, Shlomo Gazit. Political intelligence on the PLO remained a weak point.[65]

Ruthless in Gaza

To the south-west, in the Gaza Strip, Israel's struggle against the fedayeen reached a climax in the second half of 1971. 'Gaza,' wrote a foreign journalist that August, 'is the only place where the Palestine resistance, at a terrible cost and with suicidal tenacity, is worthy of the name.'[66] Conditions were radically different from the West Bank. The area, 8 kilometres wide by 48 kilometres long, was far smaller, but the population of 350,000 – nearly half of whom were refugees – was much more densely concentrated, living in appalling physical conditions that had barely changed since the great exodus of 1948. In the summer the stench of open sewage in the narrow alleyways of the refugee camps was unbearable. In the winter, the unpaved streets turned to impassable torrents of mud. Gazans had much less to lose than the West Bankers, of whom only about 10 per cent lived in refugee camps.

Under Jordanian rule serious attempts had been made to integrate the West Bank into the Hashemite kingdom, beyond Abdullah's formal act of annexation in 1950. Palestinians received Jordanian citizenship. The Egyptians, by contrast, had always fostered the Palestinian identity of Gaza. The PLO's third congress was held there in 1966 and the Palestine Liberation Army had been popular before 1967. Long after the war hundreds of weapons, mostly Karl Gustav and Kalashnikov rifles, were still circulating or hidden in secret caches. Many guns and grenades were smuggled into the Gaza Strip and sold by Bedouin who found them in abandoned Egyptian positions in Sinai. Explosives were obtained hazardously by dismantling old minefields – they fetched a handsome price. The Bedouin had a strongly developed sense of commerce but not of political loyalty: in the year that the Israeli military governor of Northern Sinai offered to pay IL10 for every grenade, 15,000 were turned in. Similar sums were promised for machine-guns, rifles, etc.[67]

In late 1968 and early 1969 Fatah and the PFLP had both managed to build up their strength, especially in the refugee camps, and the two groups often displayed bitter rivalry. The Shin Bet had operated in the strip under Avraham Ahituv after its capture in the Sinai campaign until the Israeli withdrawal in 1957. A decade later, under radically different conditions, it was again to shoulder the intelligence burden for internal security and counter-terrorism.

The Shin Bet had a lot of solid information, mostly emanating from a large network of paid informers, but was hard put to use it properly. In accordance with his policy of minimum interference in daily life, Dayan had ordered the army out of the refugee camps early in 1970, despite vigorous protests from Ahituv.[68]

One senior colleague complained:

> The result was that we effectively abandoned the camps to the sole control of the terrorist organizations and the criminal underworld at the same time. We had good intelligence, but when we told the army that there was a Fatah squad, for example, in Block C in Jabaliya, the force would leave the centre of town and by the time they got there the terrorists had been warned and had left. People would call out '*biy'u, biy'u*' [sell, sell] to show that the soldiers were coming. They were like moles. So not only did we not manage to catch the terrorists, but this also caused a lack of confidence in the Shin Bet intelligence.[69]

Curfews remained in force for long periods and in 1970 there were regular incidents of grenade-throwing and sniping at Israeli patrols, although the fighting across the Suez Canal and the civil war in Jordan tended to overshadow these events. In the course of 1970 106 Gazans were killed, ninety-four in internecine struggles, with bodies being dumped with monotonous regularity in 'Al-Jura', the putrid 'lake' in the centre of Jabaliya, the biggest camp in the Gaza Strip. Twelve Palestinians were killed by the IDF. At the end of the year, two Israeli children – the Aroyos – were killed and their mother badly injured when a grenade was thrown at their car. Dayan and Barlev decided that Gaza had to be pacified. The job was the responsibility of General Ariel ('Arik') Sharon, the bullish head of southern command, who greatly improved operational co-operation with the security service.

Working closely with the Shin Bet, the army divided the Gaza Strip into squares, which were given codenames. An elite commando unit was ordered to comb the area, square by square, until no terrorists were left. Sharon ordered that the lower branches of trees in all orchards were to be cut off, to improve the soldiers' field of vision and fire and eliminate cover. Caves and bunkers were sealed off. 'Sharon achieved his goals by working systematically and relentlessly,' his biographer has written. 'He seemed always to be there when problems arose, providing solutions, encouraging soldiers and demanding results.'[70]

Rumours circulated about the general roaming the area with a list of wanted men in his hand, crossing off the names as they were eliminated. Army units were indeed issued with regularly updated Shin Bet lists with the names – and when they were available, the photographs – of fugitive fedayeen. Ordinary 'Wanted' names were printed in black; 'Wanted and Dangerous' in red. Adult males were randomly stopped and searched; curfews were imposed on the refugee camps. In January 1971 units of Druse border policemen were brought in, and in the third week of the month alone they shot and killed five Palestinians who had failed to halt for routine searches. Allegations of brutality multiplied, as did the summary 'executions' – sometimes in broad daylight – of Palestinians suspected of collaborating with the Shin Bet and the army. But very few of the security service's real informers were targeted.[71]

The ceasefire on the Suez Canal, which had come into effect in

August 1970, had taken hold, and this allowed more regular army units to be brought into Gaza as well. Under Sharon's rule the families of wanted men were rounded up and sent to the remote Abu Zneima detention centre, on the coast of Sinai. Houses were demolished in camps like Shati and Jabaliya to widen roads and create fields of fire. 'The main thing was the shock of the demolition of a huge number of houses plus the transfer of their residents,' Gazit said later. 'That showed that the bloody Jews meant business.'[72]

As one foreign expert wrote shortly afterwards:

> The Israelis calculated that there were about 100 men on their 'wanted list' at any one time and perhaps another 100 fedayeen operating underground in the Gaza Strip who they did not know much about. Captured guerrillas seemed to talk readily, informing on their colleagues (who in turn were arrested) and excusing their betrayal by alleging that they were tortured.[73]

Ziyad Husseini, a colonel in the PLA and the acknowledged leader of the Gaza resistance, committed suicide rather than give himself up in November 1971, after hiding out in the cellar of the home of Gaza's mayor, Rashad ash-Shawwa. The local PFLP commander, known to the Israelis as 'Che Guevara' (Guevara, the Argentinian-born revolutionary killed in Bolivia in October 1967, was already a cult figure), eluded capture for a long time. Between July and December 1971 742 'terrorists' were killed or captured, often in brutal close-range firefights in hidden bunkers. In July 1971, when Sharon assumed direct control and a new Shin Bet commander took over, thirty-four terrorist incidents were recorded; in December that year there was only one. 'Before Sharon took over every officer would argue with us about how to conduct operations,' said one senior Shin Bet man, 'but the army command gradually began to understand how good the service was. Arik saw that we produced results and this improved things too.'[74] In February 1972 five senior fedayeen commanders were killed in a firefight with the army and twenty others surrendered. In March, for the first time since Gaza was conquered in 1967, no terrorist incidents were recorded.

Mossad

The spark for the Jordan–PLO crisis of 1970–71 had its origins in the gradual shift towards international operations that had been taking place in Palestinian, especially PFLP, strategy from 1968. While the Shin Bet looked after internal security inside the occupied territories, the Mossad remained responsible, as before the war, for all Israeli intelligence activities abroad. Meir Amit, who had done so much to develop the agency's interest in the military capabilities and intentions of the regular Arab armies, decided, sensibly enough under the new circumstances, to devote additional resources to the Palestinian organizations and particularly to improving security liaison with friendly foreign services. Yet it was not until after Black September that the Mossad began to closely and permanently monitor the PLO.

Reliable intelligence reports of Palestinian plans to carry their struggle abroad had reached Israel in the summer of 1968.[75] But the first hijack of an El Al plane, on a scheduled flight from Rome to Tel Aviv on 22 July, was still an unpleasant surprise. Three armed men, who were later identified as members of the newly formed PFLP, ordered the captain of the plane, a Boeing 707, to Algiers, 'to remind the world' that many Palestinians were suffering in Israeli gaols. The plane was carrying thirty-eight passengers and ten crew. The foreigners and all women and children were freed after five days; the remaining twelve Israeli men were held for thirty-nine days, and eventually released in exchange for fifteen Palestinians held in Israeli gaols.[76] It was a bitter humiliation for the Israelis and, worse, established what could have been a dangerous precedent. The Rome hijack began a new, intense and innovative period in Israel's protective security doctrine. At home the Jordan river frontier had been successfully sealed off and the fedayeen threat contained to a tolerable level. Now defensive measures had to be applied to air and sea routes to Israel and to its installations abroad. The responsibility fell to the Shin Bet's Protective Security Branch. The first steps were taken immediately, within a day or two of the Rome hijack. Armed guards were posted on all El Al planes and protective equipment installed. The cost was enormous.[77]

It was a huge and daunting task and there was no shortage of reminders of how urgent it was. Routine intelligence-gathering and the penetration of Palestinian organizations were only part of the story. However perfect the system, however extensive the cooperation of foreign intelligence and security services, the last barrier to the determined terrorist still had to be a formidable one.

The next landmark was 26 December 1968. Two PFLP gunmen opened fire on an El Al plane on the ground at Athens airport, killing an Israeli engineer. The Palestinians, who were captured by the Greeks, had arrived from, and been trained in, Lebanon. Israel's response was *ad hoc*, but no less powerful as a result. Levi Eshkol, the prime minister, called in his top military and security people for a crisis meeting the same day: Dayan, Barlev, Harmelin and Zvi Zamir – shortly to succeed Meir Amit as head of the Mossad – decided to attack Beirut airport and destroy civilian airliners on the ground. The plan had called for destroying three to four Arab-owned planes. In the end, to Eshkol's intense annoyance, fourteen aircraft were blown up, apparently because Dayan feared that anything else might be interpreted as Israeli weakness. Yet the furious international reaction to the Beirut raid shocked Jerusalem; henceforth retaliation for PLO attacks took the form of artillery barrages, air raids and ground assaults against Palestinian targets in border areas of their host countries, mostly Jordan and Lebanon. What Golda Meir (who became prime minister in March 1969 when Eshkol died) called the government's policy of 'active self-defence' meant that these attacks were carried out without reference to the timing, nature or location of specific terrorist incidents.[78]

Active self-defence

Karameh was the biggest of the Israeli raids on Palestinian targets in neighbouring Arab countries but not the only one.

From the end of 1969, when the Cairo agreement gave the PLO freedom of action in Lebanon (although ostensibly 'without compromising the overall sovereignty of Lebanon'),[79] raids against south Lebanon, especially the rugged border area that was known as 'Fatahland', became frequent. In April and May 1970 sixty-one attacks were launched from Fatahland against Israeli targets, including twenty-two settlements. The IDF used ambushes, artillery barrages and air raids in accordance with intelligence reports about PLO dispositions, but these were found to be generally ineffective. On 12 May 1970 an operation codenamed Kalahat-2 was launched against five villages in Fatahland, using tanks and APCs in difficult terrain. The intelligence component in the actual assault was significant. No fewer than forty-six trained POW interrogators were attached to the raiding battalion to question captives and examine PLO documents.[80] Lebanon became an even more frequent target for Israeli punitive raids after the final expulsion of the PLO from Jordan. A large operation was mounted in Fatahland at the end of February 1972 and a year later a long-range raid was launched against guerrilla bases in the Tripoli area. In general, though, this purely military activity had little obvious deterrent effect on Palestinian operations, although it boosted Israeli morale and created the impression of a concerted effort against terrorism. The civilian casualties suffered by the Palestinians – especially in IAF air raids – appeared to simply strengthen the resolve of the PLO to continue the struggle.

The war of the spooks

In 1969 Palestinian attacks on Israeli targets abroad were still only a tiny proportion of all those carried out inside the country and in the occupied territories.[81] On 18 February one of El Al's new skymarshals shot and killed a PFLP man who had opened fire on a passenger plane, wounding the pilot and co-pilot, on the tarmac at Zurich airport. The guard, Mordechai Rahamim, who was later acquitted by a Swiss court, became a hero in

Israel and a symbol of a new readiness to fight Palestinian terrorism abroad.

In May three Arabs and a Swede were arrested in Copenhagen on charges of a plot to murder David Ben-Gurion, the former Israeli prime minister, but they were released for lack of evidence. One of those arrested claimed later that the group had been framed by Israeli intelligence.[82]

In August 1969 the PFLP hijacked a TWA Boeing to Damascus and two Israelis on board were held for six weeks by the embarrassed Syrians, who, despite their support for the Palestinians, did not wish to be seen to be publicly supporting air piracy. Two captured Syrian pilots were quietly released later.[83] In September the Habash organization claimed responsibility for throwing grenades at the Israeli embassies in The Hague and Bonn, and at the El Al office in Brussels. In November members of the Popular Struggle Front, which had close links with Egyptian intelligence, threw a grenade at the El Al office in Athens.

By the turn of the decade the bulk of Israel's intelligence effort against the Palestinians was shifting abroad. In 1971 foreign operations accounted for just over 3 per cent of all PLO military activities. The following year the proportion went up to 12 per cent, reaching an all-time high at 30 per cent in 1973.[84] Over this period Western Europe came to supersede the Middle East as the main battleground in what rapidly became known as the 'war of the spooks' between the two sides.

Baruch Cohen, a native Arabic speaker from an old Jewish family in Haifa, was one of the Mossad's senior officers in this field. He had joined the Shin Bet in 1959, after being rejected by the police because he was under the requisite height. He had worked in the northern area, in the Arab villages of Galilee, and joined the service's investigations branch in 1966. After the 1967 war he served with the security service in Nablus – the largest city in the West Bank – until being posted to the Gaza Strip in 1969. In 1970 he was loaned to the Mossad and sent, under diplomatic cover, to the Israeli Embassy in Brussels, using the name Moshe Hanan Yishai.

Cohen's job was to keep tabs on Palestinian activities in Europe. His work took him all over the Continent, travelling from city to city to meet his contacts and informers. It was little different from the job he had done in the West Bank and Gaza, except that it was more exposed, more clandestine and more dangerous, especially since he must have been known, by sight if not by name and task, to the many Palestinians he had encountered in the occupied territories. He and a colleague, Zadok Ophir, who was shot and wounded by a Moroccan double agent who had lured him to a Brussels café in September 1972, had both been pictured in a coffee-table album of photographs published by the army in 1970 to mark 1,000 days since the Six Day War. Later, after Cohen's assassination, there were some who asked how such a grave breach of operational security could have been permitted.[85] The Arabic-speaking Ophir, like Cohen, gathered information about Palestinian activities. His attacker, a Moroccan called Muhammad Rabah, had written to the Israeli Embassy in Brussels – and other Israeli missions in Europe – while serving a sentence in a Belgian prison. Rabah offered information about Fatah and managed to escape after the assassination attempt.[86]

Black September

Baruch Cohen set up a network of Palestinian students, mostly from the occupied territories, who were used for information-gathering and penetration of fedayeen ranks.[87] By late 1971 the Israelis were starting to hear details about a shadowy new organization inside Fatah: Black September. Its targets were mostly chosen to avenge King Hussein's slaughter of the Palestinians. It made its first public appearance in Cairo on 28 November, when the Jordanian prime minister, Wasfi al-Tel, was assassinated on the steps of the Sheraton Hotel as he was about to attend a meeting of the Arab League. 'One result,' according to one very well-informed Israeli writer, 'was Jordan's willingness to cooperate with Israeli security in pursuing Palestinian terror squads and liquidating their commanders at various locations outside the Middle East.'[88] The following month an attempt was made on the life of Zeid al-Rifa'i, the Jordanian ambassador to London. In February 1972 five Jordanian Mukhabarat agents were found murdered in a cellar in Bonn. Black September sabotage attacks followed on oil refineries and industrial installations in Holland and Italy. Intelligence estimates showed that the organization comprised about 100 Palestinians and some fifteen Europeans.[89]

According to Arafat's British biographer, Alan Hart, the Mossad managed to penetrate Black September shortly after Wasfi al-Tel's killing. Abu Iyad claimed that the Israelis got their men into the organization by threatening Palestinians in Europe, especially in West Germany, that they would not have their work permits renewed unless they agreed to cooperate. Others were warned that their families in the occupied territories would suffer. 'When the Mossad agents made their approaches they usually had photographs and sometimes film of the subject's family,' the Fatah leader said. 'And from the information the Mossad agents revealed, it was clear that they knew everything there was to know about the families – names, habits, problems, weak points and so on.'[90]

Non-Arabs may also have been used by the Israelis to penetrate the Palestinian organizations. At least one, a Frenchman called Roger Coudroy, was accepted by Fatah after careful security screening in 1968. But a few weeks afterwards he was reported shot and killed in a 'training accident'. It was rumoured at the time that he had been exposed as a Mossad agent and executed. In 1969 and 1970 several hundred young European sympathizers were hosted at PLO camps in Jordan, although few received actual guerrilla training. The handful who did were mainly connected with the PFLP. In April 1971 four French nationals were arrested at Lod airport carrying explosives and detonators.[91]

The Middle East itself was not neglected in the intelligence effort against the PLO. Baruch Mizrahi, an Egyptian-born Israeli who had worked undercover before 1967 as a teacher in

Aleppo, Syria,[92] was sent to North Yemen in the early 1970s to monitor Palestinian activities there. In June 1971 a PFLP unit operating out of the Yemeni Red Sea port of Hodeida had fired rockets at an oil tanker heading northwards to Eilat. Mizrahi, masquerading as a Moroccan businessman, was captured in May 1972 while taking photographs in Hodeida. He was handed over to Egyptian intelligence and imprisoned for some time, before being released in a spy and POW exchange in 1974.[93]

The Israeli–Palestinian war escalated in 1972. In early May a Sabena airliner on a flight from Brussels to Tel Aviv was hijacked and landed at Lod airport. The hijackers demanded the release of 317 Palestinians imprisoned in Israel. Troops disguised as aircraft mechanics stormed the plane on the tarmac, killing two of the four hijackers and one passenger in an improvisation on a preplanned rescue operation codenamed 'Isotope' that had been drawn up by IDF Operations Branch.[94] Responsibility for the hijack was claimed by Black September. The commander, Ali Abu Sneineh, was the PFLP man who had led the first hijack of the El Al Boeing to Algiers in July 1968 and of a Lufthansa plane to Aden in February 1972. The two captured hijackers, Palestinian women from Bethlehem and Acre, revealed under interrogation that they had been sent on their mission by the Black September operations chief in Europe, a young man who used the codename Abu Hassan. His real name was Ali Hassan Salameh.

Worse was to come. At the end of May three members of the Japanese Red Army, who had been recruited by the PFLP, killed twenty-six people, mostly Puerto Rican nuns, and wounded seventy-six others in an indiscriminate massacre in the arrivals terminal at Lod airport. Two of the terrorists committed suicide. A third, Kozo Okamoto, was captured, tried and imprisoned.

Munich massacre

In September 1972 eleven Israeli athletes participating in the Munich Olympics were taken hostage in the Olympic Village by eight Black September men, who had been planning the operation – code-named 'Ikrit and Biram' (for two razed villages in northern Galilee) – since a meeting in Beirut in January. Two of the athletes were killed in the initial break-in to their quarters in Conollystrasse. The prime minister, Golda Meir, rejected the terrorists' demand for the release of 234 Palestinians held in Israeli gaols. 'If we should give in, then no Israeli anywhere in the world can feel that his life is safe,' she said. The German authorities refused to cancel the Olympics. Throughout the nerve-racking day of 5 September the Black Septembrists received what appeared to be coded messages from the Voice of the Palestine Revolution, broadcasting from Damascus. An Israeli anti-terrorist unit was put on standby, but time was short and the Germans refused to allow the unit to operate on their soil. The Mossad chief, Zvi Zamir, arrived on the scene at the last minute, but he was not well received; the head of the Munich police department refused to take him in his car to the military airfield at Fürstenfeldbruck, from where the terrorists were expecting to fly to freedom with their hostages.

Zamir was accompanied by an Arabic-speaking Shin Bet man, whose role in the disaster – he spoke briefly to the Black Septembrists – was seen later by the security service (which was sometimes resentful of the Mossad's more heroic public image) as underlining its own much greater experience in dealing with Palestinian terrorism.

Zamir and his aide watched helplessly from the control tower as the German authorities botched the rescue operation. 'There were huge gaps between our assessment of the Germans' ability and their planning and implementation,' the Mossad chief said later, in his first-ever public appearance. All nine of the remaining Israeli athletes were killed. Two of the terrorists were captured alive but were freed later.

Meir was bitter: 'I think that there is not one single terrorist held in prison anywhere in the world,' she said. 'Everyone else gives in. We're the only ones who do not.'[95] Munich was a deeply traumatic event: apart from the fact that the German setting of the massacre evoked painful memories, there had clearly been an Israeli security lapse of massive proportions because of the failure to anticipate the potential threat sufficiently. Repeated calls for retaliation were met by official silence, although the families of the dead athletes were told privately that their loved ones would be avenged. The massacre was only the most dramatic of a series of failures in the war against terrorism. Zadok Ophir had been attacked in Brussels on 12 September and a week later the agricultural attaché at the Israeli Embassy in London was killed by a letter bomb. Even before Munich the newspapers were full of angry articles demanding counteraction. In June Eliahu Ben-Elissar, himself a former Mossad operative, noted in *Ha'Aretz* that there were precedents for taking unorthodox initiatives against enemy violence: he recalled reports about the killing of fedayeen controllers in the 1950s and the campaign against the German scientists a decade later.[96] After the Olympics killings there was outrage. Amihai Paglin, the former operations chief of the Irgun, was arrested at the end of September after trying to smuggle weapons and explosives abroad for use in revenge attacks against Arabs.[97] The government simply seemed impotent. Abba Eban, the foreign minister, said that Israeli retaliation would be restricted to the Middle East. 'How does the foreign minister think we can fight terrorist operations in Europe by responding in the Middle East?' asked one furious pundit.[98]

In early October, following a secret inquiry into the security lapses in the Munich Olympic Village led by Pinhas Koppel, a former Shin Bet officer and commissioner of police, three senior security service executives were dismissed. Yosef Harmelin threatened to resign, but was persuaded by Meir that the sackings would help restore public confidence in the Shin Bet. Harmelin stayed on and appointed Avraham Shalom, a former Palmah man and Operations Branch officer who had been the number-two agent in the Eichmann kidnap, as the new head of the Shin Bet's Protective Security Branch.[99]

As the Koppel Commission reached its conclusions, the Shin Bet was angered by the evidence submitted by Zvi Zamir. The Mossad chief told the inquiry that his organization had received intelligence about a PLO unit flying from the Middle East to somewhere in Europe; but the report was vague almost to the point of uselessness, the security service argued, and could not have seriously been expected to change the degree of alertness already surrounding the Israeli Olympic team.[100]

Vengeance

The Munich massacre marked a turning-point in Israel's war against Palestinian terrorism. Golda Meir decided that the time had come for wholesale vengeance, not just for its own sake but as a deterrent. After consulting with Aharon Yariv, who had left the army and been appointed her special adviser on terrorism, and Zamir, who was under something of a cloud because of the repeated setbacks, she authorized the Mossad to assassinate the leaders of Black September, or at least those deemed directly responsible for Munich.

The full truth about the Israeli hit squads will probably never be known. The basis of all such operations is complete deniability, however implausible these denials may be. In this case the need for operational secrecy was twofold: to guarantee the safety of the killers and their back-up teams; and to prevent the exposure of any official connection to the assassinations. Naturally enough, the episode has generated considerable interest and a spate of books and articles over the years. Although the operational failures created a narrow opening of unwanted publicity that permitted some sketchy facts to leak out, any account must still be partial, contradictory and confusing.

The first problem is one of dating. Palestinians, especially PFLP officials, had been targeted by the Israelis long before the post-Munich wave of assassinations: in July 1970 rockets had been fired at the Beirut apartment of Wadi'a Haddad, head of PFLP foreign operations; Ghassan Kanfani, a talented novelist and Habash's spokesman, had been killed, along with his seventeen-year-old niece, in a car-bomb explosion in the Lebanese capital in July 1972. Israeli newspapers blamed him for the May massacre at Lod airport. His successor, Bassam Abu-Sharif, was badly injured by a parcel bomb several days later.

But after the Olympics massacre the pace quickened. During the ten months following the Munich débâcle, at least nine men associated by the Israelis with Palestinian terrorism were killed in violent circumstances. Some of the assassinations may have been unconnected to Munich. Wael Zwaiter, for example, who was shot dead in Rome (where he was the official PLO representative) on 16 October, was held responsible by the Israelis for organizing the first hijack of the El Al jet to Algeria in August 1968 and also for the booby-trapped tape recorder smuggled aboard an El Al plane in August 1972. Mahmoud Hamshari was blown up by a bomb planted in the telephone in his Paris apartment and detonated by remote control on 8 December. Hamshari was the PLO representative in the French capital and, like Zwaiter, more of an intellectual than a terrorist. But the Israelis believed he had been involved in several incidents, including Munich. Hussein al-Shir, assassinated in Nicosia on 25 January 1973, was described as the PLO's contact man with the Soviet KGB in Cyprus.[101] He was killed by a bomb placed under the bed in his room at the Olympic Hotel. That device was also detonated by remote control.

The following day it was Israel's turn to suffer a casualty in the 'war of the spooks'. Baruch Cohen was assassinated outside a Madrid café after his meeting with a contact – a twenty-five-year-old Palestinian who was studying medicine in the Spanish capital – was postponed for a day at the Arab's request. According to Abu Iyad, Cohen's activities were well known to Fatah/Black September, but

> what he didn't know was that several of the students he had recruited belonged to Black September and pretended to cooperate with him at the request of the organization. When he began to have serious doubts about the loyalty of those who failed to carry out the tasks assigned to them on various pretexts, it was decided to execute him. His elimination became urgent, when, in early January, shortly after Mahmoud Hamshari's assassination in Paris, Cohen announced that he was leaving Spain to take up other duties.

Abu Iyad claimed that the killing necessitated the dismantling of the entire Israeli network in Spain, because the Mossad did not know who was a Black September double agent. Cohen's three killers escaped.[102]

Baruch Cohen's death attracted little public attention at the time, but later exposure gave a fascinating glimpse of the human side of this dark period in the Israeli–Palestinian war. According to Nurit, his widow:

> Brochi wasn't a tough guy. On the contrary, he was short and very far from the image of the champagne spy. He didn't know how to dance. He couldn't drink. He was shy, very closed. But he knew how to listen. If he'd picked a different profession, he could have been a psychologist. It was a pleasure to talk to him. He'd say a word here, a word there, and the other person would open up. He exuded trustworthiness. What have these little guys got to offer if not themselves? If the Shin Bet interrogate in pairs, then Brochi was the 'good' one.[103]

Cohen's young son once spotted his father in the street talking to an Arab and asked him outright if he was a spy. The boy also found items used for disguise, like a pair of spectacles with plain glass lenses. Afterwards, his widow found no comfort in oblique hints that his death had been avenged.

> Every so often they'd come to see me and ask, as if they were being casual: 'Did you see in the paper about that guy who was killed, or that one who was blown up?' What do you think, that it comforted me? It meant that another family had been hurt, another woman left alone, a few more children who lost their father.[104]

The war continued. On 12 March 1973 Black September killed another Israeli it described as a Mossad agent, Simha Gilzer, in Cyprus[105] but the Israeli press reported unanimously that he was an elderly businessman with no intelligence connections. Baruch Cohen, by contrast, was publicly acknowledged to have been an official shortly after his death was announced. In April an Iraqi called Basil Kubaisi was killed in Paris and another Palestinian gunned down in Nicosia.

On 13 April the Israelis launched their biggest and most

dramatic retaliatory raid ever when a combined force of Mossad agents and IDF commandos killed three senior PLO officers in their homes in the heart of Beirut. Two of them, Muhammad Najjar and Kamal Adwan, were described as the two senior figures in Black September. The third, Kamal Nasser, was the PLO's chief spokesman. A second force attacked the DFLP building and two other units carried out separate assaults – one of them diversionary – on Palestinian logistics centres in the north and south of the city.[106] The operation, lyrically code-named 'Springtime of Youth', was to become a byword for Israel's ability to combine precise intelligence with military élan to strike at the very heart of the enemy camp. It was a classic of its kind. The six Mossad operatives arrived in the Lebanese capital a week before the operation on separate flights from London, Rome and Paris. Three of them were travelling on British passports. They rented cars and inspected safe houses before the assault force arrived by boat.[107] Files seized during the Beirut raid yielded a hoard of vital information about Black September operations and PLO cells – especially the well-organized DFLP – in the West Bank.[108] Israel acknowledged responsibility for the attack.

Shortly afterwards the Israelis killed three more Black September operatives. The most important of them was an Algerian called Muhammad Boudia, who had maintained the organization's operational links with a wide spectrum of European terrorist groups, including the notorious Venezuelan 'Carlos'. Some sources say Boudia worked with the PFLP rather than Black September. Whatever his precise organizational affiliation, he was blown up by a bomb placed in his car in Paris on 28 June.[109]

Fiasco in Lillehammer

In July 1973 things went badly – and very publicly – wrong. A hastily assembled team of Mossad agents, tracking a man they believed to be Ali Hassan Salameh, instead killed an innocent

Moroccan waiter called Ahmed Bouchiki in the lonely Norwegian town of Lillehammer. Six of the Israeli operatives were captured and tried in what turned out to be the most damaging exposure ever of their country's clandestine activities abroad; and to make matters worse, on the soil of a friendly country. The final identification, or rather misidentification, of Salameh was probably made by an Algerian Black September courier called Kemal Benamane, who had somehow been intimidated into becoming a double agent for the Mossad.[110]

The Lillehammer mission was headed by Mike Harari, the forty-six-year-old head of the Mossad's Operations Branch. A former Palmahnik, he had been trained as a radio operator and based in Rome for the Mossad LeAliya Bet during the post-war illegal immigration campaigns, where he was codenamed 'Alex'. In 1950, after completing his army service, Harari was recruited into the Shin Bet by Ya'akov Caroz and disappeared into the secret world. In the early 1960s he was a Mossad agent-runner in Europe (he had briefed Aharon Moshel before his mission to Egypt in 1962). By the end of the decade he was deputy head of Mossad Operations, rising to head the branch from 1970. He resurfaced only in the mid-1980s, as a close and controversial associate of the former Panamanian dictator General Manuel Noriega.[111]

Attempts to hush up the Israeli involvement failed. The team was as overconfident as it was inexperienced, itself a measure of the Mossad's difficulty in finding the right people to carry out the revenge operations. And Harari, a veteran clandestine operative, should have known better than to carry out an assassination in a small town like Lillehammer, where strangers were highly conspicuous and there had not been a murder for forty years. On 1 February 1974 Sylvia Rafael and Abraham Gehmer were sentenced to five years in prison, Dan Aerbel to five, all for second-degree murder. Marianne Gladnikoff got two and a half years and Zwi Steinberg one year. Michael Dorf, the hit-team's communications man, was freed. It was a disaster: 'The revelations of the captured agents,' two well-placed Israeli experts have commented, 'dealt a heavy blow to the undercover infrastructure of the Mossad in Europe. Agents who had been exposed had to be recalled, safe houses abandoned, phone numbers changed and operational methods modified.'[112]

The conventional wisdom is that the Lillehammer fiasco put an end to Mossad assassinations of Palestinian terrorists. This is incorrect, although the pace of attacks certainly slackened off afterwards and different methods were tried. In August 1973 Israeli fighter planes forced down a Lebanese airliner that was mistakenly believed to be carrying George Habash. Nearly six years later, in January 1979, Ali Hassan Salameh – codenamed the 'Red Prince' by the Mossad – was killed by a car bomb in Beirut. And he was not the last PLO leader to meet his end at Israeli hands.

Ideological spies

In December 1972, at the end of a bloody year in the struggle against the Palestinians, the Shin Bet exposed in Israel a small group of left-wing Jews and Arab nationalists who had cooperated in an espionage and sabotage network run by Syrian intelligence. So important was the case deemed that Baruch Cohen was called back from his Mossad job in Europe to take charge of the investigation.[113] Israeli Jews has been caught working for Soviet Bloc and Arab secret services in the past, but no previous case made the impact this one did. Syria was the most implacable of the country's enemies and the Jews involved came from the elite of Israeli society. The most prominent of them was Udi Adiv, a twenty-five-year-old Haifa University student and Mapam kibbutznik who was a star basketball player, had done his IDF service in the paratroops and fought in the Six Day War. Another leading figure was Dan Vered, a twenty-eight-year-old mathematics teacher from a wealthy Tel Aviv family. In the Israeli context, the social meaning of the case was akin to, and perhaps worse than, the treachery of the members of the British establishment who began to spy for the Soviet Union in the 'Cambridge Comintern' of the 1930s. In intelligence terms, it was of little more than marginal importance.

The network was set up by Daoud Turki, a Christian Arab who ran a political bookshop in Haifa and had long held strong Arab nationalist and communist views that made him an obvious target for Shin Bet surveillance. He met Adiv in 1970 at a meeting of the Israeli Socialist Organization, better known as Matzpen, the tiny, largely Jewish, anti-Zionist group that had emerged in the vanguard of domestic opposition to the post-1967 occupation.[114] Matzpen's ideology was a mixture of the Maoist and Trotskyist doctrines that were having such a powerful impact on the university campuses of Western Europe at the time. The 'French revolution' of May 1968, the Vietnam war and internationalist anti-colonialism provided the backdrop against which the Matzpen militants viewed the Israeli–Arab conflict. In 1970, at its peak, it had about 100 members, with a periphery of another 100 sympathizers. The organization split frequently into competing groupuscules and most of its intellectual heavyweights and founding members left the country in the late 1960s, but it acquired a reputation far out of proportion to either its Lilliputian numerical or its political strength. Reports of a 'revolutionary dialogue' with Nayif Hawatmeh's DFLP, which had recently split off from the Habash group, contributed further to Matzpen's notoriety in Israeli society. It was heavily penetrated by the Shin Bet.

Turki made contact with Syrian intelligence after seeking financial support for a new underground revolutionary organization. By the end of 1970 he had recruited several other Arab members as well as Adiv and Vered, who both secretly visited Damascus and were given training in the use of simple codes, weapons and explosives, and reported on the political, economic and military situation in Israel. Adiv said later that the information he supplied was 'trivial'.[115] It was amateurish stuff, fuelled far more by ideology than professionalism. 'Adiv and Vered emerged as the workhorses of revolution,' wrote one foreign correspondent, 'trapped by the logic of their own doctrine as they drifted leftwards from dissent to treason. Like Kozo Okamato, the Japanese gunman of Lydda, they believed that theorizing was not enough. They scorned coffee-house radicalism and took to arms.'[116]

Turki sang the Internationale when he, together with Adiv, was sentenced to seventeen years' gaol in March 1973. Both were freed in 1985, after serving twelve and thirteen years respectively. Turki was released as part of Israel's extraordinary and controversial prisoner exchange deal with Ahmed Jibril's PFLP-GC. He said later he believed that the network had been penetrated by the Shin Bet and had told Adiv so two weeks before they were arrested.[117]

Balance sheet

Palestinian resistance was effectively contained by Israel's security and intelligence services in the years that followed the 1967 war. In the West Bank armed activity by PLO groups had been virtually eradicated by the end of 1968; in the Gaza Strip by early in 1971. The Shin Bet, which had been unprepared for the consequences of the Six Day War victory, and grew vastly in size afterwards, deployed quickly and imaginatively to crush the fedayeen before they had a chance to strike roots and acquire operational experience. History, geography and organization were all on Israel's side. The sealing of the border with Jordan meant that the West Bank was almost completely cut off from the outside world; its population – a large part of the Palestinian people – isolated and controlled by their occupier. There were no 'no-go areas' for the Israelis, no 'liberated zones' where resistance could flourish. The Shin Bet, working ever more closely with the army, was relentless, fast and ruthless, sowing uncertainty by its massive use of informers and giving no quarter in the struggle.

This success prevented the Palestinians from launching a people's war at the very moment that their ideology required it. The occupied territories never became Algeria or Vietnam. Instead the Israelis constructed a security system based on the use of the 'carrot' of inducements combined with a 'stick' of often severe punishment. It was a system that was to work surprisingly well for years to come.

Yet curbing resistance inside the occupied territories had a price. After King Hussein finally expelled the PLO from Jordan in 1971, and his border with the lost West Bank was nearly hermetically closed, the Palestinians shifted their armed activities abroad. Their redeployment in Lebanon was to have profound and disastrous consequences for the future. Unable to strike at Israel from within, or from across the frontiers, radical groups like George Habash's PFLP turned to its soft underbelly – its aircraft, its embassies, El Al offices and other installations abroad. Jewish targets were hit as well, simply because they were Jewish and automatically associated with support for Israel. Combating this phenomenon required an immense effort in the field of protective security and, after terrible reminders of the urgency of the task like the Munich Olympics massacre, the Shin Bet was soon on top. Prevention required detailed and timely intelligence: obtaining information about Palestinian plans, penetrating the tiny but increasingly well-organized groups that mounted the attacks, often with the assistance of Arab states. Here too Israel was assisted by the fact that it physically controlled the occupied territories and had good intelligence resources on the ground: agents from the West Bank and Gaza could be infiltrated into PLO groups operating abroad. In the war against terrorism, Humint was, and remains, the golden key.

Israel's task was complicated, however, by the need to work on hostile or neutral territory. Mossad agent-runners in Brussels or Madrid could not operate openly, with army protection, like their Shin Bet colleagues in Nablus or Hebron. Their activities were far more dangerous and exposed and if liaison with friendly foreign security services increased in this period, no European government could tolerate defiance of its own laws. The Lillehammer disaster in July 1973 struck a severe, if temporary, blow at the Mossad's ability to function abroad.

Terrorism was an irritant – occasionally a bloody and humiliating one – but still no more than an irritant. Its propaganda effect was far more powerful than any damage it could really do to Israeli security. Yet it still required the deployment of immense human and financial resources by the intelligence community. So did the IDF's preventive and retaliatory attacks on PLO bases and refugee camps in Jordan and Lebanon. These in turn encouraged a dynamic of response and revenge that did nothing but perpetuate and deepen the conflict. By the eve of the 1973 war Palestinian resistance played only a marginal role in disrupting Israeli life. The Shin Bet and the Mossad could thus be justly proud of their achievements in making the status quo tenable – for their own countrymen at least. But the battle was far from over.

9

Mehdal:

1973

Low probability

Soon after the 1967 victory IDF intelligence assessed that it would take the Arab armies only 'a year to eighteen months' to recover, at least in terms of replenishing their lost equipment.[1] And indeed, by 1968 Egypt's military strength, at least on paper, was greater than it had been before the war.

During the immediate post-war years, which were dominated by Israel's battle against Palestinian guerrilla infiltrations along the river Jordan and by the war of attrition launched by Egypt on the east bank of the Suez Canal, military intelligence set up a network of electronic surveillance and communications-monitoring stations along the new ceasefire lines. Stone-covered, antennae-bedecked fortresses went up on Mount Hermon, on the northern edge of the Golan Heights overlooking the Damascus Plain; along the Jordan; and on the Suez Canal, with the Umm Hashiba station on the heights thirty kilometres east of the canal looking deep into Lower Egypt.

At various points along the front lines Aman managed to tap Arab military communications. In the early 1970s, near military bases along the Gulf of Suez, Egyptian counter-intelligence discovered a hollow telephone pole, containing a battery-operated transmitter which bugged calls along the line. Aman had simply replaced the original pole with this unconventional device.[2]

During the static war of attrition (1968–70), which was

characterized by constant artillery exchanges, commando raids and, in its final stage, Israeli air attacks on front-line positions and strategic targets in the Nile Valley, IDF Intelligence Branch played an important auxiliary role, supplying Israeli commandos and airmen with target sheets. Its major successes included producing the intelligence that facilitated the destruction of the Naj Hamadi bridges and electricity pylons; the IDF Armoured Corps raid along a 100-kilometre strip of Gulf of Suez coastline, using Soviet T-55 tanks and APCs; and the capture and removal by a heliborne paratroop unit on Christmas night 1969 of the latest Soviet P-12 radar, which was lifted off a hillock at Ghardaka, on the Gulf of Suez.

It was at this time that IDF intelligence began developing camera-carrying drones to monitor the Egyptian front without exposing valuable pilots to ground fire. The project was launched by an Aman major, Mordechai Brill, who persuaded his superiors to buy three remote-controlled toy aircraft in the US for $850. A trial run over an Israeli anti-aircraft battery proved that the 1.5-metre-wide drone was not easily targeted by ground-fire. A first operational run in the summer of 1969 over Egyptian positions near Ismailia was highly successful: the Egyptians did not even fire at the craft and it returned to base with good, clear photographs. A further flight over Arab Legion emplacements in the Jordan Valley was also successful.[3] Far more sophisticated drones, with long-range capabilities and television cameras, later became a mainstay of Aman intelligence-gathering over enemy territory.

The IAF was unleashed along the Suez Canal in July 1969 after the outgunned IDF infantry, armour and artillery dug in on the east bank proved unable to cope unaided with the sheer volume of Egyptian firepower. In effect, the air force served as flying artillery. In January 1970, after six months of air raids failed to silence the Egyptian gunners, the IAF, battle-testing its newly acquired F-4 Phantom fighter-bombers, began attacking army camps and strategic targets in and near the Nile Valley.

These deep-penetration bombings forced Nasser, who flew to Moscow on 24 January, to seek large-scale Soviet help in defending Egyptian air space. The Soviets responded swiftly, sending batteries of SAMs, including the latest SAM-3s, with Soviet crews, and squadrons of MiG-21s, with Soviet pilots and ground crews. Yet despite an accumulation, from October to November 1969, of intelligence pointing in the right direction, Aman failed to anticipate the arrival of the Soviet air defence units in Egypt. The Aman estimate, of 'low probability' of the deployment of Soviet troops, was backed by a similar CIA assessment.[4]

From April 1970 the Soviets flew patrols over the Nile Valley and Israel ceased its deep-penetration bombings. The Soviets then slowly began pushing their missile batteries and air patrols eastwards towards the canal to provide cover for the front-line Egyptian troops, who were still being pounded daily by the IAF. Israel responded by bombing the easternmost Soviet missile bases. The Soviets sent up MiGs to protect the missiles, and the IAF again veered away. But it was only a matter of time before Israeli and Soviet aircraft clashed. At the end of July 1970 Israeli Phantoms shot down four or five Soviet-piloted MiGs in a large-scale dogfight west of the Canal.

The worrying prospect of an escalation of Israeli–Soviet clashes brought the Americans into the picture. William Rogers, the secretary of state, drew up a plan for a ceasefire along the Canal and everyone was happy to call it quits. Nasser had long reached the conclusion that his war of attrition had failed in its objective of dislodging Israel from the Canal, and neither the Soviets nor the Israelis wanted a serious confrontation. The ceasefire went into effect on 7 August 1970.

But the Egyptians emerged with one far-reaching victory, which would have telling effect three years later. On 8 August they pushed their AA missile network eastwards, almost to the banks of the Canal. The Rogers-mediated agreement had called for both a ceasefire and a 'standstill' or freezing of the Israeli and Egyptian deployments on 7 August. In moving the AA missile network Cairo gambled that Israel would not resort to hostilities in response to their violation of the standstill provision. And the Egyptians were right: Israel gritted its teeth and did nothing.

Ironically, Aman had warned the government weeks earlier that the Egyptians would almost certainly violate the 'standstill' clause and move the missile umbrella eastwards. By October 1970 there were some fifty SAM batteries along the Suez front, sixteen of them SAM-3s manned by Soviet soldiers. When Israel complained to Washington that the Egyptians had breached the agreement, Ray Cline, the head of the State Department intelligence unit, INR, told the White House that the Israeli complaint was baseless. When Israeli ambassador Yitzhak Rabin told his military attaché, General Eli Zeira, what had happened, Zeira immediately asked Tel Aviv to send him a photographic interpreter and a set of aerial photographs showing the Egyptian deployment. These duly arrived in Washington and Zeira was summoned to the White House, where he laid out the evidence before President Nixon. Nixon, angry with Cline, then ordered the Pentagon to remove its veto on several categories of weapons the Israelis had asked for during the preceding months.[5]

'Radish' – the fateful message

For three years, between summer 1970 and autumn 1973, there was quiet along Israel's borders with Syria and Egypt. The status quo seemed to be holding. Armed Palestinian resistance in the West Bank and Gaza Strip had been effectively contained and while the PLO's spectacular terrorist attacks abroad attracted international attention, they also underlined its fundamental impotence in the face of their powerful enemy. Israel was content. But the Arabs, who continued to regard the occupation of the Golan Heights and the Sinai peninsula as an enduring insult, were determined to put an end to the impasse.

At 1.55 p.m. on Saturday, 6 October 1973, the Syrian and Egyptian armies simultaneously attacked Israel's front-line positions on the Golan and on the east bank of the Suez Canal. For all practical purposes, the IDF was caught with its pants down. The Israelis were outgunned and overwhelmed at most points within minutes or hours. It was one of the worst strategic and most unpleasant tactical surprises since Hitler's invasion of Russia in 1941. The IDF's commanders were to claim later that the army had been let down by Aman and the Mossad.

Yet Israel had had an effective thirty-six-hour warning of the impending assault. At 2.30 a.m. on Friday, 5 October, a cable reached Mossad chief Zvi Zamir with a message from the secret service's most important agent. The message said only '*tsnon*' (Hebrew for 'radish'); it was the agreed codeword for 'war is imminent' and it was exactly what the Mossad and Aman had been waiting for for a fortnight, a fortnight in which the agent, who was described by one senior Israeli as 'the best agent any country ever had in wartime, a miraculous source', had not made contact. Zamir's bureau chief, the first Israeli official to actually see the cable and digest its shattering significance, said later: 'We'd never had anything like it.' The message promised further details within the next twenty-four hours.[6]

Zamir did not tell prime minister Golda Meir, defence minister Dayan or IDF chief of staff David Elazar about the message. A few minutes later, Aman chief Eli Zeira called Zamir to inform him of the latest intelligence from Egypt and Syria; Zamir then told his military counterpart that the message from his top source had arrived. The Mossad chief said simply: 'It's war. We don't have a date, but its imminent.'[7] Yet the absence of a date or time for the attack was crucial. Again without informing the prime minister, Zamir, after a brief consultation with Zeira, decided to fly to Europe to personally rendezvous with the source and to verify the report.[8] He wanted confirmation and he needed a date. Zeira sat on the message, waiting to hear from his Mossad colleague.

Zeira did inform Dayan of the '*tsnon*' message, because later that Friday the defence minister referred to the piece of intelligence Zamir had received 'from his friend', and mentioned that the Mossad chief was soon due to receive confirmation of its contents. Zamir left his home at 5.00 a.m., flew out and met his agent at midnight. Some three to four hours are then unaccounted for. Zamir called Zeira at 3.45 a.m. on Saturday, 6

October, telling him that the Egyptians and Syrians intended to launch a war that day 'at sunset'. This dramatic telephone message was followed an hour or so later by a cable sent in cipher to both Mossad HQ and Zeira.

Zamir apparently failed to pass on immediately the information he had obtained at around midnight on 5/6 October because there was no cipher clerk on duty at the local Israeli Embassy owing to the Yom Kippur holiday. In any event, only at 3.45 a.m. did he decide to forgo elementary security precautions and telephone the information over an open line.

Zeira testified later before the Agranat Commission, which investigated the intelligence failure that preceded the war, that

> this source had, in the past, [given] a number of times and dates for the outbreak of war, and war had failed to break out. It is possible that the war did not break out then because the Egyptians noticed that we had mobilized troops on those dates. But it is also possible that this source had always misled us . . . In any event, this time [on 6 October] the source stated clearly: Today![9]

The exact source of the fateful war message still remains a closely guarded secret. Dayan described it thus: 'It was not a report on Arab activity in the field but an intelligence message regarding the Arab decision to go to war. We had received similar messages in the past, and later, when no attack followed, came the explanation that President Sadat had changed his mind at the last moment.'[10]

At about 4.30 a.m. Lieutenant Colonel Avner Shalev, head of Elazar's bureau, phoned the chief of staff and told him that 'the piece of information that they had been waiting for had arrived and was unequivocal – the Egyptian and Syrian armies intend to launch an attack on Israel at 6.00 p.m. The attack would be launched simultaneously on the Suez and Golan fronts.'[11]

The mistake or misinformation about the timing of the joint Syrian–Egyptian assault – '6.00 p.m.' – was to prove crucial, and invaluable to the Arab side. The attack in fact began a full four hours earlier, at 1.55 p.m., catching many Israeli units on the hop between rear bases and front-line positions.

The original piece of intelligence had apparently been accurate or more accurate. But, as emerged in a subsequent analysis, somewhere *en route*, before it reached Israel's military leaders, the message, which had spoken of war breaking out during 'the afternoon hours' or 'before sunset', had been distorted and turned into the far firmer '6.00 p.m.' or 'sundown'.[12] Sunset on 6 October 1973 occurred at 5.20 p.m. The Agranat Commission was to blame Zeira and his deputy, the director of the Aman Research Department, Brigadier-General Aryeh Shalev, for the wrong hour.[13]

At the Israeli cabinet meeting on the morning of 6 October prime minister Meir said that 'the war will begin at 6 o'clock this evening . . . or perhaps the meaning is 4 o'clock'. She described the arrival of the fateful message as 'miraculous'.[14] Dayan said that he assumed the Arabs would open fire at 5.00 p.m. Minister of commerce and industry Chaim Barlev, Elazar's predecessor as IDF chief of staff, questioned the 6.00 p.m. report as making no military sense. Education minister Yigal Allon, a major-general in the 1948 war, supported Bar-Lev. But Elazar was adamant that this was the message and that it was credible.[15]

The Arab war plan

Aman had been aware of Egypt's plan of assault across the Suez Canal – down to many of its fine operational details, including the composition of assault waves, timetables, armour and artillery objectives – since the end of 1971.[16] On the basis of a large-scale Egyptian canal-crossing exercise that winter and previous, smaller exercises in the preceding years, Aman's Research Department was able to piece together most of the plan. In its half-yearly analysis written in mid-1972, the department assessed that the Egyptian high command had rejected the idea of a renewed war of attrition and was planning a full-scale canal crossing, aimed at seizing chunks of Sinai eastwards as far as the strategically vital Mitla and Gidi passes.

The Egyptian plan, codenamed 'Operation Badr', called for a two-stage assault across the waterway, with five infantry divisions establishing five separate ten-kilometre-deep bridgeheads (which would eventually join together into a continuous front) and battalions of heliborne commandos disrupting the Israeli rear at key crossroads. The five divisions – the 18th, 2nd, 16th, 17th and 19th – were the lead elements of two armies, the Second Army and the Third, which also contained three armoured divisions. (A First Army, composed of two mechanized divisions and one division of Special Forces, was left behind to defend Cairo and the Nile Valley.) The infantry assault was to be followed by a second stage, in which two armoured divisions and two independent armoured brigades would cross the waterway, move through the bridgeheads and advance as far as the passes. A separate combined task force of naval units and paratroops would at the same time capture Sharm-ash-Sheikh at the southern tip of the Sinai peninsula.

By mid-1973 the plan was known to Aman almost in its entirety. On this level, where IDF intelligence went wrong was in not knowing that, contrary to standard Soviet military doctrine for crossing water obstacles, the Egyptians had imposed an artificial intermission or 'operational halt' between the first-wave crossing and consolidation and the start of the second, armoured, penetration stage. Had the IDF known this, it would not have thrown away complete tank battalions in the abortive and bloody counter-attacks on the infantry bridgeheads on 8 October, out of a baseless fear that the Egyptians intended to immediately push on to the Mitla and Gidi passes. The main lines of the plan were conceived by Sadat and General Sa'ad ad-Din ash-Shazli. Many of the details of the Syrian war plan were also known to Aman – as Zeira told a meeting of the IDF top brass on 5 October.[17]

Knowing the Arab war plan or plans was one thing; believing that the Arabs actually intended to go to war was quite another. In autumn 1973 Israel's political and military leaders proved unable to make the passage from this knowledge to this belief. Barring their way, as it were, was what became known in

Hebrew as the *'kontzeptziya'* (concept), or a cluster of interlocking false assumptions.

The 'concept', or false assumptions

Soon after President Anwar Sadat succeeded Gamal Abdel Nasser in September 1970, he began announcing his intentions to renew the war with Israel. Early in 1971 he declared that year to be 'the year of decision'. But 1971 passed without a renewal of hostilities. This and other factors persuaded Aman's Research Department, the IDF general staff and the country's political leaders that the new Egyptian leader did not really mean business. Many dismissed him as a 'buffoon'.

During the late 1960s and early 1970s a 'concept' took hold that the Arabs had no intention and were incapable, in the short and medium term, of renewing the war against Israel. This 'concept' was based on several assumptions: (1) Israel's massive defeat of the Arab armies in 1967 and its continuing control of the occupied territories, which afforded territorial depth, gave the country an unprecedented military edge, which the Arab states were fully aware of; (2) Syria on its own would not dare to risk war against Israel; (3) Egypt would not hazard going to war so long as it was weak in the air, in terms of both planes and AA defences.[18]

Aman's overall assessment of Arab designs until 5 October 1973, the day before Yom Kippur, remained that war was 'highly improbable' or 'improbable'. It was this fundamentally incorrect assumption that lay at the root of the intelligence blunder – the *'mehdal'*, to use the post-war Hebrew neologism – that almost led to disaster and changed the face of the Middle East for years to come.

Israel's dismissal of the possibility of war was grounded on overwhelming contempt for the Arabs. The Israelis blithely ignored repeated Egyptian announcements that the status quo was untenable and that war was inevitable. Zvi Zamir said later:

We simply did not believe that they were capable. In effect, that was also my personal problem, we scorned them. 'Put all their paratroops with Saggers [the anti-tank missiles which devastated Israel's armour] on a hill – and I'll wipe them out with two tanks,' one major-general told me. Even when we received reliable information about the water cannon, which they intended to use to breach the earthen banks on the Bar-Lev Line, there was the same dismissive reaction: What water cannon?![19]

In the higher reaches of the Israeli government, notably in the Foreign Ministry, there were some who did not fall for the *'kontzeptziya'*. Gideon Rafael, a senior diplomat, wrote later:

Some of us ventured to differ from this outlook. Regardless of the developments discernible from the beginning of 1973, intelligence assessments had become increasingly and infectiously self-assured. They invariably predicted the undisturbed continuation of the cease-fire. Who influenced whom is hard to tell. The question of whether it was the military who set the minds of the politicians at rest or the national mood of complacency which dulled the alertness of the military mind will remain a subject of historical and psychological speculation. At any event, it was a process of cross-fertilization breeding disaster.[20]

The Arab political deception

An important element of deception – both political and military – was built into the Egyptian–Syrian war plans. And a string of coincidental events during the months and days before the war dovetailed with the deliberate deception campaign and served to blunt Israeli appreciation of what was happening or was about to happen. These either diverted attention away from Arab war preparations or deceived Israeli watchers and listeners into believing that what they were seeing were not preparations for war. The Arab deception campaign – much to the surprise of its architects – worked.

Paradoxically, President Sadat's repeated public declarations of intent during 1972 and the first half of 1973 served to blind

Israel's leaders as to Egypt's very real preparations for war. They sounded to Israeli ears simply like more of the same. Sadat's 'year of decision' had come and gone. A similar pattern characterized the following year. On May Day 1972 Sadat declared: 'In our next war I will not make do with liberating the land. Israel's impudence and hubris these twenty-three years must cease. And as I have said already: I am willing to sacrifice a million people in this battle.' In November the president told his ruling Socialist Union party that Egypt would go to war within six months, at most a year. In December Sadat reported to his National Security Council that efforts to reach a diplomatic solution had failed: the only way 'to liberate the conquered lands' was war.[21]

Sadat's repeated threats eroded his credibility. It became a case of crying wolf. Throughout spring, summer and autumn 1973 the Israeli dismissal of Sadat was translated into a dismissal of his threats. And the dismissal of his public statements spilled over into a mistaken dismissal of the activity on the ground. This was a vital factor in the lulling of Israel.

Thus it was that Cairo Radio's announcement on 11 September 1973 that the object of the meeting then taking place in the Egyptian capital between Sadat and Jordan's King Hussein was 'to discuss the preparations for the fateful battle against Israel' was not taken seriously in Jerusalem.[22]

Sadat's speech on the anniversary of Nasser's death on 28 September 1973 – a week before the war – was utilized to deceive Israeli listeners, who by then were becoming worried about growing Egyptian and Syrian troop concentrations along the borders. There was no lengthy exposition of the need to fight Israel and it sounded like routine lip service when Sadat vaguely asserted that the liberation of land remained the first priority. 'God willing,' he said, 'we shall achieve our objective.'

Diversion at Schonau

Political deception was supplemented by diversions during the countdown to war. The most serious specific feint, which shifted

Israeli political and intelligence attention away from the Middle East to Europe for five vital days, was the Schonau Affair.

On 28 September two Arab terrorists held up at the Austrian border a train from Czechoslovakia carrying Soviet Jewish emigrants. Holding Jewish and Austrian hostages, the gunmen demanded the closure of the Schonau transit camp in Vienna, which served as a way station for Soviet Jews emigrating to Israel, as the price of the hostages' release. Austrian chancellor Bruno Kreisky capitulated quickly. Israel was outraged at this submission to terrorism and on 1 October prime minister Meir flew to Vienna to try to persuade Kreisky (a Jew who was regarded in Jerusalem as something of a 'traitor' because of his pro-PLO leanings) to rescind the Schonau closure. She failed. On 3 October she reported bitterly to her cabinet colleagues that Kreisky had not even offered her a glass of water.

But the drama of the hijacking, Kreisky's capitulation and Meir's abortive mission to Vienna all served to divert Israeli attention away from ominous developments nearer home. But was the Schonau incident actually part of the deception operation? The evidence is ambiguous. No Arab leader has claimed that it was, but then, they could hardly be expected to claim responsibility for a terrorist attack, whatever its ulterior motive. The gunmen belonged to As-Saiqa, a PLO component run by the Syrian government. It is almost inconceivable that they would have set out on such a politically sensitive mission without a green light from Damascus. And only a few days before, the organization's leader, Zuheir Muhsein, had denounced terrorist attacks abroad as 'adolescent actions'. Yet this one served usefully to rivet Israeli interest for four or five crucial days.[23]

What happened in Jerusalem and Tel Aviv because of the events on the Austrian–Czech border and in Vienna during those first days of October was, in a sense, a microcosm of the misdirection of Israeli intelligence energies that had taken place from 1970 and, more emphaticaly, from 1972 onwards. The increase in Palestinian attacks on Israeli and Jewish targets abroad gradually diverted intelligence resources away from the

Arab regular armies to fighting terrorism. This shift of focus became sharper after the Munich Olympics massacre in September 1972. Arab sources claimed later that, since the Six Day War, Israel had pulled out a large number of agents from Syria and Egypt, 'because it stopped treating the threat of war seriously, and decided to concentrate on penetrating the terrorist organizations'.[24]

An additional factor that contributed to Israeli blindness in the months before the war may have been the exposure that year of several well-placed Mossad agents in Egypt. Two of them, a senior Egyptian Engineering Corps officer and his girlfriend, were arrested in June 1973 and executed a year later after an alert Cairo postal clerk spotted what turned out to be an enciphered microdot message on the back of a stamp. It contained information about rocket bases. Another important and veteran Israeli agent in Egypt was Nabil al-Nahas, head of the Technical Department of the Afro-Asian Solidarity Organization in Cairo. He was detained in mid-November 1973 but had apparently been under lengthy surveillance and neutralized for some time before his arrest. The capture and, in some cases, execution of sixteen other Egyptians charged with spying for Israel was announced in 1974. Most had been arrested in 1973.[25]

One Israeli agent who was active until the eve of Yom Kippur was Ibrahim Shahin, who worked with his wife and later their three sons to photograph and map 'field subjects' such as the location of trenches, airports, missile bases and the deployment of various units. Shanin, a Palestinian, had been recruited by Aman in El Arish shortly after the capture of Sinai in 1967, and, typically for a low-grade agent, he was asked first to provide ostensibly innocuous information – such as details of food prices and transport fares – before being moved on to military matters and regular payment by his controllers. He provided intelligence about unusually dense troop movements in the Canal Zone area about a month before Yom Kippur, but it was claimed later that this had reached Israel only after the war. Shahin was arrested in August 1974 and hanged in 1977.[26]

In early September 1973 Egypt and Jordan renewed diplomatic relations, which had been severed by Cairo in March 1972 when King Hussein published his plan for a Jordanian–Palestinian federation. Israeli intelligence failed to link this move to Egyptian preparations for war.

Throughout most of 1973 Egyptian ministers held almost continuous talks with Western governments, where they 'spoke in pacific terms . . . while the press and radio were encouraged to play up the concern of Egypt and Syria over the search for a peaceful solution to the Middle East conflict . . .'[27] At the end of September Israeli and Arab foreign ministers agreed to meet secretly in the US in November to discuss procedures for substantive negotiations.[28]

Al-Ahram reported in early October that Egypt's defence minister, Ismail Ali, was scheduled to meet his Romanian counterpart in Cairo on 8 October.[29] On the day the war began President Sadat sent an emissary with greetings to the leaders of Egypt's Jewish community on their High Holiday, Yom Kippur.[30] But at least one Israeli analyst concludes that the Egyptians did not have very high hopes of the political deception and did not invest much in it. Sadat believed that preparing his people for battle was far more important than fooling the enemy. In visits and speeches to Egyptian units during the countdown, the president deliberately tried to create 'a clear feeling that the [coming] war was necessary'.[31]

There was also political deception by Syria: Radio Damascus announced on 4 October that President Assad would begin a nine-day tour of Syria's eastern provinces on 10 October.

The immediate military deception

Deception was one of Egypt's main weapons before 6 October, although Sadat did not make the launching of the war contingent upon the success of the deception plan. Egyptian intelligence in fact assessed that Israel would have a 'three-to fifteen-day concrete warning' of the impending attack. They expected that in the best case Israeli counter-attacks would be launched against their prospective bridgeheads on the east bank of the Canal twenty-four hours after the start of the operation; in the worst case this would happen six to eight hours after the crossing. The success of the deception certainly surprised the Egyptian High Command.[32]

The main element of deception in 'Operation Badr' was that it took place within the framework, and at the end, of a much-publicized exercise codenamed 'Tahrir 41'. Aman and Israel's other intelligence arms were deceived into believing that the massive troop movements on the Egyptian side of the canal were all part of a canal-crossing exercise rather than preparations for the real thing.[33] In 1970 the Military Research Division of the Egyptian War Ministry distributed to divisional commanders a paper on deception during a crossing of the Suez Canal – in advance of a canal-crossing exercise, codenamed 'Tahrir 41', which was to take place in October that year. The 1970 paper laid out the various means of deception to be used and explained how the 'exercise' was to be transformed into a real attack come D-Day.

The success of the 'Tahrir 41' deception was so great that Aman chief Eli Zeira repeatedly dismissed various Egyptian measures taken during the exercise (high alerts declared in the northern and central sectors of the canal area, etc.) as stemming from Egyptian fears that Israel would exploit the exercise to launch an attack. Zeira even used this argument at a meeting of senior officers on 5 October, twenty-six hours before the war broke out.[34]

'Tahrir 41' began on 1 October and was due to last until 7 October 1973. The operational order, issued on 30 September, stated that with the announcement of a prearranged code-word the exercise was to change into a real attack. Egyptian reservists were called up in September in two shifts, many of those from the first shift being ostentatiously released in the first few days of October. The High Command published advance instructions to the released reservists to return to work after 7 October. Similarly, it was announced that classes in Egypt's Staff and Command College and in its Military Academy would resume on 9 October. Instructions to officers desiring to leave during the exercise to go on the Umra, the small pilgrimage to Mecca, were announced in *Al-Ahram* and on military communications networks that were certain to be monitored by Aman. Bridging equipment was moved up to the canal weeks in advance. Some of it was then hidden in underground bunkers nearby and some was ostentatiously moved back to the main army bases along the Nile during the final days before the war. On 4 October the Egyptian media reported that 20,000 reservists had been demobilized. Immediately before the assault on the morning of 6 October, the Egyptians deployed special squads of troops along the canal; their task was to move about without helmets, weapons or shirts, and to swim, hang out fishing lines and eat oranges.[35]

The Egyptian military deception was extremely effective. At the IDF General Staff meeting of 1 October Zeira described 'Tahrir 41' at length and ruled out the idea that the giant exercise might be camouflage for a real assault. The Aman chief noted that the Egyptian High Command had instructed its units to renew leaves on 8 October, the day after the end of the exercise. Some officers had been allowed to go on the pilgrimage to Mecca, which would hardly be expected if a war was being planned.[36] And on the morning of 5 October, at a meeting of senior army chiefs, Zeira, who was still arguing 'low probability', cited a report that Egyptian officer cadets who had been sent to the canal area for the exercise had orders to return to Cairo on 8 October.[37] The picture was complete – and utterly wrong.

The Lebanese and Syrian media reported on 2 October that the Syrian army had been put on alert for fear of a possible Israeli pre-emptive strike. This reinforced Aman's natural tendency to believe that the Syrian deployment was indeed defensive. The alert declared the same day in the northern and central sectors of the canal was linked by Aman to 'Tahrir 41'.[38]

One of the main reasons for the striking success of the deception plan was that the Egyptian High Command carried it out with an eye to both Israeli monitoring and its own troops.

In the months before 1 October, as few as ten Egyptian ministers and generals and a similar number of Syrians knew about the war planned for the autumn. These included presidents Sadat and Assad, the two war ministers and commanders-in-chief, the directors of operations, the directors of military intelligence, and the commanders of the two air forces and the AA defence networks. On the Egyptian side the entire plan was apparently known only to Sadat and his war minister, Ismail Ali.[39] Egyptian army corps and divisional commanders, and equivalent General Staff officers, were told of the war only on 1 October at a meeting of the Supreme Council of the Egyptian Armed Forces.[40] Their Syrian counterparts learned of the war and D-Day at a similar meeting in Damascus. Brigade and battalion commanders in both armies learned of the imminent offensive only on 5 October or the following morning, on the actual day of the attack. The vast majority of Egyptian and Syrian officers and troops found out only an hour or two before the actual assault.

During the final days of the countdown, Syrian and Egyptian military and political leaders, who had learned the bitter lesson of Israeli Sigint interception capabilities in 1967, refrained completely from exchanging messages by telephone, radio-telephone or cables. Communications security was facilitated by a state-of-the-art Swiss–Swedish device called Cryptovox, which had been introduced into the Syrian army in 1972.[41]

The countdown to war and Israel's intelligence failure: 1972 to 6 October 1973

In mid-July 1972 Egypt expelled its army's 20,000 Soviet advisers. Aman interpreted the move as a signal of Sadat's decision not to go to war with Israel for the time being, since the expulsion also appeared to mean at least a temporary cessation of Soviet arms shipments to Egypt and a general weakening of its army. In justifying the move later, Sadat publicly berated Moscow for failing to provide Egypt with certain categories of weaponry that the Americans were willingly supplying the Israelis. This reinforced Aman's belief that Sadat was aware of his army's inferiority to the IDF and had rejected the military option. In fact, Sadat had been partly motivated by a desire to free himself from Soviet shackles; he would not allow Moscow to veto a decision to go to war.

According to Aman, Sadat's expulsion of the Soviet advisers was intended mainly to persuade the United States that Egypt had left the Soviet fold and was bent on reaching a political solution to the Middle East conflict, which only Washington could engineer or mediate. But the Americans failed to reciprocate by applying serious pressure on Israel to offer concessions.[42]

Some time that autumn Sadat reached the conclusion that war must be one of his major options. But he none the less pressed on with diplomatic moves in the hope that American or American–Soviet pressure could extract concessions from Israel and some sort of Israeli withdrawal without war. By early spring 1973 Sadat seems to have become convinced that the diplomatic option was leading nowhere. This impression was bolstered by the fruitless secret meeting between the national security advisers of the Nixon administration and the Sadat regime, Henry Kissinger and Hafez Ismail, that February. Concrete preparations for war moved into high gear.[43]

The first major sign that Sadat was seriously considering a fight came when he replaced his war minister, General Muhammad Ahmed Sadek, by General Ahmed Ismail Ali, who took over on 1 November 1972. Sadek is believed to have favoured the all-or-nothing approach embodied in the Egyptian army plans 'Granite 2' and 'Granite 3', which called for a full-scale Egyptian offensive aimed at the conquest of the whole Sinai peninsula and possibly the Gaza Strip as well. Sadat, backed by his army's chief of staff, Sa'ad ad-Din ash-Shazli, believed only in the feasibility of a limited canal-crossing war, with a halt at the Sinai passes.[44]

During the winter the Egyptians strongly reinforced their canal-side defences. The canal-crossing plan was repeatedly revised and the crucial concept of an 'operational halt' – between the first, infantry-wave crossing and consolidation, and the second, armoured, thrust inland – introduced. Hafez Ismail and the war minister, Ismail Ali, visited Moscow in January and February 1973 and concluded new arms-purchasing agreements.

Ismail also went to Damascus at least once in February to coordinate strategy with the Syrians and possibly to induce them to join in the actual attack. While the Syrians do not seem to have been initially enthusiastic, Sadat and Assad agreed on 23 April 1973 to the principle of a joint, simultaneous assault some time before the end of the year. A joint military council was set up to coordinate preparations. On 2 May the High Command of the two armies met to coordinate the air assault and other aspects of D-Day.[45]

In late August the two countries decided to launch the war between 7 and 11 September or between 5 and 11 October, and it was agreed that Egypt would give Syria five days' notice before D-Day. The date, 6 October, was apparently chosen only on 12 September, at the secret Sadat–Assad summit in Cairo (and, by some accounts, only on 1 or 2 October, at a meeting of the Supreme Council of the Egyptian Armed Forces). On 3 October war minister Ismail Ali flew again to Damascus and informed the Syrians of Egypt's final agreement to the date. At this meeting the two armies decided on H-Hour. The Syrians preferred an assault at dawn (with the sun behind their attacking columns); the Egyptians preferred sunset. The compromise struck was 2.00 p.m. The Soviet ambassador in Cairo was apparently told by the Egyptians on 3 October of Egypt's intention to 'violate the ceasefire'. The following day Assad informed the Soviet ambassador in Damascus of H-Hour.[46]

From April 1973 Israeli intelligence picked up strong signals of Egyptian and Syrian preparations for war. Early that month a squadron of sixteen Iraqi Hunter jets and a squadron of sixteen Libyan Mirages landed in Egypt to bolster the Egyptian air force. Intelligence sources – including the same high-level source who supplied the final, decisive *'tsnon'* warning to the Mossad on 6 October – indicated that Sadat had decided on 15 May as D-Day for a five-division canal-crossing assault.[47]

The IDF began preparing for the prospective attack; the operations – which included mobilizing some reserve units and reinforcing fortifications, tank traps and minefields in the north and south – were codenamed 'Kahol–Lavan' (blue and white).

At first, IDF chief of general staff David Elazar was characteristically sceptical. At the General Staff meeting on 6 April he asked: 'How many times can a leader [i.e. Sadat] repeat the same threat? In 1971 he said that year was the Year of Decision; he said that 1972 was the Year of Decision; he said that before Muhammad's birthday, the occupied territories would be liberated; he promises that the clash will be this year . . .' Elazar agreed with Aman director Zeira, who argued at General Staff meetings on 12 and 15 April that the prospect of war was remote, a 'low probability'. Aman also rejected the possibility of a simultaneous two-front (Syrian–Egyptian) offensive. The Syrians would join a war only after the Egyptians proved successful on their own; they feared the Israel Air Force, said Aman.

But at the 15 April meeting, Mossad chief Zamir was far from dismissive about Arab intentions and capabilities: there was no certainty that the Arabs would attack, but neither was there any certainty that they would refrain from doing so, he said. In any event, Egypt's preparations were worrying and there was a reasonable possibility of war. Sadat's conditions for going to war had been fulfilled: the canal-crossing divisions now had an anti-aircraft missile umbrella; they had sufficient bridging equipment; and they had an AA system for effective defence of the Nile Valley. Zamir's pessimistic approach was shared by defence minister Dayan: the Arabs intended war as they could no longer countenance the continued political–diplomatic stalemate.

The crucial meeting of Israel's leaders at this stage of the crisis took place on 9 May in the Defence Ministry war room in Tel Aviv. Zeira continued to dismiss the prospect of war. Elazar rated the possibility as 'low' but said that it was higher than at any time since 1967. He now suggested that if war did break out, it would occur simultaneously on both fronts.

In April and May Zeira repeatedly assured the General Staff and the cabinet that Israeli intelligence would, in any event, provide a 'five to six'-day advance warning of any Arab plan to launch a full-scale war; and that a minimal 'forty-eight-hour warning' would be forthcoming in a worst-case ('catastrophic') situation. Whether, when the time came, Aman would be able to supply the necessary six-day or even forty-eight-hour warning never came up for debate; no one thought it necessary to question Zeira's repeated assurances on this crucial point.[48]

But the summer months, in which new signs of the imminent war were picked up, passed without event. Zeira and Aman's Research Department emerged as the clear 'victors' over the war-fearing Mossad, and to a certain extent over Elazar and Dayan. This victory was to reinforce Aman's dominance and the massive intelligence failure the following September–October. Aman had been right in the spring; ergo, Aman was deferred to in the autumn, at tragic cost.[49]

The next major change in the military status quo came on the Golan front in August, when the normally cautious Syrians carried out a massive, unprecedented and unexplained deployment along the ceasefire lines. Even more worrying was the deployment opposite the Golan defences of a tightly packed AA missile network, which covered the Golan skies as well as the air space above the Syrian divisions. But Aman dismissed this as a defensive move to guard the approaches to Damascus against Israeli air strikes.[50] The *'kontzeptziya'* still held.

Calm before the storm

Aman's calm during August and early September remained undisturbed by Egyptian earth-moving activities along the canal. The Egyptians were seen building new access roads and training troops to breach the earth ramparts sloping down to the water. The Israelis accepted the Egyptian explanation, transmitted via the United Nations, that these activities were 'routine'.[51]

Egypt and Syria began considering Yom Kippur for D-Day, because it was assumed that on that holiest of all Jewish holidays, observed even by the secular majority of Israelis, when all public services (transportation, radio, etc.) shut down, the IDF would find it doubly hard to mobilize its reserves quickly. In addition, a full moon and Suez Canal tidal considerations made that day optimal from Egypt's point of view.[52]

On the wider, political horizon, Israel was unmoved by various warning signs, such as Libya's takeover of the Western oil companies and talk of an Arab oil embargo against the West. One senior Aman officer dismissed Saudi Arabia contemptuously: 'On top there is just sand, with some backward people, and underneath there is oil'.[53]

Then came the 13 September air battle in which IAF jets, on a reconnaissance mission over Syria, were attacked by MiGs. In the ensuing mêlée, twelve Syrian and one Israeli aircraft were shot down. The battle had the effect of stilling Israeli fears and providing a cover for Arab preparations. The alert that was immediately called in the Syrian and Egyptian air forces and in other Egyptian units was dismissed by Aman as stemming from the air battle and was therefore viewed as purely defensive.[54]

A wide-ranging review of the situation by the IDF General Staff on 17 September produced the following assessment by Zeira. The Arabs remained incapable of launching a war because of Israel's decisive air superiority – again proved so graphically only days before. If their armoured and AA capabilities improved, he argued, they might contemplate launching a renewed war of attrition – but not before the end of 1975. Zeira repeated this assessment at a closed meeting of Foreign Ministry executives on 21 September.[55]

According to one source, on 22 September Sadat informed Soviet leader Leonid Brezhnev that the war would be launched on 6 October.[56] On 24–25 September Aman monitored signs of a major new movement of Egyptian troops from the Nile bases towards the Suez Canal. These were followed by reports of boats being moved to the canal-side positions; of leaves being cancelled; and of a postponement from October to November of rank-advancement exams for Egyptian officers. Before the end of the month, Aman reported the mobilization of Egyptian reserve units.

But all this activity was dismissed by Aman's Research Department simply as preparations for 'Tahrir 41', which was due to start on 1 October. IDF intelligence predicted on the basis of past exercises that the Egyptians would move ammunition, bridging equipment and further units to the front – as, of course, occurred.[57] But the reinforcement of the units in the Hauran and the cancellation of leaves, the state of alert and the call-up of reserves in the Syrian army seemed to be more worrying.

Aman's Research Department again ruled on 26 September that Syria would not go to war alone and as Egypt was not planning war, there would be no outbreak of hostilities. But IDF OC Northern Command, Yitzhak Hofi, and defence minister Dayan were uneasy about the Syrian build-up. At the General Staff meeting of 25 September Hofi declared that there was a 'danger here of a surprise attack'. Dayan said he was afraid of a short, sharp Syrian 'grab' for a chunk of Golan land. Chief of staff Elazar said that this was unlikely as the IAF could overcome the Syrian AA system within 'half a day'.

On 24 September a combined US intelligence estimate, by the CIA, the NSA (National Security Agency) and DIA (Defence Intelligence Agency), that a joint Syrian–Egyptian assault was possible was sent to Israel. The US assessment was based on an unusual division-level Egyptian exercise, using a complex field communications network.[58] But a CIA request two days later for Israeli intelligence's appraisal of the situation elicited a 'not-to-worry' response.[59]

On 26 September, driven by Hofi's fears and Dayan's insistence, the IDF decided to reinforce its Golan Heights defences, which were manned by one under-tanked armoured brigade (the 188th) and a battalion or two of infantry, with elements of a second armoured brigade (the 7th). This reinforcement – the rest of the 7th brigade would reach the Golan shortly before the shooting started – was to prove crucial during the first days of the war; indeed, the presence and prowess of the 7th Brigade was to make all the difference between defeat and the loss of the Golan and the repulse of the Syrian invaders. The extra tanks began to reach the heights on the eve of the Jewish New Year (Rosh HaShana), 28 September.

A measure of Israel's general lack of concern was the cabinet's decision to enable prime minister Meir to address the European Parliament at Strasbourg on 30 September and to send foreign minister Eban to the UN General Assembly in New York. And the chief of staff, David Elazar, took his family to Sharm ash-Sheikh for a weekend holiday.

Yet the Syrian build-up continued to trouble the IDF. On 30 September the General Staff decided to send a further battalion of the 7th Brigade to the Golan. At that meeting the deputy chief of staff, Major-General Israel Tal, questioned Aman's tranquillizing assessments and may (the sources differ on this highly sensitive point) even have said, 'There's going to be a war.' But Tal did not to press home his opinion and did not demand a meeting with the defence minister to state his case. The General Staff, guided by Aman, continued to regard war as a 'very low probability'.[60]

Things nearly changed dramatically the following day, 1 October. In the early morning hours Aman received a report that Egypt and Syria intended to launch a full-scale attack later that day: Egypt, according to this intelligence, had decided to cross the canal, establish bridgeheads and press the superpowers to force an Israeli withdrawal from the occupied territories. The Egyptian exercise would turn into a genuine canal-crossing offensive, the report stated.

There were further signs of Arab readiness: Cairo international airport was briefly closed down;[61] more troops were called up and fresh units moved towards the canal. The IDF General Staff convened that morning. Aman's 'early morning report' notwithstanding, Zeira concluded: 'The situation is completely normal and will not develop into a war and there is no intention of turning it into war.' Zeira was referring to the start of 'Tahrir 41', which began that morning; the exercise accounted for the unusual Egyptian troop movements, he declared. A further Syrian armoured division had begun to move from northern Syria towards the Golan. But that too had nothing to do with war, because the Syrians would not embark on war without Egypt, and Egypt was not going to war, because it lacked a counterweight to the IAF. No one – the generals, Dayan or Mossad chief Zamir – demurred. The Americans were told not to worry. None the less, the rest of the 7th Brigade was ordered on to the Golan – and in the nick of time.[62]

In Strasbourg, meanwhile, Golda Meir met Western European leaders and flew to Vienna on 1 October for the 'Schonau' meeting with Chancellor Kreisky. Yisrael Galili, one of her senior ministers, called her before she left Strasbourg and mentioned the tension on the Golan Heights, but nothing more. The prime minister proceeded to Vienna, her mission supported by demonstrations in Tel Aviv and the Israeli media attacks on Kreisky and the PLO; attention was diverted away from the Middle East at precisely the moment it was most needed.

It was during this week, between Rosh HaShana (28 September) and 5 October, that Zeira decided not to employ what were cryptically described later as 'additional [intelligence-gathering] measures' with the purpose of divining Cairo's and Damascus's real intentions. For failing to employ these measures, while giving Elazar and Dayan the impression that he had done so, Zeira was severely reprimanded by the Agranat Commission the following year.[63]

On 2 October Mossad chief Zamir – more concerned by developments since May than his Aman colleagues – asked Zeira why the front lines were not being reinforced. Zeira replied: 'We are sending another brigade [i.e. the 7th] to the Golan.' On 3 October Zamir apparently tried to alert Golda Meir to the situation but the prime minister told him to talk to Dayan. That morning Egypt's Middle East News Agency reported by mistake that Egypt's Second and Third Armies had been put on a state of alert. Egyptian officials denied the report within minutes.[64]

At 11.00 a.m. on 3 October the senior cabinet ministers, including Meir, who had by now returned from Europe, and the army chiefs met to reassess the situation on the Golan front.

How should Israel react if the Syrians attacked? Zeira was ill; Brigadier General Aryeh Shalev, head of Aman Research, represented IDF intelligence. At the request of Elazar, Shalev and his namesake, Lieutenant-Colonel Avner Shalev, Elazar's *chef de bureau*, had quickly produced an analytical paper on the Syrian deployment. The two Shalevs reported that there were now between 750 and 800 Syrian tanks at the front, as compared to 250 the previous May; 550 artillery pieces, as compared to 180; thirty-one AA missile batteries, as compared to two at the beginning of 1973. And still the paper concluded that there was a 'low probability' of a Syrian attack and explained the purpose of the massive build-up as defensive.[65]

At the 3 October meeting (to which Zamir was not invited) Elazar and Dayan expressed concern at the Syrian moves; they were especially troubled by the build-up of the AA defence network, for which there was no reasonable explanation. Brigadier Shalev said:

> There is a report . . . that outlines a Syrian attack plan. According to the report, there is an intention to activate it in the near future . . . As to Egypt, there is a worrying report from a reliable source from 30 September, saying that on 1 October, two days ago, in the morning, Egypt was about to attack Sinai, and the Syrians would act simultaneously on the Golan . . .

But Shalev dismissed these reports as well as Elazar's and Dayan's fears. An Egyptian–Syrian offensive was 'not . . . likely. [War is] a low probability.' Aman's assessment continued to hold sway.[66]

That day Egyptian war minister Ismail Ali flew to Damascus for a final coordination session; no one in Aman seems to have remarked on the anomaly of his departure from Egypt during the huge 'Tahrir 41' exercise.

Voices in the wilderness

While the IDF intelligence chiefs were busy persuading the politicians that war was inconceivable, middle-ranking Aman officers in Southern Command were busy stifling the almost lone dissident who (subsequently) emerged honourably from the intelligence shambles – Lieutenant Binyamin Siman-Tov, one of the Command's junior intelligence officers. On 1 October, the day 'Tahrir 41' kicked off on the other side of the Canal, Siman-Tov wrote a memorandum entitled 'Movement in the Egyptian Army – the Possibility of a Resumption of Hostilities'. He argued that the exercise seemed to be camouflage for a real canal-crossing assault. In the absence of any reaction from his superior, Lieutenant-Colonel David Gedaliah, Southern Command's chief intelligence officer, Siman-Tov followed this up on 3 October with a second, more comprehensive analysis, entitled 'Situation Report on the Egyptian Army: 13 September–2 October 1973'. Lieutenant-Colonel Gedaliah, unimpressed, sat on the two memoranda and failed to pass them on to Aman HQ.

At one point in the commission's long proceedings, Gedaliah was asked: 'When did you reach the conclusion that it was war?'

Gedaliah replied: 'On Yom Kippur [6 October], at 2.00 p.m., I am afraid, at 2.00 p.m.'[67]

Lieutenant Siman-Tov, a lonely voice in the wilderness of the *'kontzeptziya'*, was of too low a rank to have been aware of another Aman dissident who plunged into the fray that week. He was Brigadier-General Yoel Ben-Porat, commander of Aman's Collection Department, who on 2 October had demanded that Zeira order the mobilization of his unit's reserve personnel. Zeira refused. When reports of the Soviet pull-out of 4 October began to arrive, Ben-Porat, defying Zeira's veto, mobilized dozens of his men 'on a voluntary basis', and that evening went to the Aman chief and enumerated the signs he believed pointed to war. Zeira replied: 'Stop assessing and stick to your job, which is collecting intelligence.'[68]

Warning lights in Tel Aviv

On Thursday, 4 October, the red lights began to go on in Tel Aviv. Zamir was becoming increasingly worried but failed to share his forebodings with the ministers. That evening he and Zeira held a crucial tête-à-tête at which Zamir 'wagered' that there would be war and told Zeira of the initiative he intended to take. Zeira agreed. Within hours the Mossad chief was on his way to his fateful rendezvous in Europe to try to confirm the '*tsnon*' warning.[69]

More ominous signals were picked up by Aman that day. Sigint intercepted an order from the Egyptian High Command to certain units to break off the Ramadan fast (during which Muslims refrain from eating or drinking from dawn until dusk for twenty-eight days) and the Egyptians turned off the flames emitted by the Gulf of Suez oilfields in order to reduce their vulnerability to air attack. That night first reports reached Aman and the Mossad of the hasty preparation for departure from Egypt and Syria of the families of Soviet advisers; a fleet of Aeroflot transport planes left the Soviet Union for the Middle East.

By noon on 5 October the planes were on their way back to the Soviet Union. Just after noon on 5 October Zeira reported to the IDF top brass that eleven Soviet transport aircraft had landed during the previous few hours at Damascus airport.[70]

During the previous night Aman's Research Department had completed the development and analysis of a large batch of aerial photographs taken earlier that day (Thursday) by Israeli aircraft west of the Canal. It was the first aerial reconnaissance operation since the end of September; the IDF had drastically cut back on air reconnaissance missions in order not to aggravate tension and because of the danger to the pilots from the AA missile batteries. The photographs showed that the Egyptian artillery deployment had grown, in ten days, from 800 guns to 1,100. Tank formations had taken up positions immediately behind the canal-side earth ramparts; and there was an unprecedented concentration of bridging equipment. The Research Department officers later described the 'hammer-blow' effect the photographs had had on them. The first appreciation of the photographs, written at 6.55 a.m. on 5 October, concluded with the dry but ominous sentence: 'In the canal area [the

Egyptians] have taken up an emergency deployment, larger than any deployment previously known to us.' But the initial shock wore off because in a later fuller appreciation of the aerial reconnaissance results, Lieutenant-Colonel Yona Bendman of the Research Department's Egyptian desk wrote (at 13.15 p.m.):

> (A) It is possible that the emergency deployment is one of the subjects being examined within the framework of the multi-division exercise [i.e. Tahrir 41]. (B) Although the taking up [by the Egyptians] of an emergency deployment on the canal front prima facie includes signs testifying to an offensive initiative, according to our assessment no change has occurred in the Egyptian assessment of the relative strength of our two armies. Therefore, the probability that the Egyptians intend to renew hostilities is low.

None the less, the officers of the Research Department, who met once again that Friday afternoon to discuss the situation, went home for the Yom Kippur weekend 'with a heavy heart'.[71]

The aerial photographs ate away at Aman's certainty; the departure of the Soviet families dealt it a further blow. Was the departure due to Arab fears of an Israeli attack or to Arab offensive plans? If the former, wouldn't the Soviets have approached Washington to stay Israel's hand? And 5 October provided more new and ominous signals. Soviet merchant vessels steamed abruptly out of Alexandria and Port Said for the open sea and four of Egypt Air's new Boeing aircraft flew out of Cairo International to Jedda, Saudi Arabia – to be out of harm's way.[72] Elazar declared a Stage-3 alert (the IDF's highest) on both fronts; all leaves were cancelled and the skeleton force that mobilizes the country's reserve units was held in readiness. His self-assurance shaken, Zeira now offered no objections. But neither Elazar nor Dayan called for a massive mobilization of the reserves.

At a further meeting of the political and military leaders at 11.30 a.m. on 5 October, the chief of staff admitted that he was no longer sure that war was a 'low probability'. Elazar said he still expected, if war was indeed imminent, more than a twelve-to twenty-four-hour warning; if no warning was forthcoming, it would constitute a 'complete surprise'. But at the full General Staff meeting that followed, Zeira reverted to his previous assessment: there was only a 'very low probability' of a joint Syrian–Egyptian attack. Aman's director still did not believe that war – now twenty-four hours away – was imminent. The General Staff dispersed without decision; everyone awaited new and definitive intelligence from Zamir. (Golda Meir was to say later that since those September–October days, she was 'unable to bear that word, "probability" [*sevirut*] . . . Every time I hear it, a shudder passes through me . . .')

At 5.00 p.m. on 5 October a vital piece of Sigint – a non-Arab message stating that there would shortly be war on both fronts – was intercepted. Ben-Porat passed it on to the head of Aman Research, Brigadier Aryeh Shalev, but for some reason, this vital information failed to reach the prime minister, the defence minister or the chief of staff.[73] An hour or so later, at 6.35 p.m., Zeira received word that Soviet ships were steaming out of Egypt's harbours to the open sea.[74]

Zeira was already in possession of the vital Mossad information – *'tsnon'* – relayed to Zamir from Europe at 2.30 a.m. on 5 October. But he still awaited Zamir's personal confirmation. That arrived a few hours after the midnight meeting in Europe between the Mossad chief and his agent. Zeira then set about telephoning generals and ministers with the news: it was war. The weeks of hesitation and doubt had come to an end.

The senior generals then convened, at around 6.00 a.m. on 6 October, in Elazar's office in Tel Aviv. Zeira reported that the evacuation of the Soviet advisers' families was now being followed by the exodus of the advisers themselves.[75] Zeira outlined the likely course of the Egyptian assault, in line with the long-known plans. Zeira's description was accurate. The agonizing problem was that the unmobilized IDF was in no position to exploit the information it had. At almost the same time as the decisive *'tsnon'* message from Zamir reached Tel Aviv, between 8.00 and 9.00 p.m. Washington time (around 3.00 a.m. Israel time), the head of the State Department's research unit, INR, Ray Cline reached the conclusion that hostilities were almost inevitable. But he was slow to pass this assessment on to Kissinger.[76]

The Syrian–Egyptian attack began at 1.55 p.m. while the Israeli cabinet was still in emergency session (and expecting the hostilities to begin four hours later, at 6.00 p.m.). The Syrians fielded some five divisions, with 1,400 tanks and over 1,000 artillery pieces; they were opposed by two armoured brigades, with a total of 177 tanks, a couple of infantry battalions and about fifty artillery pieces. The Egyptians fielded nine divisions, with 1,700 tanks and 2,000 artillery pieces; they were opposed by forces amounting to one armoured division, with 300 tanks and about thirty guns. The problem faced by the unreinforced Israeli troops in those first hours and days of battle was stark and obvious.

Aman's performance during the 1973 war

After the war, the Agranat Commission scathingly criticized Aman's performance during the first days of combat. A misleading or often downright incorrect picture of the Arab deployments, weaponry, lines of advance and intentions was presented by IDF intelligence to the generals conducting the battles. As Elazar was later to say of the afternoon of 6 October: 'What they knew was incorrect, and what was correct they were unable to tell me at that stage – who [which Arab unit] was where.' Aman failed to quickly discover how many bridges the Egyptians had thrown across the Canal and prematurely reported the crossing to the east bank of two Egyptian armoured divisions.

While Aman had known of the existence in Arab hands of the latest anti-tank weaponry, such as the Soviet-made Sagger missile, it had failed to assess properly its potential effect on the battlefield and to disseminate properly information about the new weapons among IDF combat units. Nor had it predicted the massive use to which these weapons would be put, or their effectiveness when employed so profusely. The Saggers and RPG-7s used by the Egyptian infantry and Syrian commando units devastated IDF armour in the first three days of the war.[77]

There was a similar failure by Aman (and the IAF) to appreciate the full effectiveness of the Soviet-built and organized AA missile screen in Syria and Egypt. Assessments were guided by the experience of the war of attrition in 1968–70, when the Israeli Phantoms had usually held their own against the Egyptian SAMs. On the morning of 6 October, with the war just hours away, IAF commander Benny Peled told Elazar that 'we allow the Syrian air force an hour in appropriate weather conditions [that is, the IAF could destroy the Syrian air force in one hour] . . . the AA missile system we can finish by noon . . . Then we can turn to Egypt.'[78] These assessments were to prove highly optimistic and indicate that the Aman/Air Force Intelligence Department evaluators had simply not done their homework properly.

As to the anti-tank weaponry, Aman quickly fathomed what had happened on the basis of the initial reports from the front. During planning for the first major IDF counter-offensive of the war on the night of October 7–8, Zeira warned against exposing the Israeli armour to the new weaponry before appropriate counter-measures were devised and deployed. But Elazar overruled him, arguing that if the situation was bad now, it could be much worse in a few days' time, when the Egyptians would have added more missiles, minefields and anti-tank obstacles to their defensive deployment on the east bank of the Canal. The attack, by Avraham Adan's and Ariel Sharon's armoured divisions, went ahead on 8 October and was repulsed by the Egyptian gunners and infantry. Adan's division suffered serious losses.[79]

One of Aman's major failures during the war was the arrival at the Golan front, without prior warning to the IDF divisions in the area and without any aerial or commando interdiction, of a large Iraqi expeditionary force. During the first days of the war, the Iraqi force, consisting of two armoured divisions (the 3rd and the 6th), with some 500 tanks, 700 armoured personnel carriers and 30,000 troops, moved undetected from bases near the Iraqi–Syrian border some 400 miles through the open desert on one or two axes to the Hauran, arriving and moving directly into battle between 12 and 19 October. The Iraqi counter-attack, though beaten off with heavy losses to the Arabs by the Israeli tankmen, stalled the IDF's momentum and gave the badly mauled Syrian units several days' respite, during which they regrouped and consolidated their defences west of Damascus. It is unclear whether Aman informed the General Staff of the impending arrival of the Iraqi force and its routes of advance and the General Staff failed to act on the information or, as some sources claim, Aman failed altogether to issue any warning or issued a warning so vague and insubstantial as to be ignored quite legitimately by its recipients.[80]

Aman did have some successes during the dark days of Yom Kippur. One of them was its prediction two days in advance of the start of the second stage of the Egyptian offensive. The Aman evaluation, submitted to Elazar on 12 October at a time when the General Staff and the cabinet were at a loss about how to proceed with the war, stated that Egypt would send its armoured divisions across the Canal and advance towards the vital Mitla and Gidi passes on 14 October. The IDF's armour was ready for them.[81]

Aman's Sigint Collection Department had a second major success on 16–17 October, when it tracked Egypt's 25th Armoured Brigade as it made its way northwards from the Third Army enclave towards the Israeli crossing-zone. The early warning of its advance enabled General Sharon's division to set a two-brigade trap along the shore of the Great Bitter Lake. The 25th Brigade was almost completely destroyed, with few Israeli losses.[82]

A telling sign of the Egyptian collapse on 14 October was the change in the quality of Egyptian army reporting from the battlefields up the chain of command. In the first days of the war, while the Egyptians were successful, that reporting had been accurate. On 14 October the Egyptian commanders transmitted outlandish lies – that their forces had 'captured Baluza', an Israeli rear base, or the Gidi Pass. Aman Sigint had picked up these transmissions and the IDF General Staff understood that the tide of battle had turned: the Egyptian high command was being misled and, without a true picture of the battlefield, had effectively lost control over its forces.

Aman also correctly predicted – contrary to its experience in 1967 – that Jordan would refrain from entering the war, an assessment that enabled the IDF to send to the Golan a division that had originally been earmarked for deployment along the Jordan river. On Sunday, 7 October, Sigint monitored the decisive message to the effect that King Hussein would sit this one out. During the first days of the war, the IDF was thus able to leave only twenty-eight tanks on the entire Jordanian front.[83]

Probably the most important piece of intelligence to reach the IDF units in the field was the location of the 'seam' between the Egyptian Second Army, which had crossed the canal around Ismailia, and the Third Army, to the south, which had crossed between Suez and the Bitter Lakes. This 'seam' represented the maximum point of Egyptian vulnerability, and was to be the place where the IDF punched through the Egyptian front on 15 October, reached the Canal at Deir Suweir and crossed over to the west bank, initiating the start of the Egyptian collapse. But by all accounts, though they differ, it was not Aman that had discovered the 'seam'.

According to Ariel Sharon, it was his division's reconnaissance battalion that found it on 9 October, when, moving northwards along the east bank of the Great Bitter Lake, it had tried to link up with surrounded Israeli positions at Deir Suweir. The same claim was made by General Shmuel Gonen (Gorodish), the OC Southern Front. Gonen said he found the 'seam' when examining IAF aerial reconnaissance photographs on the morning of 11 October.[84]

If field or combat intelligence performed poorly during 1973, Sigint nevertheless registered some significant successes. Most are still highly classified, but one notable intercept gave IDF Northern Command an accurate idea of the location and objective of a lead Syrian armoured brigade, the 47th. Aman monitored the Syrian commander reporting that he 'sees the Sea of Galilee, and in an hour's time will bathe in it'.[85]

Post-mortem: the Agranat Commission

As Aman had been Israel's principal intelligence-collecting agency and the sole assessor, evaluator and interpreter of intelligence, it was the chief victim of the purge that followed the Yom Kippur War. The Agranat Commission, set up in November 1973 and headed by the president of the Supreme Court, Shimon Agranat, produced three reports. Its interim report, issued on 2 April 1974, contained most of the Commission's main findings and recommendations. The final report, published on 30 January 1975, in general terms criticized Aman's performance in the field during the first three days of the war; it was especially scathing about the inefficiency of field intelligence before and during the unsuccessful IDF counter-offensive in the south on 8 October.[86]

The Commission recommended the removal from intelligence work of Eli Zeira, his deputy Aryeh Shalev, David Gedaliah, the intelligence officer of Southern Command, and the head of the Egyptian desk in Aman's Research Department, Lieutenant-Colonel Yona Bendman. (The Commission also 'with reluctance' recommended the removal from his post of COS David Elazar and, with lesser reluctance, OC Southern Command, Shmuel Gonen.) A few days after the publication of the interim report Zeira left the army and was replaced by General Shlomo Gazit, who had headed Aman's Research Department until 1967 and since then had been Coordinator of Operations in the West Bank and Gaza Strip. Shalev was replaced by Yehoshua Saguy, the former intelligence officer of Southern Command and commandant of the IDF Intelligence School. Gedaliah was replaced by Lieutenant-Colonel Zvi Schiller.

In the realm of organization the Agranat Commission's main recommendation was to break Aman's monopoly on the evaluation of intelligence and to introduce what it called 'pluralism in the various types of intelligence evaluations'. After publication of the interim report the Foreign Ministry's small Research Department was vastly expanded, with the aim of producing 'independent political–strategic intelligence' evaluations, and a large Research Department was set up in the Mossad. The Commission also recommended (reiterating a recommendation by the Yadin–Sharef Committee of 1963, which had been set up after the ructions of the Lavon Affair and the row over the German scientists in Egypt) that the government appoint an 'adviser to the prime minister on intelligence affairs', who, with a small 'highly skilled staff', would be able to independently assess the assessors. This recommendation was never carried out.

With the establishment of the Mossad's Research Department and the expansion of the Research Department of the Foreign Ministry, Aman's monopoly on evaluation had come to an end. But it remained in sole charge of evaluating military intelligence and in practice remained responsible for producing national strategic assessments and preventing the recurrence of a strategic surprise.[87]

In the months following the outbreak of the Yom Kippur War and the publication of the Agranat Commission's interim report there was a great deal of guilty soul-searching in Aman. A 'Pearl Harbor complex' developed and Gazit was hard pressed to boost morale. The Agranat Commission had specifically instructed Aman to reform the Research Department so that less manpower, time and energy would be expended on political intelligence-gathering and analysis and more on purely military research. The number of officers on the military side was greatly increased. The department was restructured and integrative geographical sections were set up, so that each section head was responsible for military, technological, political and economic intelligence for his region. A new and independent section – the Review Section, commanded by a senior officer – was created to act as a 'devil's advocate' in every field: its task was to present the contrary, unconventional case on every issue.[88] Junior officers were encouraged to present their own views, be they conformist or dissident. A model of warning signals for impending war was formulated. Aman evaluations, distributed regularly to the country's military and political leaders, were in future more open, less definite in tone and often included unorthodox opinions. An effort was made to keep facts clearly distinct from assessments.[89]

One of the most important findings of the Agranat Commission was that Aman had failed to distinguish properly between the 'signals' (of imminent war) and the background 'noises', in which these signals were enmeshed. It was not that the signals were missing or missed; they were there, in abundance, and were monitored by Aman and Israel's other intelligence-gathering agencies.[90] But IDF intelligence – meaning the Research Department – had failed to separate them from the background noises, some of them deliberate (deception), most incidental, that had spelled routine and a continued ceasefire.

In its interim report the Agranat Commission concluded:

> In the days preceding the Yom Kippur War, Aman (Research) had plenty of warning intelligence, provided by the Collection Department of Aman itself and by other collecting agencies of the state. Aman (Research) and the director of Aman did not correctly evaluate the warning provided by these pieces of intelligence, because of their doctrinaire adherence to the *'kontzeptziya'* and because of their readiness to explain away . . . the enemy [moves] along the front lines . . . as a defensive deployment in Syria and a multi-arm exercise in Egypt, similar to exercises that had taken place in the past.

In its final report the Commission recommended major changes in the IDF's combat or field intelligence. Aman units in the field had almost ceased to function during the first days of the war. This was especially true during the defensive engagements of 6–8 October on the southern front.

The main changes in field intelligence were the introduction of an array of drones for aerial reconnaissance at the regional command and divisional levels and the establishment of a ground observation unit employing state-of-the-art electro-optical equipment. The Aman contingents in the three regional commands (Northern, Central and Southern) were strengthened in order to render them an effective counterweight to Aman's HQ departments. A new job was created, chief intelligence officer, with the rank of brigadier-general, in order to decrease the administrative workload of the Aman director and enable him to devote more time to the branch's crucial research and evaluation functions. Aman's first chief intelligence officer was Dov Tamari, a former deputy paratroop brigade OC and former OC armoured division. The new men put the mistakes of 1973 behind them, but those mistakes would haunt them – and the entire country – for years to come.

The lessons

Israel's grand intelligence failure in 1973 offered two main lessons: that preconceptions and prejudices will often prevail over hard facts, especially when those facts point towards a bleak future; and that intelligence agencies, however well led and organized and however sophisticated their equipment, will invariably encounter difficulties in separating the wheat (good intelligence) from chaff (misleading or irrelevant intelligence), significant signals from meaningless background 'noise'. In the end it will always be up to the assessors and evaluators, and the political masters they serve, to interpret correctly the available intelligence. If they contemptuously dismiss their enemy as a bumbling, inefficient idiot when this is objectively warranted, they will in all probability do no harm; but when such an approach is unwarranted, they may lead their country to perdition.

The disaster of Yom Kippur led to greater caution and hesitation in intelligence assessments and to a less dismissive attitude towards Israel's potentially warlike neighbours. One negative effect of this, which was sharply felt in 1977, was the embarrassing degree of scepticism displayed by the intelligence community – and especially Aman – towards Egypt's peace initiative.

Despite the post-war reforms – the value of whose increased 'pluralism' was anyway questioned by many professionals – a variety of objective, geopolitical and strategic factors continued to constrain the entire Israeli intelligence community severely in ways that inevitably limited its ability to anticipate an Arab attack. Not least is the fact that the bulk of the IDF consists, now as then, of reservists who must be called up, equipped and deployed in time of war to assist the standing army of professionals and conscripts doing their national service. Israel's enemies, by contrast, maintain large standing armies which can move from defensive to offensive deployment in a matter of hours. A mistaken assessment of an Arab military threat can have far-reaching political and economic consequences for the Jewish state. And an unnecessary mobilization of the IDF's reserves – easily visible to any enemy – can in itself lead to a serious escalation of a crisis. The margins for error were, and remain, dangerously narrow.

The nature of the Arab regimes Israel faces is an unchanging factor too. Most are still autocracies in which one man, overnight, can decide on war or peace. Presidents Assad of Syria and Saddam Hussein of Iraq and King Hussein of Jordan do not require prolonged parliamentary or cabinet debate before ordering an attack. And clear knowledge of their decision is unlikely to filter out to Israeli intelligence beforehand. Sources as well-placed as the author of the heart-stopping *'tsnon'* message Zvi Zamir received on 5 October 1973 are few and far between.

Yom Kippur remains an open sore for Israel. The long-retired protagonists of the battered intelligence community continue to cross swords occasionally, defending their record, trying to clear their names when the old charges resurface, as a little more information dribbles out with each year that passes. Zvi Zamir remained virtually silent until, in 1989, he responded furiously and publicly to charges made by Yoel Ben-Porat, head of Aman's Collection Department in 1973, insisting hotly that it was IDF intelligence and not the Mossad that had failed at the most crucial moment of them all.[91]

The story of the *mehdal* is a Pandora's box of painful and

unfinished business which, once opened by the Agranat Commission, can still give out dark and embarrassing secrets. Perhaps the most intriguing of recent revelations is the suggestion that, on 25 September 1973, a full twelve days before the war began, prime minister Golda Meir received a personal warning of the impending Egyptian–Syrian assault from King Hussein of Jordan, who (apart from belatedly sending a small token force to assist the Syrians on the Golan Heights) stayed well out of the fighting once it began. Meir took that secret with her to the grave.

The importance of this claim was immense. Previously, Israel's intelligence community, not its politicians, had always borne the brunt of the blame for Yom Kippur. But if the prime minister herself had indeed received such a warning – and from such a uniquely informed Arab source – how could she have failed to pass it on to Aman and the Mossad? Yet even if she had, would it have been enough to change the fatal *'kontzeptziya'*?[92]

10

Interregnum with Peace: 1974–80

Post-war changes

The aftermath of Yom Kippur found Israel in a state of deep collective shock. By the time the 2,500 dead had been buried and the Agranat Commission had reported on the blunders and complacency that had preceded the war, the two most battered thirds of the country's intelligence community were under new management. Between publication of the commission's first and final reports, Yitzhak 'Haka' Hofi, a career soldier and former head of IDF Northern Command, had replaced Zvi Zamir, maintaining the post-Harel tradition of appointing IDF generals as heads of the Mossad. Shlomo Gazit took over from the disgraced Eli Zeira as chief of IDF intelligence. At the end of 1974 Yosef Harmelin, the only secret service chief unscathed by the pre-October failures and the post-war recriminations, was replaced as director of the Shin Bet by his deputy, Avraham Ahituv.

A new Middle East war seemed unlikely following the conclusion of the disengagement agreements negotiated in marathon shuttle diplomacy by the US secretary of state, Henry Kissinger, between Israel and Egypt (January 1974 and September 1975, known as Sinai I and Sinai II) and Syria (June 1974, on the Golan Heights). Kissinger had forced Israel to cede a small ribbon of territory round Quneitra back to Syria and to pull back from the Suez Canal to the east of the Mitla and Gidi passes, but most of Sinai and, more important, the entire West

Bank and Gaza Strip remained under occupation. Thus the Palestinian problem, which many believe is the very heart and core of the Arab–Zionist conflict, remained unresolved. Peace of any kind still seemed a remote prospect.

The shock of peace

Yet just four years after the disaster of 1973 Israel's intelligence community failed once again to provide early warning of an earth-shaking event: the *mehdal* this time was in not predicting President Anwar Sadat's peace initiative, which resulted in the signing of the September 1978 Camp David accords, the start of negotiations to solve the Palestinian question, and the Israel–Egypt Peace Treaty in March 1979, which ended nearly thirty years of conflict between the Jewish state and the largest and most powerful of its Arab enemies.

Early in 1976 Aman director Shlomo Gazit began to worry that a change of heart in the Arab world, from belligerency towards peaceful intentions, would go unnoticed in Israel.[1] After the trauma of Yom Kippur Aman had sensitized its antennae in all that related to Arab preparations for war. But were its receivers properly attuned to Arab moves towards peace? What would be the signs of an Arab change of heart? In September 1976 Gazit started to think seriously about the problem. He approached several foreign intelligence services – mainly the CIA – and asked for their views about such indicators, but their answers proved to be of little use. Gazit then turned to Israel's leading Middle East research body, the Shiloah Institute of Tel Aviv University (named after the late Reuven Shiloah), and asked the academics for a set of indicators. Eventually the Aman officers and the professors formulated two questions: (1) Has there been a change in public Arab statements about Israel? (2) Has there been a normative change in the Arab stand vis-à-vis Israel and the idea of peace?

Basing itself on these rather general guidelines, Aman's Research Department went to work and emerged in early

October 1977 – about six weeks before Sadat came to Jerusalem – with the conclusion that no change had occurred in the Arab world regarding attitudes to Israel. The Research Department believed that Sadat had reached a crossroads and could choose either peace or war. The Israeli–Egyptian Second Sinai Disengagement Agreement of September 1975 was scheduled to expire in October 1978, and Aman was convinced that Egypt would not renew it, meaning that the status quo in Sinai was in jeopardy. The Department leaned towards the opinion that Sadat would opt for war, despite Egypt's palpable unreadiness for a renewal of hostilities: since 1973 the Egyptian armed forces had been allowed to fall into rack and ruin.[2] In one of the preparatory discussions leading up to the formulation of Aman's annual 1977 national security assessment, a senior Aman officer suggested, half jokingly, that Egypt might opt for peace. 'Everyone laughed,' Gazit recalled later.

Israel's fundamental conception about Arab attitudes to the conflict made it difficult even to consider the idea of peace. 'The thirty years of conflict that preceded Sadat's visit had crystallized our thought processes in such a way that many of us saw only two possibilities, armed coexistence or war,' wrote Aluf Hareven, who had served in senior research positions with both IDF intelligence and the Mossad.[3]

In the spring of 1977 Charlotte Jacobson, the president of the US women's Zionist organization Hadassah, was invited to visit Cairo, an unusual gesture from the Egyptian regime. She asked the Rabin government for its opinion and was advised not to go because, as the Israelis put it, such a visit could be exploited by the Egyptians for propaganda. But Jacobson went. She returned to the United States via Jerusalem, where she enthused about what she had seen and heard. She told the Israeli government that the Egyptians were interested in a compromise and that she had been accorded red-carpet treatment. 'But not a word appeared about the visit in the internal Egyptian media, and this was not a good sign,' recalled Gazit. It was believed that public mention of Jacobson's visit would have implied greater warmth towards the Jewish state. So in its 1977 annual assessment, Aman concluded that while there had been some semantic changes in Egyptian media references to Israel, these were most likely 'a matter of propaganda'. There was no indicator of imminent peace. The Mossad was no wiser, despite the research department it had set up as a result of the Agranat Commission recommendations.

IDF intelligence was at a disadvantage. It had not been informed of the secret meeting in Morocco on 16 September between the foreign minister, Moshe Dayan, and Hassan Tohami, Sadat's deputy premier, and, perhaps even more significantly, it had no way of knowing that prime minister Begin would respond so favourably to an Egyptian initiative. Israel's long-standing connection with King Hassan of Morocco had rarely been so useful. Yitzhak Rabin had visited secretly as prime minister in October 1976 and had heard the king's concern about the rising tide of Arab radicalism that he feared would grow if the conflict with Israel were not resolved.[4] The Dayan–Tohami talks in Marrakesh had been arranged and attended by a senior Mossad officer (according to some sources it was the service chief himself, Yitzhak Hofi; others claim it was David Kimche), but the secret was well kept and, anyway, the talks were inconclusive. At the beginning of November the deputy prime minister, Yigael Yadin, suggested calling up the IDF's reserves to meet a possible Egyptian threat in Sinai.

So when, on 9 November 1977, Sadat announced his readiness to come and address the Knesset in Jerusalem, Aman was extremely sceptical, if not downright suspicious. It still seemed 'totally out of step with the mood and thinking in Egypt', Gazit argued. Sadat's foreign minister, Ismail Fahmi, was just as surprised and immediately resigned. The same day Gazit told Mordechai Gur dramatically: 'This is the deception of the century.'[5]

Aman had good reason to doubt the genuineness of Sadat's move. The bitter memory of 1973 had instilled in its Egyptian experts an exaggerated awareness of the role of deception in Arab strategy. Intelligence reports showed that the Egyptian army had intensified training and was preparing for war in

1978. Remarks made by Sadat on a visit to Saudi Arabia fuelled the fears of deception. 'If I believed the Israelis wanted peace I wouldn't go to Jerusalem but would pursue ordinary negotiations,' the Egyptian president had said. 'But the Israelis are extremists and that's how I want them to appear before the whole world.'

A few days later Aman suspicions translated, embarrassingly, into a published statement by the IDF chief of staff, Mordechai Gur, that Sadat's move might be a new Egyptian deception to mask real aggressive designs.[6]

On 14 November Gazit told Ezer Weizman, the minister of defence:

> It doesn't matter what the Egyptians say, we have to assume that they're preparing for war, and we will not know when. Their actions can serve as a smokescreen for war. Sadat will argue that he was prepared to go all the way and that Israel didn't respond. The decision to go to war depends on five or six people, and we can't depend on a date.[7]

But the historic visit went ahead. Sadat arrived in Jerusalem on 19 November, addressed the Knesset and dramatically opened the way to Israeli–Egyptian talks, the Camp David agreement, the fruitless search for Palestinian 'autonomy' in the West Bank and, eventually, the peace treaty and the return of Sinai to Egyptian sovereignty. Gazit was to explain later that the peace policy had been 'the result of a personal decision, a decision that had not been discussed, examined or accepted by any forum within the ruling circles of Cairo. It did not rest on any broad Arab consensus.'[8]

Gur, who greeted the Egyptian leader on the tarmac at Ben-Gurion airport ('I wasn't bluffing,' Sadat told him), remained unrepentant. 'I really thought it was a deception plan at a very high strategic level,' he said later. 'I didn't think that the Egyptian president was going to start a war during the visit or immediately afterwards. I didn't mean that kind of deception, but a deception in the sense of careful preparation for war towards 1978.' While Sadat was addressing the Knesset, Ezer

Weizman sent the chief of staff a note saying: 'Start preparing for war.'[9]

The failure of the entire Israeli intelligence community to predict the Sadat peace initiative cast a serious shadow over the post-Yom Kippur pluralistic reforms and over its capacity to foresee major political or strategic changes in the Middle East. This was not to be the last time it would display this fundamental weakness.

Israel, Iran and the Kurds: 1967–79

In February 1979, a month before the signing of the peace treaty with Egypt, Israel lost its most important ally in the Middle East. Just as it managed finally to break through thirty years of Arab hostility, the Shah of Iran fell to a coalition of Islamic fundamentalists and left-wingers, a blow primarily for the United States, but one for Israel too. The relationship between Tehran and Jerusalem had broadened and deepened since the Mossad's Foreign Relations Division had first begun to nurture it as the centrepiece of its successful 'periphery policy' in the late 1950s and early 1960s. The incumbent of the Peacock Throne bought huge quantities of Israeli weapons and was an invaluable partner in trade and the exchange of intelligence. Ayatollah Khomeini hated Jews, was opposed to the very existence of Israel and was close to the most radical of its Palestinian enemies. It was not a merely symbolic gesture when the new regime's Revolutionary Guards handed over the Israeli Embassy building in Tehran to the PLO.

By the time the Shah fell, the Israeli–Iranian relationship no longer involved the hapless Kurds. Israeli assistance for the Iraqi Peshmerga had increased dramatically after the 1967 war and it rapidly became one of the worst-kept secrets in the Middle East. The leader of the Kurdish Democratic Party, Mulla Mustafa Barzani, visited Israel in September that year and presented Moshe Dayan with a curved Kurdish dagger. A well-planned mortar attack on the oil refineries at Kirkuk in March

1969 was widely believed to be the work of the Israelis. The Egyptian journalist Mohamed Hassanein Heikal was told in 1971 that 'Israeli officers in Kurdistan were in constant radio contact with Israel and were involved in espionage inside Iraq'.[10] The Iraqi press regularly mentioned the Israeli presence.

The Shah continued to pursue a policy of weakening Iraq internally, and when the Iraqi–Soviet friendship treaty was signed in April 1972 he gained powerful new supporters. The following month the Shah secretly arranged with President Nixon and his secretary of state, Dr Henry Kissinger, for massive economic and military support of the Iraqi Kurds, so as to neutralize the Iraqi army regionally. Over the next three years more than $16 million in CIA funds was funnelled to the Kurds.[11] US sources, probably located in the State Department, which opposed the policy, reported soon afterwards that the Israelis were serving as the conduit and handing over $50,000 per month. Zvi Zamir, then head of the Mossad, paid a visit too.[12]

It was a coldly calculated arrangement, as later described by the Pike Report submitted to the US House of Representatives. 'The president, Dr Kissinger and the foreign head of state [the Shah] hoped our clients [the Kurds] would not prevail,' it said. 'They preferred instead that the insurgents simply continue a level of hostilities sufficient to sap the resources of our ally's neighbouring country [Iraq]. This policy was not imparted to our clients, who were encouraged to continue fighting. Even in the context of covert action, ours was a cynical enterprise.'[13] The same calculations applied to Iran and Israel, which substantially increased their aid to the Kurds in the summer of 1972. Golda Meir saw the Shah in Tehran just before Nixon and Kissinger arrived.[14] In August 1972 new unrest broke out in Kurdistan.

Massive quantities of Soviet weaponry captured in 1967 were transferred to the Kurds. Ya'akov Nimrodi, the highly influential Israeli military attaché in Tehran, served as the main channel. A contemporary anecdote tells how Barzani, accustomed to receiving Eastern Bloc arms, was once surprised and pleased to be given accidentally a consignment of Israeli-made mortars, which he found superior and so demanded more. Barzani had exaggerated expectations of Israeli capabilities: he had, according to one well-placed source, 'set his sights on a joint campaign in which Israel would capture Syria while he conquered Iraq'.[15] Despite their deepening involvement, the Israelis tried to keep a low profile and it is uncertain whether the ordinary Peshmerga fighters knew their identity. Sometimes the Israeli advisers wore Iranian army uniforms, but not all of them could speak Farsi.[16]

The Israelis had few illusions about the true nature of their relationship with the Shah. Towards the end of the support for the Iraqi Kurds, in 1974 and early 1975, the strain began to show. Iran wanted to harass Iraq, but not more than that, for it had always to consider the 5 million Kurds living within its own borders. Israeli representatives in Iran knew that their presence, which was never accorded full diplomatic status, was acceptable only as long as it served the interests of the Peacock Throne. Uri Lubrani, who became ambassador in September 1973, had been ambassador in Ethiopia from 1968 to 1971 in similarly fragile and 'peripheral' political circumstances; he became a regular choice for difficult jobs in sensitive places and in May 1983 was appointed coordinator of Israeli activities in Lebanon. Intelligence and security remained a vital part of the Iranian–Israeli relationship until the very end in 1979. The last Israeli ambassador to Tehran before the overthrow of the Shah was Yosef Harmelin, the head of the Shin Bet from 1963 to 1974.

According to some sources Israel asked Barzani to mount a new offensive in October 1973 to try and stop the Iraqis moving in support of the Syrian army on the Golan front. The CIA and Kissinger vetoed the plan. At the same time the Shah promised Saddam Hussein he would not take advantage of the deployment of Iraqi forces – sixty aircraft, 30,000 men and 400 tanks – to the front line against Israel. When the Iraqis were mauled on the Golan – losing twenty-one planes, eighty tanks and 125 dead – the Shah could be well pleased with his manoeuvre.

In March 1970 the Baghdad government and Barzani had

worked out a fifteen-point peace plan which was to be implemented in 1974 after a four-year transitional period. Thus the settlement of the Kurdish question in Iraq was seriously imperilled by the increased Iranian–US–Israeli support for Barzani. This international backing meant that he could continue the war. For the moment, the Peshmerga leader escalated his demands, insisting that the Kurdish region include Kirkuk and its oil wells and that the Kurds have the authority to maintain their own army and conduct their own foreign affairs. In effect, Kurdish fighters refused to relinquish their weapons and halt the civil war in March 1974, at the end of the transitional phase. The Iraqi army, increasingly equipped with Soviet weapons, was soon able to achieve military success. In early March 1975 the Iraqis accepted an Iranian offer to stop supporting the Kurds in exchange for a settlement along the Shatt al-Arab. The Kurdish rebellion collapsed and desperate pleas from Barzani to Kissinger were simply ignored. William Colby, the CIA chief, questioned the secretary of state and was told bluntly that 'secret service operations are not missionary work'.[17] Considering how widely known it was, the secret of Israel's support for the Kurds remained highly sensitive. When prime minister Begin spoke openly and proudly about the subject shortly after the outbreak of the Gulf War in 1980, he was criticized by Meir Amit – under whom the relationship had begun – for his indiscretion about past operations.[18]

If America and the West 'lost' Iran in 1979, it was not for lack of warnings by the Israelis, who were 'the first to start ringing the alarm bells'.[19] Lubrani, who was known to be extremely well informed, had been writing gloomy assessments of the Shah's chances of survival since early 1978. In early June he dispatched a long cable home, arguing that it was no longer a question of 'whether the Shah could survive', but only 'how long he would last'. The Americans dismissed his reports as alarmist, as they did those of the French SDECE, the only other Western intelligence service to predict disaster.[20] 'Having gone to Iran from Ethiopia,' Lubrani wrote later, 'I had seen a monarchy actually in the process of decay. I realized very early in my stay that the only organized infrastructure which had leeway to operate within the country was the religious community.'[21] Reuven Merhav, the Mossad representative in Tehran, reached similar conclusions.[22] Around the same time another senior Mossad liaison officer was consulting with the head of SAVAK, General Nassiri Moghaddam, about which 'troublemakers' might usefully be arrested to try and forestall further opposition to the regime.[23]

The CIA report

Another consequence of the Iranian revolution was extremely embarrassing for Israel's intelligence community. Documents seized from the US Embassy in Tehran in November 1979 included a copy of a secret CIA report entitled 'Israel: Foreign Intelligence and Security Services Survey'. The Iranians published the report. The forty-seven-page document, originally prepared in 1976 and based partly on publicly available information, was redistributed in 1979. It contained several obvious errors, but overall it was the most detailed account ever published of the structure and general priorities and performance of the Israeli secret services. The report stated that the Mossad employed 1,500 to 2,000 personnel, of whom 'about 500' were officers. The Shin Bet had 1,000 members with 550 'of officer rank'. Military intelligence employed 7,000 personnel, including 450 officers.

According to the CIA, the Mossad was divided into eight departments: (1) Operational Planning and Coordination; (2) Collection; (3) Political Action and Liaison; (4) Manpower, Finance, Logistics and Security; (5) Training; (6) Research; (7) Technical Operations; and (8) Technology. The Shin Bet also had eight departments, three operational ones – Security, Arab Affairs and Non-Arab Affairs – and five support ones – Planning and Coordination, Operational Support, Technology, Investigations and Legal/Administration.[24] Isser Harel, always ready to comment, found the report's appearance 'an act of amazing irresponsibility'. He was especially angry that it had not mentioned the Mossad's acquisition of Khrushchev's famous de-Stalinization speech of the Soviet Communist Party Congress in 1956.[25]

Iraqi interlude: bombing the Baghdad reactor

Israel had been uncertain about how to respond strategically when the war between Iran and Iraq erupted in September 1980. But there were clearly short-term, tactical opportunities to be seized. Despite the fiercely anti-Western and anti-Israel character of the Khomeini regime, arms supplies to Tehran continued in secret, and it seemed to make sense to exploit Baghdad's preoccupation with the Gulf to strike at this powerful Arab enemy.

Israel's most stunning blow came in the summer of 1981. At 5.34 p.m. on 7 June, a force of eight IAF F–16s, covered by six F–15 interceptors, swooped down on Iraq's French-built Osirak nuclear reactor at Al-Tuweitha, north of Baghdad, and bombed it to rubble. The timing of the raid, as Aman chief Yehoshua Saguy said later, had been 'meticulous': work had ended at the plant, which was in an advanced stage of construction, about an hour before.[26]

The surgical strike, in which one French technician died and nine Iraqis were killed and wounded, brought to an end months of Israeli planning to neutralize Iraq's nuclear development programme. The Al-Tuweitha reactor was due to go 'hot' – with the insertion of the uranium rods into the core – in July or September. After that a raid would have caused nuclear pollution around Baghdad, with incalculable though almost certain massive death and injury to the Iraqi population.

Israel and Iraq had been formally in a state of war since the 1948 Iraqi invasion of Palestine; unlike the other Arab combatants, Iraq had subsequently refused to sign an armistice agreement. Israel's leaders, led by Menachem Begin, believed that the nuclear programme launched by President Saddam Hussein was geared to the production of nuclear bombs and that these weapons – despite the ongoing war against Khomeini's Iran – were destined primarily for use against Israel. Begin and most of his fellow ministers thought in terms of a possible 'second Holocaust'.

Iraq's nuclear programme began in the late 1970s. Secret agreements were signed with the French government and French companies to provide the reactor, technicians and nuclear fuel. Planning for the IAF attack began in November 1979.[27]

From the start, in late 1978, both Aman chief Shlomo Gazit (later replaced by Yehoshua Saguy) and Mossad chief Yitzhak Hofi opposed the bombing plan. They believed that some years would elapse before the reactor could begin to pose a threat to Israel and feared that a strike could escalate into war, impeding or even undoing the Israeli–Egyptian peace process. They were backed, until 1981, by deputy prime minister Yigael Yadin.[28]

According to Gazit, Aman had 'reliable and authoritative' information that Iraq was bent on developing nuclear weaponry rather than pursuing benign research. But throughout the countdown to the raid, he remained convinced that Israel should try to block the Iraqi programme by non-military means. According to Viennese press reports, one of the Mossad's main sources on the state of Iraq's nuclear programme at given points in time was Roger Richter, an employee of the International Atomic Energy Agency (Richter was fired after the bombing, following Iraqi complaints that he had supplied both Israel and the United States with confidential information).[29]

Israel pursued a number of diplomatic strategies to halt the progress of the Iraqi nuclear programme. France was repeatedly approached, directly and indirectly; the United States was mobilized to pressure France. Nothing helped. On 6 April 1979 Israel took its first initiative on the ground to block the programme: Mossad agents raided the storerooms of a French nuclear plant at Le Seyne-sur-Mer, near Toulon, where the reactor core was being built. The core was blown up and the attack claimed by a previously unknown organization called the 'French Ecological Group'. The French DST security service suspected that the Mossad was the most likely perpetrator.[30]

A second effort to dissuade either the French from pressing on with their nuclear assistance or the Iraqis from continuing with the project was made in June 1980. Dr Yahya al-Meshad, an Egyptian-born metallurgist and a member of Iraq's Atomic Energy Commission, who was in Paris to complete arrangements with the French about the shipment of nuclear fuels to Baghdad, was murdered in his hotel room by unknown assailants. His body was found by a chambermaid on 14 June. He had received a large number of knife wounds though robbery was not the motive. The killing reminded many of the mysterious attacks against the German scientists working on Nasser's rocket programme in the early 1960s. A prostitute who had met the Egyptian scientist on the evening of his death and had heard voices coming from his room was questioned by the DST on 1 July. On 12 July she was killed in a hit-and-run car accident.[31]

In September 1980 Israel received help from an unexpected quarter: Iranian aircraft twice raided the Al-Tuweitha site, inflicting minor damage on the reactor's auxiliary buildings. The Iraqis stepped up security and anti-aircraft defences around the perimeter. This may well have provided the Israelis with another opportunity, this time to recruit agents on the spot. After the Iranian attacks all the French and Italian experts working at the reactor went home, returning only in February 1981. Inside sources were almost certainly found in the intervening period.[32]

On 14 October 1980 senior Israeli policy-makers and army and intelligence chiefs met in Jerusalem to discuss the reactor problem. Colonel Aviem Sella, the IAF's new head of operations, was busy working on the bombing plan. Begin forcefully pressed his view – that to destroy the site was the lesser of two evils. Yigael Yadin and interior minister Yosef Burg continued to oppose the bombing. They were supported by Hofi, Saguy and the IDF's head of planning, Major-General Avraham Tamir. Saguy argued that a strike might induce Iraq and Iran to bury the hatchet and turn their attention to Israel. Interestingly, the deputies of both intelligence chiefs backed Begin. The deputy head of military intelligence, Aviezer Ya'ari, asserted that the Baghdad bombs were being built for use against Israel; and Hofi's deputy, Nahum Admoni, argued that the strike would be a useful warning to others in the Arab world.[33]

The full cabinet debated the issue on 28 October, with Saguy and Hofi calling for a postponement of the raid to see how the Iraqi programme developed. The Aman chief argued forcefully against the 'second Holocaust' approach. Nuclear arms in Arab hands did not necessarily spell Israel's destruction. Destruction of the reactor would not halt Iraq's nuclear programme. In any case, Iraq would not be in a position to produce nuclear weapons until at least the early 1990s. Saguy was worried about possible US and Arab responses to such a strike. It could cause, he argued, 'a deep rift and severe crisis between Israel and the US'.[34] He remained convinced that Iraq's programme could be blocked by other means.[35] But the majority of ministers remained unmoved by the views of the heads of Aman and the Mossad. The cabinet decided in principle on an air strike. On 10 November 1980 David Ivri presented the IAF plan to the General Staff.

On 15 March 1981 the General Staff approved the plan. Saguy initially voiced reservations, suggesting that the IAF might fail to destroy the reactor and Israel would incur the world's wrath.[36] On 3 May the Aman chief said that the proposed raid would lead to the re-establishment of the anti-Israeli Eastern Front – Syria, Jordan and Iraq – and in any case, the Iraqi 'bomb' was still far-off.[37] Saguy's opposition almost sparked off a high-level crisis two days before the raid was at last launched (there had been repeated delays in implementation, because of a crisis in Lebanon and a summit meeting between Begin and Egypt's President Sadat, etc.). On 4 June, not having been informed of the 7 June date for the attack, Saguy had exploded, saying that he was not responsible for the operation and there would be 'no intelligence'. But he was eventually mollified.[38]

The raid went off without a hitch. The aircraft flew over Saudi Arabia and Jordan for over an hour and, taking the Iraqi AA defences by surprise, completely destroyed the reactor core and adjacent buildings. The Iraqis belatedly fired off some SAMs and sent up interceptor planes, but there was no contact and the Israeli force reached home unscathed.

And contrary to Aman and Mossad fears and warnings the raid resulted in remarkably little negative fall-out. There were condemnations by the Arab world, some half-hearted criticism in the West and a brief suspension of F-16 deliveries by the United States, but nothing more. Iraq's nuclear development programme was set back by years. And the French, giving the whole matter second thought, stopped supplying the Iraqis with weapons-grade uranium, as Israel had long demanded.

One temporary adverse effect was a decision by the United States to restrict Israel's access to US satellite intelligence on countries not directly threatening Israel or not on its borders. William Casey, the swashbuckling head of the CIA, was privately pleased that the Israelis had disposed of the Iraqi nuclear problem, and he admired their audacity, but he went along with the new restrictions and the withholding of the F-16 deliveries. A month after the bombing Saguy visited Casey; the long-term intelligence relationship between the two countries was undamaged.[39]

Begin reaped political benefit and swept to electoral victory at the head of his Likud bloc for the second time the following month. He crowed over the success and gave away far too much about the intelligence that had been available in planning the raid, volunteering incorrect information about the depth below the ground of a secret Iraqi laboratory and hinting heavily at US cooperation. The Mossad chief, Yitzhak Hofi, gave an unprecedented newspaper interview to publicly urge politicians to stop compromising contacts with friendly foreign intelligence services by revealing secret information supplied by them. 'He did not,' Begin's biographer has noted, 'need to name the politicians he had in mind.'[40]

Aman's defeat over the reactor attack – they had consistently opposed it, it had taken place and the negative fall-out they had predicted had barely materialized – had a serious effect during the following months on the input of IDF intelligence during the countdown to the invasion of Lebanon exactly one year later. Saguy, who had objected to the Al-Tuweitha operation and opposed the prospective invasion, was simply not listened to.

The PLO adjusts

Henry Kissinger had promised Israel in 1975 that Washington would not deal with Yasser Arafat's Palestine Liberation Organization unless it unequivocally accepted UN resolutions 242 and 338 and recognized Israel's right to exist. But throughout the second half of the 1970s, both before and after Anwar Sadat's dramatic journey to Jerusalem, the PLO remained a serious problem, both for the region's peace-makers and for Israel's intelligence community.

The Palestinians were unhappy with Israel's three disengagement agreements with Egypt and Syria, largely because Kissinger's successful bilateral approach to the Middle East problem was undercutting their chances of taking part in an all-party peace conference; they felt isolated and unimportant. But the PLO quickly began to adjust its strategy to the post-war situation. In June 1974 the Palestine National Council – the organization's 'parliament' – vowed to establish an 'independent national fighting authority' on any Palestinian soil liberated from the Israelis. Although explained as a tactical change, this marked, as one expert commented later, 'a real shift in the PLO position towards the occupied territories; unequivocal support for military struggle has ever since been supplemented by a willingness to consider political means as well'.[41] Implicit in this decision was a readiness to make do with Palestinian sovereignty over only a part of historic Palestine.

At the summit conference held in Rabat, Morocco, in October 1974 all the Arab countries, and most significantly Jordan, reaffirmed the status of the PLO as 'the sole legitimate representative of the Palestinian people' and secretly gave the organization veto power over any Arab peace proposal. The main effect of both these moves was to bring the occupied West Bank and Gaza Strip to the forefront of Palestinian politics and strategy. They also increased existing strains and rivalries between the different groups that sheltered under the PLO's 'umbrella'. Backed by the Ba'athist regime in Baghdad, the breakaway Fatah Revolutionary Council, led by Sabri al-Banna – better known as Abu Nidal – began to wage a war of assassinations against Arafat's Fatah organization in Europe and the Middle East. But Abu Nidal was not alone. George Habash's larger PFLP led the opposition to the PNC decisions and became synonymous with the concept of 'rejectionism', although the mainstream camp carried out its own share of bloody attacks. Before the PNC, in April 1974, three members of Ahmed Jibril's PFLP–GC killed eighteen Israelis, including eight children, in an attack on an apartment block in Kiryat Shmona. In May, as Kissinger was shuttling between Damascus and Jerusalem to try and finalize the Israeli–Syrian disengagement agreement, three members of Nayif Hawatmeh's DFLP – which supported Arafat's increasingly pragmatic line – infiltrated across Israel's northern border and took over a school in the Galilee development town of Ma'alot. The three terrorists and twenty-two children were killed and over seventy wounded in the subsequent shoot-out with the IDF. Katyusha rockets, which the Shin Bet discovered later had been smuggled across the Dead Sea, were found aimed in the general direction of Jerusalem's King David Hotel, where Kissinger was staying.

Arafat made diplomatic progress. On 14 November 1974 he addressed the UN General Assembly in New York: 'I have come bearing an olive branch and a freedom fighter's gun,' he said. 'Do not let the olive branch fall from my hand.' Less than a week later another DFLP squad struck, killing four Israelis and wounding twenty before the terrorists were themselves killed in an apartment block in Bet Shean. In March 1975 the Savoy Hotel in Tel Aviv was attacked by a seaborne guerrilla squad and there was a large bomb explosion in Jerusalem in early July.

The Lebanese civil war erupted in the summer of 1975. From the spring of 1976 Israel began to look northwards to see how the shifting constellations of Lebanese politics could be turned to its advantage in the war with the Palestinians. Terrorism was still a major priority for the country's security and intelligence chiefs and was to remain so for years to come. And, for the first time since 1967, they had to deal with armed, underground activity by Jewish extremists as well.

Rescue at Entebbe

Israel's most famous action ever in the war against terrorism took place on the tarmac at Uganda's Entebbe airport on 3/4 July 1976. The operation remains a classic example of military daring combined with precise intelligence obtained from a variety of sources in rapidly changing circumstances and on remote and difficult terrain. Aman and the Mossad both played vital roles in the planning.

The crisis began on 27 June, when an Air France plane *en route* from Tel Aviv to Paris was hijacked after a stopover in Athens, where airport security was notoriously lax. Two days later, after spending a night in Casablanca and being refused permission to land in Khartoum, the plane arrived at Entebbe. The hijackers, a mixed group of Arabs and Germans working for the Wadi Haddad faction of the PFLP, demanded the release of forty Palestinians in Israeli gaols, as well as about a dozen others from European countries. They also wanted two young West Germans, Thomas Reuter and Brigitte Schultz, who had been secretly arrested in Kenya a few months before when they tried to shoot down an El Al jet taking off from Nairobi airport with a SAM-7 rocket. The Air France plane and the passengers would be blown up if the prisoners were not flown to Uganda by 30 June.

Cabinet ministers were not enthusiastic about the military

options presented to them and initially favoured agreeing to the hijackers' demands. Prime minister Rabin, anticipating objections, ordered the Shin Bet to produce a report showing that there were precedents for freeing convicted murderers.[42] Shortly before the 30 June deadline passed, the IDF chief of staff, Mordechai ('Motta') Gur, said he could not recommend military action because of the absence of sufficient intelligence about the situation on the ground, although the separation of the Israeli and Jewish passengers from the others – who were then released – looked ominous and, for some, aroused terrible memories.

A carefully crafted cabinet statement helped buy more valuable time: ministers were authorized to continue efforts to free the hostages. The hijackers apparently assumed that their demands were to be met and postponed their deadline until 3 July to allow for the exchange of prisoners. Disinformation about Israeli intentions, deliberately leaked to third parties, may have played a role in the deception.

Military planning then went into high gear as more intelligence became available. The preparations were aided by the presence of several senior IDF officers and pilots who had served in Uganda on training and support missions for the Idi Amin regime, which had been on good terms with Israel until 1972. Officials of the Histadrut construction company, Solel Boneh, which had built Entebbe airport, were called in too. Films of Amin being received at the airport were screened, and one officer had the bright idea of using a long, black Mercedes limousine – like the one used by Amin – as a ruse to get past the Ugandan guards. 'But none of this helped us find out specific things like where the plane was, how many terrorists there were and which room they were in in the terminal,' said Major Muki Betzer, one of the planners and a participant in the assault force.[43] Amin himself was contacted by phone and this helped the Israelis understand that he was actively cooperating with the hijackers.

Mossad agents in Kenya and in Uganda itself, where the PLO had an office, helped build up a detailed picture of the situation on the ground. On 2 July, the day before the actual rescue, the planners received vital intelligence, photographs of Entebbe airport taken the previous day.[44] Mossad agents from all over Europe were called in to Paris to question the non-Israeli passengers who had been released and flown to Orly airport, and it was only then that the crucial missing information was obtained. One of them, a French Jew called Michel Cojot, was particularly adept at recalling the airport's layout and the location of the hostages, the terrorists and the explosive charges they had planted.[45]

A key coordinating role was played in this operation by Rabin's adviser on terrorism, Major-General Rehavam ('Gandhi') Ze'evi, a gung-ho former head of the army's central command who was the first incumbent of the post. In Paris Ze'evi continued talks with the hijackers via the French and he was not told that a rescue mission was under way; this added an additional element of deception to the overall plan.[46]

The rescue operation – codenamed 'Thunderball' – finally went ahead on the basis of precise intelligence about the dispositions of hijackers and Ugandan troops. One worrying problem was the existence of Ugandan MiG fighters at Entebbe airport and the possibility, 'even though of a low probability', according to the Aman chief, Shlomo Gazit, that they could be used to shoot down the Israeli C-130 Hercules transports during the flight north after the rescue. All eleven MiGs were destroyed during the raid to ensure the safe return flight of the task force and the hostages.[47]

The six-plane force flew low over the Red Sea to avoid enemy radar. The lead Hercules – a very quiet plane despite its bulk – touched down at Entebbe a few minutes after a British airliner had landed. It was all over in a few minutes: all the terrorists were killed, as well as more than a dozen Ugandan soldiers; the attacking force lost an officer, Lieutenant-Colonel Yonatan Netanyahu, and one soldier badly injured and paralysed for life. Three hostages were killed and Dora Bloch, a seventy-three-year-old passenger who had earlier been hospitalized in Kampala, was murdered by Idi Amin's troops. No plane flying to or from Israel has been hijacked since then.

The Mossad's Kenyan connection was vital in providing a forward base.[48] The rescue operation went ahead smoothly largely because of the help of Bruce McKenzie, a British businessman and former Kenyan cabinet minister who was then serving as an adviser on security and intelligence to President Jomo Kenyatta. It was McKenzie's men who had caught Thomas Reuter and Brigitte Schultz the previous January and had arranged for their secret transfer to Israel to stand trial. The two Germans were sentenced to ten years' imprisonment but were released after serving less than half their term in December 1980. McKenzie was killed in 1978 by a bomb planted on his private plane. It was widely believed that it was the work of Ugandan agents taking revenge for his role in the Entebbe rescue.

Ballots or bullets?

Nearer home, in the mid-1970s, it was a time of political change in the occupied territories. In December 1975 the Labour defence minister, Shimon Peres, announced that elections would be held in West Bank towns the following April. The Jordanian election law was amended and the franchise extended to all adults over twenty-one, for the first time ever including women. 'Peres,' according to his biographer, 'held that allowing the inhabitants of the territories a first-hand experience of the values of the democracy would give them a greater sense of self-rule and in turn mitigate the less appealing effects of the occupation.'[49] Put less generously, the defence minister also hoped to use the elections as a basis for some sort of autonomous local administration and believed that the incumbent conservative, pragmatic and mostly pro-Jordanian mayors, who, he hoped, would be returned to office, would serve as a barrier against the mounting influence of the PLO.[50] The West Bank elections turned out to be a mistake, another blunder of policy. But the decision to go ahead was taken not because of faulty intelligence but because insufficient weight was attached to known facts.

Despite vigorous opposition from the PLO, previous elections for West Bank municipalities had been held in March and May 1972, and with a little encouragement from the Shin Bet, the traditional candidates had been returned in the big cities. Cash support had not been given. The security service, which by early 1968 had contained substantially armed PLO resistance, had argued that terrorist activity was on the wane and raised no objections to giving West Bankers a limited opportunity for political expression.[51] The PLO's concerns about its position were justified: the results, which were far more favourable to King Hussein and Israel than to Yasser Arafat, mirrored the *de facto* cooperation which existed between Israel and Jordan and the increasing readiness of local leaders to cooperate with the Israeli authorities on day-to-day issues. Municipal polls had taken on an exaggerated significance since 1967, because under occupation they were the only form of democratic life. Israel's reforms made them even more important. Moshe Dayan had been the driving force behind the 1972 polls; they were held in the context of his overall approach of open bridges, open minds and regular personal contact with the Arab population.

In the countdown to polling day on 12 April 1976, the situation started to look worrying. Pressure was exerted on two of the leading traditionalists, Sheikh Muhammad Ali Ja'abri of Hebron and Haj Ma'azuz al-Masri of Nablus, to run again. On 28 March, to help Sheikh Ja'abri, his nationalist rival, Dr Ahmad Hamzi Natshe, was deported to Lebanon, along with another pro-PLO candidate running as mayor of Al-Birah. The decision was taken by the defence minister; the security service was simply asked to provide the names of suitable candidates for expulsion.[52] But the radicals still appeared to have the upper hand and there was talk of cancelling the election. On 4 April Peres told the cabinet he could 'not guarantee the results', but added that he had 'read with regret articles in the Israeli press which make it sound as if the left and the PLO have already won'.[53]

On 8 April, with just four days to go before the elections, the Shin Bet warned the defence minister 'quite specifically' that the PLO candidates were likely to win in most places.[54] But there was conflicting advice: Professor Amnon Cohen, a noted Hebrew University orientalist who was serving as adviser on Arab affairs to the West Bank military government, insisted that tradition would win out and that the interests of *hamulas* (clans) were still more powerful than modern politics. Peres's adviser, David Farhi, took a less clear-cut view.

The results were a disaster for Israel. Pro-PLO candidates, openly encouraged by the organization abroad, swept the board. Voter turnout was high (72 per cent) and the successful candidates were younger, better educated and more openly nationalist than the previous incumbents. Nablus was taken by Bassam Shak'a, a veteran Ba'athist, Hebron by Fahd Qawasma, and in Ramallah and Tulkarm the sitting radical nationalists, Karim Khalaf and Hilmi Hanoun respectively, were re-elected. Ibrahim Tawil in Al-Birah and Muhammad Milhem in Halhoul, near Hebron, were both nationalists. The cities of the West Bank were henceforth run by men who supported the PLO as their sole legitimate representative, who rejected Jordan's policies and opposed Israeli occupation.

Recriminations quickly followed, fuelled by the ever-simmering rivalry between Rabin and Peres and the division of labour between them. Rabin, as prime minister, had direct responsibility for the Shin Bet (and the Mossad); Peres, as defence minister, for the occupied territories, although he was far less involved on a day-to-day level than his predecessor, Moshe Dayan, had been. Rabin ordered the Shin Bet to supply him in future with its 'raw' intelligence in addition to the 'finished' political intelligence assessments it gave to the Defence Ministry. He accused Ahituv of working for Peres and not for him.[55] The security service was furious and protested afterwards that it had warned quite clearly that the influence of the PLO was rising. Ahituv went to Avraham Orly, coordinator of government operations in the West Bank and Gaza, and demanded that the press be briefed in such a way as to make clear that the Shin Bet had been right.[56] Rabin publicly attacked his defence minister. Peres, he said in a newspaper interview, 'erred in his assessment, and his error led the government of Israel to take steps that did nothing to enhance its prestige'.[57] Chief of staff Gur demanded the resignation of Amnon Cohen and David Farhi, the advisers on Arab affairs, but they stayed on.[58]

As had happened before the Yom Kippur War, the Israeli defence establishment had failed to anticipate events. Their inability to foresee the results of the West Bank elections was due not to a lack of adequate intelligence but rather to rigid adherence to a concept that did not include the growing influence and popularity of the PLO in the occupied territories. The official mind-set was still based on the old division of refugees and pro-Jordanians and paid insufficient attention to the far-reaching effects of the PNC decisions and the Rabat summit in 1974. In retrospect, some Shin Bet officers would argue that in the preceding years they had paid too much attention to terrorism and too little to the changing political aspects of the Palestinian problem. 'Our main priority was fighting hostile terrorist activity,' said one, 'and you could measure your successes in that. Not publicly, but at least what you had done was reflected in the newspapers. Of course politics were important, but you couldn't measure it.'[59]

Avraham Ahituv

The PLO successes in the West Bank were a rare setback for Avraham Ahituv, the Shin Bet chief. When Golda Meir was prime minister, Moshe Dayan had been given a free hand in the occupied territories, but Yitzhak Rabin's tense relations with Shimon Peres, his defence minister, made life hard for Ahituv. In July 1975 there had been an ugly incident that squeezed the security service uncomfortably between the two rival Labour Party leaders. An Arab employee at Jerusalem's Diplomat Hotel found a top-secret Foreign Ministry document lying on the dining-room floor after Dayan, by then no more than a humble Labour MP, had breakfasted there. A Shin Bet investigation revealed that Peres had given his distinguished predecessor some classified material and that Dayan had accidentally mislaid one of the papers. Since the Yom Kippur War there had been enormous public sensitivity to any involvement by Dayan in security matters and when the story was leaked to the press by the prime minister's office, Peres was put in a bad light. Worse still, Rabin ordered that he be taken off the circulation list for certain types of classified documents, although the decision was later rescinded.[60]

Until 1976, two years into his tenure, Ahituv had done very well, bringing the Shin Bet to a position of unprecedented influence in matters of internal security. Under his directorship procedures were formalized both internally and vis-à-vis the other components of the intelligence community. He oversaw the transition to a fully computerized service and helped attract bright young people into the ranks. In 1975 pay and working conditions were brought into line with the level of the regular army in belated recognition of the service's operational status in the occupied territories.[61] He appointed high flyers in their mid-thirties – mostly the protégés of Yehuda Arbel, since retired – to head various branches. 'He was known,' one expert concluded when Ahituv stepped down, 'as a man of tremendous authority who was extremely commanding and decisive.'[62] A CIA profile described him as 'extremely bright, hard-working, ambitious and thorough', although he could also be 'headstrong, abrasive and arrogant'.[63]

Ahituv joined the security service when it was still part of the IDF in 1950 and started his long career in Yosef Harmelin's military security section. He spent almost a year doing an advanced intelligence course in Jerusalem before returning to a staff job with the section.[64] Born in Germany in 1930, he was brought by his parents to Palestine five years later, on the crest of the massive wave of German-Jewish immigration known in Zionist historiography as the 'fifth *aliya*'. He received a traditional middle-class religious-nationalist education in the Tel Aviv surburb of Bat Yam, but showed a practical bent in studying metalwork and in his first job for the National Electric Corporation. During the 1948 war he was injured in an accident which left him with a lifelong limp.

He ran Shin Bet operations in the Gaza Strip between the Sinai campaign in November 1956 and the Israeli withdrawal in spring 1957, an experience that was to stand him in good stead a decade later, when the security service played such a central role in determining policy towards the Arab territories captured in the Six Day War. It was then that he met the dashing chief of staff, Moshe Dayan, with whom he always enjoyed close personal and working relations. It was largely on Dayan's recommendation that he became Harmelin's deputy in 1971.

He was based abroad with the Mossad from 1961 to 1965, and, like his colleague Yehuda Arbel, was almost certainly working on the related issues of the German scientists and rocket experts in Nasser's Egypt, and the hunt for Nazi war criminals.[65] With his religious background and fluent Yiddish, he was an ideal candidate to take part in the search for Yossele Schumacher, the little Orthodox boy whose kidnapping had diverted the secret services from their regular work. Most of Ahituv's work in Israel, however, was devoted to Arab affairs, which until the great change of 1967 meant being involved in policy towards the country's Arab minority. Shortly before taking over from Yosef Harmelin, Ahituv played a key role in the case of Archbishop Hilarion Capucci, the Syrian-born Greek Catholic prelate caught *in flagrante delicto* in August 1974, smuggling arms and explosives for Fatah. Capucci was sentenced to twelve years' imprisonment but was released in 1977.

The Shin Bet chief consistently – and wisely – refused to deal with leaks from the often sieve-like cabinet and government institutions, which would have involved the service in messy tangles with ministers, officials and journalists. Ahituv was extremely demanding with his subordinates. He once sacked a senior officer who had claimed for a fictional breakfast on his expense account. 'The moment he came into the building all you could hear was the buzzing of the flies,' one colleague said. But he was no less severe with himself. Essentially an autodidact, he completed his secondary education and both a BA and a law degree in what little spare time he had. He was given his lawyer's licence in 1971. Surprisingly, perhaps, he acquired a reputation as something of a liberal.

Jewish terror

Just after the start of the Jewish Sabbath on 2 May 1980, a four-man Fatah squad armed with assault rifles, grenades and explosive charges ambushed and killed six Israeli settlers outside Beit Hadassah, in the centre of the West Bank town of Hebron. It was one of the bloodiest and best-planned attacks carried out by Palestinians since the occupation began.[66] For the PLO, the operation was a hammer blow at the most militant of its Israeli enemies. Revenge was not long in coming. And when it did, it embroiled the Shin Bet in one of the most sensitive and difficult cases it had ever encountered.

By the summer of 1980 Jewish settlement in the West Bank had become a fact of life. Hebron, with its tomb of the Patriarchs, had powerful emotional and religious associations for observant, nationalist Jews. A small but flourishing Jewish community had lived there until sixty-nine of them were massacred by their Arab neighbours in 1929, one of the landmark events of the mandatory period.

In the spring of 1968, less than a year after the Six Day War victory, an intense and ascetic rabbi called Moshe Levinger and a group of supporters had celebrated Passover at the city's Park Hotel. Later, with permission from the army, the settlers moved into the military government building. That became the nucleus for settlement in the heart of the city, and, in September 1970, for the building of Kiryat Arba, an incongruous suburb of concrete apartment blocks on a barren hill just outside.

In 1973 Levinger was one of the founding fathers of Gush Emunim (Bloc of the Faithful), founded within the National Religious Party to underline commitment to traditional orthodoxy with the centrality of nationalism and Eretz Yisrael (the Land of Israel). The movement's first years were difficult. The Labour Party was unenthusiastic about settlement in populated

Arab areas, although many ministers, especially Yigal Allon, the former Palmah commander, turned a blind eye to, or even quietly approved of, the movement's activities. In 1969 Allon, then deputy prime minister, had formulated a plan under which, with certain exceptions, settlement would be permitted only in the Jordan Valley, which was to serve as Israel's security frontier in the event of a peace settlement. One of the exceptions was Kfar Etzion, which had been overrun by the Jordanians in 1948. In 1974 a group of settlers was evicted by the army after trying to set up a settlement near Nablus. In December 1976 they finally succeeded, starting out in an army camp and then setting up an outpost called Kadum. Ofra, near Ramallah and Ma'ale Edumium, half-way between Jerusalem and Jericho, had been established illegally in 1975. The thirty other settlements set up between 1968 and 1977 were carried out within the framework of Allon's blueprint.

The settlers' moment arrived in May 1977, when Menachem Begin came to power on a platform of increased settlement throughout the West Bank and Gaza. Begin, however, proved a disappointment, not only because of his readiness to sign a peace treaty with Egypt in March 1979 but also because he insisted that the government, not Gush Emunim, would determine the pace of settlement. The Camp David autonomy plan, which promised limited self-rule for the Palestinians in the West Bank, worried Gush Emunim too, even though the Palestinians themselves rejected it scornfully. 'Autonomy means no more than power to collect garbage and exterminate mosquitoes,' sneered one leading PLO loyalist. But the Israeli right-wingers were more worried by Jews than by Arabs, and when the settlements of Yamit and northern Sinai were handed back to the Egyptians, a dangerous precedent was established. Yet Begin kept his word. Settlement in what became known universally as 'Judaea and Samaria' began to transcend the narrow ideological confines of the Gush. Quality of life in the wide open spaces, cheap mortgages and other subsidies began to attract many non-religious Israelis, especially from the crowded suburbs of Tel Aviv and Jerusalem.

This coincided with growing militancy by the Palestinians. In October 1978, a month after the signing of the Camp David accords, a coalition of Palestinian groups and individuals founded the National Guidance Committee (NGC) to combat Begin's self-rule scheme. Its twenty-two members included pro-PLO mayors from the West Bank and Gaza Strip and representatives of trade, religious, professional and student bodies. The defence minister, Ezer Weizman, who was buoyed up by the exhilarating experience of negotiating with Egypt, hoped that the NGC might prove to be independent of the PLO and serve as a partner in Israeli dialogue with the Palestinians living under occupation. Thus the body was allowed to hold public rallies during the first months of its existence.[67] Dr Natshe, expelled to Jordan on the eve of the 1976 elections, was allowed to return home and Weizman rejected the Shin Bet's recommendation that the radical mayor of Nablus, Bassam Shak'a, be deported.

The settlers were worried. As one of them wrote:

> The new Palestinian commanders no longer bedecked themselves in tiger-striped uniforms and loaded Kalashnikovs. Rather, dressed in elegant suits and half-height shoes, they clutched microphones and incited their supporters in city squares to resist the occupation. Instead of a handful of venomous terrorists lurking in underground organizations and acting only under cover of darkness, tens of thousands of local youths enlisted enthusiastically in the new campaign, which they waged (almost) without any explosives.[68]

Gush leaders began to talk openly about stockpiling weapons if the Camp David autonomy scheme was implemented and railed at the increasing political freedom being given to the Palestinians. Stone-throwing attacks became more frequent and settlers, frustrated by the army's inaction, began to carry out reprisals. In March 1979 a Jew from Kiryat Arba was tried for the murder of an Arab schoolgirl he had shot during a demonstration in nearby Halhoul. He was acquitted but the tension was mounting perceptibly. In early 1980 Bassam Shak'a got in trouble again, because Major-General Danni Matt, coordinator of government operations in the territories, leaked to the press remarks made by the mayor, ostensibly justifying terrorist attacks. In the ensuing uproar, it was decided to deport Shak'a, but a month later the order was rescinded. Weizman was relieved and phoned the Egyptian defence minister to inform him that the peace process, which had seemed briefly to be threatened by Israeli actions in the occupied territories, could continue. Shak'a, who had been in detention, was given a hero's welcome in Nablus, and for the next few months violence again escalated in the West Bank. On 30 April, two days before the Beit Hadassah attack, a Palestinian from Tulkarm who had tried to attack the city's military governor was shot dead.

Immediately after the Hebron killings it was decided, at the suggestion of the West Bank military commander, Brigadier-General Binyamin ('Fuad') Ben-Eliezer, to expel the mayors of Hebron and nearby Halhoul, Fahd Qawasma and Muhammad Milhem, both ardent PLO supporters who had been elected in 1976, and Sheikh Ragheb al-Tamimi, the Muslim Qadi of Hebron. A month earlier all three had attended a mass rally at Hebron town hall and were therefore seen by the Israelis as in some vague way responsible for the mood of militancy which had preceded the Beit Hadassah incident. Weizman gave his backing to the expulsion decision, having rejected a more drastic proposal by Matt to deport all the members of the National Guidance Committee. Ahituv, who disliked such drastic moves, was not consulted.[69]

It was not enough for the outraged settlers. Shortly after the funerals of the Beit Hadassah victims, twenty of them met in Kiryat Arba to discuss retaliatory action. Two of their leaders, Menachem Livni and Yehuda Eztion, started to plan attacks against prominent politically active Palestinians. In addition to mayors Shak'a of Nablus, Khalaf of Ramallah and Tawil of Al-Birah, they also targeted Dr Natshe and Ibrahim Daqqaq, an engineer from East Jerusalem who served as secretary of the NGC.

The action took place on 2 June 1980, the date symbolically

chosen for being thirty days – a traditional period of Jewish mourning – after the Hebron killings. It was carried out by three-man cells composed of a driver, someone to affix the bombs to the victims' cars and a guard/look-out. In the preliminary surveillance work, the settlers banked on the fact that the appearance of Israeli civilians in West Bank towns would be linked to the Shin Bet. But they wore army uniforms for the actual operation. Shak'a and Khalaf were both maimed, the first losing both legs and the second both feet, when the bombs placed in their cars exploded. Daqqaq was not at home and a barking dog outside Natshe's house in Bethlehem deterred the team. The bomb meant for Tawil blinded an army sapper sent to defuse it.

Shin Bet investigates

Begin condemned the attacks and promised a speedy investigation. The settlers were divided in their response. Some were openly pleased, but others feared that the attacks would play into the hands of their enemies. Many suspected that the bombings had been carried out by the Shin Bet.[70]

The investigation was difficult. Before the bombings, the settler community had not been a GSS intelligence target, in the way that, for example, the Communist Party, the National Guidance Committee or a foreign embassy or consulate had been. The service had 'assets' among Jews in the West Bank and Gaza: it did not have agents or carry out surveillance. To do so would have required a decision from the prime minister, who would have been most unlikely to have agreed. What the Shin Bet knew about the settlers had been acquired as a by-product of its general monitoring of Jewish political extremism; thus the relevant information was not concentrated in any one section.[71] Ahituv's religious background made him generally sympathetic, although he had opposed the re-establishment of the Jewish Quarter in Hebron and had strong views about anyone 'taking the law into his own hands'.[72]

Avraham Ahituv and Begin got on extremely well. The Shin Bet chief was a curious feature in the Israeli landscape, an old-fashioned and rather formal man, and these were traits he shared with the prime minister. Ahituv wore dark suits, braces and shirt–bands. And Begin admired him. He was a man of broad political understanding and had been quick to respond to a request by the prime minister to present the service's views on the security implications of the autonomy scheme.[73]

Yet the investigation was still extremely sensitive. Newspaper reports alluded repeatedly to a meeting in which Ahituv asked Begin to authorize the arrest of some of the settlers as potential suspects. 'We'll break them down during interrogation,' the Shin Bet chief promised. Begin refused, but still pressed Ahituv to make progress. 'Begin wasn't stupid enough to try and stop the investigation,' one senior GSS man said, 'but he was clever enough to make clear exactly what he did want.'[74] The prime minister, a stickler for legalities, knew the case had to be pursued, but he also knew where it was likely to lead. And he had personal memories of the Shin Bet surveillance of his Herut Party in the bad old days of the 1950s, when – the Israeli right believed, and not without justification – Isser Harel ran internal security on the basis of what was good for Mapai and Ben-Gurion.

Shortly afterwards, the story erupted publicly. An American newspaper, the *Washington Star*, reported that Ahituv was about to resign because Begin had ordered him to halt the investigation into the underground. Ahituv responded, uniquely, by giving an on-the-record interview to Israel Radio and *Yediot Aharonot* in which he categorically denied the story.[75]

The security service gave the investigation high priority. Haggai Segal, one of the bombers, who later wrote a book about the affair, said: 'The GSS, it transpired, regarded catching us as a challenge and matter of prestige of the highest order, and spared no effort to find an outlet for the frustration that had accumulated . . .'[76]

The Shin Bet used a variety of methods to try and catch the

Jewish terrorists. The owner of a workshop in Kiryat Arba was picked up in a Jerusalem street and taken to a hotel for a 'chat' and the screening of a video showing him in embarrassing circumstances with a woman friend. The film had been shot in the very same hotel room and the agents threatened to show it to his wife if he did not tell them what he knew about the bombing of the mayors. Later, when he refused to cooperate, the Shin Bet arranged to delay some payments owed him by the Ministry of Defence. Pushed to the verge of bankruptcy, the man found a way of reporting to Begin what was happening. The prime minister intervened, ordering the Shin Bet to leave the suspect alone unless they had information directly linking him to the attack. Begin repeated this several times, often at the instigation of his right-wing minister of technology, Yuval Ne'eman.[77]

Business as usual

Investigating the Jewish underground became a major pre-occupation for the Shin Bet, but its routine work of dealing with Palestinian violence and political subversion continued apace. Despite its immense growth since the 1967 war, the secrecy surrounding the work of the security service in the occupied territories remained intense and there were very few circumstances in which the Israeli military censor eased his grip on this highly sensitive subject.

One form of exposure came when big PLO operations or networks were uncovered. An especially dramatic example came to light in October 1978, just at the time that Gush Emunim and the West Bank settlers were getting seriously worried about mounting Palestinian militancy: a giant explosive charge was discovered outside a cinema in central Jerusalem. The Shin Bet investigation led to several Fatah activists, who had been assisted by a Jewish criminal called Yosef (Jo-Jo) Nidam. Nidam, who normally dealt in drugs, had delivered large quantities of weapons and explosives that were smuggled across the Lebanese border. Surveillance was stepped up in this period against United Nations personnel serving with the newly arrived United Nations Interim Force in Lebanon (UNIFIL), a peace-keeping force. The UN men crossed the border freely and were an obvious target for recruitment by the PLO.

Other rare opportunities to glimpse the Shin Bet's work came when agents were killed on duty. In April 1979 an officer called Moshe Goldfarb was killed in Samaria. Unusually, his death was announced, and equally unusually, an official inquiry was ordered to examine the circumstances of his death, although its findings were never made public.

Just over a year later, in June 1980, another Shin Bet agent was killed. He was named as Moshe ('Musa') Golan, aged thirty-four, a five-year veteran of the service who had been born in Egypt. His death provided brief but dramatic exposure for the Shin Bet and extravagant praise for the 'unknown soldiers' who toiled in the shadows. The government was represented at his funeral by the prime minister himself as well as by the deputy minister of defence.

Golan was killed by a young Shin Bet informer called Bassam Mahmoud Habash, who lived in the Balata refugee camp near Nablus. Habash had provided his controller with information that had led to the exposure of two important Fatah cells.[78] The Shin Bet man had arranged routinely to meet Habash in a 'safe house' in the Israeli coastal town of Netanya. During the session, the informer suddenly threw pepper in Golan's eyes, stabbed him to death, seized his pistol and two full magazines and escaped. The PFLP announced that the Israeli agent had been executed 'by one of our groups operating in the occupied homeland' in retaliation for the recent death of a Palestinian student killed during a demonstration in Bethlehem. The PFLP claim raised the possibility that Habash had become a double agent, maintaining contact with the Israeli in order to mislead him and eventually trap and kill him. Perhaps. Or perhaps the informer simply wanted out and took the only possible route. Three days later, after an intensive chase and an emergency mobilization of all known sources by Golan's colleagues, Habash was tracked down and killed by an army unit in a shoot-out in Nablus. A curfew was imposed on Balata that night as Habash was buried. Three days later, his family's home was bulldozed into the dust, *pour encourager les autres.*[79]

Another rare form of exposure for the Shin Bet came when allegations were made, as they were with increasing regularity in the late 1970s, of brutality in the interrogation of Palestinian detainees. An official commission of inquiry established in 1987, when security service matters were very much more on the public agenda than they had been a decade earlier, said that 1971 marked the approximate point at which the Shin Bet began to lie consistently to the courts about the manner in which confessions were extracted from suspects. In June 1977 the *Sunday Times* of London published a lengthy and well-documented report about the alleged torture of Palestinian detainees.[80] Official Israel reacted furiously to the article; a decade later much of the detail it contained would be confirmed by the Landau Commission.

Ismail Ajwa, a young journalist from a village near Jerusalem, would not have been surprised by the Commission's findings. Ajwa was first detained in December 1978, at the height of Palestinian opposition to the Camp David autonomy scheme. During the first eighteen days of the ninety-four he spent in detention, Ajwa was held in the Russian Compound police headquarters in Jerusalem – known to all Arabs as the Muscubiyya – where a young Shin Bet man called 'Uzi' beat him and abused him for his alleged links with the PLO. 'Later,' Ajwa recalled, 'I was questioned very cleverly by Abu Nihad, an Iraqi of about forty-five. He spoke excellent Arabic, better than mine. He did not use violence but tried to force me to sign an agreement to leave the country, which I refused to do. The interrogators also told me that my wife was seeing other men in the village.' Ajwa alleged that he had been throttled and chained to a pipe with his hands behind his back and a mask over his head for seventy-two hours.

Whatever its methods, the Shin Bet had an impressively high success rate in solving terrorist attacks in Israel and the occupied territories. In 1980, 85 per cent of the cases it dealt with were solved.[81]

Endgame

After thirty years in the Shin Bet and six as its director, Avraham Ahituv retired in December 1980. One of his last major decisions was to persuade the government to ban a political congress by Israeli Arabs, who, it was believed, were becoming increasingly radicalized and 'Palestinian' in their outlook. Begin asked him to recommend two candidates to replace him. Ahituv proposed his deputy, Avraham ('Avrum') Shalom (Bendor), and David ('Dodik') Ronen, a Jerusalem-born veteran of the Arab Branch who had long experience in the West Bank and later wrote a remarkably detailed and revealing account of the service's activities in the early years of the occupation.[82] Shalom, who got the job, was an operations man *par excellence* and many had been surprised when he became Ahituv's number two in 1974. Ahituv, who always got on very well with Begin, preferred to deal with high politics and grand design, and wanted a practical man at his side. Wagging tongues in the secret world said that Ahituv had chosen Shalom to succeed him so that after he had gone his own tenure would seem more impressive. 'It was definitely Machiavellian,' said one official. 'He didn't appoint a successor who cast a shadow over his own achievements in the job.'

Shalom, whose parents came to Palestine from Germany in 1933, was a Palmahnik who had joined the security service in its early years. In 1960 he served as deputy to Rafi Eitan in the Eichmann kidnapping. 'He took part in every significant operation the service ever carried out, but always at the operational level, in the field,' the Israeli public learned later. 'He was a scout more than a commander, a man whose understanding was based on irreplaceable experience, a hard-working, persistent, colourless man.' Shalom appointed Reuven Hazak as his deputy.[83]

Shalom's first priority was the investigation into the Jewish underground, which was still limping along without any obvious success. And the terrorists were getting bolder. After the attack on the mayors in June 1980, several of the group's hardline members returned to an old idea of blowing up the Dome of the Rock – the Old City mosque on the site of the ancient Jewish temple – thus striking a blow against Islam in general, the Palestinians in particular and hastening the coming of the Messiah. As an added bonus, such an action would almost certainly halt the peace process with Egypt and the withdrawal from Sinai. The evacuation in April 1982 of Yamit, the first civilian settlement to be handed over to Egypt as provided for by the peace treaty, sharpened the mood among the settlers. Members of Rabbi Meir Kahane's extremist Kach Party had threatened mass suicide before they were overcome by troops and police.

The underground group struck again in the summer of 1983. After a young settler was stabbed to death in Hebron they decided on random revenge. On 26 July three underground members, wearing Arab kaffiyeh head-dresses and gloves and driving a car with false licence plates, threw a grenade and fired sub-machine-guns at a group of students at Hebron's Islamic College. Three were killed and about thirty injured. 'Whoever did this,' declared Rabbi Levinger, 'has sanctified God's Name in public.'

Begin was visibly shocked when Avraham Shalom called him to report on the Islamic College incident and he ordered the Shin Bet to spare no effort to bring the perpetrators to justice. The service had still failed to solve the 1980 attack on the mayors or the killing of an activist of the Peace Now movement, Emile Greenzweig, at a demonstration in Jerusalem in February 1983. Somehow, that summer, the restrictions on the investigation were lifted. Shalom's predecessor, Avraham Ahituv, now retired, hinted at some of the difficulties of dealing with a community that enjoyed considerable emotional and political sympathy from the higher echelons of the government.

'The failure to arrest the assailants was primarily one of

intelligence,' the former Shin Bet chief wrote. 'Operationally, they were good. Their circumspection was flawless and their immediate political surroundings protected them.' The settler community had refused to cooperate with the Shin Bet investigation, Ahituv explained, because of a sense of solidarity with the underground group – with their motives if not their methods. And the government's *ex post facto* approval for unauthorized settlement activity had meant that there could be no official justification for turning the entire community into an intelligence 'target'. The Shin Bet was not to blame. It was the politicians who had to carry the can.[84]

Shalom's men persuaded a young Orthodox Jew to serve as an agent in the underground group and he was tricked into providing the investigators with several names. A woman was recruited in Hebron's Jewish Quarter. Surveillance was mounted against the leading members of the group. Menachem Livni's army reserve unit in Lebanon was joined by a middle-aged GSS officer who had been ordered to watch the man from Kiryat Arba. A group of Shin Bet agents dressed as soldiers flagged down Livni's car in the Jordan Valley and pretended that one of them had had an accident. They managed to plant 'a listening and location device' in the vehicle.

The next operation turned out to be the underground's last. A plan to booby-trap five Arab buses in East Jerusalem was known almost in its entirety to the Shin Bet. On the evening of its execution, 26 April 1984, an extensive surveillance network was in place from Hebron to Jerusalem. A reserve soldier stationed permanently in a guard post opposite the home of Shaul Nir was equipped with sophisticated listening devices. The Shin Bet, which photographed the entire operation with hidden cameras, moved in only when the bombs had actually been planted. Twenty-seven people were detained. Rabbi Levinger was held for ten days and released.

Confessions were obtained quickly, without violence, but with much use of sleep deprivation and 'good cop–bad cop' methods of interrogation. Promises of pardons were given to encourage cooperation. The Temple Mount plot, about which the Shin Bet had known little, came out too. Fifteen Shin Bet officers testified in camera at the trial, but the substance of what they said was permitted for publication, giving unprecedented exposure to their methods of interrogation. But by the time the Jewish underground trial began, the security service – and Avraham Shalom personally – were embroiled in another dramatic and very damaging case.

11

The Lebanese Quagmire: 1978–85

Death on the highway

Early on the morning of 11 March 1978 two rubber dinghies carrying eleven Palestinians landed on a beach on Israel's Mediterranean coast, next to the Ma'agan Michael Nature Reserve. Each of them carried a Kalashnikov AK-47 assault rifle and ten magazines, four grenades and blocks of TNT.

They first shot dead an American-Israeli photographer, Gail Rubin, who was out taking pictures of birds, and then walked three kilometres to the Haifa–Tel Aviv coastal road, Israel's main highway. After firing at a few cars, they managed to stop two passing buses, full of Egged bus drivers and their families out on a picnic, and a taxi. The Palestinians crammed most of the passengers into one bus and ordered it southwards towards Tel Aviv, occasionally firing bursts out of the windows at passing cars and pursuing police vehicles. The policemen did not shoot into the bus for fear of hitting the hostages.

A ragtag force of policemen, border police and soldiers hastily assembled at the busy Glilot junction just north of Tel Aviv. As the bus careened into the crossroads, it met a roadblock and a hail of bullets, aimed first at the vehicle's wheels and then at the windows from which the terrorists were firing. Grenades exploded and the bus caught fire.

When the police and medics went in, they discovered nine dead terrorists and several dozen dead Israelis, most of them badly charred. Altogether thirty-seven Israelis were killed and seventy-eight wounded. Four survivors were badly injured.[1] The Coastal Road Massacre, as it came to be known, was a turning-point in Israeli–Lebanese relations. Given the number of Israeli casualties and the venue – Israel's main road artery, connecting Tel Aviv and Haifa – the massacre could not but be a watershed. No previous raid from Lebanon had been so damaging; none had struck at Israel's heartland with such deadly effect. Everyone understood at once that Israel would retaliate fiercely against PLO forces across the northern border.

As Aman chief Shlomo Gazit was to put it later:

> When an atrocity like the Coastal Road Massacre occurs, the Israeli government sees red. It is inconceivable that it won't react. The political leaders then came to Aman, as if they were shopping in a supermarket. We told them – these are the possible targets for retaliation – and they picked A and C and H off the shelf, as it were.

The result, five days after the attack, was 'Operation Litani'.

'Operation Litani'

'Operation Litani', in which several IDF brigades, numbering 7,000 troops,[2] invaded Lebanon up to the Litani river (save for the Tyre enclave, south of the river), was in one sense typical of large IDF operations: it unravelled into something far more ambitious, in both scope and time, than had been originally planned.

Syria was careful to keep out of the fighting. Israeli armour advanced on six axes, with artillery and air attacks first pulverizing PLO positions. Paratroops were dropped by helicopter deep inside the invaded area to cut off any enemy retreat. The Israeli forces advanced slowly and carefully to keep down casualties; but this inevitably reduced PLO casualties as well.[3]

The order was to advance some ten kilometres northwards to destroy PLO camps and installations, to briefly hold four enclaves and then, having consolidated these under the control of Israel's Christian ally, the 'Free Lebanese Army' (FLA), of Major Sa'ad Haddad, to withdraw. But the operation went so smoothly that the units swept northwards up to the Litani. 'The word Litani had never been mentioned during the planning,' Gazit said. 'And what we ended up with was a continuous Haddad-controlled strip north of the border rather than disconnected enclaves.'

The idea of a continuous strip was not adopted at first because Aman had no faith in the FLA's ability to control the largely Shi'ite Muslim population of the border strip. Gazit also feared that the Israeli right would quickly pressure the government to set up settlements in south Lebanon.[4]

The invasion led to the establishment of a new peace-keeping force, UNIFIL, which was deployed when the IDF withdrew to the border on 31 June. Haddad's zone became a continuous, ten- to fifteen-kilometre strip, just north of the international frontier, from the Mediterranean to Mount Hermon.[5]

Laying the foundations: 1975–81

Israel's invasion of Lebanon in June 1982 was the result of two processes, one that began in the late 1960s and the other that started in 1975. The first was the gradual shift of the centre of PLO operations from Amman and the Jordan river to Beirut and southern Lebanon. The second was the start of the Lebanese civil war and the forging of the Israeli–Phalange alliance.[6]

The PLO began operating out of the Palestinian refugee camps in south Lebanon from the end of 1968. The greater Israel's successes against the PLO along the Jordan, the more determined were Palestinian efforts to open up a 'second front'. The process culminated in Black September in 1970, when King Hussein's troops smashed the military power of the Palestinians in Jordan. The battered PLO moved its HQs and remaining forces to Beirut and south Lebanon, reconstructed its units and intensified strikes against Israel. Soon the PLO had set up a state within a state, stretching from the refugee camps around Beirut, through Ein Hilwe and Mieh Mieh near Sidon to Rashidiya and Nabatiyah in the south.

The PLO influx was one of the factors leading to the gradual disintegration of the Lebanese state and society during the first half of the 1970s. The organization's cross-border operations against Israeli frontier settlements brought IDF retaliation against the whole population of southern Lebanon, leading, in turn, to the flight of Shi'ite refugees to Beirut's southern suburbs. These poor Shi'ites were embittered with the Christian-dominated Lebanese establishment and turned increasingly to fundamentalist religion. They became an important element in the destabilization that eventually resulted in civil war. When that began the country's Christian communities, led by the Maronites, and their militias – dominated by the 'Lebanese Forces' of the Phalange Party – were pitted against a loose and shifting coalition of Muslims and left-wingers, including the Shi'ite Amal militia, the Druse Progressive Socialist Party fighters and the Nasserist Mourabitun. During the first phase of the civil war most of the PLO groups at one point or another assisted the Muslim–leftist coalition against the Christians.

The breakdown of the Lebanese polity, which took place against the backdrop of superpower rivalry, the Israel–Arab conflict and various inter-Arab struggles, inevitably sucked in outside contenders. As the Lebanese militias sought external allies who could finance, arm and train them, so the country's immediate neighbours were interested in backing the Lebanese to try to safeguard their own interests (such as Israel's concern about the security of its northern border and Syria's about a possible Israeli 'left hook' attack on Damascus via Lebanon's Beka'a Valley).

Soon after the outbreak of hostilities the Christians turned to the Jews, who since before 1948 had intermittently offered a 'natural' alliance between the region's two main non-Muslim minorities. Israel's interest in an alliance with the Lebanese Christians had been a central theoretical component of the 'periphery doctrine' since the 1950s; the civil war presented conditions in which theory could at last become practice. The Mossad and, to a lesser extent, IDF Intelligence Branch, were the channels through which this alliance was forged.

The Lebanese civil war began in April 1975. In September the embattled Christians made their first approach – via a Mossad station in Europe, probably Paris – to Jerusalem. Danny Chamoun, the leader of the small Christian Tigers militia and son of former Lebanese president, Camille Chamoun, asked Israel for urgent military assistance.[7] Jerusalem reacted cautiously, declining to intervene directly, but channelled some stocks of light arms to the Phalange.

The Mossad's David Kimche, who handled the service's 'Lebanese account' until the late 1970s, thought this a natural response. As he argued later:

> At the start we did the right thing. It was a long time before Sadat's visit to Jerusalem and every approach to Israel from an Arab country was important for us, especially since at that time the main quarrel of the Lebanese was with the PLO. For the first time ever our neighbours were queueing up to talk to us. The policy was that whatever happened we would not assist actively, but would help them to help themselves.[8]

The Christians' military situation continued to deteriorate. By the spring of 1976 the Phalangists were desperate. On 12 March they played the Israeli card: a party emissary, Abu Halil, set out on an IDF missile boat to Haifa to meet prime minister Yitzhak Rabin and foreign minister Yigal Allon. Abu Halil pleaded for aid. Rabin decided to send an exploratory mission, composed of a senior Aman officer (Binyamin Ben-Eliezer, known as 'Fuad') and a senior Mossad man. A few days later, the two met Bashir and Amin Gemayel, the sons of the old Phalange party leader Pierre Gemayel, on a missile boat in the harbour at Jounieh, north of Beirut. The Israelis left unimpressed.[9]

Yet permanent liaison was soon established, with one or two Mossad officers stationed in Jounieh to monitor the civil war at first hand. The relationship with the Phalange was made the responsibility of the Mossad, though Aman officers also continued to meet the militia's leaders and to produce their own reports and estimates.[10]

A team of four officers, led by Colonel Ben-Eliezer, was sent to assess Phalange needs. The team watched training, met Phalange officers and observed the Christians attack the Palestinian stronghold of Tel al-Za'atar. It reported back to Jerusalem on the militia's fragmentation and military shortcomings, but noted their sincere loathing of the PLO and recommended a substantial upgrading of Israeli arms supplies.[11]

Syria's entry into Lebanon, which began through its PLA proxies in January 1976 and became direct and full-scale that June, changed the situation radically. Although invited in by the Christians and initially serving their purposes, the Syrian entry set off alarm bells in Christian East Beirut and in Jerusalem; whatever the ostensible reason for its intervention, Syria seemed to be on the verge of gobbling up her western neighbour. Israel felt it had to act.

In August, prime minister Rabin repeatedly met Camille Chamoun on an Israeli missile boat off the Lebanese coast. A more important meeting followed, between Rabin and the Gemayels, *père* and *fils*. This did not go smoothly but the arms supply relationship nevertheless moved up several notches. Israel, Rabin explained to Chamoun, was willing to help the Christians help themselves'. Within weeks large Israeli shipments of rifles, anti-tank missiles and old Sherman tanks reached Jounieh. Responsibility for the arming of the Phalange, which had become a large logistical operation, was transferred from the Mossad to the Defence Ministry, though David Kimche remained the Israeli executive responsible for the relationship with the Lebanese Christians.[12]

Yet the Phalange wanted more. In September, during Ben-Eliezer's third mission to the Christian enclave, Bashir Gemayel pleaded with him for immediate Israeli intervention to eject the Syrians. Gemayel reiterated the plea during a visit to Israel later that month with Danny Chamoun, at which they met Rabin.

The first round of the civil war came to an end in October 1976, when a successful Syrian offensive at last ended the hopes of the Muslim–leftist–Palestinian alliance that they could crush the Christians. The following two years were a period of consolidation for the Phalange, with Bashir Gemayel emerging as the dominant military figure in the Christian camp, partly because it was he who had engineered the crucial Israeli connection.

Bashir's relationship with the Mossad blossomed. The Mossad under Yitzhak Hofi emerged as the chief advocate within Israel of a full alliance with the Phalange. IDF intelligence, by contrast, was unenthusiastic from the start about the Christian connection and regularly highlighted the shortcomings of the Phalange. Saguy was later to say critically that the Mossad 'regarded the Christians as an asset, and indeed trusted them'. Aman did not.[13]

The Phalangists maintained an uneasy relationship with Syria, but matters came to a head in June 1978, when Bashir's gunmen murdered Tony Franjieh, the head of a pro-Syrian Maronite faction, in his mountain redoubt at Zogharta. The Syrian reaction – massive shelling of the Christian strongholds in East Beirut, Jounieh and the Metn range to the east – was devastating.

In Jerusalem, meanwhile, the government had changed. The dramatic result of the May 1977 general election had pushed Rabin's Labour Party into opposition for the first time since 1948; the Likud's Menachem Begin, former leader of the pre-state group Irgun and founder of the right-wing Herut Party, was the new premier. Rabin had been cautious about Lebanon; Begin spoke openly and histrionically of Israel's commitment to prevent 'genocide' against the Christians. Aman warned the prime minister that the Phalange, not the Syrians, were responsible for the summer spiral of violence in and around Beirut, and defence minister Ezer Weizman ruled against unleashing the IAF against the Syrian artillery. The Israelis also turned down Bashir Gemayel's request that Israel land troops in Jounieh to deter the Syrians. Yet Begin made his point none the less. Israeli armour was concentrated on the Golan in a show of force and on 6 July IAF Kfirs streaked over Beirut. Begin also gave Gemayel a commitment that Israel would come to the Christians' assistance with air power should Syria unleash its own air force against the Christians. The Syrians ceased fire.[14]

A new Syrian–Phalange crisis broke in the spring of 1981. In December 1980 Phalange units had taken control of security in the Christian city of Zahle, on the Beirut–Damascus road. They quickly clashed with the Syrians, who imposed a blockade on the city. With the thaw in the Mount Lebanon snows, the two sides began digging in on the high ground around Zahle and fighting was renewed around 1 April 1981. Gemayel announced that the Christians would 'fight to the finish' as the Syrians were bent on wiping Zahle off the face of the earth and expelling its inhabitants. Gemayel sent urgent messages to this effect via the Mossad to Begin. The Israeli leader was moved: 'What is being done today to the Christians in Lebanon is exactly what the Nazis did to the Jews in the 1940s in Europe,' he told the Knesset Foreign Affairs and Defence Committee on 30 April.[15] On 8 April the Israeli cabinet's Security Committee had sent Gemayel a reiteration of its commitment to protect the Christians against Syrian air attack.[16] On 25 April Syrian heliborne commandos captured a key Phalange post on Mount Senin, overlooking Zahle and the Beka'a Valley.

The Syrians issued clear signals to Israel not to interfere: in mid-April they dug in the Beka'a a number of emplacements for anti-aircraft missile batteries but did not introduce the weaponry. The message – which was picked up by Aman – was unmistakably clear: if Israel interfered, Syria would introduce missile batteries into Lebanon, changing the strategic status quo.[17]

Yehoshua Saguy was uneasy about the progression of events in Zahle. He suspected a deliberate trap by the Christians to suck Israel into the Lebanese maw. Yitzhak Hofi soon agreed with the Aman chief that Zahle was a Phalange plot to entice Israel. But Nahik Nevot, the senior Mossad executive who in the late 1970s was given charge of the Lebanese desk and was responsible for the relationship with the Phalange, pressed for Israeli intervention. Nevot was known to the CIA as 'Peter Mandy' and was considered by his American counterparts to be 'miserly . . . dispensing bits of the Mossad's precious human-source reports only when it served Israeli interests'.[18] Nevot's predecessor, David Kimche, who had left the Mossad after rowing with Hofi over the service's Lebanon policy, said later that he also saw Zahle as a turning-point.[19]

At the crucial Israeli cabinet meeting of 28 April 1981 the IDF chief of staff, Rafi Eitan, proposed an air strike against Mount Senin. Saguy spoke against, warning that the Syrians would immediately introduce AA missiles into Lebanon and that aerial intelligence-gathering would be severely prejudiced. Several senior ministers backed Saguy. But Begin countered: 'We will not allow them to perpetrate genocide in Lebanon.'[20]

Despite the absence of a clear cabinet decision, Eitan immediately ordered the IAF into action and two Syrian supply helicopters were shot down over Mount Senin. The next day, in response, the Syrians introduced four SAM-6 batteries into the Beka'a and medium-range Scud surface-to-surface missiles were deployed near Damascus. Begin countered by pledging to destroy the missiles if they were not removed.[21]

On 30 April the scheduled Israeli air strike against the missiles was called off at the last moment because of poor visibility. Later that day the United States asked Israel to hold off to allow US diplomacy to persuade President Assad to withdraw the missiles. Begin was happy to take the exit offered. Syrian troops conquered the rest of Mount Senin.

But while US special ambassador Philip Habib shuttled between Damascus, Beirut and Jerusalem, trying to defuse the crisis, a second confrontation was looming. On 28 May the IAF began a massive bombing campaign against PLO concentrations in southern Lebanon. It was as if, frustrated *vis-à-vis* the Syrian missiles, Israeli anger was deliberately unleashed on an alternative, softer target. Eitan and Begin were itching for a full-scale 'final' confrontation with the PLO. The PLO reacted with caution and restraint, failing to fall into the Israeli trap.

But the second IAF assault, on 10 July, provoked the Palestinians beyond recall. Israeli jets hit important PLO targets in Beirut – killing over 100 people (thirty of them guerrillas) and wounding 600. The Palestinians responded with barrages against Israel's border towns of Kiryat Shmona and Nahariya, with over 2,000 shells and rockets fired (killing six and wounding fifty-nine). For two full weeks Israeli airmen and gunners traded fire day and night with the PLO batteries. More than 70 per cent of Kiryat Shmona's inhabitants fled southwards and Palestinian and Shi'ite refugees poured northwards. The constant Israeli pounding almost brought the PLO to its knees. But Begin, under heavy US pressure and shocked by the panicky Israeli civilian evacuation of the border towns, decided to call it quits.

Israel's vastly superior firepower had failed to dislodge or silence the PLO. Habib negotiated a ceasefire and the guns fell silent on 24 July. The PLO promptly set about restoring its military infrastructure in the south, adding dozens of field pieces and rocket launchers; the threat to Israel's border settlements remained as sharp as ever. 'The guns of July' were a turning-point; they were to leave a deep and lasting mark on Begin and the Israeli defence establishment, and were to serve as a reminder that an accounting would have to be made with the PLO at the earliest opportunity.[22]

In August 1981 Begin, who had served as both prime minister and defence minister since Ezer Weizman's resignation in 1980, was replaced at the Defence Ministry by the right-wing Ariel Sharon, veteran of every war since 1948, advocate of Greater Israel and a man – even his many enemies had to admit – of vision and determination. From that moment on, Sharon worked tirelessly to 'solve the problem of Lebanon once and for all', as he put it. During the following eleven months, south Lebanon was a powder keg waiting to blow up. Aman's defeat over the attack on the Iraqi nuclear reactor had seriously eroded its influence on Lebanese questions. Yehoshua Saguy was virtually ignored. The new minister's bulldozing style swept aside Yitzhak Hofi as well. 'The Mossad's involvement lost importance as soon as the Christians found their way directly to Sharon's ranch,' one senior executive said bitterly.[23]

Preparing a war

In Israeli eyes, the US-mediated ceasefire agreement with the PLO served as a screen behind which the guerrilla organization was able to rebuild and expand its military forces, which were gradually taking on the appearance of a conventional, if somewhat small and primitive, army. By the summer of 1982, according to Sharon, the PLO had an army of 15,000 men, 6,000 of them in southern Lebanon, armed with some 100 (mostly antiquated T-34 and T-54) tanks, some 350 artillery pieces and Katyusha rocket launchers, 150 armoured cars and a small AA capability.[24]

The trio that steered Israeli defence policy in the second Likud government, from August 1981, consisted of Begin, Sharon and IDF Chief of Staff Rafael Eitan. Sharon's immediate aim, which was acceptable to Begin and the bulk of the cabinet, was to remove the PLO 'threat' from Israel's northern border. His wider goal was to deliver a blow against the PLO from which it would never recover. Sharon's broader strategy was based on the premise that with the PLO humbled, Israel would find it easier to browbeat the now leaderless Palestinians of the West Bank and Gaza Strip into accepting Israeli rule, thus paving the way for eventual Israeli annexation.

Part of this grand design was the setting up of 'Village Leagues' in the West Bank to mobilize the rural sector against the PLO-dominated towns. Village League members were pro-Jordanian loyalists like their leader, Mustafa Dudin, from Hebron, and their ranks were fleshed out by dubious characters with criminal backgrounds. Many of them were given weapons by the Israeli civil administration and were viewed as simple collaborators by their fellow Palestinians. The Shin Bet had grave reservations about the scheme but had little choice other than to comply.[25]

The Lebanese component of the prospective assault was to destroy Palestinian and Muslim power so that a 'new' Lebanon could emerge under the Phalange. It could then be expected that Lebanon would become the second Arab state to make peace with Israel.

Sharon intended to achieve his objectives through an expanded or 'big' version of 'Operation Pines', an IDF contingency plan for the invasion of Lebanon that had been drawn up in April 1981. Both the original plan (or 'Little Pines'), which called for an IDF advance as far as Sidon, and 'Big Pines', which envisaged an advance to a line north of Beirut and the Beirut–Damascus highway, were reviewed in September 1981 by the new OC Northern Command, Major-General Amir Drori.[26]

From the start, Sharon thought in terms of 'Big Pines' rather than 'Little Pines', although he concealed this from his cabinet colleagues. As early as October 1981 he spoke, in a briefing to the IDF General Staff, of the inclusion of Beirut in the prospective campaign.[27]

How long would the IDF have to stay in Lebanon in order to assure the emergence of a new, Phalange-dominated regime? Sharon thought six weeks. Saguy was less optimistic and believed it would take not less than three months.[28] The plan for the new order and for the final eviction of the PLO depended in large measure on the election to the presidency of Bashir Gemayel, who announced his candidacy in November 1981. The election was due to take place the following summer.

Sharon first presented his plans to the cabinet on 20 December 1981. The defence minister did not mention 'Big Pines' by name, but the map be brought included an IDF arrow advancing to the Beirut–Damascus highway. This was the first time the ministers had heard of any intention to invade Lebanon or been told of the main lines and aims of the campaign. Many were shocked and a number objected. Sharon – and Begin – had been warned that they faced serious opposition in cabinet. The defence minister henceforward proceeded more cautiously, rarely letting his cabinet colleagues see the entire breadth of this thinking.[29]

In the second week of January 1982 Sharon, accompanied by Nahik Nevot from the Mossad and various generals and aides, paid a secret visit to Christian Lebanon and told Bashir Gemayel of the impending invasion. And he was frank that the plan had to include the expulsion of the PLO from Beirut. Saguy objected: 'We mustn't go as far as Beirut. We'll only get bogged down there,' the Aman chief said. Besides, conquering an Arab capital would raise Arab and US hackles. Sharon beat a tactical retreat. The Phalange would take Muslim West Beirut, he said. But Saguy insisted that the Christians were just not up to the task.

Later in the tour, the Phalange leaders gave indirect support to Saguy's position by displaying unmistakable reluctance to assist the IDF. Politically, as Pierre Gemayel made clear, the Israelis should not expect a peace treaty between the two countries after the invasion. The Phalange, a shocked Sharon was told, could not become 'traitors' to the Arab camp.[30]

But the plans went ahead. In February Begin sent Saguy to Washington to sound out the Reagan administration. Alexander Haig, the secretary of state, told the IDF intelligence chief that the United States would condone a full-scale Israeli attack only in reprisal for a flagrant PLO violation of the ceasefire. Saguy returned home satisfied.[31]

The same month a PLO unit was captured after crossing the border from Jordan. The Shin Bet insisted that the guerrillas had come from Amman; Eitan ignored this and stressed the responsibility of the PLO leadership in Beirut.[32] The intelligence facts were being selectively marshalled to suit the grand political and military design.

In March the chief of staff visited Beirut again. But in April a new problem surfaced. Saguy was joined by Yitzhak Hofi in objecting to the whole concept. The Mossad's Nevot was responsible for the on-going, day-to-day liaison with the Phalange; indeed, he refused to allow meetings between IDF officers and the Phalange without his presence. Nevot, thoroughly under Bashir's influence, pressed for invasion. But Hofi had come down hard behind the Aman view that the Phalange could not be relied upon. The heads of Israel's two main intelligence services were undermining Sharon's strategy.[33]

Yet still the planning continued. Israeli reconnaissance and intelligence units mapped out the invasion routes, checking bridges, passes and roads on the way to Beirut. In the spring of 1982 a series of attacks abroad, along Israel's borders and in the occupied territories almost provoked the long-planned war. On 3 April a Mossad officer named Ya'akov Barsimantov was shot dead outside his Paris home by a group called the Lebanese Armed Revolutionary Factions. Begin thought this ample provocation to launch 'Operation Pines'; but on 11 April five ministers dissented.[34] On 21 April an Israeli soldier died and two were wounded when their vehicle ran over a mine in the South Lebanese Security Zone. Later that day Israeli jets bombed PLO targets. The PLO held its fire. But a second wave of IAF raids on 9 May nearly provided the required PLO response. PLO guns and rocket-launchers sent dozens of projectiles on to the Israeli side of the border, but not one shell hit an Israeli village or town. The Palestinian message was clear: 'We're avoiding hitting Israeli civilian centres, but we are capable of doing so, and if provoked sufficiently, we shall do so.'

The Syrians, with a division entrenched in eastern Lebanon's Beka'a Valley and a brigade dug in in Beirut, had no inkling of the scope of the impending IDF assault as late as the end of April. Syrian intelligence continued to think in terms of an expanded 'Operation Litani'. The PLO leadership, on the other hand, feared precisely something along the lines of 'Big Pines'.[35]

Begin brought a watered-down version of 'Big Pines' before the cabinet on 10 May. A majority of eleven out of eighteen ministers voted in favour. Begin had tentatively scheduled the invasion for 17 May, but called it off when it became clear that the seven dissident ministers continued to oppose a large-scale ground attack. At the cabinet meeting of 10 May Sharon and Begin had presented an expanded 'Little Pines' rather than an all-out assault up to Beirut. Sharon spoke of a 'limited', 'police' operation, not war. But the deputy head of military intelligence, Brigadier-General Aviezer Ya'ari, standing in for Saguy (who was abroad), warned that the operation would mean war with Syria.[36] Henceforth, Begin and Sharon would sell the ministers a limited, 'Little Pines' assault, which could muster cabinet approval. Talk of a 'second-stage' advance up to Beirut and the Beirut–Damascus highway was carefully muted, and it was trotted out by Sharon only after the war had begun and only as 'contingency' planning, born of the exigencies of battle.

But Sharon handled his generals differently. At the General Staff meeting three days later they were treated to an unvarnished version of 'Big Pines'. The objectives were a link-up with the Phalange around Beirut and reaching and cutting the Beirut–Damascus highway. It was clear to all that the invasion would necessarily lead to a clash with the Syrians. Saguy presented Aman's case against 'Big Pines', again to no avail. The IDF intelligence chief said a major clash with the Syrians was inevitable; the Syrians would reinforce their troops and Israel would have to deal with their missiles. Saguy also predicted that the Phalange would not lift a finger to help the IDF during the invasion. Nor, he said, would the invasion succeed in destroying the PLO. Saguy warned of the superpower implications of the war and concluded that the nation, and the IDF itself, would be divided. This was no way to go into battle.[37]

Saguy could not have spoken more clearly. But his statement was made at a General Staff meeting. In the more important cabinet meetings, the IDF intelligence chief had either kept his peace or spoken far less clearly and emphatically, allowing the views of Begin and Sharon to carry the day.

Abu Nidal strikes again

Close to midnight on 3 June 1982 the cabinet militants at last had their provocation. Israel's ambassador to Britain, Shlomo Argov, was shot in the head outside London's Dorchester Hotel by a Palestinian gunman. He and his two accomplices belonged to the breakaway group led by Abu Nidal (Sabri al-Banna), a former Fatah official who was supported by Iraq and opposed Yasser Arafat's 'capitulationist' leadership of the PLO. The assassination attempt seemed designed precisely to provoke an IDF assault against Arafat's Lebanese stronghold.[38]

Begin didn't care exactly who had shot Argov or why. The cabinet was convened in emergency session on the morning of Friday, 4 June; the result, despite Ariel Sharon's absence on a secret trip to Romania, was a foregone conclusion. The previous night Begin had already ordered Eitan to send in the air force to attack Palestinian targets; the cabinet had been called merely to provide the rubber stamp.

The cabinet meeting began with a briefing by Avraham Shalom, the head of the Shin Bet, which was responsible for the security of Israeli personnel abroad. Shalom said the attack was probably the work of the Abu Nidal group. Gideon Mahanaimi, the prime minister's adviser on terrorism, was about to elaborate on the nature of the group when Begin cut him off sharply, saying: 'They're all PLO.' Rafi Eitan had taken the same view a few minutes earlier, when told by an intelligence aide that it was probably the work of the anti-Arafat group: 'Abu Nidal, Abu Shmidal,' he said. 'We have to strike at the PLO.'[39]

After the intelligence chiefs had been silenced, Eitan proposed the bombing of PLO headquarters in Beirut. Both Eitan and Saguy assessed that the likely PLO response would be to shell Israel's northern border villages. If that happened, said the chief of staff, the IDF would retaliate massively. All present understood that he was speaking of 'Operation Pines', in one of its versions. None of the ministers objected. What the cabinet did not know was that Aman and the Mossad had months before acquired copies of PLO orders to its front-line artillery units to respond automatically, with barrages against the Israeli settlements, should the IAF attack the Beirut headquarters.[40]

What ensued closely followed the expected scenario. The Israeli jets hit Beirut at 3.15 p.m. Two hours later the PLO guns and Katyusha rocket-launchers opened up on the Galilee settlements. The two sides traded bombs and shells throughout the following day. On the night of Saturday, 5 June, the cabinet reconvened at Begin's home in Jerusalem. The premier asked the ministers to approve a forty-kilometre thrust into southern Lebanon to destroy the PLO guns and rocket-launchers with the range of the Galilee settlements. No one mentioned an advance beyond the forty-kilometre arc, the conquest of Beirut or a link-up with the Phalange. 'Beirut is outside the picture,' said Sharon. He spoke of a 'twenty-four-hour' operation. Only one minister, the former Brigadier-General Mordechai Zippori, criticized the invasion plan, fearing a frontal clash with the Syrians, but he was persuaded to vote with the majority – a classic example of what sociologist Irving Janis calls 'group-think'.[41] Two Liberal Party ministers abstained. Saguy and Hofi were present, but were not invited to speak and did not.[42]

The invasion was to begin the next morning. On the night of 5 June Bashir Gemayel was hastily summoned to a meeting with Eitan and given advanced warning of the operation. The chief of staff asked the Phalangists to open fire along the Green Line, which separated Muslim West Beirut from the Christian East, and for permission for Israeli combat teams to disembark at Jounieh. The Phalange turned down both requests.[43]

Fighting a war

Israeli armoured columns began crossing the border on Sunday, 6 June. Because of Sharon's deception of his cabinet colleagues about the scope of the operation, the military commanders did not have a clear definition of their objectives. The army's moves had to be trimmed in accordance. Heliborne and seaborne forces could not, as strategy dictated, be landed deep in the enemy rear, near Beirut or along the Beirut–Damascus highway to trap the PLO and Syrian units in the south, in Beirut and in the Beka'a Valley.

The plan involved advancing northwards along four axes: a western (one-division) axis, commanded by Brigadier-General Yitzhak Mordechai, along the coast road, through the main PLO concentrations around Tyre and Sidon, towards Damour and Beirut; a central (one-division) axis, commanded by Brigadier-General Avigdor Kahalani, northwards through Nabatiya, along the mountain ridges overlooking the coast road towards Sidon; a second central (one-division) axis, commanded by Brigadier-General Menahem Einan, moving initially in Kahalani's footsteps and then driving northwards through the Shouf Mountains to the Beirut–Damascus road; and an eastern (two-division) axis, commanded by Major-General Avigdor Ben-Gal, directed at Hasbaya and Rashaya al-Fukhar, which could then push northwards towards the main Syrian concentrations in the eastern Beka'a. A fifth, seaborne, force, commanded by Brigadier-General Amos Yaron, was landed at the Awali estuary just north of Sidon. Aman had long predicted that if the IDF advanced along the central axis, the Syrians would intervene.[44]

In the west the invaders faced a ragtag army of 6,000 PLO fighters, in two brigade formations and several independent battalions; then there was a division of Syrian troops in the Beka'a and an independent Syrian brigade in Beirut. At the end of the first week of the war, the division in the Beka'a was joined by a second Syrian division.

The Palestinians along the coast and in the hills to the east did not fight in large, organized formations but they put up an unexpectedly strong and courageous resistance, delaying the overwhelmingly superior IDF by as much as seventy-two hours. Particularly strong resistance was encountered in the refugee camps around Tyre and Sidon (Rashidiye, Al-Bas and Ein al-Hilweh) and in Sidon itself.

The link-up along the coast between Mordechai's division and Yaron's amphibious force at Damour took place on the Awali estuary, just north of Sidon, on 9 June. That was also the day of the start of the frontal Israeli–Syrian clash in eastern Lebanon.

The IDF had already killed Syrian troops on 7 June and the air force had destroyed two Syrian radar stations. On 8 June Einan's tanks clashed with the westernmost Syrian positions around Jezzine, captured the town, and then took on Syrian forces of brigade strength at Ein al-Zehalta, to the north. The Syrians had decided to contest Einan's drive to the Beirut–Damascus highway. In the costly mountain-pass battle, Syrian commandos and tankmen successfully delayed the Israeli advance long enough to ensure that Einan did not reach the highway before the superpower-imposed ceasefire went into effect at noon on 11 June.[45]

Meanwhile, the three crucial orders that were to convert the forty-kilometre-deep campaign into a fully fledged war were issued by Sharon: to Yaron, to advance on Beirut; to IAF Commander David Ivri, to take out the twenty-odd Syrian AA missile batteries in the Beka'a; and to Ben-Gal, to push northwards through Hasbaya towards the Beka'a to destroy the Syrian 1st Division.

The operation against the missiles, which combined air assault, barrages of ground-to-ground missiles and long-range artillery fire, went in at 2.00 p.m. on Wednesday, 9 June; it was all over by 4.15. The first strike took thirty-five minutes; the second strike, which went in at 3.45 p.m., was a mopping-up operation. Syrian defence minister Mustafa Tlas described a three-stage assault: a massive 'blinding' operation by Israeli airborne and ground ECM systems against the Syrian radar and electronics installations; a barrage of air-to-ground missiles (fired by Israeli jets from a range of thirty-five kilometres), ground-to-ground missile and artillery fire against the AA missiles' radar and control stations; and a close-up strike by forty IAF Phantoms, Skyhawks and Kfirs. Seventeen of the Syrian batteries were wiped out. In an effort to save them, the Syrians threw in packs of interceptors and lost twenty-nine jets to no Israeli losses. The Syrians were to lose another fifty planes during the following days, again to no Israeli losses. The devastation of the Syrian air defence system in Lebanon was a major electronic intelligence and air force coup. Tlas later attributed the Israeli victory in the battle for Lebanon's skies to Israel's superior ground control, radar system and airborne early warning aircraft (Hawkeyes), and to Syria's 'radar blindness', in part stemming from the inability to deploy Syrian radar stations in various parts of non-Syrian-occupied Lebanon.[46]

Ben-Gal's force set off for the Beka'a on Wednesday afternoon, 9 June. Its aim – never achieved – was to reach and cut off the Beirut–Damascus highway south-east of Shtoura. Lack of drive, technical snags, including fuel shortages and traffic jams, and fierce resistance, especially around Sultan Yakoub, by the Syrian 1st Division prevented Ben-Gal's overwhelmingly stronger force from reaching the road before the ceasefire came into effect.[47]

Meanwhile, General Yaron's paratroops, soon joined by Kahalani's force, began their thrust northwards towards Beirut via Damour. A Phalange liaison officer joined the Israeli force on the morning of 11 June, just south of the Lebanese capital. Fighting the PLO and elements of the Syrian 85th Brigade, Yaron's paratroops slowly slogged their way through the foothills east of the Sidon–Beirut road and linked up with the Phalange forces, outside Ba'abde, at 1.00 p.m. on 13 June. The Beirut–Damascus road had finally been cut. There was a joyous meeting of Bashir and Pierre Gemayel and the Israeli generals. The IDF had reached the suburbs of Beirut.

But the city itself, defended by about 10,000 PLO fighters, assorted Muslim militiamen and the remnants of the Syrian brigade, was to prove a tough nut to crack. The IDF encirclement of Beirut turned into a siege. Israel demanded that the PLO and the Syrians leave the city; the PLO resisted. PFLP leader George Habash spoke of a 'second Stalingrad'. Begin and Sharon wanted the Phalangists to conquer West Beirut but the Gemayels refused. American ambassador Philip Habib began complex negotiations between the Palestinians, Syrians and Muslim Lebanese on the one hand and Israel on the other to obtain a peaceful evacuation of the PLO and Syrians.

For the next two months the Israeli forces shelled and bombed West Beirut, cut off water and electricity and nibbled away at the Palestinian defences in short, sharp ground offensives. A chain of lethal car-bomb explosions – attributed by the PLO and Tlas to Israeli 'agents'[48] – undermined morale in the besieged city. To the east IDF units mounted a number of short offensives northwards, to wrest further points of control along the Beirut–Damascus highway – at Aley and Bahamdoun – away from the Syrians.[49] Israeli aircraft repeatedly bombed buildings where PLO leaders were believed to be hiding, but without killing any of them,[50] and a series of ground attacks by Israeli paratroops ate away at the outlying southern districts of

West Beirut, conveying the message that the IDF was resolved to conquer the city if the PLO fighters did not leave. In the end, Lebanese Muslim pressure and the PLO's own fears that the IDF would assault West Beirut persuaded Arafat to agree to pull out. The withdrawal began on 21 August under cover of a multinational (American–French–Italian) force. Some 15,000 Palestinian fighters and Syrian troops left the city over the next few days, the Palestinians mostly boarding Greek boats for Tunis and Algeria, the Syrians travelling by truck along the road to Damascus. An Israeli sniper had Yasser Arafat in his sights as the PLO leader said his goodbyes.[51]

Throughout the war, both against the PLO and the Syrians, the IDF made effective use of drones for intelligence-gathering and electronic jamming. Drones were used to film PLO emplacements at Beaufort Castle, overlooking the Litani, over Syrian positions around Jezzine and in the lower Beka'a Valley, along Ben-Gal's routes of advance. Occasionally, as at Sultan Yakoub, the intelligence failed to reach the field commanders in time to have an effect on the battlefield.[52]

The enigma of Bashir Gemayel

Bashir Gemayel was elected president of Lebanon with the aid of Israeli bayonets and money on 23 August, two days after the start of the PLO evacuation from Beirut. Despite the inactivity of the Phalangists during the battle, all seemed set for the consummation of the Israeli–Maronite alliance. But within days Ariel Sharon's 'grand design' for an Israeli-aligned, Phalange-ruled Lebanon began to fall apart.

On 30 August Gemayel was flown to Nahariya for a meeting with Begin. A few hours earlier the United States had told the prime minister of President Reagan's new peace plan for the Middle East. It was a slap in the face for those who had believed that the destruction of the PLO in Lebanon would lead to a strengthening of Israel's hold on the occupied territories. Reagan's plan called for Israeli withdrawal from the bulk of the

West Bank and Gaza Strip and their confederation with Jordan. And as if this was not enough, Lebanon's president-elect began chafing at the bit. When Begin asked him about signing a peace treaty with Israel, Gemayel replied: 'I cannot decide on such matters alone . . . the hasty signing of a treaty is not justified, from either a political or a security standpoint . . .' Begin suggested that Gemayel pay a public visit to Israel immediately after his assumption of office and proposed a target date – 31 December 1982 – by which time the peace treaty would be signed. Gemayel asked for 'a year's grace'.

Begin suggested to Gemayel that Major Sa'ad Haddad might now be appointed commander of the southern Lebanon region. Gemayel countered that Haddad still faced a treason charge and would have to stand trial, although this was a mere formality. The Israelis wanted to leave Haddad's force and the Security Zone in place; Gemayel implied that Beirut's sovereignty would have to reach down to the international frontier. Begin then referred to colleagues of Bashir who preferred a pro-Syrian orientation for Lebanon. The Israeli prime minister suggested that these people should be avoided and offered to give Gemayel the list of names. After Bashir's departure, Begin chastised Nahik Nevot of the Mossad for failing to deliver the Phalange goods.[53]

Bashir was incensed at these slights to his independence and to Lebanese sovereignty. Back home he complained to his father that Begin had 'treated me like a child'.[54]

In the Israeli defence establishment a division of opinion had sprung up around the question of Gemayel and the Phalange. Should Israel put all its eggs in one basket and rely on the president-elect and his party as its mainstay in Lebanon? Or should it diversify its contacts, and open channels to other parties? Could the Phalange be trusted? Sharon, Eitan and the Mossad – though with the Mossad chief Yitzhak Hofi growingly disenchanted – continued to support the exclusive Phalange connection. Amir Drori and other Northern Command officers were sceptical and pressed for diversification.[55]

The movement of Haddad's troops northwards, to the Zaharani river and then the Awali river, implied that distrust of the Phalange was matched by continued faith in Haddad. Thus the vision of a 'new order', an independent, sovereign Lebanon under Gemayel, in complete control of its own house, was being curtailed by Israel's concrete need to safeguard its northern border. The Israeli–Phalange alliance was being undermined by both sides.[56]

The assassination and the massacre

Bashir Gemayel and Ariel Sharon met for the last time on 12 September 1982. Sharon, accompanied by Nevot, had initiated the meeting in order to erase the residue of bitterness left by the Gemayel–Begin meeting at Nahariya a fortnight before and to coordinate action to 'clear out the remaining terrorists' from West Beirut.

Sharon demanded that Phalange and Lebanese army units carry out the operation. Gemayel spoke of destroying the refugee camps and turning the area into 'an enormous zoo'. The Palestinians, said Gemayel, would be shipped to Syria 'in air-conditioned buses'. Sharon does not seem to have objected to the plan. As the Kahan Commission Report made clear later, Gemayel had repeatedly told the heads of the Mossad that his intention 'was to eliminate the Palestinian problem in Lebanon when he came to power – even if that meant resorting to aberrant methods . . .'[57]

On 14 September Gemayel visited Phalange HQ in Beirut's Ashrafiya district to address party activists. Since the late 1970s President Assad had come to regard Bashir as his main enemy in Lebanon; this feeling grew still more acute with the IDF invasion and Bashir's election. The Syrians decided to activate one of their Lebanese affiliates, the Syrian National Party, to eliminate the bothersome Maronite. Habib Shartouni, a secret member of the SNP, had a sister who lived on the third floor of the building that housed the Phalange branch in Ashrafiya. On 13 September Shartouni was instructed by his Syrian controller, from Rome, to assassinate Gemayel by detonating a bomb in his sister's flat, a floor above the Phalange hall.

Shartouni got his sister out of the flat, set the 300-kilogram bomb and waited with a remote control transmitter on a neighbouring roof. At 4.10 p.m., while Gemayel was in mid-speech, Shartouni detonated the bomb. The Phalange HQ collapsed in a pile of rubble. Twenty-seven Phalangists died and thirty-seven were wounded. The Syrians immediately announced that the Israelis were responsible. The Phalange arrested Shartouni and announced that Syria was behind the murder.[58] Nahik Nevot, who happened to be in Beirut, rushed to the scene and was told that Bashir had been wounded and rescued. But five hours after the explosion the Phalange leader was found dead. The news was immediately conveyed to Jerusalem.[59]

Begin and Sharon decided on the takeover of key areas and junctions in West Beirut. The city was still full of PLO and pro-Syrian 'terrorists'; the assassination of Gemayel was proof of this, if any were still needed. And Begin also spoke of the need to protect the city's Muslims against Phalange revenge. Aman's evaluations were similar. IDF intelligence argued that the assassination could lead to acts of revenge and general civil strife; and that the IDF – potentially a 'stabilizing element' – had best enter West Beirut to nip any trouble in the bud.[60]

IDF armour and paratroops moved into West Beirut at 5.00 a.m. on 15 September. One of the main axes of advance bordered on the Sabra and Shatilla camps, from where several dozen Palestinians took pot-shots at the advancing Israelis. At 9.00 a.m., at the rooftop IDF divisional command-post overlooking Shatilla, Sharon told his generals that the Phalange would go into the camps 'under IDF supervision'. Saguy, who was present, later denied that he had heard such an order being issued. Sharon and Saguy drove to Phalange HQ at Karantina. The defence minister spoke of the Phalange moving in with the IDF and said, of the remaining 'terrorists' in West Beirut: 'I don't want a single one of them left!' But Sharon apparently did not speak explicitly – then, or that afternoon at Bikfaya, where he consoled Pierre and Amin Gemayel – of the need to avenge Bashir's death.

During the afternoon of 15 September, the deputy director of Aman, Aviezer Ya'ari, said that the IDF's entry into West Beirut was viewed as crucial by the city's Muslim population: they believed that only the IDF could protect them against the vengeance of the Phalange. This, of course, had been Begin's real or ostensible reason for approving the move. Ya'ari also said that Bashir's assassination was probably the work of the left-wing, Lebanese Nasserist militia, the Mourabitun, so the Christians had no reason to take revenge on the Palestinians. The Mossad's initial evaluation of who was behind the assassination was identical.[61]

On the afternoon of 16 September, in Tel Aviv, US special ambassador Morris Draper, ambassador Sam Lewis, Eitan and Saguy discussed the IDF entry into West Beirut. Saguy said that the Phalange were likely to go in. Eitan said: 'Lebanon is at a point of exploding into a frenzy of revenge. No one can stop them . . . They're obsessed with the idea of revenge . . . I could see in the eyes [of the Phalangist commanders] that it's going to be a relentless slaughter.'

Eitan's future tense was out of date. The Phalangists had already started pushing into Sabra and Shatilla and IDF mortars soon began to provide illumination rounds. Aman officers followed the Phalangists' progress from General Amos Yaron's rooftop HQ and on radio receivers. A Mossad liaison officer was in Karantina throughout. At 7.00 p.m. the radio monitors got their first hint of the butchery that had begun. A Phalange officer asked what to do with fifty women and children he had rounded up. Eli Hobeika, the militia commander, gave a chilling reply: 'That's the last time you're going to ask me. You know what to do.'

Yaron warned Hobeika not to harm civilians, but the IDF's sensibilities were of little interest to the Phalangists. Hobeika had briefed his men before going into Sabra and Shatilla to kill young Palestinians in order to trigger a mass exodus from the camps. An hour later, at about 8.00 p.m., the radio monitor in Yaron's command-post heard a Phalange commander ask what to do with forty-five captured Palestinian men. Jesse Soker, his superior, responded: 'Do God's will.'[62]

That evening, when the cabinet met in Jerusalem to discuss the IDF entry into West Beirut, Sharon spoke of the IDF push but failed to mention the Phalange. Saguy left early, saying he was tired. Towards the end of the session, Eitan announced that the Phalange were already operating in Sabra and Shatilla. He implied that they were under IDF control. And he warned, without connecting the warning to the Phalangists' operation, of impending revenge and carnage among the Lebanese factions.

Eitan's announcement was the first time the new Mossad chief, Nahum Admoni, who had replaced Yitzhak Hofi only on 12 September, heard that the Phalange had been assigned the clean-up of the camps. Admoni echoed Eitan's warning: Christian revenge attacks were a possibility, he said.

During the night of 16–17 September several Aman officers took note of the monitored radio messages and sent disturbing reports about possible atrocities to Aman's Research (Estimates) Department and to Northern Command's forward HQ at Aley. One report spoke of '300' Palestinians, some of them civilians, killed. But the Aman duty officers in Tel Aviv decided not to wake up Saguy, and no one had a clear picture of what was happening in the camps.

The next morning, 17 September, at about 11.00 a.m., their unease got the better of Generals Yaron and Drori and they ordered the Phalange units in the camps to stop in their tracks. But in the early afternoon Yaron allowed a force of 150 Phalangists to join Hobeika's men. And at a meeting between Eitan and the Phalange commanders at 5.00 p.m. the IDF chief of staff permitted the Phalange units to remain in the camps until the following morning and to complete their mission. The Phalange would then have to leave, 'because of American pressure', Eitan explained. In the summary of the conversation made by a Mossad officer, Eitan is quoted as saying that he had received a 'positive impression ... from the statement by the

Phalangist forces and from their behaviour in the field . . .' The Phalangists asked for IDF bulldozers to raze 'illegal structures' in the camps. The Mossad representative supported the request and Eitan agreed, though only one bulldozer, without IDF markings, was supplied. Further reports and rumours of atrocities that afternoon and evening failed to evince any Israeli response and the Phalangists continued killing Palestinians and burying them under buildings with bulldozers. The Israeli generals were disturbed by the rumours but were busy with a wide range of other problems.

By about 8.00 the following morning, 18 September, the Phalange had still failed to evacuate the camps and the IDF ordered the Christian troopers out of the area. It was during the next few hours that the carnage was discovered.

Yet communications on the subject within the IDF and the other Israeli bureaucracies remained faulty. Begin learned of the massacre only at 5.00 p.m. – from a BBC broadcast. He then called Sharon, who ordered an investigation of the report. Meanwhile, the Phalangist Voice of Lebanon announced that a unit of Major Haddad's troops had carried out the massacre. Eitan met the Phalange commanders in Karantina, reprimanded them and demanded that they publicly own up to the slaughter. They refused. Aman was later to estimate that between 700 and 800 Palestinians and Lebanese Muslims had died in the massacre; the Palestinian Red Crescent Society put the death toll at 2,000; and the Lebanese special prosecutor, Assad Germanos, who investigated the affair, put the figure at 460.

At its meeting on Sunday night the Israeli cabinet tried to distance itself from the massacre by announcing that the atrocity had been committed by 'a Lebanese unit' that had entered the camps 'at a point far away from IDF positions'. The implication was that the Phalange, which was not mentioned by name, had gone in without IDF knowledge or supervision.[63]

But the Israeli public, which had been uneasy for weeks over the course of the war, exploded in outrage when the news of the massacre finally broke. Official efforts at a cover-up only stoked the fires of indignation. Eventually, after an unprecedented mass rally of 400,000 protesters in Tel Aviv, the resignation of energy minister Yitzhak Berman, dissident TV appearances by President Yitzhak Navon and the president of Israel's Academy of Sciences and Humanities, Professor Ephraim Urbach, and demands by several minor coalition partners, Begin finally acquiesced and appointed a judicial commission of inquiry, headed by Supreme Court President Yitzhak Kahan.

The Kahan Commission

The Kahan Commission, composed of Kahan, Supreme Court Justice Aharon Barak and Major-General (Res.) Yona Efrat, sat from 1 October 1982 until 7 February 1983, heard fifty-eight witnesses and read the testimony of 163 others, including Palestinians, Lebanese, Europeans who worked in the Palestinian hospitals in Beirut, and Israeli military and intelligence personnel. While authorized to examine 'all the facts and factors connected to the atrocities committed by a unit of the Lebanese Forces [the official name of the Phalange militia] against the civilian inhabitants of the Sabra and Shatilla camps', the inquiry in fact focused on the Israeli role in the killings. In a wider sense it was also an investigation of the Israeli–Phalange connection. Thus the Commission inevitably focused on the Mossad and Aman, and their relations with the Christians.

The Kahan Commission found the IDF indirectly responsible for the massacre, arguing that the officers concerned should have anticipated what was about to happen and should have stepped in and halted the operation when the first reports came in.

It attributed a 'certain degree of responsibility' for what happened to prime minister Begin and charged that foreign minister Yitzhak Shamir had erred in not following up a report about the massacre that he had been given on 17 September. But most of the Commission's findings and recommendations on the political level were directed against Ariel Sharon. The defence minister was found to have been 'remiss in his duties' by having ignored the possibility of a slaughter. The Commission recommended that Sharon 'draw the appropriate personal conclusion' (resign) or that the prime minister remove him from office. Sharon did not resign; he was removed by Begin, although he remained in the cabinet as a minister without portfolio.

As to the military, the Commission ruled that Lieutenant-General Eitan had been negligent and remiss in his duties and had failed before and during the massacre to do anything to prevent or limit the killings. But as Eitan was about to complete his stint as chief of staff, it said it would not pass judgement on his suitability to continue in office. The Commission let off OC Northern Command Amir Drori with a mild rebuke. The divisional commander responsible for West Beirut, General Amos Yaron, was found guilty of not fulfilling his duties properly. It was recommended that he be removed from any position of command for at least three years. (He was subsequently appointed Israel's military attaché in Washington.)

Yehoshua Saguy, the Aman chief, was found grossly negligent in having failed to warn his superiors before and during the massacre of what was about to happen or was already afoot. The Commission recommended that Saguy be removed from office. (He resigned and left the army, and was elected a Knesset member, for the Likud, in 1988.) The new Mossad chief, Nahum Admoni, was let off with a reprimand for not having spoken clearly at the cabinet meeting of 16 September.

The Kahan Commission found that while the division of labour between the Mossad and Aman 'was spelled out', it clearly 'left room for misunderstandings and duplication in various areas'. Both agencies had maintained contacts with the Phalange and produced evaluations about them. Underlying the clear difference of attitude displayed towards the Phalange by the two intelligence agencies, the Kahan Commission found, was the fact that 'the Mossad [was] to a not inconsiderable extent under the influence of constant and close contact with the Phalangist elite [and] felt positively about strengthening relations with that organization . . .'

In making this judgement, the Commission quoted from Nahum Admoni's testimony before them: 'The Mossad tried, to the best of its ability, throughout this period, to present and approach the subject as objectively as possible; but since it was in charge of the contacts, I accept as an assumption that subjective, and not only objective, relations also emerged. I must accept that, in contacts, when you talk to people, relationships are formed.'

To illustrate their point, the commissioners cited a report written by an Aman officer who was attached to the Mossad liaison group with the Phalange during the war and a report written at the same time by the Mossad representative. The Aman report 'gave a negative evaluation . . . of the Phalangists' policy during the war', while the Mossad officer's report 'vigorously rejected' these conclusions.[64]

Ending a war

Things truly fell apart for Israel in Lebanon in September 1982. Exactly a week after Bashir Gemayel's murder, his brother Amin was elected president with US support. The Americans declined to support the alternative proposed by Israel – a continuation of the presidency of Elias Sarkis, with the government effectively in the hands of Lebanon's chief of military intelligence, Colonel Jonny Abdu.

A proposal by General Drori to cut IDF losses and withdraw unilaterally to southern Lebanon was rejected by the government. Begin, Sharon and Eitan decided to cling on and try to extract from the Lebanese quagmire as much political and military gain as was still possible. It was another fatal error of judgement.

Israel and the United States spent the last months of 1982 and the first months of 1983 trying to coerce the new Lebanese president into meeting the commitments entered into by his late brother about the 'normalization' of relations with Israel while assuring the security of Israel's northern border. In secret talks held at Ariel Sharon's ranch in the Negev, and in open sessions between Israeli, Lebanese and US teams alternately at Khalde, south of Beirut, and in Netanya and Kiryat Shmona in Israel, the three sides negotiated a non-belligerency agreement. Gemayel was constrained throughout by his fear of Syria and its Lebanese proxies, the Druse, the Shi'ites, the Palestinians and others. The Syrians made their views painfully evident with the truck bombing, by Shi'ite militants from the Beka'a Valley, of the US Embassy in Beirut on 18 April 1983. This left sixty-one dead and 120 wounded.

In the accord, which was finally signed on 17 May 1983, Lebanon agreed to end the state of belligerency with Israel (formally in force since 1948); to a degree of normalization of relations; and to joint Israeli–Lebanese patrolling of the southern border area. Gemayel won some major concessions from Israel: the agreement was not a 'peace' treaty; it provided for a full Israeli withdrawal; and it did not allow for IDF surveillance stations and bases on Lebanese soil.

The May agreement was none the less roundly condemned by Syria and its allies, who embarked on a guerrilla campaign against the Israeli occupation forces, a concerted assault on Gemayel himself, on Phalange positions, especially in the Shouf mountains, and on Gemayel's allies. At the same time, Syria promoted a rebellion against PLO leader Yasser Arafat within his own Fatah organization, and soon Syria and the rebel Palestinians were besieging Arafat's last Lebanese stronghold, in Tripoli in the north.

In August 1983 the IDF withdrew southwards from the Shouf to a new line along the Awali river. But Assad wanted both the Israelis and the Americans out of Lebanon completely. The US Marine contingents, which had originally been dispatched in September 1982 to help assure the orderly withdrawal of the PLO, and which had been left around the capital to prop up the Gemayel presidency, soon fell victim to the Syrian proxies. On 23 October 1983 the Marines' Beirut HQ was destroyed by a Shi'ite truck bomb, causing 241 fatalities. The CIA chief, William Casey, who had a professional's appreciation of the Mossad's human intelligence assets – especially in Syria, Lebanon and the Soviet Union, and the way it ran complex, interlocking false-flag espionage operations – asked Nahum Admoni to investigate. Israel quickly traced the bombers to Syria and Iran.[65] Another truck bomb, that same day, demolished the French HQ in the capital, killing seventy-four French paratroops. Shi'ite gunmen and Druse artillerymen regularly fired at US Marines dug in around Khalde junction and at Beirut airport. The Americans responded with massive artillery barrages from the USS *New Jersey* on the Druse positions in the Shouf, although Reagan stopped short of approving air raids on Syrian positions in the Beka'a. US might was of little avail; the harassment continued. The Shi'ite–Druse alliance quickly overwhelmed the Christian units of the Lebanese Army and punched a corridor from the Shouf through to the sea, at Damour and Khalde. The Americans pulled out of Lebanon in February 1984. Israel stayed.

Fighting the Shi'ites

The Shi'ite–Palestinian guerrilla campaign against the Israelis in south Lebanon escalated in the autumn of 1983. The most painful blow was the truck bombing of the IDF–Shin Bet HQ in Tyre on 4 November 1983, in which some thirty Israelis, including five security service officers, died. Syria's desire to see Israel expelled from Lebanon meshed with the local Shi'ite population's natural wish to be rid of a foreign occupier. The southern Shi'ites, led by the mainstream Amal movement, had only reluctantly taken up arms against the IDF; many had initially greeted the Israelis as saviours, or at least given the invasion their silent approval, and had been happy with the destruction of the PLO infrastructure. 'By dismantling Palestinian power in the summer of 1982,' wrote Fuad Ajami, the community's finest historian, 'Israel had done for the Shia what they had not been able to do for themselves.'[66]

Long before the war, in the late 1970s, David Kimche had lost an internal Mossad argument about whether to try to build an alliance with the Lebanese Shi'ites as well as with the Christians. Some of the service's most promising young officers protested at the exclusive dependence on the Christian Phalange.[67] Iranian help had been sought in dealing with the Shi'ite religious establishment in the south. From the interrogation of Iranian militants captured during 'Operation Litani', Israeli intelligence uncovered details of PLO training for opposition groups in Tehran. The Shah extended aid to the Lebanese Shi'ites to prevent them from supporting Ayatollah Khomeini, who was then still in exile in France, and also to try to expose his enemies.[68] But the 1979 revolution had put an end all this.

Israel's Shi'ite option probably had little chance. As Ajami argued later:

> Unlike the Lebanese Christians, they could not openly embrace Israel. They were not that kind of people. For centuries the Maronites had played the game of inviting strangers and drawing on their resources. The Shia, on the other hand, carried with them a nervousness about encountering strangers, a fear of defilement. The peculiar Shia relationship to the larger Arab world – they were of it, but not fully – rendered them unable to come to terms with Israel. Like Caesar's wife, they had to be above suspicion. They were sure that they would not be forgiven a close association with Israel.[69]

After the 1982 invasion some Israeli officers still hoped to play the Shi'ite card. But Aman argued that Amal could not be trusted because of the presence of radical, pro-Iranian elements. Instead an effort was made to mobilize Shi'ite soldiers into Sa'ad Haddad's largely Christian militia. Psychological warfare was used to try and exploit factional and communal rivalries to Israel's advantage. As one IDF officer said later:

> There was information and disinformation. We would drop leaflets warning the Shi'ite population of the consequences of attacking Israel. We would take people in and feed them dirt about the people we were against: he's an embezzler, he's a homosexual, he's a

coward, and so on. Then we would also try and demonstrate the benefits of cooperating with Israel. We funded broadcasting stations and newspapers and got them to print articles about hospitals and medical services we were running for the people's benefit.[70]

But the oppressive conditions of the continuing Israeli occupation gradually dashed these hopes as well. On 16 October 1983, the day of Ashura – which commemorates the martyrdom of the Shi'ites' Imam Hussein – trigger-happy, nervous Israeli soldiers killed two people and wounded several others during a traditional mourning procession through the southern town of Nabatiya. The Tyre suicide bomb attack took place less than three weeks later. Early in 1984 a leading cleric, Sheikh Ragheb Harb, was killed – apparently by Israeli agents – in Jibshit. Militancy, not the community's traditional submission, became the order of the day.

IDF intelligence had predicted that if Israel prolonged its stay, Shi'ite displeasure would turn into active resistance. And so it did. Palestinian and Shi'ite fighters, working together in the National Resistance Movement, soon turned every road into a free-fire zone, every IDF position into a target, sparking an endless cycle of ambush and repression, searches, demolition of houses, mass arrests, further roadside bombs and ambushes and more Israeli retaliation, drawing more and more of the local population into the web of animosity. Short of massive collective punishments and mass expulsions, there was little the IDF could do to neutralize the guerrillas. The result was a slow but inevitable Israeli recognition of defeat and withdrawal southwards to the border 'Security Zone'.

The guerrilla compaign had begun in late 1982 with isolated attacks by a small number of Lebanese Communists and leftists and gradually came to be dominated by the Iranian-inspired (and often Syrian-paid and trained) Muslim fundamentalists of Hizbullah (The Party of God) and remnants of the PLO. These were joined in early 1984 by militiamen of the larger Amal movement. The Shi'ites were soon mounting around 100 attacks a month, altogether causing the Israeli army some 200 fatalities over two and a half years. Lacking an intelligence infrastructure in south Lebanon, the IDF was hard put to identify and trap the guerrillas, who moved easily in and out of the villages and hamlets.

Some time towards the end of 1982 the Shin Bet, which never normally operated in enemy teritory, was reluctantly mobilized to assist the IDF. Small numbers of security service personnel had gone into the Palestinian refugee camps immediately after the invasion, but this was seen as a short-term operation that was an extension of its regular work in the West Bank and Gaza. Thousands of men were detained in June and July after being identified by masked informers and taken for interrogation in camps in south Lebanon or Israel. Harrowing stories of beatings, humiliation, torture and harsh conditions became commonplace. Prisoners were made to stand for hours in the blazing sun with burlap sacks over their heads. Many Lebanese and Palestinians were shocked at the extent to which the Israelis found collaborators willing to identify suspects. 'These men are the best weapons the Israeli army has against us,' said one. 'They can turn any of us in, regardless of whether we are guilty or not. They are responsible for the lists of names with which the Israelis apprehend us.'

Interrogators were interested in any information about PLO activities and support.

> If someone gave his profession as teacher, the Israelis beat him more than the others and said: 'You haven't taught your students anything smart. You have simply organized them politically.' If one was a salesman, he heard, 'A salesman needs capital, and you got it from the terrorists or borrowed it from them.' To students the Israeli interrogating officer said: 'A student needs money to study. You got it from the terrorists.' Journalists were beaten because they had written things against Israel. And from the bank employees they wanted to know how large was the bank account of Abu al-Houl, the chief of the PLO secret service.[71]

Avraham Shalom opposed a larger deployment for the Shin Bet, but in the end he had little choice.[72] Shalom knew that no security service can operate satisfactorily without firm military control of the territory. He knew it could be a costly move, with little chance of success. Nine Shin Bet officers had died at a stroke in November 1982, when the IDF–Shin Bet HQ in an abandoned multi-storey building in Tyre collapsed following a gas explosion. Amos Rimon, a kibbutznik, was the most senior of the security service officers to die in the blast.[73] Afterwards a new HQ was set up in the town, with Yosef Ginossar, head of the service's Haifa-based northern region, named as commander for the 'Lebanese theatre of operations'.

The Shin Bet set about trying to reproduce the West Bank–Gaza model of informers, agents, safe houses and interrogation facilities. Security service personnel normally travelled in two-car convoys, using battered Mercedes with Lebanese licence plates to try and blend into the landscape. They were usually accompanied by a squad of IDF soldiers. One of many such escort operations ended in disaster in December 1983, when a Shin Bet car speeding through Sidon was fired on and an Israeli soldier was killed. Ginossar refused to take responsibility when confronted later by the dead man's battalion commander and made strenuous efforts to keep his own officers out of trouble. The story only came to light later when Ginossar was at the centre of a much bigger row.[74]

Military censors permitted very little to be published in Israel about the Shin Bet's secret war against the Shi'ites and Palestinians. But a good idea of the nature of the struggle can be gleaned from the graphic reports published by Robert Fisk, the veteran Beirut correspondent of *The Times* of London, who travelled widely and enjoyed excellent sources in the south.

Fisk described one action, which took place in mid-June 1984 in the Shi'ite village of Bidias in the notorious 'iron triangle' east of Tyre. Fifteen Shin Bet men in three Mercedes cars stopped outside a garage owned by Murshid Nahas, a local Amal commander. One of the Israelis called out Nahas's name while eight others took up positions around the garage. Two of the cars circled around the square to keep other villagers away. Nahas appeared and was dragged into the back of the Mercedes. One local woman said later that she heard an Israeli say to Nahas: 'Choose the kind of death you want.' The man's bullet-ridden body was later found nearby. Amal's commander in southern Lebanon, a schoolteacher called Daoud Daoud, was to claim later that Nahas had been approached by the Israelis and been asked to work for them. He had refused.[75]

Bidias remained a centre of anti-Israeli activity. In early January 1985 a mixed IDF–Shin Bet force again scoured the village.[76] A large amount of the Shin Bet's attention was devoted to Ma'arake, another militant Shi'ite stronghold near Tyre. The Shin Bet arrested about 100 villagers in June 1984, following repeated attacks on the IDF in the area. On 4 March 1985 a bomb concealed on the roof of the village mosque destroyed most of Hizbullah's regional command; the villagers accused an Israeli unit which had raided the village the previous day of leaving the bomb behind. Among the twelve people killed were Khalil Jeradi, Muhammad Sa'ad and Muhammad Hussein Khalil, three prominent Hizbullah commanders.[77]

The final months in Lebanon were a severe strain for the Shin Bet men, who were working long hours in dangerous, brutal and demoralizing conditions at a time when most Israelis wanted nothing more than simply to leave the whole Lebanese mess behind them. In September 1984 a security service officer named Ze'ev Geva was shot dead in an ambush near Majdal Balhis. Geva was travelling in a convoy of two cars with other Shin Bet officers and IDF guards when Shi'ite gunmen opened up with RPGs and automatic weapons. Geva and a soldier both died instantly.[78]

The Shin Bet operated at least three regional interrogation centres apart from the Tyre HQ, where dozens of prisoners died along with their captors in the explosions of November 1982 and November 1983.[79] Those considered guilty of activity in the guerrilla organizations were sent to the big Ansar detention centre, south-east of Sidon. As early as August 1982 it already contained 10,000 prisoners, according to an Amnesty International estimate. The Shin Bet often appeared to be carrying out arrests at random in the hope of gleaning some information on the guerrillas. The local population saw this as an attempt to terrorize and cow them.[80]

In trying to reproduce its *modus operandi* in the West Bank and Gaza Strip, the Shin Bet relied heavily upon locally recruited agents and informers. The service found no difficulty in enlisting agents from among Lebanon's warring religious groups – almost everyone had a personal vendetta against this or that group, organization or clan. Imad Gharbiya, a Lebanese taxi driver, was recruited at an IDF roadblock near Jezzine in 1984. He was asked to collect information on Palestinian and left-wing Lebanese groups fighting the IDF. Information he provided apparently enabled the Israelis to neutralize a roadside bomb. Gharbiya also planted a bug in a Druse village in the Shouf. He was run by a controller codenamed 'Abu Ibrahim', who met Gharbiya at least once in Cyprus and arranged for him to visit Israel, where he took courses in communications and sabotage. Gharbiya must have been a promising agent because he was also sent on espionage missions to Syria, from where he sent intelligence on the Syrian army to a cut-out in Belgium. Gharbiya was eventually tried for 'collaboration with the enemy' by a Lebanese court and sentenced to several years' hard labour.[81]

And he was one of the lucky ones. Many of the lower-level informers who worked for Israel were summarily executed later. One of these killings took place in Sidon a few days before the IDF evacuation. 'A Mercedes pulled up outside a patisserie,' the *Times* correspondent reported in his best deadpan style. 'A man wearing a yellow stocking mask climbed out of the vehicle and fired five bullets from a black handgun at the shop owner. He then coolly climbed back into the car and drove away . . .'[82]

A similar fate met Haydar Dayekh of Jouaya. Having worked with the Israelis, his name appeared in a list of forty-five 'collaborators' on wall posters distributed around the occupied zone and signed by the 'National Resistance'. In January 1985 a man pulled up outside his home and emptied a whole pistol magazine into Dayekh's stomach before driving off. Two separate Palestinian hit teams were dispensing rough justice to collaborators in Sidon during the final days of Israeli rule. One man who got away fled the port city by boat with two dozen protégés a few days before the IDF pull-out.[83]

Lebanon became a byword for brutality, and the Shin Bet's experience there was more brutal than most. Rafi Malka, head of the security service's Operations Branch, said later:

> Lebanon gave us Lebanonization, levantinization . . . In order to stay sane and stay alive, you had to do things that were unacceptable. The Shin Bet was no exception. It was a struggle in a wild west and people paid with their lives if they tried to behave according to accepted standards. The general impact was not good, to put it mildly.[84]

Malka was to have good reason, just a short time later, to reflect on just how badly the service had been affected by the war.

The Lebanese failure

Lebanon was Israel's greatest intelligence failure. The Mossad and Aman had had a hand in preparing the war, in terms both of establishing the Phalange connection and of operational advice. And the IDF had consistently failed: failed to destroy the PLO (though it did temporarily dislodge the guerrillas from Beirut); failed to dislodge the Syrians; and failed to pacify the wild south. Aman had opposed the war from the start; the Mossad was ambivalent, with senior executives like Nahik Nevot promoting the fateful alliance with the Christians, while its head, Yitzhak Hofi, tried to hold back. Yet when Abu Nidal's gunmen provided the long-awaited pretext, the war against the PLO was launched – and it failed dismally. And Israel's third intelligence agency, the Shin Bet, ended up participating in the failure in the brutal and unwinnable guerrilla war against the Palestinians and the newly militant Shi'ites. It was the defeat in that last ugly battle against the Muslim guerrillas of the south – a battle which could not have been won without using even more extreme, repressive measures than would have been condoned by Israeli society – that finally forced Israel to end its 'war of choice' in Lebanon. The scars took a long time to heal.

12
Occupational Hazards: 1984–7

Scandal time

'Affairs emerge when a nation's political realm comes to be dominated by bitter disputes over the meaning of a particular sequence of events,' an Australian historian has commented with reference to the celebrated defection of two Soviet agents, – the Petrovs, in the early 1950s. 'Affairs grow from those cases which seem to touch the most sensitive nerve-ends of a society – the fundamental issues of value and allegiance.'[1]

Starting from the early 1980s, as Israel limped home, already battered and demoralized, from its disastrous Lebanese adventure, several such scandals exploded in dizzying succession in the very heart of the country's secret world. All of them raised questions, not only about bureaucratic and personal rivalries in the intelligence community but also about the function of secret services in general, and in Israel in particular; not only about buck-passing between spymasters and politicians but also about morality, justice and responsibility. Above all they touched upon the issue of government control over its intelligence and security services, the accountability of those services for their actions and the broader question of the rule of law in a democratic society. The first of them began on 12 April 1984, just a few days before the Shin Bet's arrest and exposure of the Jewish underground.

Death in the wheat field

At 6.20 that evening four teenage Palestinians from the Gaza Strip boarded the number 300 bus in the busy Egged terminal in downtown Tel Aviv, *en route* for the southern town of Ashkelon. About half-way through the journey one of the thirty-five passengers, who had somehow become suspicious of the four Arabs and their intentions and had tried in vain to warn the driver of his fears, jumped off, shouting: 'Terrorists, terrorists'.[2]

What happened during the next twelve hours was to lead to the most serious scandal ever to rack Israel's internal security service. In its wake, the head of the Shin Bet, Avraham Shalom, would be named, exposed and forced to resign, as would other senior personnel; some of its secret methods would become public knowledge; and it would become the focus of unprecedented public attention and criticism both at home and abroad. The Bus 300 Affair or the Shin Bet Affair, as it was variously known, raised fundamental questions about the potential conflict between the rule of law and countering terrorism; about Israel and its relationship with the Palestinians. Many saw the scandal as an ugly modern version of the Lavon Affair.

It began when one of the Palestinians, Jamal Qabalan, threatened the bus driver with a knife and a hand grenade. A second hijacker, Muhammed Baraka, brandished some kind of spray can. The third, Majdi Abu Jum'a, took up position in the centre of the bus, holding a briefcase from which wires were protruding. His cousin, Subhi Abu Jum'a, stood by the rear door and said he had a grenade. 'Don't move. We have no quarrel with you,' one of the hijackers shouted. 'We just want to release our comrades from prison.' A pregnant woman passenger was allowed off near Ashdod and alerted the police. Roadblocks were erected, but the bus continued, until, a few miles south of Gaza City, on the outskirts of Deir al-Balah, soldiers shot out the rear tyres and the vehicle ground to a halt, parallel to a disused railway line. The driver escaped and was beaten by troops, who mistook him for one of the hijackers.

By 8.30 that night, when the defence minister, Moshe Arens, was informed of the incident, the police special anti-terror squad and an elite army unit were already in position around the bus, waiting for orders. The chief of staff, Lieutenant-General Moshe Levy, was there with other senior officers, including Brigadier-General Yitzhak ('Itzik') Mordechai, commander of the paratroop and infantry forces. Also present were Avraham Shalom, his deputy, Reuven Hazak, and at least five other Shin Bet personnel.

Negotiations began with Qabalan, who was still standing by the driver's seat. He demanded to see the Egyptian ambassador and the immediate release of 500 Palestinian prisoners. By this time several journalists and photographers had arrived on the scene. A second bus, identical to the hijacked vehicle, was brought to a nearby field and the army assault team began training on it. The soldiers stormed the Egged bus at 4.43 a.m. on Friday, just before dawn. An Israeli TV crew almost gave the game away by turning its lights on the attacking force at the critical moment. Qabalan and Baraka were shot and killed at close range and the troops entered the vehicle. Most of the passengers had thrown themselves to the floor, but seven were injured. One passenger, a woman soldier, died of her wounds.

The two other hijackers, Subhi and Majdi Abu Jum'a, were overpowered and badly beaten about the head and body in order to stun them. When they were brought off the vehicle Brigadier-General Mordechai questioned them both briefly about whether they had more accomplices and whether the briefcase bomb was booby-trapped. By Mordechai's own later account, he struck them several times with a pistol in his hand. The explosive charge in the briefcase was defused by a police sapper, and the two hijackers, dazed and stumbling but clearly alive, were handed over to Shin Bet men and soldiers. Four press photographers, among others, saw the two as they were being being hustled to a nearby wheat field next to the railway tracks. All the photographers took pictures.

An IDF statement issued at 6.00 that morning described the

incident in some detail but made no mention of casualties among the hijackers. Israel Radio's 7.00 a.m. radio news bulletin, however, reported that two terrorists had been killed in the assault and two others captured. But later that day, in response to repeated questioning by journalists, the IDF spokesman said that two terrorists had been killed in the storming of the bus and that the two others had died on their way to hospital in Ashkelon.

Serious doubts quickly began to emerge about the truth of the official statements. The Jerusalem correspondent of *The New York Times* ignored the restrictions of the military censor and reported suspicions that the hijackers had been killed after capture. In both the media and the IDF General Staff there was an awkward feeling that someone was not telling the whole story. On 28 April Arens appointed the defence ministry comptroller, a respected reserve general called Meir Zorea, to hold an inquiry into the affair.

Despite criticism that it was improper, Arens allowed Shalom to appoint his own man, Yosef Ginossar, to represent the security service on Zorea's inquiry board. Ginossar, head of the Shin Bet's northern region in 1982, had overseen operations in the bloody guerrilla struggle against the Shi'ites and Palestinians in south Lebanon. Shalom told the defence minister he simply wanted to prevent friction between the Shin Bet and the army. Arens found this argument 'logical'. But it became apparent later that Ginossar had used his position to leak details of the proceedings to Shalom.[3] Together, meeting nightly at the home of 'V', the service's deputy legal adviser (whose identity is still classified), they worked out the Shin Bet cover-up. A journalist who testified before the board was impressed by Ginossar's smooth, professional performance. Mordechai was questioned at length by Zorea and admitted that he had struck the two hijackers. Shalom was less forthcoming.

'I asked him,' Zorea said later, 'did you give the order to kill them or not?' Shalom lost his temper, but it transpired afterwards that this was all a show. I told him to spare me the anger and answer a simple question with a simple answer. He said he didn't give the order. And, honestly, you need a pretty fertile imagination to guess that the head of the Shin Bet is lying.[4]

The comptroller's findings were published on 20 May 1984. The inquiry found, after ordering an autopsy, that both terrorists had died of fractured skulls, and that unspecified members of the 'security forces' had committed crimes. An investigation had to be carried out, and the man chosen to conduct it was the state prosecutor, a pedantic, bespectacled lawyer called Yonah Blattman. On 29 May the new *Hadashot* newspaper, bypassing censorship, defiantly published a dramatic front-page picture of one of the Jum'a cousins being led away from the bus, very much alive. The photograph pointed graphically to some kind of cover-up, although it was unclear who was involved.

Mordechai began to suspect that he was being set up by the security service; he quickly realized that the versions of all the Shin Bet personnel questioned had been well coordinated in advance. One senior Shin Bet witness described to Blattman how he saw Mordechai standing in front of a kneeling terrorist and kicking him in the head. Another one said that the brigadier had used his pistol like a hammer. The overall effect of the Shin Bet evidence was to point to Mordechai as the prime suspect. The descriptions appeared to fit the pathological evidence perfectly. The Shin Bet witnesses were briefed by the legal advisers before appearing before the inquiry and ordered to report back to headquarters afterwards to describe what had happened. It was a highly professional job by professional secret policeman. Several press reports in this period quoted military sources as claiming that the Shin Bet was trying to frame the army.

'Itzik' Mordechai was a popular officer with a fine combat record and his friends tried to help him. Witnesses were found who, in contrast to what both Zorea and Blattman had been told, testified that Shin Bet men *had* beaten the two terrorists. Nine soldiers described how Shin Bet agents had sealed off the wheat field where they were dealing with the hijackers and later ordered military policemen to help get the Jum'a cousins, who were barely conscious by then, into the back of a Volkswagen van. Someone described what had happened that morning as an 'organized lynch'.

None of this helped the brigadier. The Blattman inquiry concluded on 12 August 1985 that there was insufficient evidence to charge Mordechai with killing the terrorists, but it recommended, nevertheless, that he, five Shin Bet men and three policemen, be tried for assault. Mordechai was acquitted after a seven-minute hearing on 18 August. Shortly afterwards he was promoted to major-general. Two weeks later a special disciplinary court run jointly by the security service and the Mossad cleared the five Shin Bet men of charges of conspiring to assault the hijackers. And the charges against the policemen were later dropped.

On 14 October Reuven Hazak went to Shalom and demanded his resignation because of the cover-up in the Bus 300 Affair and the false accusations against Mordechai. Hazak and two close friends, senior officers in the service, Rafi Malka, head of the Operations Branch, and Peleg Radai, head of the Protective Security Branch, had been discussing the issue among themselves for months. They all held ranks equivalent to that of a general in the IDF and they believed that the service's tradition of honest reporting was crucial to the Shin Bet's efficient functioning both internally and externally, in its relations with the Ministry of Justice and the courts. But Shalom refused to own up or resign.

After long and agonized deliberation, Hazak – then acting director of the Shin Bet in Shalom's absence abroad – went to see the prime minister, Shimon Peres. Peres had already been briefed by Shalom about his 'over-ambitious deputy' and he told Hazak to drop the matter and get back to work. The premier let it be known that he believed Hazak was trying to mount a 'putsch' against Shalom so he could take over the service. The prime minister failed to mention to his aides – his conduit for leaks to the press – that Hazak had offered his own resignation if that was the price necessary to obtain Shalom's removal. Later Peres suggested that Hazak retire, or at least take study leave. When Hazak left, Shalom immediately sacked Malka, who went to the High Court of Justice, appealing for his own reinstatement and Shalom's dismissal. Radai, alone and isolated, quickly resigned.

It was at this point that Hazak did the unthinkable and took the issue outside the service, to the attorney-general, Professor Yitzhak Zamir. Zamir and his aides cross-examined Hazak and the other two 'dissidents' for days. Convinced that they were telling the truth, Zamir went to Peres and demanded that he sack Shalom, Ginossar and the service's two legal advisers. The prime minister refused.

By the spring of 1986 the affair was no longer a secret. In a small country like Israel, journalists and secret servants can be friends, even though they usually agree not to talk about sensitive issues. Ido Dissentchik, the editor of *Ma'Ariv*, had studied with Radai at the Hebrew University and they were still close. And in Jerusalem, where Radai lived and led an active social life, some of his best friends were journalists, several of them with distinctly 'dovish' views.

Rumours had been circulating for months that three very senior Shin Bet men had resigned and that their resignations were somehow connected to the mystery that still surrounded the bus hijack, the killing of the terrorists and the suspicions against Mordechai. Several anonymous 'deep throats' appeared. One phoned Dissentchik, another contacted Michael Karpin,[5] a senior editor at Israel TV. Nahum Barnea, editor of the *Koteret Rashit* weekly magazine, had pursued the story doggedly from the beginning, ignoring the censor to publish Mordechai's photograph and accuse the authorities of a cover-up. Dissentchik suspected for a while that Radai was his source, but was disabused of this when, while talking to Radai on one telephone, his 'deep throat' rang again on a second line.

The stunning news finally came out on Saturday night, 24 May 1986, although it was carefully 'coded' to evade the censor. Amir Shaviv, Israel Television's legal affairs correspondent, reported that Professor Zamir intended to prosecute a very senior official in a very sensitive state service. That person was named next day as Avraham Shalom.

Now there was no stopping the scandal. The head of the Shin Bet, the whole country quickly knew, was accused of withholding information about the Bus 300 killings, putting pressure on witnesses and tampering with evidence. Nahum Barnea put it succinctly: 'The meaning of these suspicions is that the most senior officials in the State of Israel's most sensitive service are accused of conspiring to mislead two commissions of inquiry and their own superiors.'[6]

Some people felt angry. David Krivine, a veteran *Jerusalem Post* journalist who had personally crusaded against the famous *Sunday Times* torture report in 1977, sounded particularly bitter: 'Ten years ago the then head of the GSS, Avraham Ahituv, was outraged at my asking him whether his staff practised the physical brutalities described. His staff were educated men, he pointed out, with a high level of dedication. Such sadistic conduct was not conceivable.'[7]

Parallels with the Watergate scandal began to be heard in public and the awkward question of ministerial responsibility quickly arose. Yitzhak Shamir had been prime minister at the time of the incident at Deir al-Balah, but Peres had taken over as the scandal developed in the shadows after the formation of the national unity government in September 1984. Shamir was due, under the bizarre agreement to 'rotate' the premiership, to replace Peres in October 1986. The Labour Party leader had no political interest in pursuing the affair. No one in Israel ever won votes by making an issue out of two dead Arab terrorists. Peres seemed to be doing everything he could to bury the affair. So when Professor Zamir was suddenly replaced there was intense speculation that this was directly connected to his determination to prosecute Shalom.

But ultimately the Shin Bet chief had to go. Shalom finally resigned on 26 June, after it was announced that he and three other officials had been granted pardons by President Chaim Herzog, even though they had not been charged with any crime. One of the three was Ginossar and the other two were the service's legal advisers. Rumours circulated that Shalom had threatened to leak secret files that would be embarrassing both to Peres and to Herzog. And Shalom's supporters in the Shin Bet were accused of fabricating stories about a love affair between Hazak and Dorit Beinish, a senior aide to Zamir who had displayed great zeal in pursuing the case. Beinish and two colleagues in the Justice Ministry had worked closely with the Shin Bet on the Jewish underground case; they felt personally betrayed. And now that the truth was finally out, the army was furious over the way Mordechai had been framed.

With the date of rotation rapidly approaching, and both Labour and Likud spoiling for a fight over any issue big enough to stop the hand-over, the exposure of the affair seemed briefly to threaten the future of the coalition. But in August the High Court of Justice upheld the validity of the presidential pardons for Shalom and his three colleagues. A police investigation then began – the cabinet's reluctant preference to a full-scale official commission of inquiry. But then, on the basis of the first precedent, seven more Shin Bet men, apparently those who actually finished beating the Jum'a cousins to death in the back of the Volkswagen van, were also pardoned.

In mid-September Yosef Harish, Zamir's replacement as attorney-general, received the police findings, including the statements of thirty-nine witnesses. These were then examined by a team of three senior Justice Ministry officials. The findings made clear beyond doubt that the two hijackers were killed on Shalom's orders, which were given to a Shin Bet official identified only as 'Y'. Shalom claimed he gave his orders on the basis of a conversation with Shamir in November 1983, in which the treatment of captured terrorists was discussed. Shamir told the police he remembered the meeting, but added: 'Looking back, I must say that that could not be understood as permission to take prisoners, question them and then kill them.' The Justice Ministry team concluded that Shamir had not known of the order to kill the terrorists or of the subsequent cover-up. Their report stated:

In the course of the affair it has been argued that the Shin Bet operates in a grey area between the law and the vital security needs of the State of Israel, and that it was extremely difficult to conduct efficient security operations without deviating from the law. On this point we recommend that it be determined unequivocally: all government activity in Israel, including that of the security forces, is conducted, and must be conducted, within the framework of the laws of the state. Even those areas of security activity known as the 'twilight zone' must be regulated and scrutinized by the law's directives.

Because Shalom and the other protagonists had already been pardoned, Harish decided at the end of December 1986 that no further action could be taken. The case was closed.[8]

And there, were it not for luck, coincidence and the determination of sections of the Israeli press, the matter might finally have rested. In April 1987, though, the Shin Bet's nightmare began again. After weeks of rumours about another simmering scandal, Israelis learned of more dirty deeds by their secret service.

The Nafsu Affair

Izzat Nafsu, an army lieutenant who had served more than seven years of an eighteen-year prison sentence, was suddenly cleared by the High Court of charges of treason and espionage after claiming throughout a long and secret legal struggle that he had been tortured and framed by the security service. Nafsu, a member of Israel's tiny Circassian minority, was found guilty only of failing to inform his superiors of two meetings with a commander of the Fatah guerrilla group in south Lebanon in 1979. The court upheld a two-year prison sentence and demotion to the rank of sergeant-major, and ordered him freed at once.

Nafsu's Fatah contacts took place in the twilight period between 'Operation Litani' and the 1982 invasion. The PLO and the IDF were physically close on the ground. Agent-running, field intelligence and dirty tricks were common tasks in south Lebanon; Sa'ad Haddad's militiamen, UNIFIL troops, psychological warfare and special operations were the background. Lebanon was an old story that aroused bad memories. What mattered now, just as it seemed that the wounds of the Bus 300 Affair were healing, was the evidence that here too, four years before Shalom had made his fatal error in the Deir al-Balah wheat field and when Avraham Ahituv was still head of the service, the Shin Bet had tortured and abused a suspect, fabricated evidence and lied to the courts about its methods.

The Nafsu Affair became public because of the previous scandal. The prisoner himself, languishing in his cell in a military gaol, knew that he had a chance to reopen his case when he happened to see a newspaper photograph of a familiar face, although he did not know the man's name. The fleshy, bespectacled features Nafsu saw were those of Yosef Ginossar, recently appointed to head the Israel Export Institute after leaving the Shin Bet. Ginossar, everyone now knew, had orchestrated the Bus 300 cover-up with Shalom, and been pardoned, like his disgraced boss, by the president.

Izzat Nafsu had been arrested in January 1980. He was interrogated in a hotel suite rented by the Shin Bet and initially was well treated. Circassians serve loyally in Israel's security forces.[9] Like the country's Druse minority, they are widely perceived by Jews as 'better' than Arabs. His family claimed that he was given hot and cold showers and then forced to stand outside on cold January nights. But the main pressure was psychological, and was similar to the methods used later with the members of the Jewish underground. On the fourteenth day of the investigation Nafsu broke down and made a full confession to his interrogators. Two members of the Shin Bet team had their doubts, but Yosef Ginossar, who was in charge, was sure Nafsu was guilty.

The trial was held in secret. Nafsu's lawyers argued that his confession was false and had been extracted illegally. The centre of the case was the 'mini-trial' on the admissibility of the confession. The Shin Bet called as a witness the veteran head of its Investigations Department, a colourless man who was known within the service as 'Pashosh'. Ginossar testified too, but under a false name. Abu Qasim, the Lebanese informer who had implicated the army officer, was not called. Nafsu's eighteen-year sentence shocked his friends and family. Like 'Itzik' Mordechai, the young Circassian was popular and his commanders from the 'Haddadland' days tried to help. But a closely argued 2,000-page appeal was dismissed with an eleven-page verdict. Nafsu's lawyer compared his client to Alfred Dreyfus, the French Jewish army officer whose false imprisonment shook France in the 1890s and influenced Theodor Herzl's formulation of the Zionist idea. It was heady, emotive stuff, but Nafsu stayed in prison.

But by early 1987 the atmosphere had changed radically. The revelations of the Bus 300 Affair had severely undermined the trust of state prosecutors in the propriety of Shin Bet interrogations. And Ginossar had also admitted to the police that the security service had falsified testimony in other cases. Nafsu's lawyers demanded to see the Blattman report. The Shin Bet panicked and, after consulting Harish, proposed that Nafsu be pardoned. The Circassian refused; he insisted on an honourable acquittal and complete rehabilitation.

The nightmare began again. The Israeli press was suddenly packed with articles questioning the functioning of the security service. Ze'ev Schiff of *Ha'Aretz*, the doyen of the country's military correspondents, reflected the official view at the same time as suggesting that there was still an extremely serious problem:

> Suspected terrorists cannot be questioned over a cup of coffee. But it must be reiterated that the issue is by no means interrogation in torture chambers, such as are found in Syria, for example, or anything like what Stalin's KGB did. Indeed, it's doubtful whether the GSS interrogations are much rougher than those of the British against the IRA. Menachem Begin, during his time as prime minister, explicitly instructed the GSS that it was forbidden to torture persons being investigated, even if they were suspected of the gravest crimes. Those in the know explain that the deviation is from 'judges' rules', but this does not mean that every investigator can act as he sees fit.[10]

The Supreme Court had no doubts that the investigators had broken the law. The confession extracted by the Shin Bet, it ruled on 24 May, 'was devoid of any legal basis'. Notes had not been taken and 'unacceptable means of pressure' had been used. Nafsu said his interrogators had pulled his hair, pushed him to the ground, kicked, scratched and insulted him. He was ordered to strip and take a cold shower, deprived of sleep and made to stand in the prison yard for hours even when he was not being questioned. He was also threatened that his mother and wife would be arrested and that personal information about him – implying that he was homosexual – would be made public. The Circassian 'Dreyfus' was freed and given a hero's welcome in his home village. The Shin Bet's methods of interrogation were to be investigated.

Its critics, at least, were delighted. As Chaim Baram, a left-wing journalist, said:

> One of Israel's great successes has been in the false differentiation it has made between what we do and what other people do. The CIA man is a drunk, or corrupt. The American pilot in Vietnam napalms peaceful villagers. But our secret agents are blue-eyed, paperback heroes and our pilots destroy 'terrorist strongholds'. Now our elites are starting to sober up and slaughter some sacred cows. It doesn't matter that I don't believe in the Shin Bet. I never believed in them. But it is very important that the civil courts and the Justice Ministry don't believe in them any more.[11]

The Landau Commission

Shortly afterwards another commission of inquiry got under way. Judge Moshe Landau, a former president of the Supreme Court, was joined by Yitzhak Hofi, the previous head of the Mossad, and Ya'akov Maltz, the state comptroller. The Commission's brief was narrow but highly sensitive: the Shin Bet's investigation techniques in dealing with cases of 'hostile terrorist activity' were to be scrutinized and recommendations made for the future.

The Landau Commission report was released on 30 October 1987. It came out on a Friday afternoon, just as the country was closing down for the Jewish Sabbath. The time, it seemed to many, was designed to delay debate until after the weekend. The eighty-eight-page document praised the 'devotion and professionalism' of the security service, but the central point was not flattering.

For sixteen years, it concluded, Shin Bet agents had regularly lied to the country's courts about confessions obtained under physical pressure from Palestinian suspects. The Commission appeared far more concerned by the practice of giving false evidence to the courts than by the actual use of brutality and torture. It noted that in 1971 there was a 'serious change', marked by a spate of allegations that violent methods were being used to extract confessions from terrorist suspects. The report's public comments on the use of force appeared to vindicate years of charges by Palestinians and foreign organizations like the Red Cross and Amnesty International that human rights abuses were routine under Israeli occupation. It did not, however, recommend the prosecution of any Shin Bet agents.

'The methods of pressure must concentrate mostly on the non-violent, psychological pressure that results from an intensive and lengthy interrogation and from the use of tricks, including deception,' the Commission said. 'But when these do not achieve their aim, there is no way but to use a moderate amount of physical pressure.'

The Landau Commission set down detailed guidelines on the use of force – 'limited and clearly delineated psychological and physical pressures' – in the second, secret part of its report, and recommended that these should be reviewed annually. The secret section also contained charts showing the deployment of Shin Bet manpower and comparing the number of terrorist suspects with the number of interrogators, the number of attacks and the percentage of them solved on an annual basis.[12]

Security service witnesses had clearly stressed the difficulty and urgency of the task they faced. Obtaining evidence for trial of suspects was not, the Commission noted, a major priority. 'What we believe,' one senior Shin Bet official testified, 'is that investigations are a tool in our system of intelligence gathering. That also explains, very partially and perhaps unconvincingly, why we care less about trials, because when I've caught the perpetrator and explained the attack I'm already moving on to the next stage, chasing the next terrorist.'[13]

Reactions followed swiftly. One former security service officer, identified by *Ha'Aretz* only as 'Y.A.', told the paper:

> Anyone who thinks that we can conduct luxurious interrogations when we're dealing with people who are prepared to kill men, women and children is making a serious mistake. The Shin Bet is not above the law, but sometimes you have to deviate from it a bit in order to get to the truth. The Shin Bet must be allowed to lick its wounds, learn the lessons, get out of the spotlight and get back to work.

The army professed to be shocked by the revelations about false testimony. 'Had we known,' said an IDF prosecutor, 'we would not have cooperated.' One anonymous former Shin Bet chief welcomed the report: 'This is what I call a defensive report – defence of democracy without causing state security to collapse. I am convinced that at this moment the GSS is operating exactly in accordance with the instructions laid down.'[14] Ginossar was pleased with the Commission's work and Shin Bet interrogators felt vindicated.[15]

But not everyone was satisfied. Legal experts wondered why Avraham Ahituv and Shalom should not be prosecuted. 'Is the blood of GSS chiefs thicker than the blood of the chief of staff in the Yom Kippur War?' asked one.[16] Liberal critics saw the line about 'moderate physical pressure' simply as a licence to torture. A leading Israeli Arab asked:

> How many innocent children, husbands, fathers, wives and mothers are now languishing in . . . Israel's military prisons? How can we ever calculate the monumental suffering and damage that has been done to our Palestinian society – to the many families who have suffered so terribly as a result of Israel's injustice? To the children who are

permanently scarred physically and emotionally by their trauma at the hands of Shin Bet interrogators? To the families living in abject poverty because their husbands and fathers cannot provide for them from a prison cell? To those made homeless by a lying GSS which demolished their homes?[17]

There was hope, too, that the long ordeal was over. *Hadashot*, whose publication of the picture of the Jum'a cousins did so much to start the ball rolling, commented:

> The Landau Commission has given a golden opportunity to the GSS to begin a normal relationship with society and the legal system and to the head of the GSS to restore to his men the sense of mission and the morale necessary to carrying out their work. We may assume that the prolonged striptease the service has been performing for the last two years, which caused it such great damage, has come to an end. Now the GSS can return to covert activity under the protection of the law, with closer supervision.[18]

As the *Jerusalem Post* put it in its editorial: 'The ultimate question that arises is whether a democratic society burdened with the occupation of another unwilling people can, despite the best intentions, for long sustain the rule of law, whether in that circumstance the usages of violence must not inevitably eclipse the usages of justice designed to keep social violence at bay.'[19]

Harmelin returns

Avraham Shalom's ignominious departure from the Shin Bet in June 1986 created a serious problem of morale and succession in the security service. A sense of bitterness and helplessness was rife among the lower ranks, who felt that their dedication to a difficult and thankless job had been overshadowed by the witchhunt over the scandal.[20] Shalom had been in office for five years when disaster struck. The Bus 300 Affair began when he was riding high after the exposure of the Jewish underground. In finally cracking that case he had succeeded where his predecessor, Avraham Ahituv, had failed. But his achievements came to nothing once the heat was on. His able deputy and expected successor, Reuven Hazak, was forced out too, as were Rafi Malka and Peleg Radai. The solution was a simple one. Yosef Harmelin, who had headed the service for eleven years from 1963 to 1974 and was a byword for solidity and discipline, was asked to come temporarily out of retirement and clean up the Shin Bet's act until a full-time replacement could be found. He was sixty-three and agreed to do the job for one year only. In the end he stayed for almost eighteen months.[21] Harmelin's appointment remained a secret and was subject to the usual rules of strict military censorship. His successor, who took over in March 1988, was, in line with service tradition, an internal candidate.

The Pollard Affair

At 10.40 a.m. on 21 November 1985 a civilian US Navy intelligence analyst, thirty-one-year-old Jonathan Pollard, was arrested outside the Israeli Embassy on International Drive in Washington. Pollard was detained by FBI agents after being ejected from the compound, together with his wife, Anne, by security guards. She was arrested two days later. The awkward scene at the embassy gates marked the beginning of one of the most damaging intelligence scandals in Israel's history, especially since it involved spying on the country's closest ally, the United States.

Pollard, a Jew and a passionate Zionist, had worked for the US Navy since 1979. In June 1984 he was assigned to the Anti-Terrorist Alert Centre (ATAC) of the Naval Investigative Service in Suitland, Maryland. He first served as a watch officer, monitoring classified message traffic on terrorist activities, passing it on to the analyst responsible for the relevant geographic area. In October 1985 he was himself promoted to intelligence research specialist within ATAC, 'specifically responsible for analyzing classified information concerning potential terrorist activities in the Caribbean and the continental US'.[22]

He had top-secret security clearance and access to Sensitive Compartmentalized Information (SCI) about sophisticated technical systems of intelligence-gathering on a 'need to know' basis. It was understood that those with SCI access codes would not look at information that was unrelated to their duties.

In April 1984 Pollard was introduced by a mutual friend to Colonel Aviem Sella, an Israeli Air Force officer who was on leave, studying computer science at New York University. Sella was a talented combat pilot who had led the 1981 IAF attack on Iraq's nuclear reactor and had been the first Westerner to photograph the Soviet SAM-6 missile. He had also shot down a Soviet-piloted MiG-21 over the Suez Canal during the war of attrition in July 1970. Pollard made clear to Sella that he wanted to spy for Israel.

Pollard was aware that US intelligence was not cooperating fully with Israel and had realized the limitations of the relationship after being involved in two official intelligence exchanges with Israel. He told investigators later that he had decided as early as 1982 to establish clandestine contact with Israel. Sella, intrigued by Pollard but fully aware of the implications of the approach, sought and was given permission by the IAF commander, Major-General Amos Lapidot, and by the chief of staff, Lieutenant-General Moshe Levy, to continue the contact. The Mossad, which is supposed to run Israeli espionage operations abroad, reported that it knew of him and wanted nothing to do with him.[23]

Using a series of prearranged codes the two met several times and Pollard handed over documents to prove his bona fides. In November 1984 Sella accompanied Pollard and his then girlfriend, Anne Henderson, on an all-expenses-paid trip to Paris, where Pollard was introduced to his new 'handler', Yosef (Yossi) Yagur, science attaché of the Israeli Consulate in New York.

Yagur was in fact the chief representative in the US of a small and obscure component of the Israeli intelligence community. The Bureau of Scientific Liaison, known by its Hebrew acronym Lakam, had been set up in 1960, when Shimon Peres was deputy defence minister, to gather secret scientific and technological intelligence. Its very existence was anathema to Isser Harel, then head of the Mossad, who viewed it as an attempt by Peres to undermine his own authority as 'Memuneh' of the intelligence and security services. The two were bitter enemies: Harel had responded only rarely to requests from the Defence Ministry to deal in scientific spying and when he did, he complained, he got no credit for it. Meir Amit, head of Aman in the early 1960s, had welcomed Lakam's existence; that had helped to fuel the deep animosity between the two men, which came to a head over the crisis of the German scientists and ended in Harel's resignation in March 1963.[24] Lakam, run by a former Shin Bet man called Binyamin Blumberg, survived within the Defence Ministry and chalked up several notable coups: it was involved in the celebrated theft of blueprints for the French-made Mirage jet fighter in 1968, in which a Swiss engineer, Alfred Frauenknecht, was gaoled for four and a half years for espionage.[25] In the United States it maintained offices in New York, Washington, Boston and Los Angeles, and was openly listed in telephone books and government directories. Lakam, according to the ever-acerbic Harel, the only former intelligence chief prepared to comment publicly on the burgeoning scandal, was a 'bastard organization'.[26]

Rafi Eitan

On the same trip to Paris Pollard was also introduced to Lakam's director, Rafi Eitan. Eitan was a legendary figure in Israeli intelligence. A former Palmahnik who had joined the Shin Bet in the early 1950s, he had headed its Operations Branch and commanded the snatch squad that kidnapped Adolf Eichmann in Buenos Aires in 1960. In the mid-1960s, in the reorganization carried out by Meir Amit, he replaced Joe Ra'anan in a Mossad operations job in Europe. In 1968 he was part of an Israeli team that applied to visit the NUMEC nuclear processing plant in Pennsylvania shortly before the disappearance of 200 pounds of enriched uranium, enough to make six atomic bombs.[27]

Physically unprepossessing, he was a small, myopic and barrel-chested man, who had been almost deaf in one ear since an accident in the 1948 war. He was known universally as Rafi 'HaMasriah' (the Stinker). He stayed on in the Mossad until the early 1970s, rising to be deputy head of its Operations Branch, but resigning when he failed to be promoted to head the service. John le Carré used Eitan as a model for Marty Kurtz, an Israeli character in *The Little Drummer Girl* who tracks down and kills Palestinian terrorists. In 1976, when Ariel Sharon, a close friend and mentor, became adviser on security affairs to prime minister Rabin, Eitan became his assistant. When Sharon left the post Eitan went with him and into private business. He returned to security matters in July 1978, when Menachem Begin named him adviser on terrorism to replace Amihai Paglin, the former Irgun operations chief who was killed in a car accident and had not enjoyed the confidence of the intelligence services.[28] During Eitan's tenure, in 1979, the Palestinian held responsible for planning the Munich Olympics massacre, Ali Hassan Salameh – the 'Red Prince' – was finally tracked down by Mossad agents and killed in a car bomb explosion in Beirut.[29] Eitan did well as terrorism adviser; his reputation made for high-level coordination with both the Mossad and the Shin Bet, and he received all 'raw' intelligence from all field units.[30]

In 1981, when Sharon replaced Ezer Weizman as defence minister, Binyamin Blumberg was sacked and Eitan was given charge of Lakam, even though he had no scientific background. It did not look like a very important post; in fact the unit seemed to be declining. Shortly after the creation of the Labour–Likud national unity government in September 1984, the new defence minister, Yitzhak Rabin, ordered Lakam's work restricted; according to one report, he planned eventually to eliminate it altogether.[31] When the new premier, Shimon Peres, appointed an ambitious young journalist and Labour Party loyalist called Amiram Nir to replace Eitan as terrorism adviser,

Eitan stayed on in the prime minister's office. And Lakam was all he had left.

A gold-mine in Washington

After the trip to Paris Pollard began to provide Yagur with a mass of valuable intelligence. From January 1985 until 15 November, just a few days before his arrest, he made biweekly deliveries of classified documents to the home of Irit Erb, a secretary at the Washington embassy, where the material was photocopied. Sometimes he went through a car wash while transferring the papers to a special briefcase. He met Yagur and another man identified only as 'Uzi' once a month for 'tasking' on what material to obtain. Pollard supplied documents on Soviet ship movements and arms deliveries to Syria and other Arab states, including information on SS-21 and SA-5 missiles, and maps and satellite pictures of Iraqi and Syrian weapons and chemical warfare factories. Some reports maintain that he also provided information which, according to one Israeli official, 'made our life much easier' in the IAF attack on PLO headquarters in Tunisia on 1 October 1985. Rabin denied this a few weeks later: 'If we reached a point that Israeli intelligence will not have enough of its own sources to supply this kind of information for this kind of operation,' the defence minister said, 'we will really be in bad shape.'[32]

He was a gold-mine. The full extent of Pollard's penetration will probably never be known, but US officials said afterwards that in the seventeen months of Pollard's activities, more than 1,000 classified documents – 360 cubic feet of them – were compromised. The majority of these were 'detailed analytical studies containing technical calculations, graphs and satellite photographs'. Some of them were hundreds of pages long and more than 800 were classified 'Top Secret'. Some of the material compromised US intelligence-gathering methods, the damage assessors said. 'Numerous classified analyses of Soviet missile systems reveal much about the way the US collects information, including information from human sources whose identity could be inferred by a reasonably competent intelligence analyst'.

According to some reports Pollard gravely compromised US intelligence operations in South Africa by passing on to Israel unedited reports from agents and monitoring stations which contained clues about when, where and by whom particular pieces of information were gathered; there were also assessments as to the reliability of informers.[33] Given the intimate ties between Pretoria and Jerusalem, including in the field of intelligence and security, a leak of this sort of information could have been very damaging indeed to US espionage.[34] The CIA and the NSA would have to assume that some of their South African assets and operations had been exposed by the Israelis.

Pollard claimed throughout that his activities were motivated not by financial or by material gain but by a desire to help Israel in its struggle against terrorism. This argument failed to impress the FBI. 'Throughout his relationship with the Israelis,' the investigators concluded, 'the lure of money motivated and eventually consumed him.' The terrorism claim was just as insubstantial. Of the thousands of pages of classified documents he delivered, only 'a minuscule proportion' concerned terrorism. Sella, Eitan and Yagur had all told him they were not interested in US intelligence on terrorism. In one of their monthly meetings Yagur specifically instructed Pollard 'not to waste time by obtaining this type of information'. In the summer of 1985 Yagur asked Pollard to work on something that was not only nothing to do with terrorism but was also in obvious contravention of the US policy of refraining from providing any military assistance to Iran: potential Israeli arms sales to the Khomeini regime.[35] Israel was then deeply involved in trying to strengthen Iranian air defences around the key Kharg Island oil terminal, which was coming under heavy attack from the Iraqi air force. It was precisely then that the United States and Israel were starting to secretly coordinate strategy on forging an opening to 'moderate' elements in Iran to try and win the release of US hostages held by Iranian-backed fundamentalist groups in Lebanon.

Pollard's initial motives may have been idealistic, but he was soon working for people who were far more experienced than he was in the darker side of espionage. 'Money was a key element,' one well-placed source said. 'Eitan insisted that Pollard be put on the payroll to guarantee his continued cooperation. It would further tie him to Israel and make it very difficult, if not impossible, for him to walk away.'[36] Later, when Pollard began to get nervous about his activities, he was given an Israeli passport in the name of Danny Cohen. 'It's an old espionage ploy. You constantly have to reassure your spies. Their emotional state can become unstable. They can get very nervous. Eitan thought that the passport would help to ease Pollard's concerns. Occasionally he showed signs of becoming very edgy about the whole thing.'[37] The Lakam chief also asked Pollard to provide information about the electronic-eavesdropping activities of the National Security Agency in Israel and the names of Israelis spying for the United States. Eitan, a gamekeeper-turned-poacher in terms of his long expertise in both counter-espionage and espionage, wanted to catch spies as well as run them. Pollard, quietly encouraged by the more pleasant Yagur, refused.[38] Other Lakam officials had expressed grave doubts to Eitan about running Pollard: the results of a graphological analysis showed the spy to be an unstable character. Eitan's subordinates insisted he signed a document stating that he had heard their reservations. At the very least, they warned, Sella should not be involved any further. Eitan signed, but ignored them.[39]

A rogue operation?

The damage and the dangers were obvious the moment Pollard was picked up. Yagur, Ravid and Erb left hurriedly for Israel the day after the arrest. The initial official Israeli response to the news was that Pollard had been run in a 'rogue' operation by a unit that had run amok. The longer view, developed over the difficult months that followed, was that the case was a temporary 'blip' on the wider screen of US–Israeli relations. The arrest prompted a spate of retaliatory, self-justifying articles in the Israeli press about American espionage operations in Israel,[40] and in the US media about Israeli ones in the United States, dating back to the early 1950s. One of these reports described a remarkable incident when FBI agents bugging an Arab embassy in Washington met a team of Israelis who had just finished a similar job.[41]

Eitan bore most of the blame. Lakam was disbanded almost immediately, but it quickly became clear that before the scandal broke the unit's efforts had been greatly appreciated. As recently as March 1985 Eitan had reported to members of the Knesset Intelligence Services Sub-Committee on Lakam's activities and was encouraged by them to keep up the good work.[42] Yet afterwards he found few friends to defend him: 'It was no accident that Eitan was eased out of the mainline defence-intelligence establishment some fifteen years ago,' said one former Mossad colleague. 'But he returned through a back door, and his lack of sound judgment will be remembered long after we have forgotten his professional excellence.' The unit's precise purpose remained shrouded in secrecy, but it was argued that Eitan had a dangerous personal habit of 'empire-building' and that he was motivated partly by a desire to take revenge on the Americans for their hostile attitude towards Ariel Sharon's handling of the war in Lebanon.[43] Sharon himself was unrepentant. 'Israel does not receive from the US all the information it needs,' he said bluntly. 'If we compare what we gave over the years with what we got, we without doubt gave much more in much more important fields than we received.'[44] According to one theory, the Sharon–Eitan team had managed to persuade Begin that his policies should be implemented only if he sought an alternative – in Lakam – to the 'Labour Party-dominated Mossad'.[45] Sella was officially criticized for displaying 'superfluous personal initiative' in getting involved in the case. Unofficially, he was said to have liked the idea of the travel and perks that went with running a secret agent.

Pollard's own account quickly destroyed the 'rogue operation' line of defence. The Israeli government, he said in an affidavit submitted to the court:

> acted predictably by attempting to limit the damage to itself by retreating behind a plausible denial screen in which the scandal was purportedly precipitated by a group of renegade intelligence officers acting without authorization. If one takes into account both the quality and highly specialized performance expertise of the personnel involved . . . it seems unlikely that their collaboration could have been the product of random selection.[46]

Israel damned itself further by cooperating only partially with the American investigation and by publicly rewarding both Eitan and Sella. While the Shin Bet cover-up in the Bus 300 Affair simmered behind the scenes, Avraham Shalom, who was still in office, was ordered to coordinate the liaison with the US investigators. It was hard to avoid the impression that he was given the job because of what the politicians knew to be his expertise in fabricating testimony. Most of the work was done by Shalom's lawyer, Ram Caspi. To some it seemed like a bad joke.[47] The two gave the Americans just enough material to incriminate Pollard, but it was wrapped in so many lies that the Americans quickly lost faith in the Israeli version. Sella remained a secret, and the day before the US team arrived, the pilot was sent out of the country, with the exit stamp on his passport backdated.[48] The investigation took the form of what were described as 'interviews' rather than formal, sworn testimony.

Eitan, still under the patronage of Ariel Sharon – then minister of trade and industry – was appointed chairman of Israel Chemical Industries. Aviem Sella's crucial role as the man who first recruited and 'ran' Pollard stayed secret for several months, but he was finally indicted in March 1987, the day before Pollard himself was sentenced to life imprisonment and his wife to five years for possessing classified documents. To make matters worse, Sella was promoted and made commander of the important Tel Nof IAF base, the largest in the country. A secretary who issued the invitations to the promotion ceremony sent them out according to a routine list, which included the US Embassy in Tel Aviv.[49] Such insensitive behaviour hardly squared with the contrite attitude being officially displayed, and it attracted criticism. 'After Pollard was arrested,' commented the *Jerusalem Post*'s Washington correspondent, Wolf Blitzer, 'Israel should have done one of two things. It should either have hung tough and remained silent – an action which would have been understood by hard-nosed US intelligence officials – or it should have cooperated fully and accurately with the Americans. By taking a middle position – partial and misleading cooperation – Israel managed to bring upon itself the worst.'[50]

Two separate commissions of inquiry were set up in March 1987. The first was a two-man team, appointed by the inner cabinet, composed of Yehoshua Rotenstreich, a lawyer and former chairman of the Israel Press Council, and Zvi Tsur, a former chief of staff. The second was conducted by the Knesset's seven-member Intelligence Services Sub-committee, headed by Abba Eban. Both reported at the end of May but neither cast any real light on where the ultimate responsibility for the scandal lay.

Pollard's conviction was not the end of the story. Nearly a year after he began his life sentence US officials remained convinced that a second Israeli spy had been active during the same period in the Defence Department or CIA. The suspicion was based on the fact that Pollard revealed that his Israeli handlers often specified by date and document the material they wanted him to obtain. He was once shown a document to which he did not and could not have had access.[51] Despite considerable sympathy for him in Israel, and hopes that he could somehow be deported there before his gaol sentence was up, Pollard remained behind bars, and bitterly quoted Graham Greene in reference to himself: 'I've never met a man who had better motives for all the trouble he's caused.'[52]

The affair probably caused less damage than was initially feared. While congressmen and Jewish leaders expressed loud concern and indignation, the CIA, the State Department and the Pentagon were quietly conducting business as usual with Israel. Joint weapons research programmes were begun after the spy's arrest and at the height of the affair Israel was designated by the United States as a major non-NATO ally with status similar to that of Japan and Australia. 'We consider the Pollard business very compartmentalized and not having a broader effect,' one senior US official said.[53]

Nahum Admoni

The Pollard Affair came as a grave embarrassment for Israel, but the Mossad could at least say: 'I told you so.' It had known about the willing spy in US naval intelligence and decided not to deal with him. Yet for some of the service's critics, that was too easy an answer. If the Mossad never takes the initiative, they argued, then nothing could ever go wrong. But it could not fail to be touched by the scandal.

The head of the service, Nahum Admoni, had begun his tenure in difficult and demoralizing circumstances, replacing Yitzhak Hofi just days before the Sabra and Shatilla massacre in September 1982, and then facing the questions of the Kahan Commission about the Mossad's role in the Lebanon war. Admoni was precisely the sort of smooth intelligence bureaucrat who did all he could to avoid upsets, let alone scandals that rocked clandestine relationships with loyal and generous allies. Liaison with friendly foreign services and with the other components of the Israeli intelligence community was the lifeblood of men like him. Rafi Eitan and Lakam were not the sort of rivals he needed, and the unit's disbandment came as a relief. He was the very antithesis of virtuosos like Eitan. Policy, not operations, rogue or otherwise, was his forte.

Admoni was the first head of the Mossad to have risen from the ranks, but that was fortuitous. It was thanks only to the untimely death of Yekutiel Adam in Lebanon that Admoni, a compromise candidate, got the position and thus reversed the trend of 'parachuting' in politically safe IDF generals. Other more talented former Mossadniks were either unacceptable or unavailable, or both. David Kimche had left in 1980 after a bitter row with Hofi and accepted the director-generalship of the Foreign Ministry. Shmuel Goren, one of Hofi's most brilliant and widely admired deputies, was associated with a minor internal scandal in the mid-1970s and was later to take up the thankless job of coordinator of government operations in the West Bank and Gaza Strip. Nahik Nevot, who had liaised with the Lebanese Christians after Kimche quit, was another possible candidate, but he was pushed aside. Rafi Eitan had been interested too, but Begin, who admired his work as adviser on terrorism, was worried that he was too close to Ariel Sharon, who – as the Lebanon war had shown only too starkly – was already powerful and independent enough as defence minister without having secret intelligence under his fleshy wing too.[54]

Nahum Admoni was born in Jerusalem in 1929 and was educated at the city's prestigious Rehavia Gymnasium, where middle-class immigrants like his Polish parents sent their children. He served in the Shai and IDF intelligence in the 1948 war and was discharged in 1949 with the rank of first lieutenant. He then studied international relations at the University of California at Berkeley. Returning to Israel in 1954, he was given a job teaching the subject at the Intelligence Services training school, along with other young stars like David Kimche. His first foreign posting was in Addis Ababa, in the heady years when Ethiopia occupied a key place in the Mossad's 'periphery' doctrine. He was in Paris in the mid-1960s, at the height of Israel's strategic alliance with France, and had also served in Washington, working closely with the CIA. He had never been involved in the derring-do of espionage, a fact which his many detractors were always quick to recall. He was appointed as deputy to Hofi in 1976.

Irangate

After the shock of the Pollard scandal, things went from bad to worse for the Mossad. Late in 1986, when the first news emerged of the clandestine American arms deals with Khomeini's Iran, and of Israel's role in the scheme, some of Nahum Admoni's enemies argued that the Israeli end of the Irangate affair began with the gradual decline of the Mossad as the senior arbiter of the country's foreign intelligence activities.

Israel had been secretly sending arms to the Islamic Republic since the start of the Gulf War in September 1980, but had come under heavy pressure from the United States to desist after the rise of Iranian-backed Shi'ite terrorism in Lebanon in 1983. In October that year 241 US marines were killed in Beirut by a Shi'ite suicide bomber apparently assisted by an Iranian intelligence officer. The kidnapping, torture and execution in March 1984 of William Buckley, the CIA station chief in the Lebanese capital, was a further blow for Washington. Between then and June 1985 seven Americans were taken hostage in Beirut by Hizbullah or Islamic Jihad.

Israel, withdrawing gradually and painfully back across the border into a Galilee that was no more or less peaceful than before the costly and divisive war, had suffered from Shi'ite radicalism too. There was clear evidence of Iranian training, finance and inspiration for the suicide bombers, but Israel still believed its broad regional interest lay in weakening Iraq – the same argument that had been behind its support for the Kurdish rebels in the 1960s and early 1970s.

Yet its policy was unclear. No serious high-level discussion had ever been held about how the Gulf War could be positively exploited for Israel's long-range strategic purposes. The country's 'Iran lobby', composed largely of serving and former military and intelligence officials whose views had been formed at the height of the relationship with the Shah, was stronger and more influential than the 'Iraq lobby', a much smaller group of individuals who argued that Khomeini's Iran was a truly dangerous enemy; that the Baghdad regime had changed radically since it led the rejectionist camp in the Arab world in the 1970s; that it had abandoned support for hardline Palestinian terrorists like Abu Nidal and now belonged more naturally to the moderate bloc formed by its two closest Arab allies, Egypt and Jordan; and that a judicious policy could help encourage that trend and decrease the dangers of a future coalition of warlike states on Israel's 'eastern front'.

Towards the end of 1984 this vacuum was filled by a trio of wealthy and well-connected international businessmen who had more than policy on their minds. Ya'akov Nimrodi, a former Shai man, Aman agent-runner and IDF military attaché in Iran; Adnan Khashoggi, the Saudi multimillionaire; and Al Schwimmer, the American-Jewish founder of Israel Aircraft Industries and a close friend of Shimon Peres, stepped into the breach. They brought with them a mysterious Iranian arms dealer and former SAVAK agent called Manucher Ghorbanifar, who claimed tantalizingly to represent politically moderate elements in Iran who hoped to take over once the Khomeini regime was destroyed and were interested in opening a dialogue with the Americans. The CIA knew and mistrusted Ghorbanifar as a 'talented fabricator', but Nimrodi and Schwimmer believed, or perhaps wanted to believe, that he could deliver the goods. When Khashoggi persuaded the Saudis to fund a small arms deal via Ghorbanifar, an official Israeli connection was not far behind.[55]

Nimrodi and Schwimmer went straight to Peres, who, after consulting with Yitzhak Rabin, the defence minister, and Yitzhak Shamir, the foreign minister, approved continuing the contacts with Ghorbanifar, but demanded that they be managed personally by Nimrodi. The effect of this was that from the very beginning the Mossad, which was after all supposed to be in charge of running secret operations abroad, was shut out of the picture completely. The prime minister asked the Mossad for its opinion, which was negative, less for reasons of broad strategy than because of the obvious operational difficulties involved and the difficulty of assessing the chances of success. 'Peres never publicly announced this decision,' a confidant of Nimrodi's has written, 'but he chose a private merchant so that he could deny any connection with the matter should there be a snafu or early revelation.' Once the process began, neither the Mossad nor Aman were asked to provide position papers outlining their views of what was developing.[56]

It was one of many errors on the Israeli side of the scandal. And when, in May 1985, the United States began to try and clarify its policy towards Iran – and especially the painful and complex matter of Tehran's influence over the Islamic extremists holding American hostages in Lebanon – questions of intelligence came into the picture. Michael Ledeen, a pro-Israeli consultant to the US National Security Council, went to Israel to meet Peres and Shlomo Gazit, the former Aman chief who was then serving as coordinator of government policy towards Iran but quit shortly afterwards because of his conern that the Mossad was being frozen out. Ledeen also saw David Kimche, the British-born director-general of the foreign ministry and a former deputy head of the Mossad under Yitzhak Hofi.

Kimche was to become a key figure in the Irangate affair. After twenty-seven years in the Mossad the habits of secret diplomacy were second nature to him, and he had developed a close working relationship with Robert 'Bud' McFarlane, the US national security adviser. Kimche said later that his involvement began at a meeting with McFarlane at the White House on 3 July 1985, the day that Israel quietly released 300 Lebanese Shi'ite prisoners, its side of the Syrian-brokered deal in which the hijackers of a TWA jet to Beirut the previous month had freed thirty-nine hijacked Americans unharmed, after murdering one – a US Navy diver.[57]

The first US-approved shipment of ninety-six TOW anti-tank missiles went from Tel Aviv to Tehran at the end of August 1985, even though the secretary of state, George Shultz, made clear that he had strong reservations: 'Israel's agenda,' he complained to McFarlane, 'is not the same as ours, and an intelligence relationship with Israel concerning Iran might not be one upon which we could fully rely.' Defence secretary Casper Weinberger had similar doubts. A further 408 missiles went three weeks later. A few days after that Reverend Benjamin Weir, kidnapped in Beirut in May 1984, was released. By the end of 1985 the Americans were having serious second thoughts and McFarlane's successor, Admiral John Poindexter, told the Israelis formally that the secret policy was being dropped. But this, it quickly turned out, was neither a clear nor a durable decision.

In December Kimche had started to have his own doubts,[58] and when he opted out of Iranian affairs, pleading a heavy workload at the foreign ministry, he was quicky replaced as the key Israeli official involved by Amiram Nir, Peres's ambitious young adviser on terrorism. They were very different characters from very different backgrounds. Nir started out badly as far as Israel's intelligence community was concerned. When Peres appointed him to the terrorism job after the 1984 elections, replacing Rafi Eitan, both the Mossad and the Shin Bet were shocked. Admoni and Avraham Shalom preferred Gideon Mahanaimi, the genial Aman and paratroop brigade veteran who served as Eitan's deputy. Admoni went so far as to change the structure of the heads of secret services committee (which the Mossad chief traditionally chaired) to exclude the terrorism adviser.[59]

Like Amihai Paglin, Menachem Begin's controversial choice for the post in 1977, Nir found that the intelligence professionals could set the pace of cooperation with him. As a former journalist – he had been the military correspondent of Israel Television – and a political appointee, he was never trusted in the same way that Rafi Eitan, who had spent his life in the secret world, had been. Nir took up the challenge and after a few months had acquired some bureaucratic teeth and a reputation as an astute thinker with original and innovative ideas. Yet he remained frustrated by the limitations of the job. Nir persuaded the prime minister to let him handle liaison with the NSC. Most of it was with McFarlane's deputy, Colonel Oliver North.[60]

An American journalist described their relationship succinctly:

> Nir and North hit it off well. Both were young action-oriented men who faced an array of critics at home yet suddenly found themselves wheeling and dealing at a geostrategic table with the approval of their respective nations' leaders. North was a square-jawed marine and Vietnam veteran, the kind of military man with whom Nir always felt

most comfortable. Nir's job gave him immediate access to every report filed by Israeli spies and terrorism-watchers around the world, the kind of information that North could use in his duties as the NSC's resident counter-terrorism expert.[61]

When Robert McFarlane resigned at the end of November 1985 and was replaced by Poindexter, North's role became more important; and when he was ordered to coordinate the Iran initiative, the relationship with Nir, already close because of their cooperation on counter-terrorist matters, blossomed. In January 1986 came the proposal – exactly from where remains one of the central and enduring mysteries of Irangate – that the Iranians be overcharged for weapons supplied by the US and Israel and that the surplus cash be secretly diverted to the Contra rebels fighting the Sandinista regime in Nicaragua, now that Congress had cut off funding.

Nir edged Nimrodi and Schwimmer out of the Israeli side of the deal and maintained the contact with Ghorbanifar. Several more arms deliveries were made to Tehran, but no more hostages were freed until after the end of the direct Israeli involvement, nor was there any progress towards the much-discussed US dialogue with Iran. In May 1986 North, McFarlane, Nir (posing as an American) and several others visited Tehran, carrying a Bible inscribed by President Reagan, a chocolate cake and several Colt pistols as gifts for their hosts.

The Mossad was unhappy, although it remains unclear precisely how much it was told. Nir certainly felt he had to watch his back, despite the support of Rabin. Just before the trip to Tehran Ghorbanifar told the Israeli about a possible opening to a senior Libyan security official and Nir provided some relevant information from his own files. In a memo to Poindexter, North said that Nir had asked that the Libyan contacts be kept secret. 'As you know,' North wrote, 'Nir is operating without the Mossad back-up and has considerable concern about the CIA becoming more knowledgeable about his activities.' Nir's fear was presumably that the Mossad would learn from the CIA that he had been giving away too much.[62]

Nir's decision to go to Tehran astonished the Mossad and confirmed its deeply held suspicion that he was an enthusiastic amateur who was far out of his depth. He had no previous experience of intelligence operations in general or of Iran in particular. By accompanying McFarlane and the other Americans on the abortive mission he broke a cardinal rule of all clandestine activity: not only was he running a complex and dangerous operation single-handed but he had also placed the whole thing in jeopardy by going – under the flimsiest of disguises – into the very heart of the enemy camp for no obvious reason. Nir should, said one Mossad veteran, have insisted on a meeting in Geneva.[63]

Israel played a vital role in what became known as the Irangate scandal, but it remained a supporting role. The virtual exclusion of the Mossad from the process was not the reason for the policy's failure, but it at least limited the damage when awkward questions started to be asked. The Tower Commission, appointed by President Reagan to investigate the Iran/Contra affair, found that Israel could not be given more than its fair share of the blame, although it was clearly hampered by being unable to investigate exactly what had happened in Jerusalem.

The Commission concluded:

> Even if the government of Israel actively worked to begin the initiative and to keep it going, the US government is responsible for its own decisions. Key participants in US deliberations made the point that Israel's objectives and interests in this initiative were different from, and in some respects in conflict with, those of the United States. Although Israel dealt with those portions of the US government that it deemed were sympathetic to the initiative, there is nothing improper per se about this fact. US decision-makers made their own decisions and must bear responsibility for the consequences.[64]

The Hindawi Affair

On 17 April 1986 an alert El Al security guard at London's Heathrow Airport discovered 1.5 kilograms of Semtex plastic explosive concealed in the false bottom of a bag belonging to a pregnant young Irishwoman, Anne Murphy, who was about to board a scheduled Jumbo Jet flight to Tel Aviv. There were 375 people on the plane. The detonator for the device, concealed in a pocket calculator, had been primed by Murphy's boyfriend, a Jordanian called Nezar Hindawi, who had promised to join her in Israel and marry her there. Hindawi, an agent for Syrian intelligence, was arrested shortly afterwards and sentenced the following October to forty-five years in prison, the longest term ever handed down by a British court.

Elaborate conspiracy theories were woven around what seemed, on the basis of all the available evidence, to have been a fortuitous discovery based on luck, a high level of training and perhaps a heightened state of alert about possible attacks on El Al planes.[65] In the most extreme version, the Mossad had stage-managed the entire operation in order to embarrass Syria by 'setting it up' as a practitioner of state terrorism. According to this view, Hindawi was an *agent provocateur*, 'the instrument for an Israeli penetration of Syrian intelligence'.[66]

For Israel, the outcome of the Hindawi Affair was a vindication of years of costly investment in protective security, something that is immediately evident to anyone who has flown El Al in recent years.[67] It also had the useful effect of publicly exposing Syria, its most implacable Arab enemy, to unprecedented though short-lived international criticism. After Hindawi's conviction, Britain severed diplomatic relations with the Assad regime and the American and Canadian ambassadors were withdrawn from Damascus for a few months.

The affair had its immediate origins in a mistake by Israeli intelligence. Israeli–Syrian tension had been mounting over Lebanon since the end of 1985 and in February 1986 IAF fighters forced down a Libyan executive jet flying from Tripoli to Damascus after a conference of Palestinian and other radical Arab groups. The Mossad apparently believed that one of the passengers on the jet was the PFLP-GC leader, Ahmed Jibril, who had been at the conference in Libya, or possibly even the notorious Abu Nidal. Neither turned out to be on board, but

Abdullah al-Ahmar, the powerful assistant secretary-general of the ruling Syrian Ba'ath party was. Assad, hearing of the humiliating treatment of al-Ahmar and the other (mostly Lebanese) passengers during their brief and enforced stay at a military airfield in northern Israel, was furious at this slight. The actual decision to force down the plane had to be taken very quickly, defence sources said. Some critics of the operation, including Aharon Yariv, the former Aman chief, questioned the wisdom of trying to catch Palestinian leaders in such a risky way.[68]

Assad's role in what happened next remains a matter of conjecture. All agree that bringing down an Israeli civilian airliner in retaliation was not the style of a man who carefully calculated every move and knew that if such an act could be traced to Syria, it would almost certainly mean war. Many experts found it useful to compare the Syrian leader's record on terrorism with that of Libya's mercurial Colonel Qadhafi: 'Qadhafi is a clown who likes to work in centre-stage,' said one. 'Syria is more like a sniper firing from the rafters. People die but we never see the smoking gun.'[69]

Some veteran Assad-watchers maintained that it was simply inconceivable that the president had not known of the plan; his personal involvement in much less significant intelligence operations was cited. Many argued that in the Hindawi Affair matters were taken up, *à la* Thomas à Becket, by subordinates who sought to find favour by relieving Assad of a meddlesome enemy. What is clear is that the question of revenge for the Israeli move was dealt with by his trusted head of air force intelligence, General Muhammad al-Khouli, who was answerable only to the president, himself a former commander of the air force. Israeli intelligence had a grudging respect for Khouli's service, which had become Syria's main vehicle for foreign intelligence operations. The state-owned Syrian Arab Airlines was just one of the assets at its disposal. Khouli was a powerful figure, but he had rivals. Ali Duba, head of military intelligence, was one, and other powerful security chiefs vied with him for Assad's ear.

By the time Hindawi's trial opened at London's Old Bailey in October 1986, the Syrian connection was clear. Hindawi had been assisted by a Syrian Arab Airlines crew, had been warmly congratulated by the Syrian ambassador in London and had been helped to go into hiding by embassy security men. His confession had been leaked in the Israeli press as early as May[70] and the Jerusalem government was naturally quick to exploit the evidence to link Assad directly – or at least officials answerable to him – to an act of terrorism that could have had horrendous consequences for the entire Middle East. Correspondents were given background briefings by Aman officers specializing in the subject; they admitted that they had been astonished to learn that Hindawi was not working for one of the Palestinian groups but for Syria proper.

An aura of mystery continues to surround the affair. Did Israel have any prior knowledge of what Hindawi and his controllers planned? According to unconfirmed reports from Damascus late in 1986, an air force intelligence officer, Colonel Mufid Akhour, was detained on suspicion of being an Israeli agent. Akour was mentioned by Hindawi in court as a deputy to Lieutenant-Colonel Haitham Said, head of recruitment and foreign operations for General Khouli's service.

Over twenty years before Syria had been traumatized by the exposure of 'Kamal Amin Thabit' as the Mossad spy Eli Cohen and fears of Israel's intelligence capabilities had never subsided.[71] The Hindawi Affair fuelled these old suspicions about the degree of Israeli penetration of the Syrian leadership, and perhaps even of its own secret services. 'Perhaps,' said one Western diplomat in Damascus, only half joking, in a reference to the head of Assad's military intelligence, 'Ali Duba's real name is Eli Dubinsky.'[72]

This was not the only case which the Syrians – and others – attributed to the long and legendary arm of the Mossad. A story that was circulating widely in Damascus in the spring of 1988 told of an affair between Assad's fun-loving defence minister, General Mustafa Tlas, and a *femme fatale* who was widely believed to have been an Israeli agent. The story first came to light in May in an obscure Swiss newspaper, *Le Matin*. *'Encore un "coup" du Mossad'*, read the headline and told of Diane Sydney, a 'young Scottish dancer of Jewish origin'. Quoting a 'Middle Eastern intelligence service', the paper ran a picture of Tlas with his arm round the attractive blonde girl, both wearing bathing suits and broad smiles. According to the Italian weekly *Panorama*, the photograph was taken in the early 1980s when Israel was planning to invade Lebanon. Diplomatic sources said the picture was circulated by Tlas's enemies, possibly Rifa'at al-Assad, the president's exiled brother.[73]

The Vanunu Case

Just before Nezar Hindawi's trial began at the Old Bailey, Britain played a supporting role in another world-class drama involving Israel's secret services. This one began on 5 October 1986 when the *Sunday Times* of London ran a long and exclusive article entitled, 'The Secrets of Israel's Nuclear Arsenal'. It was based on information supplied by Mordechai Vanunu, a former technician at the Dimona Nuclear Research Centre in the Negev desert.

The *Sunday Times* article, written by its Insight team of investigative reporters, caused a sensation. 'Vanunu's evidence,' the newspaper said, 'has surprised nuclear weapons experts who were approached by Insight to verify its accuracy because it shows that Israel does not just have the atom bomb – which has long been suspected – but that it has become a major nuclear power.'[74] The paper concluded that Israel now ranked as the world's sixth nuclear power, that Dimona had produced between 100 and 200 nuclear weapons of different destructive force and, most critically, that the crucial process of plutonium extraction went on secretly, deep below ground, out of sight of prying spy satellites. All this rested on the testimony of one man, an inside source.

Mordechai Vanunu, who was thirty-one when the *Sunday Times* story appeared, had been born in Morocco and emigrated to Israel as a child. He worked as a technician at Dimona from November 1976 to October 1985. He signed several declarations about the need to maintain secrecy. From early 1985, according to the prosecution, he collected secret information, including codenames, pertaining to the centre, took photographs and made drawings. In January 1986 he left Israel with the pictures and notes and arrived in Sydney, Australia, in May. There he met a *Sunday Times* reporter, Peter Hounam. The newspaper, smelling a scoop, brought Vanunu to London, where he was cross-examined by nuclear physicists, who found his story credible. On 30 September, five days before the Insight story appeared, Vanunu disappeared. It became apparent later that he had been lured to Rome by a blonde woman Mossad agent, identified only as 'Cindy', drugged with a hypodermic syringe, kidnapped by two men, and taken by ship to Israel to stand trial.[75] The *Sunday Times*'s allegations about the kidnapping, said the Israeli Foreign Ministry spokesman with magnificent flippancy, 'sound like the basis for a film script'. The government insisted repeatedly that there was nothing illegal about the manner in which Vanunu was brought to Israel. It was not until 9 November, over a month after the story was published, that the government announced he was in custody.

The Israeli press, restricted on the one hand by severe censorship and emboldened on the other by patriotic fervour (increased, perhaps, by Vanunu's conversion to Christianity), wanted blood: 'Israel has to lay its hands on Vanunu,' wrote a *Ha'Aretz* columnist. 'In many other democracies Vanunu would have ended up as a corpse dumped on his father's doorstep. If Israel has not yet brought him back to this country, the government should be asked why he is still free; and if Vanunu has already been apprehended, the government should be given a free hand.'[76]

Vanunu was charged on three counts: treason, aggravated espionage and collection of secret information with intent to impair the security of the state. The trial was held entirely in camera at the Jerusalem district court, where the conditions of extreme secrecy included boarding up all the windows and erecting a large canvas awning over the entrance so that the prisoner could not be seen arriving and leaving in a van with its windows painted over. Vanunu himself was forced to wear a motorcycle crash helmet to make life difficult for photographers. Some of this was in obvious retaliation for his stubborn attempts to publicize his views and plight: in December 1986, on the way back to the maximum-security prison at Ashkelon from a remand hearing, he scrawled details of his abduction from Rome on the palm of his hand and pressed it against the window of the police van.

Attempts by his defence lawyer, Avigdor Feldman, to turn the trial into a public indictment of Israel's nuclear weapons policy and to argue that his client had a moral duty to reveal what was happening at Dimona were a dismal failure. 'I am fully aware of the difficulties of this defence line,' Feldman said, 'but this will, in effect, be the first time, anywhere in the world, that the legality of nuclear weapons has ever been debated in court. It's just a shame it had to be in Israel.'[77] Neither did he progress with the argument that Israeli courts had no jurisdiction because Vanunu had been brought illegally into the country and would almost certainly not have been extradited from Italy or Britain because of the political nature of his offence. State prosecutors argued that a public trial could harm Israel's security and its relations with other countries. After an appeal to the High Court, Vanunu himself was permitted to describe how he was apprehended and under what conditions he was held, but forbidden to say where he was caught, identify exactly where he was held or give the names of the people who apprehended and guarded him. Feldman did not even try to subpoena 'Cindy' to appear as a witness. One star witness who did appear for the defence in January 1988 was the foreign minister, Shimon Peres, who was forbidden to answer questions on five specific topics related to the trial. Peres had played a central role in setting up Israel's nuclear research programme in the late 1950s and 1960s, when he was deputy minister of defence. He was also serving as prime minister when Vanunu was kidnapped from Rome. Vanunu was sentenced to eighteen years' imprisonment in March 1988.

Like the Hindawi Affair, the Vanunu case provided fertile ground for complex theories about what really happened. Was it possible that Israeli security had been unaware of Vanunu's activities, during and after he left Dimona? Was it not likely that the technician had been unwittingly used to put an end to years of deliberate ambiguity about whether Israel really had atomic weapons? These were the sorts of question that were asked when Israel finally admitted that he was in custody and awaiting trial.

Dr Frank Barnaby, a British nuclear expert who testified for the defence, was an exponent of this conspiratorial approach:

> History shows that Mossad is a highly competent secret service. The most credible explanation of its behaviour in the Vanunu case is that it found out what Vanunu was up to and decided to give him the chance to tell his story. His abduction from London via Rome – the sort of highly efficient operation one has come to expect from Mossad – and his trial in Jerusalem have added considerable authenticity to Vanunu's account. This is just what one would expect if the Israeli authorities wanted the world to take notice of Vanunu's disclosures. If they had done nothing, the *Sunday Times* article would have very soon been forgotten. Instead, it has received considerable attention in all forms of the media.[78]

Another expert commented:

> Although the Israeli government appeared distressed by Vanunu's disclosures, the possibility remains that it deliberately planted the story. Israeli military planners have become increasingly concerned recently about Syria's highly accurate Soviet-supplied SS-21 missiles and the possibility that Syria might use them with chemical warheads. Israel may have hoped to chill Syrian adventurism by means of Vanunu's revelations, issuing a reminder of Israel's overwhelming military strength. Or, outgoing Labour prime minister Shimon Peres, about to hand over office to the conservative Yitzhak Shamir, may have hoped to sustain momentum towards Middle East peace negotiations by showing the Israeli public that the nation was so strong that it could safely offer future concessions.[79]

Disseminating rumours and spreading deliberate disinformation were familiar aspects of Israel's nuclear weapons policy: in

1969, to give one particularly brazen example, Israeli agents in the United States had openly inquired whether the F-4 jets they were purchasing could be fitted with bomb racks suitable for nuclear weapons. The request was certain to be denied, but it was also sure to be leaked to the press in Washington and elsewhere.[80]

Yet the conspiracy theorists were almost certainly wrong, because in essence the story was a simple one: a security lapse of momentous proportions had taken place and allowed what appeared to be unequivocal confirmation of what the entire world had either long known or assumed to be the case – that Israel possessed a large and independent nuclear weapons capability. Vanunu was considered a traitor who had to be caught, even at the slight risk of damaging relations with a friendly country, and punished in accordance with the law and as a deterrent to other would-be whistle-blowers or spies. 'Had Mordechai Vanunu opted for a different route – for example, a direct leak to a hostile intelligence service instead of publication in the press,' commented Ze'ev Schiff, 'it's very likely that no one would have known what he'd done.'[81]

The well-substantiated allegation of the Mossad kidnapping from Rome would have been denied, however strong the evidence to the contrary. A security officer at Dimona was dismissed, although it remained unclear whether the Shin Bet had to bear the blame for overlooking Vanunu's decidedly suspicious behaviour: his friendship with Arab students at Beersheba University, where he was doing a part time course, set the alarm bells ringing, and he was warned. 'If Mordechai Vanunu in fact wanted to signal to the Shin Bet that he was no longer fit to be employed in a sensitive position,' said one newspaper, 'he chose every conceivable means of doing so in the most public way possible.'[82] It seemed incredible after that that Vanunu could take a camera in and out of the top-secret establishment, yet the fact that he did so, and was allowed to leave the country, does not automatically turn a 'cock-up' into a conspiracy.

'It is not just a one-time slip-up,' commented Ze'ev Schiff. 'It involves a whole series of hitches, basic errors on sensitive matters, complacency and exaggerated trust bordering almost on stupidity ... It recalls, in microcosm, the situations of indifference and lack of coordination on the eve of the Yom Kippur War.'[83] At the same time, there was grudging recognition of the Mossad's professionalism in locating Vanunu and returning him to Israel so quickly and cleanly.[84]

Vanunu's motives were clearly ideological, and he was nominated for the Nobel Peace Prize by his supporters abroad. But he was treated no differently by the Israeli security establishment than more conventional spies and traitors had been. He was luckier, in some respects, than Professor Marcus Klingberg, a Russian-born scientist from the top-secret Nes Tziona chemical and biological warfare centre, who was tried in camera on charges of being a Soviet agent and whose existence was never even admitted by the Israelis. Klingberg 'disappeared' in 1983 after supposedly suffering a nervous breakdown and was said to be in a mental hospital in Switzerland. In the extraordinary degree of secrecy surrounding it – extending even to a refusal to admit his existence behind bars – Klingberg's case was reminiscent of that of Motke Kedar, the famous 'prisoner X' of the 1950s and 1960s, who was tried and gaoled secretly after committing murder while on an espionage mission abroad.

According to reports published outside Israel, Klingberg emigrated to Israel in 1948 after serving as an epidemiologist in the Red Army. His wife, Wanda, said that she knew where he was but was unable to discuss the subject. Peter Pringle, an *Observer* correspondent, stumbled across the story while researching a book about biological warfare.[85] While visiting Israel in 1985 his car was broken into and some documents were stolen from a briefcase, which was later returned by police – minus the papers. An Israeli reporter who tried to follow up the story after details were published in the *Observer* wrote a detailed 4,000-word article that was completely suppressed by the military censor. In February 1988 it was reported – again abroad – that Klingberg might be released in a complex deal that would also involve the United States halting further investigations into the Jonathan Pollard spy case.[86] (Pollard was already serving a life sentence, but Israeli officials were apparently worried that further inquiries might unearth more spies in the heart of the US administration.) The little evidence that was available suggested strongly that Klingberg had been a long-term Soviet 'mole'.[87]

Also mentioned in the spy swap story was another Soviet agent who was arrested in Israel in 1987. Shabtai Kalmanovitch, a flamboyant businessman and socialite, had emigrated to Israel from the USSR in 1971 and was tried and gaoled for nine years in 1989 on espionage charges. But his trial was held in camera and the public was never told what he had done. The little information that emerged about the case suggested that Kalmanovitch was another penetration agent, who had been trained by the KGB in the early 1970s. He worked briefly on the 'absorption' of other Soviet immigrants, then entered politics, making powerful friends in the still-ruling Labour Party. He also established a reputation as a successful showbiz impresario, which allowed him to make frequent trips abroad and bring large amounts of money into the country.[88] He had aroused suspicion as early as 1975, when the Shin Bet had been warned about him by a cabinet minister.[89]

The secret war of Ismail Sowan

In 1987 Britain provided the backdrop for yet another intelligence scandal that, hot on the heels of the Pollard Affair and Irangate, as well as the embarrassment of the Vanunu revelations and kidnapping, came as a further blow to Nahum Admoni as he eked out his final months as head of the Mossad. And this time it concerned him directly. For some time disturbing stories had been circulating in Israel about vaguely defined unrest within the organization, although the restrictions of military censorship prevented all but the broadest hints from emerging publicly.[90] The general drift was about low morale, a sense of dissatisfaction and a dulling of the service's legendary reputation and cutting-edge. In their different and damaging ways Rafi

Eitan and Amiram Nir had both shown starkly how easily the famed Mossad could be sidestepped by other parts of government or by the intelligence community. The service's critics were not satisfied with the explanation that the Mossad had not been directly involved in either scandal; it did not appear to be involved in very much at all.

In March 1987 Britain revealed a plot to supply false UK passports to Mossad agents. Eight well-forged blank British passports discovered the previous summer in a telephone booth in West Germany had been traced to the Israeli Embassy in Bonn. A strong protest was delivered and the Foreign Office sought assurances that 'such behaviour would not be allowed to happen again'. Israel gave a grudging 'half assurance' after seven different representations by the British.[91] Some argued that the criticism of the Mossad over this incident by other Israelis was exaggerated, but it was a sign of the times.[92] And then, in August 1987, a case surfaced which threw considerable light on the Mossad's techniques for penetrating and running agents in hostile organizations.

British police investigating the killing of Ali Al-Adhami, a Palestinian cartoonist whose work appeared in the Kuwaiti newspaper *Al-Qabas*, arrested another Palestinian called Ismail Sowan. Sowan, who was living in the northern coastal city of Hull, was found to be in possession of four assault rifles, hand grenades, 145 kilograms of Semtex plastic explosives, detonators, timing devices and hundreds of rounds of ammunition. This was one of the largest arms caches ever found on the British mainland. Sowan was working for the Mossad.

Sowan hailed from a small village on the outskirts of East Jerusalem and had been sent to Beirut in 1978 to study civil engineering. Like other young Palestinians, the nineteen-year-old student came under pressure to join one of the fedayeen organizations. He opted for the biggest, Fatah, and spent a week on a training course in south Lebanon, learning how to fire Kalashnikov assault rifles and throw hand grenades.

His formal relationship with the Israelis began when he went home that summer to visit his family. His elder brother, Ibrahim, warned him that he could get into trouble if the Israelis found out what he had done in Lebanon and suggested he should pre-empt any problems by offering to work for them.[93] They did tend to know a lot: Palestinians returning from abroad were often staggered by the detailed dossiers their Israeli interrogators had about the most mundane aspects of their everyday life.[94] Whether Sowan had been spotted in advance by the Shin Bet and whether his motive was simply financial remain unclear. What is certain is that at some point he met two Shin Bet officers – Captain Elias and Major Yunis were their 'worknames' – in the Bethlehem police station. Later he saw them again in a safe house near Mount Herzl in West Jerusalem and told them of his life in the Lebanese capital.

Sowan became a useful agent. When he was ordered by the PLO in Beirut to contact a Fatah man in Nablus on one of his visits home, during which he was routinely debriefed and paid, his Shin Bet controllers told him to go ahead. Sowan was given an electronic locating device before he went to the meeting. His Nablus contact was quickly arrested, but Sowan's 'cover' was not blown and he returned to Lebanon, where he was told to fake concern that the Israelis knew about him.

Sowan returned to Jerusalem in 1982. He gave up plans to study in Jordan because of the need to do military service there. Captain Elias introduced him to 'Morris' from the Mossad, who arranged for the Palestinian to go to Paris, all expenses paid. After a year there, studying French and reporting on his fellow Palestinians to a Mossad case officer called 'Adam', Sowan went on to study in Britain. Again, he was paid a generous salary – £600 per month – and expenses.

It was there that the long investment in him started to pay off in hard intelligence. By chance or design, Sowan met Abdel-Rahman Mustafa, a major in Force 17, the Fatah unit set up to provide a personal bodyguard for Yasser Arafat but which had gone operational in its own right since the Lebanon war. Mustafa, according to the British lawyer who prosecuted Sowan, was a 'ruthless, dedicated and sophisticated terrorist' who was suspected of involvement in the hijacking of a Lufthansa jet in

1972. He was nominally employed at the Arab League offices in London. Sowan had known Mustafa in Beirut and once contact was established, his Mossad controller told him to try and locate an arsenal of PLO weapons and ammunition that was thought to be in Mustafa's possession. It was an important mission, so important that a second Israeli agent, a young Druse from the Golan Heights town of Majdal Shams called Bashir Samara, was also sent to find the Force 17 man. Sowan claimed later that he was seeking in that period to sever his contact with the Mossad, partly because he had recently married an English woman and wanted to settle down, but also because he was far removed from the action. 'Albert', his case officer at the London embassy, agreed. Mustafa was best man at Sowan's wedding in August 1986.

Mustafa left Britain in April 1987 but deposited the weapons and explosives in Sowan's flat in Hull, where he had a job as a research assistant at the Humberside College of Further Education.

Mustafa returned to Britain in July, under an assumed name, and asked Sowan to store some more cases. Mustafa was in fact organizing the assassination of Ali Al-Adhami, whose biting caricatures about corruption and double standards had proved too much for his favourite target – the PLO leadership. The Palestinian cartoonist was shot down on 22 July 1987, outside the *Al-Qabas* office in Chelsea. Mustafa coordinated the fourteen-man team that carried out the murder. The gunman got away undetected.

Sowan was in Jerusalem when he heard of the killing. He knew at once that Mustafa must be behind it and that it was only a matter of time before the British police came looking for him. He decided to tell the Israelis about the incriminating suitcases that were still stored in his flat in Hull. The Shin Bet reassured him that the matter would be dealt with by 'David' from the London embassy. Someone then made a simple but serious error, forgetting to inform the police at Ben-Gurion airport passport control not to allow Sowan to leave the country.[95] He did and arrived back in Britain on 5 August. A week later he was arrested. Mustafa's suitcases were still in his flat. Bashir Samara was picked up two weeks later and questioned about the Al-Adhami killing. Like Sowan, he told the police he was working for the Mossad. He was barred from entry to Britain because his 'exclusion was conducive to the public good for reasons of national security'.[96]

One of Sowan's Mossad controllers, Ya'akov Barad, who was working under diplomatic cover, was visiting Israel at the time of the Palestinian's interrogation. A message from the Foreign Office in London made it clear that he was not welcome to return to Britain. A second Israeli official, an attaché named Aryeh Regev, was expelled after Sowan was convicted in June 1988 and sentenced to eleven years in gaol. They were the first Israeli diplomats ever thrown out of Britain. According to some reports, three other Mossad men were also expelled. The Foreign Ministry in Jerusalem was suitably embarrassed: 'We regret that Her Majesty's Government has seen fit to take measures of the kind adopted,' a spokesman said. 'Israel did not act against any British interests.'[97]

Perhaps not, but its secret intelligence service had clearly blundered in a big way. The detailed exposure of Mossad agent-running inside the PLO was bad enough, and the trial at the Old Bailey guaranteed wide publicity. The absence of an official Israeli explanation fuelled the fires of speculation, always ready to combust spontaneously in such circumstances. Why had the Mossad not simply removed Mustafa's cases from Sowan's flat? Had they done so, Sowan would probably never have been arrested and the embarrassing details of the penetration operation would never have been made public. According to one source, Mossad agents did enter the Hull flat. If so, the decision to leave the weapons cache in place must have been deliberate. The Israelis may have realized that Sowan was playing a double game, or perhaps calculated that the discovery of the weapons would so badly damage the PLO that this would more than outweigh any revelations about the Mossad's involvement. If so, it was a terrible miscalculation.

The evidence, however, points to a much more prosaic

explanation. Informed Israeli sources claimed hotly that it had been the intention to inform the British security service, MI5, about Mustafa's suitcases, but that the British simply found out first. There were angry calls for a secret inquiry into the Sowan Affair, which produced the most damaging exposure of Mossad operations since the Lillehammer fiasco in 1973. 'In terms of the results in the field, this is a miniature Pollard Affair,' one senior Israeli official said.[98]

Operation Moses

Before the spate of scandals that began with the Pollard Affair, the early 1980s brought the Mossad one dramatic coup that was a heady throwback to the days when much of Israel's political and intelligence resources were devoted to the ingathering of the exiles. Not since the Moroccan immigration of the late 1950s and 1960s had secret diplomacy and clandestine operations been applied so vigorously as they were to bring the Falashas, the mysterious black Jews of Ethiopia, to Israel.[99]

The background to the operation was difficult. After the 1973 war relations between Israel and Ethiopia – which had first been consolidated under the aegis of the Mossad during the heyday of the 'periphery doctrine' in 1958 – were severed and they were not renewed by the Marxist regime that overthrew Haile Selassie and took power in 1974. Jews suffered in the post-revolutionary chaos. In 1975 the Falashas were officially recognized as Jews by the Chief Rabbinate in Jerusalem and thus automatically entitled to Israeli citizenship under the Law of Return, but emigration from Ethiopia was restricted.

Small groups of Falashas had started fleeing to Israel via neighbouring Sudan from the end of 1977 after Menachem Begin and the Ethiopian president, Colonel Mengistu Haile Mariam, worked out a secret deal under which Ethiopia would turn a blind eye to the emigration in return for continued Israeli arms supplies. This mutually convenient arrangement ended in a welter of mutual embarrassment in February 1978 when the foreign minister, Moshe Dayan, inadvertently confirmed publicly that weapons were still going to Addis Ababa.

By the early 1980s the Falashas were being openly persecuted by the Ethiopian authorities. Severe drought and famine in Gondar province and the depredations of the war between the central government and the Tigrean and Eritrean rebels made matters worse.

The Mossad had been put in overall charge of the Ethiopian emigration effort in 1980. Bribery was used extensively to win the cooperation of the authorities in Sudan, the only viable clandestine exit route from Ethiopia. Some Sudanese officials acted out of moral conviction; others were simply bribed. Mossad agents – some speaking fluent Sudanese Arabic – forged or bought documents such as internal travel permits, rented vehicles and safe houses, and handed over money to finance the movements of increasingly large numbers of refugees. At the climax of the operation, in early 1985, there were twenty Mossad agents operating in Sudan.

By the end of 1982 the Mossad had extricated 2,000 Falashas. By the end of 1984 some 7,000 had arrived in Israel. Sudan's internal security service, Amn al-Dawla, knew all about the operation. And so, of course, did President Ga'afar Nimeiri. The Ethiopian emigration question was one of the main items on the agenda during a day-long secret meeting Nimeiri held with the Israeli defence minister, Ariel Sharon, in a third African country in May 1982, just before the invasion of Lebanon. They were brought together by the Saudi millionaire, Adnan Khashoggi.[100]

An apparatus was set up in Khartoum to coordinate the different aspects of the exodus and to provide transit facilities. It all bore a striking resemblance to how Morocco had secretly cooperated with the exodus of its Jewish community twenty-five years before. Falashas and other operatives were dropped off the Sudanese coast by Israeli Sa'ar missile boats and then made their way to the refugee camps in eastern Sudan and Ethiopia itself. In several cases, unmarked IAF Hercules transport planes landed at desert airstrips and airlifted refugees directly out of Sudan to Israel.

But the operation moved too slowly. In the early months of 1984 the steady trickle of refugees became a flood, and it was just then that the degree of Sudanese cooperation changed for the worse. Nimeiri had become much more cautious since the assassination of Anwar Sadat in October 1981 and he was especially worried that the Muslim Brothers would discover what was happening and expose his clandestine link with the Zionist enemy.

Israel applied pressure via the United States, partly, it has been argued, to try and complete the exodus without damaging the substantial Mossad assets that had been built up in Sudan.[101] Finally the arrangements were made, with the CIA and the US Embassy playing a major role: Sudan agreed to allow direct flights of Falashas from Khartoum International Airport to Belgium, thence to Israel. Dozens of flights, carrying 8,000 Falashas, went from Sudan, via Brussels, to Tel Aviv between the end of November 1984 and the first week of January 1985, when the secret of Operation Moses finally came out.

13

Intifada: 1987–90

Israel's 'war of choice' in Lebanon did not destroy the PLO although it dealt a grievous blow to the organization's operational capabilities. In the first nine months of 1984, according to the Aman chief, General Ehud Barak, 80 per cent of attacks against the IDF in Lebanon were carried out by Shi'ites, mostly members of Amal, although the mainstream group was increasingly overshadowed by the Iranian-backed Hizbullah.[1] Yet by the summer of 1985, when the IDF withdrew the bulk of its combat forces, leaving behind only a narrow, border 'Security Zone', it was clear that the Palestinian guerrillas still posed a threat, even though most of their men and leaders were scattered as far apart as Tunis, Baghdad, North Yemen and Algiers.

The secession of anti-Arafat groups had strengthened the pro-Syrian trend in the Palestinian camp and increased the inherent tendency for rivalry between the different organizations. Gradually the focus of the struggle changed: since south Lebanon was no longer an effective base for Palestinian operations against Israel, the action shifted abroad. It was similar to what happened when the PLO was expelled from Jordan in 1970, but on a much smaller scale.

A new front opened up at sea as Palestinians tried to return to Lebanon, resupply and reinforce their units there, or, less frequently, to mount seaborne attacks against Israeli targets. The Israeli navy began to play a key role in the interdiction of the motley array of vessels used by the PLO, mostly Fatah, which had a rudimentary 'naval arm'.

In March 1985 a ship called the *Khalil 1* was captured off Cyprus. Four men were detained and later tried on charges of being members of Fatah's Force 17. One of them, Abu Nur, was in charge of the Force 17 office in Tunis, which, the Israelis believed, played a key role in coordinating between the scattered elements of the PLO.[2]

In April the Israelis intercepted and sank a Panamanian-flagged merchantman called the *Atavarius* that had sailed from Algeria to mount a raid on the Defence Ministry compound in Tel Aviv on the eve of Independence Day celebrations. The Palestinians had intended to leave the mother ship on high-speed dinghies, land on a deserted beach and make their way to the target. Abu Jihad, Arafat's deputy and commander of all PLO military activities, was the chief planner. In the Israeli attack, over 100 miles from the shore, twenty passengers were killed and eight men captured and detained, then tried secretly in Israel. A combination of precise intelligence, luck and persistence brought impressive results as these seaborne interceptions continued. Two more took place in August.

What happened on the night of 11 September 1985 was more typical. An Israeli navy patrol craft stopped a boat called the *Opportunity* half-way between Beirut and Cyprus and found Faisal Abu Sharah, a senior Force 17 man, hiding below deck. The Palestinian was transferred to the Israeli ship, handcuffed and had a sack placed over his head. He underwent months of intensive interrogation by both the IDF and the Shin Bet while in administrative detention. 'Arrested on the high seas', was entered on the standard detention form signed by the defence minister. Abu Sharah was finally sentenced to eight years in prison on a charge of membership of a hostile organization.[3]

In the autumn of 1985 the secret war at sea served as the background to a series of bloody and dramatic events that was to give a new lease of life to the dying theme of Palestinian terrorism and present Israel's intelligence community with a series of novel challenges.

The Tunis raid

On the morning of Tuesday, 1 October 1985, Israeli F-15 fighter planes bombed the headquarters of the Palestine Liberation Organization at Hammam ash-Shatt, south-east of Tunis. The Israeli attack was a technical feat of great accomplishment, involving a flight of over 1,900 kilometres each way, air-to-air refuelling, political and operation nerves and extremely precise intelligence.

Considering the complexities involved, the IAF raid was mounted at short notice. It came in direct retaliation for the murder of three middle-aged Israeli tourists on a yacht in the marina at Larnaca, Cyprus, on Yom Kippur, 25 September. Three members of the PLO's Force 17, including an Englishman called Ian Davidson, killed the three in cold blood without making any of the usual demands to release Palestinians in Israeli gaols. Cyprus, with easy access to both Israel and the Arab world, had long been a sensitive and often dangerous junction in the shadowy war of terrorism and intelligence between Israel and the PLO. Yet the evidence was that the three Israelis were not, as the Palestinians claimed, Mossad agents, but simply what they appeared to be. At least one British newspaper wrongly identified the woman victim, Esther Palzur, as Sylvia Rafael, the South African-born Mossad agent caught in the Lillehammer affair in 1973.[4] Sylvia Rafael was in fact alive and well and living in Norway.

Force 17, whose headquarters were in the Jordanian capital Amman, had been threatening for some time to carry out such an attack if Israel did not release the unit's deputy commander and twelve other men who had recently been captured at sea while on their way from Cyprus to south Lebanon. The mood in Israel was ugly: 'If additional proof were needed that the Lebanon war solved no problems in the sphere of terrorism, it came in Larnaca,' *Ma'ariv* commented. 'If additional proof were required that the Palestinians are still not ripe for peace negotiations, this too has been made clear. Yasser Arafat may have disavowed the act, but it is difficult to believe him.'[5]

The inner cabinet met in special session the day after the Larnaca killings. The ministers were joined by the IDF chief of staff, Major-General Moshe Levy, General Ehud Barak, the Aman chief, and the commander of the IAF, General Amos Lapidot, who described the plan to raid the PLO HQ near Tunis. Lapidot explained that there was little chance of resistance either from the Tunisian air force or from anti-aircraft fire. The main difficulty he foresaw was the possibility of the technical problems that could arise on such a long flight. Yitzhak Rabin, the defence minister, wanted to strike quickly to exploit the rare mood of international sympathy for Israel after the Larnaca killings.

Bombs hit Arafat's headquarters and other military sites at Hammam ash-Shatt, including a building used by Force 17. Barak said later that Arafat's presence or absence 'was not a factor in the plan'.[6] As Aman had predicted, there was no interference, either from the Tunisian air force or from ground fire, possibly because the Tunisian radar was out of action, although it is unclear whether this was because of a genuine malfunction or Israeli jamming. According to Israeli figures, seventy-five people were killed, including sixty PLO men, and forty to sixty injured. Tunisian sources said the dead included a larger number of civilians.[7]

The IAF attack owed much to detailed knowledge of the layout of PLO headquarters, including Humint sources who could point out the precise function of different buildings. Tunisia had become an important Israeli intelligence target since the PLO had moved its headquarters there in 1982. According to one source, 'Some Tunisian "assets", for whom greed was the incentive, were told the truth, that they were working for Israeli intelligence. High-ranking Tunisian officials were recruited under false pretences, believing they would be helping European intelligence services.' By mid-1985 the Mossad network was extensive and included safe houses, weapons caches and a clandestine communications system.[8] When the Jonathan Pollard Affair erupted a few weeks after the attack, persistent reports claimed that the American spy had provided the Israelis with detailed intelligence about the air defence systems of both Libya and Tunisia and that this had facilitated the planning for the raid. Pollard himself certainly believed this to be the case, although Rabin firmly denied the story. As with the attack on the Iraqi nuclear reactor four years earlier, there was little serious political fall-out apart from routine condemnations of Israel at the United Nations.

The Achille Lauro *Affair*

Retaliation was not long in coming. Less than a week after the Tunis raid, on 7 October 1985, four members of the Palestine Liberation Front, a small PLO affiliate headed by Mahmoud Abbas (Abu al-Abbas), took over an Italian cruise liner called the *Achille Lauro* shortly after it sailed from Alexandria, Egypt, *en route* for the Israeli port of Ashdod. It was the most spectacular act of maritime piracy the world had seen for twenty-five years and there were 454 passengers on board to play in the drama. The four hijackers had apparently planned to sail into Ashdod, but when they were prematurely discovered by the crew, they forced the vessel to sail towards Syria. However, they were refused permission to enter the port of Tartus. They murdered an elderly, wheelchair-bound American Jew called Leon Klinghoffer, threw his body into the sea and then, on 9 October, ordered the ship to stop off at Port Said, at the northern end of the Suez Canal.

The maritime hijacking was a grave embarrassment for Yasser Arafat. The Abu al-Abbas group occupied an awkward place in the PLO: it was represented on the organization's ten-member executive committee and had attended the last session of the Palestine National Council – the PLO 'parliament' – in Amman in November 1984, when six other pro-Syrian groups stayed away. Yet Abbas was unhappy about the increasingly 'diplomatic' direction taken by Arafat, and particularly about the previous February's agreement with King Hussein of Jordan on a joint negotiating strategy for peace talks. From the moment the incident began, Israel, leaning heavily on its considerable intelligence resources and its ability to monitor events as they were taking place, did all it could to implicate the PLO as a whole.

Unlike the Force 17 killers in Larnaca, the *Achille Lauro* hijackers did demand the release of Palestinian prisoners held in Israeli gaols. They produced a list of fifty names, headed by the man who had led a four-man PLF team ashore at Nahariya in April 1979, when they had shot and killed a father and his five-year-old daughter. The man's wife, Smadar Haran, who was hiding in a back room, accidentally smothered her crying two-year-old daughter to death as she tried to keep the terrorists from finding and killing them as well.

Negotiation was out of the question, especially since the uproar over the release of 1,150 Palestinian and Lebanese prisoners in exchange for three Israeli soldiers the previous May. The massive and disproportionate deal with Ahmed Jibril's PFLP-GC had been widely criticized, and many felt it had gone ahead only because of intense pressure from the families of the captured soldiers. Some 500 of the freed Palestinians had been allowed to return to their homes in the West Bank and Gaza Strip, an element of the package that the Shin Bet had strongly opposed. One of them had been gaoled for taking part in the PLF's Nahariya operation, which the organization had commemorated afterwards in the publication of a glossy brochure.[9] The fact that there were no Israeli nationals on board the *Achille Lauro* made matters much simpler.

Israel quickly established contact with the United States, whose forces in the eastern Mediterranean had been on special alert since the hijacking was reported. Amiram Nir, Peres's energetic adviser on terrorism, maintained close liaison with Colonel Oliver North of the National Security Council, which was coordinating the American end of the crisis. Other channels included General Uri Simhoni, the military attaché at the Israeli Embassy in Washington.

The ship reached Port Said on the evening of 9 October and the hijackers, and Abu al-Abbas himself, disembarked on a small tug. They surrendered to the Egyptians and PLO officials after being promised safe conduct out of the country. Initially, the end of the drama was presented as a victory for PLO 'mediation' – 'a success story for PLO diplomacy', said an official in Tunis – but that was before Klinghoffer's death was confirmed, before Israel revealed the full extent of PLO involvement and before surveillance revealed the extent of Egyptian duplicity about the aftermath.

Monitoring of Egyptian communications by Israel and the US National Security Agency was intense and successful, although the Israeli reports were arriving in Washington fifteen minutes ahead of the US ones and were being passed directly to the Pentagon by Uri Simhoni.[10] Once the hijackers were in custody the United States made it clear that they must be brought to justice. The American ambassador to Egypt, Nicholas Veliotes, boarded the ship on 10 October and was heard to say on an open line to the embassy in Cairo: 'You tell the foreign ministry that we demand that they prosecute those sons of bitches.'[11] President Mubarak said publicly that the four Palestinians had left the country. But the intercepts, which provided nearly real-time intelligence, revealed that they were still there and that Mubarak thought that George Shultz, the secretary of state, was 'crazy' to think that Egypt, an Arab country, would dare to surrender them.[12] Mubarak arranged for the Palestinians to leave Egypt secretly on an Egyptair jet on 11 October. The plane was intercepted by four jets from the USS *Saratoga* and forced to land at the Sigonella NATO air base in Sicily. The hijackers were taken into custody by the Italian authorities, although Abu al-Abbas himself and an aide were freed. In Rome the government of Bettino Craxi fell over the row that ensued following the release.

Just how much Israeli intelligence knew was revealed a few days later in an extraordinary television appearance by the Aman chief, General Ehud Barak. Barak played a tape of part of a monitored ship-to-shore conversation between Abu al-Abbas and the hijackers. Barak explained that the exchange took place on 9 October, when it was clear that the operation had failed but before the PLO accepted responsibility for the attack and was still trying to impute it to a small Syrian-backed breakaway faction of the PLF. There was a lot of static in the background and the conversation was cryptic, but Abu al-Abbas, who according to the Israelis was using the name Abu Khaled, appeared from the tape to know the hijackers by their first names and to be aware of their original plan. He gave them instructions, which they followed once they had verified that it was indeed him speaking to them from Port Said.

In fact, what Barak revealed was not much of a secret. Journalists covering the story in Port Said had heard exactly the same exchange between shore and ship – courtesy of the local Lloyd's agent – and had noted the significance of the request one of the gunmen made to or about Abu Khaled: 'I want a sign that he is the one.' This was taken – more or less correctly, as it turned out later – to mean that the hijackers wanted to be sure that they were dealing with a friendly party.[13] The real importance – and crucial innovation – of the Israeli monitoring was to reveal that Abu Khaled was no less than Abu al-Abbas himself, a fact which made nonsense of the mediation claim.

The Aman tape was of immense political value to Israel: 'Abu al-Abbas was involved up to his neck in the planning, implementation and command of this attack,' Barak said. 'He is no marginal figure, but one of the people closest to Arafat. His headquarters are located in Tunis, in Hammam ash-Shatt, not more than 100 metres from the headquarters of Arafat himself, which were destroyed in the Tunis bombing. Abu al-Abbas is a member of the PLO's highest operational body – the ten-member executive committee.'[14]

Every intelligence agency normally goes to great lengths to conceal not only its sources and methods but also the degree of its ability to monitor the enemy, so the decision, personally approved by Rabin, to release the *Achille Lauro* tape was not taken lightly. On balance, despite the great unease of many Aman officers,[15] it was probably worth it. The only precedent was the famous monitored conversation between King Hussein and President Nasser during the 1967 war. Barak also hinted strongly that Israel and the United States cooperated closely during the crisis. Copies of the tape were passed to the Americans and the Italians. Israeli intelligence had produced the 'smoking gun'. Shimon Peres flew to Washington the day afer Barak's TV appearance and made the most of it. One of his first meetings was with the director of the CIA, William Casey.

Target Jordan

Aman's release of the *Achille Lauro* tape was the first shot fired in a new and intense stage of Israel's political and propaganda offensive against the PLO. Following the Larnaca killings and the retaliatory attack on the organization's Tunis headquarters, the government sought to press home its advantage. Arafat had been stung by the British government's cancellation of a visit to London by two of his executive committee members and his diplomatic progress seemed to have been momentarily checked. And when, visiting Cairo in early November 1985, he formally declared an end to 'all forms of terrorism', the Israelis predictably dismissed the statement as 'meaningless', especially since the PLO leader specifically excluded armed resistance in the 'occupied territories'. And only a few days afterwards this was amended by Salah Khalaf – Abu Iyad – to mean 'all of Palestine'.

Highlighting PLO terrorism remained on the agenda, but the next headline-grabbing horror came from Arafat's sworn enemy, Abu Nidal. On 27 December 1985, while much of the world was still basking in its Christmas afterglow, gunmen from the dissident Palestinian group mowed down nineteen passengers, including five Americans, at the El Al check-in counters at Rome and Vienna airports. In April 1986, in the subsequent US air raids against targets in Libya, which was believed to be supporting Abu Nidal, Israel played a full supporting role. Fighting terrorism in grand style was in vogue, and, thanks largely to the intelligence at its disposal, Israel rode the crest of the wave.

Israel went on to the offensive because the demise of the PLO presented an opportunity to prise apart the uneasy partnership between Yasser Arafat and King Hussein and to try to draw Jordan into the peace process. Jordan's conspicuous failure to join other Arab countries in condemning the US interception of the Egyptian plane carrying the *Achille Lauro* hijackers was noted with approval. Israel adopted the slogan of 'improving the quality of life' in the occupied territories to try and induce Hussein to act alone on behalf of the Palestinians. In November 1985, as part of this strategy, it approved the appointment of a Palestinian businessman, Zafer al-Masri, to replace the IDF officer who had been serving as the mayor of Nablus, the largest town in the West Bank, since the dismissal of the maimed Bassam Shak'a in 1982.

Official Israeli statements had been harping ominously for several months on the theme of the PLO's strengthened presence in Amman, and how this had adversely affected the security situation in the West Bank and Gaza. In the year between April 1985 and April 1986, 'terrorist acts' in the occupied territories increased by 52 per cent over the previous year and there was a significant rise in the use of improvised explosive devices.[16] 'The Jordanians are making a reasonable attempt to thwart the PLO's attempts to send squads and Katyusha rockets over the river,' Shmuel Goren, the coordinator of government operations in the territories, said in September 1985. 'They are not exerting themselves to prevent contacts between residents of the territories and the PLO offices . . . It's enough for someone in Jordan to give money, briefings, instructions and a communications system to lead to an increase in hostile activity.'[17]

After the *Achille Lauro*, Ehud Barak put the Aman view in greater detail:

> The presence of PLO headquarters across the Jordan is the central factor behind the rise in the number of attacks in the areas under our

> control . . . A person gets up in the morning in his house in Nablus or Hebron, makes a two-hour trip to Amman, goes to the Jabal al-Hussein neighbourhood, where there is a four-storey building . . . bearing a large sign: 'PLO – Office of the Commander in Chief', who is none other than Arafat. He meets there with Abu Jihad or Abu Tayib, heads from there to an operational apartment in Amman itself, in some residential neighbourhood, or to Abu Tayib's office in the Jabal Nuzha neighbourhood just a few hundred metres from Hussein's palace. He receives money for the operation, is briefed, reports on problems encountered in the preparatory stages. He can train, receive instructions as to how the combat material will be smuggled to him. He returns home that same evening. If anything goes wrong he can again make a quick trip to Amman, return that same evening and iron out the difficulty. This cannot be done with such ease and in such a manner from Tunisia.[18]

Barak was deliberately exaggerating and there was an obvious paradox in his carefully crafted public presentation: if Israel knew so much about how the PLO functioned in Jordan and maintained operational headquarters for activities in the occupied territories – a point the intelligence chief underlined by going out of his way to drop the names of key people and places – then surely the threat could not be that great? He conceded that attacking PLO headquarters in Jordan – as opposed to those in faraway Tunisia – entailed 'aspects which are not related to terrorism alone'.

Eventually, the Israeli warnings were heeded. In February 1986 King Hussein lost patience with Arafat, who refused to meet US conditions unequivocally and accept UN resolutions recognizing Israel. He could no longer work with the PLO leadership, Hussein declared bitterly, 'until such time as their word becomes their bond, characterized by commitment, credibility and constancy'. The Amman accord of the previous year was declared a dead letter and the repercussions followed quickly. King Hussein mended his fences with Syria, Arafat's enemy; and his military intelligence began to openly support Colonel Atallah Atallah – Abu Zaim – the Amman-based PLO rebel of dubious reputation and limited support who had demanded that Arafat be replaced as the organization's leader. A number of clumsy attempts were made to squeeze unconvincing declarations of loyalty to the king from delegations of West Bank notables. In July Jordan ordered the closure of twenty-five Fatah and PLO offices in the kingdom. Khalil al-Wazir – Abu Jihad – the deputy commander of all PLO forces, was given forty-eight hours to leave the country. 'The further away he is the better for all of us,' said Shimon Peres. Abu Jihad was also commander of Fatah's Western Sector – the group's main operational unit for activities in the occupied territories and Israel. According to Israeli intelligence, two smaller and highly secret bodies, Recruitment Committee 77 and Committee 88, also operated under his command.

Kiryat Shmona: six–one

At 10.30 p.m. on 25 November 1987 a young member of Ahmed Jibril's Syrian-backed PFLP-GC flew silently across the Lebanese border in an ultra-light hang-glider and landed in a field of thorns east of the northern Israeli town of Kiryat Shmona. In the course of the next few minutes, before being shot down himself, the Palestinian managed to kill six Israeli soldiers and wound seven others in a nearby army camp. It was a grievous blow. Despite prior intelligence about a possible terrorist infiltration provided to IDF Northern Command, insufficient precautions had been taken to meet the threat. The Night of the Hang-Gliders, as the event became known in Israel, was a badly needed fillip to Palestinian morale. It also acted as a trigger for a far more serious development.

Other events did much to forge a mood that was ripe for heightened resistance to the Israelis. That month's Arab summit conference in Amman was so preoccupied with the Gulf War between Iraq and Iran that the Palestinian issue – for so many years the very touchstone of Arab solidarity – was barely on the agenda. The occupied territories, especially the Gaza Strip, were seething.

Shin Bet personnel in Gaza had been struggling for some time with an upsurge of clandestine, occasionally violent activity by Islamic militants operating in two rival organizations, the Islamic Jihad, which was affiliated loosely with Fatah, and a larger group called the Mujam'a, which had followed the example of Iranian fundamentalists and founded a mosque-based network of social welfare and educational centres. Islamic Jihad was the more professional of the two: organized along classic cell lines, with each member knowing only his immediate commander, it succeeded in acquiring weapons and explosives, mainly bought from Jewish criminals. Clandestine communications were maintained with Jordan via letters that were wrapped in nylon and swallowed by couriers crossing the bridges. Several of its members were arrested in August 1986, but the group's leader escaped by fishing boat to Egypt. Shin Bet interest increased after three Israelis were stabbed to death in Gaza. By the end of 1986 sixty suspects were in detention.

In May 1987 six Islamic Jihad prisoners escaped from the security wing of Gaza prison. Two of them managed to leave the country, a third was captured, and the remaining three went underground to organize new attacks. Over the next few months they killed two more Israelis – a civilian contractor and a military police officer – before being gunned down themselves in a dramatic shoot-out with the army and the Shin Bet. A security service agent called Victor Rejwan was also killed.[19] Another escapee and two innocent people had been shot dead a few days earlier. Palestinians treated both incidents as deliberate massacres. 'They do not use the death penalty in Israel,' said a leading PLO supporter bitterly. 'They just kill people in the streets.'[20] On 18 November Israel ordered the deportation of Sheikh Abdel Aziz Odeh, spiritual leader of the Islamic Jihad.

On 6 December, less than two weeks after the hang-glider attack, an Israeli civilian was stabbed to death in the centre of Gaza city. Two days later four Palestinians from Jabaliya were killed and six injured in a road accident involving an Israeli truck at the Erez junction at the northern end of the Strip. That too, fed by rumour and the bush telegraph, was somehow interpreted as intentional. On 9 December extensive rioting broke out in Jabaliya, the largest refugee camp in the area. 'Kiryat Shmona: Six–One' – a triumphal victory cry borrowed from the football field – became a popular taunt in large-scale clashes between Israeli soldiers and Palestinian demonstrators. The intifada had begun.

Intifada!

The eruption of the Palestinian uprising caused a spate of recriminations between the various Israeli bodies involved in security in the occupied territories. The army pleaded that it was too busy maintaining public order to know what was happening beneath the surface. Critics of the civil administration, which was in daily contact with the Palestinian population at all levels of life, argued that it leaned too heavily on traditional sectors, such as village mukhtars, who were known for their conservative views and were generally seen as one of the few remaining bastions of pro-Jordanian feeling.

The Shin Bet was still in a state of internal disarray, despite Yosef Harmelin's takeover; and no sooner had the Landau Commission report been published than three officers were suspended for lying over the case of Awad Hamdan, a young Palestinian from Tulkarm who had died while under interrogation in July.[21] The immediate response, as the scale of the unrest became clear, was that the Shin Bet was 'good' at terrorism and 'bad' at politics. Later, the security service's small research section, which had been set up despite objections from Avraham Shalom in 1983, was expanded to try and fill the intelligence gap.[22] Shmuel Goren, the former Mossad executive who had the thankless job of coordinating government operations in the territories, was blamed for the oversight.

Yet it was several weeks before the idea of the intifada as something radically different from previous bouts of disturbances took hold in Israeli minds. Political leaders, particularly the defence minister, Yitzhak Rabin, pointed out repeatedly that the PLO had been surprised by the spontaneous eruption, as if that also excused Israel's own surprise and discomfort.

Rabin was visiting the United States in the second week of December, and it was not until the end of the month that it was decided to stream reinforcements into the West Bank and Gaza, by which time the initial momentum of the unrest had gathered force. Decision-making was haphazard and policy coordination poor: for weeks the army used crowbars to force striking shopkeepers to open their premises, further radicalizing previously passive sections of the population which had been either galvanized into action by the generally militant atmosphere or simply intimidated by the young men of the Shabiba – the Fatah youth movement – who quickly became the foot-soldiers of the intifada. Rabin announced a policy of 'force, might and beatings', and TV screens across the world showed pictures of Israeli soldiers using batons and stones to break the limbs of demonstrating Palestinians.

The Shin Bet seemed helpless to deal with the unprecedented mass resistance, but its monitoring of militants was used to try to neutralize key leaders. In January 1988 came the first deportations of nine selected individuals, although in each case the expulsions were followed by more rioting as well as international criticism, most painfully from the United States.

It quickly became apparent that many of the 600 prisoners who had returned to their homes in the occupied territories after their release in the controversial exchange with Ahmed Jibril's PFLP-GC in May 1985 were active participants in the intifada; several of these became candidates for one-way trips across the Lebanese border. Jibril al-Rajub, who was arrested at the end of December 1987, was fairly typical. He had been sentenced to life imprisonment in 1970 for Fatah activities. He came from Dura, a large village in the Hebron hills, and while in prison wrote a best-selling book about his experiences, revealing much about how the inmates' loyalty to the different PLO organizations continued and indeed dominated life behind bars. After his release in the Jibril exchange Rajub went to work under Faisal Husseini at the Arab Research Centre in East Jerusalem, one of the most important of the network of PLO-inspired institutions created in the occupied territories over the last decade.

Take us to your leaders

The main problem for the security service was locating the body that became known as the United National Leadership of the Uprising. From early in 1988 leaflets signed by the UNLU began to appear with instructions to the Palestinians about what to do: when to hold strikes, when to open shops, when to observe anniversaries, when to boycott Israeli goods, to resign from the civil administration, to attack collaborators, etc. The Shin Bet had some successes. In February a van carrying thousands of leaflets was stopped at a routine army roadblock near Ramallah. The subsequent arrest of several members of the DFLP – one of the smallest but perhaps the best organized of the PLO groups in the occupied territories – led investigators to a small but modern commercial printing press in Issawiyah, near Jerusalem. But the picture that emerged was not encouraging: the leaflets were produced in several locations after being drafted by an *ad hoc* committee of representatives of the different groups that comprised the UNLU. Even after thousands of arrests, the leaflets were still appearing regularly. Later, the text of leaflets would be broadcast by the PLO radio station in Baghdad, copied down by hand or on word processors and distributed locally.

Some of the leaflets seemed to be fakes. One that was distributed in Hebron by local merchants called for an end to strikes because of the impossibility of doing business. 'The Zionist enemy has begun issuing forged leaflets . . . in order to create confusion, silence the intifada and divert it from the correct path,' warned an apparently genuine counter-leaflet that appeared in the West Bank city a few days later.[23] Others gave different dates for strike days or attacked named groups in an apparent attempt to increase divisions in Palestinian ranks. Palestinians were quick to charge that the Shin Bet was responsible for these forgeries. The Islamic Resistance Movement (Hamas, from the Arabic acronym), which had grown out of the Mujam'a network in the Gaza Strip and often expressed hostility to the more secular-oriented PLO, began to issue its own instructions. Few Arabs claimed that the organization was 'run' by the Israelis since it quickly came to represent a threat of its own to the occupation authorities. In June 1989 Hamas was declared an illegal organization.

Months of unprecedented Israeli repression failed to sever the links between the UNLU and the PLO outside. Arab citizens of Israel helped with the transfer of the limited amount of funds necessary to finance what was essentially a low-cost enterprise. Emergency funding by the UNRWA relief agency was of great help to refugees, especially in the Gaza camps, where long curfews were repeatedly enforced and breadwinners could not get to work in Israel. Several large sums of money were seized at the Jordan bridges, and amounts larger than $1,000 had to be declared. The cutting off of international telephone lines from the occupied territories did not seem to help either. Alongside the stone and the petrol bomb, the facsimile machine became a symbol of the intifada: faxes were used extensively to send drafts of documents – including leaflets – to PLO offices in Europe and Cyprus, from where they could be sent on to the organization's headquarters in Tunis or Baghdad. Abu Jihad, head of Fatah's Western Command, used his networks to maintain contact with the people of the occupied territories. But it was rarely clandestine activity in the traditional operational sense. It involved ideas, money and public relations, not guns and bombs. It forced the Shin Bet, as two well-placed Israeli writers have astutely observed, to change, 'the gist . . . being the difference between a security service and a secret police'.[24] The intifada was a new experience for both sides, even though old habits died hard.

Death in Limassol

As the Shin Bet struggled against the intifada in the occupied territories, the Mossad escalated the secret war against the PLO outside. On 14 February 1988 it struck a heavy blow against the hard core of Fatah operations. A powerful bomb planted in a Volkswagen Golf in the Cypriot port of Limassol killed three of the organization's top military men. It was clearly the work of experts.

Marwan Kayyali was a colonel on the PLO's military council, headed by Abu Jihad. PLO sources said his main task was to supply Palestinians in Lebanon with 'everything from bread to bullets'. Muhammed Buhais was an official of the PLO's Occupied Homelands Office, which was also responsible to Abu Jihad and was closely involved in the intifada.

But the main target of the Limassol bombing was assumed to be Lieutenant-Colonel Muhammed Tamimi, ostensibly another official of the Occupied Homelands Office. Tamimi, codenamed 'Hamdi', was in fact the head of one of Fatah's most important operational and intelligence branches, known as Recruitment Committee 77, described by one expert as 'the most covert nucleus within an already clandestine system'. One of its main tasks was coordination with the Islamic Jihad organization in Gaza. Tamimi, a cool professional with a distinct *modus operandi*, was held personally responsible for the planning of the Beit Hadassah massacre of six settlers in 1980 and for the throwing of grenades at soldiers at Jerusalem's Wailing Wall in October 1986. The 1980 killings in Hebron, which led to the creation of the Jewish settler underground, were Tamimi's revenge for the Mossad's assassination in Cyprus of his friend Ibrahim Barghouti, head of the Western Command's 'Hebron Committee'.[25]

The Limassol killings attracted surprisingly little attention at the time, largely because the victims' names meant nothing to anyone except their families, their colleagues in the inner recesses of PLO operations and Israeli intelligence. 'Recent history has taught us something about the manner in which different Palestinian actions and splinter groups square accounts with each other,' said the standard Israeli denial. Yasser Arafat, speaking in Kuwait, hinted strongly that his Cairo Declaration about restricting terrorism might have to be reviewed in the light of the Israeli offensive. He blamed the Mossad for the attack.[26]

No one had any doubts about who was responsible for the blow that came the following day. On 15 February a limpet mine disabled the *Soi Phryne* in Limassol harbour and ended the most ambitious public relations exercise ever mounted by the PLO. The Greek passenger vessel had been bought to serve as the 'ship of return' which would sail to Haifa in support of the intifada; it was to be a dual reminder, both of the Palestinians' 'right to return' to their homeland and of the Jewish refugee boats that ran the British blockade of Palestine in the late 1940s. Israel had already made clear that the ship would not be permitted to enter its territorial waters, and clearly preferred a pre-emptive, casualty-free underwater strike to what, it was easy to predict, would turn into an embarrassing and media-saturated spectacle the moment the PLO boat was intercepted and turned back.

As a Western reporter wrote:

> Palestinians grudgingly acknowledge that the Cyprus bombings were masterpieces of tradecraft – surgical operations that quickly and cleanly accomplished their objectives. They express particular professional admiration for the precision of the remote-controlled car bomb. Just enough explosive was placed under the driver's seat to kill the three men while avoiding harming others. Detonation was delayed until the car reached a retaining wall on one side of the driveway and an open field on the other.[27]

. . . and in Tunis

The next blow against the PLO was far more important. On 16 April 1988 Israeli commandos assassinated Abu Jihad in his Tunis home. It was a ruthless operation of unsurpassed technical brilliance that combined thorough intelligence with flawless execution.

Seven Mossad operatives, using false Lebanese passports and speaking the right Arabic dialect to match, formed the advance party. The detailed reconnaissance of the PLO leader's villa and the route to it was carried out long before. The Mossad agents hired the three vehicles that had been used to bring the commandos – members of Sayeret Matkal (the elite reconnaissance unit attached to the IDF general staff) – from the beach where they landed in rubber dinghies that launched from a missile boat waiting safely offshore. An IAF Boeing 707 electronic warfare plane – Israel's DIY equivalent of the American AWACS – flying in international air space on flight path Blue 21 between southern Sicily and northern Tunisia, served as a command and control centre, linking the hit team with its mother ship.

On board the plane commanding the operation was General Ehud Barak, the former head of military intelligence and then the deputy chief of staff. The Mossad was represented by the deputy head of its Operations Branch. Jamming equipment was used on the ground to disrupt telephone and radio links in the Sidi Bou Said area, where Abu Jihad lived, ensuring the raiding party a safe retreat after the killing.

Considering the scale of the operation and the risks involved, it was mounted at fairly short notice. The plan was first mooted on 9 March, three days after three Palestinians who had infiltrated from Egypt seized a civilian bus in the Negev desert, near the Dimona nuclear reactor, and killed three of its passengers before dying themselves in the ensuing Israeli assault. The Israelis said that Abud Jihad had planned that and scores of other terrorist attacks, including the abortive *Atavarius* operation in April 1985. His killing was finally given the go-ahead on Wednesday, 13 April, three days before its execution.[28] The Tunis raid was strikingly similar to the operation codenamed 'Springtime of Youth' in April 1973, when a larger commando force, again guided by Mossad agents, landed in Beirut and killed three top PLO men.

Israel followed its usual practice and refused to admit officially that it was responsible for the killing. Yet the denials convinced no one. And when, contrary to normal practice, the censor permitted for publication press reports about the victim and the operation, this was universally taken to imply confirmation. The Mossad, responsible for targeting and producing psychological profiles of PLO leaders, did not underestimate Abu Jihad. A secret graphological test carried out on a sample of his handwriting five years earlier had found him to be a perfectionist of high intelligence with a precise and analytical mind.[29]

Unusually too, the killing of Abu Jihad met with considerable public criticism. 'We are trying to find Palestinians to talk to us,' said Ezer Weizman, the most 'dovish' member of the cabinet. 'We are trying to get the US to bring the two sides together. I don't think the assassination contributes to this. Liquidating individuals will not advance the peace process.' Weizman pointed out that the Tunis killing had come at a time when the intifada appeared to be waning as a result of Palestinian exhaustion and unprecedentedly tough Israeli countermeasures. Weizman had no compunction about shooting terrorist leaders. But, like other liberal Israelis, he recognized that Abu Jihad, who was on the right wing of the PLO and represented that awkward combination of violence and pragmatism that made the organization so morally and practically awkward to deal with, might, under the right circumstances, have become a man of compromise.

Others argued that it made better sense to talk to one's enemies rather than simply to kill them. As the *Ha'Aretz* columnist Yoel Marcus wrote:

> The Abu Jihad operation may make us feel good, may be good for our egos, but it does not in itself really address the weighty problems this country should be struggling with. The killing of Abu Jihad is a symbolic illustration of what is happening to us. It was an operation made for a nostalgia movie about the good old days of brilliant punitive raids – because it does not advance us one inch towards a solution of the problems that have produced this or that 'Abu'.

The killing had no obvious short-term results. What mattered was the message that had been sent: a combination of Israel's long and deadly arm with the useful addition of encouraging fear and suspicion of spies and traitors in Palestinian ranks. Amnon Shahak, the Aman chief, said in June: 'I believe it will take some time until all the roles he fulfilled are performed by others. I doubt they will be performed with the same, let's call it efficiency, or quality, with which Abu Jihad carried them out.'[30] Other officials privately admitted later that the effect of the killing was far less than had been expected.[31]

Protecting sources

One of the greatest difficulties for the Shin Bet as the uprising took its course was a spate of attacks on its network of collaborators. The Palestinians themselves knew far better than the outside world just how much the Israelis depended on them for information, in prison or outside, and the Popular Committees and 'Striking Forces' that had sprung up throughout the West Bank and Gaza Strip quickly targeted suspects.

Palestinians, like Israelis, had noticed the way in which some of the security service's dirty linen was being washed in public in the course of the Bus 300 scandal. Early in 1987, several months before the intifada began, an unsigned four-page Arabic leaflet, distributed in the militant Balata refugee camp in Nablus, reported in detail on the methods used by the Shin Bet and on how to take care to avoid falling victim to them.[32]

Special attention was devoted to sexual entrapment, in which photographs of young women were taken in compromising positions and then used to blackmail the subjects into collaboration. Women were warned not to frequent dress shops and beauty parlours where they did not know the owners, in case hidden cameras had been installed in dressing-rooms or drugs were used on unsuspecting victims. Threats to publish such pictures were clearly powerful weapons in a traditional Muslim society. Visits to the civil administration to receive licences or permits could be exploited by the Shin Bet, as could full-scale interrogations. Pretending that a prisoner or detainee had become an informer to expose him/her to the revenge of fellow inmates was said to be a common method.[33]

The High Court of Justice had ruled in July 1986 that the prison authorities had the right to keep a prisoner in solitary confinement for his own safety, even if the prisoner did not want to be isolated and felt no danger from his companions. Muhammad Hammad, a well-known informer, had decided to mend his ways, but was punished for doing so and kept in solitary. The lesson seemed to be: 'The authorities intend that a collaborator should remain a collaborator and they want to conceal the fact that for collaborators there is a way back.'[34]

The Bus 300 Affair had given some credibility to the authors of such anonymous leaflets and if they exaggerated the cunning or cruelty of their Israeli enemy, their accusations at least deserved serious examination. Another one that appeared in the same period accused the Shin Bet or its agents of the deaths of seven Palestinians who had been found dead in mysterious circumstances.[35]

Several well-known cases were strikingly similar. Bilal Najjar, a student at An-Najah University in Nablus, had disappeared in April 1984 and his headless corpse was found two weeks later. The police claimed he had died while handling explosives. Two other men were reported to have met their deaths in the same way near Nablus in July 1985. The same explanation was given for the death of Hassan Al-Faqiyah from Qatana in October 1985, even though many Palestinians found this explanation incredible. Faqiyah, half-blind and almost crippled, was a journalist who had been working on the sensitive issue of land sales to Israelis in the West Bank. He had been threatened by Palestinians from nearby Beit Sureik, where a lot of land had been sold to Israelis. Another Qatana man, Issa Shamassneh, was killed in similar circumstances in August 1986. A month later Hassan Alayan, a former prisoner from Gaza, was killed by an explosion while he worked in his fields. He had taken his mother with him, which suggested that an attempt to prepare a bomb was unlikely. Palestinian sources said he had been warned by the Shin Bet to stop his political activities. An American journalist who questioned a unnamed 'senior official' about some of these cases and the suspicions of foul play received the tantalizing answer: 'Maybe some of those who blew themselves up while preparing bombs received a little "help". So what? I prefer not to know.'[36]

Collaboration quickly became an important item on the agenda of the intifada. When the uprising began, Al-Quds, the PFLP-GC radio station operating from southern Syria, began regularly to broadcast the names and addresses of alleged collaborators. By April 1989 one-third of the 2,700 attacks carried out since the intifada began were perpetrated against mukhtars, mayors and other suspected collaborators.[37]

As one foreign journalist noted:

> Collaborators have long been part of the political and social landscape of the West Bank, as are the well-connected Arab intermediaries who, for a fee, arrange building and travel permits for residents, and the local Arab police or town officials who lead Shin Bet men after midnight to the houses of those targeted for arrest ... For many Palestinians, life under occupation seems a constant series of bottlenecks. At each bottleneck stands a Shin Bet agent who has the power to say yes or no. Anyone who wants to buy land, or build an addition to his house, or start a business or travel abroad must have a permit or a document. Often the price . . . is willingness to give information.[38]

The system was extensive and efficient: West Bank teachers seeking employment at Arab schools in East Jerusalem, for example, had to have a clean bill of health from the Shin Bet.[39]

Collaboration was a painful subject for the Palestinians, although some took comfort in the fact that it was a phenomenon common to all foreign occupations and one in which individual circumstances, far more than ideology, were the determining factor. As the British historian Richard Cobb wrote in his masterly study of France during the Second World War:

> Often there is only a very thin line between commitment to collaborationism, to resistance or to gaullisme; one should not exclude the

elements of luck and of chance, especially in the lottery of wartime that puts a special premium on unpredictability and that may hand out, with equally blind impartiality, the winning number or the tarot card of death.[40]

Lynch in Qabatiya

In some cases, especially in remote villages, collaborators were simply driven out by other Palestinians and forced to seek refuge in the cities or in Arab communities inside the green line. This happened in Yamoun, near Jenin, as early as January 1988. A turning-point came in Qabatiya, north of Nablus, on 24 February 1988, when one 'heavyweight' collaborator, Muhamad Ayad, was killed and his dead body strung up from a power pylon.[41] Ayad, who was typically recruited by the Shin Bet in the late 1960s while in prison for a security offence, was widely known to be working for the Israelis and often boasted about it. Six months previously someone had tried to plant a bomb in his car, but he chased away the perpetrators with the Uzi sub-machine-gun he was licensed to keep for his protection. Ayad was killed after opening fire on a hostile crowd, killing a child and wounding several others. More than ninety people were arrested and charged with taking part in what became known as the Qabatiya lynch.

Afterwards, following a call from the local mosque, several other collaborators turned in or publicly destroyed their weapons and swore on the Koran never to work for Israel again. Similar incidents were reported in Jenin and Tulkarm. In Beit Sahour, a prosperous Christian town near Bethlehem, collaborators begged forgiveness at church services.[42] Some penitents went to great lengths to prove that they had mended their ways: several cases were reported of former collaborators participating enthusiastically in attacks on members of the security forces. One such man from the West Bank village of Arraba shot and wounded two policemen before being gunned down himself.[43] The Shin Bet had warned of the possibility of attacks on collaborators and the army was blamed for having moved too slowly to save Ayad and prevent what one expert called 'the gravest development since the uprising broke out'.[44]

The Qabatiya warning was quickly heeded. Rapid deployment units were put on standby to help collaborators in distress. Some were equipped with radio transmitters or special phone lines linked to the nearest army headquarters.[45] In March 1988 the army blew up three homes in Bidiya, near Nablus, after an attack on a suspected collaborator. 'We will do everything we can to protect everyone,' declared Brigadier-General Shaike Erez, commander of the West Bank civil administration. 'We will hit back immediately at those who try to attack them and we will settle accounts with the attackers afterwards. The houses in Bidiya were blown up to make it clear to the whole village that we will not let anarchy prevail in Judaea and Samaria, and that we will not let people working with us get hurt.'[46]

Many collaborators were former members of the Village Leagues, founded in the late 1970s and beefed up when Ariel Sharon was defence minister in 1981 in an abortive attempt to turn the more backward rural areas of the West Bank against the PLO-dominated towns – an appendage to the grand strategy of which the invasion of Lebanon was the centrepiece. In mid-August Tahsin Mansour, chairman of the organization in the Tulkarm area and the mukhtar of nearby Azun, opened fire on youths he saw about to throw Molotov cocktails at Israeli vehicles.[47] Ten days later his car was stoned and he opened fire, wounding a youth in the crowd.[48] In a Christian village in the Jenin area a Village League man and his son terrorized other residents for months on end with their Uzis.[49]

In March 1988 the intifada took a dramatic step forward when Palestinian employees of the civil administration began to respond to calls by the PLO to resign from the posts 'and stop betraying their people before it is too late'. Here too violence and intimidation played a role. By mid-month, after the murder of an Arab policeman near Jericho, half the Arab policemen in the West Bank and Gaza Strip had resigned. Tax collectors quit too.

In April the acting mayor of Nablus threatened to resign and in June someone stabbed the mayor of Al-Bireh, one of about a dozen Palestinians appointed by the Israelis to replace nationalists who had resigned or been sacked in previous years. Some eighty-five village councils were also headed by Israeli appointees.

The attacks continued. Late in August 1988 a collaborator was hacked to death in Yatta, near Hebron. Four more were killed in September. These included As'ad Abu Ghosh, a Nablus man and former prisoner who was widely believed to be a Shin Bet informer. The bloody corpse of another Nabulsi was left hanging from a meat hook in the heart of the Old Casbah. Two more collaborators, including the mukhtar of Bidiya, were killed in October. It was the third attempt on his life. That month's other victim was shot dead in the Israeli Arab town of Umm al-Fahm, where he had fled from his home village in the West Bank after opening fire when his car was stoned.

Another effect of the attacks against collaborators was to expose further some of the nastier methods used by the Shin Bet to recruit them. Before the uprising these had been mentioned only in clandestine leaflets of limited circulation. But after it began Palestinians in Nablus, where the local security service commander, who went by the name of 'Abu Shawki', was well known, claimed repeatedly that these techniques included sexual entrapment and blackmail as well as the use of drug dealers and other underworld and criminal elements. Two prostitutes who were brutally murdered in the city in April and June 1989 were widely suspected of working for the Shin Bet and recruiting young girls to act as informers.

A typical case was that of Musalam Sharbati, an East Jerusalem man. He was arrested in March 1988 and claimed he faced deportation because he had refused to cooperate with the GSS. Sharbati had left for Jordan in 1976, served a prison sentence for drugs offences and returned to Israel in 1985. Seeking to renew his residence permit, he was sent to the

Russian Compound police HQ in Jerusalem, where a Shin Bet man called 'Abu Samir' told him he could stay in the country only if he agreed to serve as an informer. He refused and was forced to leave again for Jordan. When he returned to Jerusalem in 1987, he was arrested and appealed to the High Court.[50]

The Israeli public got a good look at this unsavoury subject in October 1989, when a Gaza man called Muhammad Halabi, who was a well-known drug dealer and pimp, was arrested for the murder of seven people in the shadowy criminal underworld in the slums of Jaffa and southern Tel Aviv. Halabi, a resident of the Jabaliya camp, had once worked as an informer for the Shin Bet, and the police let it be known that the security service had been wrong to give him permission to live inside Israel once his cover had been blown.[51]

Attacks on collaborators came in waves. At least twenty were recorded in April 1989 alone and of these at least eight ended in death; others almost certainly remained unreported. Leaflet number 38 issued by the United Leadership of the Uprising had designated 26 April as a 'day of reckoning' for collaborators. That month's targets included Israeli-appointed municipal or local council members, employees of the civil administration, mukhtars, bus or taxi drivers who transported Palestinians to work in Israel, an employee of Israel Radio and several other ordinary people accused of working with the authorities.

Palestinian activists identified several distinct categories of collaborators: land dealers, Shin Bet agents, police informers, people who maintained contact with the civil administration, mukhtars and other Israeli-appointed officials.[52] Generally, these were thankless positions to be in. 'Israel,' said one, 'treats collaborators like lemons: it squeezes the juice out of them until the last drop, and when it can make no further use of them, throws the skin away.'[53] 'Until the beginning of this intifada,' complained another, 'no one dared hurt us. The power was in our hands and they were afraid of us. But since the intifada started we don't know where we stand.'[54] Some 'heavyweight' collaborators became more aggressive the more uncertain the future looked. In July 1989 a group of armed collaborators entered Ya'abed village near Jenin and imposed a curfew.[55]

In some cases the accusation of collaboration clearly served simply as an excuse for the settling of accounts on personal or criminal grounds. But several allegations of rape were vigorously denied by Popular Committees or the Strike Forces charged with meting out punishment to collaborators. One Israeli newspaper found that charges of sexual abuse of the prostitutes who were later killed in Nablus and Gaza were baseless and that these were probably deliberate disinformation, designed to smear the image of the intifada.[56]

The spate of attacks in the spring of 1989 was linked by some observers to the fact that as the army withdrew some of its forces and relied less on physical presence and more on traditional intelligence-gathering and the use of special undercover military units, networks of Shin Bet informants were being reactivated or enlarged. When the army left Idna, near Hebron, in February 1989, several collaborators protested and Jewish settlers living nearby warned the Shin Bet that the consequences could be grave. 'As these [collaborators] pose a potentially deadly threat,' one Western correspondent wrote, 'they face correspondingly higher penalties from their own people.'[57] In an attempt to curb the phenomenon, the army began systematically to hunt down activists who attacked collaborators. Israel denied the existence of two IDF 'death squads' codenamed 'Cherry' (*duvdevan*) and 'Shimshon' (operating in the West Bank and Gaza Strip respectively), but Israeli newspapers documented several cases of the use of unmarked, unregistered civilian vehicles for special operations.[58] By December 1989, two years into the intifada, at least 150 Palestinians had been killed for collaboration, imagined or real.

Foot-soldiers of the uprising

The intifada was an unfamiliar phenomenon for the Israelis. Apart from the first few months after the 1967 war, there had never been anything approaching it for mass resistance and mobilization, and although there were periods of relative calm and a drop in the number of mass demonstrations, the iron-fist policy laid down by Yitzhak Rabin did not seem to work. 'This is not like Gaza in 1970, when there was a list of 300 wanted men and Sharon and his people crossed them off, one by one, until they got to the end,' said a senior security official. 'This is a mass movement, and when one name is crossed off another one or two take its place.'[59] Everyone realized this basic fact fairly quickly. 'Until the intifada,' said an intelligence officer with the Minorities Squad of the Jerusalem Police – which worked closely with the Shin Bet and carried out arrests on its behalf – 'we didn't need to be escorted by the Border Police to go into East Jerusalem. We just had to appear, two or three of us, and people would cross over to the other side of the street. Now things are different. They're not afraid, and that includes everybody, but mainly the children.'[60]

Salah Musa, a nineteen-year-old Palestinian from Jenin, was fairly typical of the generation that had grown up under Israeli rule and become the young activists of the uprising. He had worked in Israel and been a member of the Shabiba. In June 1988 he was asked by his local popular committee to build up a small cell, with general instructions to paint slogans, distribute leaflets and help organize attacks on collaborators – one of hundreds of similar groups that became known as the 'Striking Forces'. It was then that he came to the attention of the Shin Bet as a potential troublemaker. What he did could hardly be classified as clandestine activity. There were no codenames, no 'compartmentalization'; and when Musa decided to act, all he had to do was pop round the corner to collect his friends. On 30 August 1988 he and five others threw petrol bombs at the homes of several local people who were known to be cooperating with the civil administration. On 15 September they destroyed the premises of a shopkeeper accused of selling Israeli produce and disobeying the UNLU leaflets. A month later they assaulted an Arab policemen who had defied orders to resign and then attacked and wounded an Israeli driver in a chance encounter.

It was then that Musa formally entered the Shin Bet's 'wanted' category. He was arrested in early December, along with seven other youngsters from Jenin.[61]

By the end of the first year of the intifada, the security service was boasting that it had apprehended the perpetrators of nearly all attacks, either against collaborators or against Israelis. The Shin Bet, with a little PR help from friendly local journalists,[62] began to regain its poise. In a rare departure from normal practice (use of the generic and misleading term 'security forces' or 'security services'), the military censor allowed, and seemed even to encourage, the full mention of its formal name, the General Security Service.

In early December 1988, a day before the first anniversary of the outbreak of the uprising, Rabin publicly thanked the anonymous head of the Shin Bet for solving nearly ninety attacks and making over 600 arrests in October and November alone. The publication of Rabin's fulsome text was an unusual move that was seen as being designed to improve Shin Bet morale and advertise its deterrent ability. 'I see you in your daily work, in the alleys of Nablus, in Tulkarm, in Gaza and Khan Yunis,' Rabin wrote. 'I follow your efforts, your daring, resolution, courage, as well as the sophistication and resourcefulness you employ to apprehend murderers and terrorists.'

The organizational breakdown of the detailed figures issued by the defence ministry was highly revealing: ninety-three 'terrorist cells' were discovered from 1 October to 30 November. Sixty-two were in the West Bank, twenty-seven in the Gaza Strip and four inside Israel proper. Of these ninety-three, twenty-nine were Fatah cells, five DFLP, three PFLP, five Hamas, three Islamic Jihad and one Abu Nidal. The remaining forty-seven – almost exactly half – were described as 'local'. This statistic, more than anything else, attested to the unique, grass-roots nature of the intifada. The bulk of Palestinian resistance to Israeli occupation had become independent of the PLO and its organizational structures. Fighting that resistance meant fighting something far bigger than the Shin Bet, the army or anyone else had ever encountered before.

Politics, intelligence and the intifada

It was not only the mass character of the unrest that made the intifada different from any previous challenge to Israeli rule over the West Bank and Gaza Strip. The uprising set in train a series of events that were to change the political character of the Palestinian question in radical and unforeseen ways. Those changes in turn strengthened the spirit of Palestinian resistance, curbed Israel's ability to crush it and maintained a dynamic in which Israel's traditional twenty-year combination of carrot and stick, of security and collaboration, seemed increasingly ineffective.

The first landmark came at the end of July 1988, when King Hussein of Jordan finally severed his ties with the West Bank. The king's anger with the PLO had been growing since the collapse of the Amman Accord in February 1986, and this had been expressed in the subsequent closure of Fatah offices and the expulsion of Abu Jihad to faraway Tunis.

The cancellation of Jordan's ambitious development plan for the West Bank and its decision to dissolve parliament and end representation for West Bankers seemed like a victory for the intifada and final, grudging recognition from Amman that there really was no longer any 'Jordanian option' for making peace with Israel. The message was that in future the PLO would really have to go it alone.

In November 1988 the Israeli general election resulted in the creation of another national unity government, but this time without the rotation agreement produced by the deadlock of 1984. After weeks of tortuous and cliff-hanging coalition negotiations, the Likud's Yitzhak Shamir became prime minster again and the Labour leader, Shimon Peres, opted for the finance ministry. Foreign affairs were given to the Likud's Moshe Arens, who was no more flexible on the future of the West Bank than Shamir was.

On 15 November, while the coalition bargaining was still going on, the Palestine National Council met in Algiers and unilaterally declared Palestinian independence. Likud and

Labour buried their differences to dismiss this as a PR gimmick, even though by the end of the month over fifty countries, including the Soviet Union, had recognized the phantom state. The PNC's political statement called for a comprehensive solution based on the pre-1967 borders. It represented the clearest indication ever that the PLO would settle for a state in the West Bank and the Gaza Strip. In December Yasser Arafat, continuing his extraordinary peace offensive, addressed a special session of the UN General Assembly in Geneva, after Israel had persuaded the United States not to grant him a visa to go to UN headquarters in New York.

It was in Geneva that the PLO changed its spots – not enough to satisfy Israel, but sufficiently to convince the United States. Washington decided that the PLO had finally met the conditions laid down by Henry Kissinger in 1975; that Arafat, having denounced terrorism and accepted UN resolutions 242 and 338, which were generally interpreted as recognizing Israel, could take part in the regional peace process. The US decision came as a body blow to Israel, not only to the outgoing government in Jerusalem but also to a forty-year tradition of trying to solve the conflict with the Arabs with everyone but the Palestinians themselves.

Although the PLO had not initiated the uprising and despite its lack of total control over it, the intifada was the organization's most valued political asset. It had become, in the words of one perceptive Israeli expert, 'a sort of substitute for the loss of its Lebanese stronghold'.[63] And Israel seemed unable to stop it. The United States and the PLO began a 'substantive dialogue' just before Christmas.

'A monumental deception'?

As the intifada continued and the PLO started reaping diplomatic successes, some familiar questions began to be asked in Israel about the relationship between intelligence and policy-making. Were the Palestinian uprising and its far-reaching consequences another example of an intelligence blunder or oversight, an event that should or could have been foreseen? Yoel Ben-Porat, still crusading for full publication of the lessons of the great *mehdal* of 1973, thought it was: 'The intifada,' the former Aman officer argued, 'is a conceptual surprise that attacked the remnants of arrogance and conceit that prevailed in Israel on the eve of the Yom Kippur war.'[64] Yet it remained unclear quite where the precise responsibility lay for intelligence assessment pertaining in part at least to an area under Israeli rule. Brigadier Haim Yavetz, a senior officer in Aman research in the late 1970s, believed it was the job of the Shin Bet or the civil administration. Was it the task of military intelligence to predict the existence of a new Jewish underground? he asked rhetorically.[65] In any event, General Amnon Shahak, the new head of IDF Intelligence Branch, did not believe that he had committed any error. 'It was not within the sphere of Aman's responsibility to assess this development,' he insisted.[66]

Intelligence assessments, however, did not stand still. For several months, despite the restrictions of military censorship, Israeli newspapers had managed to hint at disagreements between IDF intelligence and the government, or at least its Likud wing under Yitzhak Shamir, over how to deal with the Palestinians, beyond the immediate and pressing question of the uprising.

The official position of the government, formulated after Arafat's dramatic appearance in Geneva, was that he and his organization were engaged in a 'monumental deception' and that the people of the occupied territories would still welcome an alternative to the PLO. IDF intelligence thought otherwise and had done for some time: 'Even if the PLO leadership is not directing the intifada,' General Shahak said in June 1988, 'it is certainly a participant. The residents here and the PLO leadership have one vision, and I don't think they are arguing amongst themselves about the shared goal. They speak the same language and believe in the same objectives.'[67]

In a verbal presentation of parts of Aman's semi-annual national intelligence assessment presented to the cabinet in

March 1989, Shahak told ministers that the PLO had indeed undergone a process of moderation; that the dialogue with the United States was likely to continue; and that no sane Palestinian in the West Bank or Gaza Strip would agree to act as a substitute for the PLO. An earlier Aman report, submitted to the cabinet in December 1988, had resulted in an official complaint from Shamir's office to both Shahak and Rabin.[68]

Details about the Aman assessment were leaked to journalists and created a political sensation that travelled abroad quickly. First reports concentrated on the view that Washington would not halt its dialogue despite attempts by the foreign minister, Moshe Arens, to persuade the Americans to do so. *Ha'Aretz* accurately reflected the Aman view. 'All recent intelligence assessments dealing with the PLO point to substantial changes in the organization's position,' the paper said, 'and there are differences only over Arafat's ability to win broad support for his strategy and for further concessions, especially concerning negotiations with Israel about an interim settlement in the occupied territories.'[69]

Shahak was defensive and somewhat self-effacing about the revelations:

> The political echelon makes political decisions based on the intelligence assessment. And Intelligence Branch does not recommend decisions or directions which the State of Israel should take. We do not recommend to the political echelon what to do. Our job is to provide the political echelon with the information with which to decide what to do . . . None of us has ever been part of a system that dealt with political matters beyond intelligence issues.[70]

The estimate submitted by the Mossad to the prime minister was less clear-cut than the Aman assessment, leading some experts to argue that the post-1973 intelligence pluralism had never proved really effective and that bet-hedging was still the dominant theme in its approach.[71]

Neither was the fourth and junior branch of Israel's intelligence community immune to these difficulties. In the summer of 1989, as the intifada reached its eighteenth month and the

PLO showed no signs of reverting to type, officials of the Foreign Ministry's Political Research Division expressed concern that the division's assessments on Jordan and the PLO 'were influenced by the political expectations of the ministry's senior echelons and no longer formed an objective analysis'.[72] 'The PLO may have changed eight points on a scale of ten,' said one official. 'But according to the Foreign Ministry's Jordan–PLO desk it's changed only two, and that's only in tactical terms.'[73]

Members of other branches of the intelligence community were surprised at the argument of the senior Foreign Ministry analyst in charge of Jordan and the PLO – that the PLO had not undergone any substantive change. This was precisely the position adhered to religiously by the foreign minister, Moshe Arens, and his deputy, Binyamin Netanyahu. Netanyahu, a rising star in the Likud, had been Israel's ambassador to the United Nations and was a self-styled expert on international terrorism, not least, his critics said, because his brother, Yoni Netanyahu, had died in the legendary Entebbe rescue operation in 1976.

Secret servants, public images

If the Israeli intelligence community had a stormy time in the 1980s, this was partly because it had been forced, in spite of itself, to emerge slightly from the shadows and had thus become increasingly exposed to public scrutiny. Even the legendary Mossad had its share of scandals. The Bus 300 Affair, it seemed to many, was the result of the central role the Shin Bet had come to play in Israeli life, or at least in Palestinian life, since the 1967 war. The Lebanese experience showed just how badly things could go wrong, and how badly the secret servants could behave. The security service, which had once worked quietly and virtually unaccountably behind the scenes and had been almost unknown to the Jewish public, was seen to have become the dominant body dealing with the occupied West Bank and Gaza Strip, creating a strangely close, almost intimate, relationship with the people it ruled.

Towards the end of the decade a perceptive Israeli writer, Yigal Sarna, looked at the unclassified evidence that had been gathered during a Shin Bet interrogation of Faisal Abu Sharah, a Force 17 officer from Dahariya near Hebron who had been captured by the Israeli navy at sea while sailing from Lebanon to Cyprus:

The file fascinated me, because it opened a window on to a world which we barely know, a world of hidden struggle where the Israeli and the Palestinian fight their battle of life and death. If someone were to take everything that's been written about the Palestinians in the State of Israel since the beginning of the conflict – details of lives, families, daily routine – literature will lag far behind the archives of the security forces. The archive of the Shin Bet will give a very precise picture, from its own particular angle, and far more comprehensive than what is available in Hebrew literature. The security service, more than any other Zionist body, is the strongest link between us and them.[74]

This rough intimacy was given powerful expression in the summer of 1987, when Israeli newspapers and magazines, as well as the vast Jerusalem-based foreign press corps, were marking the twentieth anniversary of the 1967 war with endless special supplements and in-depth features. David Grossman, a talented young novelist, wrote a series of articles, later expanded into a best-selling book, about life on both sides of the green line two decades after it was erased by the Israeli victory. Grossman devoted an entire chapter of *The Yellow Wind* to 'Gidi', known as 'Abu Deni' to the Palestinians, a young Shin Bet officer serving in the West Bank. Grossman caught something of the constricting closeness of the unequal relationship between Israelis and Palestinians from 'Gidi's' peculiar angle, as well as the deep hostility lurking just beneath the surface.

Grossman's 'Gidi'

thought that he did not want to be there, in the twilight area created when two peoples turn their dark, corrupt sides toward each other, and the thought startled him, because he loved his work and believed in it, and felt that it gave him the necessary rules with which to navigate through his life. But he also knew clearly that when two apples touch one another at a single point of decay, the mold spreads over both of them.[75]

The Yellow Wind became a cult, and its translation into English, Arabic and other languages won it a deserved place as a sharp and sensitive portrayal of the realities of occupation. Grossman wrote the Shin Bet chapter, called 'A Swiss Mountain View', as fiction, partly to evade the censor, who would have been unlikely to permit such a revealing interview with a real security service officer, but he made clear that it was based on documentation.[76] In the original Hebrew edition, *HaZman HaTsahov*, the chapter was subtitled 'A story – perhaps'.

Opening the closet door a little sometimes served the purposes of the secret services themselves. When Yosef Harmelin stepped down in March 1988 after completing his interim tenure, and the Shin Bet was embroiled in the intifada, the service's new director – an internal candidate unscathed by the ructions of the Bus 300 scandal – adopted a new high-profile approach that must have made some of his more discreet predecessors shudder.

In February 1989 he was given a surprise party at the Israel Museum in Jerusalem, where he did nothing more sinister than celebrate his forty-fifth birthday and play the trumpet. Yossi Sarid, a voluble member of the 'dovish' opposition Citizen Rights Movement, was one of many guests who enjoyed the party, especially the birthday boy's five-minute rendering of Gershwin's 'Summertime'. 'I'd rather have a Shin Bet chief who plays his trumpet into the microphones than one who plants microphones,' Sarid quipped.[77] It was, the gossip columnists said afterwards, the social event of the week, a secret policeman's ball to which only the select were invited.[78] The journalist Nahum Barnea put the party into neat and amusing historical perspective:

Some of the guests said that if Yosef Harmelin, the former Shin Bet chief, had been there, he would have had the shock of his life, to say nothing of Avraham Ahituv, who'd have sacked the lot of them, or Avraham Shalom, who would have ordered them beaten to death. And Isser Harel? He would have sent letter-bombs to all the guests, and then written a vicious book about them.[79]

There was even talk in this period of glasnost of appointing an official spokesman for the security service, and several leading journalists were discreetly consulted about how this could best be done. One of them, ironically, was the editor of *HaOlam HaZeh*, Uri Avneri, who had attacked the Shin Bet, when Isser Harel and Amos Manor were in charge back in the 1950s, as the 'apparatus of darkness'.[80]

At around the same time an unusual blow was struck at the secrecy surrounding the Mossad. The High Court of Justice authorized for publication an article in the Tel Aviv weekly paper *Ha'Ir* which cast doubts on the competence of the Mossad chief, Nahum Admoni, but preserved his anonymity. It was the first time ever that the military censor had been overruled by a court, and legal experts believed that the judgment could have far-reaching implications.[81]

The *Ha'Ir* article was first submitted to the censor in August 1988 and was banned. Several amended versions were also banned, until one was finally approved, although with thirty-two passages deleted. The banned sections contained a description of the Mossad chief, criticism of his performance and details about his planned replacement. Brigadier-General Yitzhak Shani, the chief censor, argued that if the article were published, it might diminish the Mossad's ability to operate. The court ruled that the article must omit any details which might identify the Mossad chief, but went on: 'The way to achieve a balance between security and freedom of speech is to maintain freedom of speech and to apply restrictions only when there is absolute certainty of a real threat to the country's security and when no alternative is available.'[82]

Admoni paid the price for years of excessive secrecy and the virtual lack of external control or supervision of the Mossad. The *Ha'Ir* article and the spate of others that followed blamed him for six years of unimaginative leadership in which caution had been the driving spirit. 'Imagine appointing a good adjutant to be the IDF chief of staff,' one of his enemies said. On the eve of the Jewish New Year, Rosh HaShana, Admoni had gathered his employees in the Mossad canteen and said: 'I wish us all a year without mistakes.' Another critic explained: 'If you are looking for one sentence that characterizes his style and method, that's the one.'[83]

The service's failures since the war in Lebanon – the Ismail Sowan case and the expulsions of Mossad men from the UK, forgetting the forged, blank British passports found in a West German phone box, the embarrassments of the Pollard Affair and Irangate – were all detailed by the scandal-hungry Israeli press. But its successes went unmentioned. The censor did not allow the new wave of publicity to extend very far. *Hadashot* headlined its story 'And who liquidated Abu Jihad?', but was able to make no mention of the event itself, nor, for that matter, of the bombing of PLO headquarters in Tunis.[84] The little new information that did come out was neither flattering nor significant. *Yediot Aharonot* revealed that Admoni was a snappy dresser who was known by insiders as 'Mr Gucci'.[85] Admoni was also blamed for an incident in Athens in 1988 when a PLO official had spotted a man and woman trying to photograph him in the street and had complained to the police, who had quickly discovered that the two – named as Menachem Zim and Daliya Eyal – were Mossad agents.[86]

Shortly after the *Ha'Ir* article was finally published, on 13 January 1989, it was announced that Admoni was about to retire. His replacement was an internal candidate – only the second time this had happened in the service's history. The new Mossad chief was a veteran of Sayeret Matkal, the famed IDF General Staff Reconnaissance Unit, had joined in the 1960s and, unlike his predecessor, spent most of his career 'on the dark side of the house', running some successful covert operations.[87]

Until he left, Nahum Admoni's name had remained classified, and Israeli newspapers and foreign correspondents based in the country were permitted to quote only from a foreign source which had, a few years earlier, mistakenly published the Mossad chief's names as Nahum Adnoni. The error was finally corrected after the High Court judgment, but Israel's most secret service crawled back into its shell.

Just how anxious it was to stay there became apparent in a uniquely embarrassing way in September 1990. As the world was preoccupied by the Iraqi occupation of Kuwait – the Mossad, like other intelligence agencies, failed to predict it – Israel applied to a Canadian court to halt publication of a book called *By Way of Deception: The Making and Unmaking of a Mossad Officer*.

Its author, a Canadian-born Israeli called Victor Ostrovsky, had served as a Mossad collection officer – a *katza* (the Hebrew acronym for *katzin issuf*) – for just seventeen months, from October 1984 to March 1986, when he was dismissed. The book was the single most comprehensive exposure ever of the agency's structure and operations. It contained the names of dozens of personnel (there were, it claimed, just 1,200 in all) and station chiefs, gave codenames of units and locations of premises, and described operational methods including assassinations, sexual blackmail and other ways of recruiting agents.

Yet the book owed its success largely to Israeli ineptitude. The government's decision to take legal action to prevent its appearance, first in Canada, and then in the US, was doomed to failure. All that was necessary was to contemplate the prolonged and ultimately abortive attempt by the British government to halt publication of *Spycatcher*, the memoirs of the former MI5 officer Peter Wright. In the US there was outrage from civil liberties groups. And the New York court which overturned a restraining order against publication ruled that Israel had provided no concrete evidence that its national security would be harmed if *By Way of Deception* was allowed to appear. The short but high-profile legal battle provided undreamed-of publicity for Ostrovsky: 15,000 copies were sold within hours of the court decision.

Former heads of the Mossad, like the ever-garrulous Isser

Harel, spoke angrily of the grave damage the book would cause, just as he had when American newspapers published the classified CIA report on Israel's intelligence community that had been captured from the US Embassy in Tehran after the Iranian revolution of 1979. Others disagreed with this knee-jerk reaction: 'There is nothing true in that book that wouldn't be known to rival intelligence services anyway,' one political source said. 'The problem is how much will be believed by US politicians and what effect it would have on American public opinion.'

With the Pollard affair a fading memory, Ostrovsky revived the old question of spying on allies. He described a super-secret 27-member Mossad unit – codenamed 'Al' – used for espionage operations in the US, and said: 'Their primary task is to gather information on the Arab world and the PLO as opposed to gathering intelligence about US activities, but the dividing line is often blurred and, when in doubt, Al does not hesitate to cross over it.'

He touched an especially raw nerve with the claim that the Mossad had forewarning of the Shi'ite terrorist truck-bomb attack on the US Marines headquarters in Beirut in 1983, in which more than 240 American servicemen were killed, but that it failed to notify Washington in the hope that the attack would ruin US–Arab relations. Ostrovsky said that the Mossad had specific information that the Hizbullah organization was preparing a Mercedes lorry packed with explosives for the attack. Nahum Admoni, he revealed, decided not to pass this intelligence on, and told his men: 'We are not here to defend the Americans. They're a big country. Just send them the normal information.' Thus the Americans were given only a routine and general warning, one of scores they received in Lebanon in this period. Admoni did not respond to the charge, but Yehoshua Saguy, Aman chief during the Lebanon war, vigorously denied it.

Generally, though, such claims were impossible to either prove or refute. Ostrovsky's account was given verisimilitude by the sprinkling of names of personnel, codewords of units and secret locations throughout the book. But his revelation that the Mossad training centre was located at Glilot, on the coast north of Tel Aviv, surprised few Israelis. No one was convinced by his claim that orgies involving women soldiers were a regular feature of its courses. Nor was his credibility enhanced by the unlikely allegation that it was the Mossad which had brought about the resignation of the then Labour Prime Minister, Yitzhak Rabin, in 1977, by leaking information about an illegal bank account maintained by his wife in Washington. The *Ha'Aretz* journalist involved, Dan Margalit, denied the entire story.

Ostrovsky became the object of a concerted smear campaign in the Israeli press. It was argued that because of the 'compartmentalization' of diffferent Mossad departments and the application of the 'need-to-know' principle, the short period he had spent on full-time employment in the service could simply not have been enough for him to have learned so many secrets. The implication was that he was a talented fabricator.

Yet many of his stories had the ring of truth about them, especially when they confirmed previous suspicions or allegations. His account of Mossad operations against Iraq's nuclear programme, for example, or assassinations of Palestinians, fitted in with what was already widely known and has been described here and elsewhere. His claim to have been involved in the surveillance operation which led to the mistaken forcing-down of a Libyan jet in 1986 – and, in revenge by Syria, to the Hindawi affair – was credible. It was his role in that case that led to his dismissal.

Ostrovsky was an embittered man anxious to convey the impression that his motives were idealistic, that he had a duty to expose his former employers as evil. But, in Israel at least, he convinced no one. For an idealist, much of his exposure was gratuitous and transparently cynical: when he wrote that thousands of Jews all over the world routinely volunteered to help Mossad operations, he claimed to be motivated by concern for their safety. When he described and even named Arabs who had worked for Israel – in Syria, Iraq, Libya and inside the PLO –

he quite clearly endangered their lives. And he seemed to be confused: for the Mossad, he conceded in interviews, was necessary to Israel's security.

Ostrovsky hurt the Mossad in the same way that Mordechai Vanunu hurt the security of the country's nuclear capability. He provided what appeared to be inside confirmation of suspicions, which, however strong, could not be publicly confirmed except by someone who was prepared to be a whistle-blower and to accept the possible consequences. His book was embarrassing: if an intelligence agency cannot manage to keep its own innermost secrets, especially ones whose publication might adversely affect its liaison with friendly services, how effective can it be? It did not really matter that units and personnel had been identified, for code or cover names can be, and routinely are, changed: it was of little importance, for example, that what he described as the Mossad's 'assassinations unit' was called *Kidon*, Hebrew for 'bayonet'; what mattered was that an inside source had described the existence of such a unit, even if no one was really surprised by the revelation.

Shin Bet recovers

Towards the end of the decade, the Shin Bet continued its new high-profile approach, basking in the considerable successes it notched up as its most pressing preoccupation, the intifada, continued. By the time the uprising reached its second anniversary, in December 1989, the security service's performance was definitely improving. As the Palestinians in the West Bank and Gaza Strip tired of their long struggle and the human and economic sacrifices it required, the character of the unrest gradually changed. The mass stone-throwing demonstrations of the first year gave way to hit-and-run attacks by small groups of young masked activists. And when it came to these smaller numbers of people, who were organized in classic cell-like structures, the Shin Bet's intelligence system still worked, despite the killing of so many alleged informers. Its heavyweight sources, it seemed, had been virtually untouched by the internecine bloodletting in the enemy camp.[88] It operated ever more closely with the army, which appointed special liaison officers to maximize the use of intelligence about fugitives;[89] as happened in Gaza in the early 1970s, soldiers were issued with long lists of wanted men. Because of the multidigit identity card numbers that accompanied the names, the Palestinians became known as 'bingos'.

In the final months of the year Shin Bet agents working with the army tracked down and killed or captured the members of two small Fatah-affiliated armed groups, Black Panther and the Red Eagle, both linked to the PFLP, that had operated in Nablus, largely against collaborators. It was announced that the head of the Shin Bet had personally visited the West Bank city to congratulate his men there on a job well done. Several months before that the service had made hundreds of arrests and broken up the entire military wing of the Hamas movement in the Gaza Strip, although some Palestinians argued that the Islamic militants, who were less accustomed than PLO veterans to the ways of clandestine struggle, were a relatively easy target. Interrogations in the Shin Bet wing of Gaza gaol, where three detainees died (under torture, according to their lawyers and relatives) during the intifada, were said to be especially brutal.[90] Two service interrogators were suspended and charged with manslaughter in one of these Gazan cases, giving rise to grave doubts as to whether the recommendations ('moderate physical pressure') of the Landau Commission were really being implemented.[91] Prisoners continued to be a vital source of intelligence. At the end of 1989 10,000 Palestinians were still in detention.

These successes were not quite a throwback to the first years after the 1967 war, when the security service had so comprehensively crushed the first signs of armed resistance to the occupation, but they at least gave the impression that things were not, after all, out of control. The numbers of prisoners alone attested to the degree to which participation in the intifada was still a mass phenomenon.

And in the longer term, too, there was mounting concern about the effect of the uprising on the country's 18 per cent Arab minority living inside the pre-1967 borders. The Shin Bet was still responsible for monitoring their activities, and the signs of the community's increasing radicalization – the rise of Islamic fundamentalism and identification with the goals of the PLO – were a factor that could not be ignored in any national strategy for the future.[92] The service repeatedly argued that the government should grant full rights and supply equal services to try and blunt dissent among Arab citizens.[93]

In the first months of 1990 the Shin Bet showed that it was still capable of holding down Palestinian resistance in the West Bank and Gaza Strip to a tolerable level and that its long-tried *modus operandi* had not been neutralized by the intifada. By early summer 280 collaborators had been resettled, for their own safety, inside the 'green line.'

And the uprising, already waning, suffered blow after grievous blow. In May, after an abortive seaborne attack on the Israeli coast by the Palestine Liberation Front – led by Abu al-Abbas of *Achille Lauro* fame – the US halted its dialogue with the PLO, robbing the organization of the greatest political achievement of the 'war of stones.' That this coincided with the collapse of Israel's rickety Likud–Labour national unity coalition and its replacement by a new right-wing Likud government was another nail in the coffin of Palestinian aspirations. In August 1990, when Iraq invaded Kuwait, Palestinians everywhere – including in the occupied territories – lined up in enthusiastic support for Saddam Hussein. The Gulf crisis caused them grave political and economic damage, battering their dialogue with the Israeli left, halting vital financial support from Arab countries, and further overshadowing their own struggle.

All this made life easier for the Shin Bet. It went on, galvanized by the conviction that internal security had to be maintained so that Israel, if it ever came to that, could negotiate from strength, not weakness, about the future of the West Bank and Gaza. The security service was held in high esteem by the country's political leaders, but its job was to assist and advise the government, not to make high policy. Yet, like the IDF, it had growing doubts as to just how long it could manage without the achievement of that most elusive of goals, a political solution to the Arab–Israeli conflict.

Conclusion

Israelis began to re-examine some of their more enduring myths in the 1980s, and the country's intelligence community was no exception. Hebrew literature – as good a guide as any to self-images, if not to reality – caught up belatedly with the development of the spy story elsewhere and portrayed the secret agent as a flawed, not a perfect hero. Ambiguities and ironies crept in. Amos Oz, Israel's most famous living novelist, created a Mossad man, warts and all, lost in the moral no man's land of agent-running, as dishonest in his private life as he was in his secret profession.[1] Fictional Shin Bet agents, like David Grossman's 'Gidi', began to have their doubts about the job.[2] Yitzhak Ben-Ner drew a picture of an ageing and embittered security service officer troubled to the core of his being by having to deal with the Palestinian intifada in the occupied territories.[3] The literary secret servants, in short, were losing their legendary touch.

These images owe much to the dismal exposure of Israeli intelligence in recent years; yet they may be misleading. For a history that oscillates violently between astonishing successes, blighting failures and explosive public scandals cannot be complete until all the secrets – or at least the important ones – finally emerge. And between the dramatic coups and the bitter recriminations lies a long, grey, silent routine of watchfulness whose full story will never be told.

How is it possible to understand fully the history of the Second World War without knowledge of the Ultra operation that enabled the Allies to crack Axis codes and anticipate enemy moves? How can one comprehend the crucial role of British counter-intelligence without understanding the now famous 'Double-Cross System', in which Nazi agents in Britain were successfully 'turned' in their prison cells and forced to feed false information to their unsuspecting controllers?

Questions of a similar scale and importance must trouble any honest student of Israeli intelligence. In their different ways the strange cases of Ismail Sowan, Nezar Hindawi and Jonathan Pollard each illuminated some very dark, sensitive and contemporary corners: the degree of penetration of the PLO and the armed forces and secret services of Arab states; the extent of intelligence cooperation with the United States. Until the archives of Israel's secret services are opened, questions about subjects as vital as these simply cannot be answered in a definitive way. And publicly, of course, they may well never be.

Yet these are definable gaps in our knowledge – all historians face them – not insurmountable barriers to understanding. Although the picture that emerges from this overview of half a century of clandestine warfare is complex and variable, and is still fuzzy and unclear at some important points, certain firm conclusions about different periods, including the present day, are still inescapable. Even the tips of icebergs help us envisage something of the unseen mass beneath the surface.

Israel has consistently been good at human intelligence, the oldest form of spycraft, which remains, despite sophisticated surveillance satellites, computer cryptanalysis and the other vast technological advances of recent years, the best way to find out what an enemy is doing, thinking and planning. This achievement is all the more remarkable in the Israeli context, for the circumstances of the state's birth and existence present unusual problems. The classic ideological spy, motivated by a belief in the system of his own country's enemy, does not exist in the Middle East conflict. There are no closet Arab Zionists, no Syrian, Iraqi, Egyptian or Palestinian Kim Philbys who believe that the transformation of Palestine into Israel, the dispossession and partial exile of an Arab people, is a good and positive thing. Yet still the agents and their controllers meet in their safe houses and communicate via dead-letter boxes. Ezra Danin, the Shai pioneer who began recruiting Palestinian informers to follow the course of the general strike of 1936, would feel quite at home with his Shin Bet successors trying to penetrate cells of intifada activists in 1989. In the 'second oldest profession', like the first, some things never really change.

Ingenuity, ruthlessness and dishonesty have played their part in this history, as they have done, and continue to do, to a greater or lesser degree, in the work of all intelligence and security services everywhere. 'False flags' can be used for recruitment, agents can be blackmailed, pressured and coerced. They can also be, and more often are, paid handsomely for their services. Dangerous enemies can be killed, without any obvious moral qualms. Lies are told, at home and abroad. Denials may often be implausible, but the only crime is being caught. '*A la guerre*,' as the French say, '*comme à la guerre*.'

Another vital strand is Israel's unique ability to staff its secret services with men and women who can pass convincingly for the nationals and speak the languages of most countries on earth, including all its Arab enemies. The Palmah Mist'Aravim of the 1940s represented a modest beginning for a long and fruitful tradition, although concern has been expressed in recent years that the absence of new Jewish immigrants from elsewhere in the Middle East and the declining interest in Arabic language and culture – itself a reflection of the continuing conflict – is damaging that ability.

A paradox leaps out of these pages across all the years. Israeli intelligence has a fine reputation that is based justly on some of the famous world-class coups that have been described here. Remember the acquisition of Krushchev's de-Stalinization speech; the theft of the Iraqi MiG and the Mirage production secrets from Switzerland; the meticulous intelligence preparations that guaranteed the dazzling success of the decisive Israeli air strike in June 1967; the almost total defeat of armed Palestinian resistance in the late 1960s and the subsequent containment of terrorism at home and abroad to tolerable dimensions; the legendary Entebbe rescue in 1976.

And then recall the repeated failures, usually of early warning, when it came to the major test of war and strategic change. The Shai failed to accurately predict or chart the Arab invasion of Palestine in 1948. Aman misread the meaning of Egyptian and Jordanian moves in May 1967 and failed to provide adequate warning of the Arab onslaught in October 1973, even though the Mossad controlled a remarkable agent who was sufficiently well informed to know almost exactly when the attack would begin. IDF intelligence and the Mossad helped shepherd Israel into the disastrous war against the PLO in Lebanon in 1982, gambling fatally on the Christians and then gravely underestimating the hostility of the Shi'ite Muslims. Both agencies emerged sullied by their failures. This grim catalogue may do little more than highlight the known limits of intelligence and the dangers, especially apparent in the Mossad's Lebanese experience, of mixing collection and analysis with actual operations. Nevertheless, these are still striking failures. Good, even excellent organizations failed to deliver precisely at those crucial moments for which they were created.

Israel's failure in a related field, to foresee the end of the Gulf War between Iran and Iraq in 1988, was widely taken as a warning sign that could have more worrying implications elsewhere. Nearer home, on a smaller but no less significant scale, the outbreak and persistence of the Palestinian uprising in the West Bank and Gaza Strip in 1987 was a failure by the Shin Bet and Aman to read the changing political and psychological map of the enemy camp. This too raised old questions about the ability of intelligence agencies to see the wood when so many trees, often individual branches and even leaves, are so comprehensively monitored. Tactical virtuosity is one thing; strategic blindness another.

Another theme worth noting is the varying role of Israel's intelligence chiefs at different times. 'Little' Isser Harel dominated security for fifteen years because he had Ben-Gurion's ear and also a keen sense of the value of his own advice about domestic political matters as well as about foreign espionage. Harel also enjoyed a deserved reputation as a rare genius of clandestine operations: the kidnapping of Adolf Eichmann helped salve the terrible wounds of the Nazi Holocaust with a strong dose of Israeli persistence and derring-do. In the early 1950s the Aman director Yehoshafat Harkabi had his doubts about the efficacy of the IDF's reprisal raids in deterring fedayeen attacks, but his thought had little effect on policy.

When the towering figure of David Ben-Gurion disappeared into the political wilderness in 1963, the role of Israel's intelligence community in national decision-making increased significantly. Meir Amit of the Mossad fought and won against Levi Eshkol over the Ben Barka Affair. And his contemporary as Aman chief, Aharon Yariv, had a crucial impact on policy in the tense days before the 1967 war. Both the Mossad and the Shin Bet – especially the latter – enabled Israel to hold on to the occupied West Bank and Gaza Strip by containing Palestinian resistance to an acceptable level. Success bred complacency and the political solutions were left – as was only proper – to the politicians. But those solutions were never found.

The great disaster of 1973 sapped confidence in intelligence. In 1976 the politicians ignored the advice of the Shin Bet and let pro-PLO candidates sweep to victory in the West Bank elections. And the following year the same agencies that had failed to foresee the Yom Kippur War failed to foresee Anwar Sadat's peace initiative, despite the wide-ranging reforms ordered by the Agranat Commission. In 1982 Menachem Begin and his ministers knowingly chose to ignore the fact that the attempt on the life of the Israeli ambassador in London had been carried out not by the PLO but by Yasser Arafat's arch-rival, Abu Nidal. Begin invaded Lebanon anyway. Politics and intelligence do not always make comfortable bedfellows.

Israel's secret services have always gone far beyond the traditional tasks of espionage and counter-espionage. Early operational versatility – a product of the circumstances in which the Yishuv laboured towards statehood from the mid-1930s – was carried over into the years of independence. Clandestine immigration and arms acquisition did not end in 1948. The operations to bring Iraqi and Moroccan Jews to Israel in the 1950s and 1960s were mirrored by the exodus of the black Jews of Ethiopia in the 1980s. Such activities were made possible by, and were a powerful spur to, the Mossad's unique tradition of maintaining secret links with countries – including Arab states like Morocco and Sudan – which cannot or will not establish open diplomatic ties with it.

Obtaining weapons and advanced technologies secretly, and often illegally, and denying them to enemies remain a preoccupation. In 1948 Shai agents sank a boat taking war material to Syria, hijacked the one sent to replace it and then stole its cargo of weapons. In the 1950s Aman exploited its intelligence capabilities to supply France with priceless information about the Algerian rebels and constructed a pivotal alliance with Paris to update Israel's arsenals and acquire an independent nuclear capability. In the early 1960s the Mossad waged a ruthless secret war of threats and assassinations against German scientists building rockets in Nasser's Egypt. In 1981 Israel stunned the world by bombing Iraq's nuclear reactor. In 1989 the Mossad mounted a campaign against scientists building rockets for Iraq and Egypt. *Plus ça change* . . .[4] Using the media to disseminate stories and warnings that help Israeli operations and undermine the country's enemies has long been a speciality.

In the last decade of the twentieth century, over forty years into Israel's existence, the main function of its intelligence services remains the assessment and prediction of Arab military intentions and capabilities. Much of that is carried out by Aman, using the advanced technologies now at its disposal. Israel is surrounded on land by countries with which it is formally in a state of war – Syria, Jordan and Lebanon – and it still rules over rebellious Palestinians, who are probably closer today than ever before to achieving the independence that for so long has been beyond their grasp. Beyond the immediately hostile countries lie large and powerful Arab or Muslim states that continue to pose a threat. Israel's secret wars go on. Yet if there is a single lesson in this turbulent history it is that the importance of intelligence can be overrated. It is, in the final analysis, no more than a tool – one whose capabilities and limitations must be recognized precisely by those who use it –

not a substitute for policy. In a more perfect world, knowing one's enemies would be used to try and make peace with them. Until then – in Israel and elsewhere – the spies will have their day.

Glossary

(H.) Hebrew
(A.) Arabic
(acr.) acronym

AHC: Arab Higher Committee
Al-Asifa: (A.) military wing of Fatah ('The Storm')
Aliya: (H.) immigration to Israel ('ascent')
Aman: (H. acr.) Agaf HaModi'in (IDF 'Intelligence Branch')

BGA: Ben-Gurion Archives
Biyun: (H.) intelligence, espionage
BND: Bundesnachrichtendienst (West German foreign intelligence service)
Bricha: (H.) escape

CIA: Central Intelligence Agency (USA)
CID: Criminal Investigation Department (Britain)
CZA. Central Zionist Archive

DFLP: Democratic Front for the Liberation of Palestine
DST: Direction de la Surveillance du Territoire (France)

ECM: Electronic countermeasures
EIMAC: Egypt-Israel Mixed Armistice Commission

FAHA: (H. acr.) Pe'ilut hablanit 'oyenet (Hostile Sabotage Activity)
Fatah: (A. acr.) Reverse acronym of Harakat al-Tahrir al-Filastiniya (Palestine Liberation Movement)

Fedayeen: (A.) guerrillas ('self-sacrificers')
FLN: Front de Libération Nationale (Algeria)

GSS: General Security Service (see Shabak)

Haganah: (H.) Pre-state underground army ('defence')
Hamas: (A. acr.) Harakat al-Muqawama al-Islamiya (Islamic Resistance Movement)
Histadrut: labour federation
Hizbullah: (A.) Party of God

IAF: Israel Air Force
IDF: Israel Defence Forces
IL: Israeli Lira – official name of old Israeli currency
Intifada: (A.) uprising
Irgun: (H.) right-wing Zionist underground group
Irgun Bet: Precursor of Irgun
ISA: Israel State Archive

JAE: Jewish Agency Executive
Jihad: (A.) holy war
Jihaz ar-Rasd: (A.) 'Surveillance Apparatus', PLO counter-intelligence
JNF: Jewish National Fund

Katam: (H. acr.) Katzin leTafkidim Meyuhadim ('Special Duties Officer')
KMA-PA: Kibbutz Meuhad Archives-Palmah Archive

Lakam: (H. acr.) Lishka LeKishrei Mad'a ('Scientific Liaison Bureau')
Lehi: (H. acr.) Lohamei Herut Yisrael ('Fighters for the Freedom of Israel'), a small, radical terrorist group that broke away from the Irgun in 1940–41, the better to pursue the struggle for national liberation against the British. Also known as the Stern Gang.

Mapai: (H. acr.) Mifleget Po'alei Eretz Yisrael (Israeli Labour Party)
Matkal: (H. acr.) Mate Klali (IDF 'General Staff')
Mehdal: (H.) blunder or oversight
MI5: British Security Service
MI6: British Secret Intelligence Service
MI9: British organization that helped POWs escape from Germany

Mist'Aravim: (H.) Palmah Arab Platoon ('Arabizers')
Modi'in: (H.) intelligence
Mossad: (H. Mossad LeBiyyun U'Letafkidim Meyuhadim) ('Institute for Espionage and Special Duties')
Mu'aradun: (A.) opposition
Mufti: (A.) Muslim religious leader
Mukhabarat: (A.) security police

NGC: National Guidance Committee
Nokmim: (H.) Avengers
NSA: National Security Agency (USA)

OAS: Organisation de l'Armée Secrète (France)
OSS: Office of Strategic Services (USA)

Palmah: (H. acr.) Plugot Mahatz ('Striking Companies')
Peshmerga: Kurdish guerrilla fighters
PFLP: Popular Front for the Liberation of Palestine
PFLP-GC: Popular Front for the Liberation of Palestine-General Command
PLA: Palestine Liberation Army
PLF: Palestine Liberation Front
PLO: Palestine Liberation Organization
PNC: Palestine National Council
PRO: Public Record Office

Qadi: Muslim religious judge

RAF: Royal Air Force
Rekhesh: (H.) clandestine arms procurement
Rigul: (H.) espionage
Rigul negdi: (H.) counter-espionage

SAVAK: (Farsi acr.) Sazman-e Amniyat va Ittilaat e-Keshvar (Iran)
Sayeret Matkal: (H.) General Staff Reconnaissance Unit
SDECE: Service de Documentation Extérieur et de Contre-Espionnage (France)
SDO: Special Duties Officer (*see* Katam)
Sephardim: Oriental Jews

Shabak: (H. acr.) Sherut HaBitachon HaKlali ('General Security Service'/GSS) *or* Shin Bet
Shahar: (H.) Palmah Arab Platoon ('The Dawn')
Shai: (H. acr.) Sherut Yediot ('Information Service')
Sherut Mod'in: (H.) Intelligence Service
Sherut Yediot: (H.) *see* Shai
Shin Bet: (H.) *see* Shabak
SIS: Secret Intelligence Service (Britain)
SNS: Special Night Squads
SOE: Special Operations Executive (Britain)
Stern Gang: *see* Lehi

TNSS: Turkish National Security Service

UAR: United Arab Republic
UNDOF: United Nations Disengagement Observer Force
UNEF: United Nations Emergency Force
UNIFIL: United Nations Interim Force in Lebanon
UNLU: United National Leadership of the Uprising
UNRWA: United Nations Relief and Works Agency
UNSCOP: United Nations Special Commission on Palestine
UNTSO: United Nations Truce Supervision Organization

Yishuv: literally 'settlement', but more generally used for the Jewish community in Palestine

Notes

Introduction

1 Phillip Knightley, *The Second Oldest Profession*, London, 1986.
2 Christopher Andrew and D. Dilks (eds.), *The Missing Dimension*, London, 1984.
3 Dennis Eisenberg, Eli Landau and Menachem Portugali, *Operation Uranium Ship*, Tel Aviv, 1978.
4 For a particularly nasty example see Sa'ad al-Bazzaz, *Al Harb as-Siriya*, London, 1987 (al-Bazzaz is a former Iraqi diplomat).

1 Origins: 1936–46

1 *Sefer Toldot HaHaganah*, Vol. II, p. 632.
2 Uri Milstein, *Toldot Milhemet HaAtzmaut*, Vol. I, Tel Aviv, 1989, p. 155.
3 Leo Kohn to Arthur Lourie, 21 April 1936, CZA S25/3252.
4 Moshe Shertok diary, 5 August 1936, CZA S25/443.
5 Chaim Weizmann interview with Stanley Baldwin, 19 May 1936, CZA S25/7559.
6 Ezra Danin, *Tsioni BeKhol Tnai*, Jerusalem, 1987, p. 118.
7 Ibid., p. 123.
8 Ibid., p. 146.
9 Asa Lefen, 'HaShai', in *Modi'in VeBitachon Leumi*, p. 100.
10 Danin, op. cit., p. 124.
11 Ezra Danin to Reuven Zaslani, 8 August 1936, ISA 4373/1.

12 Yehoshua Porath, *The Palestinian Arab National Movement, 1929–1939*, London, 1977, p. 179.
13 Ezra Danin memorandum, 29 August 1936, ISA 4373/1.
14 Reuven Zaslani to Haim Sturman and Nahum Horowitz, 2 February 1937, ISA 4373/3.
15 Teddy Kollek, *Jerusalem Post*, 4 May 1984.
16 Marcus Sieff, *Don't Ask the Price*, London, 1987, pp. 105–6.
17 *Guardian*, 7 July 1987.
18 Reuven Zaslani to Dr Dov (Bernard) Joseph, 15 July 1938, ISA 4373/3.
19 Reuven Zaslani papers, ISA 4373/3/.
20 Porath, op. cit., p. 238.
21 Ezra Danin to Reuven Zaslani, 3 October 1938, ISA 4373/3.
22 Ezra Danin to Reuven Zaslani, 30 January 1939, ISA 4373/3.
23 Danin, op. cit., pp. 137–9.
24 Ezra Danin to Reuven Zaslani, 26 November 1938, ISA 4373/3.
25 Danin, op. cit., p. 144
26 M., Haifa, to Reuven Zaslani, 5 June 1939, ISA 4373/3.
27 *Sefer Toldot HaHaganah*, Vol. III, pp. 242–5.
28 Danin, op. cit., p. 154.
29 Interview with Shimshon Mashbetz.
30 Interview with David Karon.
31 Interview with David Karon.
32 Interview with Ya'akov Shimoni.
33 Interview with Ya'akov Shimoni.
34 Lefen, op. cit., p. 102.
35 Yisrael Amir, *Derekh Lo Slula*, Tel Aviv, 1988, pp. 92–3.
36 Interview with Josh Palmon.
37 *Te'udot VeDmuyot*, 2nd edn, Magnes Press, Jerusalem, 1981, pp. 11–20.
38 Lefen, op. cit., p. 103.
39 Interview with David Karon.
40 Shabtai Teveth, *Ben-Gurion: The Burning Ground*, Boston, 1987, pp. 711–18.
41 Reuven Zaslani testimony, 18 April 1958, ISA 4373/5.
42 Yeruham Cohen, *LeOr HaYom U'Vamahshakh*, Tel Aviv, 1969, pp. 25–46.
43 Reuven Zaslani testimony.
44 Julian Amery, *Approach March*, London, 1973, pp. 281–2.

45 C. M. Woodhouse, *Something Ventured*, London, 1982, p. 16.
46 Reuven Zaslani report, 27 November 1944, CZA S25/205.

2 The Test of Battle: 1947–9

1 'Capture of the Shahar Men in Jaffa', 1 January 1948, to 'Tene (Ayin)', Shai Arab Department, KMA-PA 101-56.
2 ? to Tene (Ayin), 26 December 1947, KMA-PA 109-85; 'Mo'atza' (Palmah HQ) to 'Hillel' (Yisrael Galili), 29 December 1947, KMA-PA 109-91; Ezra Danin to Eliahu Sasson, 23 December 1947, CZA S25/4057; Tene (Ayin) to 'Sasha' (Yigal Allon), 25 December 1947, KMA-PA 109-87; and translation of a story in the Jaffa newspaper *Ash-Sha'ab* about the arrest of 'Sami', with minutes by 'Luria' and 'Sasha', KMA-PA 109-86.
3 Benny Morris, *The Birth of the Palestinian Refugee Problem, 1947–1949*, Cambridge, 1988.
4 Report by 'Sasha' (Allon), 27 May 1947, KMA-PA 103-3.
5 Yoav Gelber, *Gari'n LeTzava Ivri Sadir*, Jerusalem, 1986, p. 397; and 'Sergei' (Nahum Sarig) to battalions, ? March 1948, IDF Archives 960/10/1-12/.
6 Palmah HQ to 'Sasha' (Allon), ? August 1947, KMA-PA 101-77.
7 Yeruham Cohen, *LeOr HaYom U'Vamahshakh*, Tel Aviv, 1969, pp. 60-61; and 'Report of the Mist'Arev in Beirut', 18 January 1948, KMA-PA 101-54.
8 Note by 'Hillel' (Galili), 6 May 1948, KMA-PA 109 gimel-72; Palmah HQ to 'Hillel', 13 May 1948, KMA-PA 102-30; and *Yediot Aharonot*, 27 April 1982.
9 Yigael Yadin to brigades, city commanders, 3 February 1948, KMA-PA, 102-38.
10 'A Shahar patrol in Quncitra', 15 November 1947, KMA-PA, 101-42 and 44.
11 *Yediot Aharonot*, 20 April 1977.
12 'Gideon' to Yiftah Brigade/Palmah HQ, 13 May 1948, KMA-PA 109 gimel-138.
13 Yeruham Cohen, *Ma'arachot*, January 1985.
14 O.C. Shahar, 'Report on the Hijacking of a Car', undated, KMA-PA 107-19; and 'Information' (daily report, Palmah HQ to Haganah General Staff), 28 January 1948, KMA-PA 109 gimel-43.

15 Palmah HQ to Yigael Yadin, 29 February 1948, KMA-PA 101-111; Palmah HQ to 'Knesset' (Haganah General Staff), 'Daily Report', 28 February 1948, KMA-PA 109 gimel-91; and *Sefer HaPalmah*, Vol. II, pp. 137-9. See also O. C. Shahar 'Report on the Kidnapping of Kamal Kubalak by the Shahar', 3 April 1948, KMA-PA 101-3.

16 Palmah HQ to 'Amon', 23 January 1948, KMA-PA 107-80; Palmah HQ to Haganah General Staff, 19 February 1948, KMA-PA 109 gimel-80; and 'Report on a "Zarzir" [i.e. assassination] Operation – Against Sheikh Nimr al-Khatib', undated, unsigned, KMA-PA 101-55.

17 Yigael Yadin to Yigal Allon, undated, KMA-PA 101-99; Yigal Allon to Yigael Yadin, 8 February 1948; and minute by Yigael Yadin, KMA-PA 101-97.

18 Isser Be'eri to Yigal Allon, 26 August 1948, KMA-PA 102-96; and Palmah HQ to Intelligence Service, 6 September 1948, KMA-PA 102-97.

19 *Yediot Aharonot*, 27 April 1984; and *Ma'ariv*, 20 February 1984.

20 Repeated attempts to retrieve Buqa'i's body from Jordan failed (*Yediot Aharonot*, 15 April 1990).

21 Ben-Gurion diary, entry for 3 April 1947, quoted in Gelber, op. cit., p. 394.

22 Uri Milstein, *Toldot Milhemet Ha'Atzmaut*, Vol. I, Tel Aviv, 1989, pp. 170–72.

23 Interview with Isser Harel.

24 Isser Harel, *Bitachon VeDemocratia*, Tel Aviv, 1989, p. 89.

25 Hezi Salomon, 'Hashpa'at Irgunei HaModi'in', in 'Shel HaYishuv Al Ha'Arachat HaMatsav Shel Ben-Gurion, 1946–1947', *Ma'arachot*, 309.

26 Gelber, op. cit., pp. 395–6.

27 Ibid,, pp. 397–8.

28 David Ben-Gurion, *YoMan HaMilhama*, Vol. I, Tel Aviv, 1982, p. 36, entry for 10 December 1947; p. 112, entry for 4 January 1948; and p. 169, entry for 21 January 1948.

29 Asa Lefen, *HaShai*, pp. 103–6.

30 Milstein, op. cit., pp. 168–70.

31 Pinhas Pick, 'HaReshet HaTsvait Ha'Anti-Britit Shel HaHaganah BeYerushalyim', *Eidan*, 2, 1983.

32 Interview with Shmuel Toledano; and Lefen, op. cit., pp. 103–6.

33 Harel, op. cit., p. 93.
34 Milstein, op. cit., p. 175.
35 Ben-Gurion, op. cit., p. 35, entry for 10 December 1947; and CZA S25-426, Political Department, 'Protocol of the Meeting, 25 March 1948'.
36 Interview with Shmuel Toledano.
37 Ben-Gurion, op. cit., p. 246, 26 February 1948; *Sefer Toldot HaHaganah*, Vol. III, p. 1915; Gelber, op. cit., pp. 406-7; and CZA S25/9664, 'Protocol of the Meeting of the Arab Division, 22 April 1948'.
38 'Protocol of the Meeting on "Shem" [i.e. Arab] Affairs, 1–2 January 1948', KMA-Yisrael Galili Papers; Yisrael Galili to brigades, 18 January 1948.
39 'Protocol of a Meeting of the Political Department, 25 March 1948', CZA S25/426.
40 Gelber, op. cit., pp. 399–400.
41 Ibid., p. 400.
42 'Protocol of the Meeting of the Arab Division, 22 April 1948', CZA S25/9664.
43 Quoted in Gelber, op. cit., p. 411.
44 Ibid., pp. 411–12, quoting 'Information on the Arab Armies – Invasion', 9 May 1948, by Operations/Intelligence Department.
45 Ibid., pp. 413–14.
46 'The Arab Armies', 25 May 1948, by Shmuel Ya'ari, ISA FM 2564/6. A revised, expanded version of this report was produced by the Foreign Ministry Middle East Affairs Department, Research Division, on 25 June 1948.
47 Gelber, op. cit., p. 414.
48 Ibid., p. 418.
49 Ben-Gurion, op. cit., Vol. II, p. 294, entry for 7 June 1948.
50 Ibid., p. 548, entry for 24 June 1948.
51 Ibid., p. 583, entry for 12 July 1948; and Gelber, op. cit., p. 419.
52 Ya'akov Berdichevsky, Ministry of Minority Affairs representative in the South, to Gad Machnes, Minority Affairs Ministry director-general, Tel Aviv, 4 November 1948, ISA Minority Affairs Ministry 297/60.
53 'Hiram' to 'Da'at (Ayin)' (Foreign Ministry Political Division, Arab Department), 17 June 1948, ISA FM 2569/13.
54 'An Arab Spy', 6 January 1949, Middle East Affairs Department, Foreign Ministry, ISA FM 2569/12.

55 'Hiram' to 'Da'at', 3 August 1948, ISA FM 2569/13, See also 'Report from Informants Who Returned from a Trip via Nazareth–Irbid–Zarka–Amman–Jericho–Nablus–Nazareth', 15 September 1948, ISA FM 2569/13.

56 Research Division to Ya'akov Shimoni, 23 July 1948, ISA FM 2569/13.

57 Ibid., 19 July 1948.

58 Political Department to Ya'akov Shimoni, 27 July 1948, ISA FM 2569/13; and Ya'akov Shimoni to Eliahu Sasson, Paris, 19 August 1948, ISA FM 2570/11. See also Gelber, op. cit., p. 421.

59 *Yediot Aharonot*, 7 April 1988.

60 Ibid.

61 Ben-Gurion, op. cit., Vol. III, pp. 968–9, entry for 8 February 1949.

62 Gelber, op. cit., p. 428.

63 Teddy Kollek, *For Jerusalem*, Tel Aviv, 1978, p. 57.

64 Eli Peleg, Rome, to Moshe Shertok, Tel Aviv, 26 May 1948, ISA Reuven Shiloah Papers 4373/7.

65 For example, Jefferson Patterson, Cairo, to Secretary of State, 20 July 1948, dealing with the North African Arab contingents fighting in Palestine, with a covering note in Hebrew from 10 August 1948, ISA, Boris Guriel Papers. The files contain a great many raw intelligence cables from 'Yanai' (Paris Operations) to 'Da'at' (Political Division) from the period 1948–52 that include intelligence collected by an agent or agents in Algeria and Morocco.

66 Eliahu Sasson (Paris) to Ya'akov Shimoni, 21 July 1948, ISA FM 3749/1.

67 Eliahu Sasson, Paris, to Ya'akov Shimoni, 23 August 1948, ISA FM 3749/1.

68 For example, see 'Report from Mrs Yolande Harmer on the Situation in Egypt', 18 October 1948; and 'Report on an Interview between Mrs Yolande Harmer and Senator Mahmoud Abd al Fath', Paris, 25 October 1948, both in ISA FM 2565/15.

69 Eliahu Sasson, Paris, to Ya'akov Shimoni, 16 October 1948; Ya'akov Shimoni to Eliahu Sasson, Paris, 12 November 1948, both in ISA FM 3749/1; Yolande Harmer, Paris, to Eliahu Sasson, Tel Aviv, 5 November 1948; and Mahmoud Mahlouf to Yolande Harmer, 10 March 1949, both in ISA FM 3749/2.

70 'Report on the Meeting of the "Paris Branch" of the Middle East Affairs Department, 2 February 1949', ISA FM 3749/2; and Eliahu Sasson, Tel Aviv, to Arazi and Shmuel Divon, Paris, 2 February 1949, ISA FM 3749/2.
71 'Report from Yusuf Sabbagh . . .', 24 June 1948, ISA FM 2408/16.
72 Eliahu Sasson, Paris, to Ya'akov Shimoni, 23 July 1948; and Eliahu Sasson, Paris, to Ya'akov Shimoni, 20 August 1948, both in ISA FM 3749/1.
73 'Report to "Da'at" from Limassol, 25 December 1948', ISA FM 3749/1.
74 Eliahu Sasson, Paris, to Ya'akov Shimoni, 9 September 1948, ISA FM 3749/1.
75 Yitzhak Levy, *Tish'a Kabin*, Tel Aviv, 1986, pp. 392–3; and Munya Mardor, *Shelihut Aluma*, Tel Aviv, 1957, pp. 200–261.

3 Birth Pangs: 1948–51

1 Isser Harel, *Bitachon VeDemocratia*, Tel Aviv, 1989, p. 171.
2 Haggai Eshed, *Mossad Shel Ish Ehad*, Jerusalem, 1988, p. 122.
3 Ibid., pp. 126, 129, 130.
4 David Ben-Gurion, *YoMan HaMilhama*, Vol. III, Tel Aviv, 1982, p. 888, entry for 20 December 1948.
5 Harel, op. cit., p. 170; and interview with Isser Harel.
6 BGA, diary entry, 30 June 1950.
7 Teddy Kollek, *For Jerusalem*, Tel Aviv, 1978, p. 49.
8 Richard Deacon, *C, The Life of Sir Maurice Oldfield*, London, 1984, pp. 69–70.
9 Kollek, op. cit., p. 58.
10 Anthony Verrier, *Through the Looking Glass*, London, 1983, p. 97.
11 Idit Zertal, '*La 5ième Côté du Triangle*', in I. Malkin (ed.), *La France et la Méditerranée*.
12 Ya'akov Shimoni to Eliahu Sasson, Paris, 19 August 1948, ISA FM 3749/1.
13 For early Zionist–Druse relations see Ian Black, *Zionism and the Arabs, 1936–1939*, New York, 1986, pp. 336–53.
14 Ya'akov Shimoni to Eliahu Sasson, Paris, 12 July 1948; and Ya'akov Shimoni to Eliahu Sasson, Paris, 19 August 1948, both in ISA FM 3749/1.

15 Ya'akov Shimoni to Eliahu Sasson, Paris, 19 August 1948, ISA FM 3749/1.
16 Ya'akov Shimoni to Eliahu Sasson, Paris, 16 September 1948, ISA FM 3749/1.
17 Eliahu Sasson to Ya'akov Shimoni, 27 September 1948; Ezra Danin to Tuvia Arazi, Paris, 21 September 1948; Eliahu Sasson to Ya'akov Shimoni, 6 October 1948; and Ezra Danin to Eliahu Sasson, 24 October 1948, all in ISA FM 3749/1.
18 'Summary of a Meeting', 2 January 1949; and Political Department to Ya'akov Shimoni, 10 January 1949, both in ISA FM 2570/20.
19 Stewart Steven, *The Spymasters of Israel*, New York, 1980, p. 37.
20 Eshed, op. cit., pp. 130–31.
21 'Conference of Ministers of Israel', 17–23 July 1950, Tel Aviv and Jerusalem, ISA FM 2463/2.
22 Eshed, op. cit., p. 129.
23 *Ha'Aretz*, 7 August 1981.
24 Harel, op. cit., p. 173.
25 Ibid., p. 174.
26 Eshed, op. cit., pp. 132–3.
27 Yoav Gelber, *Toldot HaHitnadvut*, Vol. IV, Jerusalem, 1979–83, p. 350.
28 Harel, op. cit., p. 147.
29 Eshed, op. cit., p. 134.
30 Tom Segev, *HaYisraelim HaRishonim*, 1949, p. 144, quoting the GSS vetting report of 14 August 1949.
31 Abbas Shiblak, *The Lure of Zion*, London, 1986, p. 120.
32 Ibid., p. 114.
33 Shlomo Hillel, *Operation Babylon*, passim.
34 'Dekel' to Reshut (Mossad), 22 May 1951, ISA FM 2569/10.
35 Reshut Green (Mossad), to 'Nuri', Tehran, 23 May 1951, ISA FM 2569/10.
36 Shmuel Divon to the 'Adviser on Special Duties' (Shiloah), 23 May 1951, ISA FM 2569/10.
37 'Yoav'-'Dekel' to Reshut (Mossad), 24 May 1951, ISA FM 2569/10.
38 'Yoav'-'Dekel' to Reshut (Mossad), 24 May 1951, ISA FM 2569/10.

39 'Dov'-'Dekel' to 'Or', Mossad LeAliya Bet, 'Ruth', Mossad, 27 May 1951, ISA FM 2569/10.
40 See 'From Oren: 28', ISA FM 2569/10. In a letter to *Ha'Aretz*, 23 November 1983, the former IDF quartermaster-general, Major-General (Res.) Mattityahu Peled, linked 'Salim' with Mordechai Ben-Porat ('Menashe Salim') and implied that the Iraqis had released Ben-Porat because he had turned in his fellow agents.
41 'Yehuda Tajjar', an undated Mossad report, probably from the end of 1955, ISA FM 2387/5, bet.
42 'Dov'-'Dekel' to the Jewish Agency Department for Oriental Jewry, 29 May 1951, ISA FM 2569/10.
43 E. Nedad, director of the Department for Oriental Jewry, to 'Yoav' ('Dov'), 30 May 1951, ISA FM 2569/10.
44 E. Nedad, director of the Department for Oriental Jewry, to 'Yoav', Baghdad, 30 May 1951, ISA FM 2569/10.
45 'The Situation in Iraq', a summary produced by the Mossad, 5 July 1951, ISA FM 2569/10.
46 *Ha'Aretz*, 12 January 1984.
47 Wilbur Crane Eveland, *Ropes of Sand*, New York, 1980, pp. 48–9.
48 'The Baghdad Trials', unsigned, undated, probably a Mossad document, ISA FM 2387/7.
49 *Ma'Ariv*, 1 March 1968.
50 Eliahu Sasson to the foreign minister and the director-general of the Foreign Ministry, 5 February 1952, ISA FM 2563/6.
51 Harel, op. cit., p. 178.
52 Isser Harel to David Ben-Gurion, 8 December 1960; Isser Harel to Haim Ya'ari, Ya'akov Caroz and Shmuel M., 16 November 1960 (a letter of appointment); and Haim Ya'ari, Ya'akov Caroz and Shmuel M., 'Investigating Committee [Report] – the Iraqi Bombs Affair', 7 December 1960, all in Yisrael Galili Papers, Kibbutz Meuhad Archives, 47/3.
53 Segev, op. cit., p. 120.
54 'Nuri' to Reshut, 20 May 1951, ISA FM 2569/10.
55 'Nuri' to Reshut, 20 May 1951, ISA FM 2569/10.
56 'Nuri' to Reshut, 24 May 1951, ISA FM 2569/10.
57 'Nuri' to Reshut, 27 May 1951, ISA FM 2569/10.
58 Eshed, op. cit., p. 136; and interview with Isser Harel.
59 BGA, Ben-Gurion diary, entry for 24 May 1952.

60 *Jerusalem Post*, 29 April 1960.
61 Harel, op. cit., p. 224.

4 From War to War: 1949–56

1 Aviezer Golan and Danny Pinkas, *Shula: Codename the Pearl*, New York, 1980, pp. 82, 113. Shula was well known to the Lebanese authorities and was arrested several times before finally leaving the country. Shmuel Moriah, an Iraqi-born Israeli agent who visited Beirut and Damascus in this period, actually introduced himself – as an Israeli – to the head of the Lebanese internal security service, Amir Farid Shehab, and lived to tell the tale (*Ma'ariv*, 4 July 1986).
2 Interview with Shmuel Toledano.
3 Oded Granott, *Tzahal BeHeilo*: *Hayl HaModi'in*, Tel Aviv, 1981, p. 34.
4 Israeli files contain a translated copy of a letter from a German military expert serving in Syria to a friend in Germany, from 1 February 1952. The unnamed adviser on armoured warfare, working in Damascus under 'a former colonel of the [German] General Staff, Kriebel', reported he was one of about thirty former 'professional officers . . . all back in our old grades, but [we] do not wear uniforms . . .' The officer added: 'I am very surprised at the great sympathy they have here for us Germans . . . In many stores and private homes they have a picture of Hitler and seem to like him as in former days.' The copy of the letter is in ISA FM 2565/13, forwarded to Jerusalem by the Israeli Embassy, London.
5 *Ha'Aretz*, 28 May 1982.
6 Report, headed 'Most Secret', 7 January 1950, ISA FM 2565/13.
7 Moshe Sasson, Middle East Affairs Department, to Yosef Fogel, undated, ISA FM 2565/13.
8 IDF Intelligence Department, 'The Reactions of the Arab States and the Great Powers to the Events in Syria', 14 December 1951, ISA FM 2565/13.
9 Patrick Seale, *The Struggle for Syria*, London, 1965, p. 134.
10 Gideon Rafael to the Foreign Minister, 21 February 1954, ISA FM 2408/20.
11 Seale, op. cit., p. 135.

12 Moshe Sharett, *YoMan Ishi* (personal diary), Vol. 2, Tel Aviv, 1978, p. 333, entry for 1 February 1954.
13 IDF Intelligence 10, Northern Base, 'The Clash in Jabal Druse', 18 May 1954, ISA FM 2569/1 bet.
14 IDF Intelligence Branch to the Prime Minister, Minister of Defence, etc., 'A Summary of the Events in Syria and Egypt, a Special Intelligence Report', 2 March 1954; Perlin, Intelligence 10, to Israel Embassy, Washington, and Israel Legation, Ankara, 2 March 1954; and Pinhas Lavon to the Foreign Minister, 9 March 1954, all in ISA FM 2565/1 bet.
15 Sharett, op. cit., pp. 374–5, entry for 25 February 1954.
16 Seale, op. cit., p. 137.
17 Haim Auerbach, Katam North, to Intelligence 10 HQ, 14 February 1951, ISA FM 2565/12.
18 Shmuel Divon, Foreign Ministry, to Yehoshafat Harkabi, IDF Intelligence, 19 February 1951, ISA FM 2565/12.
19 E. Sheloush to Middle East Affairs Department, Foreign Ministry, 16 May 1951, ISA FM 2565/12. See also ISA FM 2565/12, E. or A. Ilani, in the name of the director of the GSS, to the Middle East Affairs Department, Foreign Ministry, 2 May 1951.
20 E. Sheloush to Middle East Affairs Department, 31 October 1951, ISA FM 2565/11.
21 S. Ben-Elkana to Middle East Affairs Department, 20 September 1951, ISA FM 2565/11.
22 *Yediot Aharonot*, 20 April 1977; and Grannot, op. cit., p. 31.
23 *BaMahane*, 28 June 1989.
24 Isser Harel, *Bitachon VeDemocratia*, Tel Aviv, 1989, p. 172.
25 Interview with Yehoshafat Harkabi.
26 IDF Intelligence 5 to ?, 10 January 1955, ISA FM 2387/7. Elad's role in the affair is exhaustively described, from his recruitment to 131, through his activities in Egypt, to his ultimate arrest and imprisonment, in his book, *Ha'Adam HaShlishi*, Tel Aviv, 1976. Despite its obvious lack of impartiality, Elad's apologia remains a basic text for unravelling the affair.
27 *Ha'Aretz*, 18 March 1975.
28 Interview with Yehoshafat Harkabi.
29 Granott op. cit., p. 38, gives text of Yehoshafat Harkabi to Isser Harel, 18 February 1954.
30 Interview with Yehoshafat Harkabi. A lawyer who served as legal

adviser to the Mossad in the 1960s liked to tell the following story to illustrate the problems of finding spies of the right moral fibre. An Israeli agent stationed in an Arab port used to transit through Rome on his rare visits home. There he befriended an Italian woman of dubious respectability. One day, when the agent was in place, the woman turned up in Haifa, with a small baby, and complained to the police that the father of her child was an Israeli spy. She knew the whole story – codewords, cover names, etc. Rotenstreich was called in to deal with the crisis and took the matter to Ben-Gurion, who asked angrily: 'Just what kind of people do you recruit as our spies?' Rotenstreich tried a joke. 'Prime Minister,' he said, 'we tried to get Shai Agnon [the Nobel Prize-winning Hebrew novelist] to go, but he refused.' After Suez relations between the Mossad and Aman were also soured by the case of Mordechai ('Motke') Kedar, one of the most sensitive – and sensational – scandals ever to rack Israel's intelligence community. Kedar had a criminal past; he was suspected of bank robbery and possibly murder as well. He was recruited to Unit 188 – the revamped Unit 131 – in a deal with the police and on the recommendation of a psychologist who believed he had the necessary qualities for clandestine work. In March 1957 he was sent to Argentina to develop a cover story before being sent to an enemy country. He lived in the home of a prosperous local Jew and had an affair with his daughter. Kedar stabbed his host to death after getting $80,000 which he said he needed to set up a secret meeting between Israeli and Egyptian officials. Kedar fled to Paris, but was lured back to Israel, where, in early 1962 he was tried *in camera* in a military court and sentenced to life imprisonment. He was freed in 1974 after serving seventeen years. In Ramle gaol, where he was held in conditions of utter secrecy, he was known as 'Prisoner X'. (Harel, op. cit., pp. 271–84, 288–90). For Kedar's own version see *Yediot Ahanorot*, 2 February 1990.

31 The operation itself is described authoritatively by Haggai Eshed, *Mi Natan et HaHora'a*, Jerusalem, 1979, pp. 17–32. A fuller, personalized account, from the viewpoint of the Jewish participants, is given by Aviezer Golan, *Operation Susannah*, New York, 1978, pp. 29–105.

32 Colonel Gibli to director general, Foreign Ministry, and the director of the Mossad, 1 November 1954, ISA FM 2387/7.

33 Private information.
34 *Ha'Aretz*, 1 January 1988.
35 *Ha'Aretz*, 18 March 1975; and *Ha'Aretz*, 23 April 1980.
36 'Heads of Agreement', 26 October 1954, ISA FM 2387/7.
37 Colonel Gibli to Defence Minister, IDF Chief of Staff, 27 October 1954; and Colonel Gibli to Defence Minister, IDF Chief of Staff, ? October 1954, both in ISA FM 2387/7.
38 IDF Intelligence 5 to ?, 11 January 1955, ISA FM 2387/7.
39 *Ha'Aretz*, 7 July 1989.
40 Eshed, op. cit., remains the most detailed study of the bureaucratic in-fighting and the political aftermath of the affair. Eshed, who was hired by Ben-Gurion to investigate and document the affair, enjoyed unprecedented access to all the relevant Aman, Mossad and cabinet material.
41 Private information; and *Ha'Aretz*, 23 April 1980.
42 *Ma'ariv*, 13 April 1982.
43 Gideon Rafael, Jerusalem, to Reuven Shiloah, Washington, 1 February 1955, ISA FM 4374/22.
44 Gideon Rafael to the Foreign Minister, 14 June 1955, ISA FM 2446/1.
45 'Arab Infiltration of Israel', Foreign Ministry Research Department – Zvi Ne'eman, 10 July 1952, p. 10, ISA FM 2474/13 aleph.
46 Ehud Ya'ari, *Mitzra'im VeHaFedayin*, Givat Haviva, 1975, pp. 10–11.
47 Radi Abdullah, Cairo, to Arab Legion Chief of General Staff, Amman, report on 'Incidents on the Egyptian–Israeli Boundaries', 5 September 1955, PRO FO 371/115905.
48 Katam Base, Jerusalem, to IDF intelligence, 1 April 1954, ISA FM 2453/7.
49 UN Observer, Major Rosenius, to Chairman, EIMAC, 4 December 1954, ISA FM 2402/12.
50 IDF Intelligence Department, 'Infiltration in 1952 (a Summary of the Months January-November 1952)', undated, ISA FM 2428/4 aleph. The summary's Appendix A included a list of border villages that served as infiltrators' bases on the Syrian–Lebanese, Jordanian and Egyptian fronts. The first village listed on the Jordanian front was Qibya.
51 See, for example, IDF Intelligence Department, 'The Activity on the Borders, Summaries and Conclusions for the Month of January

1952', 13 February 1952, p. 1, ISA FM 2428/7; the Foreign Ministry Research Department, 'The Arab Infiltration into Israel', 10 July 1952, p. 10, ISA FM 2474/13; Yair Elgom, Foreign Ministry Research Department, to Mordechai Gazit, Israel Embassy, London, 25 May 1953, ISA FM 2592/18; and Foreign Ministry Research Department, 'Glubb Demands the Punishment of Infiltrators', 26 March 1954, ISA FM 2453/6.

52 A. Eilan to Gideon Rafael, 4 January 1954, ISA FM 2474/13 aleph.

53 Research Department, 'Glubb Demands the Punishment of Infiltrators', date of information 1 February 1954, date of distribution 26 May 1954, ISA FM 2453/6.

54 Foreign Ministry Research Department, 'Concerning the Murder in Ma'ale Akrabim', date of information 21 March 1954, date of distribution 23 March 1954, ISA FM 2453/6.

55 'Statements by the Director of Military Intelligence, Colonel Yehoshafat Harkabi, at a Meeting with Journalists on 7 October 1955', ISA FM 2440/7.

56 Ya'ari, op. cit., pp. 27-31. The description is based on the report of the Egyptian commission that investigated the affair.

57 'Statements by the Director of Military Intelligence, Colonel Yehoshafat Harkabi, at a Meeting with Journalists on 7 October 1955', ISA FM 2440/7.

58 *Ma'ariv*, 12 June 1986; and E. L. M. Burns, *Between Arab and Israeli*, London, 1962, pp. 164-5.

59 Yair Elgom, Foreign Ministry Research Department, to Mordechai Gazit, Israel Embassy, London, 25 May 1953, ISA FM 2592/18.

60 IDF Intelligence Branch, 'The Establishment of a Fedayeen Organization in Jordan', undated, together with covering letter from the Israel Embassy, London, to M. Ofer, Foreign Ministry, Jerusalem, 1 June 1956, ISA FM 2592/18.

61 IDF Intelligence Branch, 'Special Report: The Gaza Incident – Summary and Assessment of the Situation', 22 March 1955, ISA FM 2454/5.

62 Granott, op. cit., pp. 45–6; and Raymond Cohen, 'Israeli Military Intelligence before the 1956 Sinai Campaign', in *Intelligence and National Security*, Vol. 3, No. 1, January 1988, pp. 100–140. Cohen states that 'the weak point of Aman's operation in the period preceding the 1956 Sinai Campaign was the absence of authoritative evidence on Egyptian thinking at the highest level

or . . . a lack of "really reliable sources in the heart of Egypt"'.

63 Quoted in Cohen, op. cit., p. 130.

64 See Elad, op. cit., passim, for his various visits to Egyptian military bases in 1953–4.

65 BGA, Ben-Gurion diary, entry for 15 September 1956. The prime minister was an avid and admiring reader of IDF intelligence reports. But he could be pedantic; in May 1955 he asked Aman to make sure that it used the correct Hebrew spelling of the names of months (David Ben-Gurion to Chief of Staff and Aman, 7 May 1955, BGA).

66 Quoted in Selwyn Lloyd, *Suez 1956*, London, 1980, pp. 34–5.

67 Head of Mossad (Isser Harel) to ?, 23 December 1955, ISA FM 2450/7.

68 Moshe Sharett, *YoMan Ishi*, Vol. 5, Tel Aviv, p. 1372, entry for 12 March 1956.

69 Ibid., Vol. 6, p. 1572, entry for 18 July 1956.

70 Harel, op. cit., p. 403.

71 Interview with Isser Harel.

72 *Boston Globe*, 14 December 1986.

73 *Ma'ariv*, 20 January 1989.

74 *Yediot Aharonot*, 23 January 1989.

75 Mohamed Heikal, *Sphinx and Commissar*, London, 1978, p. 93.

5 Enemies Within: 1948–67

1 Isser Harel, *Bitachon VeDemocratia*, Tel Aviv, 1989, p. 162.

2 Interview with Isser Harel; and *Sefer Toldot HaHaganah*, Vol. 3, Part 2, p. 1082.

3 BGA, Ben-Gurion diary, entry for 29 January 1951.

4 Ibid., entry for 1 February 1951. Until 1954 the official exchange rate was IL1.8 to US$1.

5 Ibid., entry for 18 September 1951; see also entry for 21 September 1950.

6 *HaOlam HaZeh*, 8 June 1957.

7 *Ma'ariv*, 29 June 1980.

8 Moshe Sharett, *YoMan Ishi*, Vol. 1, Tel Aviv, 1978, p. 91, entry for 28 October 1953.

9 Interview.

10 Interview with Isser Harel.

11 *Jerusalem Post*, 27 September 1963.

12 Interview with Amos Manor.
13 Interview with Ephraim Levy.
14 *HaOlam HaZeh*, 20 July 1988.
15 Private information.
16 Isser Harel, *HaEmet al Retzah Kastner*, Tel Aviv, 1985, p. 133; and Yoav Gelber, *Toldot HaHitnadvut*, Vol. III, Jerusalem, 1979–83, biographical notes.
17 *Hadashot*, 6 November 1987.
18 Harel, *Bitachon* op, cit., p. 166.
19 Yeshayahu Levite, *Milhemet HaTslalim*, Tel Aviv, 1969, p. 30.
20 Interview with Ya'akov Caroz.
21 Harel, *Bitachon* op. cit., p. 164.
22 Interview.
23 Sharett, op. cit., Vol. 1, pp. 145–6, entry for 12 November 1953.
24 Walter Schwarz, *The Arabs in Israel*, London, 1959, p. 23.
25 Interview.
26 M. Alon, GSS, to Foreign Ministry Middle East Department, 16 January 1951, ISA FM 2565/20, 2565/12.
27 Eliahu Sasson to GSS, 13 November 1950.
28 Schwarz, op. cit., p. 141.
29 Interview.
30 BGA, Ben-Gurion diary, entry for 19 December 1957.
31 Schwarz, op. cit., pp. 89-90.
32 Interview with Ya'akov Caroz.
33 Levite, op. cit., p. 67.
34 *Jerusalem Post*, 14 November 1958.
35 Interview.
36 Yeshayahu Lavi (ed.), *Parshiot Ne'elamot*, Tel Aviv, 1961, pp 7–29.
37 Levite, op. cit., p. 89.
38 *Matara*, August 1988; and Ya'akov Caroz, *The Arab Secret Services*, London, 1978, pp. 125-8.
39 Caroz, op. cit., p. 148.
40 Ibid., p. 155.
41 Levite, op. cit., pp. 147-8.
42 *Ma'ariv*, 6 June 1986.
43 Caroz, op. cit., p. 165.
44 Israeli intelligence and security officials, including the Memuneh, Isser Harel, dismissed the story as nonsense. Egypt revealed the

spy's existence only in the mid-1980s, and the story was dramatized in a popular television series. *Observer*, 6 July 1988, *Ma'ariv*, 5 July 1988.

45 Levite, op. cit., pp. 70–75.
46 Caroz, op. cit., pp. 73–6.
47 Ilya Dzhirkvelov, *Secret Servant*, London, 1987, pp. 246–9.
48 Isser Harel, *Rigul Sovieti*, Tel Aviv, 1987, p. 14.
49 Interview with Isser Harel.
50 According to Ion Pacepa, *Red Horizons*, London, 1989, p. 284, Romanian intelligence ran a highly successful agent who lived at the Romanian Church's Mission in Jerusalem.
51 Ray Brock, *Blood, Oil and Sand*, Cleveland, 1952, p. 69.
52 Sharett, op. cit., Vol. 5, Tel Aviv, 1978, p. 1393, entry for 13 April 1956.
53 Ibid., p. 1398, entry for 27 April 1956.
54 Ibid., Vol. 6, p. 1629, entry for 13 August 1956.
55 Avri Elad, *Ha'Adam HaShlishi*, Tel Aviv, 1976, pp. 283–6.
56 Levite, op. cit., p. 99
57 BGA, Ben-Gurion diary, entry for 12 January 1952; and Michael Bar-Zohar, *Ben-Gurion*, Vol. 2, Tel Aviv, 1987, p. 924.
58 Harel, *Kastner*, op. cit., p. 17.
59 BGA, Ben-Gurion diary, entry for 26 July 1950.
60 Harel, *Bitachon*, op. cit., pp. 207–12; and *Ha'Aretz*, 8 June 1973.
61 Interview; and *HaOlam HaZeh*, ? June 1957.
62 Bar-Zohar, op. cit., pp. 927–8.
63 *HaOlam HaZeh*, 8 May 1957.
64 Knesset statement, 19 June 1957.
65 BGA, Ben-Gurion diary, entry for 19 June 1957.
66 Harel, *Bitachon*, op. cit., p. 215.
67 BGA, Ben-Gurion diary, entry for 29 July 1957.
68 Ibid., entry for 22 November 1957.
69 Interview with Rudi Avneri.
70 Yosef Almogi, *HaMa'avak al Ben-Gurion*, Tel Aviv, 1988, p. 26.
71 Uri Avneri to David Ben-Gurion, BGA, 6 December 1953.
72 Sharett, op. cit., Vol. 4, Tel Aviv, 1978, p. 1036, entry for 1 June 1955.
73 Teddy Kollek, *For Jerusalem*, Tel Aviv, 1978, p. 53.
74 Noah Lucas, *The Modern History of Israel*, London, 1974, pp. 327–8.
75 *HaOlam HaZeh*, 20 March 1957.

76 Harel, *Kastner*, op. cit., pp. 264, 353.
77 Interview with Uri Avneri.
78 Sharett, op. cit., Vol. 6, p. 1636, entry for 17 August 1956; p. 1685, entry for 4 September 1956; and p. 1704, entry for 17 September 1956.
79 Ibid., Vol. 7, p. 1882, entry for 27 November 1956.
80 Ibid., Vol. 8, p. 2314, entry for 18 September 1957.
81 *HaOlam HaZeh*, ? June 1957.
82 Avner Bar-On, *Ha Sipurim Shelo Supru*, Jerusalem, 1981, p. 110.
83 Harel, *Rigul*, op. cit., pp. 26-9.
84 Ibid., p. 92.
85 Ibid., p. 26.
86 Yisrael Beer, *Bitachon Yisrael*, Tel Aviv, 1966, p. 17.
87 Harel, *Rigul*, op. cit., p. 93; and Beer, op. cit., pp. 9–50.
88 Interview with Ephraim Levy.
89 Sharett, op. cit., Vol. 5, p. 1349, entry for 14 February 1956.
90 Harel, *Rigul*, op. cit., p. 105.
91 Walter Laqueur, *A World of Secrets*, New York, 1985, p. 213.
92 Miles Copeland, *The Game of Nations*, New York, 1969, pp. 104–5.
93 Reinhard Gehlen, *The Service*, New York, 1972, p. 260.
94 Harel, *Rigul*, op. cit., p. 120; and *HaDashot*, 19 April 1989.
95 *Yediot Aharonot*, 9 March 1990.
96 *Hadashot*, 19 April 1989.
97 Interview with Isser Harel.
98 *Ma'ariv*, 25 April 1964.
99 *Guardian*, 8 December 1982.
100 *Ma'ariv*, 6 June 1986.
101 Avi Shlaim, *Collusion across the Jordan*, Oxford, 1988, p. 232.
102 *Guardian*, 18 April 1987.
103 *Yediot Aharonot*, 8 December 1989.
104 David Ronen, *Shnat Shabak*, Tel Aviv, 1989, p. 27.
105 Eitan Haber, *HaYom Tifrotz Milhama*, Tel Aviv, 1987, p. 131.
106 *Jerusalem Post*, 26 March 1978.
107 Interview.
108 Interview with Shmuel Toledano.
109 Harel, *Bitachon*, op. cit., p. 443.

6 *Great Leaps Forward: 1956–67*

1 *Haggai Eshed, Mossad Shel Ish Ehad*, Jerusalem, p. 165. See also *Boston Globe*, 14 December 1986, for Angleton's special relationship with the Mossad.

2 Isser Harel, *Bitachon VeDemocratia*, Tel Aviv, 1989, pp. 382–3.

3 Interview with Isser Harel. The Shin Bet's debriefing of recent immigrants from behind the Iron Curtain and the orderly transmission of the information collected – on Soviet industrial and military and other strategic installations – to the CIA seems to have begun in June or early July 1951. On 20 July 1951 Shiloah, the head of the Mossad, told the American ambassador to Tel Aviv, Monnett B. Davis, that 'much useful information is already being made available to the US'. Davis, reporting to the secretary of state, commented that his embassy knew nothing of this arrangement, 'but it is the second time he [Shiloah] has given assurances that his government was cooperating in supplying information derived from immigrants'.

A few weeks later Shiloah was a little more cagey at a meeting with Davis's subordinates, the deputy head of mission, Erwin P. Keeler, and Steven Zagorski, an embassy attaché. Keeler probed the Mossad chief about 'an earlier remark by [Shiloah] that the Israel government sometimes obtained very important information, and that it reached the proper sources [*sic*: should be agencies] – did this mean that we could assume that it reached the US government, whether through diplomatic or other channels? Mr Shiloah offered no reply to the first query, and to the second said he was not at liberty to divulge channels; however, he spoke vaguely of Ben-Gurion's, Sharett's and his [Shiloah's] broad circle of acquaintances in the US and elsewhere.' (See National Archive (Washington), RG84, Tel Aviv Embassy Classified General Records, 1950–52, Trevi and Peripheral Security Correspondence, 350., Davis to Secstate (60), 20 July 1951, and 'Memorandum of Conversation' (Shiloah, Keeler, Zagorski), 13 September 1951 and covering note by Davis, 21 September 1951).

Shiloah's revelations to the American diplomats in Tel Aviv were occasioned by the embassy's own secret information-gathering operations – Trevi and the Peripheral Reporting project. Zagorski and Keeler were respectively responsible for the two operations, whose purpose was to collect information on various Soviet and Eastern Bloc realities, including persecution of religious dissidents, the 'denial of human rights' behind the Iron Curtain and 'forced labour' camps. The embassy collected this information by interviewing recent Jewish immigrants from the Eastern Bloc, scanning local newspapers and journals and culling from Israeli government press releases and communiqués. The Trevi and Peripheral Reporting operations severely worried Israel's leaders, who feared that word of them would get back to the Soviet and Eastern Bloc authorities. Specifically, Shiloah and the other Israeli leaders feared that these operations 'would disrupt existing arrangements or embarrass future arrangements with Iron Curtain governments, whereby latter permit emigration Jews to Israel'. Shiloah imposed severe curbs on the Trevi and Peripheral Reporting information-gatherers.

Nonetheless, Zagorski's and Keeler's customers back in Washington were happy with the product. As Harold Vedeler, the officer in charge of the Office of Polish, Baltic and Czechoslovak Affairs at the State Department, wrote to Zagorski in the spring of 1952: 'I wish to tell you that we have been following closely the peripheral reports on Poland and Czechoslovakia which have come from Tel Aviv ... excellent reports ... I have in mind particularly the despatches prepared on subjects discussed with a former member of the Ministry of Czechoslovak Foreign Affairs ... The Peripheral Unit's despatch No. 451 of 5 December 1951 dealing with the fall of Rudolph Slansky proved quite illuminating about the possible motives in the recent Czechoslovak purges. We were also very interested in having your impressive account of the suffering and wretched conditions of forced labor in the Soviet Union ...'

Another despatch from Washington gives an idea of the type of detail Zagorski's customers were interested in: 'I am about to write a report on the current status of the Romanian Workers' Party (Communist),' wrote one research division officer to Zagorski, 'with emphasis on the control it exercises on all phases of the political, economic, social, military and religious institutions of the country. I would, therefore, appreciate anything you can obtain on the subject. Concrete examples on how the cell organizations effect their manifold controls in an industrial plant, a school, a military or police unit, a local people's council, a collective farm etc., would be of great help to me to attempt to estimate the power of the party over the life of the average Romanian . . .' (See NA RG84, Tel Aviv Embassy, Classified General Records, 1950–52, Trevi and Peripheral, Security Correspondence 350. (61), Davis to Secstate, 20 July 1951; Harold Vedeler to Steven Zagorski, 15 April 1952; and Stephen Peters, Division of Research for USSR and Eastern Europe, Department of State, to Steven Zagorski, 12 February 1952. Other documents in this bulging file elucidate further aspects of Trevi and Peripheral, operations conducted also out of other American embassies in countries absorbing substantial numbers of Eastern bloc emigrants).

4 BGA, Ben-Gurion diary, entry for 23 February 1952.

5 Harel, op. cit., p. 388.

6 *Yediot Aharonot*, 24 November 1985.

7 Eshed, op. cit., p. 164; and Moshe Sharett, *YoMan Ishi*, Tel Aviv, 1978, passim, for references to 'Jim'.

8 Thomas Powers, *The Man Who Kept the Secrets*, New York, 1979, p. 100.

9 Teddy Kollek, *For Jerusalem*, Tel Aviv, 1978, p. 99.

10 Sharett, op. cit., Vol. 5, p. 1420, entry for 8 June 1956.

11 Interview with Isser Harel.

12 Interview with Ya'akov Caroz.

13 *Ma'arachot*, 306-7, December 1986 – January 1987, pp. 28–37.

14 Interview with Yehoshafat Harkabi.

15 Oded Granott, *Tzahal BeHeilo: Hayl HaModi'in*, Tel Aviv, 1981, pp. 53–6.

16 Interview with Mordechai Bar-On.

17 Alistair Horne, *A Savage War of Peace*, London, 1977, pp. 157–8; and Moshe Dayan, *The Story of My Life*, London, 1977, p. 235.

18 Roger Paligot and Pascal Krop, *La Piscine*, pp. 109–18.

19 *Guardian*, 30 October 1986.

20 Matti Golan, *Shimon Peres*, London, 1982, p. 36.

21 *Ha'Aretz*, 29 September 1989.

22 Harel, op. cit., pp. 291–6.

23 *Yediot Aharonot*, 10 February 1989.

24 Eliezer Shoshani (ed.), *Teisha Shanim Mitoch Alpayim, Shlihuta Shel Yisrael BeGalut Maroko BaShanim 1955–1964*, 1964, p. 42; and Shmuel Segev, *Mivtza Yachin*, Tel Aviv, 1984, pp. 34–5. *Teisha*

Shanim is the official joint Mossad – Jewish Agency history of the Moroccan *aliya* operation. The volume is still classified. A copy is deposited in the Yisrael Galili Papers, Box 50, Kibbutz Meuhad Archives, Ef'al, Israel.

25 Segev, op. cit., p. 70.

26 *Yediot Aharonot*, 22 January 1988.

27 Shoshani, op. cit., p. 21.

28 Segev, op. cit., p. 108.

29 *Yediot Aharonot*, 28 December 1988.

30 *Yediot Aharonot*, 22 January 1988; and Shoshani, op. cit., pp. 19–20, 242.

31 *Guardian*, 29 December 1988.

32 Segev, op. cit., p. 114. A letter by S. Z. Shragai, the director of the Jewish Agency's Immigration Department, to World Jewish Congress chairman Nahum Goldmann, 27 August 1956, referred to in a forthcoming study by Dr Yaron Tsur of the Mossad and the Moroccan *aliya* operation, tells of a meeting three days before with the British governor of Gibraltar and casts light on the British role and attitudes at this time to the Israeli operation.

33 *Yediot Aharonot*, 22 January 1988.

34 Guttman, who worked with Arthur Ben-Natan in Mossad LeAliya Bet in Vienna, was one of the Nokmim (Avengers), the band of Haganah and ex-British Army soldiers who hunted down and executed SS officers in parts of Europe occupied by the Allies immediately after the Second World War. Later he joined the Irgun. In 1949 he was involved in a plot to kill Nazi war criminals in Spandau prison, but the plan was aborted.

35 Shoshani, op. cit., pp. 105–7, reproduces Isser Harel to the commander of the Misgeret, Paris, 20 February 1961.

36 Shoshani, op. cit., pp. 103–4, reproduces Isser Harel to the commander of the Misgeret, Paris, 27 February 1961.

37 Segev, op. cit., p. 251.

38 Arye Lyova Eliav, *Taba'ot Eidut*, Tel Aviv, 1984, pp. 99–119.

39 *Ma'ariv*, 19 February 1988.

40 Harel, op. cit., p. 409.

41 Interview with Ya'akov Caroz.

42 Segev, op. cit., p. 93.

43 Interview with Ya'akov Caroz.

44 Harel, op. cit., p. 178.

45 Eshed, op. cit., p. 282.
46 Harel, op. cit., p. 409.
47 CIA report, 1976.
48 Shmuel Segev, *HaMeshulash HaIrani*, Tel Aviv, 1981, p. 214; and Granott, op. cit., p. 66.
49 Eliav, op. cit., pp. 156–64.
50 Segev, *HaMeshulash*, op. cit., p. 215.
51 Ezra Danin, *Tsioni BeKhol Tnai*, Vol. 2, Jerusalem, 1987, p. 547.
52 Marvin Zonis, *The Political Elite of Iran*, Princeton, 1981, p. 85.
53 Gideon Rafael, *Destination Peace*, New York, 1981, p. 78.
54 See Sharett, op. cit., Vol. 4, p. 1138, entry for 18 August 1955; p. 1182, entry for 30 September 1955; and p. 1292, entry for 8 November 1955.
55 BGA, Ben-Gurion diary, extract for 19 August 1956; and Sharett, op. cit., p. 1160, entry for 21 September 1955; p. 1190, entry for 5 October 1955; and Vol. 5, p. 1430, entry for 12 June 1956.
56 Anthony Sylvester, *Sudan under Nimeiri*, London, 1977, pp. 159–61.
57 Michael Bar-Zohar, *Ben-Gurion*, Vol. 3, Tel Aviv, 1987, p. 1322.
58 Benjamin Beit-Hallahmi, *The Israeli Connection*, London, 1988, p. 52.
59 Bar-Zohar, op. cit., passim; and *Yediot Aharonot*, 11 January 1974.
60 BGA, record of meeting with R. Timor of the Foreign Ministry, 15 May 1961.
61 Avner Bar-On, *HaSipurim Shelo Supru*, Jerusalem, 1981, p. 135.
62 F. Halliday and M. Molyneux, *The Ethiopian Revolution*, London, 1981, p. 232.
63 Eshed, op. cit., p. 264.
64 Bar-Zohar, op. cit., p. 1327.
65 Eshed, op. cit., p. 275.
66 CIA report.
67 Interview with Israel Carmi; and Modechai Naor, *Laskov*, Tel Aviv, 1988, pp. 139-50. Another team of Nokmim operated more or less independently, under the poet and former partisan leader Abba Kovner. They penetrated British and American POW camps holding SS troops and poisoned inmates *en masse*, though it is unclear how many Nazis died in these operations.
68 Michael Bar-Zohar, *The Avengers*, London, 1968, p. 172.

69 Isser Harel, *Kam Ish Al Ehav*, Jerusalem, 1982, p. 20; and Isser Harel, *The House on Garibaldi Street*, New York, 1975, p. 40.
70 Malchin, an explosives expert, had joined the Shin Bet in 1950 and had spent his first years in the service instructing Israeli Embassy personnel abroad how to deal with letter bombs (interview with Zvi Malchin).
71 Uri Dan and Peter Mann, *Eichmann BeYadei!*, Tel Aviv, 1987, describes the kidnap operation from the point of view of Zvi Malchin; see also *Yediot Aharonot*, 15 September 1989.
72 Gerland L. Posner and John Ware, *Mengele*, New York, 1986, p. 194.
73 Zvi Aharoni to Ya'akov Caroz, 25 September 1979.
74 Harel, *Bitachon*, op. cit., pp. 339–47.
75 Ibid., pp. 340–41.
76 Interview with Shmuel Toledano.
77 *Yediot Aharonot*, 15 December 1980 and 30 May 1986.
78 Michael Bar-Zohar, *Spies in the Promised Land*, New York, 1972, p. 237.
79 Isser Harel, *Mivtsa Yossele*, Tel Aviv, 1982, passim.
80 Kollek, op. cit., p. 154.
81 Isser Harel, *Mashber HaMadanim HaGermanim*, Tel Aviv, 1982, passim.
82 *Yediot Aharonot*, 4 May 1979.
83 Eitan Haber, *HaYom Tifrotz Milhama*, Tel Aviv, 1987, p. 61.
84 Bar-Zohar, *Ben-Gurion*, op. cit., pp. 1529–30.
85 Peter Malkin and Harry Stein, *Eichmann in My Hands*, New York, 1990, pp. 79–103.
86 Golan, op. cit., p. 114.
87 Harel, *Mashber*, op. cit., p. 42.
88 Similar charges were made when Israel launched its first experimental satellite in September 1988, just before that year's Knesset elections.
89 Harel, *Mashber*, op. cit., pp. 19–26.
90 Rafael, op. cit., p. 108.
91 Haber, op. cit., p. 61.
92 Yair Kotler, *Joe Hozer El HaOr*, Tel Aviv, 1988, p. 31.
93 Private information. Shamir's first reaction when Harel called him in for an interview was that the Memuneh suspected him of being involved in some new underground activity and he was

'amazed' when he was offered a job with the Mossad. 'I had ten very great years of dangers, adventures and difficult experiences, but a wonderful feeling of intense satisfaction,' Shamir said afterwards (*Yediot Aharonot*, 26 February 1988 and 6 October 1989). On Herzl Amikam, see Shulamit Livnat, *HaShamayim Krovim Yoter*, Tel Aviv, 1989, pp. 61–72.

94 Harel, *Mashber*, op. cit., p. 41.

95 Bar-Zohar, *Hunt*, p. 196.

96 Bar-Zohar, *Ben-Gurion*, op. cit., pp. 1534–5.

97 Wolfgang Lotz, *The Champagne Spy*, London, 1972, p. 12.

98 Antony Parsons, *They Say the Lion*, London, 1986, p. 60.

99 Lotz was arrested by the Egyptians in February 1965. He was tried and convicted on espionage charges, although he maintained his 'false flag' cover as a German agent. He was released after the 1967 war.

100 *Matara*, September 1989.

101 Moshel was probably mistaken; the magazine was the French edition of the well-informed London-based *Jewish Observer and Middle East Review*. Both were edited by Jon Kimche, David's elder brother. Moshel was offered a higher salary than the one paid by his newspaper, and was trained in communications, the use of dead-letter boxes and other forms of tradecraft. His Mossad boss in the French capital – then headquarters of the Mossad's European operations – was Yitzhak Shamir, who was using the cover name 'Samuel Singer'. (Shamir also used the cover names 'Markovitz', 'Barzilai' and 'Limon' – *Yediot Aharonot*, 9 April 1990.) Before leaving for Cairo late in 1962 Moshel went to Amsterdam – Holland was a favourite base for Israeli intelligence operations – to be briefed on Egypt and the Middle East in general by another Mossad officer called Mike Harari, who was to end his espionage career with a spectacular failure in Norway just over a decade later. Moshel was a tricky agent; he was an enthusiastic bisexual and Shamir once found him in a Paris hotel room with a well-endowed Hungarian night porter hidden in the wardrobe. 'Your Hungarian is one of our people,' Shamir told him, 'I knew that he was with you. I only wanted to know how you'd behave when things got hot.' (Aharon Mosehl, *Die Viper*, Hamburg, 1989, pp. 114–15.)

102 Moshel, op. cit., p. 145.

103 Harel, *Mashber*, p. 61.
104 Rafael, op. cit., p. 109.
105 Haber, op. cit., p. 61.
106 Kotler, op. cit., p. 46.
107 Haber, op. cit., pp. 60–65.
108 Interview with Isser Harel.
109 Harel, *Mashber*, op. cit., p. 123.
110 Kollek, op. cit., p. 154.
111 Private information.
112 *Yediot Aharonot*, 13 November 1987.
113 Haber, op. cit., p. 64.
114 Faligot and Krop, op. cit., pp. 231–8.
115 Steward Steven, *The Spymasters of Israel*, New York, 1980, p. 239.
116 *Hadashot*, 29 February 1989.
117 *Time*, 29 December 1975.
118 Interview.
119 Yoram Peri, *Between Battles and Ballots*, Cambridge, 1983, p. 242.
120 Harel, *Bitachon*, op. cit., pp. 451–2; and Steven, op. cit., pp. 248–50.
121 Peri, op. cit., p. 243.
122 *Yediot Aharonot*, 19 October 1987.

7 Six Days in June: 1967

1 Yair Kotler, *Joe Hozer El HaOr*, Tel Aviv, 1958, pp. 12–21. In January 1964 an Egyptian pilot defected to Israel with his Yak training aircraft. He eventually settled in Argentina, but was caught and executed in Egypt two years later.
2 The best single account of the MiG-21 episode is in *Ha'Aretz*, 14 May 1982. The article is based in part on foreign sources.
3 Interview with Aharon Yariv.
4 Donald Neff, *Warriors for Jerusalem*, New York, 1984, p. 128, quoting from the NSC protocol of the meeting.
5 Yitzhak Rabin, *The Rabin Memoirs*, Jerusalem, 1979, pp. 43–4.
6 Ezer Weizman, *On Eagles' Wings*, London, 1976, p. 207.
7 Interview with Aharon Yariv.

8 Eitan Haber, *HaYom Tifrotz Milhama*, Tel Aviv, 1987, p. 147; and David Kimche and Dan Bawly, *The Sandstorm*, London, 1968, p. 136. See also Shlomo Gazit, 'Intelligence Estimates and the Decision-Maker', in *Intelligence and National Security*, Vol. 3, No. 3, July 1988; and Ze'ev Schiff, *A History of the Israeli Army*, London, 1987, pp. 199–200.

9 Transcript of Binyamin Geist interview with Aharon Yariv, 19 September 1973, kindly given by Geist to the authors.

10 Haber, op. cit., pp. 133–4.

11 Interview with Aharon Yariv.

12 Moshe Dayan, *The Story of My Life*, London, 1977, p. 309.

13 Samir A. Mutawi, *Jordan in the 1967 War*, Cambridge, 1987, p. 95.

14 Neff, op. cit., pp. 53, 176.

15 Dayan, op. cit., p. 309; and Walter Laqueur, *The Road to War*, London, 1969, p. 85. Neff, op. cit., p. 59, says that the Podgorny warning to Sadat was delivered as early as 29 April. This seems unlikely. Yariv believes that the Soviets 'informed' the Egyptians of the Israeli designs on Syria in part, at least, in order to obtain an Egyptian withdrawal of its troops from Yemen. Kimche and Bawly, op. cit., p. 115, hint that Israeli intelligence was 'absolutely convinced' that the Soviets knew that their warnings to Syria and Egypt of Israeli troop concentrations were false, According to Kimche – at the time of writing *Sandstorm* a senior Mossad executive – and Bawly, the Soviets feared for their client regime in Damascus and believed that the continued Palestinian raiding would provoke a major IDF response. Yet they were unable to persuade Damascus to rein in the guerrillas. The Soviets hoped that the Israeli troop concentration warning would scare Damascus into at last stopping the Palestinian incursions. According to Kimche and Bawly, p. 88, the 'second Soviet warning' pinpointed the date and hour of the prospective IDF assault on Syria: '04:00 on 17 May'.

16 Patrick Seale, *Asad*, London, 1988, p. 126.

17 Neff, op. cit., p. 150.

18 Haber, op. cit., p. 147–51.

19 Ibid., p. 149; Oded Granott, *Tzahal BeHeilo: Hayl HaModi'in*, Tel Aviv, 1981, pp. 77–8; and Rabin, op. cit., p. 53.

20 Neff, op. cit., pp. 58–9.

21 Granott, op. cit., p. 78.
22 Ibid., p. 79.
23 Rabin, op. cit., p. 54.
24 Michael Brecher, with Benjamin Geist, *Decisions in Crisis, Israel 1967 and 1973*, Los Angeles, 1980, p. 107.
25 Rabin, op. cit., p. 55.
26 Haber, op. cit., p. 153.
27 Transcript of Binyamin Geist interview with Aharon Yariv, op. cit.
28 Granott, op. cit., p. 80; and Haber, op. cit., p. 164.
29 Yariv believes today that 'Nasser did not [in May-June 1967] intend to go to war. At worst, he thought that Israel would attack his forces dug in in Sinai and that the Egyptian army would repel the attack' (interview with Aharon Yariv). Arab military cooperation and coordination could only be expected to grow. Egypt's 4th Armoured Division began to move into Sinai on 24 May. Indeed, Aman's Research Department, headed by Shlomo Gazit, wrongly assessed on 25 May that Nasser would attack the following day – out of fear that Israel intended to mount a pre-emptive air strike against Egypt's military airfields.
30 Interview with Aharon Yariv. The Berlin-born 'Biber' joined the Palmah at the age of sixteen and began his intelligence career preparing maps and entries for the 'villages files'. At the end of the war of independence, in May 1949, Biber was transferred to IDF Intelligence Department, where he was placed in 'Section Gimel', responsible for Jordan. He remained on the Jordanian desk until 1974, when he moved over to the computer department. He was Israel's 'man in Amman' (a town he never visited), and his intimate, detailed knowledge of Jordan, the Arab Legion and Hussein's government and court became legendary. At intelligence meetings he spoke 'in the name of Hussein', presenting the king's thinking, usually with remarkable prescience. His identification with Jordan was so complete that when the Syrian army invaded Jordan in September 1970, Biber lowered the Jordanian flag on his desk in Tel Aviv to half-mast. When the Syrians withdraw, he raised it again. Hussein's birthdays were formally celebrated each year at the Jordanian desk, with cakes and wine, with Biber presiding. He was personally hurt by Hussein's partnership with Nasser in the 1967 war. Later, in 1973, Biber was to

predict – accurately – that Hussein would stay out of the war (*Yediot Aharonot*, 15 September 1985. See also Haber, op. cit., pp. 227–8). Hussein was indeed deeply unhappy in 1967 at the prospect of war with Israel. Jordanian intelligence had reported to him that the Egyptian president had walked into a trap set for him by Syria, but as the crisis escalated, the king felt he had no choice (Mutawi, op. cit., pp. 98–103).

31 *BaMahane*, 28 June 1989.

32 David Ronen, *Shnat Shabak*, Tel Aviv, 1989, pp. 23–4.

33 Binyamin Geist interview with Meir Amit, 23 July 1973. Amit said: 'You can never be 100 per cent certain, because there exists the irrational factor. True, this factor has to be taken into account, and perhaps [in 1967] a mistake was made in not taking sufficient account of irrational criteria.'

34 Haber, op. cit., pp. 205–6.

35 Haber, op. cit., p. 209. Seale, op. cit., pp. 136–7, dismisses Israel's alleged anxiety and regards the whole countdown to war as a huge and successful deception aimed at gaining world support for the subsequent assault. Seale says that, from the start, Israel knew of the Arabs' glaring military inferiority and that the campaign would be a pushover. It 'knew that the Egyptians had walked into a trap. It read Egyptian radio traffic, noted the plaintive cries for water and fuel, and observed the traffic jams and the supply columns going astray . . . It was because the situation on the ground in Sinai was so beckoning that the Israeli generals could barely restrain themselves.'

36 Haber, op. cit., pp. 216–7. For the Amit trip to Washington, see Brecher, op. cit., pp. 153–4, 157, 163–4, 235, 347, 349.

37 Neff, op. cit., p. 182. According to Binyamin Geist's interview with Meir Amit, Amit said he had gone to the United States 'to tell [the Americans] that we were going to war, and to hear their reaction'. He also told them that while welcoming material aid, political support and 'the neutralization of the Russians', Israel did not want Americans 'to die in Israel' – i.e. to fight for Israel.

38 Neff, op. cit., p. 190; and Binyamin Geist interview with Meir Amit, (AS 33).

39 Mutawi, op. cit., pp. 111–12.

40 Haber, op. cit., p. 219.

41 Neff, op. cit., pp. 194–5.

42 Dayan, op. cit., pp. 351–4. Neff, op. cit., p. 203, gives slightly different estimates of Egyptian air strength and losses.
43 Hussein of Jordan, *My 'War' with Israel*, p. 66.
44 Ibid., p. 55.
45 Interview with Aharon Yariv.
46 Rabin, op. cit., p. 77; and Hussein of Jordan, op. cit., p. 102.
47 Neff, op. cit., p. 202; and Hussein of Jordan, op. cit., pp. 102–3.
48 Rabin, op. cit., p. 82.
49 Schiff, op. cit., p. 200.
50 Interview with Aharon Yariv. Schiff, op. cit., p. 200, writes that the major was shot by Israeli troops as he tried to cross over to the Israeli lines 'to give himself up'. Another version appears in Uri Dan and Yoel Ben-Porat, *The Secret War*, New York, 1970, pp. 161–6. It was later suggested that the whole story was a fabrication put out by Aman to safeguard another less obvious source.
51 Hussein of Jordan, op. cit., pp. 69–70.
52 *Ha'Ir*, 10 March 1989.
53 Ya'akov Caroz, *The Arab Secret Services*, London, 1978, p. 119.
54 Interview with Aharon Yariv.
55 Ibid.
56 Wolf Blitzer, *Territory of Lies*, New York, 1989, pp. 101–2.
57 Shmuel Segev, *Boded BeDamesek*, Tel Aviv, 1986, is the best book on Cohen's life and death.
58 Hussein of Jordan, op. cit., p. 105.
59 Ibid., p. 81.
60 Over the years this conversation has appeared in a number of variations in a number of publications. This version, the most accurate available, is taken from the IDF's weekly magazine, *BaMahane*, 4 January 1989. See also Haber, op. cit., pp. 238–9.
61 Mutawi, op. cit., pp. 151–2.
62 See Neff, op. cit., p. 219, citing a CIA report apparently based on a Sigint intercept of a message by the Soviet officer from the first days of the war, reporting that he had seen aircraft with US markings overflying Ismailia. See also Hussein of Jordan, op. cit., pp. 83–84, which 'explains' why Nasser, and perhaps he himself, believed at the time that American and British aircraft had participated in the Israeli air strike.
63 Interview.
64 Interview with Aharon Yariv.

65 Timing of interception according to General (Res.) Yoel Ben-Porat in *Ha'Aretz*, 5 June 1987. Rabin, op. cit., p. 84, says that the order was given only on 'the evening of 6 June'. It is possible that the discrepancy between '2.00 p.m.' and 'the evening' was due to the time it took the order to pass down the Egyptian chain of command.
66 Schiff, op. cit., p. 194.
67 Ibid., p. 200.
68 IDF Intelligence Branch, 'The Syrian Intelligence Keep the Russian Military Advisers in Syria under Surveillance', July 1967.
69 IDF Intelligence Branch, 'Syria Deployed Forbidden Forces in the Defence Zone and Fooled the UN Observers', July 1967.
70 The affair is well summarized in Steven, op. cit., pp. 252–66.
71 For the full story of the Cherbourg boats, which went on to win stunning victories against the Egyptian and Syrian navies in October 1973, see Abraham Rabinovich, *The Boats of Cherbourg*, New York, 1988.

8 Palestinian Challenges: 1967–73

1 Shlomo Gazit, *HaGezer VeHaMakel*, Tel Aviv, 1985, p. 291.
2 Interview with Aharon Yariv.
3 Aharon Yariv, statement, 8 February 1989.
4 *BaMahane*, 28 June 1989.
5 Interview with Shlomo Gazit.
6 Ze'ev Schiff and Raphael Rothstein, *Fedayeen*, New York, 1972, p. 63.
7 Gazit, op. cit., p. 283.
8 Interview.
9 Eitan Haber, *HaYom Tifrotz Milhama*, Tel Aviv, 1987, pp. 289–90.
10 Gazit, op. cit., pp. 14, 96.
11 David Ronen, *Shnat Shabak*, Tel Aviv, 1989, p. 13.
12 *Ma'ariv*, 4 December 1987.
13 Sarah Lazar, *Yehuda*, p. 36.
14 *Koteret Rashit*, 3 September 1986; and *Ma'Ariv*, 4 December 1987.
15 Moshe Dayan, *Living with the Bible*, London, 1978, p. 48.
16 Schiff and Rothstein, op. cit., p. 12.
17 Alan Hart, *Arafat*, London, 1984, pp. 241–3.

18 Helena Cobban, *The Palestinian Liberation Organisation*, Cambridge, 1984, p. 37.
19 Shabtai Teveth, *The Cursed Blessing*, London, 1970, p. 235.
20 Abu Iyad-Eric Rouleau, *My Home, My Land*, p. 56.
21 *Yediot Aharonot*, 21 September 1984.
22 Haber, op. cit., p. 323.
23 Interview.
24 Interview.
25 Amnon Cohen, *Miflagot Politiot BeGada HaMa'aravit*, Jerusalem, 1980, p. 3.
26 Interview with Shlomo Gazit.
27 Interview.
28 *BaMahane*, 28 June 1989.
29 *Yediot Aharonot*, 9 April 1990.
30 Cobban, op. cit., p. 275.
31 Ronen, op. cit., p. 117.
32 Hart, op. cit., pp. 248–9.
33 David Pryce-Jones, *The Face of Defeat*, London, 1974, p. 34.
34 Moshe Dayan, *The Story of My Life*, London, 1977, p. 405.
35 Pryce-Jones, op. cit., p. 36.
36 *Kol Ha'Ir*, 9 December 1988.
37 Ronen, op. cit., pp. 197–8.
38 Ibid., pp. 59-60.
39 Gerard Chaliand, *The Palestinian Resistance*, London, 1972, p. 73.
40 Interview.
41 Ronen, op. cit., pp. 182–8.
42 *Yediot Aharonot*, 21 September 1984.
43 Meron Benvenisti, *Jerusalem, the Torn City*, Jerusalem, 1976, p. 218.
44 General Security Service, *West Bank Information Digest*, 21 December 1967, KMA, Yisrael Galili Archives, 65/1.
45 Teveth, op. cit., pp 247–55
46 *Kol Ha'Ir*, 9 December 1988.
47 Avner Bar-On, *HaSipurim Shelo Supru*, Jerusalem, 1981, p. 217.
48 John Cooley, *Green March, Black September*, London, 1973, p. 100.
49 Haber, op. cit., p. 338.
50 Ronen, op cit., p. 196.
51 Hart, op. cit., p. 265.

52 Ehud Ya'ari, *Strike Terror*, New York, 1970, p. 141.
53 Benvenisti, op. cit., p. 224.
54 Hart, op. cit., p. 266.
55 Steve Eytan, *L'Oeil de Tel Aviv*, Paris, 1972, p. 72.
56 Interview.
57 Ronen, op. cit., pp. 140-48.
58 Interview.
59 Ya'ari, op. cit., p. 277. See also Michael Bar-Zohar and Eitan Haber, *The Quest for the Red Prince*, New York, 1983, p. 100.
60 Ya'akov Caroz, *The Arab Secret Services*, London, 1978, pp. 413–15.
61 Samir A. Mutawi, *Jordan in the 1967 War*, Cambridge, 1987, pp. 169–70.
62 Interview; and *Ha'Aretz*, 11 July 1985.
63 Edgar O'Ballance, *Arab Guerrilla Power, 1967-1972*, London, 1974, p. 181.
64 Eytan, op. cit.
65 Interview.
66 *Observer*, 1 August 1971.
67 Interview.
68 *Ha'Aretz*, 15 December 1980.
69 Interview.
70 Uzi Benziman, *Sharon, an Israeli Caesar*, New York, 1985, p. 115.
71 Interview.
72 Interview with Shlomo Gazit.
73 O'Ballance, op. cit., p. 197.
74 Interview.
75 Haber, op. cit., p. 324.
76 *Yediot Aharonot*, 30 August 1988.
77 Haber, op. cit., p. 324.
78 Ariel Merari and Shlomo Elad, *Fahah Hul*, Tel Aviv, 1986, p. 116.
79 Helena Cobban, *The Making of Modern Lebanon*, London, 1985, pp. 109–10.
80 Moshe Bar-Kochba, *Markavot HaPlade*, 1989, pp. 229–61.
81 Merari and Elad, op. cit., p. 97.
82 Cooley, op. cit., p. 186.
83 Leila Khaled, *My People Shall Live*, 1973, pp. 131–57.
84 Merari and Elad, op. cit., p. 97.
85 *Monitin*, February 1988.

86 *Ma'ariv*, 29 September 1972.
87 Iyad-Rouleau, op. cit., pp. 112–13.
88 Ze'ev Schiff, *A History of the Israeli Army*, London, 1987, pp. 172–3.
89 Israeli TV film, *Sportaim al Capaim*, 4 September 1983.
90 Hart, op. cit., pp. 309–10.
91 Cooley, op. cit., pp. 187–9.
92 Shmuel Segev, *Boded BeDamesek*, Tel Aviv, 1986, p. 14. According to Segev, Mizrahi went to Yemen and was arrested *before* 1967, while watching the performance of the Egyptian army.
93 *Ma'ariv*, 19 October 1977 and 6 May 1981.
94 Hanoch Bartov, *Dado*, Tel Aviv, 1978; and Bar-Zohar and Haber, op. cit., p. 4.
95 *Sportaim al Capaim*, op. cit.
96 *Ha'Aretz*, 1 June 1972.
97 *Jerusalem Post*, 25 September 1972; and *Yediot Aharonot*, 17 November 1989. Paglin, whose underground codename was 'Gidi', had manufactured the furnace used to cremate the body of Adolf Eichmann. In 1977 he was appointed prime minister's adviser on terrorism.
98 *Ha'Aretz*, 13 October 1972.
99 *Hadashot*, 23 September 1987.
100 Interview.
101 David B. Tinnin, *The Hit Team*, Boston, 1976, p. 84.
102 Iyad-Rouleau, op. cit., pp. 112–13.
103 *Monitin*, 113, February 1988.
104 Ibid.
105 Iyad-Rouleau, op. cit., pp. 112–13.
106 Bartov, op. cit., pp. 227–31.
107 Steven, op. cit., pp. 327–31.
108 Interview; and Rafik Halabi, *The West Bank Story*, New York, 1981, p. 87.
109 Colin Smith, *Carlos*, London, 1976, pp. 100–107, 129–3.
110 Tinnin, op. cit., *passim*.
111 *Hadashot*, 29 April 1988; and *Yediot Aharonot*, 12 January 1990.
112 Bar-Zohar and Haber, op. cit., p. 200. For a convincing account of the post-Munich hit-squad operations, purportedly based on an inside Israeli source, see also George Jonas, *Vengeance*, London, 1984.

113 *Monitin*, 113, February 1988.
114 Aryeh Bober (ed.), *The Other Israel*, New York, 1972.
115 *Hadashot*, 8 December 1989.
116 *Guardian*, 26 March 1973.
117 *Hadashot*, 2 December 1988.

9 *Mehdal: 1973*

1 Oded Granott, *Tzahal BeHeilo: Hayl HaModi'in*, Tel Aviv, 1981, p. 92.
2 *Aviation Week*, 30 June 1975.
3 Granott, op. cit., p. 100.
4 *Yediot Aharonot*, 7 October 1983. According to Brigadier-General Yoel Ben-Porat, an internal commission of inquiry in Aman investigated this lapse but the report was eventually shelved.
5 Interview.
6 *Yediot Aharonot*, 24 November 1989.
7 Ibid.
8 Dennis Eisenberg, Uri Dan and Eli Landau, *The Mossad: Inside Stories*, New York, 1978, p. 251.
9 Shlomo Nakdimon, *Sevirut Nemucha*, Tel Aviv, 1982, pp. 79–80, 105; and Moshe Dayan, London, 1977, *The Story of My Life*, p. 463. See also *Monitin*, October 1988; and *Yediot Aharonot*, 8 October 1989 and 24 November 1989.
10 Dayan, op. cit., p. 463.
11 Hanoch Bartov, *Dado*, Vol. I, Tel Aviv, 1978, p. 9. Eric Rouleau, *Le Monde*'s veteran Middle East correspondent, asserted that Dayan was informed of the impending war not by the Mossad or Aman but by 'a high CIA official' (*Sunday Times* Insight Team, *The Yom Kippur War*, London, 1977, pp. 121, 128). This is unlikely.
12 Bartov, op. cit., Vol. II, p. 9.
13 According to a later version, Zamir's cabled summary of the '*tsnon*' warning reached Israel at 6.00 a.m. on 6 October and read: 'Resumption of combat towards last light, today, 6 October 1973. Coordinated and simultaneous attack by the Egyptian and Syrian armies.' (*Yediot Aharonot*, 8 October 1989.)
14 In her autobiography, *My Life*, London, 1976, p. 358, Golda Meir wrote that her military secretary had woken her at around 4.00 a.m., saying that the intelligence was that the attack would be launched 'late in the afternoon'.

15 Nakdimon, op. cit., p. 107; and Michael Brecher, *Decisions in Crisis, Israel 1967 and 1973*, Los Angeles, 1980, p. 202. Brecher suggests that the mistake in the intelligence report occurred because the word 'before', which should have preceded 'sunset', had been omitted.
16 According to Aryeh Hashavia, *Milhemet Yom HaKippurim*, Tel Aviv, 1974, p. 15, American intelligence obtained a copy of the 'Egyptian plan' in April 1973.
17 Nakdimon, op. cit., pp. 29, 92. Patrick Seale, in *Asad*, pp. 199–200, maintains that the Syrian (and Egyptian) war plans were delivered at the end of August or beginning of September 1973 by a 'Syrian major-general' to an unnamed Arab intelligence service, which then promptly turned them over to Washington and Jerusalem. The plans, he says, were complete in every detail, save that H-Hour was designated as 6.00 a.m. Seale does not identify his source.
18 The mid-1972 bi-annual Aman assessment of Arab strength and intentions made the activation of the Egyptian plan to cross the Canal contingent upon 'the increase of the capability of the Egyptian air force'. There are two variations of this element of the '*kontzeptziya*'. The Agranat Commission, in its Interim Report in April 1974, mentioned the belief that Egypt would refrain from war until it 'first possessed an aerial capability to attack Israel in depth, and especially Israel's main airfields, in order to neutralize the Israel Air Force'. Other sources have laid greater emphasis on the inadequacy of Egypt's anti-aircraft missile defences as the 'aerial' leg of the '*kontzeptziya*'.
19 Bartov, op. cit., Vol. I, p. 237.
20 Gideon Rafael, *Destination Peace*, New York, 1981, p. 282.
21 Nakdimon, op. cit., p. 23.
22 Ibid., p. 48. President Assad of Syria was also in town at the time and he met repeatedly with Sadat and, possibly, Hussein, but his presence was kept secret.
23 Meir, op. cit., pp. 347–52; and *Sunday Times* Insight Team, op. cit., pp. 101–2.
24 Hashavia, op. cit., p. 55.
25 Ya'akov Caroz, *The Arab Secret Services*, London, 1978, pp. 235–6.
26 After Shahin's execution his wife and children were freed from gaol and managed to get to Israel, where they were resettled and

given new identities. However, they remained disgruntled about their treatment by the authorities and went public with their story in 1989, giving cheque-book journalism a bad name by selling their 'exclusive' story simultaneously to several newspapers (*Jerusalem Post*, 28 November 1988).

27 Mohamed Heikal, *The Road to Ramadan*, London, 1976, p. 15.
28 Brecher, op. cit., pp. 55–6, fn 11.
29 Heikal, op. cit., p. 30.
30 Hashavia, op. cit., p. 57.
31 Shmuel Bar, *Milhemet Yom HaKippurim Be'Einei Ha'Aravim*, Tel Aviv, 1986, pp. 40–41.
32 Bar, ibid., p. 40.
33 As early as 1969 the then deputy director of Aman's Sigint/Comint Collection Department, Yoel Ben-Porat, had written a report suggesting that any enemy exercise from division level and above should be treated by 'Collection' as possible camouflage for a real offensive. Ben-Porat had based the report on the Soviet-East Bloc preparations from May 1968 for the invasion of Czechoslovakia in August 1968. That invasion had taken place after, and under the guise of, a prolonged exercise and had effectively deceived NATO (as well as Czech) intelligence (*Yediot Aharonot*, 7 October 1983).
34 Nakdimon, op. cit., pp. 82, 92.
35 Hashavia, op. cit., pp. 56–7; Zvi Lanir, *HaHafta'ah HaBesisit*, Tel Aviv, 1983, p. 81; Heikal, op. cit., pp. 14, 30; and Granott, op. cit., pp. 135–7.
36 Nakdimon, op. cit., p. 61.
37 Ibid., p. 81.
38 Bartov, op. cit., Vol. I, p. 303; and Granott, op. cit., p. 122.
39 Hashavia, op. cit., p. 19, states that of the Arab leaders outside Egypt and Syria, only Houari Boumedienne knew of the war plans and the date of the attack. Hashavia says that on 3 October a secret alert was declared by Algiers, barring diplomats on home leave, senior officials, army officers and journalists from leaving the country.
40 Bar, op. cit., p. 108.
41 Hashavia, op. cit., p. 58; and Seale, op. cit., pp. 205–6.
42 *Sunday Times* Insight Team, op. cit., pp. 54–9.
43 Henry Kissinger, *White House Years*, pp. 1300, 1474.
44 Bar, op. cit., p. 27.

45 Seale, op. cit., pp. 192–3.

46 Bar, op. cit., pp. 42–5; and Seale, op. cit., pp. 193–4.

47 Bartov, op. cit., Vol. I, p. 240.

48 Ibid., Vol. I, pp. 233, 241–3, 246–7, 262–5, 278; Breacher, op. cit., p. 69; and Nakdimon, op. cit., p. 30.

49 Brigadier (Res.) Yoel Ben-Porat maintained that the Syrians and Egyptians had planned to go to war in May but had been pressured to defer it by the Soviets, who were intent on holding a quiet summit with the Americans. Ben-Porat maintained that in May Aman had three pieces of intelligence 'from excellent sources' that explained the deferment (*Monitin*, September 1988).

50 Bartov, op. cit., Vol. I, pp. 280–81; and Granott, op. cit., p. 112.

51 Granott, op. cit., p. 112.

52 Nakdimon, op. cit., p. 48.

53 Bartov, op. cit., Vol. I, p. 281.

54 Granott, op. cit., p. 112; and Bartov, op. cit., Vol. I, pp. 282–3.

55 Bartov, op. cit., Vol. I, p. 287; Granott, op. cit., p. 112; Nakdimon, op. cit., p. 53; and Rafael, op. cit., p. 282.

56 Nakdimon, op. cit., p. 54.

57 Granott, op. cit., pp. 120–21.

58 Brecher, op. cit., p. 75, fn. 4.

59 The American intelligence track record during the countdown to the Yom Kippur War was somewhat better than that of its Israeli counterparts. In May 1973, while Aman had completely written off the Arab preparations, the State Department's own assessment unit, the Bureau of Intelligence and Research (INR), produced a paper examining the possibility of a joint Egyptian–Syrian attack on Israel during the following six months. The paper had rated the chance that such an assault would take place as just less than even – a '45 per cent chance', as one Washington analyst put it. This INR paper was followed quickly by another, at the end of May, which now rated the chance of war during the autumn 'better than even'. The CIA apparently agreed, although it was uncertain about the timing. As the war clouds gathered in the autumn, the newly installed secretary of state, Henry Kissinger, asked the INR for an updated evaluation. On 30 September INR replied that the Syrian and Egyptian build-ups and moves were 'inconclusive'. The CIA produced a similar assessment; while the Egyptian build-up was designated potentially 'very ominous', the

agency's conclusion was '10 per cent less alarmist than the INR'. The CIA had been strongly influenced by the Aman input. But the National Security Agency, the US Sigint organization, had picked up clear signals pointing to war. One of them indicated Soviet concern about the possible outbreak of war, because of the presence of thousands of Soviet advisers and their families on Syrian and Egyptian soil. (*Sunday Times* Insight Team, op. cit., pp. 69–71, 92, 104; and Nakdimon, op. cit., p. 57.)

60 Bartov, op. cit., Vol. I, pp. 297–8.

61 Heikal, op. cit., p. 32, says the closedown of the airport and the evacuation from Cairo of Egypt Air's new Boeings were the initiative of a senior Egypt Air official who sensed that war was coming – and earned General Ismail's rebuke.

62 Bartov, op. cit., Vol. I, p. 299; *Yediot Aharonot*, 7 October 1983; and Granott, op. cit., p. 122. Yoel Ben-Porat, who was notified of the 1 October piece of intelligence at 3.00 a.m. by an officer in Aman's Collection Department, Colonel Menachem Digli, says that from that moment on he was convinced that war was imminent, and he immediately issued a war alert order to his department personnel.

63 Bartov, op. cit., Vol. I, p. 304.

64 Bartov, op. cit., Vol. I, pp. 304–5; Heikal, op. cit., p. 26; and Brecher, op. cit., p. 75.

65 Bartov, op. cit., Vol. I, p. 305.

66 Nakdimon, op. cit., p. 67; and Bartov, op. cit., Vol. I, pp. 306–7.

67 Bartov, op. cit., Vol. I, p. 323; Granott, op. cit., p. 137; and Agranat Commission Report, p. 37.

68 *Monitin*, September 1988. Ben-Porat spent the mid 1980s writing a classified and highly detailed analysis of the 1973 intelligence failure, submitting it to Aman OC Amnon Shahak in 1987. It is probably the definitive study of that failure.

69 Bartov, op. cit., Vol. I, pp. 314, 316.

70 Lanir, op. cit., p. 81; *Ha'Aretz*, 9 March 1979; Nakdimon, op. cit., p. 93; and *Yediot Aharonot*, 7 October 1983.

71 Agranat Commission Report, p. 36; Bartov, op. cit., Vol. I, p. 314; and Granott, op. cit., pp. 125–7.

72 Hashavia, op. cit., p. 34.

73 A few months later, following an internal inquiry, Lou Tordello, deputy head of the American NSA, was fired – according to some

sources because of his failure to intercept this crucial, non-Arab message.

74 Bartov, op. cit., Vol. I, p. 320; Nakdimon, op. cit., p. 5; and *Yediot Aharonot*, 21 October 1983.

75 Bartov, op. cit., Vol. II, p. 15.

76 Nakdimon, op. cit., p. 98.

77 Some analysts reject this assessment, arguing that Aman did know of the new weapons, had thoroughly warned the IDF training and field units of their use and effects, and had even predicted their possible use in large quantities. See discussion of this important point, in relation to both the anti-tank and anti-aircraft missiles, in Lanir, op. cit., pp. 48–52. Lanir rightly points out that in three border skirmishes between Israel and Syria in 1972–3, before the Yom Kippur War, the Syrians had twice used Sagger missiles against Israeli tanks, on the first occasion destroying one tank with a forty- to fifty-missile broadside. The IDF quickly learned the lesson. Aman's Technical Division sent out a detailed circular on the new weapon. In the third skirmish, IDF countermeasures had neutralized the Saggers and no Israeli tanks were hit. Aman, says Lanir (p. 52), had also long known about Egypt's powerful water cannon, with which holes were punched in the earthen ramparts along the Canal on 6 October.

78 Nakdimon, op. cit., p. 122.

79 Bartov, op. cit., Vol. II, p. 79.

80 Moshe Bar-Kochba, *Merkavot HaPlada*, Tel Aviv, 1989, pp. 329–30. Yoel Ben-Porat maintains that Aman did have advance knowledge of 'the routes, size and intentions of the Iraqi expeditionary force', and the air force and commandos were sent into Jordan to interdict it – but for some reason failed to do so.

81 *Ha'Aretz*, 2 October 1987. The author, Brigadier-General Aharon Levran, was deputy head of Aman's Research Department in 1973.

82 Interview.

83 *Ha'Aretz*, 2 October 1987.

84 Bartov, op. cit., Vol. II, p. 213.

85 Bar-Kochba, op. cit., p. 284.

86 The Tel Aviv publishing house Am Oved published the three parts of the Agranat Commission Report – the 2 April 1974 'Interim Report', the 10 July 1974 'Additions to the Interim Report' and

the 30 January 1975 'Third and Final Report' – in one volume in 1975. The full document, covering thousands of pages, was designated top-secret and remains classified, with only senior ministers, army brass and intelligence chiefs having access. The Commission was composed of Agranat, another justice of the Supreme Court, Moshe Landau, the state comptroller, Yitzhak Ernest Nebenzahl, and two former IDF chiefs of general staff, Yigael Yadin and Chaim Laskov.

87 Agranat Commission Report, pp. 29–33; and Lanir, op. cit., pp. 90–92. The reorganization of the intelligence community went ahead over the objections of the new Aman director, Shlomo Gazit. Gazit argued that: (1) the multiplicity of evaluating agencies would reduce Aman's responsibility for 'the big picture' and would reduce the sense of responsibility among the branch's officers; (2) the additional research bodies, which would necessarily feed off the same material as Aman's Research Department and would be manned by officers from the same socio-cultural environment, would almost inevitably produce similar conclusions and assessments as Aman itself; (3) Israel's main problem was still interpreting the broad strategic–military picture, and for this Aman was suitably trained – while the Mossad and Foreign Ministry Research departments were not, and would almost inevitably bow to Aman's assessments; and lastly (4) there was a fixed, limited pool of potential Middle East experts and intelligence talent in the country, and to recruit from this pool for three separate agencies would inevitably lower the calibre of Aman's researchers. The duplication would waste manpower and other resources. Gazit argued, but to no avail. He pointed out later that all the research departments – Aman's, the Mossad's and the Foreign Ministry's – were taken equally by surprise by Sadat's peace initiative of November 1977 (interview with Shlomo Gazit).

88 An analysis of the work of the Review Section is to be found in 'The Imperative of Criticism', by Lieutenant-Colonel 'Shmuel', in the *IDF Journal*, Vol. II, No. 3, 1985; and *Ha-aretz*, 9 March 1979.

89 Granott, op. cit., p. 140.

90 David Elazar, the dismissed COS, wrote in a memorandum submitted to the cabinet in May 1975 that in the months before the

war Aman had monitored at least 400 'significant [raw] items of information pointing to the possibility of war'. But most of these were never brought to his attention (Brecher, op. cit., p. 55).

91 *Yediot Aharonot*, 24 November 1989.

92 *Yediot Aharonot*, 8 October 1989; and *Ha'Aretz*, 27 October 1989.

10 Interregnum with Peace: 1974–80

1 Interview with Shlomo Gazit.

2 Oded Granott, *Tzahal BeHeilo: Hayl MaModi'in*, Tel Aviv, 1981, pp. 144–5; Ze'ev Schiff, *A History of the Israeli Army*, 1987, p. 204; and *Ha'Aretz*, 22 October 1978.

3 *Davar*, 11 September 1987.

4 Eitan Haber, Ze'ev Schiff and Ehud Ya'ari, *The Year of the Dove*, New York, 1979, p. 9.

5 *Davar*, 27 November 1987.

6 Gazit said that Gur's statement, for which the general was reprimanded by defence minister Ezer Weizman, was a mistake. Gur had given the interview four days before its publication, at a time when everyone was still unsure whether Sadat was really coming. The chief of staff gave the interview in order to conceal his plans to visit Iran secretly. The publication of the interview while he was in Tehran was designed to cover his unexplained absence from Israel. Later, Gur argued that he had merely been trying to warn the Israeli public against a possible Egyptian ruse as the whole subject of the Sadat visit had never been properly discussed between the political leaders and the military (*Davar*, op. cit.).

7 *Davar*, op. cit.

8 Shlomo Gazit, 'Intelligence Estimates and the Decision-Maker', in *Intelligence and National Security*, Vol. 3, No. 3, July 1988, p. 280. See also Zvi Lanir, *HaHafta'ah HaBesisit*, Tel Aviv, 1983, pp. 88–90.

9 *Davar*, op. cit.

10 Shmuel Segev, *HaMeshulash HaIrani*, Tel Aviv, 1981, p. 214.

11 Seymour Hersh, *The Price of Power*, New York, 1983, p. 542.

12 *Washington Post*, 17 September 1972.

13 Gerard Chaliand, *People without a Country*, London, 1980, pp. 184–5.

14 Segev, op. cit., p. 128.

15 Matti Golan, *Shimon Peres*, London, 1982, p. 150.
16 Interview.
17 Chaliand, op. cit., p. 189.
18 *Jerusalem Post*, 8 October 1980.
19 Mohamed Heikal, *The Return of the Ayatollah*, London 1981, p. 149.
20 Michael Ledeen and William Lewis, *Debacle*, New York, 1981, p. 126.
21 *The Times*, 16 April 1985.
22 *Yediot Aharonot*, 8 December 1989.
23 Miles Copeland, *The Game Player*, London, 1989, pp. 251–2.
24 CIA Report, *Washington Post*, 1 February 1982.
25 *Ma'Ariv*, 5 February 1982.
26 Shlomo Nakdimon, *First Strike*, New York, 1987, p. 219. Nakdimon, a former spokesman of prime minister Menachem Begin, was given access to a variety of top-secret papers and protocols, including cabinet and IDF General Staff minutes, in the preparation of his book.
27 David Ivri, 'Ikifat HaKur HaGari'ini BeIraq – Yuni 1981', in Ze'ev Klein (ed.), *HaMilhama BaTerror*, Tel Aviv, 1988; and Nakdimon, op. cit., p. 109. Ivri was the commander of the IAF from 1977 to 1982 and deputy chief of staff from 1983 to 1985.
28 Nakdimon, op. cit., p. 95.
29 Ibid., pp. 100, 179; and *Ha'Aretz*, 21 July 1981.
30 Amos Perlmutter, Michael Handel and Uri Bar-Joseph, *Two Minutes over Baghdad*, London, 1982, pp. 69–70.
31 Ibid., p. 72.
32 'From an intelligence point of view it is easier to penetrate underdeveloped and less industrialized countries which depend heavily on foreign experts whose loyalties they cannot fully check or control and whose private goals are to make as much money as possible in the shortest possible time' (ibid., p. 103).
33 Nakdimon, op. cit., pp. 160–61.
34 *Ha'Aretz*, 18 August 1983.
35 Nakdimon, op. cit., pp. 165–6.
36 Ibid., p. 184.
37 Ibid., p. 190.
38 Ibid., p. 208.
39 Bob Woodward, *Veil*, New York, 1987, pp. 160–162.
40 Eric Silver, *Begin*, London, 1984, p. 220.

41 Shaul Mishal, *The PLO under Arafat*, Yale, 1986, p. 115.
42 Golan, op. cit., p. 180.
43 *Hadashot*, 30 December 1988.
44 *Jerusalem Post*, 4 July 1986.
45 Stewart Steven, *The Spymasters of Israel*, New York, 1980, p. 381.
46 'Gandhi' did better than his successor, Amihai Paglin, the former Irgun operations chief appointed by Menachem Begin when he became prime minister in May 1977. Paglin was virtually boycotted by both the Shin Bet and the Mossad, not least because he had been convicted in 1972 on charges of trying to smuggle weapons abroad to mount anti-Arab attacks (*Koteret Rashit*, 15 June 1988).
47 Gazit, op. cit., p. 262.
48 *Ha'Aretz*, 3 April 1981.
49 Golan, op. cit., p. 177.
50 Moshe Maoz, *Palestinian Leadership on the West Bank*, London, 1984, p. 134.
51 Interview.
52 Interview.
53 Golan, op. cit., p. 178.
54 Interview.
55 Interview; and *Ha'Aretz*, 7 May 1976.
56 *Ma'ariv*, 10 May 1976.
57 *Ha'Aretz*, 12 May 1976.
58 Interview with Mordechai Gur.
59 Interview.
60 Golan, op. cit., pp. 167–8.
61 *Ma'ariv*, 6 June 1986.
62 *Jerusalem Post*, 15 December 1980.
63 *Washington Post*, 1 February 1982.
64 *Yediot Aharonot*, 15 December 1980.
65 *Ha'Aretz*, 15 December 1980.
66 On the planning and the operation's background, see *Koteret Rashit*, 24 February 1988.
67 Pinhas Inbari, *Meshulash Al HaYarden* Jerusalem, 1983, pp. 44–53.
68 Hagai Segal, *Dear Brothers*, New York, 1988, p. 97.
69 *Ma'ariv*, 19 December 1980.
70 Segal, op. cit., p. 10.

71 Interview.
72 *Ha'Aretz*, 15 December 1980.
73 *Ma'ariv*, 10 December 1980.
74 *Ha'Aretz*, 15 December 1980.
75 *Yediot Aharonot*, 8 August 1980.
76 Segal, op. cit., p. 122.
77 Ibid., p. 124.
78 *Al-HaMishmar*, 4 July 1980.
79 David Ronen, *Shnat Shabak*, Tel Aviv, 1989, pp. 223–32.
80 *Sunday Times*, 19 June 1977.
81 *Yediot Aharonot*, 15 December 1980.
82 *Ma'ariv*, 8 December 1989.
83 *Hadashot*, 23 September 1987.
84 *Davar*, 20 August 1983.

11 The Lebanese Quagmire: 1978–85

1 For a Palestinian view of the operation, see Abu Iyad (Salah Khalaf), *Lelo Moledot*, Tel Aviv, 1979, pp. 294–5; for an Israeli view, Avner Yaniv, *Dilemmas of Security*, New York, 1987, 1971.
2 Yaniv, op. cit., p. 72.
3 Mustafa Tlas, *HaPlisha HaYisraelit LeLevanon*, Tel Aviv, 1988, pp. 50–60.
4 Interview with Shlomo Gazit.
5 Yaniv, op. cit., pp. 73–5.
6 The Phalange Party, set up by the Maronite Christian Gemayel family in the 1930s, represented Christian interests in Lebanon. The Israeli–Phalange relationship was born in 1948 and continued, with interruptions, through the 1950s and 1960s. But these links, which involved some Israeli subsidies and other aid, turned into a fully fledged alliance only in the mid-1970s. From the 1930s the Zionist movement had looked to the Lebanese Christians, a 'fellow' minority in the Muslim-dominated Middle East, as a potential ally. The start of the Lebanese civil war in 1975 increased the attractiveness of the Phalange in the eyes of Israeli politicians and generals. For the early years, see Benny Morris, 'The Birth of the Israeli–Phalange Relationship, 1948-1951', in *Studies in Zionism*, spring 1984; and Ian Black and Neil Caplan, 'Israel and Lebanon: Origins of a Relationship', *Jerusalem Quarterly*, spring 1983.

7 Yaniv, op. cit., p. 57.
8 *Hadashot*, 17 February 1989.
9 Ze'ev Schiff and Ehud Ya'ari, *Israel's Lebanon War*, London, 1986, p. 14.
10 Brigadier-General Zvi Inbar, 'Va'adat Kahan', in Ze'ev Klein (ed.), *HaMilhama BaTerror*, Tel Aviv, 1988, pp. 113–23; and *Ha'Aretz*, 7 June 1985.
11 Schiff and Ya'ari, op. cit., p. 18.
12 Ibid; and Reuven Avi-Ran, *HaMeuravut HaSurit BeLevanon* (1975–1985), Tel Aviv, 1986, p. 67. According to one estimate, the Rabin government spent $150 million arming the Maronites between 1975 and 1977. Phalange officers and NCOs were brought to Israel for short IDF training courses. One young Arabic-speaking IDF officer who took part in the covert operation recalled later that the Lebanese militiamen used to boast about their participation in massacres of the Muslims and Palestinians (Yoram Binur, *My Enemy, My Self*, New York 1989, p. 36).
13 Inbar, op. cit., p. 113; Schiff and Ya'ari, op. cit., pp. 22–23; Yaniv, op. cit., pp. 63–4, 83–4; and Avi-Ran, op. cit., p. 291.
14 Schiff and Ya'ari, op. cit, p. 26; and Avi-Ran, op. cit., p. 136.
15 Avi-Ran, op. cit., pp. 139–40.
16 Ibid., pp. 138–9.
17 Yaniv, op. cit., p. 86; and Avi-Ran, op. cit., p. 139.
18 Bob Woodward, *Veil*, New York, 1987, p. 380.
19 *Hadashot*, 17 February 1989.
20 Schiff and Ya'ari, op. cit, pp. 34–35.
21 Yaniv, op. cit., p. 86; Avi-Ran, op. cit., p. 134; and Schiff and Ya'ari, op. cit., pp. 34–35. See also Itamar Rabinovich, *The War for Lebanon 1970–1983*, New York, 1984, pp. 114–20.
22 Yaniv, op. cit., pp. 88–9; Schiff and Ya'ari, op. cit, pp. 35–8; and Major-General Yehoshua Saguy, 'Hitmasdut HaTerror VeHaHitdarderut LaMilhama', in Klein, op. cit., pp. 37–9.
23 *Ha'Aretz*, 18 November 1988.
24 Ariel Sharon, 'Tfisat HaBitachon UMilhemet Shlom HaGalil', in Klein, op. cit., pp. 43–57.
25 Interview.
26 Major-General (Res.) Amir Drori, 'Oranim Mitgalgel [Rolling Pines]', in Klein, op. cit., pp. 73–87; and Schiff and Ya'ari, op. cit., pp. 45–6.

27 Schiff and Ya'ari, op. cit., pp. 42–3.
28 Ibid., p. 46. Schiff and Ya'ari's book remains the best and most comprehensive account yet published of the Lebanon war, and its narrative has served as the basis for parts of this chapter. For a more general, political overview, see Rabinovich, op. cit., pp. 121–52.
29 Schiff and Ya'ari, op. cit., pp. 47–8; and Yaniv, op. cit., p. 107.
30 Schiff and Ya'ari, op. cit., pp 48–51.
31 Ibid., pp. 67–8; and Yaniv, op. cit., pp. 108, 139.
32 Uzi Benziman, *Sharon, an Israeli Caesar*, New York, 1985, p. 233.
33 Schiff and Ya'ari, op. cit., p. 53; and *Monitin*, June 1986.
34 Yaniv, op. cit., p. 108.
35 Avi-Ran, op. cit., pp. 147–8.
36 Schiff and Ya'ari, op. cit., pp. 59–60.
37 Ibid., pp. 56–7.
38 Yaniv, op. cit., pp. 109–10. The head of the London hit team, Nawwaf Rosan, was an East Bank Jordanian who had been with Abu Nidal since being recruited by Iraqi intelligence in Jordan in the early 1970s. Another member of the team was Marwan al-Banna, from Nablus, a second cousin of the terrorist leader. Rosan was known to have been in close contact with the Iraqi Embassy in London. One theory was that Iraq had ordered or at least encouraged the attack on Argov to provoke an Israeli invasion of Lebanon as a diversion from its own serious losses against Iran in the Gulf War. Iraq 'responded' to the assassination attempt by calling for a ceasefire. Tehran rejected the call and accused Baghdad of being behind the London shooting. (*Guardian*, March 7 1983).
39 Interview with Gideon Mahanaimi; Schiff and Ya'ari, op. cit., pp. 97–8.
40 Ibid., p. 101.
41 Described in Yaniv, op. cit., pp. 110–13.
42 Schiff and Ya'ari, op. cit., pp. 103–6. Lieutenant-General Rafael Eitan, 'Milhemet Shlom HaGalil, Pe'ula Yabashtit Rehava', in Klein, op. cit., pp. 63–71, claims that the cabinet meeting of 5 June had not limited the operation to a 40-kilometre arc and had approved a thrust as far north as the Beirut–Damascus highway and a link-up with the Phalange around Beirut.
43 Schiff and Ya'ari, op. cit., pp. 106–7; and Drori, op. cit., p. 76.

44 Schiff and Ya'ari, op. cit., p. 112.
45 Tlas, op. cit., pp. 143–59.
46 Ibid., pp. 173–93, also ascribed the success of the Israeli anti-missile offensive to a total blanketing of Syrian radar and electronics in the Beka'a with electronic jamming by specially equipped Boeing 707s, Skyhawks, Hawkeyes and ECM ground stations. He singled out such a station on Mount Hermon in this context. Specially equipped drones were used for diversion, jamming and surveillance, and were sent in to attract the first salvo of missiles (ibid., pp. 188–9). Tlas's is the fullest description yet published of the Israeli anti-missile strike.
47 For full descriptions of Ben-Gal's campaign and the Syrian resistance, see ibid., pp. 195–224; and Schiff and Ya-ari, op. cit., pp. 171–80, which focuses on the dramatic trap at Sultan Yakoub.
48 Rashid Khalidi, *Under Siege*, Columbia, 1986, pp. 88, 93–4, 202; and Tlas, op. cit., p. 233.
49 Tlas, op. cit., pp. 163-8.
50 Khalidi, op. cit., pp. 93–4, maintains that the PLO security service captured seven 'Israeli agents' (all Arabs) out of twenty-four sent in to locate and signal to the IAF the whereabouts of these PLO leaders. Ten of these agents died in Israeli bombings, says Khalidi, quoting Abu Iyad. Eitan was later to claim (in Klein, op. cit., p. 70) that the IAF could have killed Arafat a number of times, but did not because doing so would have meant killing many civilians as well.
51 The siege of Beirut and the PLO evacuation is described in detail in Khalidi, op. cit.
52 Schiff and Ya'ari, op. cit., pp. 124, 157, 174; Avi-Ran, op. cit., p. 157; and in Klein, op. cit., p. 104.
53 *Monitin*, June 1986.
54 Schiff and Ya'ari, op. cit., pp. 233–6; and Yaniv, op. cit., p. 152.
55 Schiff and Ya'ari, op. cit., pp. 236–7.
56 Ibid., p. 239.
57 This quotation and the bulk of what follows is based on the Kahan Commission Report, which appeared in full, save for a secret twelve-page appendix, in the *Jerusalem Post*, 9 February 1983. See also Schiff and Ya'ari, op. cit., pp. 246–7; and Yaniv, op. cit., pp. 152–3.
58 Tlas, op. cit., p. 311; and Avi-Ran, op. cit., pp. 174–5.

59 Schiff and Ya'ari, op. cit., pp. 247–9; and *Monitin*, June 1986. Israel cooperated closely with the United States in the investigation of Gemayel's assassination. The Mossad supplied the CIA with information from its 'best Syrian agents, surveillance reports and electronic intercepts' (Woodward, op. cit., p. 219).
60 Kahan Commission Report.
61 Ibid.; and in Klein, op. cit., p. 114.
62 Kahan Commission Report.
63 Schiff and Ya'ari, op. cit., pp. 277, 279–80.
64 Kahan Commission report; Lanir, op. cit., pp. 156–9; and Schiff and Ya'ari, op. cit., pp. 282–4.
65 Woodward, op. cit., pp. 160–61, 286.
66 Fuad Ajami, *The Vanished Imam*, New York, 1986, p. 200.
67 *Washington Post*, 6 August 1989.
68 Shmuel Segev, *The Iranian Triangle*, New York, 1988, pp. 117–18.
69 Ajami, op. cit., p. 201.
70 *Independent*, 29 September 1989.
71 Detailed testimonies apear in Franklin P. Lamb (ed.), *Israel's War in Lebanon*, Boston, 1984, pp. 633–800.
72 Interview; *Yediot Aharonot*, 29 May 1987.
73 *Ma'ariv*, 15 November 1982.
74 *Koteret Rashit*, 20 April 1988.
75 *The Times*, 6 July 1984; and *Ma'ariv*, 10 July 1984.
76 *The Times*, 14 January 1985.
77 *The Times*, 10 July 1984 and 14 January 1985; *Guardian*, 14 February 1985; and *The Times*, 5 March 1985 and 6 March 1985.
78 *Ma'ariv*, 25 September 1984.
79 *Ma'ariv*, 21 June 1984, quoting from *Le Monde*; and *The Times*, 7 March 1985.
80 *The Times*, 7 March 1985, 12 March 1985 and 14 March 1985.
81 *Hadashot*, 1 May 1988.
82 *The Times*, 24 December 1984.
83 *The Times*, 14 January 1985 and 25 January 1985; and Moshe Arens, 'Hidush HaHaskama HaLeumit Benosei Bitachon', and Lieutenant-General Moshe Levy, 'MiLevanon Lesdeh HaKrav Ha'Atidi', in Klein, op. cit., pp. 141–7.
84 *Hadashot*, 18 March 1988.

12 *Occupational Hazards: 1984–7*

1 Robert Manne, *The Petrov Affair*, Sydney, 1987, p. xi.
2 *Ma'ariv*, 18 July 1986.
3 For Ginossar's version see *Yediot Aharonot*, 8 January 1988.
4 *Hadashot*, 23 September 1987.
5 *Ma'ariv*, 18 July 1986.
6 *Koteret Rashit*, 25 May 1986.
7 *Jerusalem Post*, 4 June 1986.
8 *Koteret Rashit*, 23 April 1987.
9 Amina Mufti, a Circassian woman recruited by the Mossad, served as an agent in Beirut from early 1973 until 1976, when she was captured by the PLO, and released in a prisoner exchange in 1980 (see Steve Posner, *Israel Undercover*, New York, 1987). She was swapped for two top Fatah men, William Nassar and Mehdi Bseiso (*Jerusalem Post*, 27 February 1980).
10 *Ha'Aretz*, 8 May 1987.
11 *Guardian*, 27 May 1987.
12 *Ha'Aretz*, 1 November 1987.
13 Landau Commission Report, p. 14.
14 *Ha'Aretz*, 4 November 1987.
15 *Ha'Aretz*, 1 November 1987.
16 *Ha'Aretz*, 4 November 1987.
17 Statement by Canon Riah Abu el-Assal of Christ Evangelical Episcopal Church, Nazareth, 3 November 1987.
18 *Hadashot*, 1 November 1987.
19 *Jerusalem Post*, 1 November 1987.
20 *Ha'Aretz*, 5 September 1986.
21 *Hadashot*, 28 March 1988.
22 US Government Memorandum in Aid of Sentencing, 6 January 1987.
23 Wolf Blitzer, *Territory of Lies*, New York, 1989, pp. 8–9, 13.
24 Interview.
25 Blitzer, op. cit., p. 10.
26 The 1976 CIA report, 'Israel: Foreign Intelligence and Security Services', did not mention Lakam. But it stated that 'collection of scientific intelligence in the US and other developed countries was the third priority of Israeli espionage'. 'The Israelis devote a considerable portion of their covert operations to obtaining scien-

tific and technical intelligence,' it said, 'This included attempts to penetrate certain classified defense projects in the United States and other Western nations' (*Washington Post*, 1 February 1982).

27 The plant had a history of 'poor record keeping, lax security, missing uranium and close ties with Israel' (*Boston Globe*), 14 December 1986. See also *International Herald Tribune*, 6 June 1986. This episode and related clandestine Israeli attempts to acquire uranium have been described in a heavily disguised 'factional' manner in Dennis Eisenberg, Eli Landau and Menachem Portugali, *Operation Uranium Ship*, Tel Aviv, 1978, and in Elaine Davenport, Paul Eddy and Peter Gillman, *The Plumbatt Affair*, London, 1978.

28 *Koteret Rashit*, 15 June 1988.

29 See Michael Bar-Zohar and Eitan Haber, *The Quest for the Red Prince*, New York, 1983.

30 *Miami Herald*, 26 August 1986.

31 *Hadashot*, 25 March 1987.

32 Statement by Yitzhak Rabin, 3 December 1985. One Israeli expert has speculated that it may be more than coincidence that Pollard was encouraged to intensify his espionage activities in a period of 'blindness' in intelligence-gathering about Syria. Between May 1985 and January 1986 eight Syrian nationals were reported by the Syrian media to have been executed on charges of spying for Israel (Raymond Cohen, *Threat Assessment in Military Intelligence: The Case of Israel and Syria, 1985–86*, Intelligence and National Security, Vol. 4, No. 4, October 1989, pp. 755–6). Apparent confirmation of the 'blindness' theory is provided by a 76-part Aman questionnaire about different aspects of Syrian military preparedness given to the Mossad for the use of a high-ranking Syrian agent prior to his return home from Europe, in late 1984 or early 1985 (Victor Ostrovsky and Claire Hoy, *By Way of Deception: the Making and Unmaking of a Mossad Officer*, New York, 1990, pp. 350–6).

33 *Sunday Times*, 29 March 1987.

34 See James Adams, *The Unholy Alliance*, London, 1984.

35 *Jerusalem Post*, 26 December 1986.

36 *Jerusalem Post*, 14 December 1986.

37 *Jerusalem Post*, 14 December 1986.

38 Blitzer, op. cit., p. 92.

39 *Koteret Rashit*, 4 February 1988.
40 *Ha'Aretz*, 26 November 1985; and *Ma'Ariv*, 29 November 1985.
41 *Washington Post*, 15 June 1986.
42 *Ha'Aretz*, 27 March 1987.
43 *Ha'Aretz*, 24 March 1987.
44 *Time*, 23 March 1987.
45 *Koteret Rashit*, 11 June 1986.
46 *Jerusalem Post*, 1 March 1987.
47 *Hadashot*, 23 September 1987.
48 *Koteret Rashit*, 27 January 1988.
49 *Ha'Aretz*, 5 March 1987.
50 *Jerusalem Post*, 6 March 1987.
51 *International Herald Tribune*, 20 February 1988.
52 *Jerusalem Post*, 13 March 1987.
53 *The New York Times*, 15 March 1987.
54 *Hadashot*, 13 January 1989.
55 Shmuel Segev, *HaMeshulash HaIrani*, Tel Aviv, 1981, pp. 14–15.
56 *Ma'ariv*, 19 March 1987; *Al-HaMishmar*, 24 March 1987; and Segev, op. cit.
57 *Hadashot*, 17 February 1989.
58 *Hadashot*, 17 February 1989.
59 *Ha'Ir*, 13 January 1989.
60 *Hadashot*, 9 December 1988.
61 *Miami Herald*, 20 January 1987.
62 Segev, op. cit., pp. 259–60.
63 *Ha'Aretz*, 18 November 1988.
64 Tower Commission Report, New York, 1987, pp. 83–4.
65 *Guardian*, 15 November 1986.
66 Patrick Seale, *Asad*, London, 1988, p. 480.
67 *Ha'Aretz*, 11 July 1986, for a monologue by an El Al security officer.
68 *Guardian*, 6 February 1986. It does seem to have been an unreliable method of catching wanted Palestinians. The same had happened in August 1973, when a Lebanese passenger plane was forced down in the mistaken belief that George Habash of the PFLP was on board.
69 *Miami Herald*, 27 July 1986.
70 *Ha'Aretz*, 10 May 1986.
71 A Syrian journalist who wrote a book about the Cohen case in

the mid-1980s was forced to leave the country and settle in Iraq (*Yediot Aharonot*, 11 April 1988).

72 Interview. In May 1985 six Syrians were publicly executed after being convicted of 'passing classified information and jeopardizing state security to the Israeli enemy' (*Guardian*, 15 May 1985).

73 *Jerusalem Post*, 6 July 1988.

74 *Sunday Times*, 5 October 1986.

75 *Sunday Times*, 9 August 1987.

76 *Ha'Aretz*, 28 October 1986.

77 Interview.

78 Frank Barnaby, *The Invisible Bomb*, London, 1989, p. xi.

79 Leonard S. Spector, *Going Nuclear*, New York, 1987, p. 138.

80 See George H. Quester, in Jed C. Snyder (ed.), *Limiting Nuclear Proliferation*, p. 49.

81 *Ha'Aretz*, 14 November 1986.

82 *Al-HaMishmar*, 4 November 1986.

83 *Ha'Aretz*, 14 November 1986.

84 *Al-HaMishmar*, 24 March 1987.

85 *Observer*, 8 September 1985.

86 *Yisrael Shelanu*, 25 February 1988; and *Guardian*, 26 February 1988.

87 *Independent*, 26 February 1988.

88 *Yediot Aharonot*, 15 January 1988.

89 *Ma'ariv*, 12 January 1988.

90 *Monitin*, September 1987.

91 *Sunday Times*, 15 March 1987.

92 *Al-HaMishmar*, 24 March 1987.

93 Ibrahim Sowan was to suffer for his reputation. In March 1990 he was found murdered during a spate of killings of Palestinians suspected of collaborating with the Israelis (*Hadashot*, 23 March 1990).

94 Another Palestinian who became a valued Israeli agent in the first half of the 1970s was originally approached when he returned home for his father's funeral. He was told he would be permitted to bring his family back from Jordan to the West Bank if he cooperated. The man was employed at the Saudi Arabian Embassy in Amman and had a close relative in one of the PLO groups in Syria. His Israeli controller knew the man's file in

detail long before their first meeting. For a heavily disguised account of a true story, see *Ma'ariv*, 6 June 1980.

95 *Ma'ariv*, 13 January 1989.

96 Full accounts of the Sowan case appear in *Ha'Aretz*, 24 June 1988; and *Jerusalem Post*, 24 June 1988.

97 *Guardian*, 16 June 1988.

98 *Yediot Aharonot*, 29 July 1988.

99 The best general accounts of the Falasha exodus and the Mossad's role are in Tudor Parfitt, *Operation Moses*, London, 1985; and Louis Rapoport, *Redemption Song*, New York, 1986.

100 Ariel Sharon, *Warrior*, p. 417; and *Yediot Aharonot*, 24 February 1989.

101 The Mossad may have been cashing in on a favour; according to unconfirmed reports, Israeli commandos freed a senior CIA agent who had been kidnapped in Ethiopia at the end of 1983 (*Ha'Aretz*, 12 August 1987, quoting from the *New York Post*).

13 Intifada: 1987–90

1 Interview with Ehud Barak, *Davar*, 5 October 1984.

2 Ze'ev Klein (ed.), *HaMilhama BaTerror*, Tel Aviv, 1988, p. 163.

3 *Yediot Aharonot*, 20 January 1989.

4 *Daily Telegraph*, 26 September 1985.

5 *Ma'ariv*, 26 September 1985.

6 Interview with Ehud Barak, Israeli TV, 16 October 1985.

7 The Israeli figures appear in the IAF Historical Branch version of the Tunis raid in Klein, op. cit., pp. 167–9.

8 *Washingtonian*, June 1988.

9 On the negotiations with Jibril, including the psychological warfare waged by the Shin Bet to increase Palestinian pressure on the Palestinian leader, see *Yediot Aharonot*, 19 April 1989.

10 David C. Martin and John Walcott, *Best Laid Plans*, New York, 1988, p. 248.

11 *Guardian*, 11 October 1985.

12 Bob Woodward, *Veil*, New York, 1987, pp. 414–17.

13 *Guardian*, 10 October 1985.

14 Interview with Ehud Barak, Israeli TV, 16 October 1985.

15 *Ha'Aretz*, 23 October 1985.
16 *Ha'Aretz*, 17 April 1986.
17 *Davar*, 6 September 1985.
18 Interview with Ehud Barak, Israeli TV, 16 October 1985.
19 *Davar*, 19 August 1988.
20 *Guardian*, 26 October 1987.
21 For a summary of the Hamdan case, see *Ha'Aretz*, 24 September 1989.
22 *Yediot Aharonot*, 2 December 1988.
23 United National Committee, 10 February 1988. See also Shaul Mishal, *Avanim Ze Lo HaKol*, Tel Aviv, 1989, for a comprehensive study of the leaflet phenomenon.
24 Ze'ev Schiff and Ehud Ya'ari, *Intifada*, New York, 1990, p. 161.
25 *Koteret Rashit*, 24 February 1988; and memorandum on PLO, Office of the Adviser on Countering Terrorism, 12 December 1988.
26 *Guardian*, 17 February 1988.
27 *Washington Post*, international edition, 24 February 1988.
28 David Halevy and Neil C. Livingstone, *Washingtonian*, June 1988.
29 *Ha'Aretz*, 17 April 1988.
30 Israel Radio, 9 June 1988.
31 Interview.
32 *Ha'Aretz*, 5 May 1989.
33 'Let Us Foil the Intelligence Methods of the Enemy and Struggle against Them with Determination', unsigned, undated leaflet, Arabic.
34 *Alternative Information Centre Bulletin*, 7 August 1986.
35 Committee for the Defence of Palestinian Human Rights, 'How These Fighters were Killed by Zionist Intelligence and Its Agents', undated leaflet, Arabic.
36 *Los Angeles Times*, 6 July 1986. Death by deliberately doctored, unstable explosives or detonators was a method that other security services had considered, if not employed. Peter Wright of Britain's MI5 once suggested 'examining the possibilities of planting booby-trapped detonators' on the Provisional IRA in Northern Ireland; the proposal was rejected (Peter Wright, *Spycatcher*, New York, 1987, p. 359).
37 *Hadashot*, 4 April 1989.
38 *International Herald Tribune*, 2 March 1988.

39 *Ha'Aretz*, 2 December 1987.
40 Richard Cobb, *French and Germans, Germans and French*, p. 162.
41 *Davar*, 29 February 1988.
42 *International Herald Tribune*, 2 March 1988.
43 *Hadashot*, 18 May 1989.
44 *Ha'Aretz*, 3 March 1988.
45 *Ha'Aretz*, 21 May 1989.
46 *Jerusalem Post*, 13 March 1988.
47 *Ma'ariv*, 16 August 1988.
48 *Jerusalem Post*, 26 August 1988.
49 *Davar*, 12 December 1988.
50 *Hadashot*, 12 May 1988.
51 *Guardian*, 1 November 1989.
52 Interview.
53 *Yediot Aharonot*, 28 April 1989.
54 *Kol Ha'Ir*, 5 May 1989.
55 *Hadashot*, 28 July 1989.
56 *HaOlam HaZeh*, 3 May 1989.
57 *Independent*, 12 May 1989.
58 *Hadashot*, 5 June 1989.
59 *Yediot Aharonot*, 2 December 1988.
60 *Yediot Aharonot*, 30 June 1989.
61 *Hadashot*, 30 December 1988.
62 *Yediot Aharonot*, 19 December 1988.
63 *Davar*, 19 December 1988.
64 *Ha'Aretz*, 30 June 1988.
65 *Ha'Aretz*, 23 March 1989.
66 Interview with Amnon Shahak, IDF Radio, 9 June 1989.
67 Interview with Amnon Shahak, Israeli TV, 9 June 1988.
68 *Davar*, 9 February 1989.
69 *Ha'Aretz*, 16 March 1989.
70 Interview with Amnon Shahak, IDF Radio, 9 June 1989.
71 *Yediot Aharonot*, 24 March 1989. Shortly after his retirement from the Mossad in March 1989, Nahum Admoni said he believed that the PLO was still 'fundamentally' a terrorist organization. 'I presume that if the PLO decides it needs to advance its achievements, and if the political process is slowed, it will renew its path of terror in order to get the process moving and to achieve additional aims,' he said (IDF Radio, 21 July 1989).

72 *Yerushalayim*, 23 June 1989.
73 *Yerushalayim*, 30 June 1989.
74 *Yediot Aharonot*, 20 January 1989.
75 David Grossman, *The Yellow Wind*, New York, 1988, p. 144.
76 Interview with David Grossman, Israeli TV, 7 June 1987.
77 *Yerushalayim*, 24 February 1989.
78 *Guardian*, 11 March 1989.
79 *Yediot Aharonot*, 24 February 1989.
80 *Yerushalayim*, 17 February 1989.
81 *Hadashot*, 13 January 1989.
82 *Guardian*, 12 January 1989.
83 *Ma'ariv*, 13 January 1989.
84 *Hadashot*, 13 January 1989.
85 A French magazine published in Lebanon quickly seized on this harmless snippet but was apparently baffled by problems of transliteration from Hebrew through Arabic into French, announcing that the Mossad chief's '*nom de guerre*' was '*Monsieur Godschi*'.
86 *Yediot Aharonot*, 13 January 1989.
87 *Washington Post*, 6 August 1989.
88 Interview.
89 *Ha'Aretz*, 5 October 1989.
90 Interview, *Ha'Aretz*, 21 December 1989.
91 *Ha'Aretz*, 18 March 1989 and 5 April 1989.
92 Interview.
93 *Yediot Aharonot*, 30 March 1990.

Conclusion

1 Amos Oz, *LaDa'at Isha*, Tel Aviv, 1988. See also Amon Jakont, *Pesek-Zman*, Tel Aviv, 1982; and Shlomo Frankel, *Sodi BeYoter* Tel Aviv, 1988.
2 David Grossman, *HaZman HaTsahov*, Tel Aviv, 1987.
3 Yitzhak Ben-Ner, *Ta'atuon*, Tel Aviv, 1989.
4 *Davar*, 28 April 1989.

Sources

Primary Sources

Ben-Gurion Archive (Sdeh Boqer)

Ben-Gurion diary and correspondence

Central Zionist Archive (Jerusalem)

Jewish Agency Political Department Papers

Israel State Archive (Jerusalem)

Foreign Ministry Papers
Prime Minister's Office Papers
Minority Affairs Ministry Papers
Reuven Shiloah Papers

Kibbutz Meuhad Archive (Ef'al)

Yisrael Galili Papers
Palmah Archive

Public Record Office (London)

Foreign Office Papers

Boris Guriel Papers (Jerusalem)

National Archive (Washington)

Newspapers and Journals

BaMahane
Davar
Ha'Aretz
Hadashot
Jerusalem Post
Koteret Rashit
Ma'Archot
Ma'ariv
Monitin
Yediot Aharonot

Select Bibliography

Abu Iyad, *Lelo Moledet*, Tel Aviv, 1979.
Adams, James, *The Unholy Alliance*, London, 1984.
Agranat Commission Report, Tel Aviv, 1975.
Ajami, Fouad, *The Vanished Imam*, New York, 1986.
Al-Bazzaz, Sa'ad, *Al Harb as-Siriya*, London, 1987.
Almogi, Yosef, *HaMa'avak al Ben-Gurion*, Tel Aviv, 1988.
Amery, Julian, *Approach March*, London 1973.
Amir, Yisrael, *Derekh Lo Slula*, Tel Aviv, 1988.
Andrew, C., and Dilks, D., *The Missing Dimension*, London, 1984.
Avi-Ran, Reuven, *HaMe'uravut HaSurit BeLevanon* (1975–85), Tel Aviv, 1986.

Bar, Shmuel, *Milhemet Yom HaKippurim Be'Einei Ha'Aravim*, Tel Aviv, 1986.
Bar-Kochba, Moshe, *Merkavot HaPlada*, Tel Aviv, 1989.
Bar-On, Avner, *HaSipurim Shelo Supru*, Jerusalem, 1981.
Bar-Zohar, Michael, *The Avengers*, London 1968.
— *Ben-Gurion*, Tel Aviv, 1987.
— *Spies in the Promised Land*, New York, 1972.
Bar-Zohar, Michael, and Haber, Eitan, *The Quest for the Red Prince*, New York, 1983.
Barnaby, Frank, *The Invisible Bomb*, London, 1989.
Bartov, Hanoch, *Dado*, Tel Aviv, 1978.

Beer, Yisrael, *Bitachon Yisrael*, Tel Aviv, 1966.
Beit-Hallahmi, Benjamin, *The Israeli Connection*, London, 1988.
Ben-Gurion, David, *YoMan HaMilhama*, Tel Aviv, 1982.
Ben-Ner, Yitzhak, *Ta'atuon*, Tel Aviv, 1989.
Ben-Yisrael, Yitzhak, *Dialogim Al Mada VeModi'in*, Tel Aviv, 1989.
Benvenisti, Meron, *Jerusalem, the Torn City*, Jerusalem, 1976.
Benziman, Uzi, *Sharon, an Israeli Caesar*, New York, 1985.
Binur, Yoram, *My Enemy, My Self*, New York, 1989.
Black, Ian, *Zionism and the Arabs 1936–1939*, New York, 1986.
Black, Ian, and Caplan, Neil, 'Israel and Lebanon: Origins of a Relationship', *Jerusalem Quarterly*, spring 1983.
Blitzer, Wolf, *Territory of Lies*, New York, 1989.
Bober, Aryeh (ed)., *The Other Israel*, New York, 1972.
Brecher, Michael, *Decisions in Crisis. Israel 1967 and 1973*, Los Angeles, 1980.
Brock, Ray, *Blood, Oil and Sand*, Cleveland, 1952.
Burns, E. L. M., *Between Arab and Israeli*, London 1962.

Caroz, Ya'akov, *The Arab Secret Services*, London, 1978.
Chaliand, Gerard, *The Palestine Resistance*, London, 1972.
— *People without a Country*, London, 1980.
Cobban, Helena, *The Palestinian Liberation Organisation*, Cambridge, 1984.
— *The Making of Modern Lebanon*, London, 1985.
Cohen, Amnon, *Miflagot Politiot BaGada HaMa'aravit*, Jerusalem, 1980.
Cohen, Raymond, 'Israeli Military Intelligence before the 1956 Sinai Campaign', *Intelligence and National Security*, Vol. 3, No. 1, January 1988.
Cohen, Yeruham, *LeOr HaYom UvaMakshakh*, Tel Aviv, 1969.
Cooley, John, *Green March, Black September*, London, 1973.
Copeland, Miles, *The Game of Nations*, New York, 1969.
— *The Game Player*, London, 1989.

Dan, Uri, and Ben-Porat, Y., *The Secret War*, New York, 1970.
Dan, Uri, and Mann, Peter, *Eichmann BeYadai!*, Tel Aviv, 1987.
Danin, Ezra, *Te'udot U'Dmuyot*, Jerusalem, 1981.
— *Tsioni BeKhol Tnai*, Jerusalem, 1987.
Davenport, Elaine, Eddy, Paul, and Gillman, Peter, *The Plumbatt Affair*, London, 1978.

Dayan, Moshe, *The Story of My Life*, London, 1977.
— *Living with the Bible*, London, 1978.
Deacon, Richard, *'C'*, London, 1984.
Dzhirkvelov, Ilya, *Secret Servant*, London, 1987.

Eisenberg, Dennis, Dan, Uri, and Landau, Eli, *Mossad: Inside Stories*, New York, 1978.
Eisenberg, Dennis, Landau, Eli, and Portugali, Menachem, *Operation Uranium Ship*, Tel Aviv, 1978.
Elad, Avri, *Ha'Adam HaShlishi*, Tel Aviv, 1976.
Eliav, Ayreh Lyova, *Taba'ot Eidut*, Tel Aviv, 1984.
Eshed, Haggai, *Mi Natan Et HaHora'a*, Jerusalem, 1979.
— *Mossad Shel Ishi Ehad*, Jerusalem, 1988.
Eveland, Wilbur Crane, *Ropes of Sand*, New York, 1980.
Eytan, Steve, *L'Oeil de Tel Aviv*, Paris, 1972.

Faligot, Roger, and Krop, Pascal, *La Piscine*, Oxford, 1989.
Fisk, Robert, *Pity the Nation*, London, 1990.
Frenkel, Shlomo, *Spector: Sodi BeYoter*, Tel Aviv, 1988.

Gazit, Shlomo, *HaMakel VeHaGezer*, Tel Aviv, 1985.
— 'Intelligence Estimates and the Decision-Maker', *Intelligence and National Security*, Vol. 3, No. 3, July 1988.
Gehlen, Reinhard, *The Service*, New York, 1972.
Gelber, Yoav, *Toldot HaHitnadvut*, Jerusalem, 1979–83.
— *Gar'in LeTsava Ivri Sadir*, Jerusalem, 1986.
Gilad, Z. (ed.), *Sefer HaPalmah*, Tel Aviv, 1955.
Golan, Aviezer, *Operation Susannah*, New York, 1978.
Golan, Aviezer, and Pinkas, Danny, *Shula: Codename the Pearl*, New York, 1980.
Golan, Matti, *Shimon Peres*, London, 1982.
Granott, Oded, *Tzahal BeHeilo: Hayl HaModi'in*, Tel Aviv, 1981.
Grossman, David, *HaZman HaTsahov*, Tel Aviv, 1987.
— *The Yellow Wind*, New York, 1988.

Haber, Eitan, *HaYom Tifrotz Milhama*, Tel Aviv, 1987.
Halabi, Rafik, *The West Bank Story*, New York, 1981.
Halliday, F., and Molyneux, M., *The Ethiopian Revolution*, London, 1981.
Harel, Isser, *The House on Garibaldi Street*, New York, 1975.

Harel, Isser, *Mivtsa Yossele*, Tel Aviv, 1982.
— *Kam Ish Al Ehav*, Jerusalem, 1982.
— *Mashber HaMad'anim HaGermanim*, Tel Aviv, 1982.
— *HaEmet Al Retzah Kastner*, Tel Aviv, 1985.
— *Rigul Sovieti*, Tel Aviv, 1987.
— *Bitachon VeDemocratia*, Tel Aviv, 1989.
Hart, Alan, *Yasser Arafat*, London, 1984.
Hashavia, Aryeh, *Milhemet Yom HaKippurim*, Tel Aviv, 1974.
Heikal, Mohamed, *The Road to Ramadan*, London, 1976.
— *Sphinx and Commissar*, London 1978.
— *The Return of the Ayatollah*, London, 1981.
Hersh, Seymour, *The Price of Power*, New York, 1983.
Hillel, Shlomo, *Ru'ah Kadim*, Jerusalem, 1985.
Horne, Alistair, *A Savage War of Peace*, London, 1977.

Inbari, Pinhas, *Meshulash Al HaYarden*, Jerusalem, 1983.

Jackont, Amnon, *Pesek-Zman*, Tel Aviv, 1982.
Jonas, George, *Vengeance*, London, 1984.

Kahan Commission Report, Jerusalem, 1983.
Khaled, Leila, *My People Shall Live*, London, 1973.
Khalidi, Rashid, *Under Siege*, Columbia, 1986.
Kimche, David, and Bawly, Dan, *The Sandstorm*, London, 1968.
Klein, Ze'ev (ed.), *HaMilhama BaTeror*, Tel Aviv, 1988.
Knightley, Phillip, *The Second Oldest Profession*, London, 1986.
Kollek, Teddy, *For Jerusalem*, Tel Aviv, 1978.
Kotler, Yair, *Joe Hozer El HaOr*, Tel Aviv, 1988.

Lamb, Franklin P. (ed.), *Israel's War in Lebanon*, Boston, 1984.
Lanir, Zvi, *HaHafta'ah HaBesisit*, Tel Aviv, 1983.
Laqueur, Walter, *The Road to War*, London, 1969.
— *A World of Secrets*, New York, 1985.
Lavi, Yeshayahu (ed.), *Parshiot Ne'elamot*, Tel Aviv, 1961.
Ledeen, Michael, and Lewis, William, *Debacle*, New York, 1981.
Levite, Yeshayahu, *Milhemet HaTslalim*, Tel Aviv, 1969.
Levy, Yitzhak, *Tish'a Kabin*, Tel Aviv, 1986.
Livnat, Shulamit, *HaShamayim Krovim Yoter*, Tel Aviv, 1989.
Lloyd, Selwyn, *Suez 1956*, London, 1980.

Lotz, Wolfgang, *The Champagne Spy*, London, 1972.
Lucas, Noah, *The Modern History of Israel*, London, 1974.

Malkin, Peter Z., and Stein, Harry, *Eichmann in My Hands*, New York, 1990.
Manne, Robert, *The Petrov Affair*, Sydney, 1987.
Maoz, Moshe, *Palestinian Leadership on the West Bank*, London, 1984.
Mardor, Meir (Munya), *Shelihut Aluma*, Tel Aviv, 1957.
Martin, David, and Walcott, John, *Best Laid Plans*, New York, 1988.
Meir, Golda, *My Life*, London, 1976.
Merari, Ariel, and Elad, Shlomi, *Fahah Hul*, Tel Aviv, 1986.
Milstein, Uri, *Toldot Milhemet Ha'Atzmaut*, Tel Aviv, 1989.
Mishal, Shaul, *The PLO under Arafat*, Yale, 1986.
— *Avanim Ze Lo HaKol*, Tel Aviv, 1989.
Morris, Benny, 'The Birth of the Israeli–Phalange Relationship, 1948–1951', *Studies in Zionism*, spring 1984.
— *The Birth of the Palestinian Refugee Problem, 1947–1949*, Cambridge, 1988.
Moshel, Aharon, *Die Viper*, Hamburg, 1989.
Mutawi, Samir A., *Jordan in the 1967 War*, Cambridge, 1987.

Nakdimon, Shlomo, *Sevirut Nemuha*, Tel Aviv, 1982.
— *First Strike*, New York, 1987.
Naor, Mordechai, *Laskov*, Tel Aviv, 1988.
Neff, Donald, *Warriors for Jerusalem*, New York, 1984.

O'Ballance, Edgar, *Arab Guerrilla Power, 1967–1972*, London, 1974.
Offer, Zvi, and Kober, Avi, *Modi'in VeBitachon Leumi*, Tel Aviv, 1987.
Oz, Amos, *LaDa'at Isha*, Tel Aviv, 1988.

Pacepa, Ion, *Red Horizons*, London, 1989.
Parfitt, Tudor, *Operation Moses*, London, 1989.
Parsons, Anthony, *They Say the Lion*, London, 1986.
Pelai, Doron, *Pitaron Mivtsai*, Tel Aviv, 1990.
Peri, Yoram, *Between Battles and Ballots*, Cambridge, 1983.
Perlmutter, Amos, Handel, Michael, and Bar-Joseph, Uri, *Two Minutes over Baghdad*, London, 1982.
Pick, Pinhas, 'HaReshet HaTsvait HaAnti-Britit Shel HaHaganah Be-Yerushalayim', *Eidan*, No. 2, 1983.

Porath, Yehoshua, *The Palestinian Arab National Movement, 1929–1939*, London, 1977.
Posner, Gerald L., and Ware, John, *Mengele*, New York, 1986.
Posner, Steve, *Israel Undercover*, New York, 1987.
Powers, Thomas, *The Man Who Kept the Secrets*, New York, 1979.
Pryce-Jones, David, *The Face of Defeat*, London, 1974.

Rabin, Yitzhak, *The Rabin Memoirs*, Jerusalem, 1979.
Rabinovich, Abraham, *The Boats of Cherbourg*, New York, 1988.
Rabinovich, Itamar, *The War for Lebanon 1970–1983*, New York, 1984.
Rafael Gideon, *Destination Peace*, New York, 1981.
Rapoport, Louis, *Redemption Song*, New York, 1986.
Ronen, David, *Shnat Shabak*, Tel Aviv, 1989.

Schiff, Ze'ev, *A History of the Israeli Army*, London, 1987.
Schiff, Ze'ev, and Rothstein, Raphael, *Fedayeen*, New York, 1972.
Schiff, Ze'ev, and Ya'ari, Ehud, *Israel's Lebanon War*, London, 1986.
— *Intifada*, New York, 1990.
Schwarz, Walter, *The Arabs in Israel*, London, 1959.
Seale, Patrick, *The Struggle for Syria*, London, 1965.
— *Asad*, London, 1988.
Segal, Hagai, *Dear Brothers*, New York, 1988.
Segev, Shmuel, *HaMeshulash HaIrani*, Tel Aviv, 1981.
— *Mivtza Yachin*, Tel Aviv, 1984.
— *Boded BeDamesek*, Tel Aviv, 1986.
— *The Iranian Triangle*, New York, 1988.
Segev, Tom, *1949: The First Israelis*, New York, 1986.
Sharett, Moshe, *Yoman Ishi*, Tel Aviv, 1978.
Shiblak, Abbas, *The Lure of Zion*, London, 1986.
Shlaim, Avi, *Collusion across the Jordan*, Oxford, 1988.
Sieff, Marcus, *Don't Ask the Price*, London, 1987.
Silver, Eric, *Begin*, London, 1984.
Slutszky, Yehuda, *Sefer Toldot HaHaganah*, Tel Aviv, 1964.
Smith, Colin, *Carlos*, London, 1976.
Spector, Leonard S., *Going Nuclear*, New York, 1980.
Steven, Stewart, *The Spymasters of Israel*, New York, 1980.
Sunday Times Insight Team, *The Yom Kippur War*, London 1977.
Sylvester, Anthony, *Sudan under Nimeiri*, London, 1977.

Teveth, Shabtai, *The Cursed Blessing*, London, 1970.

— *Ben-Gurion: The Burning Ground*, Boston, 1987.
Tinnin, David B., *The Hit Team*, Boston, 1976.
Tlas, Mustafa, *HaPlisha HaYisraelit LeLevanon*, Tel Aviv, 1988.
Tower Commission Report, New York, 1987.

Verrier, Anthony, *Through the Looking Glass*, London, 1983.

Wald, Emmanuel, *Kelalat HaKeilim HaShvurim*, Tel Aviv, 1987.
Weizman, Ezer, *On Eagles' Wings*, London, 1976.
Woodhouse, C. M., *Something Ventured*, London, 1982.
Woodward, Bob, *Veil*, New York, 1987.
Wright, Peter, *Spycatcher*, New York, 1987.

Ya'ari, Ehud, *Strike Terror*, New York, 1970.
— *Mitzraim VeHaFedayin*, Givat Haviva, 1975.
Ya'ari, Ehud, and Haber, Eitan, *The Year of the Dove*, New York, 1979.
Yaniv, Avner, *Dilemmas of Security*, New York, 1987.

Zonis, Marvin, *The Political Elite of Iran*, Princeton, 1971.

Index

(NOTE: Personal names beginning *al-*, *as-*, *ash-*, *el-* are entered under the name that follows, with prefix retained.)